EARLY LIFE IN UPPER CANADA

EARLY LIFE IN
UPPER CANADA

BY

EDWIN C. GUILLET, M.A.

*With 302 illustrations selected and arranged
by the Author*

SEAL OF UPPER CANADA,
GEORGE III, 1791-1817

UNIVERSITY OF TORONTO PRESS

PRINTED IN THE U.S.A. BY OFFSET LITHOGRAPHY

To my wife, Mary Elizabeth, whose interest and co-operation made extensive research possible and greatly increased the enjoyment of the work.

FOREWORD BY THE MINISTER OF EDUCATION FOR ONTARIO

This book has been written partly to provide a work of reference in the field of social and economic history equal in scope and authenticity to those already available in the constitutional and political departments of the subject. It has, however, an even more important purpose,—to interest our people in the lives and times of their forefathers: men and women who toiled unremittingly amidst primitive conditions to lay the foundation of our present civilisation, not only in its material aspects but in every moral and spiritual phase of the national life.

Geo. Henry

PREFACE AND INTRODUCTION

"The historians of Canada (with the conspicuous exception of Garneau) have been literary balloonists. Ascending to a high altitude, they have observed what was on the surface, whilst the character of the Canadian people and its changes in different stages of growth, from the present settlements of the eighteenth century to the confederate nation of today—all this has not yet been written. The people of Canada have been left out of Canadian histories. Those who are the authors have given us some fair narratives of events, with the addition, in some instances, of parliamentary annals and biographical sketches. . . . No work deserving to be called a history of the Canadian people has yet been written."

GEORGE SANDFIELD MACDONALD.[1]

IN the half century which has elapsed since the above statement was made there have been important contributions to the social and economic history of Canada; but, at least as far as the Province of Ontario is concerned, little of a comprehensive nature has been written concerning the life of the inhabitants of former times. We have a most romantic and colourful history, but it may be discovered only with great difficulty—if, indeed, events have not in many instances gone entirely unrecorded, or the records of them lost by unappreciative contemporaries.

The present work, undertaken at the suggestion of the Department of Education of Ontario, is an attempt to assemble the scattered fragments of our heritage of the past, and every effort has been made to extend the search to the most remote and, in many instances, hitherto untouched sources; and while the writer makes no pretence that it contains by any means a complete social history of the province, yet care has been taken to present, insofar as it is possible, an authentic and comprehensive account of such subjects as are covered, and it is hoped to continue the work in future volumes which will appear as speedily as the circumstances of a very busy life permit.

The book has been written with two main objects in view: primarily, to arouse interest among the citizens of

[1] *The Literary Aspect of the Keltic Settlement in the Counties of Stormont and Glengarry.* In *Transactions* of the Celtic Society of Montreal, 1884-7, p. 131. George Sandfield Macdonald is the only surviving son of John Sandfield Macdonald, Prime Minister of the Canadas in 1862-4, and the first Premier of Ontario after Confederation.

Canada in the early history of Ontario, and in pioneer life generally; and secondly, to provide for libraries, schools and colleges a work of reference which will enable a broader view of social and economic history than it is possible to obtain in text books or general histories. It has been part of the scope of the undertaking to include many quotations from early diaries and letters, newspapers and essays, travellers' accounts and local histories. There is but little of this material that might not be adequately paraphrased, but, since almost all of the sources are obscure, if not rare, there is an obvious advantage in the presentation of the original. Only in the largest libraries may one locate many of the historical treasures of early times, and consequently their quotation becomes the one means by which the vast majority of people will ever have access to them. In quoting these it has occasionally been considered advisable to alter the spelling and punctuation in order to correct obvious errors, or to conform with the best English usage. This has not been done in the case of proper names, nor in other instances where, because of their quaintness or for other special reasons, the variations are of historic interest.

Care has been taken to make the sections concerning transportation and pioneer life representative of the province as a whole, and examples have consequently been chosen from various localities. There has been no intention of unduly stressing any one district, though, of course, more material is available on early life in some counties than in others. The section best covered by contemporary writers is undoubtedly Peterborough County, for nowhere else is there available so much and such authoritative information as has been provided by "the literary Stricklands"—Colonel Samuel and his sisters, Mrs. Susanna Moodie and Mrs. Catharine Traill,—by Thomas Need, John Langton, Frances Stewart, and the almost contemporary local historian, Dr. Thomas Poole.

The topical method of treating history has much to commend it, though some repetition is inevitable where subjects overlap. It enables the presentation in one place of all the essentials in a manner impossible by any other means; and since most of the topics covered in the present work have never before been treated in a comprehensive manner it was considered well worth while to enter into exhaustive research. The subject matter of each chapter is independent of all others, which, it is hoped, will greatly facilitate their use for reference purposes. There is usually much more in a chapter than the name of the subject might suggest. Wherever closely-related matter may be treated without any serious digression this has been done, and the subject-matter may be seen at a glance in the Table of Contents.

The organisation of the material of most of the sections has entailed a vast amount of care, for in several instances upwards of one hundred distinct sources have been used in connection with one chapter. The task was further complicated by the general lack of comprehensive bibliographies of historical works. Much thought has been given to the method of presentation of each subject, in order that its interest and value should be the greatest possible. As a general rule the material has been developed chronologically, but this has occasionally been varied where another means of approach better suited the purpose. While by far the greater part of every topic is restricted to early life it has been considered of value to round off such subjects as relate also to modern times by giving a general description of the trend of recent developments. Care has been taken throughout the work to avoid general statements which are not well backed by the evidence. Those who are unfamiliar with the life of early times may consider that the author has unduly stressed unpleasant aspects, or omitted to mention mitigating circumstances; but every effort has been made to present an accurate picture of the past without either exaggeration or extenuation. It is, perhaps, unnecessary to add that no one is in any way responsible for opinions expressed in the work except the writer and such authorities as he cites.

The word "pioneer" is a much-abused one, but it is capable of more exact use than it often receives. There is a tendency at times to forget that the founders of Upper Canada number hundreds of thousands of men and women of many nationalities, and include fur traders, lumbermen and *voyageurs* as well as settlers—even if one omits the Indians, who contributed greatly to the development of early Canada, though their honesty and loyalty were frequently rewarded only by debauchment at the hands of individual traders and settlers. The first actual settlers were not Loyalists, but several hundred Frenchmen who were located along the shores of the Detroit during the last half century of the French period. Some 5,000 Loyalists and "late Loyalists" entered Upper Canada during the last fifteen years of the eighteenth century; but many others arrived during the same period, including a considerable contingent of German mercenaries who were engaged in the American Revolutionary War in the service of George III. For nearly three-quarters of a century pioneers continued to come in large numbers to the unsettled regions in the rear of the earliest settlements, and they suffered hardships even greater than those experienced by the Loyalists, most of whom received rations and supplies for three years, as well as generous grants of land. These immigrants of the later periods of colonisation, of English, Irish, Scotch, French, German, Dutch and American origin—to mention only the more important—were no less founders of the section of the province in which they settled than the worthiest of earlier times; and all have contributed, though not equally, to our culture.

We are still comparatively close to the days of the establishment of Upper Canada. There is at least one man still living, Monroe Lawson, near Brighton, whose father was a veteran of the War of 1812; while Dr. James Coyne of St. Thomas, one of our venerable historians, knew intimately the late Dr. Henry Scadding, who was personally acquainted with Mrs. John Graves Simcoe, wife of the first Lieutenant-Governor of Upper Canada, 1791-6. To carry the analogy still farther it may be mentioned that Mrs. Simcoe's father was one of General Wolfe's aides-de-camp and was killed at the capture of Quebec in 1759. Mrs. Simcoe lived until 1850, and within the span of her life and that of many people still living has occurred the entire British period, and the formation of Upper Canada and its progress from a wilderness to its present state.

In spite, however, of our apparent closeness to the period of the settlement of this province, the characteristics of our modern civilisation are very rapidly removing the remains and memories of pioneer days. Contemporary newspapers to the contrary notwithstanding, there are now no pioneers of communities along "the front", and very few even in more remote districts. The oldest inhabitants of the early-settled portions of Ontario can now recall only such memories of the days of first settlement as were communicated to them by father or grandfather; consequently the present is an appropriate time for the appearance of a work on "the early days". Other considerations point in the same direction, for only in recent years has the face of the country lost most of its former appearance. The introduction of electric lighting, the telephone, and—more recently—the radio have resulted in great changes in both urban and rural life; while the motor-car, with the accompanying "permanent" highways, has effected in the last fifteen years a remarkable transformation of the countryside, as is apparent to anyone who can recall even such recent times.

The "literary remains" of the pioneer period are not as voluminous as one could wish. Innumerable letters and diaries, newspapers and periodicals, have disappeared entirely, and the invaluable historical material which they contained is lost. No copies are extant of many pamphlets known to have been published, while there were doubtless hundreds of others of which there is not even a record of publication. Few remain even of books which must have had a fair circulation, while some are known to have been printed of which no copy now exists. In spite, however, of frequent fires, and a rather general attitude of carelessness in the preservation of records, there has come down to us a very considerable heritage of Canadiana.

In the earliest periods education was not widely diffused, and there is consequently a distinct lack of contemporary sources for the Loyalist period; fortunately this has been to some extent made up by the researches of such accurate historians as William Canniff, Walter S. Herrington and W. S. Wallace. Throughout the later periods of settlement the most authoritative accounts have been written by men and women of the half-pay officer class, and to these may be added a number of good books of reminiscences. In the late eighteen-seventies many counties were provided with historical atlases through the enterprise of certain publishers and printers. The value of the historical material in these is sometimes considerable, though it depends largely upon the accuracy of the men selected in each community to write the sketches of village and township history. Smaller gazetteers appeared much earlier in certain of the older counties, and they contain the names of inhabitants of early times as well as other material of local historic interest. In addition to the works mentioned many sections of the province have been satisfactorily covered by good local historians, though in other districts but little of the past has been recorded in any form.

The travel literature of the times is fortunately quite extensive, and, like contemporary newspapers, it is indispensable to the historian. When due allowance is made for individual prejudices, much of the best material on early life is contained in the excellent accounts of such writers as La Rochefoucauld-Liancourt, Isaac Weld, John Ogden, George Heriot, John Howison, John Bigsby, Basil Hall, Joseph Pickering, Thomas Hamilton, Patrick Shirreff, Adam Fergusson, Anna Jameson and Sir Richard Bonnycastle, to mention only a few of the best. While certain early British travellers in Canada almost invariably disliked everything they saw, (and particularly if they had first visited the more advanced United States), others were as extreme in their praise. There were many discriminating visitors, however, who may always be depended upon to give an accurate description of their experiences; and even those who found fault with the backwardness of Canada may be excused, for the inhabitants long laboured under material disadvantages which left them far in the rear in the march of progress.

Topographical descriptions of Upper Canada, and the many "Emigrant's Guides" which were produced, are in general fairly and accurately written, provided that they were not published for purposes of propaganda. Bouchette's *British Dominions in North America* and Gourlay's *Statistical Account of Upper Canada* are among the most valuable works of the former type. As for the guide-books for intending emigrants, those writers who told the truth, like John McDonald and the Rev. William Bell, found it bitter enough in many respects; while upon the whole it is probable that he hit the nail on the head who stated, with particular reference to emigration propaganda, that "all the truth which had been written and printed respecting Upper Canada would not cover one-half of the lies which have been told".

Diaries and journals kept by the inhabitants of an earlier day are still coming to light from time to time, as are also collections of letters. Contents of a personal or controversial nature have prevented the possessors of many of these documents from publishing them, or even allowing access to them; while the comparatively scant support accorded *belles-lettres* in this country does not encourage initiative in this respect. The most notable recent addition to Canadian diary literature is *The Diary of Mrs. John Graves Simcoe,* published in a limited edition in 1911 by John Ross Robertson, an enthusiast the value of whose historical researches is not yet generally appreciated. Without this journal of the wife of the first Lieutenant-Governor of Upper Canada, and its accompanying contemporary sketches, our knowledge of the period 1791-96 would be much more fragmentary than it is. A number of other diaries of importance have been published, usually by historical or other learned societies, or in periodicals; while a few notable journals of pioneers, as, for example, that of the Rev. William Bell of Perth, are still withheld, but, we may hope, will eventually be allowed to come to light. Among journals which have appeared in print in whole or in part may be mentioned the Jones, Proudfoot, and Willcocks diaries, all of which contribute considerably to our knowledge of the times; while among those still awaiting a publisher is that of John Thomson, an early settler on the shores of Lake Simcoe, a journal which contains material of great interest.

Among collections of letters which have been published those of John Langton and Frances Stewart stand out prominently. Many individual letters of considerable interest may be found in emigration propaganda, though they are almost always lacking in charm, and occasionally in truth and accuracy. Large numbers of historically valuable letters have unfortunately been burned, but some have found their way to the public archives, where he who is willing to dig deep may be rewarded.

With further reference to archives material it may be said that a great deal of research may be made into it without much tangible result. In some instances the collections of letters and miscellaneous papers have been indexed, while in many others they have not, and one may wade through twenty volumes of material without knowing beforehand whether there is likely to be anything to the purpose. In public libraries and private collections may also be found valuable manuscripts of historical interest. In a few instances the writer has derived assistance from unpublished material which may eventually be printed in book form; this has been gratefully acknowledged in the notes.

Reminiscences are notoriously unreliable, for most old people like to tell a good story. Where, however, the person who gives them is dependable, and he who takes them down is careful, the result is usually of value. Among recent collections of reminiscences, that of W. L. Smith, *Pioneers of Old Ontario*, has been most valuable to the present writer. The Coventry Papers in the Public Archives of Canada have also contributed some material of interest, though it would appear that the reminiscences are frequently inaccurate. Those citizens who write down their own recollections contribute not a little to the history of the country, particularly if they have been people of importance in the community, are aided by diaries and letters, and do not wait until they are too old to do more than give to the subject a rambling and inconsequential treatment.

The files of Canadian newspapers have been more frequently destroyed than preserved. Where any remain they are usually, in the earlier years at least, only partial, and in many instances only fugitive copies, if any at all, remain to testify to the existence of the publication. Newspapers provide the local historian with his best source; while they are invaluable to the economist and the writer of social history in that advertisements, market reports and accounts of amusements and other community activities are frequently to be found nowhere else.

It is impossible to mention here many modern historical

works that have been of value to the author either in content
or by the suggestion of source material; these are all listed
in the bibliography, and many of them are cited in the notes.
One book, however, which should be in every library,
(though it is now out of print), is Emily Weaver's *The Story
of the Counties of Ontario*. Another writer who is deserving
of credit for historical researches upon various aspects of
Canadian history is Fred Williams, whose short contributions which appear daily in the Toronto *Mail and Empire*
have done much to arouse an interest in history, and have
frequently been provocative of valuable material from
correspondents.

The publications of the learned societies listed in the
bibliography are in most instances the result of the researches of our contemporaries. The *Papers and Records*
of the Ontario Historical Society have, of course, provided
more of value than have the *Transactions* of the Royal
Society of Canada and other bodies in which history is not
the prime interest. The *Canadian Historical Review* is not
given over entirely to Canadian history, nor are there many
contributors who have concerned themselves with social and
economic history, which is the main subject of this work.
Some of the more valuable essays for the present purpose
were hidden away in the records of the proceedings of
associations long since defunct. A few writers have made
frequent and notable contributions to the publications of
learned societies, and among them may be mentioned Dr.
James Coyne, General Cruikshank and Mr. Justice Riddell.

The published papers of the province's local historical
societies vary in value with the enthusiasm and acumen of
their writers. Considered as a whole they yielded less than
was confidently expected. While many valuable contributions towards the history of the province may be found,
yet a considerable amount of the material lacks either interest or authenticity: while there is a tendency among
other contributors to rehash stale historical information
which is available in better form elsewhere. Upon the
whole, however, the records of the past would be much the
poorer if a few enthusiasts in the various parts of the
country had not organised historical societies. If more attention were given by the members to the careful recording

of reminiscences of reliable men of importance in the community, to the collection of accurate historical data upon outstanding local events, and to the assembling of full biographical details concerning natives of, or residents in the district who have taken a prominent part in local or national affairs, the result could not but be of immense value to future historians, who would not then have to search among fallen tombstones and fugitive copies of newspapers for meagre and unsatisfactory details of important personages and occurrences. A great deal of valuable work might also be done by the members in editing diaries and letters, either from local sources or from the archives collections.

Local history is, perhaps, the least authenticated, for it not infrequently depends upon the reminiscences of unreliable citizens and the observations of prejudiced travellers. Frequent important discrepancies occur in the sources, and, though an effort has been made to verify or qualify disputed material, it is, perhaps, too much to hope that no errors remain. Where any reader believes he has found one, or knows of any important variations which appear to have been ignored, he will confer a personal favour by communicating with the author, and at the same time he will render more accurate our knowledge of the past.

With reference to the chapters upon settlement, pioneer life and transportation it is necessary to point out that the subject matter has been dug up in very small portions,—a reference here, a few sentences there, and, somewhere else, a summary concerning one locality; only in very few instances has anything been found which gives an adequate account of most phases of a subject. Yet it may be said without exaggeration that, while hundreds of sources have been consulted in compiling these chapters, the great mass of the indispensable material upon social and economic conditions has been provided by a few dozen books of travel, diaries and letters, supplemented by still fewer good local and sectional histories and early settlers' accounts of pioneer life, and by the files of newspapers.

The section of the present work which treats of notable events in political or military annals is intended to fill a need for detailed information upon subjects merely mentioned or dismissed in a paragraph in text books and general histories. It seems to be well-nigh impossible for one to describe such events in an unbiased manner; nor, indeed, is the writer who does so beloved by his fellow-countrymen, for most people hate to have their prejudices disturbed. But in spite of any criticism which may ensue, it has been attempted to treat military events in a manner fair to all the participants—even rebels and Fenians!

The work of early artists has survived better than that of early writers. While many a rare book has been burned or allowed to mould away, pictures have been framed and kept for years, often by people who recognized neither their subject nor their value. While cultural efforts were not entirely absent in the early pioneer period, they were limited in scope by the primitive conditions which surrounded the inhabitants, and by far the greater part of the artistic works which have come down to us were executed by soldiers, engineers or travellers. Many officers of the Regular Army were specially trained in cartography, and were by no means unskilled in the use of the brush and palette. Some of their efforts were, perhaps, not impeccable from the point of view of artistic craftsmanship, but they give us remarkably true representations of contemporary life. Among these artists may be mentioned Ensign Peachey, Lieutenants Bainbrigge and Stretton, and Major-General Sir James P. Cockburn. Engraving and lithography had reached superb heights at that time, and a few artists, notably W. H. Bartlett, published collections of their works in the form of lithographs or steel engravings which could not be produced at all today. There were, too, travellers like George Heriot and J. J. Bigsby who illustrated their own narratives by sketches or paintings which show no mean artistic ability. By far the greater part of the early work, however, depicts settlements or events along "the front", for the officers were stationed at the garrison towns, and but few visitors were daring enough to endure the ordeal of "backwoods" travel. On that account contemporary illustrations of remote settlements are rare, and many localities have nothing whatever which has remained to convey to later generations an impression of the appearance of the settlement in the pioneer period.

The illustrations in this book have been chosen with a view to their portrayal of places and events described in the text. As far as they are available contemporary illustrations have been used, for, if executed by capable artists, they are undoubtedly preferable even to superior works of art of those who have drawn from imagination. Among the reproductions will be found a few drawn by some of the more gifted of early settlers, the work of Anne Langton being of outstanding interest. In using old sketches it has been considered preferable to reproduce them as they are, rather than to destroy any of their originality by redrawing them. Many illustrations have been included which are representative of the most excellent historical work of modern artists. A large proportion of the total number are reproduced for the first time, and among these are some of the most recent and successful efforts of foremost Canadian painters.

The notes have been in general restricted to the tabulation of authorities directly quoted in the work. In most instances these and the bibliography furnish sufficient evidence of the range of the source material; where it has been considered of value, however, a bibliographical note gives the chief authorities. Some reliance ought to be placed in the judgment of the author of a work of this kind, for if every important statement were to be annotated the footnotes would soon outrun the patience of the great majority of people, and the book would be read only by a few scholars and antiquarians, a condition that would militate against the prime purpose of the work. An effort has been made to have the text self-explanatory as far as possible, but footnotes have been appended wherever essential. Since no work of the kind has previously been published, the annotations will be of value to the student of history; while the general reader may, if he so wishes, ignore them.

In general, first editions of publications are quoted, but this policy has not been followed in the case of a few works of which a recent edition has appeared; these reprints, though not always free from errors, have the advantage of a fairly wide circulation, while the originals are usually exceedingly rare. For the benefit of those unaccustomed to the use of annotations it may be explained that, except where several works by one author might cause confusion, a work is only quoted once in full, the Latin abbreviations *ibid.* (*ibidem*—in the same place), and *op. cit.* (*opus citatum*— the work cited) being used to designate the source after its first citation. Each chapter is treated independently in this respect in order to enable easier reference. In the same connection it may be pointed out that the abbreviations *infra* (below), *supra* (above), *et seq.* (and following), and fn. (foot-note) are used. It may also be mentioned here that the terms "backwoods", "the bush", and "the front" are employed in this work in the sense in which they were so commonly used by early inhabitants.

A great deal of care has been taken to make the index of the greatest possible value for reference purposes. Every person mentioned in any way in the work is fully indexed, as well as everything which rises above the trivial. The illustrations and the artists, which are separately listed, are not repeated; but where additional information of importance has been included with the illustrations this has been incorporated in the index. An explanatory note at its commencement describes the system upon which the index is based.

The bibliography is very extensive, and should prove of value to those who are interested in the source material of Canadian history; for, apart from a few specialised lists prepared by public librarians, but little of a comprehensive nature has previously been available. Wherever possible the date of original publication is given in the bibliography, and if a later edition has been quoted it is so stated in the notes.

A word addressed particularly to teachers will not be out of place. Canadian history as a school subject has been "killed" by insistence upon a study of the political and constitutional phases by minds too immature to grasp their significance, a misfortune due in large measure to the traditional history text book, the contents of which until recent years have been almost entirely restricted to political, military and constitutional history. It is impossible for the average person to wax enthusiastic over the terms of the Constitutional Act or the ramifications of the Clergy Reserves problem. It is the writer's opinion that such history is not calculated to create interest in one's country, but should be studied only in the upper years of the high school and in the university, where it might be appreciated by those whose historical background had been nourished in earlier years by the teacher's emphasis upon more interesting aspects of the subject. History, like literature, should be a cultural study in our schools. It would be of inestimable value from the point of view of citizenship if the men and women of our country were intensely interested in the heritage of the past, instead of frightened away from it by ineffective presentation and a false sense of historical values. If boys and girls were introduced to the story of their native land by a presentation—with their own aid— of the history of their town or township, and a general account of the conditions under which the pioneers lived and worked and established their homes and the nation,—history would then be a delight, and an interest would be aroused which would survive a study in later years of even the comparatively dry and abstract theories of responsible government.

The writer gratefully acknowledges the co-operation which he has received from many sources. The Hon. George S. Henry, Prime Minister and Minister of Education, has taken a great interest in the production of the book, and has kindly written a foreword for it. Mr. George F. Rogers, Chief Director of Education, and Mr. H. W. Kerfoot, General Editor of Text Books, have also taken an active part in the work. Dr. A. H. U. Colquhoun's extensive knowledge of Canadiana has been of great value in tracing rare material, and his intense interest in history has been an inspiration. Several gentlemen have been good enough to read sections of the manuscript and to offer valuable suggestions: Dr. James H. Coyne, Mr. T. A. Reed and Mr. C. H. J. Snider have approved the chapters upon which they are acknowledged authorities,—the Talbot Settlement, the early history of Toronto, and the Sailing-ship, respectively; while Mr. Donald French and Professor W. S. Wallace have made suggestions which have proven of value with relation to the form and arrangement of the material. Archivists and librarians have co-operated to the full in making available the books and manuscripts which have provided the basis of the work. The author's thanks are extended particularly to Dr. George Locke, Miss Staton and staff of the Public Reference Library, Toronto; Mr. Arthur Wilgress, Miss King and staff of the Legislative Library of Ontario; Mr. W. S. Wallace and staff of the University of Toronto Library; Dr. Louis Barber, Miss Baker and staff of Victoria University Library; the Hon. Martin Burrell and M. Joseph Tarte of the Library of Parliament, Ottawa; Dr. A. G. Doughty, Dr. J. F. Kenney, Colonel G. T. Hamilton and staff of the Public Archives of Canada; Colonel Alexander Fraser, Dr. J. J. Talman and staff of the Archives of Ontario; and M. Pierre-Georges Roy, Archivist of Quebec.

The author owes a debt of gratitude to Dr. J. F. Kenney, Director of Historical Research and Publicity, Public Archives of Canada, whose interest and co-operation made possible the inclusion among the illustrations of a large number of reproductions of valuable works in the Archives collection. Mr. H. O. McCurry, Assistant Director of the National Gallery of Canada, Mr. Fred Haines and Miss Rogers of the Art Gallery of Toronto, and the staffs of the Royal Ontario Museum, the Archives of Ontario, and the Motion Picture Bureau of Ontario have also aided greatly in the assembling of the illustrations. The Canada Steamships Lines has granted permission for the reproduction of illustrations in the Manoir Richelieu Collection of Canadiana and the Marine Historical Collection, and has loaned several plates for reproduction. Similarly the John Ross Robertson Collection has provided a number of excellent illustrations, while for the reproduction of others the author is indebted to corporations and individuals, to whom credit is duly given where they appear. Assistance was rendered in this connection by the librarians of the Legislative Library of Ontario and the Public Reference Library, Toronto, who kindly granted the author permission to photograph illustrations in many rare books. Particular care has been taken to avoid the infringement of the copyright of any artist's work, and to secure the right of reproduction; but as the illustrations in most old books have no present owner they have been credited to the publications in which they appear, and to the artists if they are known.

Many others who have graciously extended favours during the writing of this book have been thanked personally. My wife has undertaken the greater part of the arduous labour of preparing an exhaustive index, and has also co-operated in seeing the book through the press, as well as in many other respects during the course of the preparation of the work; and my father has aided greatly in assembling rare illustrations and other materials of interest. The T. H. Best Printing Co., Reed-Canadian Engravers, Ltd., and The Ontario Publishing Company have co-operated to the fullest extent in the technical production of the book. The list of acknowledgments would be incomplete, however, if the respects of the author were not extended to several generations of historians, editors, artists, travellers, diarists and letter-writers, without whose care in recording past events or present impressions this work would have been impossible.

E. C. GUILLET.
Toronto, January, 1933.

CONTENTS

SECTION I.—EXPLORATION AND ADVENTURE

SECTION II.—SETTLEMENT

xxv

r

CHAPTER XI.—PIONEER SPORTS—CURLING - - - - 359

SECTION IV.—TRAVEL AND TRANSPORTATION

CHAPTER I.—INDIAN TRAILS, LOYALIST ROUTES AND CHANNELS OF TRADE - - - - - 373

CHAPTER II.—THE CANOE - - - - - - - - 395

ILLUSTRATIONS

FACING
PAGE

SECTION I
EXPLORATION AND ADVENTURE

CHAPTER I

CHAMPLAIN AND THE HURON COUNTRY

"In Champlain alone was the life of New France. By instinct and temperament he was more impelled to the adventurous toils of exploration than to the duller task of building colonies. The profits of trade had value in his eyes only as means to these ends, and settlements were important chiefly as a base of discovery. Two great objects eclipsed all others,—to find a route to the Indies, and to bring the heathen tribes into the embraces of the Church, since, while he cared little for their bodies, his solicitude for their souls knew no bounds."

FRANCIS PARKMAN.[1]

IN 1567 Samuel de Champlain was born of sea-faring parents in Bretagne, or Brittany, on the west coast of France. In early life he went to sea, and later served in the French army. At the close of the century he spent two years in the West Indies in the service of Spain, and upon returning to France wrote an interesting account of the Spanish colonial system. His advocacy of a canal across the Isthmus of Panama is a typical example of the wisdom and penetration which were such prominent characteristics of the man.

Champlain was a skilful sea-captain and hydrographer, qualifications which later led to his being sent to Canada by the king. On one occasion in later years he sailed his ship, the *Don de Dieu* of 100 tons, from Honfleur to Tadoussac in eighteen days, a record which remained unbroken for a century.

In 1603 a colonising expedition was sent by the king of France to Nova Scotia. The leader was Aymar de Chaste, but a more important member was Champlain, who had been chosen by the king for the special purpose of exploring the French possessions and reporting the results of his investigations. While a settlement was being established at Port Royal under the leadership of De Monts and Lescarbot, Champlain was engaged in a careful survey of the Atlantic coast to the south and north of the new settlement, work in which he was more interested.

[1]Francis Parkman: *Pioneers of France in the New World.* 25th Edition, 1885, pp. 365-6.

3

The colony at Port Royal was not a permanent success, and in 1608 Champlain established his headquarters at Quebec, to which most of the remaining settlers at Port Royal removed. Here he was frequently visited by his Indian allies, the Hurons, who brought furs to the new trading-post, and told Champlain fascinating tales of their great country to the westward. A young Frenchman, Nicholas Vignau, spent the winter of 1612 on the Ottawa and returned with a glowing account of a great inland sea which he claimed he had discovered. The sea referred to was probably Hudson Bay, but Vignau had not penetrated beyond the Upper Ottawa, where the Indians had told him of the existence of the great body of water. Always an explorer at heart, Champlain did not need much persuasion to make plans for an expedition to this wonderful land.

On May 27, 1613, Champlain, Vignau, two other Frenchmen and one Indian set out from St. Helen's Island on a journey to the Ottawa country. During the next two weeks they proceeded up the Ottawa, surmounting great difficulties in their bark canoe. The site of the capital of Canada is described by Champlain in his account of his trip. He refers to a tributary on the south side of the river, "at the mouth of which is a marvellous fall. For it descends a height of twenty or twenty-five fathoms with such impetuosity that it makes an arch nearly 400 paces broad. The savages take pleasure in passing under it, not wetting themselves, except from the spray that is thrown off."[2] Like almost all rivers and rapids in the early period of our history, the Rideau Falls was much larger then than it is now, though one must allow for some exaggeration in many French explorers' accounts of Canadian waterfalls.

When the party reached Morrison's Island in Lac des Allumettes a band of Algonquins exposed Vignau's lying and wished to kill him so that he could lie no more. It was then certain that Vignau had wintered among them and had not approached within several hundred miles of Hudson Bay. Champlain had previously asked the Indians for canoes and guides to the Nipissirini (Nipissing) district, but, on hearing of Vignau's falseness, and finding the In-

[2]Samuel de Champlain: *Voyages.* (The Prince Society, 1878-82, Vol. III, p. 60).

A. Sherriff Scott

MADAME CHAMPLAIN TEACHING INDIAN CHILDREN

Reproduced from a Mural in the Chateau Laurier, Ottawa   C. W. Jefferys, R.C.A

CHAMPLAIN ON THE OTTAWA, 1613

Reproduced from a Mural in the Chateau Laurier, Ottawa   C. W. Jefferys, R.C.A.

INDIANS PAYING HOMAGE TO THE SPIRIT OF THE CHAUDIÈRE

dians unwilling to guide him farther, he decided to postpone further explorations until the next year, though it was then only June 10th.

Another reason for Champlain's return to Quebec so early in the season may have been the loss of his astrolabe, though he makes no reference to it in his journal. This was an instrument used by early travellers to locate their position, while the compass indicated direction. In August, 1867, 254 years after Champlain's journey, an astrolabe on which was marked "Paris, 1603" was found in the woods at a point where Champlain is known to have made a difficult portage. As C. W. Jefferys points out, this was in all probability Champlain's astrolabe, the assumption being the more certain because Champlain does not record his latitude in the last stages of his journey as he had done at frequent intervals previously.[3]

Champlain describes a peculiar Indian ceremony which he witnessed at the Chaudière Falls. At this portage the Indians had often been surprised by their enemies, so they took care to appease the evil spirit.

"After carrying their canoes to the foot of the falls, they assemble in one spot, where one of them takes up a collection in a wooden plate, into which each one put a bit of tobacco. The collection having been made, the plate is placed in the midst of the troupe, and all dance about it, singing after their style. Then one of them makes a harangue, setting forth that for a long time they had been accustomed to make this offering, by which means they are insured protection against their enemies; that otherwise misfortune would befall them, as they are convinced by the evil spirit. This done, the maker of the harangue takes the plate, and throws the tobacco into the midst of the caldron, whereupon they all together raise a loud cry."[4]

On July 9, 1615, Champlain, Etienne Brûlé, an interpreter, a servant and ten Indians embarked in two birch canoes on a second expedition, an advance party of thirteen French, including the Recollet priest, Father Le Caron, having previously set out for the Huron country. They continued past the Algonquin villages which marked the

[3]C. W. Jefferys: *Dramatic Episodes in Canada's Story.* 1930. p. 17.
[4]Champlain, *op. cit.*, Vol. III, p. 83.

end of the voyage of 1613, through the two lakes of the
Allumettes, and on until the tributary waters of the
Mattawan were reached. Here Champlain and his party
turned left and ascended the Mattawan some forty miles,
and then portaged over an Indian trail to Lake Nipissing.
After paddling through the lake they spent two days with
the Nipissing Indians, called the Sorcerers by the Jesuits,
and here they feasted on fish, deer and bears. The expedition then continued down the French River, where provisions ran short and blueberries and raspberries had to be
relied upon for food. In this district Champlain met a
troop of 300 Indians who had a peculiar manner of dressing their hair but wore no clothes whatever, though they
were tattooed and painted on various parts of the body.
Although of such savage aspect, they were engaged in the
quiet and peaceful work of gathering blueberries. to store
away for the winter.

From the mouth of the French River Champlain proceeded along the shore of Georgian Bay to Thunder Bay,
just west of Penetanguishene, passing through Byng Inlet,
Franklin Inlet, Parry Sound and Matchedash Bay *en route*.
The Hurons led him by way of the Severn River, Sparrow
Lake and Lake Couchiching to Cahiaqué, the capital of
their nation. This village was located near the present
town of Orillia; and seventeen other villages, well-protected
by palisades, were scattered throughout the district north
of Lake Simcoe. The Hurons lived in huts, of which
Cahiaqué contained about two hundred. They grew a considerable quantity of corn, beans, pumpkins and sunflowers,
the seeds of the last-named plant providing them with oil.

Champlain took careful note of the manners and customs of the Huron nation, who are said to have numbered
thirty thousand at that time. They built the white chief
a bark lodge similar to those which they used, and in it
raised for him a simple altar, before which, on August
12th, was said the first mass among the Hurons. At
Cahiaqué Champlain met the Huron chiefs, and as a result
of the meeting an expedition was planned against the Iroquois south of Lake Ontario. Feasts and war dances enlivened the period of waiting, until finally the tardiest bands
of Indians arrived to join the war party.

The main force was to proceed eastward, but Etienne Brûlé left Lake Simcoe with twelve Indians on a recruiting expedition for Champlain. Brûlé reached Lake Ontario by way of the Humber portage trail. He is thought to have been the first white man to see Lake Ontario, just as on a later journey, in 1622, he was the first of his race to visit Lake Huron and Lake Superior. From the mouth of the Humber Brûlé and his men are believed to have crossed the lake, perhaps visiting Niagara Falls, for Champlain refers to its existence.

Meanwhile, on September 8th, Champlain left the shores of Lake Simcoe, accompanied by a large number of Huron warriors. The Trent system of lakes and rivers was the route followed to Lake Ontario. ˙In his journal Champlain wrote: "We continued our journey towards the enemy, and went some five or six leagues through these lakes, when the savages carried their canoes about ten leagues by land. We then came to another lake, six to seven leagues in length and three broad."[5] This was either Balsam or Sturgeon Lake, probably the latter. The remainder of the Trent system is called "a river which discharges into the great lake of the Entouhonorons" (Ontario); but he describes this river, on which he travelled about sixty-four leagues (160 miles), as containing in its course "five falls and several lakes of considerable size, through which the river passes".[6] The river is now called the Otonabee above Rice Lake, and the Trent below it, while the most important of the lakes in the system are, in the order that Champlain would reach them, Pigeon, Buckhorn, Chemong, Lovesick, Stoney and Rice.

It is unlikely, however, that the war party traversed all of these lakes and rivers. There was a well-known portage between Chemong Lake and the Otonabee, and it would appear probable that the Indians would travel over this carrying-place of five miles, and so avoid the many miles of paddling and numerous tiresome portages which a trip through Stoney Lake and adjacent waters would necessitate. Champlain was much impressed with the beauty of the whole district, now a favourite summer resort.

"It is certain that all this region is very fine and

[5]*Ibid.*, p. 124-5.   [6]*Ibid.*, p. 125.

pleasant. Along the banks it seems as if the trees had been set out for ornament in most places, and that all these tracts were in former times inhabited by savages, who were subsequently compelled to abandon them for fear of their enemies. Vines and nut trees are here very numerous, ... and stags and bears very abundant. As to smaller game there is a large quantity of it in its season. There are also many cranes, white as swans, and other varieties of birds like those of France."[7]

On reaching the mouth of the Trent the expedition continued through the Bay of Quinté, crossed Lake Ontario by a protected route among the islands, hid their boats in the woods, and proceeded on foot to attack an Iroquois stronghold south of Lake Oneida, probably near the present city of Syracuse. The village was well protected by four concentric rows of palisades formed of trunks of trees thirty feet high, while its location made it naturally easy of defence. The Hurons made movable parapets, a large tower and wooden shields, and under Champlain's direction assaulted the stronghold. Their lack of discipline was soon apparent, however, and Champlain was unable to keep them under his control, with the inevitable result that after a three-hour attack they were repulsed by the Iroquois. After waiting five days for promised allies the disheartened Hurons withdrew from the Iroquois country.

The result of the expedition was an intense hatred between the two races of Indians, ending in the destruction of the Huron nation in 1648-1650, and the use of their land as an Iroquois hunting-ground. The French, too, suffered many terrifying raids on their small settlements along the St. Lawrence, and the torture and martyrdom of the Jesuit missionaries among the Hurons.

Champlain had been injured in the knee during the attack on the Iroquois, and he was carried with other wounded in baskets built for the purpose. This method of transporting disabled men may have been convenient, but it was not pleasant for the wounded, who were placed within them folded together and bound with cords in such a manner as to deprive them of all motion. Champlain wrote that the pain which he suffered from his wound "was

[7]*Ibid.*

CHAMPLAIN'S FIRST BATTLE WITH THE INDIANS, 1609

CHAMPLAIN ARRIVING AT QUEBEC, 1608
Based upon the Tercentenary Pageant at Quebec, 1908

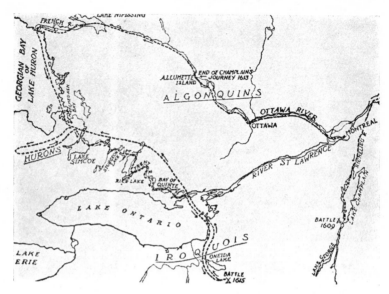

MAP OF CHAMPLAIN'S EXPLORATIONS

From the Prince Society's *The Voyages of Champlain*

A FRENCH CONCEPTION OF AN INDIAN DEER HUNT

nothing in comparison with that which I endured while I was carried bound and pinioned on the back of one of our savages."[8]

The expedition re-crossed Lake Ontario at the eastern end, and appears to have ascended the Cataraqui (Rideau) River some distance, and then worked its way twenty-five miles in a north-westerly direction. Here the Hurons planned to halt until the lakes should freeze up, whereupon travel would be easier. Champlain wished to return to Quebec, and asked for a guide and a canoe, with which the Hurons had agreed to furnish him when he was first persuaded to accompany them on the war-path; but they refused his request and insisted that he remain with them.

The location of their temporary camp is uncertain, but a study of the locality and of Champlain's narrative suggests to the historian of Lennox and Addington, W. S. Herrington, that it was somewhere between Long and Crotch Lakes.[9] Champlain gives a good description of the camp and the preparations for a deer-hunt:

"Twenty-five savages set to building two or three cabins out of pieces of wood fitted to each other, and the chinks of which they stopped up by means of moss to prevent the entrance of the air, covering them with the bark of trees. When they had done this they went into the woods to a small forest of firs, where they made an enclosure in the form of a triangle closed up on two sides and open on one. This enclosure was made of great stakes of wood closely pressed together, from eight to nine feet high, each of the sides 1,500 paces long: at the extremity of this triangle there was a little enclosure constantly diminishing in size, covered in part with boughs, and with an opening of only five feet, about the width of a medium-sized door, into which the deer were to enter. They were so expeditious in their work that in less than ten days they had their enclosure in readiness."[10]

The French leader relates in detail how the Indians by beating with sticks drove the frightened deer into the enclosed area, where they were easily killed. "I assure you,"

[8]*Ibid.,* p. 135.
[9]W. S. Herrington: *The History of Lennox and Addington.* 1913. p. 5.
[10]Champlain, *op. cit.,* Vol. III, p. 138.

he wrote, "that there is a singular pleasure in this chase."[11] The Indians feasted upon the deer, reserving the fat for winter use as a sort of butter. On another occasion Champlain saw 500 Indians drive the deer to the end of a woody point; when they took to the river, men in canoes killed them with spears and arrows almost as easily as in the stockaded enclosure.

While encamped in this district awaiting the freezing up of the lakes, Champlain was hospitably treated by one of the principal chiefs of the Hurons, D'Arontal. On one occasion he was lost for three days when he wandered too far into the woods in pursuit of "a certain bird, which seemed to me peculiar. It had a beak like that of a parrot, and was the size of a hen. It was entirely yellow except the head, which was red, and the wings, which were blue, and it flew by intervals like a partridge."[12]

On December 4th Champlain set out with D'Arontal and some 2,500 Hurons for Cahiaqué, following a route some distance north of the Trent system. He gives an interesting account of his difficult journey, "walking on the rivers, and ponds, which were frozen, and sometimes through the woods. Thus we went for nineteen days, undergoing much hardship and toil, both the savages, who were loaded with a hundred pounds, and myself, who carried a burden of twenty pounds, which in the long journey tired me very much."[13]

They experienced a thaw *en route,* and the trip of some 160 miles through water and melting snow, or over ice, would certainly cause great exhaustion and hardship to one unaccustomed to it. For part of the distance, however, the loads were hauled over the ice on *trainées de bois,* a type of sledge made of boards six or seven feet long cut with great difficulty from the trunks of trees by the use of stone axes, aided by fire. These rude sleighs were only about a foot wide, and could thus be drawn by a leather strap through the trackless forest, wherever a man could walk. The expedition reached its destination on December 23rd.

During the winter Champlain employed himself in visiting not only the Huron villages but also those of the Algonquins near Lake Nipissing. On one occasion he had a

[11]*Ibid.*   [12]*Ibid.,* p. 140.   [13]*Ibid.,* p. 143.

difficult duty to perform, when two tribes quarrelled over an Iroquois prisoner. By exercising considerable diplomacy he fulfilled the arduous task of a judge among savages. In the spring he learned that a new expedition was being planned against the Iroquois, so he persuaded some Indians to accompany him, and with Pierre Joseph secretly embarked on May 20th for Quebec, where he arrived on July 11, 1616. Here, with short intermissions, he continued to guide the destinies of Canada until his death on Christmas Day, 1635.

His life and work have been eulogised by many writers. E. F. Slafter summarises his achievements in these words:

"The explorations made by Champlain early and late, the organisation and planting of his colonies, the resistance of avaricious corporations, the holding of numerous savage tribes in friendly alliance, the daily administration of the affairs of the colony, of the savages, and of the corporation in France, to the eminent satisfaction of all generous and noble-minded patrons, and this for a period of more than thirty years, are proof of an extraordinary continuation of mental and moral qualities."[14]

Perhaps Charlevoix admired him most completely:

"Champlain died at Quebec, generally and justly regretted. M. de Champlain was, beyond contradiction, a man of merit, and may well be called 'The Father of New France'. He had good sense, much penetration, very upright views, and no man was ever more skilled in adopting a course in the most complicated affairs. What all admired most in him was his constancy in following up his enterprises, his firmness in the greatest dangers, a courage proof against the most unforeseen reverses and disappointments, ardent and disinterested patriotism, a heart tender and compassionate for the unhappy, and more attentive to the interests of his friends than his own, a high sense of honour and great probity. His memoirs show that he was not ignorant of anything that one of his profession should know, and we find him a faithful and sincere historian, an attentively observant traveller, a judicious writer, a good mathematician and an able mariner."[15]

[14]*Ibid.*, Vol. I, pp. 203-4.
[15]Pierre Charlevoix: *Histoire et description générale de la Nouvelle France.* 1744. Vol. II, pp. 88-9.

CHAPTER II

FATHER HENNEPIN AND THE FALLS OF NIAGARA

"On the 6th, St. Nicholas day, we entered the beautiful River Niagara, which no bark had ever yet entered. Four leagues from Lake Frontenac there is an incredible Cataract or Waterfall, which has no equal. The Niagara River near this place is only the eighth of a league wide, but it is very deep in places, and so rapid above the great fall that it hurries down all the animals which try to cross it, without a single one being able to withstand its current. They plunge down a height of more than five hundred feet, and its fall is composed of two sheets of water and a cascade, with an island sloping down. In the middle these waters foam and boil in a fearful manner. They thunder continually, and when the wind blows in a southerly direction, the noise which they make is heard for from more than fifteen leagues."

LOUIS HENNEPIN (1678).[1]

WHEN Jacques Cartier visited Canada for the second time, in 1535, he heard from the Indians at Hochelaga that a great waterfall carried the waters of the interior into Lake Iroquois, from which flowed the mighty St. Lawrence. In the next century Champlain referred to the Falls of Niagara in his account of his explorations;[2] he did not see it, though Etienne Brûlé, one of his men, may have journeyed there when he separated from the main expedition at Lake Simcoe. Brébeuf and Chaumonot were in the vicinity in 1640, and Dollier de Casson, accompanied by Bréhan de Galinée, visited the Niagara district in 1669, though it is unlikely that any of them saw the Falls. Galinée's narrative states that the Indians told them that the Falls was "one of the finest cataracts or waterfalls in the world; . . . . the river fell in that place from a rock higher than the tallest pine trees, that is about 200 feet".[3] The first description by an eye-witness is that of Louis Hennepin, a Recollet friar, who visited the Falls in 1678.

Father Louis Hennepin, the years of whose life are thought to be 1640-1710, came to Canada with La Salle, and shared in his scheme of sailing to China by way of

[1]Louis Hennepin: *Description de la Louisiane*. 1683. pp. 71-2.
[2]Samuel de Champlain: *Voyages* (Prince Society, 1878-82, Vol. I, pp. 271-6.
[3]René B. de Galinée: *Exploration of the Great Lakes, 1669-70*. (J. H. Coyne's translation, in Ontario Historical Society, *Papers and Records*, Vol. XXVII, pp. 38-41.)

the western lakes and the Mississippi River. A few years later Hennepin laid claim to the discovery of the entire Mississippi region, an account of his explorations appearing in several languages before the end of the century. His claim is not, however, admitted by historians, who give La Salle the honour of first exploring the Mississippi basin, and discredit a considerable amount of Hennepin's narrative; one writer refers to him as belonging to "that school of writers who state the truth by accident and a lie by inclination".[4]

On November 18, 1678, Hennepin and La Motte sailed from Fort Frontenac in a *brigantine* of ten tons with a crew of sixteen men. In his account Hennepin describes the lake through which they sailed:

"The Lake Ontario received the Name of the Lake Frontenac from the Illustrious Count de Frontenac, Governor-General of Canada. . . . . It is likewise called in the Iroquois Language, Skanadario; that is to say, a very pretty Lake. . . . . The Water is fresh and sweet, and very pleasant to drink; the Lands which border upon it being likewise very fertile. It is very navigable, and can receive large Vessels: only in Winter it is more difficult, because of the outrageous Winds which are frequent there."[5]

The weather was cold and stormy during the voyage on Lake Ontario. Hennepin ran up the Humber River for shelter, and visited the Indian village Taiaiagon to the west of its mouth. The inhabitants, though astonished at the white men's appearance, were hospitable and supplied provisions, chiefly corn, in exchange for goods. Upon setting out again on December 5th Hennepin found his small ship frozen in the ice, and the cargo had to be considerably lightened and the ice chopped away before the boat could be floated. On the following day the party reached the Niagara River, landing first at the point where Fort Niagara was later built. Proceeding up the river until their course was blocked by the rapids, they landed on the eastern bank. La Motte commenced the erection of a large fort, but the neighbouring Indians objected, so a smaller

[4]K. M. Lizars: *The Valley of the Humber.* 1913. p. 28.
[5]Hennepin: *Nouvelle Découverte d'un Pais plus grand que l'Europe.* 1697. Thwaites Edition, Vol. I, pp. 51-3.

palisade was constructed to signify French control over the land. Near the present site of Lewiston Hennepin built a bark chapel, and held the first Christian service on the east bank of the Niagara since Brébeuf's visit to the district in 1640.

Some Indians who were encamped in the vicinity guided the *voyageurs* to the mighty Niagara, of which Father Hennepin proceeded to make a sketch and write a description. While the sketch has not much merit as a work of art, yet it is of great interest since it is our earliest representation of the Falls. His description of the cataract, as published in the English edition of 1698, is much less reliable than that which appears in the *Description de la Louisiane* of 1683. The following from the 1698 account is of interest, however:

"Betwixt the Lake Ontario and Erie there is a vast and prodigious Cadence of Water which falls down after a surprising and astonishing manner, inasmuch that the Universe does not afford its parallel. . . . This wonderful downfall is compounded of two great Cross-streams of Water, and two Falls, with an Isle sloping along the middle of it. The Waters which fall from this vast height, do foam and boil after the most hideous manner imaginable, making an outrageous noise, more terrible than that of Thunder; for when the Wind blows from off the South, their dismal roaring may be heard above fifteen leagues off."[6]

Evidently the cataract made a deep impression on the minds of the visitors for they estimated its height at 600 feet, almost four times what it actually is. At that time, in addition to the two great falls, there was a crossfall which Hennepin depicts in his sketch pouring over Table Rock, a cliff which projected about 200 feet into the river. The cross-fall disappeared before the middle of the eighteenth century.

The Niagara portage trail was well-beaten even at that early date. Hennepin gives an interesting description of it: "Four leagues from this cataract or fall, the Niagara River rushes with extraordinary rapidity, especially for two leagues, into Lake Frontenac. It is during these two

[6]*Ibid.*, pp. 54-5.

Father Louis Hennepin

The Earliest Sketch of The Falls of Niagara, 1678

W. H. Bartlett

Niagara Falls from the Ferry, 1837

Before the *Maid of the Mist* was launched in 1846 a rowboat conveyed
the adventurous in front of the Falls

VIEW BELOW TABLE ROCK, NIAGARA FALLS, 1837

leagues that goods are carried. There is a very fine road, very little wood, and almost all prairies mingled with some oaks and firs, on both banks of the river, which are of a height that inspires fear when you look down."[7]

The exploration of Niagara Falls did not end with Hennepin's investigations. Millions of people have visited the great cataract since that time, and for the first century and a half new wonders continually presented themselves to the curious who were willing to surmount the natural difficulties which prevented easy access. Early visitors after Hennepin were influenced by his writings: Baron Lahontan, for example, who saw the Falls in 1688, considered the height to be between 700 and 800 feet.[8] The first reliable visitor appears to have been Charlevoix, who saw the Falls in 1721 and immediately realised the gross exaggeration of former descriptions. He made a very close estimate of the height at 140 to 150 feet.[9]

Peter Kalm, an eminent Swedish botanist, visited the Falls in 1750, and a letter of his contains the earliest account of the cataract written in English. Kalm made some very keen observations on the district. He learned that Goat Island had first been approached by human beings about 1739, when Indians using iron-shod poles had crossed to the island to rescue two of their number who had been marooned there for nine days when their canoe was swept down the rapids.[10]

In 1753 M. Bonnefons was probably the first to make the dangerous descent to the foot of the Falls, and to enter what was later called the Cave of the Winds. He made his way down with the utmost difficulty by catching hold of bushes and roots; and upon entering the cave he was drenched by the spray, and remained deaf for two hours after he had returned.[11] Towards the close of the French period Captain Pouchot of Fort Niagara first observed the

[7]Hennepin: *Description de la Louisiane*, pp. 71-2.
[8]Louis Lahontan: *Nouveaux Voyages dans l'Amerique Septentrionale*. 1703. Vol. I, p. 137.
[9]Pierre Charlevoix: *Journal d'un Voyage fait par ordre du Roi dans l'Amérique Septentrionale*. 1744. English Edition, 1761, Vol. I, pp. 345-356.
[10]See letter of Peter Kalm, in the *Gentleman's Magazine*, January, 1751.
[11]J. C. Bonnefons: *Voyage au Canada, 1751-61*. 1887. pp. 57-61.

possibility of crossing the river in bateaux just below the Falls.[12]

During the first fifty years of the British period there were many developments which increased the accessibility of the region. As early as 1765 a crude Indian ladder was in use on part of the descent to the base of the Falls, while in 1785 the first person penetrated behind the Horseshoe Fall. At this period a journey to Niagara Falls necessitated travel through a wilderness, no matter from which quarter it was approached; but by 1816 it was more easily accessible to tourists, a fact noted by Lieutenant Francis Hall.[13]

Isaac Weld, who visited Niagara in 1796, describes Mrs. Simcoe's Ladder,—a stairway down the cliff built especially for her convenience a few years earlier; but he found its use "no trifling undertaking, and few ladies, I believe, could be found of sufficient strength of body to encounter the fatigue of such an expedition".[14]

It is, perhaps, not generally known that the Niagara district was infested with adders, black snakes and rattlesnakes in the days of early settlement. Mrs. Simcoe, who considered the Falls the "grandest sight imaginable", states that she "did not see any rattlesnakes, though many ladies are afraid to go to the Table Rock, as it is said there are many of these snakes near it. There are crayfish in very small pools of water. Mr. McDonnell said that pounded crayfish applied to the wound was a cure for the bite of a rattlesnake."[15] In a later entry in her diary Mrs. Simcoe describes a snake five and one-half feet long that had been stuffed at Queenston.[16] The rattlesnakes were practically exterminated by the swine of the first settlers, who fought and killed them at every opportunity. They were commonly

[12]François Pouchot: *Memoir upon the Late War in North America, 1756-60.* See Hough Edition, 1866, Vol. II, pp. 153-6 and 173-9.

    Descriptions of the Niagara region written by visitors during the French period are most readily available in C. M. Dow: *Anthology and Bibliography of Niagara Falls.* 1921. Vol. I, pp. 17-62.

[13]Francis Hall: *Travels in Canada and the United States in 1816-17.* 1818. pp. 232-3.

[14]Isaac Weld: *Travels through the States of North America.* 1799. p. 316.

[15]*Diary of Mrs. John Graves Simcoe,* July 30, 1792.

[16]*Ibid.,* June 29, 1793.

found in several other parts of Upper Canada in the same period, and we find references to large numbers of them being killed at the head of Lake Ontario.

In 1794 a point of interest at Niagara was the "Burning Spring", located about two miles above the Falls, and "emitting a gas, or inflammable air, which, when confined in a pipe, and a flame applied to it, will boil the water of a tea-kettle in fifteen minutes".[17] In 1793 a visitor, the first of a considerable number, expressed disappointment in the Falls. In the winter of 1837 Mrs. Anna Jameson was similarly affected, and calls herself, among other names, "an ass-head, a clod and a wooden spoon" for being unable to be pleased.[18] She felt differently after a summer visit, however, and appreciated "their loveliness, their inexpressible, inconceivable beauty".[19] Even at this time it required, especially in winter, "the more robust frame of the male sex" to reach positions where the best views of the Falls were obtainable.

Most visitors agreed on the grandeur of the scene, though their impressions vary. Many have been affected as deeply as Robert Sutcliffe, who, in 1805, spent two hours "contemplating this astonishing natural curiosity".[20] Similarly George Heriot, who saw them in 1801, considered that the Falls "surpass in sublimity every description which the powers of language can afford of that celebrated scene, the most wonderful and awful which the habitable world presents".[21]

In the early years of the century a small bateau or skiff began to be regularly used to cross the river below the Falls. John Howison describes a trip in this rowboat in 1818, and also refers to lying flat on Table Rock and stretching out his arm until he could plunge his hand into the Falls; but the experiment was "truly a horrible one, and such as I would not wish to repeat".[22] Among other interesting objects, he saw a dog which "was carried over the

[17]John Ogden: *A Tour through Upper and Lower Canada.* 1799. p. 112.
[18]Anna Jameson: *Winter Studies and Summer Rambles in Canada.* 1838. Vol. I, p. 83.
[19]*Ibid.,* Vol. II, p. 36.
[20]Robert Sutcliffe: *Travels in North America, 1804-6.* 1811. p. 156.
[21]George Heriot: *Travels through the Canadas.* 1807. p. 159.
[22]John Howison: *Sketches of Upper Canada.* 1821. 3rd Edition, 1825, p. 109.

Great Fall some years ago, and suffered no injury except the fracture of two of its ribs".[23]

In 1833 Patrick Shirreff visited the Falls and describes how he penetrated 153 feet to Termination Rock, in what is now called the Cave of the Winds.[24] Almost every visitor was an explorer, for it was only the adventurous who could see the most interesting beauty spots. Among the amusements usually "taken in" a century ago was the Camera Obscura, a device stated to be "always worth a visit" because it beautifully reflected the Falls.[25] Another point of interest which attracted many visitors was Barnet's Museum. A contemporary writer says that "all that have visited it have departed pleased and gratified. It is one of the best collections of birds and animals anywhere to be met with. They are preserved in a very superior style".[26]

Everyone admired the remarkable bridge to Goat (formerly Iris) Island, referred to as "one of the most singular pieces of engineering in the world"; it was a wooden bridge, some seven hundred feet long, resting on wooden piers, and thrown across one of the worst parts of the rapids.[27] Judge Porter's first bridge was built in 1817, but had to be replaced the following year. Goat Island is one of the beauty spots of the district, and the view from a tower and from other points on the island is described by travellers as exceedingly fine.

Almost a century has elapsed since the first suspension bridge was constructed across the river below the Falls; this was later replaced by a larger structure, and now there are three railway or highway arch bridges over the river. The development of the beauties of the district is shown by the enlargement of the park area from 154 acres in 1885 to more than 1,700 acres in 1932.

Soon after the coming of the Loyalists, mills were in operation along the Niagara River, and it was even suggested in 1799 by D. W. Smith, Surveyor-General of Upper Canada, that mills be built at Table Rock![28] After the War

[23]*Ibid.*, pp. 116-17.
[24]Patrick Shirreff: *A Tour through North America*. 1835. p. 91.
[25]S. De Veaux: *The Falls of Niagara*. 1839. p. 135.
[26]*Ibid.*, pp. 135-6.
[27]See Howison, *op. cit.*, p 118; and Basil Hall: *Forty Etchings, from Sketches made with the Camera Lucida in North America in 1827-1828*. 1929. Number V.
[28]D. W. Smith: *A Short Topographical Description of His Majesty's Province of Upper Canada* . . . . 1799. pp. 31-2.

of 1812 extensive commercialisation of the district began, and most travellers deprecated it as detracting from the natural beauty. Captain Basil Hall observed in 1827 that the scenery had been "rendered less attractive by the erection of hotels, paper manufactories, saw-mills, and numerous other raw, staring, wooden edifices".[29] Captain Marryat, in 1838, noted that "a mill has already been erected, which is a great pity. It is a contemptible disfigurement of nature's grandest work".[30]

By 1845 the region had assumed a still more business-like appearance, Sir Richard Bonnycastle observing that the beauty had been "materially injured by the Utilitarian mania". In addition to hotels and mills Bonnycastle noted the "gin palaces", refreshment booths, and numerous varieties of fakirs.[31] For many years it remained characteristic of the Falls region that visitors were exploited by those who owned cabs and other conveniences, or who operated the various amusements and "concessions" in the vicinity.

In 1841 Charles Dickens journeyed to the Falls and found in the sight "nothing of Gloom or Terror . . . ., but Peace and Beauty".[32] Many other notable visitors have added their impressions to the long list, but after 1840 there is noticeable a distinct diminution of literature on visits to the Falls. This is probably to be explained by the increased accessibility of the region, which enabled a great many more people to see its beauties rather than to depend upon reading about them. In the forties and fifties it was the custom to keep public albums at Table Rock and other points for the recording of visitors' impressions. They were, of course, filled largely with literary rubbish, though occasional true poetry was to be found.

To attract visitors to Niagara at night efforts were made in later years to illuminate the falls. The first attempts by gas were unsuccessful, but in modern times batteries of powerful electric lights have produced a beautiful effect. That the illumination was not necessary to obtain a view of the Falls even on a very dark night may be seen

[29]Basil Hall: *Travels in America in 1827-1828.* 1829. Vol. I, p. 190.
[30]F. Marryat: *Diary in America.* 1839. p. 59.
[31]Sir Richard Bonnycastle: *Canada and the Canadians.* 1846. Vol. I, p. 235.
[32]Charles Dickens: *American Notes for General Circulation.* 1842. Gadshill Edition of Dickens' *Works,* Vol. XXVIII, p. 238.

from the fact that a visitor observed that "the milky white-
ness contrasted so strongly with the surrounding darkness
that the Falls became distinctly visible when we were more
than half a mile distant".[33]

From time to time there have been extensive falls of
rock at Niagara, due to the undermining of the foundation
by the force of the torrent. In 1828 a large mass estimated
at half an acre in area fell from the centre of Horseshoe
Falls, and smaller but considerable falls occurred in 1818,
1843, 1847, 1852, and 1871, in addition to several in recent
times, the latest of which was in January, 1931.

In 1767 a large piece of Table Rock broke off, but until
1850 it remained one of the most remarkable points of interest at the Falls. On June 25th of that year practically
all of the huge projection suddenly broke away and fell
with a mighty crash into the gulf below. For many years
it had been customary for stage-coaches to drive out upon
Table Rock and remain there while the passengers alighted
and enjoyed the beauties of the park. The coachman had
unhitched his horses and was washing his stage when he
heard a warning rumble below; he made his escape just in
the nick of time, but the coach disappeared into the abyss
with hundreds of tons of rock.[34] It is estimated that the section which fell was 200 feet long, 60 feet wide and 100 feet
deep.

On March 29, 1848, another remarkable event occurred
at Niagara Falls,—a natural phenomenon that has never
been known to have happened before or since. It had been
an extremely cold winter and the ice in Lake Erie was
consequently very thick. The warm weather of early
spring loosened the ice along the shores, and a strong east
wind blew the field up the lake. About sunset the wind
suddenly changed, and a gale from the west brought the ice
down with great force and dammed up the neck of the lake
to such an extent that the flow over Niagara was impeded.
The water below Black Rock soon drained over the Falls,
and by morning the American and British channels were
only fair-sized creeks, while the water surrounding Goat

[33]Samuel Strickland: *Twenty-seven Years in Canada West.* 1853. Vol.
II, p. 248.
[34]The author does not vouch for the authenticity of the details of this
story, which may be found in John Ross Robertson: *Landmarks
of Canada.* 1917. p. 219.

James Pattison Cockburn

NIAGARA FALLS, SHOWING TABLE ROCK, ABOUT 1830

De Veaux's *The Falls of Niagara*. 1839

THE BURNING OF THE CAROLINE, 1837
The end of Mackenzie's Provisional Government on Navy Island

BLONDIN CROSSING THE NIAGARA RIVER ON
A ROPE, AUGUST 17, 1859

The great French tight-rope walker (whose real
name was Jean François Gravelet) carried
Henry Colcord on his back

Island had almost disappeared. Bare black rocks, never seen before, were now in evidence; the "thunder of waters" had departed, and the great Falls had practically gone dry. Many explorers walked about on the river bed among the huge rocks, some even salvaging timber with horses and carts. Those fortunate enough to be at Niagara on that day experienced a sensation that was unique.

Characteristic of Niagara Falls in winter is the colossal ice formation which is usually found below the Falls. This is a source of wonder to visitors, the more daring of whom make a perilous exploration of the natural bridge. The ice usually breaks up in early spring with a suddenness that makes journeys upon it foolhardy. This was tragically demonstrated some years ago when three people went to their death on cakes of floating ice, while many watched from the shore and the suspension bridges, unable to give effective aid.

Numerous spectacles of an artificial nature have been arranged at Niagara to provide additional "thrills" for visitors. On two occasions about a century ago the tavern-keepers in the vicinity purchased old schooners and sent them over the Falls to attract customers and amuse the public. From 15,000 to 20,000 people, a large crowd for the days of transportation by stage-coach, assembled in 1827 to see the first of these exhibitions. A number of animals—bears, foxes, buffaloes, cats, dogs and geese—were callously placed on the *Michigan* and it was started down the river; but as a spectacle it proved a failure, for the boat broke up in the rapids well above the Falls, a few of the poor animals reaching shore. In 1829 the schooner *Superior* was similarly sent over the Falls. The desire for such shows seems to have been very great. The man who owned the winding stairs at Table Rock once advertised that he would blow up a large section of the rock with gunpowder; and the only thing that appears to have stopped him from doing so was the objection of a business associate, who disliked the idea because it might put an end to the Cave of the Winds, where he made money conducting visitors!

An event somewhat similar to the schooner episodes occurred a few years later. On December 29, 1837, the steamship *Caroline,* used as a supply ship for Mackenzie's rebel camp on Navy Island, was cut loose by Canadian soldiers and sent in flames down the river. Samuel Strickland wrote a few years later: "Those who saw the flaming ship illuminating the country and lighting up the Falls, over which the irresistible force of one of the greatest powers of nature was impelling her, describe the scene as one of unequalled sublimity. The night was intensely dark, yet every surrounding object was distinctly visible in the wild glare caused by the *Caroline* as she rushed into the thundering abyss below".[35]

The most remarkable thing about this event, however, is that modern historical research seems to prove that the *Caroline* never reached the Falls, but broke up in the rapids a mile or two above the cataract, and that even if she had remained afloat that far, the Goat Island Bridge was low enough to have stopped her progress.[36] But the evidence that the ship sank in shallow water not far below Schlosser Landing is opposed by a large amount of contemporary evidence that the boat did go over the Falls, though it is certain that these accounts were greatly exaggerated.

In 1846 the first *Maid of the Mist,* one of the early propeller steamships in Upper Canada, began to operate in the comparatively quiet water at the foot of Niagara, where a rowboat had long carried the adventurous. In 1854 the second *Maid of the Mist* was built, and continued to run below the Falls until 1861, when the owners became involved in financial difficulties. A notable deed of daring resulted, for it was decided that an attempt would be made to run through the rapids and whirlpool in order to avoid seizure by the sheriff of the town of Niagara Falls. On June 6, 1861, the boat, in command of Captain Joel Robinson, made this extremely hazardous trip in full view of hundreds on the banks of the river, and reached Queenston in safety. It is said that Captain Robinson appeared twenty years older after his perilous ordeal.

The mighty Falls seems to inspire men to deeds of daring. Throughout the years they have continually at-

[35]Strickland, *op. cit.,* Vol. II, p. 254.
[36]See A. Watt: *The Case of Alexander McLeod.* (In *Canadian Historical Review,* Vol. XII, June, 1931.). The facts of the case were, however, similarly presented many years ago; for example, by J. C. Dent in his *The Story of the Upper Canadian Rebellion* (1885.), Vol. II, p. 55.

tempted to go over the cataract in barrels, to perform feats on a tight-rope, or to swim the Whirlpool Rapids; and while some have succeeded, numerous lives have been wasted in foolhardy attempts. In former days, too, Niagara had its records and its tragedies. It is a tradition that twenty Ottawa Indians, pursued by the Iroquois, plunged into the torrent to escape the torture which would be their lot if captured; and one man is said to have survived after going over the Falls.

In modern times many notable feats have been performed in the vicinity of Niagara Falls. On July 24, 1882, Captain Matthew Webb, the first man to swim the English Channel, lost his life while attempting to swim the Whirlpool Rapids. In 1886 Kendall, using a life-preserver, made this crossing, though he was almost exhausted at the finish. In the following year the Whirlpool was successfully navigated in a lifeboat of special construction; while in 1901 a woman made the first trip over the Horseshoe Falls in a barrel. But among the many acts of daring which have occurred in the history of Niagara, none reaches the heights of skill and nerve attained by the celebrated Frenchman, Blondin. In 1859 he performed remarkable feats on wire cables stretched across the gorge, and the following year, in the presence of the Prince of Wales, reached the acme of perfection in tight-rope walking when he carried a man on his back across the Whirlpool Rapids.

From the days of Champlain down through the centuries several thousand publications have described the Falls from one point of view or another. Some tell of individual experiences, and of the beauty of the district; others set forth the more material possibilities of power development or business activity; but perhaps the thoughts of Colonel Strickland have come to the minds of most visitors:

"Misty clouds rise from the boiling deep, while bright rainbows span the river. The more we gaze the more grand and magnificent does the scene appear. Who can behold the mighty Niagara and say 'There is no God', or forget Him 'Who hath measured the waters in the hollow of His hand, and meted out heaven with a span, and comprehended the dust of the earth in a measure, and weighed the mountains in scales, and the hills in a balance'?"[37]

[37]Strickland, *op. cit.*, Vol. II, pp. 249-50.

CHAPTER III

ALEXANDER HENRY, FUR TRADER

"Plain, unaffected, telling what he has to tell in few and simple
words, and without comment—the internal evidence of truth—render
not only the narrative, but the man himself, his personal chaɪacter,
unspeakably interesting. Wild as are the tales of his hairbreadth
escapes, I never heard the slightest impeachment of his veracity. . . .
He is the Ulysses of these parts, and to cruise among the shores,
rocks and islands of Lake Huron without Henry's *Travels*, were like
coasting Calabria and Sicily without the *Odyssey* in your head or
hand."

ANNA JAMESON.[1]

ALEXANDER HENRY, the first of a noted company of
Scottish merchants to enter the western fur trade, was
born in New Jersey in 1739. In 1760 he accompanied General Amherst's expedition against Montreal, and lost his
three bateaux, laden with goods, in the descent of the Cedars
Rapids. Undismayed by this misfortune, he returned to
Albany and secured another supply. At Montreal he heard
of the great fortunes being made at the Mackinac, and decided to enter upon an expedition thither. Though General
Gage had already granted a passport for that post to Henry
Bostwick, he finally agreed to allow Henry the same rights
in the trade, then for the first time open to British merchants because of the capture of Quebec and Montreal.

The fur traders' route to the upper lakes followed the
course of Champlain's explorations in 1615, that is, up
the Ottawa River and across to Georgian Bay by way of
Lake Nipissing and the French River; this was not only
shorter than the lake route but it avoided Lakes Ontario,
Erie and Huron, too large and open for successful navigation by birch canoe. Henry knew nothing of the fur
trade, but arranged with an experienced French-Canadian
named Campion to accompany him. The narrative of his
experiences, *Travels and Adventures in Canada and the
Indian Territories between the Years 1760 and 1776,* has a
charm similar to that of the works of Francis Parkman.

It was a particularly dangerous journey to undertake at

[1]Anna Jameson: *Winter Studies and Summer Rambles in Canada.*
1838. Vol. III, pp. 17-18.

this time, for no treaty of peace had been made with the Huron Indians, traditional allies of the French. To make matters worse, the Indian leader, Pontiac, had already aroused most of the western tribes against the British. Alexander Henry knew no fear, however, and the expedition of several heavily-laden canoes left Montreal in August, 1761. The voyage up the Ottawa, and westward to the mouth of the Rivière des Français, was uneventful, though the Indians were not always friendly. While coasting among the islands of Lake Huron Henry came upon a large village of Hurons, and small articles were here bartered for fish and dried meat. The Indians were friendly until they learned that Henry was an Englishman, whereupon they intimated "that the Indians at Michilimackmac would not fail to kill me, and that, therefore, they had a right to a share of the pillage. Upon this principle, as they said, they demanded a keg of rum, adding that if not given them they would proceed to take it. I judged it prudent to comply; on condition, however, that I should experience, at this place, no further molestation."[2]

In order to avoid, if possible, all trouble in the future, Henry decided to follow the advice of his friend and companion, Campion, to disguise himself and imitate the French *voyageur*. So he laid aside his English clothes, and covered himself "only with a cloth, passed about the middle; a shirt, hanging loose; a molton, or blanket coat; and a large, red, milled worsted cap. The next thing was to smear my face and hands with dirt and grease; and this done, I took the place of one of my men, and, when Indians approached, used the paddle with as much skill as I possessed. I had the satisfaction to find that my disguise enable me to pass several canoes without attracting the smallest notice."[3]

Michilimackinac Island, long the centre of the western fur trade, is situated near the south shore of the strait connecting Lakes Huron and Superior. The centre of the island is high, in form somewhat resembling a turtle's back, so the name Michilimackinac, "the Great Turtle", was given to it. The fort was originally established by Father Marquette about 1670, on the north side of the strait; but

[2]Alexander Henry: *Travels and Adventures in Canada and the Indian Territories, 1760-76.* 1807. pp. 33-4.
[3]*Ibid.*, pp. 34-5.

it was deserted in 1706, and six years later rebuilt, but on the south side.

In the early autumn of 1761 Henry arrived at Michili-mackinac, where he found a body of hostile Chippawa Indians encamped on the island, and the French-Canadian traders at the fort no less jealous of his presence. His position was fast becoming very dangerous when the fortunate arrival at the fort of a British force entirely changed the attitude of the Indians, most of whom immediately departed. During the next two years Alexander Henry engaged in the trade under the protection of the British garrison of one hundred men.

In 1763 there were rumours of hostile designs on the part of the Indians, but the garrison did not take them seriously. The Indians were daily assembling from every quarter in unusual numbers, and on June 4th, the birthday of George III, they announced that two tribes would play a match at baggatiway, called by the French *le jeu de la crosse*. This game was played with bat and ball, and each side had its post, planted in the ground, often a mile or more distant from the opponent's goal. At the commencement of the sport the ball was placed midway between the posts, and the game consisted in keeping the ball out of one's own territory and advancing as far as possible into that of the adversary. The course of this particular contest, and the ensuing events, are well described by Alexander Henry:

"I did not go myself to see the match because, there being a canoe prepared to depart on the following day for Montreal, I employed myself in writing letters to my friends. The game of baggatiway is necessarily attended with much violence and noise. In the ardour of the contest the ball is struck in any direction by the adversary, and nothing could be less liable to excite alarm than that the ball should be tossed over the pickets of the fort, and should be followed by all engaged in the game. This was, in fact, the strategem which the Indians employed to obtain possession of the fort.

"To be still more certain of success they had prevailed upon as many of the garrison as they could to come outside the fort. Suddenly I heard an Indian war-cry and a noise of general confusion. Going instantly to my window, I saw a crowd of Indians within the fort, furiously cutting down and scalping every Englishman they found. Amid the slaughter which was raging I observed many of the French-Canadian inhabitants of the fort calmly looking on, neither opposing the Indians nor suffering injury."[4]

When the massacre was over it was found that Lieutenant Jemette and seventy British soldiers had been killed, and the remainder of the garrison taken prisoners. Bostwick, Ezekiel Solomon (another English trader), and some 300 French-Canadian *voyageurs* were also among the captured, and another trader, Tracy, was killed. Soon afterwards the small garrisons at St. Joseph's and Green Bay were similarly compelled to surrender. Had it not been for the good offices of the French trader Cadotte at Sault Ste. Marie it is unlikely that the Chippawas would have released their prisoners.

After the capture of the fort, Henry hid for a day or two with a French family, but he was finally discovered by the Indians, who had known of his presence before the massacre. They intended to kill him, but after many hairbreadth escapes from death he was finally saved by the intervention of a chief, who adopted him into his family. At the end of a year of adventurous life in the wilds among the Indians he accompanied a band of them to civilisation by way of Georgian Bay, the Severn River, Lake Simcoe and Toronto (the name of the portage[5] ending at the mouth of the Humber River). He proceeded to Niagara, where he joined General Bradstreet's force and returned to the Mackinac *via* Detroit, hoping to recover some of his goods. Michilimackinac was captured by this expedition and remained in British occupation until 1781, when a new fort, more easily defensible, was erected on Michilimackinac Island, and the old fort allowed to decay. After the American Revolutionary War, this district became part of the United States.

Alexander Henry was long known to the Indians, and in France, as "the handsome Englishman". After his experiences at Michilimackinac he was for a time associated

[4] *Ibid.*, pp. 78-9.
[5] See the commencement of Section IV, Chapter I, for Henry's account of this part of his journey.

as a partner with trader Cadotte (or Cadot, at the post named after him, now known as Sault Ste. Marie. Cadot was the only French trader of any importance to remain in the upper country after the close of French rule.

In 1765 a regulation was adopted prohibiting white men from trading west of Detroit without a license. Henry's persistence was rewarded by the monopoly of the Lake Superior trade, and he immediately purchased four freighted canoes at twelve months' credit for 10,000 pounds of beaver, then worth 2s. 6d. a pound. He engaged twelve paddlers at 100 pounds of beaver each for the season, bought for their provision fifty bushels of Indian corn at ten pounds of beaver a bushel, and the usual allowance of tallow, and pushed westward. At Chagouamigon Bay, an arm of Lake Superior where the French had once had a trading-post, he found a destitute band of Indians, and advanced them goods to the value of 3,000 beaver skins. The Indians went off to hunt, and fully repaid this and other loans made to them, being remarkably honest in all their dealings with Henry. By 1768 he had succeeded in establishing a trade route between Michilimackinac and Kaministiquia on Lake Superior.

During the autumn of 1768 the provisions of his trading party ran short, and Henry, three French-Canadians and an Indian woman lived for over a week on a lichen "which the Chipeways call *waac* and the Canadians *tripe de roche*. . . . The woman was well acquainted with the mode of preparing the lichen for the stomach, which is done by boiling it down into a mucilage, as thick as the white of an egg. In a short time we obtained a hearty meal; for though our food was of a bitter and disagreeable taste, we felt too much joy in finding it, and too much relief in eating it, not to partake of it with appetite and pleasure. As to the rest, it saved the life of the poor woman; for the men, who had projected to kill her, would unquestionably have accomplished their purpose. One of them gave me to understand that he was not absolutely a novice in such an affair; that he had wintered in the north-west, and had been obliged to eat human flesh".[6] The same lichen saved the lives of Sir John Franklin and his party during their

[6] Henry, *op. cit.*, pp. 221-2.

THE RUINS OF FORT MICHILIMACKINAC, 1850

Paul **Kane**

WHITE MUD PORTAGE, WINNIPEG RIVER

ALEXANDER HENRY AT THE LAKE OF THE
WOODS, 1775

ALEXANDER HENRY (1739-1824)

Famous as fur trader and author

dangerous journey in 1821 across the barren lands in the vicinity of the Coppermine River.

In 1768 Henry met at Michilimackinac Alexander Baxter, from England, and formed a partnership with him with the intention of working copper mines at Ontonagan, on the shores of Lake Superior. The Duke of Gloucester and others were soon after associated with Henry and Baxter in a company for the same purpose, but the venture was not a success and ended in 1774.

On June 10, 1775, Alexander Henry, accompanied by Cadotte, left the Sault to visit the western plains, then known as the Indian Territories. The expedition consisted of "goods and provisions to the value of £3,000 sterling, on board twelve small canoes and four larger ones".[7] On July 30th they reached the Lake of the Woods by way of the Grand Portage; but it had taken seven days to carry the goods above the rapids on Pigeon River, and from its headwaters they crossed the height of land to Rainy Lake, following its course and that of Rainy River to the Lake of the Woods. Here they found an Indian village, with the inhabitants of which they traded, obtaining large quantities of wild rice and fish from the Indians. When they had made a pile of all the food they could spare, the Indians led Henry to it, and the chief addressed him in a very formal speech. Having given him the best of their stores, the chief exhorted him to give as much as possible in return: "Our white brother will not, then, forget that we are in want of everything, and especially ammunition and clothing. Having given food to our brother, he will not leave us naked and cold. Moreover my young men desire milk (rum), and beg that the white brother will share his supply with them."[8] Henry gave them a keg of gunpowder, some shot and other articles, and a keg of the coveted rum.

Coasting up the west side of Lake of the Woods he saw La Vérendrye's old fort in ruins. On August 4th the party reached the Portage du Rat, a name originating from the habit of muskrats crossing there in great numbers. They then followed the Winnipeg River to its mouth and visited an amicable tribe of Indians, the Cristinaux, on the shores of Lake Winnipeg. These Indians considered it an honour

[7] *Ibid.*, p. 236.   [8] *Ibid.*, p. 243. (paraphrased).

to lend their wives to friends, so "some of my men entered into agreements with the respective husbands, in virtue of which they embarked the women in the canoes, promising to return them the next year. The women so selected consider themselves as honoured; and the husband who should refuse to lend his wife would fall under the condemnation of the sex in general".[9]

After leaving this tribe Henry was joined by the Frobisher brothers, Paterson, and Peter Pond, one of the earliest English-speaking fur traders to enter the North-West. Together they proceeded to the Saskatchewan River, the united fleet numbering thirty canoes manned by 130 men. They ascended the Saskatchewan, reaching Cumberland House, post of the Hudson's Bay Company, on October 26th. Here they separated, Pond travelling to Fort Dauphin, Cadotte to Fort des Prairies, and the Frobishers and Henry, with ten canoes, towards the Churchill River.

On January 20, 1776, their provisions were exhausted except for one cake of chocolate. This misfortune resulted from a very heavy fall of snow, which prevented their progress for many days. Surrounded by vast herds of wolves, the indomitable traders made a breakfast of hot chocolate and marched onward.

"Despair is not made for man. Before sunset we discovered on the ice some remains of the bones of an elk, left there by the wolves. Having instantly gathered them, we encamped; and, filling our kettle, prepared ourselves a meal of strong and excellent soup. The greater part of the night was passed in boiling and regaling on our booty; and early in the morning we felt ourselves strong enough to proceed."[10]

Although he did not know it, Henry had penetrated almost as far as the great Athabasca River system. The trade was brisk and lucrative in the vicinity of the Churchill and Lake Arabuthcow (Athabasca); from twenty to thirty Indians arrived daily at his post, and he purchased some 12,000 beaver skins, besides many other choice pelts of otter and marten. The Indians described to him the Peace River country, the Stony or Rocky Mountains, "from which the distance to the salt lake, meaning the Pacific Ocean, was not great".[11]

[9]*Ibid.*, p. 249   [10]*Ibid.*, p. 271.   [11]*Ibid.*, p. 324.

On July 4th, the trade having been completed, Henry and Frobisher set out on their return journey to the Grand Portage, from which they proceeded to Montreal, where they arrived on October 15, 1776. Alexander Henry had been absent from Montreal for fifteen years and two months. After a visit to Europe he continued his interest in the fur trade and carried on business as a general merchant until his death on April 4, 1824. He was for many years prominent in public life. In 1807 he published an account of his adventures, which stand out among the most perilous in the annals of the Canadian fur trade.

SECTION II
SETTLEMENT

CHAPTER I

THE GLENGARRY HIGHLANDERS

"I beg to state that the County of Glengarry has on every occasion been distinguished for good conduct, and will on any emergency turn out more fighting men in proportion to its population than any other in Her Majesty's dominions."[1]

BETWEEN 1750 and the outbreak of the American Revolution a large number of families from the Highlands of Scotland emigrated to New York State where they settled in the Mohawk Valley near Johnstown, the home of Sir William Johnson. Many of these Highlanders were Jacobites, whose previous activities are thus summarised by the historian of Glengarry:

"Conspicuous among the Jacobites were the people of Glengarry. With other Scottish Cavaliers, they had rallied around Montrose, and 'throughout his campaigns were one of the mainsprings which kept up the astonishing movements of the chivalrous enterprise'; they were foremost among the Highland forces under John Graham of Claverhouse, the Viscount of Dundee, and bore the brunt at Killiecrankie, when that great leader fell; in greater number than almost any other Highland Clan they joined the Earl of Mar in 1715. . . . In 1745 their leaders were the most trusted adherents of Prince Charles, and their men as brave as the bravest of his soldiers; they paid the penalty like men of valour as they were, some in death, others in expatriation, and all, from the proud Chief to the humblest of the clansmen, in the devastation of their homes.

'They stood to the last, and when standing was o'er,
All sullen and silent they dropped the claymore,
And yielded, indignant, their necks to the blow,
Their homes to the flame, and their lands to the foe'."[2]

The Highland emigration to the State of New York was caused largely by the distress in Scotland. Chieftains were

[1]Lieut.-Colonel Carmichael to Lieut.-General Sir James Macdonell, December, 1840.
[2]J.A.Macdonell: *Sketches of Glengarry in Canada.* 1893. pp. 6-7.

no longer able to keep a large retinue of retainers, and dispossessed their tenants, turning their estates into sheep farms. Particularly during the Napoleonic Wars the Imperial Government prevented emigration, and, many of those who attempted to leave the country were pressed into the army or navy; others wandered about in search of employment and food. The same causes led to the movement at the close of the eighteenth century and afterwards to settle Highlanders in Canada.

During the Revolutionary War most of the Scots in New York State remained staunch Loyalists, large numbers of them taking up arms against the rebels. As a result they were ill-treated during the last years of the struggle, and sought permission to come to Canada where they could remain under the British flag. As early as 1779 a petition of twenty-four families was forwarded to the British Government asking that some arrangement be effected to enable them to emigrate; and in succeeding years further memorials were sent. In his *Reminiscences* Alexander Macdonell stated that the first Highlanders in Upper Canada numbered about 300, the followers of an Irish priest named McKenna. By 1776 they had arrived at Orange (Albany), in New York State, and came to Canada some time later in order that they might enjoy the Roman Catholic religion without interference.[3]

It was not, however, until the Revolutionary War was over, in 1783, that it was possible to disband the King's Royal Regiment of New York (usually known as the Royal Yorkers), and the Royal Highland Emigrant Regiment. The officers and men of the First Battalion of the former unit, with their families, had been stationed at the close of the War at Isle aux Noix and Carleton Island; these Highlanders, 1,462 in number, settled in 1784 in the first five townships west of the Quebec boundary—Lancaster, Charlottenburg, Cornwall, Osnabruck and Williamsburg. This regiment was Sir John Johnson's corps, and most of its members had been his dependents and retainers in the Mohawk Valley. Most of the Second Battalion of the same regiment settled farther west, in Lennox and Prince Edward Counties. Many men of the 84th, or Royal High-

[3]Alexander Macdonell: *Reminiscences*. 1888. p. 13.

land Emigrant Regiment, also settled in Glengarry and vicinity. Williamstown was the centre of the settlement along the front of Glengarry, and New Johnstown (Cornwall), in Stormont, was the main government depot for the whole district; the latter village had a few inhabitants as early as 1776.

The approach of the Loyalists to the St. Lawrence was often made under difficulties which caused extreme hardship. Many men, women and children walked long distances through swamp and forest, suffering innumerable privations. An example of the experiences of these refugees is related by John MacLennan:

"A man whom I knew as an useful member of the community was the subject of the following incident. His mother carried two young children on her back. In the weary journey through the woods she thought her burden had become lighter, and discovered that she had dropped one. On retracing her steps for some distance, she found the youngster quietly sleeping beside a decayed log over which she had passed, with hands begrimed with earth. He lived to an old age, well-known by the name of 'Spogan Dubh' (black paws)—the exclamation of his mother on finding him. One of the party, coming all the way from Georgia, told the story of the company feasting on a dog, to avoid starvation—his meagre share being a paw."[4]

The last part of the Loyalists' trek was in some cases slightly easier. Those who approached Canada by way of Lake Champlain were sometimes met by military bateaux, which transported them to the St. Lawrence *viâ* the Richelieu River. From Sorel they made the laborious and tedious trip up the St. Lawrence in similar open boats, and upon their arrival at New Johnstown they encamped in tents until the land which the government agent awarded them had been properly surveyed.

The generous land grants which were made to these soldier Loyalists were based upon the rank that each man had held in the army. Each private soldier received one hundred acres on the river front and two hundred acres remote; fifty acres were allowed in addition to his wife and to each child, while each son and daughter upon coming of

[4]Cited in John MacLennan: *The Early Settlement of Glengarry* in *Transactions* of the Celtic Society of Montreal, 1884-7. p. 114.

age was to receive an additional two hundred acres. Officers' grants were considerably larger, as much as five thousand acres being given to field officers. The settlement of Glengarry County was probably military to a greater extent than that of any other section of the province. Each township was assigned to a corps, the lots were then numbered and placed in a hat, and each soldier in turn drew his grant and went immediately to his future home. Occasionally some of the settlers afterwards exchanged lots in order that old comrades might be alongside one another. As in other parts of Upper Canada, Roman Catholics and Protestants were, as a general rule, located separately.

The government dealt generously with the Loyalists in respect to supplies as well as land. Most of them had had all their possessions in the United States confiscated, and came to their new home with little or nothing. That their sacrifices were appreciated by the Imperial Government was very apparent in the plans made for their reception in Canada. Difficulties of transportation, however, made it impossible to give the St. Lawrence Loyalists as much as was distributed to those in the Maritime Provinces. The latter settlers received lumber, bricks, ploughs and even church bells, but such things were not given to the Glengarry Highlanders. Hoes and spades had to be substituted for ploughs in almost every case, and each settler had to obtain most of his building material from the forests.

For three years they were supplied with most of the necessaries of life,—food, clothes, seed, farm animals and implements. Coarse cloth suitable for trousers was supplied, and Indian blankets for coats; boots were made out of skins or heavy cloth. In addition to a hoe, a mattock and a spade, an axe was given to each settler, and a crosscut saw and a whip-saw to every two families, or, in some instances, to every four. It was intended to give a cow to each two families but the supply was insufficient. Each group of five families received a set of tools, and a "firelock" or musket; muskets were later given to every family.

A few ploughs were brought into the settlement soon afterwards, and agents were sent even to the United States to obtain supplies of seed-wheat for distribution. Portable corn-mills, run by hand, were given out, and efforts made to erect saw-mills and grist-mills as soon as possible. Some settlers were allowed to borrow military tents for temporary purposes, and boats were provided at convenient points along the river for their use. The Imperial Government ordered a reduction in the rations soon after the beginning of the settlement along the river, but Governor Sir Frederick Haldimand disobeyed the instructions and continued the supplies in full.

Pioneer life was similar along the St. Lawrence to that in all other early settlements. The inhabitants met in "bees" to help one another in the erection of rough log shanties, which were plastered inside and out with clay. An ample hearth made of flat stones was always prominent, and as no boards to make a door were available at first, a blanket suspended from the inside frequently took its place. After a time four small panes of glass were fitted into a rough sash for the one small window, and the shanty was complete. The staple food was pork, and wolves were then so numerous that it was unsafe to smoke the meat outside during the night.

Prominent among the families or clans in the Loyalist immigration to Glengarry were the Macdonells, no less than eighty-four men of that name receiving grants of land. For many years the men of this clan filled most of the important positions, both civil and military, in the district, two of them, the brothers John and Hugh, being members of Simcoe's first parliament, 1792-96. Sir John Johnson became at the close of the Revolutionary War Inspector-General of the Six Nation Indians, and never permanently settled along the St. Lawrence. A large piece of land between Glengarry and Stormont was offered to him, and reserved for the Indians when he declined it. He accepted some land near Stone House Point, in the front of Glengarry, and also owned a large tract near Williamstown, so named by him in honour of his father. He built the first mills there, and gave twelve acres of land as the site of a fair-ground for the counties, a location which later became the grounds of the Glengarry Agricultural Society. Sir John lost 200,000 acres of land in the United States, undoubtedly the heaviest sacrifice made by any Loyalist. He died in 1830 in the 89th year of his age.

The settlement of Stormont and Dundas was closely connected with that of Glengarry, though in Stormont nearly one-third of the first settlers were German Loyalists. In Dundas, too, there were many of these worthy men, refugees from the banks of the Rhine at the commencement of the eighteenth century, who had emigrated to England and then to New York State. Afterwards many removed to the Mohawk Valley, where they were soon to serve in Sir John Johnson's Loyalist regiment; and at the close of the Revolutionary War they were once more forced to migrate, this time to the banks of the mighty St. Lawrence.

In honour of the chief of the Macdonnells the most easterly county of Upper Canada was called Glengarry. Similarly the Loyalist and later Highland immigrants named most of the settlements after the neighbourhoods in Scotland from which they had come. Breadalbane, Dunvegan, Eigg, Glenelg, Strathglass, Uist and Little Knoydart were among the early names of sections of various townships, while post office and village were called McCrimmon, Athol, Glen Roy, Glen Donald, and many another appellation dear to the Scottish heart; Alexandria, formerly called Priest's Mills, was named in honour of Bishop Macdonell, Martintown after a lieutenant in the Royal Yorkers; and so one might go through a long list of place-names in the Highlander settlements.

In 1792, when Lieutenant-Governor and Mrs. Simcoe were travelling up the St. Lawrence into the newly-created province of Upper Canada, the Glengarry Highlanders demonstrated their loyalty by holding a reception:

"At a small inn on the Pointe au Bodet we found the principal inhabitants of the Township of Glengarry (Highlanders in their national dress). They came to meet the Governor, who landed to speak to them. They preceded us in their boat, a piper with them, towards Glengarry House, Mr. McDonell's, where the gentlemen went."[5]

The Macdonell referred to by Mrs. Simcoe was Colonel John, once a captain in Butler's Rangers; his home at Glengarry Point was one of the first stone houses in Upper Canada. The Simcoes had breakfast with Colonel Macdonell next day, and then proceeded to St. Regis, where

[5]*Diary of Mrs. John Graves Simcoe*, June 24, 1792.

they inspected the Iroquois Indian village in which the Rev. Alexander Macdonell had laboured as a priest for five years.

Towards the close of the eighteenth century a large number of Scottish Highlanders left their native land owing to the general badness of the times, and were induced by the presence of their Loyalist compatriots in Canada to locate in Glengarry County. The first of these settlers, 500 in number, arrived in 1786 in charge of their priest, the Rev. Alexander Macdonell. They were chiefly relatives of their leader, and came from Knoydart in Glengarry. These immigrants were located on land in the back townships of Roxborough and Finch, in Stormont, and Lochiel (then part of Lancaster) and Kenyon, in Glengarry, which were later filled up by subsequent settlers, almost all Highlanders. In 1792 a number of the Macdonells of Greenfield arrived in Glengarry, and from time to time numerous other settlers, among them many McLeods, Camerons, McPhersons and Macmillans, who came in 1796. Lochiel received most of its first inhabitants at this time, though the name of the township, commemorating the noted chief of the Camerons, was given in 1816 when the township was formed by cutting off the northern part of Lancaster.

At the close of the century there was hardly a Scottish clan that was not represented in Glengarry. But the early inhabitants of the district were not entirely of Celtic origin: Lancaster Township received its name from natives of Lancashire, England, who were early settled there; and among other nationalities were Hessian soldiers of George III who had come into the front of Charlottenburg in May, 1785.

For many years the Rev. Alexander Macdonell ministered to the Roman Catholics of Glengarry and Stormont, and in 1787 erected the "Blue Chapel" in the parish of St. Raphael in the former county. His successor, another Alexander Macdonell, later became a bishop and was well-known throughout the province, becoming even more important than his predecessor in the work of settlement along the shores of the St. Lawrence.

Presbyterianism was established in Glengarry in the same year that Alexander Macdonell erected the first Roman

Catholic church. In 1787 the Rev. John Bethune, Chaplain of the First Battalion of the Royal Highland Emigrant Regiment, organized a congregation at Williamstown, and preached also at Lancaster, Cornwall and Martintown. The first church of this denomination in Glengarry, and, in fact, in Upper Canada, was a frame building erected in Lancaster in 1796.

In 1803 the Rev. Alexander Macdonell, first Roman Catholic Bishop of Upper Canada, superintended a large emigration to Glengarry, consisting of Highlanders, "mostly Macdonells, and partly disbanded soldiers of the Glengarry Fencible Regiment, with their families and immediate connections".[6] Many of these men had had a chequered career. In 1792 an emigrant ship from the Island of Barra was damaged in a storm in the Hebrides, and put in the port of Greenock, landing the emigrants in a helpless condition without any provision for their maintenance. The Rev. Alexander Macdonell, then a missionary in Scotland, persuaded some manufacturers of Glasgow to give these people employment, though there were great difficulties in doing so owing to the dislike of Roman Catholics arising from the recent Lord George Gordon riots. Some 600 secured employment until British exports were reduced as a result of the war with France, whereupon they were again destitute.

Macdonell then petitioned the king that a regiment be formed of these men, and the result was the establishment of the first Glengarry Fencibles, the first Roman Catholic regiment since the Reformation; of this unit the young priest was gazetted chaplain, although it was at that time against the law for any Roman Catholic to hold such a position. Between 1795 and 1802 the Fencibles saw service in Guernsey and Ireland, but the Peace of Amiens closed the French War and the corps was disbanded.

Macdonell wished to settle the men in eastern Upper Canada and was finally successful in obtaining permission to do so, after he had refused suggestions that they be sent to Trinidad, Nova Scotia, New Brunswick and Sault Ste. Marie. In addition to the members of the regiment the emigration included their families and some other High-

[6]Lord Hobart, Secretary of State for the Colonies, to Lieut.-Governor Hunter of Upper Canada, March 1, 1803.

landers closely connected with them. According to the instructions of Lord Hobart, Secretary of State for the Colonies, the land was to be granted to them "in the proportion of 1,200 acres to Mr. Macdonell and 200 to every family he may introduce into the colony".[7] In the same year that the Fencibles arrived a shipload of 1,100 emigrants, chiefly from Glenelg and Kintail, joined their compatriots in Glengarry after a voyage of four months during which they had run into wintry weather off the coast of Labrador. These emigrations gave to Canada a large number of prominent men, noted in parliamentary and industrial life as well as in military annals.

Both religion and education received an impetus in 1803 when John Strachan, later Bishop of the Church of England, was ordained and appointed to Cornwall. In addition to his parochial work he commenced taking pupils, gradually forming the famous Cornwall Grammar School. Here were educated many men later influential in public affairs, among them Chief Justice Robinson, the Hon. J. B. Macaulay, the Hon. Jonas Jones and the Hon. Archibald McLean. The *Upper Canada Gazette* of August 24, 1805, contains an account of one of the earliest Public Examinations of the pupils of this school. On July 31st many notables were present at Cornwall, and a program typical of early private schools was staged.

"The students underwent a rigid examination as well at the instance of the gentlemen of learning who attended, as of the Revd. preceptor, in the following order:

"The Latin classics, Arithmetic, Book Keeping, Elements of Mathematics, Elements of Geography, of natural and civil History. The boys acquitted themselves with great credit. . . . . The whole was interspersed with different pieces of poetry and prose, many of the most humorous cast, composed for the occasion."[8]

While many of the Loyalist Highlanders and the later immigrants had received little or no schooling, yet the inhabitants of Glengarry were among the first in Upper Canada to take active steps to secure the advantages of education for those who could ill afford to attend private schools. In 1804 the Rev. John Bethune and ten other men

[7]*Ibid.*   [8]*Upper Canada Gazette*, August 24, 1805.

of the county petitioned the legislature of Upper Canada
to establish common (public) schools. The government refused, however, and the principle of elementary education
was not approved until 1816, though provision had earlier
been made for grammar (secondary) schools. In 1817 the
Township of Charlottenburg alone had twelve common
schools, a large number in comparison with most other sections of Upper Canada.

Among other enterprises in which Glengarry men were
prominent was the North-West Company. Among the
partners of this great Scottish organisation were Duncan
Cameron, later member for Glengarry in the Assembly,
John MacGillivray, afterwards a member of the Legislative Council, John Macdonell, Angus Macdonell, Alexander G. Macdonell, Hugh McGillis, and the noted explorer,
David Thompson; all of these men were closely associated
with Glengarry by birth, family connection or residence.

Lumbering was early an industry of paramount importance in the counties fronting the St. Lawrence, and the
wild and turbulent life of the lumberjack is vividly described in Ralph Connor's *The Man from Glengarry*.
Many of the Highlanders neglected their farms to engage
in the more adventurous and more remunerative lumber
trade. Pine trees over one hundred feet in height and
weighing twenty-five tons were hauled by from twelve to
sixteen teams of horses or oxen to the riverside and floated
to Quebec, where there was a ready market for masts. Oak,
elm and ash trees were often used by the settler for various
purposes, but it was customary to burn beech and maple
logs as worthless except for their ashes, which were usually
carefully gathered and sold to merchants to be made into
potash.

The pioneers occupied their summers in burning piles
of logs, and in making the land ready for wheat, which was
hoed in by hand in the fall. Winters were long and steady,
and during them every man was in the woods felling trees
and clearing the way for more fallow land. Though not a
few of the inhabitants were primarily interested in lumbering, John Howison, who visited Glengarry in 1818, believed that "every farmer will certainly soon become independent." He considered, however, that the inhabitants

A. Sherriff Scott

Courtesy of the Lake of the Woods Milling Company

THE LANDING OF THE UNITED EMPIRE LOYALISTS AT
ST. JOHN, N.B., 1783

THE CORNWALL GRAMMAR SCHOOL IN 1845

THE GLENGARRY CAIRN

Erected on a small island in Lake St. Francis to commemorate the
patriotism of Glengarry during the War of 1812 and the Rebellion of
1837

were "blunt and uncultivated", and noticed that few had
over fifty or sixty acres of land cleared, while most had
little more than half that amount; he disliked their homes,
too, finding that "a very great majority are built of logs
and contain only one apartment."[9]

To exemplify the general development of the more settled
sections along the St. Lawrence at that time may be taken
the condition of Charlottenburg Township. From a report
prepared by the chief inhabitants on January 5, 1818, at the
request of Robert Gourlay, we learn that this township
had twelve common schools, one church and three meeting-
houses of the Church of Scotland, one church and one meeting-house of the Roman Catholic Church, one minister, two
priests, two medical practitioners, twelve stores, eighteen
taverns, six saw-mills, a carding-mill and four grist-mills.
In June, 1816, the township had 500 inhabited houses and
2,500 inhabitants. [10]

During the lifetime of the early settlers in Glengarry
Gaelic was in general use. In 1819 John Goldie recorded in
his diary that he entered Glengarry, "of which the Highlanders boast so much", and observed that they retained all
the habits and customs of the Highlands of Scotland.[11]
The use of the national costume and language continued
many years longer. In fact such importance did the inhabitants attach to Gaelic that "a knowledge of it was considered a necessary qualification for the Presbyterian
pulpit."[12] In 1852 Colonel Alexander Chisholm compiled a
census of the inhabitants of Glengarry, and his tabulation
shows a great predominance of Scots. He enumerated the
people of the various Highland clans then living there.
There were 3,228 Macdonells or McDonalds, and thirty other
clans numbered from fifty to 545 each.[13]

Owing to the lowness of the ground along the river
front, land transportation developed slowly in Glengarry,
and on that account comparatively few early travellers
visited the county. When the Simcoes passed through in

[9]John Howison: *Sketches of Upper Canada.* 1821. 3rd Edition. 1825,
   pp. 34-39.
[10]Robert Gourlay: *A Statistical Account of Upper Canada.* 1822.
   Vol. I, pp. 559-64.
[11]John Goldie: *Diary*, June 7, 1819.
[12]MacLennan, *op. cit.*, p. 120.
[13]Colonel Chisholm's census may be found in J. A. Macdonell, *op. cit*,
   pp. 156-8.

1792 such roads as had been opened along the St. Lawrence were largely of log construction, and Mrs. Simcoe noted the dangerous corduroy bridges "which we everywhere met with".[14] Ox-cart and lumber-wagon on land followed canoe and bateau on the river as means of transportation. But in 1825 the three counties (Glengarry, Stormont and Dundas) had progressed, for within their boundaries were eleven two-wheeled gigs, eleven "pleasure wagons" with leather springs, and one closed carriage. Brightly-coloured stage-coaches were soon in operation; but the great event in the district occurred in 1834, when Chief Justice Robinson cut the first sod of the Cornwall Canal. It took eight years to complete, but as a result of its commencement there were many improvements in the district long before it was finished.

Glengarry was among the earliest counties to develop battalions of militia. The Glengarry Light Infantry took part in the defence of York in April, 1813, as well as in many other engagements during that war. This regiment was raised by the Macdonells, one of whom, Colonel John, was aide-de-camp to Sir Isaac Brock during the first months of the campaign of 1812, and fought and died beside "The Hero of Upper Canada" at Queenston Heights. During the war large numbers of the able-bodied men of the three counties were under arms in distant fields, and as a result Cornwall was occupied by American troops in 1813. Brigades of bateaux were continually attacked while proceeding up the St. Lawrence, resulting in great inconvenience to the settlers in the district. In the last weeks of 1813 hard-fought battles at Chateauguay and Chrysler's Farm resulted in British victories which cleared the district of the invaders. "Red George" Macdonell was one of the most heroic officers engaged in the St. Lawrence region.

Not only in the War of 1812 but also during the Rebellion of 1837-38 were the regiments of militia from the shores of the St. Lawrence conspicuous for their gallantry. As a memorial of Glengarry's patriotism the inhabitants erected, at the close of the Rebellion, an immense cairn of stones on one of the small islands in Lake St. Francis. This monument was sixty feet high, and was surmounted by a

[14]Simcoe, *op. cit.*, June 26, 1792.

flagstaff inserted in the muzzle of a cannon placed in an upright position. The Glengarry Cairn is a notable historical landmark, remaining to this day to commemorate the enthusiasm of the men, women and children who had united in its erection.

CHAPTER II

CARLETON COUNTY AND BYTOWN

"As Bytown is not overrun with Americans it may probably turn out a moral, well-behaved town, and afford a lesson to its neighbours."[1]

"Ottawa is a sub-arctic lumber-village converted by royal mandate into a political cock-pit."[2]

THE settlement of the County of Carleton is to some extent connected with Philemon Wright's American colony across the river. Wright, a native of Massachusetts, made exploration trips up the Ottawa River in 1796 and succeeding years, and was attracted by the magnificent forests in Hull Township, where he determined to found a settlement. In 1800 he conducted a party of thirty settlers, well-provided with implements, horses and oxen, to this district; the journey up the Ottawa was made over the ice in covered sleighs, and a slow trip it was, for great precautions had to be taken to make certain that the ice was thick enough to bear the weight of the settlers and their supplies. Wright established his settlement first near the Chaudière Falls, and later on the present site of Hull, of which he was the founder.

The Indians were displeased at the idea of having white neighbours, but withdrew their objections on being paid $20 in cash. Between 1802 and 1804 a grist-mill, a saw-mill, a hemp-mill and a tannery were erected in the village very appropriately called Wright's Mills. In 1807 Wright inaugurated the lumber industry in the Ottawa Valley when he took his first raft of squared timber down to Quebec from the Gatineau River. Wright's Mills, later named Hull, grew rapidly, containing in 1828 nearly 1,000 inhabitants, almost all of them Americans. Wright spent the rest of his life surveying and clearing the land, building roads, and improving his settlement, and died in 1839 at the age of seventy-nine.

Carleton County was named in honour of the second British Governor of Canada, Sir Guy Carleton (Lord

[1]John MacTaggart: *Three Years in Canada.* 1829. Vol. II, p. 219.
[2]Goldwin Smith.

Dorchester), and within its confines there are at present ten townships—Fitzroy, Gloucester, Goulbourn, Huntley, March, Marlborough, Nepean, North Gower, Osgoode and Torbolton,—most of them named after English nobility. Several of these were not created until some years after their settlement. Previous to the organisation of Carleton County, Marlborough and Nepean belonged to the County of Grenville, while Gloucester and Osgoode were part of Russell; and the present County of Lanark was originally a part of Carleton, the boundaries of many of the counties of Upper Canada being frequently altered for election purposes, or to suit the whim of someone in authority.

For some years the south side of the river opposite Hull was avoided by settlers because of the rocky cliffs which are characteristic of the district. Many lots in Nepean Township were drawn by United Empire Loyalists who never settled upon them. The first resident in the district appears to have been Jehiel Collins who erected, about 1809, a small store and dock near the foot of the canoe portage on the south side of the Chaudière Falls. Some years later he sold out to Caleb T. Bellows who built a larger wharf, and Nepean Point was known as Bellows' Landing until 1811, when, with the establishment of the village of Richmond a few miles away, it took the name Richmond Landing.

Rice Honeywell drew land in Nepean in 1792 and gave his son Ira 1,000 acres on the condition that he would settle on it. In November, 1810, Ira chopped four acres and built a log hut three miles above Chaudière Falls, near the bank of the river, the exact location being known as "Lot 26, Concession 1, Ottawa Front." After he had prepared his future home Honeywell travelled to Prescott, married, and returned in February, 1811, with his wife and some household effects. The difficult journey was made in a jumper, or ox-sled, and they travelled through the bush by way of the Putnam Settlement, near Merrickville, and down the Rideau River to the falls known as the Hog's Back, from which Honeywell cut out a trail to their home. The Honeywells were the first permanent residents of Nepean Township, and were without neighbours until settlers arrived in 1814 and subsequent years. Early in 1818 only ten families had settled in Nepean.

The first settler in Gloucester Township was Bradish Billings, formerly an employee of Philemon Wright in the lumber industry. Billings built a log house in 1812, and the following year married Lamira Dow, a teacher at Merrickville. For six years the Billings were the only settlers at Gloucester. Mrs. Billings and a young child on one occasion shot the Hog's Back Rapids in a canoe, a feat never attempted even by Indians and raftsmen.

In the early summer of 1818 the first extensive emigration to Carleton County was arranged. The 99th Regiment of Foot, including the former 99th and 100th Regiments, was stationed at Quebec after having served in Wellington's Peninsular Campaign and in the latter part of the War of 1812-14. The condition of post-war Britain was unfavourable for their return, so they were offered the chance to settle in Canada and chose the Upper Province. A military settlement had already been established in the vicinity of Perth-on-the-Tay early in 1816, and during 1817 and 1818 settlers had begun to come over the forest trails to Beckwick Township in Lanark, and to Goulbourn in Carleton, although there was as yet no decision by the government to push settlement eastward into Nepean.

Towards the end of August, 1818, however, arrangements had been made to disband the 99th Regiment, and several hundred settlers left Lachine and proceeded up the Ottawa, disembarking at Richmond Landing. Their families lived here in tents for some weeks while the men were engaged in blazing a road to the headquarters of the settlement, to be known as Richmond in honour of the Governor-General. Having located their land, transported supplies, and blazed a trail through to Chapman's Ranch, three miles distant, the men removed their families to the vicinity of the government store at this point. Grants of land had been made, varying from 100 acres to a private to 800 acres to a captain. Free transport of themselves, their families and possessions had been provided, and a small pension of from 6d. to 1s. a day. Army rations were allowed for the first year, and each head of a family was given an axe, a broad-axe, a mattock, a pickaxe, a spade, a shovel, a hoe, a scythe, a draw-knife, a hammer, a handsaw, two scythe stones, two files, twelve panes of glass and a pound of putty, twelve pounds of nails, a camp kettle, and a bed tick and blanket. A cross-cut saw, a whip-saw and a grindstone were allotted to every five settlers, and two complete sets of carpenter's tools were provided for the use of the settlement generally. Provision was made for the supply of a schoolmaster, a man named Read being sent out early in 1819 and paid £50 *per annum* by the government. He was the first teacher in Carleton County. Among the members of this military settlement was Captain Lyon, who built on the Jock River the first mill in the county.

Previous to this immigration there had been but few settlers in Nepean Township. Chapman had arrived as early as 1815, and William Bell had opened a log tavern where Bell's Corners is to-day. Richmond was located on the Jock, or as it was now named in honour of one of the English estates of the new Governor-General, the Goodwood River. By 1820, six years before the village of Bytown began its existence, Richmond was quite a flourishing village containing about a dozen general stores, four breweries and two distilleries, a saw-mill, a grist-mill, a carding-mill, and numerous trade workshops. It had a town hall, which still stands, and when the village was first planned six acres were set aside for a park, and "grants of two, four and six acres each for the residence of the clergy, for the church and for the graveyard of each of the three 'established' churches—the Anglican, Presbyterian and Roman Catholic, no 'dissenters' being deemed worthy".[3]

In the vicinity of Richmond tragically died the Duke after whom it was named. In the summer of 1819 he paid the settlement a visit and was bitten by a pet fox which proved to be in a rabid state, the bite causing his death soon after. This once important village, like many another stirring settlement of pioneer days, was fated to dwindle into insignificance. It has long been "a quiet hamlet, sleeping in the summer days on the bank of the River Jock, whose waters, with the disappearance of the forests that with such a beautiful luxuriance then covered the low banks of the stream, have dwindled in the shallow reaches almost to disappearance".[4]

[3]Andrew Haydon: *Pioneer Sketches of the Bathurst District.* 1925. p. 69.
[4]*Ibid.,* pp. 69-70.

In addition to the soldier settlers in the district, another group of immigrants, from Perthshire, Scotland, entered the same region in 1818, but they were settled chiefly in Beckwith Township, in Lanark. These families paid their own passage to Quebec and were conveyed the rest of their journey at the expense of the government.

The religious life of the entire region was largely in charge of the Roman Catholic, Presbyterian and Methodist clergy. The Rev. Alexander Macdonell, of Glengarry fame, and after him Father Heron, made periodic visits to Richmond until 1825-26, when the first Roman Catholic church was erected. The first resident minister was the Rev. Glen, a Presbyterian. There were no regular Anglican services until 1819, when the Rev. Michael Harris of Perth began to make periodical visits to Richmond. Methodism found its way to the district from the Rideau and Perth circuits, and in later years the Rev. Ezra Healy became a resident preacher.

The settlement of Goulbourn and March Townships took place at about the same time and in much the same fashion as that of Nepean. Officers, non-commissioned officers and men arrived in 1819-20, the officers taking most of the land along the Grand River, as early settlers delighted to call the Ottawa, and the men filling the rear concessions. The soil of March Township is the poorest in the county, and the locations appear to have been chosen largely because of their excellent situation in the vicinity of the noted beauty spot, Chats Falls. Some of the retired military and naval officers who came to March received grants of from 1,600 to 5,000 acres. The first to settle was Captain Monk, who arrived in June, 1819, before the township had even been surveyed. One of the most progressive and enterprising of the the early inhabitants was Hamnet Pinhey, who was well-to-do when he came from England, and who used his wealth for the betterment of the district by establishing a grist-mill, a saw-mill and a church.

Osgoode Township was settled later than the others, and chiefly by Scots, while in the rest of the country the various British nationalities were to be found—English, Irish, Scotch and Welsh. A considerable number of the soldier settlers in all townships did not remain long on their

MARCH TOWNSHIP, LAKE CHAUDIÈRE, 1840
The log building at the left was the post office

THE HOG'S BACK RAPIDS IN THE THIRTIES

BYTOWN, ABOUT 1830

This picture originally belonged to Colonel By, and was presented to the Dominion Archives by Bishop Roper

land,—in fact some sold their portion as soon as they had drawn it. The business of gambling in land grants was early established in Upper Canada, and the purchase and sale of Loyalists' or soldiers' rights was of very common occurrence, such speculation usually tending to retard actual settlement.

In the development of Carleton County the lumber industry has been of paramount importance, and for many years the most characteristic sight along the Ottawa was the large rafts of squared timber making their way to Quebec. A considerable part of the population of Bytown and of the other settlements was transient in early times, many lumbermen spending the summer there and wintering in the woods. Whisky was plentiful, and the life of the lumberman was never conducive to peace and quietness; but there were many settlers who were interested in the advancement of the county, and these were foremost in establishing schools and churches.

The county's first church was opened in March Township in 1819, and by 1851 there were thirty in Carleton. Most of the early public schools in the district were conducted by ex-soldiers, who received about $100 a year, usually payable in wheat, and who boarded with the scholars' families in turn, free of charge. That teachers often had great difficulty in collecting their salaries may be seen from the experience of Lamira Dow (Mrs. Billings). Her salary was $7 a month in notes payable in wheat at Brockville. On one occasion she walked there from Merrickville to collect her money, but was refused as the wheat had not arrived; so she returned, gathered the wheat from the settlers, took it to Brockville, and collected her account in goods! In the early days many people taught their own children, and Mrs. Honeywell, wife of one of the first settlers, educated her neighbours' children as well; but educational facilities gradually became available in the form of common and grammar schools. In 1850 there were seventy-five common (public) schools in the county, and Richmond had a grammar school in 1854, in addition to the one at Bytown.

The Hon. James Sheard was long a leading spirit in the development of fairs, and in agricultural advancement gen-

erally. The first fair in Carleton County was held in Bytown in 1829, and though it is described as the greatest, yet

"'Twas not to buy or sell they came;
They all assembled, wild and free
To have a ranting, roaring spree!"[5]

The fair ended in a horse-race, and then a fight between
"grangers" (lumbermen) and "shiners" (Irish labourers),
so the event was withdrawn for some years. A few years
later Richmond had two fairs annually, described as "the
occasions of wild brawls between the lumbermen and ex-
soldiers, when excited with drink; but at times a gigantic
Irish priest, Father Peter Smith, used to scatter the com-
batants with a long whip".[6]

Pioneer life was, of course, much the same in Carleton
as in the rest of the province. There were bees for logging
and numerous other purposes, when the settlers "killed the
fatted calf; . . . . and the young ladies, having got through
the dish-washing, looked as bright as bottled ale. . . . .
Dancing followed as a matter of course, till the short hours
passed and the young gentlemen each saw 'his Nellie'
home".[7] There were hardships, too: the wife of Captain
Monk once used a large tin tray to shelter her baby in its
cradle from the rain pouring through the roof; many a man
carried seed wheat on his back forty miles from the Rideau
to Fitzroy and Huntley, while some of the early settlers had
to "canoe it" to Montreal for their goods, often making the
laborious trip entirely alone, as did Ira Honeywell on several occasions.

The first road in the county was an improvement of the
Chaudière portage trail; the next (the first worthy of the
name) was the Richmond Road from Richmond Landing,
now Chaudière Flats. This road was built by the government from the unlimited road material to be found close at
hand. In later years road companies took charge and
macadamised (or said they did) many of the earlier roads.
In 1819 the first steamship came up the Ottawa River to
Hull, and was joyfully welcomed by the settlers along the

[5] W. P. Lett: *Recollections of Bytown and its Old Inhabitants.* 1874.
   p. 87.
[6] Emily P. Weaver: *The Story of the Counties of Ontario.* 1913,
   pp. 140-1.
[7] J. L. Gourlay: *History of the Ottawa Valley.* 1896. p. 11.

shores. Railway communication was first furnished by the
Bytown and Prescott Railway, which was in operation in
1854.

The site of the capital of the Dominion of Canada was
drawn by two brothers named Burrows in 1816, and one of
them, John, (who changed his name to J. B. Honey), arrived on the land in the following year, and shortly afterwards built a house near the corner of the present Lyon
and Victoria Streets. Honey then sold most of his land to
Nicholas Sparks, who had been an employee of Philemon
Wright for many years, and had saved enough out of his
earnings to pay $240 for the land. One who knew Nicholas
Sparks described him in the following terms:

> "Now first among our old landmarks,
>   Comes Laird of Bytown, Nicholas Sparks ,
>   Who came across in '26
>   From Hull, his lucky fate to fix
>   Upon a bush farm which he bought
>   For sixty pounds—and little thought
>   While grumbling at a price so high,
>   That fortune had not passed him by.
>
> 'Tis not my business here to flatter,
>   Or with enconiums to bespatter
>   The shadows of departed men
>   Whom we shall never see again.
>   Yet I may say, who knew him well,
>   And of him would not falsehood tell,
>   That as poor human nature ran,
>   He was an honest upright man."[8]

Sparks built a log shanty on the south-east corner of the
present Sparks and Bay Streets, where in later years the
Wellington Ward Market was located. The most populous
and wealthy section of Ottawa was destined to develop on
Sparks' land. Near Caleb Bellows' store and dock at Richmond Landing was a tavern kept by Isaac Firth in the
vicinity of the Slides Bridge. Apart from these rude
structures the entire site of Ottawa was covered by a cedar
swamp, and the district was still largely in its primeval

[8]Lett, *op. cit.*, pp. 60-61.

state when the Imperial Government chose the spot as the northern terminus of the proposed Rideau Canal, which was to be built to afford a second route between Montreal and Kingston in case war with the United States made the St. Lawrence route impracticable.

In 1826 Colonel By was placed in charge of the work, and the settlement which rapidly developed was appropriately named Bytown. The poet-historian of the capital recalls the stalwart and soldierly colonel in the words:

"As o'er the past my vision runs,
Gazing on Bytown's elder sons,
The portly Colonel I behold
Plainly as in days of old,
Conjured before me at this hour
By memory's undying power;
Seated upon his great black steed
Of stately form and noble breed;
A man who knew not how to flinch,
A British soldier, every inch:
Courteous alike to low and high,
A gentleman was Colonel By."[9]

Colonel By first camped in the forest near Nepean Point, and later occupied a house on Major's Hill. When operations commenced on the canal a large number of sappers, miners, engineers of the Regular Army, labourers, tradesmen and merchants immediately poured into Bytown. In 1827 the corner stone of the locks was laid by John Franklin, the noted Arctic explorer, and the Rideau was completed in 1832 at a cost of about $5,000,000. Until the St. Lawrence canals were built most of the trade between Upper Canada and Montreal passed over the circuitous route of the Rideau Canal and Ottawa River, and many immigrants made their way westward in the same manner, thus avoiding the more tedious bateau trip up the St. Lawrence.

By 1827 there was a considerable settlement in Lower Bytown, particularly on Rideau, Sussex and Wellington Streets, together with a double row of labourers' huts from Sappers' Bridge southwards. Among those who arrived in

[9]Ibid., p. 7.

From a Mural in the Chateau Laurier, Ottawa   C. W. Jefferys, R.C.A.

THE BUILDING OF THE RIDEAU CANAL. 1826-32

W. H. Bartlett

THE RIDEAU CANAL AT BYTOWN, 1840

WELLINGTON STREET AND BARRACK HILL, BYTOWN, ABOUT 1842

A MODERN LUMBER RAFT ON THE OTTAWA
In the background are the Dominion Parliament Buildings

that year was Daniel O'Connor, who first dispensed justice in Bytown, and whose daughter was the first child born there; he was in later years treasurer of Carleton County. In his diary he describes his arrival at Bytown:

"We put up for the night at the little stopping-place kept by Nicholas Sparks. Mr. and Mrs. Sparks received us kindly. . . . I had an interview with Colonel By, who pressed me very hard to stay, and gave me every encouragement to do so. He at once allotted to me building lot No. 31 on the North side of Wellington Street, then all bush and stumps. . . . I employed men to cut down the timber and take out the stumps. . . . After the lot was cleared I had a small but comfortable building erected, and again entered actively in business pursuits."[10]

Bytown grew rapidly in population, though the streets remained for some years such muddy trails that cows which came home through them had to be washed before they could be milked. In 1827 the bridge from Bytown to Hull was constructed; at the time this bridge was the largest in Canada, and its erection was considered quite an engineering feat. By 1828 there were about forty stores or tradesman's shops, a brewery and nine bars in Bytown, while four years later there were 150 houses, built chiefly of wood.

At this time perhaps the chief characteristic of Bytown was lawlessness. Escape to the woods was easy, so fights and brawls among the various elements of the population—grangers, shiners and ex-soldier farmers—were quite usual. Isaac Firth's hotel on Nepean Point was early notorious as a place of entertainment for lumbermen; there, too, the Scotch settlers of the district used to gather to celebrate St. Andrew's Night. Every gathering by a section of the heterogeneous population of Bytown and vicinity was commonly the occasion of a drunken brawl. On St. Patrick's Day, 1828, some 200 Irish labourers celebrated by a parade. It is said that "all were drunk, dancing and fighting",[11] and one man was killed and many seriously injured.

These labourers on the canal lived near the site of the old City Hall, the district being known to the early inhabitants as Corkstown. In this interesting locality were

[10]Daniel O'Connor: *Diary.* 1901. pp. 29-30.
[11]A. H. D. Ross: *Ottawa, Past and Present.* 1927. p. 110.

"Two rows of cabins in the swamp
Begirt by ponds and vapours damp
And aromatic cedar trees."

Mother McGinty kept the most noted tavern in Corkstown, and was well able to take care of her own interests:

"She kept the reckoning, ruled the roost,
And swung an arm of potent might
That few would dare to brave in fight;
Yet she was a good-natured soul
As ever filled the flowing bowl;
In sooth she dealt in goodly cheer,
Half pints of whisky, quarts of beer.
And when a man had spent his all
She chalked the balance on the wall.
And woe to him, who soon or late
His tally did not liquidate."[12]

During the first ten years of Bytown the Irish shiners
were the most lawless section of the population, and this
disturbing element "terrorised many peaceable citizens by
such playful antics as going to an enemy's home, stripping
the children of their clothing and making them run through
snow drifts, scattering the furniture over a radius of a
hundred yards, or blowing up the little home with gunpowder".[13] After the completion of the canal and other
public works many of the shiners were without work. Some
went to the lumber camps, and others roamed about in
gangs, attacking any "canallers" (traders) or others who
aroused their enmity. Many a man was marked as deserving a "lacing", and always received it; while these
ruffians did not hesitate to attack and insult women.

Nearly all the prominent shiners were sooner or later
hanged, murdered, or came to some other violent end,
which, we might almost add, was fortunate in that it served
the ends of justice, though always too long delayed.[14] Crime
of all kinds became so common that the law-abiding citizens
of Bytown united, in 1837, to form "An Association for

[12]Lett, *op. cit.*, pp. 82-3.   [13]Ross, *op. cit.*, p. 113.
[14]In the Toronto *Globe* of December 11 and 25, 1856, appear letters
signed "Chaudière", which describe the activities of the shiners
and give a rambling account of some aspects of early settlement. Typewritten copies of the letters are in the Public
Archives of Canada.

Preserving the Public Peace"; but even this did not end lawlessness. Constables who did their duty and arrested riotous raftsmen were often attacked or had their homes burned. The nearest jail was in Perth, fifty-three miles away, and not until Bytown had a jail of its own, in 1841, was there an improvement in the observance of the law.

In early elections at Bytown the voters were restricted to those citizens who had purchased land from Nicholas Sparks or from Theodore Besserer; thus in 1841 only ninety voted out of 600 who should have been eligible. Elections were always the occasion of excitement, and sometimes of riots. One of the most notable outbreaks in Bytown occurred in 1849 and was long remembered as "Stony Monday Riot". The occasion of the trouble was the proposed visit of Lord Elgin to Bytown, and to arrange a suitable reception a meeting was unfortunately called. The Governor had just previously signed the Rebellion Losses Bill, and there was a great divergence of opinion as to the suitability of a reception under the circumstances. Wagonloads of farmers, who were always opposed to the inhabitants of Bytown, came in force from the neighbouring townships, and some 1,500 people assembled at North Ward Market. The mob could not agree upon a chairman, each section standing out for a man who would represent themselves. An uproar resulted from the disagreement and no one was able to restore order.

"Props under the platform were pulled out, and the speakers were precipitated to the ground. . . . Angry words soon led to blows, and in about three minutes every loose stone on the market square was hurtling through the air. In the midst of the *mêlée* a shot was fired, and a general run for arms took place. The farmers were plentifully supplied from a store on Rideau Street, and the inhabitants of Bytown supplied themselves as best they could."[15]

One man was killed and twenty wounded before two companies of rifles put an end to the affair. The same force prevented a recurrence of the trouble two days later when a second meeting was attempted and hundreds of both parties came fully armed with guns and bayonets.

Meanwhile Bytown had developed greatly. Nicholas

[15]Ross, *op. cit.*, p. 118.

Sparks was soon one of the wealthiest inhabitants, for his investment of $240 eventually yielded him a profit of some $2,000,000. He sold many lots to the government or to settlers; but he was a generous man and gave away a number of valuable sites for municipal or religious purposes. A Roman Catholic priest held services in the village as early as 1827. The first Scotch kirk was built in 1828 on land given by Sparks, and within five years the same benefactor enabled the erection of Methodist and Anglican churches.

At this period most schools in Upper Canada were privately conducted, and the first school in Bytown was one of this type which opened on Rideau Street in 1827. In 1848 the common (public) school system commenced in Bytown, and there was a separate school in 1856. As in the rest of the province, secondary education developed earlier, the Dalhousie Grammar School being established in 1843. In 1834 the town's first newspaper, *The Bytown Independent and Farmers' Advocate*, was established, and it was followed in 1836 by *The Bytown Gazette and Ottawa and Rideau Advertiser*. The population grew from 2,400 in 1834 to 6,000 in 1847, when Bytown was incorporated as a town. Eight years later it became a city, and the more dignified "Ottawa" replaced the earlier name.

In 1857 the county assumed a much greater importance when Queen Victoria chose Ottawa as the site of the future capital, in preparation for which the beautiful Parliament Buildings were commenced two years later. The site chosen for the buildings was originally a densely-wooded hemlock ridge, long known as Barrack Hill, because, during the building of the canal, the military barracks were established there. The Parliament Buildings, which, on February 3, 1916, were partially destroyed by an incendiary fire, were of modified twelfth century Gothic architecture, and were constructed of limestone, cream-coloured sandstone, and marble, quarried in the vicinity and near Chats Falls. The corner-stone was laid by the Prince of Wales (later Edward VII) in 1860, and the cost of the completed block was nearly $5,000,000. The first session of parliament was held in the beautiful buildings in 1866, and the following year, with the inauguration of Confederation, Ottawa became the capital of the Dominion of Canada.

Reproduced by Courtesy of the Confederation Life Association

J. D. Kelly

PRIME MINISTERS OF CANADA, IN THE HOUSE OF COMMONS, OTTAWA

PREMIERS OF THE DOMINION OF CANADA. LEADERS AND PROMINENT MEMBERS
OF THE OPPOSITION SINCE CONFEDERATION

1. The Rt. Hon. Sir John Macdonald. From July 1, 1867 to Nov. 6, 1873, and from Oct. 17, 1878 to June 6, 1891.

2. The Hon. Alexander Mackenzie. From Nov. 7, 1873 to Oct. 16, 1878.

3. The Hon. Sir John J. C. Abbott. From June 16, 1891 to Nov. 24, 1892.

4. The Hon. Sir John S. D. Thompson. From Dec. 5, 1892 to Dec. 12, 1894.

5. The Hon. Sir Mackenzie Bowell. From Dec 21, 1894 to April 27, 1896.

6. The Hon. Sir Charles Tupper, Bart. From May 1, 1896 to July 8, 1896.

7. The Rt. Hon. Sir Wilfrid Laurier. From July 11, 1896 to Oct. 9, 1911.

8. The Rt. Hon. Sir Robert L. Borden. From Oct. 10, 1911 to Oct. 12, 1917, and from Oct. 12, 1917 to July 10, 1920.

9. The Rt. Hon. Arthur Meighen. From July 10, 1920 to Dec. 29, 1921, and from June 29, 1926 to Sept. 25, 1926.

10. The Rt. Hon. William Lyon Mackenzie King. From Dec. 29, 1921 to June 28, 1926, and from Sept. 25, 1926 to Aug. 7, 1930

11. The Hon. George Brown.

12. The Hon. Sir Richard John Cartwright.

13. The Hon. Edward Blake.

14. The Hon. George E. Foster.

15. The Hon. Sir Hector Langevin.

16. The Rt. Hon. Wm. S. Fielding.

17. The Hon. Clifford Sifton.

18. The Rt. Hon. R. B. Bennett. From Aug. 7, 1930.

J. D. Kelly

GOVERNORS GENERAL OF CANADA, IN THE SENATE CHAMBER, OTTAWA

GOVERNORS GENERAL OF CANADA SINCE CONFEDERATION
1867 TO 1928

1. The Right Hon. Viscount Monck, K.C.M.G.
   1867-1869

2. The Right Hon. Lord Lisgar, G.C.M.G. (Sir John Young).
   1869-1872

3. The Right Hon. the Earl of Dufferin, K.P.K.C.B., G.C.M.G.
   1872-1878

4. The Right Hon. the Marquess of Lorne, K.T., G.C.M.G., P.C.
   1878-1883

5. The Most Hon. the Marquess of Lansdowne, G.C.M.G.
   1883-1888

6. The Right Hon. Lord Stanley, of Preston, G.C.B.
   1888-1893

7. The Right Hon. the Earl of Aberdeen, K.T., G.C.M.G.
   1893-1898

8. The Right Hon. the Earl of Minto, G.C.M.G.
   1898-1904

9. The Right Hon. Earl Grey, G.C.M.G.
   1904-1911

10. Field Marshall H.R.H. the Duke of Connaught, K.G.
    1911-1916

11. The Right Hon. the Duke of Devonshire, K.C.
    1916-1921

12. General the Right Hon. Baron Byng of Vimy.
    1921-1926

13. The Right Hon. Viscount Willingdon.
    1926-1929

CHAPTER III

PETERBOROUGH COUNTY

A HAPPY HUNTING-GROUND

"These waters plenty fish afford,
The perch, and pike, and cat;
And there the spotted salmon swims,
And sturgeon stored with fat.

There various furs for caps are found:
The beaver, coon, wild cat;
Otter, marten, rabbit, mink,
Gray fox, ground chuck, muskrat."[1]

THE County of Peterborough is a region of forests and rocks, rivers and lakes, a noted summer resort district in modern times and just as highly prized by the Indian in pre-settlement days. In 1818, when the first settlers pushed northward from Cobourg and settled in Smith Township, the Indians claimed the ownership of large sections of this beautiful lake country and attempted to regulate the activities of those who sought to invade their territory. One of the noted beauty spots, Salmon Trout (later Stoney) Lake, is said to have been used by the Indians as a natural hospital, where sick and wounded braves recovered their health. Certain it is that the natives were very jealous of any encroachment upon Stoney Lake and told stories of wild beasts and rattlesnakes to keep people away; for they obtained their wampum-grass there, the best birch bark for their canoes, and game, fish and berries for food. The first settlers in the district found that the many hundred islands of the lake were "covered with huckleberries, while grapes, high- and low-bush cranberries, blackberries, wild cherries, gooseberries, and several sorts of wild currants grew here in profusion".[2] At that time a chief known to the early settlers as "Handsome Jack" Cow was overlord of the Stoney Lake region, and he is commemorated by the names Jack's Creek and Jack's Lake.

The first man to take up residence within the limits of

[1]*The Methodist Magazine.* 1828. p. 74.
[2]Susanna Moodie: *Roughing It in the Bush.* 1852. Edition of 1923,
    p. 334.

Peterborough County was an Indian fur trader, Herkimer (or Herchimere), who, in 1790, followed Peter Smith in the trade at Pemiscutiank or Smith's Creek (Port Hope), and three years later removed northward to the shores of Rice Lake. He carried his goods through the woods on horseback, presenting the log cabin he had inherited from Peter Smith to Myndert Harris, head of one of the four families of permanent settlers who arrived at Smith's Creek in the summer of 1793. Harris was something of a mechanic for we find that he constructed two primitive ox-carts for Herchimere, the first having wheels entirely of wood, while for the second some iron was available to bind the wheels. Herchimere's trading-post on the north shore of Rice Lake was at the mouth of the Otonabee River, near the present Indian village Hiawatha, which, in the early days of Methodist missionary zeal, produced the noted native religious leaders, Peter Jacobs and John Sunday. In later years Herchimere was succeeded in the trade by Major Charles Anderson.

The first township in Peterborough County to be surveyed was Smith, in 1818, and in that year a number of English immigrants from Cumberland made their way thither *via* Rice Lake and the Otonabee River. They erected a temporary log house near the site of the city of Peterborough, and all lived in it until a small shanty had been built on each lot. They suffered great privations before they were able to grow potatoes and wheat on a few small patches of cleared land. These pioneers, the first white settlers in the country, were William Dixon and his five sons, Joseph Lee and his two sons, Robert Millburn, Robert Walton, John Walton, Walton Wilson, Thomas W. Millburn, and John Smith and his son. During the same year some settlers moved back to Smith and North and South Monaghan Townships from older settlements along Lake Ontario, but these families were more accustomed to bush life.

In 1819 Otonabee Township was surveyed, and in May of that year a number of enterprising men, most of them from Port Hope, entered the district. They were Adam Scott, John Farrelly (a surveyor), John Ward, Charles Fothergill, Barabas Bletcher and John Edminson, and almost all of them were men of importance in the district in later years. In 1820 about twenty families and eight single men entered the township, and in the next few years a number of half-pay officers arrived, some of them conducting settlers to the new land. Captain Charles Rubidge, R.N., obtained his land in 1819 and arrived in May, 1820, being the first man in Otonabee to perform his settlement duties and secure a deed to his land. Another officer, Captain Spilsbury, brought in some settlers, but all except one of them, George Kent (the first settler in the township), found the life too arduous and left for older settlements.

A considerable amount of land in the front of this township was held by absentee half-pay officers, who hired men to perform their settlement duties. At this time there was no road from Port Hope, and the only means of access in summer was by a trail from Cobourg to Rice Lake, and thence northward by the Otonabee River. Grain and cattle had to be carried in small bateaux, the dangerous journey of fourteen miles down Rice Lake being made by one settler with four head of cattle in his boat.

Adam Scott was an ambitious young man, and erected a crude saw- and grist-mill on the Otonabee, later adding a distillery when the arrival of other settlers created a demand for cheap whisky. His small establishment was in operation in 1821, and Scott's Mills or The Plains formed the nucleus of the city of Peterborough, though until the Irish under Peter Robinson arrived in 1825 Scott and two or three workmen made up the total population. The miller was seldom daunted by difficulties: he used to walk to Cobourg or Port Hope when the occasion demanded, and once when the 250-pound crank-shaft of his mill broke down he carried it thirty miles through the woods to Port Hope to be repaired, and a few days later trudged back to his mill in triumph. The journey was the more remarkable because it occurred in the spring when the trail was at its worst.

Scott's small grist-mill was, however, inadequate to supply even the limited requirements of the few settlers in the county, and many of them continued to carry their grain to the mill at Port Hope, or to a small establishment on Galloway's Creek in Cavan Township, which had been in operation before Scott's. Some families were forced to go for weeks without bread. Jacob Bromwell stated to Sir Peregrine Maitland in 1826 that he had resorted to the expedient of chewing corn so that it might be soft enough to bake for his children's food. It was not long before milling facilities were better, however, for in 1827 Bromwell opened a small mill in Smith Township, and during the same year the government established a good one at the village of Peterborough.

The Methodist circuit-rider was the first to bring the consolation of religion to many settlers in the backwoods of Upper Canada. In 1824 the Rev. Anson Green, stationed at Cobourg, covered a circuit of several hundred miles on horseback, under the most adverse conditions. He describes a visit to Smith Township in terms which leave no room for doubt as to the hardships of the zealous men who contributed so much towards the alleviation of the suffering and loneliness of the early settler:

"On the 28th of September I started for the Township of Smith, passing through where the town of Peterborough now stands; but there was only one house there then, and that one down on the river's bank quite out of my sight. My path was a winding Indian trail, where no wheel carriage had ever passed. I was obliged to jump my horse over logs, ride him through deep mud-holes and bridgeless streams, guided sometimes by marked trees. When I got a short distant beyond Peterborough I entered a clearing with two or three log cabins in view. In one of these lived a godly old Yorkshire woman, who received me joyfully. Her house was covered with hollow logs, halved, and so arranged as to shelter its inmates from rain and snow. The room was about fifteen by twenty feet in size, and it served for our kitchen, bedroom, parlour, dining-room, and church. Here I preached to a congregation of eight souls, and was happy. O how these people in the bush value the Gospel, and love the messengers who deliver it to them."[3]

In 1822 Thomas Stewart and his brother-in-law, Robert Reid, obtained large grants of land in Douro Township, then entirely unsettled and not even surveyed; they were

[3]Anson Green: *Life and Times.* 1877. pp. 50-51.

men of a superior type and in future years became leaders in public life, Mr. Stewart being a member of the Legislative Council. The men came in ahead to supervise the construction of their log houses, and their families soon joined them by travelling in sleighs through the woods over the trail from Port Hope, which had been blazed but a short time before. For two years these families endured the hardships of pioneer life without neighbours, but in 1825 they were encouraged by the report that a large emigration from their native Ireland was being brought to the county by the Hon. Peter Robinson. Stewart had 1,200 acres in Douro, and Reid 2,000 acres, and they also received permission to control settlement in the township for five years; but they were only too glad to relinquish their right when the prospect of having neighbours was possible of fulfilment through the colonisation efforts of a member of the Legislative Council.

Peter Robinson, member of a well-known Loyalist family, was born in New Brunswick in 1785. His parents removed to Upper Canada in 1792, settling first at Kingston, and then, in 1798, at York. During the war of 1812 he commanded a volunteer rifle company, and in later years represented East York in the Upper Canadian Assembly. He was appointed to the Legislative Council, and in 1827 became Commissioner of Crown Lands, a position which he held until his death in 1838. He took a prominent part in encouraging emigration to Upper Canada, and particularly to the counties of Lanark and Peterborough, the latter of which was named after him.

Economic conditions in the south of Ireland were causing the Imperial Government a great deal of concern, and in 1823 Peter Robinson supervised an emigration of the surplus population to lands near the Mississippi River, in Lanark County. In the early summer of 1825 the experiment was repeated when 2,024 inhabitants of County Cork, chiefly Roman Catholics, sailed for Canada. Most of the emigrants were very poor, and approximately one-third of them were children. The ocean voyage was made under the usual adverse conditions of the days of sailing-vessels, and the death of over a dozen children during the crossing was not above the average. The bateau trip up the St. Lawrence proved equally as tedious as the thirty-one day ocean voyage, and there was an unfortunate delay at Kingston, resulting in 300 cases of fever and thirty-three deaths among the immigrants.

The immigration travelled in sections, and it was October before settlement on the land was under way. The first division landed at Cobourg on August 12, 1825, and the remainder followed at intervals of about one week. The 500 members of the leading section camped in tents on the beach at Cobourg, and proceeded inland about thirteen miles to Rice Lake, over an almost impassable road. About ten days' work had been put upon this road with the aid of £50 which the Quarter Sessions of the Newcastle District contributed towards defraying the expense. Further repairs were necessary as the immigration proceeded over the road, and it was then possible for ox-carts to carry the baggage and supplies, though the men and women had to walk.

Three large bateaux were also portaged to Rice Lake, but it was discovered upon arrival at Sully that the water of the Otonabee was too low to enable them to be used; so eight days were spent building a large flat-bottomed scow, sixty feet long and eight feet wide, which easily carried a heavy load without drawing more than a few inches of water. One immigrant was drowned when he ventured out upon the lake during the stay at Sully. The first party to proceed to Scott's Mills was made up of twenty old settlers and thirty of the healthiest of the Irish; but all of them suffered from ague and fever, and two died.

After many trips had been made across the lake and up the river the first section of the immigration reached Scott's Mills, which was to be the headquarters in distributing the settlers throughout the neighbouring townships. Some of them were accommodated in log buildings which had been erected at the village, but most of the immigrants immediately set to work to build themselves temporary shelters—rude wigwams of branches, sod and slabs of wood.

A settler previously mentioned, Captain Charles Rubidge, helped greatly in the actual settlement of the immigrants; for, since he himself had been a pioneer on the north shore of Rice Lake, he knew the difficulties to be surmounted. Almost all the members of the immigration were located in five townships of Peterborough County, and one (Emily, including Ops) in what is now Victoria County. The number of heads of families placed in the various townships was as follows: Asphodel 36, Douro 60, Emily 142, Ennismore 67, Otonabee 51, and Smith 34. These townships had previously been inspected by Robinson and Colonel McDonell, and suitable lots chosen. Asphodel had been surveyed in 1820, but at the time of the Irish immigration only about a dozen families were settled there; of the other townships all of them excepting Smith had even fewer settlers, or none at all.

The cost of the emigration totalled £21 5s. per head, but this included the munificent grant to Peter Robinson of £29,000, "for the emigration and settlement of 2,024 persons". The district under settlement was soon a hive of industry: settlers already located in the vicinity obtained from Robinson profitable contracts to blaze bush roads, to build log huts, and to act as guides and transportworkers in settling the newcomers on their lands.

The Irish settlers suffered greatly from disease during the early months, but not to the extent which some people would like to have believed. Among those who exaggerated the number of deaths was Colonel Thomas Talbot, who started a rumor that they were dying at the rate of thirty a day. Sea-sickness, ague, dysentery and fever exacted a heavy toll, but the highest number of deaths at any one time was when eleven were buried in one day at Kingston; while the total deaths from the time the emigration left Ireland to March, 1826, was only 102, not much more than three times the daily rate circulated by Talbot.

During the winter of 1826-27 Sir Peregrine Maitland, Lieutenant-Governor of Upper Canada, Colonel Talbot, the Hon. John Beverley Robinson, the Hon. Zacheus Burnham and James Gray Bethune of Cobourg travelled by sleigh to Rubidge's house near what is now the village of Keene, where they were welcomed by Peter Robinson, Captain Rubidge and many of the settlers. The Lieutenant-Governor visited some of the Irish in Ennismore, and received deputations from other townships at "Government House",—Robinson's commodious dwelling at Scott's Mills.

Almost the only grievance voiced by the settlers was "the want of clergymen to administer to us the comforts of our Holy Religion, and good schoolmasters to instruct our children".[4] The visit of these notables was long remembered, and the appearance of the eccentric Colonel Talbot, "clad in a remarkable sheep-skin costume, with boots of the same material",[5] aroused great interest. A grand dinner was held in honour of the official party, and the *élite* of the district—especially the ladies—were invited to meet the important men. No wonder cedar boughs were strewn in the path of these notable visitors when they honoured with their presence the backwoods village of Scott's Mills!

The Irish immigration attracted others to the district. It was stated before a committee of the British Parliament that "speculators flocked to the neighbouring townships in all directions—mills were built—stores opened—and life, bustle and civilisation went on with spirit".[6] The government provided for the Irish most liberally; in fact many experienced settlers were of the opinion of Captain Rubidge, that they "did too much for them. . . . While the rations last, many of the immigrants make little exertion, and dispose of food they have not been used to, such as pork, for whisky, thereby injuring their constitutions and morals, and fixing for a time habits of idleness. . . . This would certainly not have been the case had they been less lavishly supplied".[7]

This opinion was well-founded, for a hundred acres of land had been given to each of 415 families, and the same amount to every son who was of age; a log shanty was built on each lot at a cost of $10, and for a year and a half daily rations of one pound of pork and one pound of flour for each adult, and half that amount for children, were dispensed at government expense; while each family received a cow, an axe, an auger, a hand-saw, 100 nails, two gimlets,

[4]Appendix to the *Report of the Select Committee of the British Parliament.* 1826. p. 299.
[5]Frances Stewart: *Our Forest Home.* 1889. 2nd Edition, 1902, p. 90. The visit of the Lieutentant-Governor's party is described on pp. 88-94.
[6]Evidence of Captain Rubidge. See Sir R. W. Horton: *Ireland and Canada.* 1839. p. 41.
[7]Captain Rubidge to Basil Hall, quoted in Basil Hall: *Travels in America in 1827 and 1828.* 1829. Vol. I, p. 336.

three hoes, one kettle, one frying-pan, one iron pot, five bushels of seed-potatoes and eight quarts of Indian corn. No wonder Adam Scott found many of the newcomers anxious to trade some of their numerous recent acquisitions for cheap whisky!

Most of the Irish settled down on their land, however, and succeeded fairly well in a strange country, under conditions very different from those to which they had been accustomed in Ireland. At the end of the first year a total of 1,386 acres of wild land had been cleared, and the settlers had produced crops and live stock to the value of £12,525. Perhaps too many of the immigrants still continued in after years to reside in the typical low-roofed Irish shanty; and undoubtedly a mixed settlement of the various British nationalities would have been preferable, for Captain Rubidge stated in his evidence before a Select Committee of the British Parliament in 1847 that the immigrants were more prosperous in townships, such as Otonabee, where they were mixed with English and Scotch settlers, than in others almost exclusively occupied by themselves.[8] But the emigration scheme, often derided at the time as unsatisfactory, proved a success in later years. In 1830 John Richards was sent out by the British Government as a commissioner to learn how the Irish emigrations of 1823 and 1825 had progressed. He wrote to Sir R. W. Horton: "I was two or three days at Peterborough, during which time perhaps thirty or forty settlers, and some with their families, came in to see Mr. Robinson, and the manner in which they met him was quite affecting; it was more to bless him as a benefactor than to receive him as a visitor."[9]

When Captain Basil Hall travelled in the district in 1827 he took the trouble to visit many of the Irish settlers to learn their views upon the success of the settlement. He found "universal satisfaction expressed by these people", who praised the Hon. Peter Robinson, the government, and all concerned in the management of the emigration.[10] Many years later another shrewd observer (who was not at first favourably impressed) considered that "a great improve-

[8]Minutes of Evidence before the Select Committee, Question 2680.
[9]John Richards to Sir R. W. Horton, March 1, 1831, quoted in Horton, *op. cit.*, p. 22.
[10]Hall, *op. cit.*, Vol. I, p. 294.

ment is perceptible in the morality, industry and education of the rising generation".[11]

Captain Hall inspected also the earlier settlement of Englishmen, many of them miners, who first pushed into Smith Township in 1818. These men had paid a deposit of £10 each for their land, and it was not refunded until several years later; they bore their own expenses in addition, receiving no help whatever from the government; but they had become very prosperous in the nine years that had elapsed. This led Hall to hope that if he re-visited the county nine years later, "I should find my friends, the poor Irish settlers, living in the ease and comparative affluence now enjoyed by the inhabitants of Smith's Town."[12]

Upon the whole, however, it may be stated without fear of contradiction that the Irish were much better off in the new land than they could ever have hoped to be in the old. An excellent estimate of the success of the emigration describes their condition in Ireland as most unfortunate, for they were "mainly small farmers who had been ruined by the fall in the price of produce or recently dispossessed by their landlords, labourers out of employment, or tradesmen in poor circumstances from the general badness of the times. Many of them had known what it was to be in actual need of food; it was necessary to provide most of them with clothes and bedding before sailing. They were taken from a a district where life and property had not been safe for many years, where it had been impossible to preserve order even by the continual presence of soldiery and the frequent exportation of offenders to the convict colonies". A few months later they were satisfactorily located "in a new land where a certain living could be obtained by industry, and where disorder and murder were almost unknown. According to their own testimony they were removed 'from misery and want and put into independence and happiness'."[13]

Among the Irish in Peter Robinson's emigration were Patrick Young and his nine children. He located in Smith Township, at the rapids between Clear Lake and the

---

[11]Samuel Strickland: *Twenty-seven Years in Canada West.* 1853. Vol. I, p. 138.
[12]Hall, *op. cit.*, Vol., I, p. 294.
[13]Helen Cowan: *British Emigration to British North America.* 1928. p. 115.

The Shanty in the Bush

Fifteen Years after Settlement

Thirty Years after Settlement

THE EVOLUTION OF A CANADIAN FARM

These illustrations were probably prepared as emigration propaganda

Sketch made with the Camera Lucida by Captain Basil Hall

PETERBOROUGH, U.C., IN 1827

Reproduced by Courtesy of members of the Stewart family.

AN EARLY SKETCH OF PETERBOROUGH

Adam Scott's primitive mill may be seen on the shore of the Otonabee

Katchewanoonk, the fourteen-mile trip from Scott's Mills taking one and a half days. He erected a rude saw- and grist-mill at this excellent location, but for some years he was without neighbours, and subsisted entirely by hunting and fishing and raising a little potatoes and wheat on the few fertile spaces he could find on his rugged lot, which is described by a contemporary visitor as the wildest and most romantic spot that could have been chosen anywhere in that wild district.[14] Young's Point is now a quiet little settlement, and though most of its ruggedness has disappeared with the advance of civilisation, the Youngs are still the most important inhabitants. The original log house of 1825 remained standing for 102 years, but at last it suffered demolition—the usual fate of old buildings which have escaped fire and decay. The Youngs of to-day are not millers and hunters, but have for many years operated the only line of passenger steamships between Lakefield and Stoney Lake.

The few buildings at Scott's Mills in 1825 were considerably augmented as a result of the Irish immigration which made the small settlement its headquarters. Peter Robinson erected five buildings for his use—one for Dr. Reade, surgeon to the immigrants, two as storehouses, one as a business office where all transactions concerning the immigration took place, and the fifth and largest a dwelling-house for the use of Robinson, Colonel McDonell and a surveyor, John Smith. Dr. Reade's house served also as a church, where mass was said by Father Crawley, who arrived in 1826 and was the first resident priest in Peterborough County. Most of these log buildings were located on the west side of Water Street, near the crude mill erected in 1821 by Adam Scott.

The first merchant in the village was one Stewart, who opened shop in the latter part of 1825; by 1827 there were two larger stores. In 1826 Bailey's Tavern was built, and in the following winter a log schoolhouse was opened and both lower and higher learning taught by the first Anglican clergyman, the Rev. Samuel Armour. In 1827 the name of the settlement was changed to Peterborough in honour of Peter Robinson, and there were then twenty log

[14]Moodie, *op. cit.*, p. 323.

houses in the village. The mills which had been erected
by the government were described by John Smith, Deputy
Provincial Surveyor, who visited them in 1827, as "on an
extensive scale, being calculated to pack forty barrels of
flour, and the saw-mill to cut 3,000 feet of boards *per
diem.*"[15]

In 1827 there was built a bridge across the Otonabee
River at Peterborough, but it was destroyed during the succeeding winter and the inhabitants had to revert to a more
primitive means. Until a second bridge could be built by
public subscription the river was crossed "by means of a
large scow, sustained in the current by a long rope or cable,
to one end of which it was attached, while the other was
secured to a point on the bank at some distance above. By a
proper application of the helm, the current was made to
transport the scow from one bank to the other, a reversal
of its position after each crossing being all that was
required".[16] In subsequent years, as other immigrations
arrived in the county, Peterborough increased rapidly in
size and importance, a development due largely to the
valuable lumber trade which centred in the village.

In 1823 the Township of Dummer was surveyed, but no
attempt to settle it was made until 1831, when 1950 British
emigrants of a high type, many of them from Wiltshire,
arrived in the county. All of these came at their own expense excepting 150 whose emigration was arranged by the
Marquis of Bath, and 100 commuted pensioners and their
families who were sent out by the British Government.
They were in charge of agents during their passage, and
their settlement on the land was under the direction of
Captain Rubidge, whose importance in the development of
the county is hardly second to that of Peter Robinson.

Most of these immigrants were located in Dummer, but
some were placed in neighbouring townships. Their settlement was arranged in a very business-like manner. Guides
conducted an advance party to examine the land, and, upon
a selection being made, the agent issued location tickets to
the immigrants, entitling each to 100 acres of land when

[15]Report of John Smith, quoted in Andrew Picken: *The Canadas.*
    1832. pp. 158-9.
[16]Thomas Poole: *Early Settlement of Peterborough and Peter-
    borough County.* 1867. p. 23.

he had fulfilled the conditions of settlement. About £1 in money was given to each man who needed it, and he was soon settled in his shanty, which was erected with the help of his neighbours.

The Provincial Government supplied living rations to the members of this immigration while they were travelling through the country and during the time of location. Grants of 100 acres were made to heads of families and grown-up sons on condition that an annual amount of 1s. per acre would be paid each year for four years, the payments to commence after the expiration of the first four years on the land. At the end of eight years' actual settlement, and upon payment of £80, the settler would receive the title to his lot. The government was lenient, however, and an extension was granted to those who could not meet their obligation at the specified time.

The land upon which these immigrants settled was generally poorer, in some cases containing a good deal of rock which it was difficult or impossible to remove; nor did they receive the cows, farm implements and supplies which were so lavishly distributed among the Irish. In spite of these disadvantages, however, they accomplished more in a short time than had the Irish. Colonel Strickland, who was familiar with both settlements, noticed that "an air of comfort and cleanliness pervades their dwellings, and there is a neatness about their farms and homesteads which is generally wanting in the Irish settlements."[17] In 1832 other settlers were sent out to the same district by a Scottish emigration society, which, with the consent of the Canadian Government, offered each man a grant of fifty acres and the opportunity to purchase as much more.

The immigrants who arrived in Dummer in the early thirties aided one another in the work of settlement, and, like almost all other pioneers, their first years in "the bush" were filled with incessant toil under the most unfavourable conditions. All the roads were mere trails over which it was usual to walk long distances carrying heavy loads, amid swarms of black flies and mosquitoes. Many of the settlers had neither horses nor oxen for several years, and had to clear their land by the laborious "hand-log" method.

[17]Strickland, *op. cit.*, Vol. I, p. 138.

Auger holes sometimes served for windows in their pioneer shanties, and they had nothing but an open fire for heating and cooking. The English and Scotch inhabitants of Dummer and neighbouring townships were, however, very thankful for whatever small aid was given them, and their enterprise was rewarded by the assistance of men prominent in the Newcastle District who were interested in its development.

In 1834-35 the first grist-mill in Dummer Township was erected on the shores of Squaknegossippi Creek (Indian River) by the Hon. Zacheus Burnham of Cobourg. In 1838 he increased the water supply for his mills by blasting a canal several hundred feet through a ridge of rock between Stoney Lake and White Lake. As a result of these activities Dummer Mills (Warsaw) was soon one of the most important settlements in the county. Prominent among the early inhabitants of the village was Thomas Choate, cousin of Burnham; he was postmaster at Warsaw when the first office in that part of the county was established in 1839. The Burnhams and Choates were of "late Loyalist" stock from New Hampshire.

Meanwhile a considerable number of English and Scotch immigrants of a superior type had taken up land in other parts of the county. Many of these were half-pay officers, among whom the best known was Major Strickland, who settled near Scott's Mills in 1826 when he was but twenty years of age. A few years later, after he had spent three years in the employ of the Canada Company in opening the "Huron Tract" for settlement, he sold his land and moved ten miles northward into the bush, the trip taking two days to accomplish. His log house on the shores of Katchewanoonk Lake was the commencement of the village of Lakefield, at first called Nelson's Falls, and later Herriot's Falls and Selby.

In 1832 Strickland's sisters, Mrs. Moodie and Mrs. Traill, whose husbands were retired officers, settled in the district, and "the literary Stricklands" became famous for their influence in elevating the general tone of society around them, as also for the books they wrote, which undoubtedly form the most valuable contribution made by any family in our province in recording the experiences of pioneer life.

In 1839 another Irish emigration was brought to the county under the supervision of Captain Rubidge. These settlers numbered 183 and were chiefly from Colonel Wyndham's estates in Clare and Limerick, in the south of Ireland; they were located in the back concessions in much the same manner as the earlier Irish immigrants.

Meanwhile the village of Peterborough was rapidly increasing in importance. When Patrick Shirreff visited the district in 1833 he disliked the "mean houses", but he noted that Peterborough had the reputation of containing "a number of military and naval half-pay officers of Britain, and the society to be the most brilliant and polished in Canada".[18] John Langton, who settled on the shores of Sturgeon Lake in 1833, often visited Peterborough, the nearest supply depot. He noted that it was "a very pretty, picturesque, thriving village . . . with near thirty genteel families within visiting distance".[19] He refers in his letters to attending Bachelors' Balls there in evening dress, and remarks: "I certainly never expected on coming to Canada that I should be one of the Bachelors who gave a ball to between eighty and ninety, and meet with two of the best waltzers I ever figured with."[20]

Thomas Need, whose settlement between Sturgeon and Pigeon Lakes formed the nucleus of the village of Bobcaygeon, was another of "the rank and fashion" who were admitted to the exclusive society of Peterborough. In August, 1833, Need noticed that a rapid improvement had taken place in the village of Peterborough during that summer: "New houses had been built, new shops opened, and a large influx of inhabitants had arrived."[21] On April 24, 1834, he found the progress even more noticeable:

"The necessity of purchasing garden seeds and household stores took me to Peterborough, where a surprising alteration had been effected during the winter months; many new houses had been built, fresh stores opened, and a large number of settlers enrolled among the inhabitants.

[18]Patrick Shirreff: *A Tour through North America*. 1835. p. 123.
[19]John Langton: *Early Days in Upper Canada, Letters of John Langton*. 1926. p. 21.
[20]*Ibid.*, p. 82.
[21]Thomas Need: *Six Years in the Bush*. 1838. p. 70.

It then contained a church, post office, bank, agency office, circulating library, and two comfortable inns, with several private houses, where board and lodging might be procured on reasonable terms."[22]

Four years later there were four churches, a schoolhouse, several distilleries, stores and taverns in Peterborough, and its 150 houses accommodated a population of 900.

Most of the northern townships of the county were settled in later years, if at all, though Harvey contained a few homesteads as early as 1832, when a few "gentlemen" built fancy log houses on Pigeon Lake. On Sturgeon Lake were the settlers referred to by John Langton as six in number, four of whom "have been at an university, one at the military college at Woolwich, and the sixth, though boasting no such honours, has half a dozen silver spoons and a wife who plays the guitar."[23] The land was poor, but there was plenty of game, and this appears to have been the main attraction of the district. Within a few years some of these people had left because of their inability to make the soil productive, together with inconveniences arising from the remoteness of the settlement and the lack of good roads and bridges by which they might communicate with Peterborough, the source of supplies and centre of trade.

One traveller, who had heard the vicinity of Peterborough highly recommended, went there to see for himself, and was "at a loss to conceive what was the great inducement; and naturally inquired if there were any good practical farmers settled in the neighbourhood: of these there are very few, the principal settlers around it being half-pay officers and others who generally consider not whether the locality they fix upon is likely to be profitable, but whether it be beautiful, and likely to contribute to their pleasures." He also learned that it cost 6d. a bushel to transport produce to Cobourg, the most convenient port, and this was considered a great objection to settlement in the Peterborough district, when land a few miles from Lake Ontario could be obtained as cheaply.[24]

The outlying townships of Peterborough County were

[22]*Ibid.*, p. 88.   [23]Langton, *op. cit.*, p. 22 .
[24]Letter of William Hutton, dated at Belleville, June 20, 1834. (In *The British Farmer's Magazine*, April, 1835, p. 104).

settled chiefly by descendants of the pioneers, and it took about half a century to accomplish even a scattered settlement. In 1850 the total population of the county was 12,589, of which Harvey had 150, Burleigh only 46, and Belmont and Methuen none at all. In 1860 the Burleigh Road was blazed through a rugged wilderness to enable settlement to be pushed north of Stoney Lake towards Apsley and beyond; but for several years the district was burned over annually by forest fires, destroying all the bridges along the road.

In 1861 Giles Stone became the first white settler within the present confines of Burleigh Township, and two years later John Goulbourne erected a grist-mill on Eel's Creek, which empties into the eastern end of Stoney Lake; in the same year C. J. Vizard built a saw-mill on the same creek, and a few settlers entered the district. Even at present, however, all of the northern townships are but sparsely settled because of the rugged nature of the region, many parts of which are entirely useless for agriculture, and produce little but scrub timber, marsh hay and blueberries.

Peterborough County included what is now Victoria County until 1861. In still earlier times the entire district was known as the north riding of Northumberland County, which, with Durham, composed the old Newcastle District. Many interesting developments occurred in the County of Peterborough from time to time. Norwood and Hastings in Asphodel Township gradually grew into important villages, Hastings being known for twenty years as Crooks' Rapids after the Hon. James Crooks, whose house and mill formed the only building in 1835. Keene, in Otonabee Township, was part of the land of Thomas and Andrew Carr in 1819; but Dr. John Gilchrist built a grist-mill there in 1825, and five years later there was also a general store. In 1856 some 400 people lived in the village, which had been connected with Peterborough and Rice Lake by the Keene Road, opened under the direction of Captain Rubidge in the thirties. Another important advance in transportation facilities was the appearance on Rice Lake and the Otonabee in 1832-33 of two "fire-ships", as the Indians called them, the *Pemedash*[25] and the *Northumberland*.

[25]The complete name of this early steamship was *Pem-e-dash-cou-tay-ang* (Lake of the Burning Plains), the Indian appellation for Rice Lake.

In the fifties two railways, the Cobourg and Peterborough, and the Port Hope, Lindsay and Beaverton, were built to the thriving town of Peterborough, although they were due almost entirely to the initiative of the inhabitants of Cobourg and Port Hope, who hoped to make large profits in the transportation of lumber, grain and other produce to the front. Their expectations were not realized, however, largely because the competition between the lines prevented the success of either; but the railways were a valuable factor in Peterborough's development into an important city. In 1860 the Prince of Wales paid a fleeting visit to Peterborough, but the following year there was a very different visitation when three severe fires laid waste a large section of the town.

In the early eighties the Stricklands and Traills established summer homes on Stoney Lake, whose attractions had much earlier induced campers to its shores. The beauties of the Kawartha Lakes district were further brought to the attention of the public by the choice of Stoney Lake for the 1883 meet of the American Canoe Association, which comprised members from all parts of the continent. Since that time the region has become increasingly famous as a summer resort. The city of Peterborough is perhaps best known to the average person to-day as the site of the notable Lift Lock, opened in 1904, and as the home of the famous "Peterborough canoe", which calls one back to the days of Handsome Jack and the Indian Plains.

CHAPTER IV

ROUILLÉ—TORONTO—YORK, 1750-1803

FORT TORONTO

"Here, when the treasures of the forest vast,
Of meadows, streams and pools met their wide gaze,
The Frenchmen built a post, that here might come
Those wily craftsmen that could circumvent
The laws of Nature, and beguile her wealth
Into their packs; . . . .
And here they came—to Rouillé, through the vales
That skirt yon river with rich woods and deep
From source to sea."

MRS. S. A. CURZON.[1]

THE birth of the city of Toronto is so closely related to the history of the fur trade that some preliminary account of the events of an earlier period is essential. The lower lakes remained virtually unexplored until the last half of the seventeenth century, though a slight knowledge of Lake Ontario was gained by Champlain and Brûlé in 1615. Hennepin and La Salle led an expedition of exploration westward from Fort Frontenac in 1678, and early in the following year La Salle erected a stockade at the mouth of the Niagara River to facilitate trade between Michilimackinac and Montreal; by 1725 this post had become a more solid fortress.

In 1722, the British established, with the permission of the Iroquois, a trading-post at the western side of the mouth of the Oswego River; and from this post, called Chouéguen (Oswego), there was communication to the ocean by way of the Mohawk and Hudson Rivers. In 1728 a fort of stone was erected at Chouéguen, and it was the first British military post on Lake Ontario. It was to divert the trade from Chouéguen that the French decided to build a fort near the carrying-place of Toronto, over which the Indians brought their peltries from the northern hunting-grounds.

The attacks made by the Huron Indians, led by Champlain, against the Iroquois tribes south of Lake Ontario

[1] Mrs. S. A. Curzon: *Fort Toronto*. (In the Toronto *Mail and Empire*, September 6, 1887, the day the memorial column replacing the cairn was unveiled. The poem is reprinted in Dr. Scadding's pamphlet, *History of the Old French Fort at Toronto, and its Monument*. 1887. Appendix, pp. 43-5.)

were amply avenged at the middle of the seventeenth century, when the Iroquois practically exterminated the Huron nation in the Lake Simcoe region, as well as the Neutrals north of Lake Erie. As a result the entire territory was for a century or more the hunting-ground of the Iroquois.

From the Holland River southwards the Indians followed the Humber trail to Lake Ontario. The first suggestion of a fort at "the pass at Toronto" was made by Governor-General de Denonville in 1686, but it was to be situated at the Lake Huron end, and was to be a military post to keep the British from the district; this suggestion was not, however, acted upon. When it was seen during the second quarter of the next century that most of the trade went to the British post at Chouéguen, where better value was given in trade, it was suggested that the French traders cut prices at Detroit, Niagara and Frontenac in order to attract the Indians to these posts; if attempted at all, this did not have the desired effect of forcing the British to abandon Chouéguen. The French also sent men each spring to trade with the Indians of the village near the mouth of the Credit River, and they were often given ammunition and provisions on credit, making payment the next season with their furs.

The British continued to receive most of the commerce, however, and, in an effort to consolidate the Credit trade with that coming over the main portage route at the Humber, and the lesser trade down the Don and Rouge, (all of which passed along the north shore of Lake Ontario *en route* to Chouéguen), Governor Jonquière and Intendant Bigot wrote in the autumn of 1749 to Colonial Minister Rouillé proposing the establishment of a post near the mouth of the Humber, and "to send thither an officer, fifteen soldiers and some workmen to construct a small stockade fort there. The expense will not be great: the timber is at hand (*à portée*), and the remaining requisites can be conveyed by boat from Fort Frontenac. Too much care cannot be taken to prevent these Indians continuing their trade with the English; and to furnish them at this post with all their necessaries as cheap as at Chouéguen".[2]

[2]Jonquière and Bigot to Rouillé, October 9, 1749. Public Archives of Canada: Correspondance Générale, Series F, Vol. 93, p. 46.

F. S. Challener, R.C.A., O.S.A.

FORT ROUILLÉ

ELIZABETH POSTHUMA GWILLIM (MRS.
JOHN GRAVES SIMCOE) IN WELSH
DRESS

From Scadding's *Toronto of Old*

THE SITE OF FORT ROUILLÉ IN 1873

On April 15, 1750, Rouillé wrote that he was in complete agreement with the suggestion; he believed that it would very appreciably lessen the English trade at Chouéguen, though he considered that the British fort would be destroyed only if the Iroquois could be aroused to see "that such a post is contrary to their liberty and a usurpation which the English presume to make use of to acquire ownership of their lands".[3]

If any doubt remains that Rouillé was built in 1750, and not in 1749, (as marked on the column in the Canadian National Exhibition grounds), it is incontrovertibly dispelled by La Jonquière's letter to Rouillé dated August 20, 1750. In it he notes the Count's approval of his proposition, and states that, "to avoid loss to the King, I resolved to order Chevalier de Portneuf, an ensign serving at Fort Frontenac, to go there with a sergeant and four soldiers. He set out from the said fort on the 20th of May last, and at the same time a clerk appointed by the Intendant departed from Montreal with the necessary goods. . . . On arriving at Toronto Portneuf had a little palisaded fort built, and a small house to keep the King's goods in safety, and he remained there until the 17th of July last, when he left to rejoin his regiment, and the clerk went down to Montreal with the packages of peltries."[4]

To show that the barter had been satisfactory, even though the French were too late to obtain any of the early spring trade, La Jonquière states that seventy-nine packages, valued at about 18,000 livres, were sent to Montreal;

[3]Rouillé to Jonquière and Bigot, April 15, 1750. Series B, Vol. 91, p. 86.

[4]Jonquière to Rouillé, August 20, 1750. Series F, Vol. 95, p. 171. In Dr. Scadding's time the French correspondence quoted herein was either not available or was not used, the only authority for the building of Fort Rouillé being the *Documents Relative to the Colonial History of the State of New York*, 15 Volumes, edited by E. B. O'Callaghan, 1856-87. On page 201 of Volume X occurs a part of the above letter, defective both in translation and interpretation. This has consequently led Dr. Scadding and other historians into the error of dating the building of Fort Rouillé from 1749 instead of 1750. Recent French-Canadian historians who have had access to the original documents are correct in their account of the establishment of the Toronto post. See André Chagny: *Un Defenseur de la Nouvelle France*. 1913. pp. 148-9; and Pierre-Georges Roy: *Les Petites Choses de notre Histoire*. 1919-31, Vol. III, "Le Fondateur de Toronto", pp. 210 *et seq.*

and that more than 150 packages might have been obtained if the post had had a greater supply of cloth, brandy and bread to give in trade. The Indians promised that they would patronise the post in greater numbers the next year.[5]

The first Fort Rouillé, (named in honour of Antoine Louis Rouillé, Count de Jouy, the Colonial Minister), was but a temporary structure which was considered too small to resist a possible attack by unfriendly Indians; so La Jonquiére wrote that he would have "a fort built of double pickets, eighty feet by (indecipherable), not counting the throat of the bastions, with a lodging for the officer at the right side of the fort gate, and a guardhouse for twelve to fifteen soldiers at the left. The store will be placed along the parallel curtain where the clerk will live, and a bakery will be built in one of the bastions."[6]

Fort Rouillé was erected at the foot of the present Dufferin Street, near the lake shore. The location of the post as described by La Jonquière was "on the point of the bay of the peninsula at about a quarter of a league to the north of Toronto River, where the boat from Fort Frontenac can moor safely very close to land, and bring there all the needs for the fort and the trade". The anchorage is further described as "sheltered from all winds except the south, from which we could protect it by having a little jetty built"; and a captain with experience in navigating the river "engages to take the boat there without danger".[7]

In order that the post might be ready by April, 1751, La Jonquière and Bigot dispatched a carpenter and three helpers to Toronto to cut and square the timbers. The clerk, a baker, a cooper, and five or six men to help in the trading activities were also sent, and some twenty Indians who were good hunters and lived in the vicinity were probably expected to aid in supplying game as well as peltries during the winter.

Over a year later, on October 6, 1751, La Jonquière wrote to Rouillé that the men at the Toronto post worked all the previous winter, though hindered by illness; and that when Portneuf arrived there on April 23rd the build-

[5]Ibid.   [6]Ibid.
[7]Ibid. The word "north" in this description of the location of the fort must be an error for "east",

ings were sufficiently advanced, though not complete. Since there was no place to store the powder, Portneuf had stone prepared to build a magazine. He also informed the Governor that "the situation is very advantageous for the establishment of a saw-mill, the stream furnishing water in abundance all the year round". With regard to the success of the trade La Jonquière stated that "it will return the funds that the King spent for this fort and to supply the store".[8]

The post at the pass of Toronto seldom received the name which had been conferred upon it, but was more generally called Fort Toronto, the name being also (though less frequently) spelled Taronto, Tarontha, Toranto, Torronto, Toronton, Toreto and Tarento. This appellation had first been applied to Matchedash Bay, had later penetrated inland to Lake Simcoe, and then to the Trent system as a whole, which frequently went by the name Toronto Lakes. It is most generally accepted that "Toronto" is derived from the Huron tongue, and signifies "a place of meeting", as almost any part of the portage route from Lake Ontario to Lake Huron might well be. An Indian town of the Mississagués was early located on Lake Simcoe (which was known at various times as Lake Le Clie, Lac aux Claies, Quentironk, Sheniong, Torento and Toronto). The word Toronto as applied to this lake or the settlement on its shores signified "the populous region", and the name apparently spread in various directions to indicate the trail leading to Toronto Lake, for the village was but a small one after the Iroquois invasion at the middle of the seventeenth century.

Authorities do not even agree, however, upon the Indian language from which the word originates, much less as to its interpretation. There are several other places in North America which have the name Toronto, and experts in etymology find that the derivation "place of meeting" suits by no means all of them. The chief other suggested origin of "Toronto" is that it signifies "an opening into a lake"; this would apply equally well to the "Baie de Toronto" (Matchedash) and to the location of our own city, as well

[8]Jcnquière to Rouillé, October 6, 1751. Series F, Volume 97, p. 107.

as to several other localities where the name was early in use.[9]

Fort Rouillé was never a first-class trading-post. In 1754 there were five soldiers, one officer, two sergeants and a storekeeper, and only five canoes were needed to transport thither annually about 35,000 livres ($5,833) worth of goods. This was sufficient to trade for 1,700 pounds of good beaver, at a rate varying from three livres ten sous to five livres per lb. Dr. Scadding describes how the region just west of the mouth of the Humber "would be dotted over with numerous temporary wigwams; and a double file of traffickers, male and female, would be seen on the track leading eastward toward the stockade on the cliff a little way down the Bay,—some going, eager to effect sales, others returning pleased, or the contrary, with terms secured, or gloating over some useful or showy purchase just made."[10]

There are but few descriptions of Fort Toronto as it appeared during the nine years of its existence. On June 26, 1752, Father François Picquet, founder of the Oswegatchie mission at Ogdensburg, across the river from Prescott, was making a tour of Lake Ontario in a "King's boat", and visited Fort Toronto. He found "good bread and good wine, and everything necessary for the trade",[11] something that could not always be said of the other posts.

Captain Pouchot, the last French commandant at Niagara, described Fort Toronto's location as "at the end of the bay, on the side which is quite elevated and covered by flat rock, so that vessels cannot approach within cannon shot". In appearance the post was "a square of about 180 feet on a side externally, with flanks of fifteen feet. It

[9]Among other suggestions as to the origin of the name is one which gives the interpretation "trees in the water", and another which traces "Toronto" back to Champlain's Huron friend, D'Arontal. The former of these is generally considered to be a misinterpretation of an Indian word; while the latter is rendered most improbable by the fact that there is hardly an instance where place-names have been given by the Indians in honour of one of themselves,—and there are, in addition, the localities in other parts of America named Toronto, which certainly could have no connection with D'Arontal. It appears likely, however, that the source of the name will always remain a matter of individual opinion, though some opinions are infinitely better than others.
[10]Henry Scadding: *History of the Old French Fort at Toronto, and its Monument.* 1887. p. 16.
[11]André Chagny: *Un Défenseur de la Nouvelle France.* 1913. p. 149.

was very well built—piece upon piece, but was only useful for trade". Concerning the Humber portage route Pouchot says: "A league west of the fort is the mouth of the Toronto River, which is of considerable size. This river communicates with Lake Huron by a portage of fifteen leagues, and is frequented by the Indians who come from the north."[12]

The post at Toronto was generally considered unnecessary by the French, and during the Seven Years' War those at the fort were kept in a state of anxiety because the English were continually stirring up the natives against them. In 1757 about ninety Mississauga Indians on the way to Montreal formed a plot to pillage the fort in order to get the stores of brandy. M. de Noyelle, in charge of the ten men and storekeeper then at the post, learned secretly of the proposed attack and informed Captain Pouchot at Niagara, who immediately sent two bateaux armed with swivel guns, which speedily intimidated the Indians encamped near the fort.

In 1756 Montcalm had captured Chouéguen, but two years later it was recovered by Colonel Haldimand; in 1758 occurred also the capture of Fort Frontenac by Colonel Bradstreet. As a result of these reverses Governor-General de Vaudreuil wrote to France at the time: "If the English should make their appearance at Toronto, I have given orders to burn it at once, and to fall back on Niagara."[13] This order was carried out in the summer of 1759, and when Sir William Johnson sent some thirty men in three whaleboats from Niagara to Rouillé on July 27th, they found only "five heaps of charred timber and planks, with a low chimney-stack of coarse brick and shattered flooring at its foot, made of flagstones from the adjoining beach, the whole surrounded on the inland side by three lines of cedar pickets more or less broken down and scathed by fire".[14]

The charred ruins of Fort Toronto remained distinguishable for over a century, and for fifty or sixty years were quite a prominent landmark. On September 30, 1760, the year after the burning of the post, Major Robert Rogers visited the ruins and noted that 300 acres around the fort

---

[12]François Pouchot: *Memoir upon the Late War in North America, 1755-60.* 1866. Vol. II, p. 119.
[13]Quoted in Scadding, *op. cit.*, p. 22.
[14]*Ibid.*

had been cleared,[15] probably for fuel during the ten years of the post's existence, and for pickets and other defences; the space would also be a protection against sudden attack. In 1788, when Captain Gother Mann's *Plan of the Proposed Toronto Harbour* was made, the remains of Fort Toronto were still prominent. Mrs. Simcoe visited the ruins several times during her residence in York, 1793-96; while in 1813, when York was captured by the Americans, reference is made by their commander to "the ruins of the ancient French fort Tarento".[16] Until 1878 there were visible shallow trenches where the palisades had been, and irregularities in surface were conspicuous, though by that time part of the old site had fallen into the lake, the remainder being enclosed by a rough fence in a bad state of repair. In that year the ground was levelled and a pillar erected to mark the spot, largely through the efforts of the venerable historian of Toronto, the late Dr. Henry Scadding.

In the early British period the Humber-Holland trail continued to be the usual route to the upper lakes. That the carriage of furs over the portage was considerable may be judged from the statement of Sir William Johnson in a dispatch to the Earl of Shelburne in 1767 that, if the trading-post were restored, "traders would be willing to give as much as a thousand pounds for the monopoly of a season's trade with the Indians". In 1770 a *coureur de bois*, Jean Baptiste Rousseau, (commonly known as St. John), was given a license to trade there. His post, located on the east side of the mouth of the Humber, with an orchard of cherry trees in the rear, was probably built many years earlier, for the Humber was known as St. John's Creek as early as 1756. St. John, who might be called the last French and first British citizen of Toronto, was not, however, the only trader in the locality, for in 1761-3 at least two others, Bâby and Knaggs, were debauching the Indians by the rum trade. British troops under orders from General Gage seized Knaggs and his supplies in 1763.[17]

[15]Robert Rogers: *Journal of Major Robert Rogers*. 1765. p. 206.
[16]Dearborn to the Secretary of War, April 28, 1813.
[17]The details of these nefarious activities are to be found in the unprinted correspondence of General Amherst in the Public Records Office, London, England. See letter of W. B. Kerr in Fred Williams: *Do You Know?*, in the Toronto *Mail and Empire*, December 12, 1932.

In 1787 the British Government recognised the importance of the trade route by buying a considerable amount
of the land from the ruins of Rouillé northward, the tract
being the second district in Upper Canada to be purchased
from the Indians, though the sale was not entirely completed when the first palaver was held at the Carrying
Place, Bay of Quinté. On August 1, 1805, a second meeting
with the Indians took place at the Credit River, when
250,808 acres, made up largely of York, Etobicoke, Vaughan
and King Townships, was transferred to British control for
£1700 sterling.

Joseph Bouchette visited the site of Toronto in 1793,
before the founding of York, and afterwards wrote with
reference to his survey of the harbour: "I distinctly recollect the untamed aspect which the country exhibited when
first I entered the beautiful basin, which thus became the
scene of my early hydrographical operations. Dense and
trackless forests lined the margin of the lake and reflected their inverted images in its glassy surface. The
wandering savage had constructed his ephemeral habitation beneath their luxuriant foliage—the group then consisting of two families of Mississaugas—and the bay and
neighbouring marshes were the hitherto uninvaded haunts
of immense coveys of wild-fowl."[18]

The wigwams in which the two families of Mississaugas
lived had probably been constructed many years earlier, and
had been used by various Indians passing back and forth
over the trade route; for there is no record of a permanent
Indian settlement on the site of Toronto, though the village
Taiaiagon, west of the Humber, was in existence at least as
early as 1678, when Hennepin passed that way.

Previous to the creation of the Province of Upper Canada the British Government had decided to establish a town
at Toronto. In 1788 Surveyor-General Collins reported the
harbour to be "capacious, safe and well-sheltered",[19] and
three years later Augustus Jones, Provincial Land Surveyor,
was busy examining the same district. The first capital
of the province, however, was Niagara (Newark), although

[18]J. Bouchette: *The British Dominions in North America*. 1831. Vol.
    I, p. 89 fn.
[19]Quoted in Scadding: *Memoirs of Four Decades of York, Upper
    Canada*. 1884. p. 10.

Kingston desired the honour, and the Governor himself would have preferred the present site of London when he learned that Fort Niagara, close by the infant capital, was in United States territory and about to be garrisoned by American troops. This first choice of Simcoe's, "Georgina-upon-Thames", was made during his first tour of the Western District in February, 1793; but the Governor-General, Lord Dorchester, disallowed it, and Simcoe had to content himself with Toronto.

From Mrs. Simcoe's diary we obtain a knowledge of the Governor's arrival at Toronto, and of early life there, that was not available when Dr. Scadding wrote his *Toronto of Old*. On May 2, 1793, the Governor made his first visit to Toronto, accompanied by seven officers, the expedition following the shore line in a bateau around the head of Lake Ontario. Governor Simcoe was immediately impressed by the fine harbour, and selected the location as the site of his future capital. On May 13th Mrs. Simcoe wrote in her diary: "Colonel Simcoe returned from Toronto, and speaks in praise of the harbour, and a fine spot near it covered with large oaks, which he intends to fix as a site for a town."[20]

On July 29th Mrs. Simcoe sailed to Toronto on the sloop *Onondaga*, and the party camped in tents just east of the present Old Fort. While the soldiers were clearing away the trees and preparing the "canvas houses", the Governor's wife "went in a boat two miles to the bottom of the bay, and walked through a grove of oaks, where the town is intended to be built".[21] Soon after, Augustus Jones surveyed a series of lots on the shore of the lake from St. John's Creek (the Humber) eastward, leaving spaces for proposed roadways. In his notes he mentions "the Blacksmith's old house", which Dr. Scadding suggests was a forge near the ruins of Fort Rouillé, where the Indians and traders had repaired their implements and guns.[22]

On August 26, 1793, the Governor changed the name from Toronto to York in honour of the Duke of York, who had won a notable victory over the French; at noon the

[20]*Diary of Mrs. John Graves Simcoe*, May 13, 1793.
[21]*Ibid.*, July 30, 1793.
[22]See Scadding: *History of the Old French Fort*, p. 29.

John Ross Robertson Collection   Mrs. John Graves Simcoe

Castle Frank in the Summer of 1796

From Scadding's *Toronto of Old*

York Harbour, from the Blockhouse East of the Don, 1813

THE GARRISON AT YORK, 1796
The small building on the shore is the magazine

THE GARRISON AS IT IS TODAY
This building, the Officers' Mess, was commenced in 1840

following day the first royal salute was fired from the garrison of Toronto and responded to by the shipping in the harbour in commemoration of the change in name. Some people objected to Simcoe's policy of anglicising the place-names of Upper Canada: for instance, Isaac Weld, who travelled in Upper Canada in 1796, wrote: "It is to be lamented that the Indian names, so grand and sonorous, should ever have been changed for others. Newark, Kingston, York are poor substitutes for the original names of the respective places Niagara, Cataraqui, Toronto." Weld also mentions that before he arrived in Niagara "orders had been issued for the removal of the seat of government from Niagara to Toronto" (Weld would not use the new names!) ; and he says that "the projected change is by no means relished by the people at large".[23]

The first official plan of York was drawn in 1793 for the Governor by Alexander Aitkin, and shows the site of the town to the west of the Don, the proposed location of the battery on Gibraltar Point (Hanlan's), and the barracks at the eastern end of the present Exhibition grounds. Simcoe tried to prevent York from becoming a straggling village by setting aside the entire waterfront of the western section of the Bay as a Garrison Reserve, and to his action we owe the availability of the land for the great Fair over three-quarters of a century later. Until modern times the island was a peninsula, joined to the mainland at the foot of the present Woodbine Avenue. The small sandy connection was gradually weakened, and in 1858 the waters of Lake Ontario broke through during the course of a heavy wind, and the island was created.

In Simcoe's time the boundaries of the town were George Street on the west, Ontario Street on the east, Duchess Street on the north and Palace (Front) Street on the south. The main thoroughfare was King Street. Ontario Street appears to have followed the course of the trail leading to the canoe landing, where it was usual to carry small boats across the narrow neck of land between the lake and the bay. Palace Street was so called because of the plans to erect a residence for the Governor there, though the

[23]Isaac Weld: *Travels through the States of North America.* 1799. p. 296.

structure became the Parliament Buildings; and from 1797
to 1824 the seat of government was located at the corner
of Parliament (now Berkeley) and Palace Streets.

We owe to Mrs. Simcoe's artistic ability the only pictures of York before 1800, and from her diary we catch a
glimpse of life there during the first years of the town.[24]
She describes rides she took on the peninsula, and along
the north shore of the lake "till we were impeded by large
trees on the beach"; of rowing in "Mr. Grant's (the surveyor's) boat to the highlands of Toronto. They appeared
so well that we talked of building a summer residence there
and calling it Scarborough".[25]   On another occasion she
"walked two miles to the old French Fort, but there are no
remains of any building there".[26]   One day some Ojibway
Indians "brought the Governor 'a beaver blanket to make
his bed', as they expressed themselves, ... and invited
him to visit their country".[27]   On September 11, 1793, Mrs.
Simcoe "rowed six miles up the Don to Coons', who had a
farm under a hill covered with pine".[28]   The diary contains
a detailed account of the Governor's trips northward to the
Lake Simcoe region, expeditions which were made by canoe,
or on sleds in winter.[29]

During the spring of 1794 Castle Frank, a combined
summer residence and Government House, was built; it
was a frame building, on the heights overlooking the Don
Valley, just beyond the northern boundary of the present
St. James' Cemetery. The location was very dear to the
Simcoes, but after they left Canada the building was but
little used, and in 1829 was burned by a fire left by careless
fishermen.

The first bridge over the Don was known as Playter's
because it was on the land granted to Captain George
Playter, an early Loyalist settler in York. It was located at
the foot of Winchester Street. Mrs. Simcoe thus describes
it: "I passed Playter's picturesque bridge over the Don;
it is a butternut tree fallen across the river, the branches

[24]John Ross Robertson, the editor of Mrs. Simcoe's diary, reproduced
most of her Canadian sketches. The volume, published in a
limited edition in 1911, is now comparatively scarce.
[25]*Diary*, August 4, 1793.   [26]*Ibid.*, August 5, 1793.
[27]*Ibid.*, August 9, 1793.   [28]*Ibid.*, September 11, 1793.
[29]*Ibid.*, September 25, 1793, *et seq.*

still growing full leaf. Mrs. Playter being timorous, a pole
was fastened through the branches to hold by. Having
attempted to pass it I was determined to proceed, but was
frightened before I got half way."[30] Mrs. Simcoe had another adventure in June, 1796, when she and her little
daughter Sophia accompanied the Governor on a lake trip
during a severe storm. They were proceeding east from
Burlington in a canoe and were surprised how well their
frail boat rode the waves; but Mrs. Simcoe felt much more
at ease when they landed at the mouth of the River Credit,
where "numbers of Indians resort to fish for salmon".[31]

Governor Simcoe wished York to be a very English
town, but under his *régime* it developed chiefly as a military
establishment. The garrison of some 200 Queen's Rangers
formed the great bulk of the population, and these men
were set to work constructing buildings and opening up
roads, especially Yonge and Dundas Streets. The fort of
Simcoe's day was on the lake shore, with Garrison Creek on
two sides of it. It is believed that the building long called
No. 1 blockhouse dates from 1798, though it was to some
extent reconstructed in 1815-16. Several others among the
group at the foot of Bathurst Street were built soon after
the close of the War of 1812, but there have been alterations to most of them at one time or another.

Advertisements in Upper Canada's first newspaper give
us some knowledge of the early development of York. In
the Niagara *Upper Canada Gazette, or American Oracle*
of July 10, 1794, appears the following: "Wanted—Carpenters for the public buildings to be erected at York.
Applications to be made to John McGill, Esq., at York, or
to Mr. Allan MacNab, at Navy Hall."[32] John Ogden visited
York, "called by the natives Torento", and observed the
preparations: "A town is here in great forwardness, and
should the seat of government be removed from Newark
thence, as is contemplated, it will soon become a flourishing place".[33]

In 1796 work was proceeding on the Parliament Buildings, modest halls built of brick, one for each legislative

[30]*Ibid.*, July 6, 1796.   [31]*Ibid.*, June 16, 1796.
[32]*Upper Canada Gazette*, July 10, 1794.
[33]John Ogden: *A Tour through Upper and Lower Canada*, 1799 pp.
       100-2.

body. A landing-pier and a canal or navigable opening into Garrison Creek was also being constructed, a warrant being signed by the Lieutenant-Governor authorising the Commissioner of Stores, Mr. McGill, "to supply from time to time from the Government stores such quantities of rum as may be required to be given to the men (Queen's Rangers) employed on the wharf and canal at York".[34]

From a report[35] concerning public property in Upper Canada, issued by the Hon. Peter Russell in 1799, we learn the extent of the first military works at York. A saw-mill had been erected on the Humber to supply boards and other materials. Round log huts were constructed in 1793 and 1794 as quarters for the Queen's Rangers, as well as a similar structure in the latter year for the commissary of stores. Canals, locks and wharves were built at the Garrison to aid in landing provisions and supplies safely, and to provide a shelter for the three bateaux. A bridge was also constructed there, and a roadway pushed westward as far as the Humber, presumably as part of Simcoe's projected highway, Dundas Street.

In 1795 a powder magazine of squared hemlock logs was erected, and the intervals between the log huts were gradually stockaded; a similar protection was raised in front of the huts on the Parade, and gates with locks and bars were put up. A large blockhouse barracks was also constructed and occupied by the soldiers, and a storehouse of two storeys for the Indian presents. The Hon. Peter Russell states that 40,000 bricks had been supplied at one time or another for the building of new bakeries, chimneys and ovens.

Two one-storey brick buildings, originally intended as the wings of a residence for the Lieutenant-Governor, were erected in the town. They were each twenty-five feet by forty, and were about 100 hundred feet apart. The houses in their rear were advanced to the front as guardhouses, and some of them were later incorporated into a sort of gallery or passageway between the brick wings; here it was that the sessions of the second parliament of Upper

---

[34]Quoted in Scadding: *Four Decades of York*, p. 21.
[35]Report concerning public property in Upper Canada, 1799. (Unpublished).

Canada were held, and the building served also as a court
of justice.

In 1795 La Rochefoucauld-Liancourt, a French duke,
found about twelve houses in York, chiefly located along the
Bay near the Don. One of these was the Scadding cottage,
erected in 1796 on the east side of the Don; this is the York
Pioneers' log house now located in Exhibition Park. The
Duke shared in the love of his nation for the United States,
and consequently grasped the opportunity to cast a slur on
William Berczy's settlers in Markham Township, who had
in the previous year abandoned the Pulteney settlement
across the lake, in the Genesee River district, and had come
to Upper Canada. In describing York he says: "The inhabitants do not possess the fairest character. One of them
is the noted Baty, the leader of the German families. . . .
In a circumference of 150 miles the Indians are the only
neighbours of York."[36] The reference was undoubtedly intended, therefore, to apply to the German settlers up Yonge
Street, though it must be admitted that there were some
inhabitants of York to whom it would have been more
applicable.

When the Simcoes left York on the *Onondaga,* on July
21, 1796, Mrs. Simcoe felt so badly that she cried all day,
for the town was about to take on a new importance as
the capital of Upper Canada, the climax of the plans of the
Governor and his wife who had so thoroughly enjoyed themselves in the little garrison settlement in the wilds; they
had been the founders of the town which was soon to be
variously called "Little", "Muddy", or "Dirty" York.

One of the noted achievements of Governor Simcoe was
the opening of Yonge Street to Lake Simcoe. The road had
been commenced both by the Rangers and by Berczy's
settlers in 1794, but it was not open for the whole distance
until February 16, 1796. Augustus Jones was the surveyor
in charge of this work, as of many other early surveys in
Upper Canada. Simcoe's dream of a highway across the
province from east to west was not realised until long after

---

[36]La Rochefoucauld-Liancourt: *Travels through the United States of
    North America.* 1799. Vol. I, p. 269. "Baty" is presumably a
    translator's error for "Berczy".

his death, though a start was made in 1793 on some sections of Dundas Street west of Burlington Bay.

After Simcoe's departure, Acting-Governor Russell wrote from Niagara to an official in York that, as the legislature would meet there on the 1st of June, "you will therefore be pleased to apprise the inhabitants of the town that twenty-five gentlemen will want board and lodgings during the session, which may possibly induce them to fit up their houses and lay in provisions to accommodate them".[37] The officials of the government sailed in the *Mohawk* for York, at the end of May, 1797. Perhaps they were not all taken care of satisfactorily, for a traveller who visited the town in 1798 described it as "a dreary dismal place, not even possessing the characteristics of a village. There is no church, schoolhouse, nor in fact any of the ordinary signs of civilisation. There is no inn; and those travellers who have no friends to go to, pitch a tent and live there while they remain."[38]

In the early years of the new century all the buildings in York were of wood except the government buildings and Quetton St. George's general store; and almost all were of log construction, though frame clap-board houses were occasionally found. The residence of the Lieutenant-Governor is described as "likewise formed of wood, in the figure of a half square, of one story in height, with galleries in the centre. It is sufficiently commodious for the present state of the province, and is erected upon a bank of the lake, near the mouth of Toronto Bay."[39]

In 1797 York consisted of twelve city blocks immediately north of the Parliament Buildings, which were located close to the water front at the foot of Parliament (now Berkeley) Street. Six of these blocks were on the north and six on the south of the present King Street, and most of the street names were in honour of the Royal Family. At that time even Church Street was remote from the business district of York, while the present corner of King and Yonge Streets was not even a cross-road! Upper Yonge Street was ap-

[37]Scadding: *Four Decades of York*, p. 28.
[38]Memoirs of Mrs. Breakenridge, daughter of Dr. W. W. Baldwin, quoted in William Canniff: *History of the Settlement of Upper Canada*. 1869. pp. 530-1.
[39]George Heriot: *Travels through the Canadas*. 1807. p. 138.

proached by a trail along the route of the present Parliament Street, the section of Yonge Street below Yorkville having fallen into disuse soon after it was opened by Surveyor Jones. Hospital (Richmond) Street and Lot (Queen) Street were the usual routes by which one entered the town. Russell Abbey, the residence of the President of the Provisional Government of Upper Canada, was located at the corner of Palace and Princess Streets.

The material development of York between 1797 and 1803 was very gradual, but many events are of interest for they form the very foundation stones of a great city. "Our Town of York", as the governors called it in their proclamations, remained a very small settlement for a quarter of a century. Officials, merchants and tradesmen gradually occupied the original townsite and spread westward along the shore towards the Garrison, but at no point did the straggling town extend northward more than a few hundred feet. Dr. Scadding describes the course of development as commencing at the government buildings, "the Westminster of the New Capital", and spreading along its "Strand" towards the fort: "Growing slowly westward it developed, in the customary American way, its hotel, its tavern, boarding-house, wagon factory, tinsmith shop, bakery, general store, its lawyer's office, printing office and places of worship."[40]

The mud and the numerous stumps in the streets, added greatly to difficulties of transport. One man wrote to the Niagara *Canada Constellation* in 1799 that "if any gentleman will come forward and pledge his honour (he being perfectly sober at the time) that he will introduce a bill in the House of Assembly for the purpose of a Stump Act for the city of York he shall have my vote at the ensuing general election".[41] This type of law appears to have been effective in Vergennes, Vermont, where each drunk was forced to remove one stump from the streets. In the following year a Stump Act was in force in York, and many a root was removed by topers, who might be sentenced to eradicate one or more stumps from the highways of the town.

[40]Scadding: *Toronto of Old.* 1873. p. 28.
[41]Niagara *Canada Constellation*, December 14, 1799. See also *ibid.*, December 20, 1800, quoted *infra*, p. 282.

The inconvenience of having to reach Yonge Street by following a trail along Parliament Street led to the re-opening of that part of Yonge from Lot (Queen) Street to the three-mile post. The York *Gazette* of December 20, 1800, gives an account of a meeting held to consider the matter:

"A number of the principal inhabitants of the town met together in one of the Government Buildings to consider the means of opening the road to Yonge Street, and enabling the farmers there to bring their provisions to market with more ease than is practicable at present. . . . The Hon. the Chief Justice (Elmsley) was called to the chair. . . .

"A paper was then produced and read, containing a proposal from Eliphalet Hale to open and make the road, or so much of it as might be required, at the rate of twelve dollars per acre for clearing it, where no causeway was wanted, four rods wide, and cutting the stumps in the two middle rods close to the ground, and 7s. 6d. Provincial currency per rod for making a causeway 18 feet wide, where a causeway might be wanted. Mr. Hale's proposal was accepted; . . . . and a petition of the Legislature lies for signature at Mr. McDougall's Tavern, and subscriptions will be received by Messrs. Allan and Wood."[42]

This work was completed in June, 1802, and was for some years known as "the road to Yonge Street".

York, in common with other municipalities, was governed by officials appointed by the citizens at the town-meeting. The most important offices to be filled were those of clerk, collector and assessor, but there were also path-masters or overseers of the roads, fence-viewers, pound-keepers and town wardens. One of the pathmasters of York, John McDougall, was publicly complimented in the *Gazette* for his "great assiduity and care in getting the streets cleared of the many and dangerous (especially at night) obstructions therein". Three weeks later, on July 20, 1799, Mr. Clark, pathmaster for the west end of the town, was similarly congratulated.[43]

In 1797 George Street was the western boundary of the

York, the New Capital of Upper Canada, 1803

The "Baie de Toronto" from the Island, 1932

town, but in June of that year D. W. Smith drew up a
Plan for the Enlargement of York by which Peter Street
was the new boundary. For some years, however, comparatively few of the inhabitants lived west of George
Street. A small wharf stood at the foot of Frederick
Street, and above the beach, on an embankment some ten
or fifteen feet high, was a path often used as a promenade.
The shores of the Bay were in most parts well covered with
a growth of small cedars, while the waters abounded with
rushes and seaweeds. Mosquitoes were consequently very
numerous, and the inhabitants of York were frequently
stricken with intermittent fever carried by the mosquitoes
and aggravated by the general dampness of the climate,
which also led to severe colds, or agues, as they were long
called. At the mouth of the Don was an extensive marsh,
and early plans of the town note that the inhabitants are
permitted to cut the hay in these beautiful meadows.

Soon after York replaced Niagara as the capital the
official publication of the government was transferred to
the town. The original name of the newspaper was *The
Upper Canada Gazette, or American Oracle,* and the first
number to be printed in York appeared on October 4, 1798.
Another result of the increased importance of York was
that a post office was established there in 1799. The public
mail was brought at infrequent intervals by couriers or
other travellers on foot, horseback or in sailing-ship, though
a purely governmental service by Schenectady boat began
in the summer of 1794, and was carried on weekly during
the season of navigation. The York postmaster appears
to have had his share of troubles, and announces his resignation in 1801:

"To prevent disappointment and trouble, the public is
requested to take notice that some time ago Mr. Willcocks
resigned his place as Postmaster for York, his reasonable
charges for the rent of an office, stationery, fire, candles,
and a servant to attend being disputed; although by his
assiduity and attention the revenue was productive beyond
expectation, as appears by the accounts he rendered, and the
money he remitted to the Postmaster-General at Quebec."[44]

[44]*Ibid.,* December 19, 1801.

As no newspaper was published in York until October 4, 1798, we have little or no record of the development of business and trade prior to that date. The announcements in the *Gazette*, (the word "advertisement" would be considered too vulgar in those days!), are invaluable in that they enable the compilation of at least a partial list of the first business men of the town.

Abner Miles' Inn was the most important, if not also the first hotel in York. His day-book for 1798 survived the ravages of time at least long enough for the noted antiquarian, Dr. Henry Scadding, to make excerpts from it which add considerably to our knowledge of early life in the town. Some of the gentry were accustomed to give little dinners at Miles', and the charges for these and for liquor were frequently left unpaid for many months. Messrs. Bâby and Hamilton and Commodore Grant are jointly billed in July, 1798, for "twenty-two dinners at Eight shillings, £8 16s. Sixteen to Coffee, £1 12s. Eight Suppers, 16s. Twenty-three quarts and one pint of wine, £10 11s. 6d. Eight bottles of porter, £2 8s. Two bottles of syrup-punch, £1 4s. One bottle of brandy and one bottle of rum, 18s. Altogether amounting to £26 5s. 6d." (The amounts are in New York Currency, in which the shilling was seven pence half-penny.)

Among other events in Miles' Hotel was a "St. John's Dinner", for which Thomas Ridout, Jonathan Scott, Colonel Fortune, Surveyor Jones, Samuel Heron, Mr. Secretary Jarvis, Adjutant McGill and Mr. Crawford are each charged 16s. Chief Justice Elmsley was a prominent patron of the establishment, as was also Judge Powell. A reverend traveller's call at the inn is entered: "Priest from River La Tranche, 3 quarts corn and half-pint wine. Breakfast, 2s. 6d.", a notably frugal order in comparison with the others. Those interested in the names of the drinks of other days will find charges entered in the day-book for "gin slings", "rum slings", "sour punch", and "syrup-punch". The genial landlord occasionally advanced cash to his customers, and carried on in his inn a general store from which butter, eggs, beef, leather, buttons, "cassimere", lumber and other commodities were supplied at the prevailing high prices.

His tavern was also the rendezvous for auction sales, town-meetings and club dinners.[45]

One of the first general stores in York was that operated by O. Pierce & Co., who announce in 1799 that they have for sale spirits, rum, brandy, port wine and gin by the gallon, puncheon or barrel, at prices varying from 18s. to 22s. per gallon; also "teas, Hyson, 19s. per lb.; Souchong, 14s.; Bohea 8s.; sugar, best loaf, 3s. 9d. per lb.; lump, 3s. 6d.; raisins 3s.; figs 3s.; salt, six dollars per barrel, or 12s. per bushel. Also a few dry goods, shoes, leather, hats, tobacco, snuff, etc., etc."[46] P. Mealey also kept a general store in 1800; while in 1802 Quetton St. George & Co., at the north east corner of Frederick and King Streets, advertise a line of groceries and goods of a general nature.[47] This store was at the house of William Willcocks, said to have been the second brick building in York.

William Cooper's "Toronto Coffee House" was advertised on December 12, 1801, as ready for business. This combined inn and general store was probably located on Wellington Street. Customers were promised "genteel board and lodging", and "the best liquors, viands, etc."[48] In November, 1802, Cooper inserted the following advertisement in the *Gazette*:

"Toronto Coffee House—William Cooper begs leave to acquaint his friends and the public that he has erected a large and convenient stable on his own lot opposite the Toronto Coffee House, and stored it well with hay and oats of the very best quality. Travellers will meet with genteel and comfortable accommodation at the above house, and their horses will be carefully attended to.

"He has just received from New York a large supply of the best wines, brandy, Hollands, shrub, fresh lime juice, London porter, oysters, anchovies, red herrings, Devonshire, Navy and Cavis sauces, segars, pipes and tobacco. He has also received a very general assortment of groceries

[45]See Scadding's *Toronto of Old*, pp. 44-7.
[46]*Upper Canada Gazette*, July 13, 1799.
[47]*Ibid.*, December 11, 1802. Interesting lists of various types of commodities advertised by St. George as "just arrived from New York" may be found in Scadding's *Toronto of Old*, pp. 190-91.
[48]*Upper Canada Gazette*, December 12, 1801.

and dry goods, which he will sell cheap for cash or exchange for country produce."[49]

In early times it was believed that the inhabitants of Canada would derive great wealth from the ginseng that grew in the swamps, for in China it was worth its weight in silver, since it was considered a kind of "all-heal". In 1801 Jacob Herchmer was among those who were buying ginseng, which was then worth 2s. per pound dried, or 1s. if green. Hemp was another product which was early expected to add greatly to the profits of Canadian farmers, and at the same time, in this instance, to supply the British navy with sail-cloth and rope. The Hon. John McGill, the Hon. D. W. Smith and Thomas Scott were commissioners in York to distribute hemp seed gratis to farmers.

There is no record of the operation of any breweries or distilleries in York during the early years of the town. Imported wines were probably more in favour with the gentry, and there was, moreover, a considerable manufacture of birch beer, a very popular drink among those who did not aspire to social heights. The making of candles by the chandler, and of soap and potash in a potashery, were typical manufactures of the pioneer period. There was a great trade with England in wood ashes and potash, which is recalled by the following advertisement:

"Ashes wanted. Seven pence, Halifax currency, per bushel for house ashes will be given delivered at the Potash Works (opposite the jail) and five pence, same currency, if taken from the houses; also eight pence, New York currency, for field ashes delivered at the works. It is recommended to those persons who have ashes to be careful in keeping them dry, otherwise they will not be taken. Any quantity will be received at a time by W. Allan, York."

W. Allan held in the following year (1801) the offices of Collector of Duties and Inspector of Pot and Pearl Ashes and Flour, and in later years he was Postmaster; but he was not the only dealer in ashes, for Duke Kendrick erected a potashery on lot No. 7, west side of Yonge Street, in December, 1799. Under the heading "Ashes! Ashes! Ashes!" he advertises the price he is prepared to pay, with the explanation (which had often to be made in pioneer

[49]*Ibid.*, November 27, 1802.

days) that "he conceives it his duty to inform those who may have ashes to dispose of, that it will not be in his power to pay cash, but merchandise at cash price".[50]

It was never easy to collect debts in a period when money was very scarce and barter was the usual means of carrying on business. John Horton, in an announcement in the *Gazette*, "requests all those who are indebted to him, and whose accounts ought to have been paid long ago, to make payment in the course of one month from this date, or unpleasant measures will be recurred to; evasive answers from those whose accounts have been given in will not satisfy *his* creditors; he therefore hopes that this notice will be productive of something more than promises from those whose accounts remain unpaid."[51]

It was a time when a man frequently found it necessary to be a jack-of-all-trades if he was to support his family. In addition to all his other activities William Cooper became one of the first auctioneers in York, and announces his new profession in the following notice:

"William Cooper begs leave to inform his friends and the public in general that he has lately received License as Auctioneer for this Town. That he has appropriated a part of his house in Duke Street for the purpose of an auction room, which will be made as commodious as possible; where every attention will be paid to such articles as his friends may be pleased to honor him with the disposal of. He flatters himself that the tenor of his conduct heretofore will entitle him to the confidence and patronage of the public; secrecy will be strictly observed on his part.

"He will sell by auction at the house of Mr. John M'Dougall, between the hours of 11 and 12 o'clock on Monday, the 22nd instant, 4 barrels of prime tobacco, 1 do. of pork, a well assorted library of books in different languages; some of the most fashionable coloured fine and refine cloths, together with sundry other articles too tedious to mention."[52]

At least as early as 1799 York had a fashionable tailor, for one glorying in the unique name of Evean Eveans, with

---

[50]Allan's advertisement appears in the *Gazette* of November 22, 1800; Kendrick's in that of December 21, 1799.
[51]*Ibid.*, November 4, 1801.   [52]*Ibid.*, September 13, 1800.

the added lustre of coming from London, announces his business in a very neat note:

"Evean Eveans, taylor and habit maker, (From London), having taken a room in a small building belonging to Mr. Willcocks for the purpose of prosecuting the duties of his trade, begs leave to inform the ladies and gentlemen of York that he has commenced the above business, and to those who may honor him with their commands he flatters himself, from his experience, to afford satisfaction."[53]

One Rock calls to our attention that there was at least one hairdresser in York in 1800. In a day of wigs and beards, puffs and curls, the hairdresser had little of the barber about him.

"Rock, Hair Dresser, from London, begs leave to inform the ladies and gentlemen of York and its vicinity that he will open shop on the 25th instant, in Mr. Cooper's house, next the Printing office. All orders left for him at said place will be punctually attended to. N.B.—Shop customers and others will be dressed on the most reasonable terms."[54]

One of the first bakers in York was Paul Morin, though he was not the first, for he refers to a predecessor in his announcement of November, 1801:

"Paul Morin begs leave to inform his friends and the public that he has declined carrying on the baking business for Mr. Beaman and now carries it on in all its branches on his own account at the house formerly occupied by Mr. Beaman, where they may be supplied with bread at the rate of four lbs. for a shilling; biscuits, buns, cakes, etc. He hopes by assiduity and attention to his business to merit encouragement.

"N.B.—Any person sending flour to be baked by him will receive seven lbs. of bread for every six lbs. of flour."

Morin (or Marian) was contemporary with another baker, François Belcour, who, though slightly outbid by Morin in the amount of bread given to those who brought flour to be baked (for he advertised only "pound for pound"), was yet perhaps a little ahead of him in service for he *delivered* bread, cakes and buns, and also baked meat in his bake-oven for any who wished.[55]

[53]*Ibid.*, June 8, 1799. [54]*Ibid.*, April 5, 1800.
[55]*Ibid.*, November 14, 1801, and in many other issues of the *Gazette* between 1801 and 1804.

Even a watchmaker was established in the diminutive capital of the province:

"Elisha Purdey—Watchmaker—begs leave to inform his friends and the public that he has taken a room in the house of Mr. Marther, where he repairs and cleans watches of all kinds in the best manner and on the most reasonable terms. All orders left for him at said house will be duly attended to. He has a small but elegant assortment of jewellery for sale."[56]

The first carpenters and builders in Upper Canada were the soldiers, and, upon the arrival of settlers, every man was his own builder. The construction of log houses did not call for much specialised skill, and there was in the earliest pioneer period but little variation in the architecture or appearance of home, workshop, store, church or mill. One of the first skilled tradesmen in York was Eliphalet Hale, who announces in the *Gazette* of March 30, 1799, that he will come from Newark (Niagara) to York "to receive proposals for, and commence bricklaying, lathing and plastering."[57] Hale was a very important and useful citizen of the early town, building many houses of improved construction, as well as receiving a number of contracts for the building of roads and bridges, the removing of stumps from the streets, and similar work.

Perhaps Daniel Tiers was the first chairmaker in York. Most manufactured articles were brought from Montreal by bateau, but Tiers announces that he is enlarging his business and can supply customers with "armed chairs, settees, and dining ditto; fan-back and brace-back chairs." The interesting fact is also mentioned that "he very shortly expects a quantity of different paints; it will then be in his power to finish his chairs in the best manner."[58] Paint, it may be explained, was not easily obtainable in early times.

In the days when many people were illiterate, trade symbols were commonly affixed to the entrance of shops, and in York customers were led inside not by a signboard indicating the name of the owner but by such old English emblems as the Pestle and Mortar, the Crowned Boot, the Tea-chest, the Axe, the Saw, the Fowling-piece, the Plough,

[56]*Ibid.*, April 19, 1800. [57]*Ibid.*, March 30, 1799.
[58]*Ibid.*, January 30, 1802.

the Golden Fleece, the Anvil and Sledge-hammer, and the Horse-shoe. There was one, too, which was not an English survival,—that of the Indian Trapper, which indicated the dealer in furs.

Relations between employer and employee more closely approximated the conditions which obtained under the mediæval guild system than those of modern times. Apprentices were indentured for a period of seven years, and were to a considerable extent the property of the master. Several notices concerning escaped apprentices are to be found in the *Gazette*, and rewards of from 6d. to $10 are offered for their return.[59] There were also a number of slaves in Upper Canada during the first years of its existence, for the Act of the first parliament, while providing for the gradual extinction of slavery, did not free the slaves then in the province. Among notices concerning slaves is the following, offering a negro woman for sale in York in 1800:

"To Be Sold—A healthy, strong Negro Woman, about 30 years of age; understands cookery, laundry and the taking care of poultry. N.B.—She can dress ladies' hair. Enquire of the printers."[60]

On January 26, 1797, occurred the first recorded fire in York when "the dwelling-house of his Honour the Administrator, lately built at York, and in considerable forwardness, took fire by some accident, and was entirely consumed".[61] This house, in which the Hon. Peter Russell was to live, was located on the north side of Palace (Front) Street, near Princess Street. The fire was of course, by no means the first in York, for fires were very frequent in the days of wooden buildings, and laws were passed both by the Provincial Government and the town-meeting to lessen the possibilities of a general conflagration.

In 1800 it was ordered, in pursuance of an act of the Legislature entitled *An Act to Guard against Accidents by Fire*, that "every housekeeper in the Town of York shall, on or before the first day of October next ensuing, provide and keep TWO BUCKETS for carrying water when

[59]See, for example, the *Gazette* of May 31, 1797, and of August 25, 1798.
[60]*Ibid.*, December 20, 1800.
[61]*Ibid.*, February 8, 1797.

The First Parliament Buildings at York, 1797

YORK BARRACKS, U.C., MAY 13, 1804

Among the interesting activities being carried on by the soldiers may be seen men engaged in "stumping", and in sawing planks with a whip-saw, one man standing in a pit in this typical pioneer work.

any house shall happen to be on fire, which buckets shall be made either of wood, leather or canvas, painted on the outside and covered with pitch on the inside, and shall hold at least two gallons of water. And the said buckets shall be marked with the Christian and surname of the housekeeper to whose house they belong, and shall not be used for any other purpose than the extinguishing of fires". The regulation was also adopted that every house-holder "shall keep two ladders, the one to reach from the ground to the eaves of the house, and the other to be properly secured and fixed with hooks or bolts on the roof near the chimney".[62] In Lieutenant Stretton's water-colour of the York Barracks may be seen these ladders on the roofs of the log buildings.

In 1802 Governor Russell presented a fire-engine to the town; whereupon the citizens, to show their gratitude, erected a fire-hall by subscription "for the preservation of the engine; and such measures will be immediately adopted as are best calculated to procure the most easy access to the engine at all hours of the day and night".[63] For many years fire-fighting remained everybody's busi-ness, buckets of water being carried from the Bay or the nearest cistern or well to the scene of the conflagration. In 1813 the Americans carried away a fire-engine belonging to York, possibly the one presented by Governor Russell, or a military engine used at the barracks; this relic of early York is in an American military museum.

From time to time local laws and regulations were adopted by the town-meeting. On March 3, 1800, the annual meeting was held at Abner Miles' Tavern, and after the election of the usual municipal officials matters of general interest to the inhabitants were discussed. The regulations adopted on these occasions show how primitive and how rural were conditions in early York. One deals with that old English custom of allowing hogs to be scavengers and garbage collectors:

"It is agreed by a majority of the inhabitants of the town that no hogs, of any description, shall be allowed to run at large within the limits of the city, from and after the first day of May next ensuing, and it is further

[62]*Ibid.*, April 12, 1800.   [63]*Ibid.*, December 18, 1802.

agreed by a majority that every person or persons shall
be liable to pay the sum of five shillings lawful currency
for each time, and for each hog found running at large.
It is further agreed that all persons who keep hogs shall
cause them to be marked, which mark shall be registered
with the town clerk."[64]

In April of the same year a notice signed by T. Ridout,
C.P., announces that anyone obstructing the streets by
piles of wood and stone, or by digging pits, will be prose-
cuted.[65] Two years later the law with reference to hogs
was amended by the following resolution of the inhabitants
at the annual town-meeting, held on March 1st at Myles'
and Playter's Hotel:

"With respect to hogs (under three months old) running at large in the country it was voted by a majority
that they should be at liberty to run at large without yokes.
And in the town it was agreed that all hogs shall have
liberty to run at large, provided they be yoked and ringed,
but if found without a lawful yoke and ring to the nose,
shall be subject to impoundage until the owner pays one
dollar for each hog. This restriction to commence on the
1st day of May next."[66]

At this meeting it was also decided "that all lawful
fences shall be the height of five feet, and that there shall
be no space through the fence of more than four inches".[67]
This appears to have been a matter of considerable importance in early York, for thefts were quite common, and
men would even break down fences to revenge a grudge,
or perhaps merely for the amusement. The following advertisement, signed by Robert Gray, the Solicitor-General,
appeared in the Gazette, under the heading "$20 Re-
ward":

"Twenty dollars reward will be paid by the subscriber to
any person who will discover the man who is so depraved
and lost to every sense of social duty as to cut with an axe
or knife the withes which bound some of the fence round
the late Chief Justice's farm on Yonge Street, and to throw
down the said fence. Independent of the said inducement
it is the duty of every good member of society to endeavour

[64]Ibid., March 8, 1800.   [65]Ibid., April 12, 1800.
[66]Ibid., March 6, 1802.   [67]Ibid., July 9, 1803.

to find out who the character is that can be guilty of such an infamous act, in order that he may be brought to justice."[68]

In 1802 a number of recommendations of a nature similar to those adopted by the town-meeting were presented by the Grand Jury. One was that taverns should not sell intoxicating liquors or allow disorderly behaviour on the Sabbath, particularly during the hours of divine service. The Grand Jury also considered that the butchers of York "should be obliged to bury the garbage and useless offal of their slaughtered cattle, or to remove from the town or otherwise dispose of the same, so that it may cease to be (what it now is) a public nuisance". They suggested in addition that "joiners, cabinet-makers, carpenters and other descriptions of workers in wood, by whose trade shavings are made, should be obliged to burn or otherwise destroy the same on the Wednesdays and Saturdays of every week, at or about the hours of sunset".[69]

The first school in York appears to have been a small one established by William Cooper in 1798. Private tuition in the home, or the occasional visit of an itinerant schoolmaster, previously served the needs of the town in a rather unsatisfactory manner, while a few of the sons of the officials were sent to Lower Canada or the United States, where educational facilities were more advanced. Cooper advertised in the *Gazette* of November 3, 1798, that "he intends opening a school at his house in George Street on the 19th instant for the instruction of Youth in Reading, Writing, Arithmetic and English Grammar. Those who chuse to favour him with their Pupils may rely on the greatest attention being paid to their virtue and morals".[70] In the summer of 1799 Cooper passed an examination before the Rev. John Stuart, a step necessary because the government had decided that "itinerant characters" should not in future be allowed to impose upon the inhabitants of the country.[71]

Six years later, on January 3, 1803, a school of somewhat greater pretensions was commenced by Dr. William Warren Baldwin. He had emigrated with his father from

[68]*Ibid.*, July 23, 1803.   [69]*Ibid.*, July 10, 1802.
[70]*Ibid.*, November 3, 1798.   [71]*Ibid.*, July 6, 1799.

Ireland in 1799, settling first near Baldwin's Creek, in the Township of Clarke. In 1803 he married Phoebe Willcocks, daughter of William Willcocks of York, and they resided in a cottage at the corner of Palace and Frederick Streets. The school was first held at Willcocks' house on Duke Street, a much more pretentious building than Baldwin's small cottage. Dr. Baldwin's announcement of his school first appears in the *Gazette* of December 18, 1802, and contains a number of interesting particulars:

"Doctor Baldwin, understanding that some of the gentlemen of this town have expressed much anxiety for the establishment of a Classical school, begs leave to inform them and the public that he intends on Monday the 3rd day of January next to open a school in which he will instruct 12 boys in Writing, Reading, and Classics and Arithmetic. Terms for each boy eight guineas *per annum*, to be paid quarterly, one guinea entrance, and one cord of wood to be supplied by each boy on opening the school.

"N.B. Dr. Baldwin will meet his pupils at Mr. Willcocks' house in Duke Street."[72]

While the erection of a church in York was not considered until 1803, the Anglican service had for several years been held in the Government Buildings. At first the schoolmaster, William Cooper, read the service; and later the Rev. Thomas Raddish resided in York for eight months. The first permanent incumbent was the Rev. George Okill Stuart, who came to York in 1800 as missionary, and remained in charge until 1812. On July 9, 1803, a meeting of the subscribers to the proposed St. James' Church was held, and it was decided that the church should be of stone, and pine and oak planks;[73] this decision was changed, however, for the church was constructed entirely of wood. The building, which was not in use until 1807, had no steeple and was much like a house. Space was left for a burial-ground around it, and a few years later it was surrounded by a split rail fence.

In the autumn of 1803 Lieutenant-Governor Peter Hunter issued a proclamation establishing a market in

---

[72]*Ibid.*, December 18, 1802.
[73]*Ibid.*, July 16, 1803. A preliminary meeting was held in January of that year.

York. The document sets forth that "great prejudice hath arisen to the inhabitants of the Town and Township of York, and of other adjoining townships, from no place or day having been set apart or appointed for exposing publicly for sale cattle, sheep, poultry and other provisions, goods and merchandise brought by merchants, farmers and others for the necessary supply of the said Town of York". Realising the advantages which would arise from a weekly market, the Governor and his Executive Council "ordained, erected, established and appointed a public open market to be held on Saturday in each week and every week during the year within the said town of York, the first market to be held on Saturday, the 5th day of November, in the year of our Lord one thousand eight hundred and three".[74] The first market-house was only 36 feet by 24, and was within the square formed by Market, New, King and Church Streets, an area of five and a half acres having been set aside for the market-place. In later days the St. Lawrence Market came to be not only a centre of trade but also of public meetings, entertainment, and social life generally.

The inhabitants of York at the close of the century consisted largely of the garrison and the official class. In addition to the merchants and tradesmen who have been mentioned, there were also a few members of the professions and a number of negroes, some of whom were slaves of the officials, while others had escaped from the United States. Among the earliest families to settle in or near York were the Denisons, Baldwins, Allans, Ketchums, Crookshanks and Playters; while the official class included Peter Russell, John McGill, John Small, Thomas Ridout, Captain Lippincott, William Jarvis and William Willcocks.

In 1797 the first Law Society was established in York when four men were designated by proclamation as "fit and proper persons to practise the profession of law", after having been duly examined by Chief Justice Osgoode; William Dummer Powell, afterwards Chief Justice of Upper Canada, was one of these. A few years later Dr. Baldwin added the profession of law to those of medicine and teaching, which presumably had not proven sufficiently

[74]*Ibid.*, October 29, 1803.

remunerative. He was admitted to the bar in 1803, and carried on all his professions for some years. In 1800 Chief Justice Elmsley presided over the Court of King's Bench, and he was assisted by Mr. Justice Powell and Mr. Justice William Henry Alcock.

The magistrates of York were William Jarvis and William Willcocks, and it would appear that they had many crimes and misdemeanours to deal with. The *Gazette* contains numerous notices of robberies, even the magistrates and high officials being the victims on some occasions. In the issue of June 5, 1802, Mr. Justice Alcock offers $40 reward for the conviction of the person who stole from his "farm near the Garrison a number of iron teeth from two harrows". He states that the culprit was thought to have been a deserter from the garrison, who had sold the teeth to two blacksmiths in York.[75]

In 1803 Peter Russell offered five guineas reward for the apprehension of the thieves who stole from his barn near the town "a turkey hen, with her brood of six half-grown young ones";[76] while Magistrate Jarvis announced that he would pay $50 for information leading to the conviction of the persons who stole from his "improved grounds" a number of fruit trees.[77] John McGill once had a quantity of onions and melons stolen from his garden, while Sarah McBride missed "a fine ruffled shirt" from her house.

The punishments of the time were, as in Europe, very severe. The death penalty was in force for a large number of crimes, including forgery and counterfeiting. In 1800 a man was executed in York for forging a note, and it is recorded that "with unparalleled fortitude he approached the place of execution! and to the last appeared much resigned to his unhappy fate".[78] Two years earlier, in November, 1798, a man was sentenced to be burned in the hand for grand larceny,[79] the law as to branding being part of the English criminal code adopted in Upper Canada on the formation of the province. Whipping was a common

---

[75]*Ibid.*, June 5, 1802.　　[76]*Ibid.*, August 20, 1803.
[77]*Ibid.*, May 10, 1800.　　[78]*Ibid.*, May 17, 1800.
[79]*Ibid.*, November 17 and December 1, 1798.

punishment for petty larceny, while in August, 1801, a
thief was banished from Upper Canada for seven years.[80]

The old English punishment of standing in the pillory
was also in vogue in early York. Elizabeth Ellis was
sentenced in 1804 to six months' imprisonment, and in addition "to stand in the pillory twice during the said imprisonment, on two different market days, opposite the Market-
House in the town of York, for the space of two hours each
time".[81] The stocks, or framework in which people stood
when sentenced to the pillory, remained in the market-
place until 1834, when, with the whipping-post, they were
destroyed during a riot occasioned by the particularly wild
elections at the time of the creation of the city of Toronto.

There are, of course, records of tragedies in the town
of York and its environs. It was not uncommon at that
time to redress private grievances by resort to duels, and
on January 3, 1800, Upper Canada's first Attorney-General,
John White, was fatally injured in a duel with John Small,
Clerk of the Executive Council; Small appeared in court,
but was acquitted. Joseph Willcocks of York was engaged
in a duel in 1801, but before it had proceeded far he was
arrested by Sheriff Alexander Macdonell. It is interesting
to know that Willcocks succeeded Macdonell as Sheriff
in 1805, but was dismissed from his office in 1807 because
he was too outspoken against the government. During the
War of 1812 Willcocks fought gallantly in the British army
at Queenston Heights, and then, angered at the persecution to which he was subjected by his political enemies,
turned traitor and joined the American forces, being killed
in action at Fort Erie on September 5, 1814.

Duels of another variety are occasionally recorded in
the *Gazette*. Though no court of marital relations existed
at that early period, nor were any divorces granted, yet
an occasional notice of the following kind was necessary, for
human nature has varied but little through the centuries:

"Whereas my wife Sarah refuses to go live with me on
my farm on Yonge Street, where I have for her a comfortable house, and as I am not able to support her in town,
from the high price of provisions and the heavy expense

---

[80]*Ibid.*, August 29, 1801.
[81]Quoted in Scadding's *Toronto of Old*, p. 42.

of house rent, I therefore caution the Public not to harbour
or credit her on my account, as I will pay no debt of her
contracting from this date.

his
Abraham X Matice.
mark

York, March 1, 1800."[82]

It was a time of great frankness in such announcements,
one man stating that "my wife Nancy refuses living with
me without any manner of cause, she being influenced by
her vile parents".[83] On one occasion, at Niagara, when a
husband issued a notice warning people that he would not
be responsible for his wife's debts, the wife retaliated with
the retort that any such announcement was a joke, for
everyone knew that her husband was worthless, and that
she had frequently paid his bills; consequently she directed
merchants to take notice that she would not be responsible
for *his* debts! A series of such announcements and replies
led Hebsebah Burton, one of the wives concerned, to write
the editor of the *Niagara Herald* that "husbands advertising wives and wives advertising husbands has become no
small part of your business". It would appear that the
wives were usually in the right in these disputes, and some
of them sent very spirited retorts to the press.[84]

Newspapers of that day contained comparatively little
local news, but here and there one may find something
of interest. A short sermon on the disastrous effects of
love is given in the *Gazette* under the caption "Suicide",
with reference to a Yonge Street tragedy:

"How powerful, and how irresistible is the influence of
love! When it reigns predominant it is too frequently
productive, in many instances, of fatal consequences to the
unhappy one whom it has made subservient to its extremes! Which was the case a few days since on Yonge
Street: one of the French emigrants, it is said, shot himself because a young lady, whom he admired in the extreme,
discarded him."[85]

[82]*Upper Canada Gazette*, March 1, 1800.
[83]*Ibid.*, November 3, 1798.
[84]See *Niagara Herald*, December 14, 21 and 28, 1799; also the *Gazette*,
    May 1 and 15, 1802.
[85]*Upper Canada Gazette*, August 10, 1799.

A notice of a drowning at the Humber recalls the primitive conditions of transportation; most rivers were without bridges and it was necessary to use a ferry, or swim your horse across:

"Drowned, on Friday the 2nd instant, at the mouth of the River Humber, one of the Rangers, in attempting to swim across it on horseback."[86]

The social life of York was much like that of an English town of the period. Alexander Macdonell, Sheriff of the Home District, resided in York in 1799, and describes in his diary how the members of the official class spent their time. Office duties usually ended at 2 p.m., and dinner was served at 3 o'clock. From Joseph Willcocks' diary we learn that an ordinary dinner included "a salmon, a fillet of veal, a pair of roast fowl and a bread pudding";[87] while on Christmas Day, 1800, a good old English dinner of "soup, roast beef, boiled pork, a turkey, plumb pudding and minced pies"[88] was served at the Willcocks' home. During the evening, whist, conversation, dancing, and wine provided the main entertainment.

Some of the higher officials of the government had extensive estates on the outskirts of the town, where they carried on farming and experimented in the growth of cherries, melons, and peaches, in addition to many typically English vegetables and flowers which their gardeners produced. Their stables were noted for spirited horses, suitable for the pleasures of carrioling, the race-track and the hunt. A few of the wealthier inhabitants had yachts and were able to enjoy sailing on the Bay. Even in Indian days the peninsula (now the island) was a resort for the purpose of regaining health; and, among the early citizens of York, a favourite ride or walk.

Many of these pleasures were developed during Simcoe's *régime* in York. A letter written by Peter Russell to John McGill in December, 1796, expresses the hope "that the ladies may be able to enjoy the charming carrioling which you must have on your Bay, and up the Yonge Street Road, and to the Humber, and up the Don to Castle Frank, where

---

[86]*Ibid.*   [87]*Diary of Joseph Willcocks*, October 6, 1800.
[88]*Ibid.*, December 25, 1800.

an early dinner must be picturesque and delightful".[89] There were picnics on the peninsula and along the Don and Humber, and dances for the social set at Castle Frank, Russell Abbey, or in the Government Buildings.

From time to time notices appear in the *Gazette* concerning the York Assemblies, or dances. The first of these announcements is in the issue of December 8, 1798, and asks "the gentlemen of the town and the garrison" to meet at Miles' Hotel to make arrangements for the winter, and pay their subscription.[80] It may be presumed that similar social events were held during previous winters, when York had no newspaper in which the announcement might be inserted.

The gentlemen of York also engaged in field sports— hunting, fowling, hawking and fishing. Many a canoe might be seen on the Bay in the evening, its occupants intent upon the exciting sport of spearing fish by jack-light. In the winter of 1801 William Jarvis held a fox hunt on the ice of the Bay, and when the fox was unbagged, "the chase was followed by a number of gentlemen on horseback, and a concourse of the *beau monde* of both sexes in carriole and sleigh".[91]

Occasionally there would be a public holiday in York, and a special demonstration of loyalty sometimes occurred upon the receipt of war news from England. On August 1, 1798, was fought the battle of the Nile, but it was over five months later, on January 3, 1799, that the news reached York. A celebration was immediately planned, however, and took place the following day. It is said that William Willcocks was the only inhabitant who did not light up his home in honour of the occasion, so a mob led by one Thomas Smith smashed the windows of his house.

On June 4th the King's birthday was always celebrated. The *Gazette* of June 8, 1799, notes that the Queen's Rangers fired three volleys, the militia assembled on the beach, and a Royal Salute of twenty-one guns was fired by the Royal Artillery; after which, "at night the Government Buildings were superbly illuminated, at which place His Honour the

[89]Scadding: *Four Decades of York*, p. 23.
[90]*Upper Canada Gazette*, December 8, 1798.
[91]*Ibid.*, February 14, 1801.

From Scadding's *Toronto of Old*

York in 1803

John Ross Robertson Collection

The First Church in York (Toronto): St. James', Opened in 1807

Courtesy of the John Ross Robertson Collection and the Canadian Pacific Railway

JORDAN'S YORK HOTEL, 1801, AND THE ROYAL YORK HOTEL, 1929

A famous pioneer inn contrasted with an $18,000,000 hostelry, the largest in the British Empire

President gave a splendid ball and supper".[92] Another notable event occurred in 1803, when the Duke of Kent visited the little town, staying at "Oakhill", the residence of General Aeneas Shaw, to whose daughter Sir Isaac Brock was later engaged. General Shaw's frame cottage was one of the first buildings in York of other than log construction.

Hotel accommodation in the town was considerably improved in 1801 by the opening of Jordan's York Hotel. For many years Jordan's was the most fashionable inn in Upper Canada; and in it was held a session of parliament in 1814, after the destruction of the Government Buildings during the American occupation of the previous year. The hotel was located on the south side of King Street, between Berkeley and Ontario Streets. A few blocks from Jordan's York Hotel has recently arisen the Royal York Hotel, the largest hostelry in the British Empire.

A pleasant description of York as it appeared in the early years of the century is given by George Heriot, Deputy Postmaster-General, who wrote that the town, "according to the plan, is projected to extend to a mile and a half in length. . . . The advancement of this place to its present condition has been effected within the lapse of six or seven years, and persons who have formerly travelled in this part of the country are impressed with sentiments of wonder on beholding a town which may be termed handsome, reared as if by enchantment in the midst of the wilderness". Viewed from a point near the Don, "the scene is agreeable and diversified; a blockhouse, situated upon a wooded bank, forms the nearest object; part of the town, points of land cloathed with spreading oak trees, gradually receding from the eye one behind another, until terminated by the buildings of the garrison and the spot on which the governor's residence is placed, compose the objects on the right. The left side of the view comprehends the long peninsula which encloses this sheet of water, beautiful on account of its placidity, and rotundity of form; the distant lake, which appears bounded only by the sky, terminates the whole".[93]

Yet "Little York" (as Americans called it) was little better than in the wilds at the opening of the nineteenth

[92]*Ibid.*, June 8, 1799.   [93]Heriot, *op. cit.*, pp. 138-9.

century, for there were occasional depredations of bears and wolves. Bay Street is said to have once borne the name Bear Street because Mr. Justice Boulton's horses attacked a bear in their pasture in the vicinity. Joseph Willcocks' letters contain descriptions of similar events. On November 3, 1800, he wrote: "There was a great depredation committed the night before last by a flock of wolves that came into the Town. One man lost 17 sheep; several others lost in proportion".[94] He also describes how "two great bears . . . . took away two pigs. They carried the pigs in their arms and ran on their hind legs".[95]

At the close of 1803 the town plot of York measured 420 acres, and there were 456 inhabitants within its limits. The total value of the property was £14,871, and the taxes collected reached the staggering total of £62, a sum which would nowadays hardly pay a month's salary to a minor civic official; but it is a far cry in every respect from the York of 1803 to the Toronto of a century and a quarter later.

[94]Joseph Willcocks to Richard Willcocks, November 3, 1800, quoted in W. R. Riddell: *Life of John Graves Simcoe*. 1927. Notes to Chapter XX, p. 292.
[95]*Ibid.*, August 31, 1800.

CHAPTER V

COLONEL TALBOT AND HIS SETTLEMENT

"Wherever I went ashore I was quite enchanted by the beauty and variety of a landscape which was terminated by the noblest forests in the whole world."

PIERRE CHARLEVOIX (1721).[1]

"Charlevoix was, I believe, the true cause of my coming to this place. You know he calls this the 'Paradise of the Hurons'. Now I was resolved to get to paradise by hook or by crook, and so I came here."

COLONEL TALBOT TO ANNA JAMESON.[2]

THOMAS TALBOT, who was destined to play a most important part in the settlement of Upper Canada, was born on July 19, 1771, at Malahide Castle, Ireland, the seat of the Talbots for many centuries. In accordance with the system of patronage in vogue at that time he was started upon a career in the army by being given a commission at the age of eleven, though he was not on active service until 1790, when he joined the 24th Regiment at Quebec.

The first Lieutenant-Governor of Upper Canada, Colonel John Graves Simcoe, spent the winter of 1791-2 at Quebec, and at that time Talbot joined his staff as private secretary. He accompanied the Governor to Upper Canada in 1792, and early in the following year was a member of the official party which explored the Western District and visited Detroit. At that time the region between Niagara and the Detroit River was largely a wilderness, inhabited only by Indians and an occasional trader or settler. While travelling along Indian trails on the north coast of Lake Erie, Talbot was greatly impressed with the beauties of the country and the possibilities of settlement, and conceived the idea of establishing a colony in the region. For eight years longer, however, he remained in the army; but on Christmas Day, 1800, he surprised the fashionable society in which he moved in Britain by selling his commission. Various reasons are given for this move, the most generally

[1]Pierre Charlevoix: *Journal d'un Voyage fait par ordre du Roi dans l'Amérique Septentrionale.* 1744. Kellogg Edition, 1923, Vol. II, p. 3.
[2]See Anna Jameson: *Winter Studies and Summer Rambles in Canada.* 1838. Vol. II, p. 199.

accepted being that he had fallen in love with a member of the Royal Family, and, as marriage appeared impossible, he decided to banish himself to the fertile district in the backwoods of Upper Canada which he had explored in 1793.

Accordingly he returned to Canada in 1801 with the object of securing a township for himself; but regulations concerning land grants were considerably more strict than they had been in Simcoe's day, and he was not immediately successful. Proceeding westward along the Erie shore he reached a point which he called Skittiewaaba, (Ojibway for "fire-water"), probably at or near the present Port Stanley; here he commenced a clearing, and on May 16, 1801, wrote to the Duke of Cumberland, who had previously promised to aid him, asking that he procure for him the grant of the Township of Houghton, or some other adjacent one.[3] The scheme was that the Duke should ask his father, the King, to grant him the land free of all fees and obligations, whereupon the Duke was to transfer the property to Talbot. Although Cumberland and his brother, the Duke of Kent, made representations in Talbot's interest to Lord Hobart, Colonial Secretary, yet nothing was done at the time.

In October, 1802, Talbot was back in London, volunteering information to the government as to the capabilities of the soil of Upper Canada, and the desirability of diverting British emigration from the United States. He offered to supervise arrangements with regard to guiding settlers to their destination, and again pushed his claim to a grant of land; he was seconded in his efforts by ex-Governor Simcoe, who was then in London. They desired that his grant should be in Yarmouth Township, since Talbot had learned that hemp could be satisfactorily grown there. A few days later Talbot was given a letter by Lord Hobart directing Lieutenant-Governor Hunter of Upper Canada to arrange the matter, though there were modifications in the terms and conditions of the grant.

A considerable part of Yarmouth had already been granted to the Bâbys, so Talbot chose the Township of Dunwich as the location of his 5000 acres; and as soon as

[3]Talbot to the Duke of Cumberland, May 16, 1801. See *The Talbot Papers*, edited by James H. Coyne, Section I, pp. 75-77. (*Transactions* of the Royal Society of Canada, 1909).

the necessary preliminaries had been arranged at York he proceeded to his land. The grant was not for Talbot's exclusive use, however, as it was intended that the first hundred settlers should receive their lots in that section, each one being given fifty acres, while 150 went to Talbot for his supposed expense and trouble in locating them. A part of the township was reserved for allotment to him accordingly. Under this arrangement Talbot could not obtain more than 20,000 acres for himself, but, as Dr. Coyne points out, he actually succeeded in securing grants amounting to upwards of 65,000 acres.[4] While it was possible for settlers to purchase 150 acres additional at three dollars an acre, yet few of them were ever able to see the equity of their being given only fifty acres while the Colonel obtained the lion's share for doing little or nothing except acting in an imperious manner.

On May 21, 1803, Colonel Talbot arrived with four followers at the mouth of a small, sluggish stream in Dunwich Township, thereafter known as Talbot Creek. He seized an axe and, chopping down the first tree, inaugurated the new settlement. The location which he chose for his abode is one of the hilliest and roughest parts of the entire region, yet there he was content to build his home on the top of the cliff, a log house of three rooms, to which were later added several separate log or frame buildings. It is likely that Talbot chose this situation because of the good soil and the picturesqueness of the site, characteristics which applied equally to his earlier choice of Port Stanley. When he erected his rude residence overlooking the lake the nearest settlements were eighty miles to the west and sixty miles to the east, while at the north was unbroken forest.

While Port Talbot never amounted to much either as a harbour or a village, (for Talbot would tolerate no other settlers near him), yet its appearance during the early years of the War of 1812 was very different from that of later times. Lewis Burwell's map of the port in 1813 shows a fort (in which some twenty men were stationed), as well as a grist-mill with accompanying dam and bridge, and a number of other structures. American raiders burned in 1814 all except Talbot's residence, probably leav-

4Introduction to the *Talbot Papers*, p. 32.

ing it as a trap in which they hoped to catch him later. The remains of several of the burnt buildings have been located by excavation during the present year (1932).

There was one settler in Elgin County as early as 1796, for James Fleming located on the Thames in Aldborough Township in that year. The first person to be given a lot by Colonel Talbot was George Crane, who had come with him as an employee in 1803, and was granted land in Dunwich in 1806. Three years later several families moved in, being welcomed by Talbot at the mouth of Talbot Creek, where they landed from small boats; the Pearces, Storeys and Pattersons, who composed this small immigration, numbered thirteen in all, and were Pennsylvanians of Irish descent. The blazing of the Talbot Road in 1809-11 by Mahlon Burwell enabled the rapid settlement of the townships east of Port Talbot.

Colonel Talbot did not go out of his way to secure settlers, but accepted (or rejected) those who came to him. In his famous speech of 1832 he stated that when he undertook the formation of his settlement, "it was in the hope that I should have none other but sound British subjects, so as to ensure peace and good fellowship amongst us, and I took every pains to select characters of that description".[5] In general he followed the plan of placing those whom he liked least as far away from himself as possible, and on the worst locations.

Settlers of the various British nationalities found their way to the Talbot Settlement. Scotch predominated in Aldborough, while English, Irish and Americans were to be found in various sections. Pennsylvania Quakers were among the earliest arrivals, and other Americans came in from time to time, though always regarded with suspicion by Talbot. In a letter to the Hon. Peter Robinson, Commissioner of Crown Lands, regarding the location of settlers along a new road, he advised him to "avoid placing Highland Scotch on it, as of all descriptions they make the worst settlers for new roads. English are the best".[6] In another communication he suggests a dislike for aristocratic set-

---

[5] See *Talbot Papers*, Section II, pp. 124-6, for Talbot's draft of his St. Thomas speech.
[6] Talbot to the Hon. Peter Robinson, July 4, 1831. *Talbot Papers*, Section II, p. 114.

tlers by the statement, "Pestered with half-pay officers,
pray don't introduce any of them to me."[7]. It may be
presumed that such men frequently had too much spirit
to submit quietly to injustice. Dr. Coyne summarises the
distribution of nationalities as follows:

"Generally speaking, the three townships of Aldborough,
Dunwich and South Dorchester, and the North of Yar-
mouth, were settled by Highlanders; Talbot Road East,
including the North Branch in Southwold, by a miscel-
laneous immigration from the United States, the Long Point
settlement, the Niagara district, Southern England and
elsewhere; the south of Yarmouth by members of the
Society of Friends from Pennsylvania and New Jersey;
Malahide by settlers from New York State, Long Point and
Nova Scotia, and Bayham by immigrants from all quarters;
London Township by immigrants from Ireland under
Richard Talbot, a very distant connection of the Colonel."[8]

While most of the Scotch settlers were from Argyllshire, some had come from the United States, and other
families had returned from the Red River Settlement. The
Argyllshire Highlanders arrived chiefly in 1819, and so
numerous were they, "that when their descendants presented an address at St. Thomas in 1881 to the son of the
great MacCallum More, the Marquis of Lorne, then Governor-General, they assembled by thousands". An address
in classical Gaelic was presented to the Marquis, and in his
reply he stated that he had never, even in Argyllshire
itself, seen so many Argyllshire people present at one
time.[9]

The government's intention in granting Talbot 5000
acres for the purposes of settlement was to create a compact colony, the mere existence of which would attract
others to the region; but he ignored the stipulations contained in the grant, dropped also his proposal to grow hemp,
and worked out a scheme of settlement for his own benefit,
which inevitably retarded the development of the entire
district. The advantage which Dunwich and Aldborough
possessed in having no clergy reserves was more than offset by the founder's lands, for he systematically withheld
them from settlement, sale, or even improvement, and until

[7]Talbot to Robinson, July 23, 1832. *Talbot Papers*, Section II, p. 143.
[8]Introduction to the *Talbot Papers*, p. 40.   [9]*Ibid.*, p. 42.

after his death large areas of primeval forest and swamp remained to discourage the development of neighbouring lots and prevent the building of good roads.

In other townships, east and west, Talbot was the rather inconsistent enemy of non-resident owners, and reserved lands generally; he was consequently held in somewhat higher esteem by the settlers of these localities. But in Dunwich and Aldborough all except a few residents in the vicinity of Tryconnel, (who had been kindly treated by Talbot in 1809-10), were his inveterate enemies. Many of the original inhabitants spoke only Gaelic, and so indignant were they at the manifold injustice to which they were subjected that even in 1903, when the Talbot Centennial was held, their descendants so abhorred the name of Talbot that they refused to enter into the celebration until assured that the pioneers in general were being honoured, rather than the founder of the settlement.

Colonel Talbot entered enthusiastically into "backwoods" life. Old settlers recalled seeing him dressed in coarse homespun, working at various domestic tasks.[10] Mrs. Jameson learned from him that "for sixteen years he saw scarce a human being except the few boors and blacks employed in clearing and logging his land; he himself assumed the blanket-coat and axe, slept upon the bare earth, cooked three meals a day for twenty woodsmen, cleaned his own boots, washed his own linen, milked his own cows, churned the butter, and made and baked the bread."[11].

His plain clothes were proverbial in the Settlement and wherever he travelled. When the Americans raided Port Talbot in 1814 the Colonel's escape was due largely to the fact that he appeared to be a labourer. On his trips to York each winter in his famous high box-sleigh, to present his accounts and hand over the money he had collected from the sale of land, he usually wore a sheepskin coat and a fur cap, and was an object of curiosity wherever he went. Even in the backwoods of Peterborough County his eccentric costume, "with boots of the same material", was considered "remarkable".[12] When he visited England he lost no

[10]Reminiscences of Mrs. Amelia Harris, quoted in the introduction to the *Talbot Papers*, p. 45.
[11]Jameson, *op. cit.*, Vol. II, pp. 189-90.
[12]Frances Stewart: *Our Forest Home*. 1889. 2nd Edition, 1902, p. 90.

opportunity to display clothes of Port Talbot manufacture, and to claim their superiority over English cloth. Although his faults were many, at least it cannot be said that he was not proud to be a Canadian farmer.

His farm was perhaps at its best when Joseph Pickering was in charge of it in 1825-26; he describes in his journal, Talbot's stock, garden, and, incidentally, his interest in farming.

"The Colonel has about 150 sheep, shut up in a pen at night to preserve them from the wolves, (this is not done in old settlements). They are various breeds, some with and some without horns. Twenty-five milch cows; four yoke of oxen broken in, besides one yoke killed this fall; fifty or sixty head of young cattle, which run in the woods all the summer; twenty-three weanling calves; four horses of the nag kind, with uncut long tails, the only sort in this country, and are generally pretty good, but want a little more blood; four sows and a number of store pigs, which also get their living in the woods through the summer, and during the winter, when there are plenty of nuts and acorns. . . . .

"Colonel Talbot has a garden pretty well stocked with shrubs, fruit trees, etc., in better order than most in America, yet not like a good common one in England. There are cherries, plums, apricots, peaches, nectarines, goose-berries, currants, etc., also water-, or musk-melons, and cucumbers, fine and plenty—cabbages and other vegetables thrive very well. A patch of Swedish turnips (or ruta-baga) of good size, notwithstanding the dry season. A few hills of hops at one corner of the garden look remark-ably well; they are gathered at the beginning of September.

"There are also a few bunches of English cowslips, but none wild in the woods. There is a species of the violet in the fields, with less fragrance than the English ones. The Colonel has likewise extensive orchards; some of the fruit fine, yet the great proportion raised from apple kernels, and remain ungrafted; although they bear well, their fruit is small and inferior to those grafted, except for cider. A great portion were suffered to hang too long on the trees, until the frosts came and spoiled them. . . .

"The Colonel has his thrashing all done by the flail, but

a great deal of the grain of the province is trodden out by either horses or oxen. . . . Colonel Talbot has just received a sample of long wool from Lancashire, and intends procuring some of that breed of sheep, as he says government have removed all restrictions respecting the exportation of sheep."[13]

In later years the Talbot property deteriorated from lack of care. Patrick Shirreff, who visited Port Talbot in 1833, saw the Colonel standing on his "poorly-kept property" and intended to speak to him, but he doubted, "from accounts received in the neighbourhood", that the interview would be pleasant, so he did not approach closer. He describes Port Talbot as "a cluster of mean wooden buildings, consisting of dwelling-houses, stables, barns, pigstyes and cattle-shades, constructed and placed seemingly without regard either to convenience or effect".[14] In 1837 Mrs. Jameson observed the slovenly management of the farm, and excused the Colonel because he was "not quite so active as he used to be, and does not employ a bailiff or overseer".[15]

The group of low log and shingle buildings[16] which composed the Castle of Malahide were approached by a beautiful winding road. On his Dutch "stoop" were found just as many farm implements and farm animals, harness and skins as any other settler's home might display. Plain furniture comprised the equipment of a plain house; but the cellar was well stocked not only with choice whisky for the Colonel and his settlers, but also with double casks of selected wines from Montreal for guests of higher pretensions. The list of distinguished visitors included noblemen and governors, generals and judges, and travellers of every variety, both male and female.[17]

Talbot was reasonably strict with his settlers in demanding that the usual settlement duties be performed before he gave them their certificates. The opening of a roadway, the erection of a log house, and the clearing of five acres

13Joseph Pickering: *Inquiries of an Emigrant.* 1831. August 16, 1825; April 2, 1826; and July 1, 1826.

14Patrick Shirreff: *A Tour through North America.* 1835. pp. 182-4.

15Jameson, *op. cit.,* Vol. II, p. 197.

16See Mrs. Jameson's description (Vol. II, pp. 195-6), *infra,* The Pioneer Home (Section III, Chapter I, p. 171).

17See Dr. Coyne's introduction to the *Talbot Papers,* pp. 44-5.

COLONEL THOMAS TALBOT

ST. PETER'S CHURCH,
TYRCONNEL, ERECTED 1828

COLONEL TALBOT'S RESIDENCE, PORT TALBOT

This early sketch of Talbot's home was sent to England in 1806 and
copied by Mrs. Simcoe

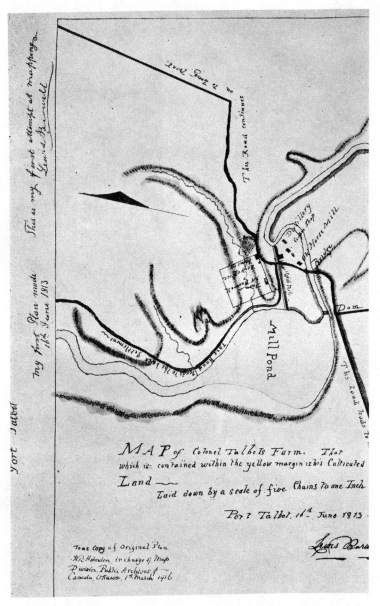

Port Talbot

My first Plan made 16th June 1813

This is my first attempt at map-making. Lewis Burwell

This Road continues

This Road goes to 40

Distillery Cooper Shop

old Horse Mill

Bridge

old Mill

Dam

Mill Pond

The Road leads to the Lake

This Road leads to

MAP of Colonel Talbots Farm. That which is contained within the yellow margin is his Cultivated Land ——— Laid down by a scale of five Chains To one Inch

Port Talbot. 16th June 1813

True Copy of Original Plan.
H.R. Holmden, in charge of Map
Division, Public Archives of
Canada, Ottawa, 1st March 1916

LEWIS BURWELL'S MAP OF PORT TALBOT, 1813

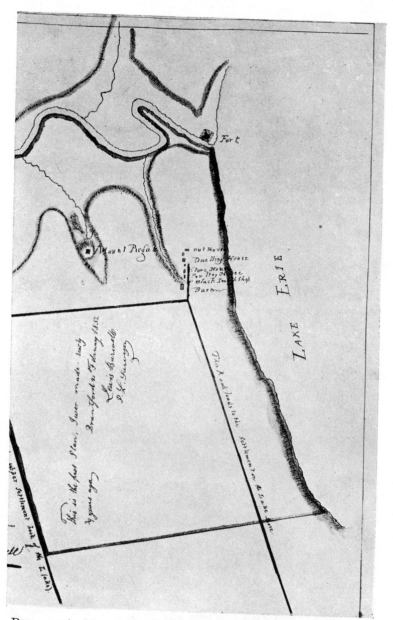

Fort

Mount Pisgah

out House

Due Wing House

Pork House
Poultry House
Black Smith Shop
Barn

LAKE ERIE

This Road leads to the Settlement on the Lake Erie

This is the first Plan, I ever made forty years ago

Brantford 21 February 1852

Lewis Burwell
P.L. Surveyor

upper Settlement Road 7 M. E. (A4)

Burwell's Map Shows Port Talbot at the Height of
its Development

From Young's *Reminiscences of Galt and Dumfries*

SHADE'S MILLS (GALT) IN 1820

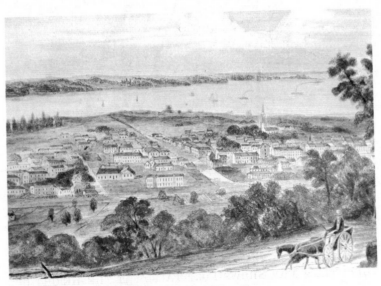

John Ross Robertson Collection

HAMILTON IN 1845

This early sketch was not carefully drawn and is inaccurate in detail

during the first year of actual settlement were insisted upon. After receiving Talbot's certificate the settler might pay the survey and patent fees and obtain his deed; but thousands neglected to do so, frequently because of the money involved, and the Provincial Government was inclined to blame Talbot for all such delinquencies on the part of his settlers. In 1827 investigation showed that the average farmer in the Talbot Settlement had cleared from twenty to twenty-five acres of land during the first three years of occupation. If a man was located on his lot in June, Talbot thought he should be able to sow five acres before the frost came, and support his family within a year if he sowed corn and potatoes.

There were hardships enough in the early years when grain had to be taken to the mill at Long Point, for Talbot's grist-mill was not rebuilt after its destruction by the Americans in 1814. Jonathan Doan's mill at Sparta was erected soon after, and was for some years a rendezvous of settlers for many miles around. Just previous to 1820 John Howison lived in the settlement for several months. He praised Talbot very highly, but was rather disgusted with the general appearance of the inhabitants and their farms, though he found the settlement "a democracy . . . where the utmost harmony prevails, . . . and the intercourse of the people is characterized by politeness, respect and even ceremony. . . . A few years' toil and perseverance has placed them beyond the reach of want".[18]

In later years there were probably many who found Canada a paradise in comparison with conditions in the Old Land. A day labourer in the Settlement wrote in 1830: "Here you have no rent to pay, no poor-rates and scarcely any taxes. No game-keepers or Lords over you. Here you can go and shoot wild deer, turkeys, pheasants, quails, pigeons, and other sort of game, and catch plenty of fish without molestation whatever. . . . Cyder is sold at 5s. per barrel; it is a land of liberty and plenty. . . . I would rather be so here than in England with £100 in my pocket."[19]

In doing business Colonel Talbot did not trouble himself

[18]John Howison: *Sketches of Upper Canada.* 1821. Edition of 1825, pp. 182-93.

[19]Letter of Philip Annett, May 24, 1830. See Andrew Picken: *The Canadas*, 1832. Appendix, pp. xxxvi and xxxvii.

to be particularly careful or accurate in method. His own
caprice usually decided the location which an applicant received, while in transferring property a pencil mark on the
Colonel's map was considered a sufficient record of the
transaction. Joseph Pickering, who lived with Talbot for
some months, considered that "as the Colonel takes no fee
for his trouble in giving out the government land, and people are continually going to him for information respecting
new lots to draw, as well as exchanging them (sometimes
repeatedly) for others, it cannot be surprising that he
should sometimes assume a severity of manner not natural
to him, to prevent vexatious applications".[20] It would appear, however, that Talbot was never very agreeable, and
not infrequently was quite insulting to those who applied
for land. Negotiations were always commenced by the
Colonel's shouting in no tender tones, "What do you want?",
which was usually followed by all manner of personal questions, if, indeed, the interview was not ended earlier by
"Devil a sod will you get here!", or some equally decisive
pleasantry.[21] A good story is told of how he came to change
his business methods:

"The Colonel transacted business in a room in his log
house; he was curt, and at times uncivil to applicants for
land. A stalwart Highlander named Duncan Patterson
called upon him to enter his name for a fifty-acre farm.
The Colonel said something that offended Patterson, who by
way of punishment put his arms around the Colonel's waist,
carried him out and laid him on his back on the lawn, where
he left him; ever after this incident the Colonel transacted
his business with applicants for land through an open
window."[22]

The name of Duncan Patterson, who used such an effective means to obtain the lot he desired, is held in honour
to this day by those who have heard from their forbears of
the autocratic manner in which the Colonel carried on deal-

[20]Pickering, op. cit., July 29, 1826.
[21]Many anecdotes concerning Colonel Talbot may be found in the
    preface to Edward Ermatinger's Life of Colonel Talbot and the
    Talbot Settlement. 1859. They are, however, to some extent
    restricted, owing to the author's avowed purpose "to transmit
    to posterity whatever is praiseworthy in his conduct and char-
    acter. . . . The faults require no biographer".
[22]Archibald McKellar: Recollections of Colonel Talbot and his Times.
    (Wentworth Historical Society, Publications, Vol. I, p. 118).

ings with his settlers. It might be added, however, that it was hardly practicable for others to imitate Patterson's conduct, for if slamming down the shutter of the window was not sufficient to convey to the applicant that his presence was no longer desired, the Colonel had a way of calling to his manservant: "Jeffrey, set on the dogs!"

For many years the Talbot Anniversary Dinner, instituted in 1817, was an interesting annual event in the settlement. Mrs. Anna Jameson found that it was the only occasion when Colonel Talbot condescended to mix with his settlers.[23] The affair was usually held in the village of St. Thomas or its vicinity, and was "generally well attended by storekeepers and people of various trades and callings, as well as the more respectable farmers".[24] Mrs. Jameson noted that at this "festive meeting of the most respectable settlers, the Colonel himself opens the ball with the ladies, generally showing his taste by selecting the youngest and prettiest".[25]

A complete description of one of these gatherings is found in a contemporary newspaper published at York, the account having been sent in by A. H. Burwell, the secretary of the organization, at the direction of those present at the celebration at Ross's Tavern, Talbot Road, on May 21, 1822. It was "numerously attended by the most respectable class of gentlemen and ladies from different parts of the district. John Backhouse, Esquire, chairman of the Quarter Session, was appointed President, and John Rolph, Esq., Vice-President. At four o'clock the party sat down to dinner under a booth of green branches erected for the occasion, after which the following toasts were drunk, accompanied by music:

1.—The King, with four times four.
2.—The Governor and the Executive of the province.
3.—The Hon. Colonel Talbot.

Upon the President giving this toast the whole assembly rose and drank it with three times three.

4.—The ladies of the Talbot Settlement.
5.—The Talbot Anniversary,—may it be celebrated every year with increasing festivity!

[23]Jameson, op. cit., Vol. II, pp. 177-8.
[24]Pickering, op. cit., May 27, 1826.
[25]Jameson, ibid.

6.—The representatives of the County of Middlesex.

7.—Agriculture and commerce.

8.—The Province of Upper Canada.

9.—The president.

10.—The Memory of General Brock.

11.—The health of the gentlemen from Long Point, who have honoured us with their company.

"The company then proceeded to the apartments, which were richly ornamented with green branches and wild flowers from the forest, and at 8 o'clock dancing commenced by the President and Mrs. Neville leading off the first figure, and continued till late in the evening, when the company retired without an instance of disorderly conduct."[26]

The Colonel appeared to appreciate the honour done him by the annual celebration, and always concluded his reply to the toast with the words "God bless you all". The most prominent opponent of the institution was Colonel Mahlon Burwell, who issued a manifesto on the subject at its inception in 1817. He believed such a celebration "premature", and with reference to Talbot he considered it sufficient to say "We know him", the meaning of which was not at all ambiguous. He took the stand that "far-fetched Anniversaries, public festivities, cordial unions, etc., as they are called in the Prospectus, . . . would have a tendency to lead us imperceptibly to scenes of dissipation", and could only result in what "the observing world would be obliged to call prostitution to flattery".[27]

With the exception of a few Irish families at Tyrconnel, the settlers of Dunwich and Aldborough Townships were always conspicuous by their absence from the Talbot Anniversary celebration. In later years, commencing during the troublous times of the Rebellion, the presence of a garrison in St. Thomas added to the glamour of the ball; but the "rank and fashion" who attended the anniversary in the late thirties were the cause of its end soon after, for the

[26]The *York Gazette and Weekly Register*, June 1, 1822. A somewhat less-detailed account of another Anniversary Celebration may be found in Edward Ermatinger, *op. cit.*, pp. 79-83, from which it is quoted in Judge C. O. Ermatinger's more readily obtainable work, *The Talbot Regime*, 1904, pp. 117-18.

[27]*Talbot Papers*, Section II, pp. 187-8.

settlers themselves (even those of respectability!) felt out of place in such company.

The Talbot Settlement was quickly extended far beyond its original bounds, for in 1811 the control of most of the London and Western Districts was given to Talbot by the Provincial Government. This enabled him to complete the Talbot Road from Delhi to Sandwich, with a cross-road between Port Talbot and the site of London. As settlement along it progressed the road gradually improved until at the time of the Rebellion it was the best in the province. In 1822, and again in 1826, Talbot sought compensation for his work,—not from the Government of Upper Canada, but from the Imperial Government, from which he always considered he had derived his power. In 1822 he stated that there were at least 12,000 people in his settlement, "the most populous and flourishing in Upper Canada";[28] while in 1826 he renewed his request for financial consideration, stating he had lost a great deal during the War of 1812, and had expended £20,000 on his colony during the twenty-three years which he had devoted to it; he estimated the population at that time at 20,000.[29] Previously he had received only an allowance of three *per cent.* for selling School Lands and Crown and Clergy Reserves in the London District, but he was successful in obtaining in addition a pension of £400, which he drew from January 1, 1826, until his death.

By 1824 Colonel Talbot had been given control of twenty-eight townships, totalling 540,443 acres; they ranged from the most westerly sections of Norfolk County to the Detroit River, including those north of the Thames from Zone, in Kent, to London Township, inclusive. In 1831 Talbot estimated the population of his domain at nearly 30,000, and in 1837 at 50,000 inhabitants. He was in continual conflict with successive governors of the province, who objected to the independent power he exercised over his colony; but he made occasional trips to England, where his influence was such that he was usually the victor. Then, as Mrs. Jameson puts it, "from these occasional flights he returns like an old eagle to his perch on the cliff, whence

[28]Memorial to the British Government. See C. O. Ermatinger, *op. cit.*, p. 94.
[29]Talbot to Lord Bathurst. *Ibid.*, p. 95.

he looks down upon the world he has quitted with supreme contempt and indifference, and around on that which he has created, with much self-applause and self-gratulation".[30]

In 1826 London was founded on the site chosen by Lieutenant-Governor Simcoe in 1793 for his future capital, which he intended to name Georgina-upon-Thames, and through which his projected trans-provincial highway, Dundas Street, was surveyed. The new village became the judicial capital of the district. On one occasion the Talbot Anniversary celebration was held there, but the Colonel's relation to London was negative: to enhance the value of his own estates he accelerated settlement along Talbot Street, and to some extent retarded the growth of London.[31] In spite of him, however, the village grew rapidly. Peter McGregor built the first house there in 1826, but seven years later a traveller, Patrick Shirreff, found "three or four large hotels, many well-filled stores, and a court-house of which the inhabitants feel proud".[32]

St. Thomas, (named in 1817 after the Colonel, though he was no saint!), had at that time a general store at Kettle Creek, and another on the hill above. Eight years later Joseph Pickering passed that way while walking from the Niagara district to Port Talbot, and he observed "the new small village of St. Thomas, rather pleasantly situated on the banks of Kettle Creek; it has a church, two taverns, a mill, two stores, and an academy".[33] Patrick Shirreff wrote in 1833 that the village "consisted three years ago of thirteen houses, but now there are about fifty".[34] When Mrs. Jameson visited "Colonel Talbot's capital" in 1837 she found that the population was 700, and had doubled in two years: "I was very struck with this beautiful and cheerful little town, more, I think, than with any place I have yet seen."[35]

The region as a whole was extensively advertised by the government, and its founder had no hesitation in say-

---

[30]Jameson, *op. cit.*, Vol. II, p. 205.
[31]See James H. Coyne: *Colonel Talbot's Relation to the Early History of London.* (Ontario Historical Society, *Papers and Records,* Vol. xxiv.)
[32]Shirreff, *op. cit.*, p. 180.   [33]Pickering, *op. cit.*, July 29, 1825.
[34]Shirreff, *op. cit.*, p. 181.
[35]Jameson, *op. cit.*, Vol. II, pp. 175-6.

ing that "there is no other settlement in North America
which can for its age and extent exhibit as compact and
profitably-settled a portion of the New World as the Talbot
Settlement".[36] This statement was at variance with the
truth, however. We have already seen how reverse of compact Dunwich and Aldborough were, and the same was
frequently true, though for other reasons, in surrounding
townships. At a meeting of the inhabitants of Malahide at
the house of William Summers, Talbot Road, on December
10, 1817, it was resolved that "the lots reserved for the
crown and clergy constitute two-sevenths of the township,
and prevent the settlement from becoming compact." Similar reports were adopted by the inhabitants of Yarmouth,
assembled "at Justice Wilcox's Inn, Talbot Road"; by those
of Southwold, at Alexander Ross's home; and at Singleton
Gardiner's in Dunwich Township, which at that time,
December 11, 1817, was stated to have one mill and about
500 inhabitants.[37]

Conditions had somewhat improved by the thirties,
however, and the Talbot Settlement was doubtless no worse
off with respect to reserved lands than the rest of the
province. Shirreff, though a farmer himself, was used to
the orderly, long-established English farms, and saw little
to approve in Talbot's domain except the roads, which he
found a great improvement over "the horrid roads of the
Huron Tract".[38] Civilisation was in prospect, however, for
he found a number of material advances: a steamboat was
just inaugurating a service between Buffalo and Port
Stanley, while between the latter port and St. Thomas
"there is a carding-, grist- and saw-mill, and a distillery
and brewery".[39]

The Reform agitation of the early thirties was a source
of great annoyance to Colonel Talbot, and all who held
broader political views than his extreme conservatism could
comprehend were branded with such pleasant names as
"diabolical wretches" and "sheep with the rot". Petitions
concerning grievances were denounced as "treason and sedi-

[36]Talbot to Sir John Colborne, 1831, quoted in Dr. Coyne's introduction
to the *Talbot Papers*, p. 37.
[37]The reports were prepared for Robert Gourlay, and appear in his
Statistical Account of Upper Canada. 1822. Vol. I, pp. 341
et seq.
[38]Shirreff, *op. cit.*, p. 181.   [39]*Ibid.*

tion founded on falsehood, fabricated for the purpose of creating discontent and, in the end, rebellion in this province". Radicals, Ryersonians and Rebels were one and the same to the Colonel, and it was popular to lay most of the blame for Reform activities upon "Hickory Quakers", "Ryersonian strolling demagogues", and "damned Cold Water Drinking Societies", all of which were anathematised the more by Talbot because they originated in the United States.[40]

The trouble between the Colonel and his settlers came to a head in the spring of 1832. The Reformers made up the great majority of the electorate, but the Family Compact party, with control over "purse and place," continued to oppose the wishes of the Assembly. On March 19, 1832, Talbot distributed a fly-sheet to his settlers announcing that, since a number of meetings had been held "on the subject of imagined grievances", he was calling "a general meeting of my Settlers on St. George's Day, the 23rd of April next, at the King's Arms at St. Thomas, at noon, when I shall attend". He signed the document as "Father of the Talbot Settlement".[41]

The result was a large gathering of electors, numbering about 2,000, many of them armed with bludgeons, and ready, if the occasion demanded, to fight the matter to a finish in the approved pioneer method. The Reformers predominated in numbers, but the Colonel's supporters made the most noise, their enthusiasm increasing as their opponents' demonstration diminished. Talbot's famous speech[42] began with the characteristic command "Silence and Attention", and was punctuated by the applause of his faction, and occasionally by interruptions of another nature:

"At one point in his address there was some noise in the outskirts of the crowd, which made the orator pause for a moment. Taking out his snuff-box, giving it the usual formal tap, he administered a large dose of the powdered tobacco to his nostrils, shook his extended fingers a few inches from his nose, and called out: 'Gentlemen, I am an

[40]See the *Talbot Papers*, Section II, pp. 117-138, for the documents relative to the Reform agitation,
[41]*Ibid.*, Section II, p. 117,
[42]*Ibid.*, pp. 124-6.

P. V. W.

LONDON, CANADA WEST, ABOUT 1839

George R. Dartnell

LONDON, CANADA WEST, 1839

ST. THOMAS IN 1830

GUELPH, U.C., IN 1840

old man—but tough'. His admirers spoke of him familiarly afterwards as 'Tommy Tough'."[43]

The laughter which greeted his reference to the "sheep with the rot—and very black they are," seemed to please him; and the amusement which was created by his jocular reference to certain of his settlers, and to Americans, Methodists (which he called "Westlians"), and Temperance Societies, undoubtedly aided greatly in the achievement of the desired result, which was the adoption of a loyal address to the King. Talbot regarded his success as the crowning triumph of his career, and its influence upon public opinion in both Canada and Britain was widespread.

Much has been written about the personal character and eccentricities of Colonel Talbot. No visitor was ever sure just how he would be welcomed at the Castle of Malahide, and, as they knew its owner by reputation, few were surprised at a cold, not to say rude reception. Thomas Need met him returning in triumph from the famous St. Thomas meeting, "which he and his friends had, by a series of counter-resolutions, converted into a loyal and constitutional one". Need learned that "report pronounces him very rich, but habit and taste have confirmed him in the simple mode of life of the Bush; and if happiness consists in wanting but 'little here below', he may be pronounced truly happy."[44]

A notable example of the impoliteness with which he occasionally treated his guests is furnished by the record of Sir James Alexander's short but remarkable visit in 1842.

"The Colonel's silent and melancholy-looking domestic, Jeffreys, received us at the door, and conducted us through an outer room garnished with flour barrels, in some of which hens were engaged hatching. In the sitting-room there was a long table, a heavy press, shelves with books, and several ancient portmanteaus. At a small fire, though it was in July, sat the Colonel occupied with his newspapers, who received us courteously and with his usual hospitality. He was a short and strong-built man, with a ruddy face, an aquiline nose, and was dressed in a white jacket and trousers. . . .

"We dined in a room with red paper and gilding, unusual ornaments. We had a well-dressed dish of roast meat

---

[43]*Ibid.*, introduction, p. 52.
[44]Thomas Need: *Six Years in the Bush*. 1838. p. 17.

and mashed potatoes, and a good bottle of port. The host, being of the old school of hospitality, pressed us to drink, which we declined after having had a couple of glasses, evidently very much to his annoyance, for when we went into the next room he followed us, and, rather to our surprise, said quietly: 'I have ordered your wagon; I don't wish you to be late in getting back to St. Thomas!' "[45]

Sir James says he left about 3 p.m., "and laughed a good deal at the singular manner of our exit, on account of following principles of temperance". But it was afterwards current in the district that the guests were not even allowed to finish their meal before their horses were brought up by Jeffrey Hunter.

Talbot's attitude toward the use of intoxicating liquors arose from his own personal appetite, together with his antipathy towards all things of American origin, as temperance organisations were. In his reference to the "damned Cold Water Drinking Societies" he was voicing an opinion which was held by the average Englishman of his class and period, for it is well-known that the early Societies were in many districts composed largely of the rank and file of the Reform party, and of the members of the non-conformist churches.

Colonel Talbot, in spite of his hard-drinking propensities, did not wish to die a drunkard, and, believing a saying that he who drank early in the morning would fill a drunkard's grave, he consistently waited until 11 a.m. before commencing the round of dissipation. He devised, however, an ingenious system whereby no time would be lost:

"He placed a mark on an out-building, showing where the sun would cast his shadow at 11 o'clock. Long before the hour the Colonel would sit in his arm-chair gazing intently at the moving shadow. Precisely when it reached the mark Jeffrey was ordered to produce the decanter, and the rest of the day was devoted to indulgence. To have ample time for this dissipation he had an inflexible rule that no business should be transacted after 12 o'clock. Settlers who had walked scores of miles following a blazed track in the woods to get their land found on their arrival that they

[45]Sir James Alexander: *L'Acadie, or Seven Years' Explorations in British America.* 1849. Vol. I, pp. 144-7.

could not see the great man bacause the noon hour had
struck. Back they had to trudge to the nearest inn, two
miles or more, or sleep in the woods, so as to be on hand to
interview the distinguished Government Agent next
morning."[46]

Talbot had the reputation of being a woman-hater, but
it appears that he had female domestics in his house in both
the early and late periods of his residence at Port Talbot.
His man-of-all-work, Jeffrey Hunter, married while in his
employ, and though there were at first objections to his
wife's presence in the household, she was shortly allowed to
take up her abode with her husband, and remained there
during the remainder of the Colonel's life at Port Talbot.
His dislike of women has probably, therefore, been greatly
exaggerated, if it is not, in some respects, entirely untrue.

Talbot's antipathy to Scots doubtless arose to a considerable extent from the mutual dislike between him and
the Aryllshire Highlanders in Aldborough. The treatment
meted out to the Colonel by Duncan Patterson could hardly
have been expected to increase his fondness for Scotchmen
in general, though it must have enhanced his respect for the
race!

In spite of the boorishness which must in all fairness be
said to have been characteristic of Talbot, and his
"despotic habits" and "total disregard, or rather total
ignorance of the feelings of others", which no less an
admirer than Anna Jameson felt constrained to admit,[47]
there were many who looked upon him as a gentleman
beneath a rough exterior, a man "with much natural
benevolence and generosity",[48] whose disposition had been
soured by the worry and toil of a long life among social
inferiors, under conditions of governmental opposition particularly galling to one of a family of such aristocratic
traditions. Those whose idea of a gentleman comprehended
merely a sort of outward chivalry and courtesy to social
equals—a man of the type portrayed by Lord Chesterfield
in his letters to his son—and whose reception by the
termagant Colonel was reasonably cordial, found that he
had "in his features, air, and deportment, that something

[46]Introduction to the *Papers*, p .49.
[47]Jameson, *op. cit.*, Vol. II. p. 201.
[48]*Ibid.*

which stamps him gentleman", a character derived "from blood and birth".[49]

Judge Ermatinger considered that an estimate of Talbot's personal character depended entirely upon the point of view; he found him of a type not unusual in the eighteenth century:

"It is hoped that what has been written will enable the reader to form a just estimate of the man who was the central figure of the Settlement during its first half century. Much depends upon the point of view from which he is regarded—whether from the standpoint of the commencement or the close of the nineteenth century. Judged by the standard of the latter, he appears to have been autocratic and intolerant in his opinions and public acts and in the performance of his official duties, and in his private life irreligious, blasphemous and, in his later years especially, well-nigh besotted. Judged by the standard of the times in which he lived, to so stigmatise him would be regarded as unjustly severe and attributable to either political rancour or private spleen."[50]

In the early years at Port Talbot the Colonel held religious services each Sunday and expected his settlers to attend; in fact he himself read the Anglican form of service, and as an inducement "to ensure punctuality of attendance, the bottle was passed around at the close. The result, it is hardly necessary to add, was satisfactory on both sides".[51] Talbot's interest in church services was more a survival of garrison discipline than a sincere belief in religion. The erection of St. Peter's Church, Tyrconnel, in 1828, put an end to his ministrations, though as a magistrate he frequently performed the marriage ceremony and, it is said, sometimes baptized children. For the last twenty years of his life there was not even a pretence of religious observance, and the Colonel is known to have treated with scant respect such clergymen as visited him, and especially non-Anglicans.[52]

The public duties that Talbot was supposed to perform were either carried out with indifference, or not at all.

49*Ibid.*, Vol. II, p. 185.
50C. O. Ermatinger, *op. cit.*, p. 312.
51Introduction to the *Papers*, p. 46.
52See Edward Ermatinger, *op. cit.*, pp. 116-17.

Though he was a member of the Legislative Council after 1809, there is no record of his presence at a meeting; he similarly neglected attendance at the Quarter Sessions and the Court of Requests. No summons or warrants were ever issued by him in his capacity of magistrate; nor did he ever condescend to vote at provincial elections. Dr. Coyne points out that for generations Dunwich, the township in which Talbot lived, was the most consistently Liberal in the county, and for no other reason than opposition to the Colonel.[53]

Even to his admirers it was apparent that Talbot's old age would not be pleasant. In 1837 Anna Jameson, comparing him to a king—"a great man who has done great things,"—considered him then an old and lonely man: "Where is to him the solace of age? He has honour, power, obedience; but where are the love, the troops of friends, which also should accompany old age? . . . . His sympathies have had no natural outlet, his affections have wanted their natural food."[54] George McKay, who lived near Port Talbot, recalled him as a "feeble old man, bent nearly double, and creeping about the old place, laboriously leaning on a stout walking-stick".[55] Such were the closing days of the Talbot *régime* on the shores of Lake Erie, a pathetic end for the once fiery and omnipotent ruler of the entire region.

The desire to leave his extensive estates to someone of his family who might carry on the dignity of the Talbots led to attempts to interest some of his relatives in residence at Port Talbot. Two of his sister's sons visited him, and one of them, Colonel Richard Airey, came with his family in the autumn of 1847 to reside with him, though the Aireys lived first, for a short time, in a house at Burwell's Corners. When they moved to Port Talbot the Colonel built for himself a small house close by, but he usually took his meals with the Aireys. In the summer of 1848 Talbot spent a few months in England and Ireland, and when he returned to Port Talbot he found his old home entirely renovated, the various buildings rearranged and

[53]Introduction to the *Papers*, p. 50.
[54]Jameson, *op. cit.*, Vol. II, p. 201.
[55]Reminiscences of George McKay, cited by Dr. Coyne in his introduction to the *Papers*, p. 57.

made compact, and the whole elegantly furnished. This so enraged the fiery Colonel that he erected a log cabin some distance off and lived there by himself until 1850. After further clashes with his nephew, Talbot decided to retire from his estate and end his days in England, and Airey was left in possession of the old homestead and 600 acres of land, though he does not appear to have been given legal ownership of it.[56] Talbot appointed George Macbeth administrator of his estate during his absence.

At Apsley House he renewed his friendship with his boyhood chum, the Duke of Wellington; but the old man had lost all touch with formal society and found no happiness amid conditions so vastly different from his fifty years' life in the Bush. He returned to Canada in 1852, but only to find that Colonel Airey and his family had departed, and the estate rented to John Sanders. Though Sanders offered to vacate, Talbot, ill in body and broken in spirit, chose to live in the small house of Mrs. Hunter, widow of his faithful servant. Here he resided, cooped up in a single room within sight of his former home on the cliff, while Mrs. Hunter attended to the needs of one who had but few friends in his old age.

George Macbeth, who had been for some years the manager of Talbot's estate, resided for a time with the Colonel at Mrs. Hunter's, and was made sole legatee of Talbot. Macbeth spent most of his spare time at the Sanders', however, and soon married one of the daughters, removing thereupon to London. Talbot gradually became weaker and more infirm, until finally Mrs. Hunter was unable to take care of him, and he was removed to Macbeth's home in London; there he spent his last days—just outside the bounds of his settlement. He died on February 5, 1853, in his 82nd year. The details of his funeral are not pleasant. On the 9th

[56]Miss Ella Lewis, the indefatigable Secretary of the Elgin Historical Society, gave an address to its members on September 24, 1932, incorporating therein the results of intensive research into the ownership of, and alterations in the Talbot property. It is her opinion that the Colonel actually gave the property to Airey, though he probably did not execute a deed of conveyance. In any case Airey appears to have rented the property to Sanders, and after Talbot's death to have sold it to him. In 1879 George Macbeth's son, Talbot Macbeth, purchased it from Sanders for $15,000.

his body was conveyed by sleigh to Fingal, a stop being made at Smith's Tavern, St. Thomas, until those in charge had drinks. Scant respect was paid to the Father of the Settlement, for at Fingal the body was first placed by the drunken undertaker in the barn of the Commercial Hotel. A niece of the innkeeper, Chauncey Lewis, states, however, that her uncle "made them yield to better treatment, and the body was brought into the hotel and put in a back bedroom; but, some of the help objecting, a storeroom was made ready, and some visitors in the hotel assisted in removing the coffin into this place, where it remained all night".[57]

The following day, "the little procession went on to Burwell's Corners, and thence over hill and dale by the winding road through 'The Colonel's Woods' to Port Talbot. Here the body lay for a short time in the old familiar home. St. Peter's Church is four or five miles farther west. There the brief service for the dead was recited. It was a bitterly cold day, and comparatively few were present. Near by, on the cliff overlooking the lake, is the final resting-place of many of the brave pioneers. There, in their midst, under a plain slab, lie the mortal remains, as the epitaph bears witness, of

'The Honorable Thomas Talbot,
Founder of the Talbot Settlement.' "[58]

[57]Ella Lewis to E. C. Guillet, June 26, 1931. Edward Ermatinger penned the following somewhat Johnsonian comment upon the "outrage" (See p. 224): "We are willing to believe that no intentional disrespect was premeditated, but neither the annals of civilisation nor the traditions of barbarism could probably furnish an instance of such lamentable inattention to the unburied remains of a departed friend."
[58]Dr. Coyne's introduction to the *Papers*, p. 56.

CHAPTER VI

ON THE SHORES OF THE DETROIT

"When the French penetrated into these regions a century ago
they brought with them not only their national courtesy, but some
of their finest national fruits,—plums, cherries, apples, pears, of the
best quality—excellent grapes, too, I am told—and all these are now
grown in such abundance as to be almost valueless . . . . It was
quite curious to find in this remote region such a perfect specimen of
an old-fashioned Norman peasant—all bows, courtesy and good-
humour. He was carrying a cart-load of cherries to Sandwich, and
when I begged for a ride the little old man bowed and smiled, and
poured forth a voluble speech, in which the words *enchanté!*
honneur! and *madame!* were all I could understand; but these were
enough. I mounted the cart and seated myself in an old chair surrounded with baskets heaped with ripe cherries."

ANNA JAMESON (1837).[1]

THE cradle of settlement in Upper Canada is the Detroit
River district, where there were several hundred settlers
before the close of the French period,—at a time when the
rest of this province was still a wilderness. The earliest
explorations along the Detroit were by Louis Joliet in
1669, and by Father Galinée in the following year; while
in 1679 La Salle and Hennepin observed large numbers of
wild turkeys, swans and deer on the shores.[2] The first
settlement arose out of the fur trade, for the European
demand for beaver skin hats led French and British to push
farther into the wilds. The British used their new Fort
Orange (Albany) as a base, and the French trade at
Michilimackinac began to fall away, for the British could
give twice as much rum in trade as their rivals could afford
of the more expensive brandy. In consequence the French
determined to establish in a suitable location a strong
military post to intercept the trade.

Antoine Laumet de la Mothe Cadillac had been for
several years commandant at the Mackinac, and his experience in the western fur trade suggested his appointment to
establish the new post. On June 5, 1701, twenty-five
canoes manned by fifty soldiers and fifty *voyageurs,* and

[1]Anna Jameson: *Winter Studies and Summer Rambles in Canada.*
1838. Vol. II, pp. 315-16.
[2]See Thwaites Edition, 1903, Vol I, p. 109, of Louis Hennepin:
Nouvelle Découverte d'un Pais plus grand que l'Europe. 1697.

a number of smaller Indian canoes, set out from Montreal and followed the fur trader's route to the west, *viâ* the Ottawa and Georgian Bay. Forty-nine days later, after making some thirty portages, the expedition reached the region suggested as the most strategic for the post, and Detroit, "City of the Strait", came into being.

The chosen location was very suitable for the days of Indian warfare, for it was defended on three sides by a waterfront, and commanded a full view up and down the river. Within a few hours Fort Pontchartrain, as the post was named in honour of the French Minister of Marine, was being planned by Cadillac and his assistants, Captain Tonty and Lieutenants Chacoruacle and Dugne. Twenty-foot posts, sharpened at the smaller end, formed the palisade, and the Church of Ste. Anne, as well as all the houses for almost a century, were erected in the same manner by inserting the logs side by side four feet into the ground. The walls of the church were set in place on the first day, and Ste. Anne's still exists after being twice burned and twice moved. By September 1st the entire settlement was enclosed by a stockade; the enclosure had an area of about thirty-seven acres, and a century later it had expanded to less than a square mile. In the summer of 1702 the first women arrived at the settlement when Madame Cadillac and Madame Tonty, escorted by *voyageurs*, made the long journey from Quebec. The historian of the city draws an interesting word-picture of life in the settlement during French control:

"Old Detroit was a quaint sort of place in early days. The stockade of unpainted timber soon began to show signs of decay, and occasionally rotten palings had to be replaced with sound timber. The houses, all unpainted and rudely constructed, took on a weather-beaten and rather dilapidated appearance. Some of the roofs sagged and walls became out of plumb, giving the older buildings a staggering effect; but the happy-go-lucky Frenchmen cared little for appearances as long as they were kept dry and warm within. . . .

"Ste. Anne's Church fulfilled the double function of supplying the souls of the inhabitants with grace, and their minds with the news of the day. After morning mass the leading acolyte would hastily doff his robe and take his stand on the little platform at the church door, where he would relate to the assembly gathered in the street all the news of the town and shore, giving notices of dances that were to be held during the week and of the horse-races to be held after dinner Sunday afternoon.

"They were mostly a carefree, jovial lot. The streets of the town were noisy day and night with the folk-songs of the old homes across the ocean. The sound of violins could be heard from many houses, and dancing was the popular amusement in which young and old joined with equal zest. The Indians loved to gather on the common, east of the fort, to play lacrosse and football. And often there were contests between the reds and the whites. . . .

"The homes were kept very clean. The fare, though simple, was well-cooked. Many houses had small looms in which the women wove coarse linens and woollens. Over their beds they hung pictures of the Madonna, and a lead crucifix always adorned the wall of the main room. . . . All along the river front, before each house, was a tiny landing-wharf with a birch canoe tied to it and sometimes a larger bateau for freighting goods. . . . Along the ridge now marked by the course of Jefferson Avenue was a rude trail by which the farmers came to the fort."[3]

For over half a century the settlement had often to fight for its existence against various tribes of Indians, jealous of one another and of the French. A body of Hurons was located near the post, a village of Ottawas was soon established on the present site of Walkerville, and another on the opposite side of the river; while to the west and south were the Miamis and Pottawatomies, and to the north on the Straits of Mackinac lived the warlike Chippawas or Ojibways. The most notable of the Indian attacks on Detroit was that under Pontiac in 1763. After his success against other western posts the Indian leader beseiged Detroit for 153 days; but, though food was often scarce, the garrison held out until October 12th, when the Indians fortunately abandoned the siege.

Under the protection of Fort Pontchartrain, settlements were gradually made on both sides of the river. In 1728 a

[3]G. B. Catlin: *The Story of Detroit.* 1923. pp. 24-6.

OLD FORT PONTCHARTRAIN, 1701

A SEIGNEUR SUPERINTENDING THE CLEARING OF HIS LAND

DETROIT WATERFRONT IN 1812

THE MONTREUIL WINDMILL, SANDWICH
Built about 1815, this mill operated until 1852 and was demolished
about 1875

Jesuit priest arrived at Detroit, and soon after established
a Huron mission on the opposite shore, where the village of
Sandwich grew up many years later. The mission-house,
part of which remained until the early years of the present
century, was built partly of hewed pine and partly of sawn
lumber, and measured thirty by forty-five feet. In later
years a church was erected, and also a priest's residence,
a storehouse for furs and one for provisions, and a blacksmith shop.

The settlement of the Canadian shore of the river was
most extensive during the last thirty years of the French
period. Numerous land grants were made between 1734
and 1756 to prospective settlers, many of them ex-soldiers,
and these men erected their small homes in straggling
shore settlements, as in Quebec. The land was held under
feudal tenure, and, in addition to his manor-house, each
seigneur was required to erect a grist-mill and blockhouse
The combined windmill forts consequently became common
on both sides of the river. Patrick Shirreff, in 1833, observed them in operation, and one, the Montreuil Windmill
at Sandwich, was a picturesque landmark until about 1875,
when it was demolished. When there was a good wind one
of these mills could grind one hundred bushels of wheat in
twenty-four hours. The settlements along the shore were
arranged in long, narrow ribbons of land with a frontage
on the river, and a group of these was called a *côte*; between
Amherstburg and Sandwich, for example, was located
Petite Côte, a name which long survived but without its
original significance.

At the time of the British conquest of Canada the
French settlements on the Detroit were considered to be
in a prosperous condition. In Detroit itself there were
some 300 dwellings and 2,000 inhabitants, and French
farmers were scattered up and down the shore from the
mouth of the River Raisin to L'Anse Creuse Bay, Lake St.
Clair. On the eastern shore of the Detroit there were
several hundred settlers, most of whom lived between the
present site of Windsor and the River Canard.

It was almost the end of the eighteenth century before
Detroit had many English inhabitants. After the American
Revolutionary War Governor Sir Frederick Haldimand in-

tended to establish a large colony of Loyalists there, but the problem of transporting them proved too great, though some of Butler's Rangers arrived in the vicinity in 1783 and succeeding years. After 1791 the number of British settlers considerably increased; for some years longer, however, the inhabitants of Detroit itself were chiefly French-Canadians. John Ogden, who visited the district in 1794, considered that the British Loyalist settlements on the Canadian side of the river exhibited a higher state of civilisation than the French settlements at Detroit, "but the French have fine orchards from which Niagara is at present supplied with cyder and apples".[4]

Though the Revolutionary War came to an end in 1783, Detroit remained in British control until 1796, when by the Jay Treaty it was transferred to the United States. On that account a new fort was hastily erected eighteen miles below, at the mouth of the river, and to this fort, called Malden, were removed the guns and military stores from Fort Detroit. Isaac Weld visited the district just after the building of Fort Malden, and found about twenty houses near the fort. He states that there were also a few dwellings at the lower end of the district, and that the Detroit River was "crowded with Indian canoes, bateaux and sailing-ships, and several pleasure boats of the officers of the garrison of the new Fort Malden".[5]

A large number of the inhabitants of Detroit moved into Upper Canada in 1796, preferring to remain under the British flag. Owing to the exodus the population of the town dwindled from 2,200 to 500. Some of these Loyalists settled near Lake St. Clair, or along the Thames, but most of them merely moved across the river to Sandwich, which was laid out for their reception. Among those who came to Sandwich was John Askin, whose grandson, Major John Richardson, became a noted author, among his writings being a history of the War of 1812, in which he fought, and a historical novel, *Wacousta*. In 1796, the first year of the settlement of Sandwich, a log building was erected to

---

[4]John Ogden: *A Tour through Upper and Lower Canada*. 1799. p. 113.
[5]Isaac Weld: *Travels through the States of North America*. 1799. p. 343.

serve as a church, and St. John's was the first Protestant
church in the Detroit River district. As lots were given
free to persons who would construct dwellings, Sandwich
soon became a flourishing settlement.

In 1804-5 the Rev. Nathan Bangs, pioneer Methodist
missionary, visited the Detroit River settlements. He
preached at Sandwich and Malden on the Canadian side,
and in the Council-House at Detroit. Bangs made three
visits to Detroit, but "it seemed to be a most abandoned
place, only a few children coming to the place to worship,
and no one appearing to take any interest in hearing the
gospel preached there; so our missionary shook off the dust
of his feet as a testimony against them, and took his departure from them. In about four weeks after this the
town was consumed by fire. The report was that it took
fire from a man smoking a segar in a stable, and the houses
being chiefly built of wood, the flames spread so rapidly
that nearly every house on each side of the main street was
consumed".[6]

The fire of June 11, 1805, destroyed practically the entire town for "when night fell there was but one un-
important warehouse and a few tottering stone chimneys
left standing above the glowing embers of what had once
been the incorporated town of Detroit".[7] But, like the great
fire of London in 1666, the burning of the town was in
reality a blessing. Many another pioneer conflagration—
such as those in Toronto, Lindsay and Peterborough—resulted in improved buildings and better streets. In fact
a traveller was assured "that whatever might be the private
loss or suffering, a fire was always a public benefit in
Toronto—a good brick house was sure to arise in the place
of a wooden one".[8] However that may be in theory, few
fires were ever a benefit to individuals in a day when
insurance was unusual; but the Detroit fire resulted in great
improvements, and the town was soon a thriving community
again.

Meanwhile a considerable number of Loyalists had taken
up land in Essex County, the first of them arriving in 1784.

[6]George F. Playter: *History of Methodism in Canada.* 1862. p. 82 fn.
[7]Catlin, *op. cit.,* p. 118.   [8]Jameson, *op. cit.,* Vol. I, p. 111.

In the absence of anything more regular they became mere squatters on the land. In 1788 a Government Land Board for the District of Hesse was created, and lots were granted to these Loyalists in the usual manner. A number of pacifists, largely Pennsylvania Germans, (commonly called "Dutch Tories"), arrived during the same period.

The change from French to British rule had made but little variation in the daily life of the French inhabitants on the Canadian shore of the Detroit. Travellers considered that they were in general somewhat more backward than their British neighbours. D. W. Smith gives a pleasant picture of the riverside settlements in the late seventeen-nineties:

"There are several windmills on the Detroit, and an orchard adjoining almost every house. The settlers are numerous, and the improvements handsome and extensive. When the fruit trees are in blossom, the prospect as you pass through the strait is perhaps as delightful as any in the world."[9]

During the War of 1812 Fort Malden figured prominenty, being the base from which Detroit and the American army under Hull were captured by the British forces. From this fort later in the war occurred the retreat of General Proctor to Moraviantown, during which the gallant Indian chief, Tecumseh, was killed. The village which grew up near Malden had been named Amherstburg in commemoration of General Lord Amherst, British commander in the Seven Years' War. For nearly two years, 1813-15, Amherstburg was occupied by American troops, the British under Proctor having partially destroyed the village and fort before their retreat.

The remains of Fort Malden existed until about 1875. The old fort was very useful during the Rebellion of 1837 and the disturbances along the border in 1838. In a rare book Robert Marsh describes how he and twenty-eight other insurgents from the United States were imprisoned in Fort Malden. They were captured after the "battle of Windsor",

[9]D. W. Smith: *A Short Topographical Description of His Majesty's Province of Upper Canada* . . . . 1799. p. 33.

and Marsh states that the twenty-nine were kept in irons in one small room for seven weeks.[10]

One of the first British retired officers to settle near Amherstburg was Colonel Matthew Elliott, who had served in the Revolutionary War and had received from the British Government a grant of 2,500 acres in Malden Township. With a number of slaves from Virginia he took up his residence on the river road below the site of the present town. He was a personal friend of Brock, Proctor and Tecumseh, and in 1813, when eighty years of age, led the Indians at the assault of Fort Niagara. The ruins of his house and the slave quarters may still be seen at Elliott's Point. One of the oldest landmarks in Amherstburg itself is Christ Church (Anglican), a red brick edifice constructed shortly after 1800.

The development of Malden Township was very slow for many years, the blame for which was placed by the inhabitants on the extensive government reserves of land. In 1817 many of the chief landowners met at William Searle's Hotel and drew up a report at the request of Robert Gourlay. The document is signed by William Caldwell, J.P., and A. Maisonville, Secretary, and gives considerable information as to the condition of the township:

"The first improvement was made in the year 1784. At present there are 108 inhabited houses and 675 persons, one Catholic chapel, and a Roman Catholic clergyman, two medical practitioners, three schools, twelve stores, five taverns, two windmills . . . . The chief reason that the township is not more settled is that, independent of the extensive crown and clergy reserves, which are common throughout this province, there is a large tract of excellent land (on which there are one or two mill-seats) reserved for the Huron Indians in the upper part of the township; a great part of this last reserve, it is presumed, might be purchased by government, and settled. Another drawback on the improvement of this township arises from a quantity of the lands being in the hands of individuals who are not

[10]Robert Marsh: *Seven Years of My Life, or Narrative of a Patriot Exile.* 1848. This book is exceedingly rare. Frank H. Severance of Buffalo found one copy after fifteen years' search, and gives a summary of Marsh's story in his *Old Trails on the Niagara Frontier.* 1903.

inclined to sell, and also large tracts belonging to minors, who cannot convey."[11]

When Patrick Shirreff visited the village of Amherstburg in 1833 he found three churches, several schools and a population of 500. He noticed that the houses were mostly of wood, "almost all bespeaking meanness and poverty. Everything, with the exception of two handsome residences below the town, seems in a state of listless decay".[12] Four years later Mrs. Anna Jameson described the village as "containing about 600 inhabitants but not making any progress".[13] Shortly afterwards another traveller was similarly impressed, for he considered that Amherstburg might be called "a finished town, for there is not a house built in it once a year. Its principal trade is in tobacco, of which about 1,000 hogsheads are raised in the neighbourhood yearly".[14]

The site of Windsor was in 1812 a meadow, forming part of Colonel Francis Bâby's farm. The farmhouse was located near the corner of the present Church and Sandwich Streets. It was a frame building and remained standing until the mid-seventies, when almost all of the old landmarks in the district appear to have been demolished. Windsor, established as a stage-coach village in 1828, was originally called "The Ferry", a log canoe being used to carry passengers and freight to Detroit; the only opposition in this service was another log canoe a little farther along the shore, and the fare charged was 25c. for the round trip. Canoe and rowboat as ferries were gradually replaced owing to the initiative of citizens of Detroit. The first advance in methods of transport was the use of a horse-boat in 1825, and this continued until 1827, when it was replaced by the small and "cranky" steamship *Argo*.

In 1833 Shirreff found in Windsor fifteen or twenty wooden houses, as well as several of brick in process of erection. He expressed the opinion that the village would "soon eclipse Sandwich and may rival Chatham".[15] When

[11]Robert Gourlay: *A Statistical Account of Upper Canada*. 1822. Vol. I. pp. 281-3.
[12]Patrick Shirreff: *A Tour through North America*. 1835. p. 215.
[13]Jameson, *op. cit.*, Vol. II, p. 317.
[14]J. Abbott: *The Emigrant to North America*. 1844. p. 80.
[15]Shirreff, *op. cit.*, p. 216.

Cornelius Krieghoff

THE HABITANT FARM

Lieutenant Philip Bainbrigge

VIEW OF AMHERSTBURG, 1838

THE OLD JESUIT MISSION-HOUSE AT SANDWICH
The building was erected in 1746, and part of it remained until 1912

COLONEL JAMES BÂBY'S RESIDENCE, SANDWICH
Built in 1790 for the North-West fur trade, this brick and frame
building is one of the most noted historical landmarks in
Upper Canada

Mrs. Jameson paid it a visit in 1837 the place was known as Richmond. Like Shirreff, she was greatly impressed by the difference in the development of the two sides of the Detroit. She noted that Detroit was a bustling and beautiful city, having a harbour crowded with large vessels, while Richmond was, on the other hand, "a little straggling hamlet, with one schooner, one little wretched steamboat, some windmills, and a Catholic chapel or two".[16] In 1858 this straggling hamlet was incorporated into the town of Windsor.

A traveller who visited Windsor in the early forties advanced an interesting reason for the founding of the village, and one that has a very modern flavour. In a letter to his brother he wrote that "the village of Windsor is a new place, formed in consequence of the American tariff, to enable the inhabitants to smuggle British goods across the river. The village, therefore, consists of two classes of men, store-keepers and tailors, the former to violate the laws of the United States, the latter to evade them; for a man coming over from Detroit buys cloth for a suit of clothes, gets them made, and then marches back to Detroit with the new clothes on his back, and the old ones in a bundle, under the very nose of the Collector of Customs".[17]

About two miles below Windsor was the village of Sandwich. Here in 1790 was erected Colonel James Bâby's house, the first brick building in the Western District; it was built for the North-West fur trade, and still remains at the corner of Russell and Mill Streets. The foundation of this interesting landmark is of stone, while the framework and beams are of walnut. In the large hallway, which was the trading-room, was hung an iron hook from which were suspended massive scales capable of weighing 2,000 pounds of furs. This house is the most notable relic of the past in the district. During the War of 1812 it was at various times occupied by the British generals, Brock and Proctor, and by the Americans, Hull and Harrison.

On December 18, 1817, the resident landowners of Sandwich Township prepared a report on the condition of the

[16]Jameson, *op. cit.*, Vol. II, p. 314.
[17]Abbott, *op. cit.* p. 80.

district at the request of Robert Gourlay. The statement reads in part: "The Township of Sandwich contains at present about 200 inhabited houses and about 1,000 souls. The front of the river only is settled, with the exception of a few houses in the interior, and notwithstanding its nearness to market, and natural advantages, we do not know of one additional settler for this number of years."

The report goes on to say that there was one Roman Catholic church and two priests, but no Protestant church or chapel, the only one in the township having been destroyed by the Americans during the War of 1812. Among the inhabitants were an Anglican preacher, two doctors and one good school teacher, who was paid £100 *per annum* by the Provincial Government and received tuition fees in addition: there were also two inferior schools, the teachers of which received £25 each and moderate fees. The township contained at that time thirteen stores, eight taverns, eight windmills and one water-mill. But the inhabitants considered that "the want of some incentive to emulation, the reserve of two-sevenths of the land for the crown and clergy, must for a long time keep the country a wilderness; a harbour for wolves; a hindrance to a compact and good neighbourhood".[18]

When Patrick Shirreff was travelling in the district (1833) Sandwich was but a small village. He states that the houses were built in an irregular manner along the shore, that its trade was "more limited even than that of Amherstburg, and its only importance in being the county town".[19] Mrs. Jameson writes that its population in 1837 was about 500, and that it was considered the chief town in the Western District.[20]

In his progress through Essex and Kent, Shirreff travelled eastward from Sandwich along the road to Chatham. This highway he found very poor, even for travel on horseback. His references describe the condition of this section of Essex County at the time. He states that the inns along the road offered but poor accommodation for travellers, not even having hay for the horses;

18Gourlay, *op. cit.*, Vol. I, p. 275.
19Shirreff, *op. cit.*, p. 216.
20Jameson, *op. cit.*, Vol. II, p. 317.

that many negroes, mostly escaped slaves, were settled along the road, and considerable tobacco grown; but "the greater part of the inhabitants are descendants of the French and still retain the language, appearance and many of the customs of their ancestors. They seldom engage in commerce or manufactures. The houses are generally brick but occasionally frame".[21]

Shirreff, a farmer himself, was interested in the grist-mills of the district, of which he found one variety "propelled by oxen walking on an inclined plane", and another driven "by oxen or horses attached to a large wheel, moving horizontally a few inches above the ground". He considered these poor machines; but he heard that a steam-power grist-mill was about to be built at Sandwich.[22]

Among the settlers of importance in the vicinity of the Detroit River after 1820 were negroes from the United States. Joseph Pickering observed in 1826 that "black slaves, who have run away from their masters in Kentucky, arrive in Canada almost weekly, where they are free and work at raising tobacco; I believe they introduced the practice. One person will attend and manage the whole process of four acres, planting, hoeing, budding, etc., during the summer. . . . There are some hundreds of these people settled at Sandwich and Amherstburg, who are formed into a volunteer corps and trained to arms".[23] A traveller noted that in the early forties that there was "a settlement of industrious Irish in the rear of Sandwich, who, though their land was originally wet, have made it highly productive by draining. It is the most prosperous settlement I have yet seen in the Western District".[24]

For a long time the progress of Essex County was slow when compared with developments across the border, and with settlements farther east. In 1824 the total population was only 4,274, but it had doubled by 1837 in spite of a depression due largely to the unsettled conditions incident to the Rebellion. In the forties there was little improvement, but in later years the development was rapid, and Essex

[21]Shirreff, *op. cit.*, p. 201.   [22]*Ibid.*, p. 213.

[23]Joseph Pickering: *Inquiries of an Emigrant.* 1831. September 10 and 12, 1826.

[24]Abbott, *op. cit.*, p. 80.

became one of the most thickly-populated counties in the province. Towards the close of the century this exceedingly flat district, in which it is hard to find a hill, developed wells of natural gas; these, and the tobacco fields, are characteristic of Essex to-day.

The first member of the Provincial Assembly for Suffolk (Elgin) and Essex was David William Smith, later Surveyor-General of Upper Canada, who was sent to Simcoe's first parliament in 1792. Francis Bâby and William Macomb represented Kent in the same parliament, while James (Jacques) Bâby was a member of both the first Executive Council and the first Legislative Council. Kent County had been created on July 16, 1792, and included all the present State of Michigan as well as territory on the Canadian side of the Detroit. One of the members for Kent, William Macomb, was a Detroit Loyalist. On July 11, 1796, the laws of the United States were for the first time in force in Detroit, the town being a part of Upper Canada until that date.

The border settlements on the Detroit were twice raided in 1838 by so-called Patriots, belonging to Hunter's Lodges. These secret anti-British societies with republican sympathies were organised in the United States. The first of the attacks was on Point Pelee Island, thirty-five miles south-east of Amherstburg; the second was directed against Richmond (Windsor). Both invasions were repulsed by a few British Regulars and Canadian militia, and the invaders withdrew hurriedly to the United States. Since that time the proximity of the great Republic has been the chief reason for the increasing importance of the Border Cities and the district generally.

SECTION III
PIONEER LIFE

CHAPTER I

THE PIONEER HOME

"The orders of architecture baffle all description: every one builds his cottage or house according to his fancy, and it is not a difficult thing, in passing through the country, to tell what nation the natives of the houses 'hail from,' if we are aware of any of the whims and conceits that characterize them."

JOHN MACTAGGART (1829).[1]

THE first homes in Ontario were those erected along the Detroit River by several hundred disbanded French soldiers, who were settled there in the last forty years of the French period. Their *côtes*, or long, straggling villages, resembled in appearance the settlements along the St. Lawrence in Quebec. The *habitants'* cottages were low buildings with steep roofs, projecting eaves, and, as a general rule, dormer-windows. Sometimes they were built of logs, sometimes of rough stone if it were readily available, but in either case it was usual to cover the outer walls with pine boards which, when whitewashed, gave the cottages a neat and pleasing appearance. A windmill, or a cross, was quite frequently attached to the chimney of the house. An observer described the French-Canadian's home as "a little house with verandahs all round, few windows and few fancies; everything done with an air of humble comfort."[2] Barns were built of rougher materials, usually logs, while root-houses and bake-ovens were constructed of rocks and clay. The home of the *habitant* had from one to three rooms on the ground floor, and the high-pitched roof provided a loft which was reached by a ladder and used as a sleeping-room. As in other pioneer homes, the floors were commonly made of timbers smoothed off with the axe, but the French often partly covered them with hand-woven rugs. Like those in Quebec, the Detroit River settlements were under the control of seigneurs, who lived in manor-houses varying but little, except in size, from the homes of the peasants.

The first English-speaking settlers in Upper Canada

[1]John MacTaggart: *Three Years in Canada.* 1829. Vol. I, p. 308.
[2]*Ibid.*, pp. 310-11.

were almost entirely United Empire Loyalists, about 5000 in number. Most of the Loyalists came to Canada without worldly goods, their possessions having been either destroyed or confiscated by the revolutionists, or proving impossible to carry with them on their long and laborious trek to their new home in the wilderness. As they reached the government depots at Halifax and St. John in the Maritimes, Sorel, Chambly, Yamachiche, Cornwall and Kingston in the St. Lawrence region, and Niagara and Detroit in the west, they received their "location tickets," supplies and rations, and proceeded to their lots at the first opportunity. A considerable number of German mercenaries who had fought for George III in the Revolutionary War came to Canada at the same time and under the same circumstances as the Loyalists.

Those approaching Canada from the east were conveyed by bateaux up the St. Lawrence, proceeding in brigades of twenty or more. The head of each family held a location ticket, describing the general position of his future land, and as the bateaux were laboriously worked up the rapids the occupants eagerly scanned the wild shores, comparing their appearance with the well-developed farms that they had left behind in order to remain British. Many of the Loyalists were soldiers, and almost every family had a military tent, capable of accommodating eight or ten persons in a very crowded manner. Each night the tent was pitched on the shore, and in the morning the monotonous voyage continued. When they had reached their location it was often necessary to remain encamped for some time, while the surveyors completed their division of the land into lots; and as the tents would not accommodate all, some had to sleep beneath the trees. In some instances the summer had passed before the first "drawings" of land were made; this delay greatly increased the hardship of the first winter in the woods.

At last the surveyor, with his map in front of him, checked off each lot as its number was drawn from a hat. The officers received their lots first, usually the best locations along the waterfront, while the private soldiers and civilians drew theirs from the "back township" locations. Occasionally lots were exchanged so that old comrades in

Ensign James Peachey

ENCAMPMENT OF LOYALISTS AT NEW JOHNSTOWN (CORNWALL), JUNE 6, 1784

A LOCATION TICKET, 1816

BEGINNING A HOME

the same regiment might be near-neighbours. The families, or sometimes the men only, then proceeded to their lot, carrying the tent, such tools and supplies as they had been issued, and a few days' rations. It was often a difficult matter to identify the boundaries of their land, for the forests were full of matted undergrowth and fallen trees, and the undrained swamps and bridgeless streams presented still more formidable difficulties; but the tent was pitched and camp meals were cooked, while a suitable spot was chosen for the shanty after a general idea of the lay-out of the land had been obtained.

Co-operation among settlers was a prominent feature from the first; neighbours helped one another in erecting their crude log shanties, the more difficult of construction because the short-handled ship-axes in general use were but little heavier than hatchets, and only a few other tools of use in the work were available. The log shanty was constructed in the same manner in the later pioneer periods as in Loyalist days; it might be as large as twenty by fifteen feet, but it was very often considerably smaller. The usual shanty was about ten feet long, eight feet wide and six feet high, with the roof sloping to the back, where the wall was frequently not more than four feet high. Round logs, often of basswood or pine, formed the walls. Under the base-logs large rocks were placed for support, and the logs were roughly notched at the corners so that they would fit into one another.

When the log walls had been run up to the desired height the rafters were set in position and the shanty roofed in. The slanting roof was sometimes composed of thick slabs of basswood overlapping one another; other settlers used strips of elm bark about four feet long and two feet wide, placed in overlapping layers and fastened by withes to the poles; while another variety of roof consisted of small hollowed basswood logs laid like tile. When the rude house had been completed, the appearance of its interior varied with the possessions of the owner, and his efforts to make it homelike. Thomas Need's shanty is an example of the success of a bachelor in making his home in the backwoods comfortable, even if crude.

"The next few days were occupied in building a shanty,

or rude hut. . . . It consisted of one apartment, 14 feet by 12 feet in the clear, and contained in the way of furniture a camp bedstead, a chest of drawers, and a well-filled book-case; it had also the somewhat unusual luxury of a chimney, pegs for the suspension of guns and fishing implements, and shelves for my scanty kitchen utensils: a hole in the planks served to admit light, and air found free entrance through numberless cracks and crevices; such as it was, however, it served my purpose well; and when the evening closed I used to light my lamp and sit down to my books with a great feeling of comfort. Several of the classics, which on their shelves at Oxford were rather looked at than into, were now treated with the attention they deserve; and in the solitude of the Bush it was no light pleasure to re-peruse scenes and passages, every one of which was pregnant with some cherished association of school or college."[3]

The roof was usually improved at a later date. Need wrote in his journal on August 7, 1833: "The original roof of my shanty being only of rude logs, I thought it expedient to new-roof it entirely, after the most approved fashion, with thin pieces of deal cut into squares like slate."[4] This roof of cedar, though evidently considered an advanced type, was not satisfactory, for three months later Need states that the rain came through it in many places owing to the laths being warped by the sun. He expected that the rain would restore the roof to its original condition; but "meanwhile the house was a perfect vapour bath".[5]

After a shanty was built the ends of the logs were sawn off, and the cracks chinked with wedge-shaped pieces of wood and plastered with clay inside and out, moss often being used temporarily where clay was unobtainable. Not a nail or screw was used in the construction of these shanties, which were commonly of one room only; though occasionally a partition was later erected at the centre. There was no cellar or foundation, but sometimes a small excavation was made, which was reached by a trap-door and a short ladder. A hole in the roof formed the first exit for the smoke from the open fire in the centre of the room. Before winter set

[3]Thomas Need: *Six Years in the Bush*. 1838. pp. 58-9.
[4]*Ibid.*, p. 70.   [5]*Ibid.*, p. 79.

in an effort was sometimes made to construct a fireplace at one side of the shanty, though many a pioneer family lived for several years without one. Samuel Strickland found that "four thick slabs of limestone, placed upright in one corner of the shanty with clay well packed behind them to keep the fire off the logs, answered very well for a chimney, with a hole cut through the roof directly above to vent the smoke."[6]

The log house was an elaboration of the shanty. The usual building was about twenty feet long, eighteen feet wide and from nine to twelve feet high, and its construction was similar to that of the shanty. White oak or white pine was frequently used for the walls of the log house, and the logs were morticed at the ends and finished as in the shanty, the holes between them being "stubbed" or chinked with chips, moss and mud; where the materials were available, a better job was done by the use of a plaster made of clay mixed with lime or sand. Many an early settler burned limestone during a logging bee in order to secure sufficient lime for this purpose.

It was not usually possible to complete one's home before occupation, and many a house remained in an unfinished condition for two or three years. Those who wished their home to have a finished appearance spent many days hewing down the logs on the inside walls. A log house could not be erected too high or the logs might decay and fall in, but both shanty and log house were occasionally raised a few feet in later years to create a small loft or upstairs bedroom, quite often used as a sleeping-room for the children; this loft was approached by a ladder, often from the outside.

The roof of the log house was usually of a more permanent nature than that of the shanty, though the bark of the pine, spruce, oak, elm or ash could easily be peeled from the trees in summer and used as a temporary covering, to be replaced as soon as possible by a better roof. The hollowed slab or half-log of the basswood formed a common roof, the convex form of one piece overlapping the edges of the concave forms of the slabs on either side. Shingles

[6]Samuel Strickland: *Twenty-seven Years in Canada West*. 1853. Vol. I, p. 92.

of split pine, cedar or spruce, often made by hand, were used in place of the cruder roof whenever they were available.

In a log house a large fireplace was usually erected. The foundation was of stone, and flat stones formed the hearth. The chimney consisted of a framework of small sticks, two or three inches in diameter, laid in the form of a hollow rectangle, and well plastered inside and out with clay mixed with straw. The wood in these chimneys sometimes caught fire when frost had prevented the clay from becoming hard. On that account ladders were occasionally built on the roofs of log houses, near the chimneys, to enable fires to be put out quickly. Many chimneys were poorly built, and some of the smoke found its way out through holes in the roof or walls.

A variation from the usual construction of chimneys was observed by a traveller in western Upper Canada in the early thirties: "On the boundary of the Huron Tract, next to the London District, we passed a negro settlement. The houses of the coloured people appeared of a particular construction, having the chimney-stack on the outside of the log house, and which stack is composed of thin, sawn timber, placed horizontally and mixed with clay."[7]

The fireplace of the pioneer home was usually a huge affair, eight feet or more wide, and provided the only means of heating and cooking in most early houses; in the earliest pioneer period it also furnished the chief method of lighting the house during the long winter evenings. An effort was made to keep the fire always burning, for it was not easy to strike a light in the days before the lucifer match came into common use, which was many years after 1829, when it was invented. When the fire went out, live embers were sometimes carried from the nearest neighbour's, but this was no easier than striking a light. The huge back-logs which burned slowly in the fireplace were sometimes so large that they had to be drawn into the house by oxen.

The floor of the pioneer home varied with the period and with the economic condition of the settler. In Loyalist times the floor was sometimes merely the hard earth. Sawn lumber was then very scarce, and few settlers were fortunate enough to be able to procure boards. Bark,

[7]Patrick Shirreff: *A Tour through North America.* 1835. p. 178.

and boards sawn by hand with a whip-saw were sometimes used for flooring, but more usually it was made
of timbers roughly squared with axe or adze. Split
logs, called puncheons, three or four inches in thickness,
often composed the floor of early homes in the Niagara
district. Most floors were very rough, for the unseasoned
wood soon warped; consequently it was usual to relay them
after the wood had dried. To clean these crude floors
sand and plenty of hot water, applied with a heavy splint
broom and a mop, was found to be quite satisfactory. Those
who painted their floors were considered to be imitating
the "Yankee" fashion. The most prosperous settlers, particularly the residents of towns and villages, used carpets
to cover the inequalities of the flooring.

Crude substitutes for doors and windows were used
where milled lumber was not available. As a general rule
the openings were sawn or chopped out after the house
had been raised. Some settlers used the laborious whip-
saw to obtain a few boards for a door, while others split
them roughly with a broad-axe. Pioneers are known to
have used a blanket to cover the doorway until something
better was available. Some log houses were built without
windows, the construction of the house being easier when
they were left out; while in many cases the doorway and
the cracks in the walls were considered to let in more than
enough cold air in winter. It was not unusual for settlers
to bore holes in the wall to provide a little additional light
and air, while wooden pegs fixed in similar holes provided
a place to hang utensils and clothing.

Hinges and locks of doors and windows were made of
wood. The wooden latch of the door was on the inside,
and could be lifted from outside by a leather latch-string
passing through a hole a few inches above; this string
might be pulled in at night, but as a general rule it was
left out, and the old saying "the latch-string is always out"
signified the hospitality of our pioneer settlers. The ingenuity which characterised many of those who set up a
home in the wilderness is well exemplified by the methods
which one settler used to construct and hang the door of
his log house:

"A man and his wife, with two children, moved into the

Township of Ops, into a dense forest, eight miles from the nearest settler. For months he chopped away at the forest trees, all alone, and succeeded at length in making a clearing in the forest, and erecting a log house for himself and his family. The logs were peeled and notched at the ends, and laid up squarely, each tier making the house the diameter of a log higher. A hole was cut through for a doorway, and another for a window. To form a door he split some thin slabs from a straight-grained cedar, and pinned them with wooden pins to cross slats.

"The most ingenious parts of the construction, however, were the hinges. Iron hinges he had not, and could not get. With the auger he bored a hole through the end of a square piece of wood, and sharpening the other end with his axe he then bored a hole into one of the logs of the house, constituting in part a door-jamb, and drove the piece of wood into this hole. This formed the top part of the hinge, and the bottom part was fashioned in exactly the same way. Now to the door, in like manner, he fastened two pegs of wood with holes bored through their ends. Placing the ends of the hinges above one another they presented the four ends with holes leading through them, the one above the other. Next he made a long pin with his handy jack-knife, leaving a run at one end of it, and making it long enough to reach from the top to the lower hinge. Through the holes at the ends of the hinge this long pin was placed, and thus the door was hung."[8]

The log house had seldom more than one window, and often had none at all. Until a sash could be obtained, or a rough one made with a jack-knife, a blanket, or a wooden shutter fitted in grooves, covered the opening. From four to six panes of glass, usually seven inches by nine, were inserted in the sash by the Loyalists, for glass and putty were issued to most of them. Some settlers, however, used oiled paper in their windows until glass could be procured; while others preferred to stuff waste material such as old clothes into the opening, rather than use the very brittle American glass which was often all that was available.

Such were the log houses of the pioneers, rude homes in which many of the first generation passed the rest of

[8]Thomas Conant: *Upper Canada Sketches.* 1898. pp. 59-61.

From Egerton Ryerson's *The Story of My Life*   Mrs. E. Carey

THE OLD CREDIT MISSION, 1837

School   Council-House   Church   Peter
                                                                 Jones'
                                                                 Study

SIR JOHN A. MACDONALD'S BOYHOOD HOME
Located west of Kingston, four miles north of Adolphustown

From Geikie's *Life in the Woods*

OUR HOME IN THE WOODS

"Dens of dirt and misery which would be shamed by an English pigsty."—Susanna Moodie

J. E. Loughlin

INTERIOR OF A SETTLER'S HOME IN 1812

their lives; structures which were commonly raised in one day at the expense of a few gallons of whisky for the refreshment of those who came to help. But the average log house was neither a thing of beauty nor a joy forever. Mrs. Moodie's indictment of the emigration propaganda of the times does not mince words:

"In 1830 the great tide of emigration flowed westward. Canada became the great landmark for the rich in hope and poor in purse. Public newspapers and private letters teemed with the unheard-of advantages to be derived from a settlement in the highly-favoured region . . . . They talked of log houses to be raised in a single day, by the generous exertions of friends and neighbours, but they never ventured upon a picture of the disgusting scenes of riot and low debauchery exhibited during the raising, or upon a description of the dwellings when raised—dens of dirt and misery, which would, in many instances, be shamed by an English pig-sty."[9]

The extreme hardship of living under such conditions cannot easily be imagined. Many families were so disheartened at the prospect that they would have returned to the Old Land immediately if that had been within the realm of possibility. Instead of the meadows and lanes which the Englishman loved there were unending forests and swampy trails through the bush. The great loneliness which most settlers felt, but bravely suppressed in the hope of better days to come, is shown in the plaintive lament of an anonymous resident of Otonabee Township.

MY HAME

"I canna ca' this forest hame,
    It is nae hame to me;
Ilk tree is suthern to my heart,
    And unco to my e'e.

If I cou'd see the bonny broom
    On ilka sandy know';
Or the whins in a' their gowden pride,
    That on the green hill grow:

[9] Susanna Moodie: *Roughing It in the Bush*. 1852. Introduction to the 3rd Edition, 1854.

If I cou'd see the primrose bloom,
  In Nora's hazel glen;
And hear the linties chirp and sing,
  Far frae the haunts o' men:

If I cou'd see the rising sun
  Glint owre the dewy corn;
And the tunefu' lavrocks in the sky
  Proclaim the coming morn:

If I cou'd see the daisy spread
  Its wee flowers owre the lee;
Or the heather scent the mountain breeze,
  And the ivy climb the tree:

If I cou'd see the lane' kirk yard,
  Whar' frien's lye side by side:
And think that I cou'd lay my banes
  Beside them when I died:

Then might I think this forest hame,
  And in it live and dee;
Nor feel regret at my heart's core,
  My native land for thee."[10]

As settlement spread in later years into "the wild lands" of the older counties, and to the vast unopened territories back from the lakes, the log house continued to be the pioneer home of the settler. Conditions under which it was raised were not usually as primitive as in earlier times. Some settlers were able to hire workmen to build their houses, though the "raising bee" was much more usual. In organized emigrations arrangements were sometimes made to have the log shanties for the incoming settlers constructed before their arrival. The Irish emigrants brought out to Peterborough County in 1825 by the Hon. Peter Robinson had their houses built at the expense of the government by men hired for that purpose, and the cost per house was only $10. Captain Basil Hall, an English traveller who investigated conditions in this settlement two years later, describes these log huts (to build which two men were

[10]*Cobourg Star*, December 27, 1831.

sufficient to cut down the trees and erect the entire house in two days) as about twenty feet by twelve, and seven feet high. The roof of each was made of logs split into four lengths and hollowed out; they overlapped like tiles, "so that each alternate log formed a gutter or channel to carry off the rain".[11] The openings between the logs in the walls were filled with mud and moss; sometimes the house had a window, sometimes not. While these homes were mere shanties, yet the hardship of settling in the new land was mitigated to the extent that the bewildered settler had at least a roof over his head when he began the great adventure in the backwoods of Canada.

The temporary homes of these Irish settlers when they first arrived at Scott's Plains (Peterborough) were even more primitive than the log shanty. Immediately upon their arrival they set to work upon the construction of "rude huts or wigwams, composed of slabs, bark, or the branches of trees, and sods, to shelter them from the weather during the interval which must elapse before they could be located upon their lands in the neighbouring townships".[12] The five log buildings which Peter Robinson erected to serve as his headquarters were of a comparatively advanced type, with square gables and shingled roofs. The logs of the walls and partitions were hewed to a level surface in the interior of the buildings, and, considered as a whole, they were long regarded "as first class houses, and models of taste and perfection in the youthful town".[13]

In some districts Building Societies were established as joint-stock companies; these lent money to settlers on the security of their lands, and enabled many a man to erect or improve his home.[14] Most emigrants, however, continued to come individually and unassisted, and constructed their

[11]Basil Hall: *Travels in North America in the Years 1827 and 1828.* 1829. Vol. I, p. 292.

[12]Thomas Poole: *Early Settlement of Peterborough and Peterborough County.* 1867. p. 5.

[13]*Ibid.*, p. 16.

[14]In the Douglas Library, Queen's University, Kingston, is a pamphlet, published in 1847, descriptive of the Kingston Building Society. An account of the Newcastle District Building Society, including lists of shareholders and members, may be found in E. C. Guillet: *Cobourg,* in the *Cobourg Sentinel-Star,* July 28, 1932.

log homes with the help of their neighbours. As Walter Riddell puts it:

"A settler would come in and either draw or buy a lot, chop down a few large trees and put up a shanty, covering it with bark or split basswood logs. Leaving for a short time, he would come back bringing his wife with him, the young couple having taken their wedding jaunt over a blazed track through the woods, carrying all their worldly possessions on their backs, making their bed of cedar or hemlock boughs, setting themselves down in the forest to subdue the wilderness and by patient industry and perseverance hew out a home."[15]

Those whose means enabled them to hire workmen might have a house erected at no great expense, for a book published in 1822 says that the cost to an immigrant "for building a log house, with a shade for his oxen, and pig-stie" was only £7 10s. ($30) ; and it is further stated that "for this sum his house may have two apartments, a stone chimney and hearth, and two glazed sash windows".[16]

While the initial hardships of pioneer life were sometimes not as severe as in the Loyalist period, yet they were often very great. The Reids and Stewarts were settlers of an excellent type who received land in Peterborough County and arrived on their lots in 1823. A mason had been hired to construct chimneys, but the frost prevented the completion of the work, and the Reid family lived all winter in "merely a shed or hut made of logs, and roofed with slabs hollowed out of logs to turn the wet; the shanty was quite open at one side, and in front was a great log fire".[17] The snow during that winter was from three to four feet deep, but "the little children, from two years old and upwards, sat around the fire, heavy snow falling all the time; . . . . yet they were never so healthy or so lively".[18]

Even in houses of improved type and construction the cold was often very intense. Mrs. Traill describes how cold it was in her home during the winter of 1833: "The mercury

[15]Walter Riddell: *Historical Sketch of the Township of Hamilton.* 1897. p. 7.
[16]Charles Fothergill: *A Sketch of the Present State of Canada.* 1823. p. 57.
[17]Thomas Stewart to Basil Hall, quoted in Hall, *op. cit.,* Vol. I, p. 313.
[18]*Ibid.*

was down to twenty-five degrees in the house; abroad it it was much lower. The sensation of cold early in the morning was very painful, producing an involuntary shuddering, and an almost convulsive feeling in the chest. Our breaths were congealed in hoar-frost on the sheets and blankets. Everything we touched of metal seemed to freeze our fingers."[19]

Owing to the poor means of heating the homes, the cold was felt in town houses almost as much. From the days of early settlement many of the homes of Kingston were of limestone because of the abundance of it in the vicinity; but even in these houses, and others of the better types in the towns, water commonly froze in one's bedroom during the night. Letters of a century ago contain frequent references to the coldness of the houses in winter; and even those who had stoves had difficulty in their erection and management. The letters between Ann Macaulay in Kingston and her son, John, in Toronto, contain many allusions to stove pipes, the buying of wood, the use of candles because of the dearness of oil, and other related matters. John Macaulay wrote to his mother in November, 1837: "We live in a very airy house. The wind almost blows through it;"[20] his mother, referring to the previous winter, wrote: "If I may judge by the quantity of ashes, I burnt an immensity of wood, for in February I was obliged to take out 12 bushels as the ash-house was quite full, which never happened since I kept house."[21]

From time to time improvements to the log house were made by the more enterprising settlers: perhaps a coat of whitewash was applied (paint was very scarce); later on a verandah or stoop might be added, with vines growing up the posts to soften the rough appearance of the home. The average house in Upper Canada, however, was still of a poor type when compared with the homes in Britain and the United States in the same period; this accounts in a large measure for travellers' descriptions of "the miserable

[19]Catherine Traill: *The Backwoods of Canada*. 1836. Edition of 1929, p. 161.
[20]Macaulay Papers; John Macaulay to Ann Macaulay, November 22, 1837. (Archives of Ontario).
[21]*Ibid.*; Ann Macaulay to John Macaulay, November 6, 1837.

log houses" to be found in all parts of the province. The appearance of every farmhouse varied, however, with the energy, thrift and natural abilities of the owner.

Nationality played an important part in the type and general appearance of the home. Dutch settlers were particularly fond of stoops; while Americans who could afford them preferred large, white frame houses with green blinds for the windows, like the fine old "Colonial" home of the United States. These houses are somewhat jocularly described by a writer in the early thirties as "painted white, with nine windows and a door in front, seven windows in either gable, and a semi-circular one above all, almost at the top of the angle of the roof, the blinds painted green, the chimney-stalks highly ornamented, and also the fanlight at the door. . . . . It is almost needless for me to say that this is the mansion of Jonathan, or the U. E. Loyalist from the United States."[22]

The liking for frame houses was not, however, restricted to settlers of American origin. As Dr. Dunlop said: "When a man gets on a little in the world, he builds a frame house, weather-boarded outside, and lathed and plastered within."[23] Frame houses usually cost from $1000 to $2500, but it was difficult to make them air-tight, and consequently some people objected to them because they were "as hot as an oven in summer, and as cold as an open shed in winter."[24] In 1823 a traveller visited Johnson's Inn, near the site of the present town of Barrie. He describes the inn, as "a clap-boarded house, square in shape and rather large, standing upon a gravelly bank close to the lake. It contained a good kitchen, three or four sleeping-rooms, partly in the roof, two good parlours, and a bed-chamber for guests of quality. I have had worse at the best hotels in Washington."[25] He observed, however, that "so new was the wood when the house was put together, or so hot are the summers in Kempenfeldt Bay, that it had shrunk most grievously. The kitchen and parlour might

[22]MacTaggart, *op. cit.*, Vol. I, pp. 309-10.
[23]William Dunlop: *Statistical Sketches of Upper Canada.* 1832. p. 108.
[24]*Ibid.*, p. 109.
[25]J. J. Bigsby: *The Shoe and Canoe, or Pictures of Travel in the Canadas.* 1850. Vol. II, p. 71.

Anne Langton

Anne Langton

TWO INTERIOR VIEWS OF JOHN LANGTON'S "BACHELOR"
ESTABLISHMENT, STURGEON LAKE, 1833

Reproduced by Courtesy of Mrs. Andrew Doole   Mary Adams

THE PRESTON HOMESTEAD NEAR LAKEFIELD
A typical "second" or "third" home, after prosperity had rewarded
the toil of the pioneer

THE DECEW STONE HOUSE, NIAGARA, AS IT APPEARED IN 1903
The headquarters of Fitzgibbon before the Battle of Beaver Dams

almost be called parts of a cage, so well were they ventilated".[26]

Some of the Irish settlers, on the other hand, varied the log shanty until it was similar to the homes in common use in rural Ireland. The chief characteristic was the high earth embankment against the walls of a low house, which sometimes gave it the appearance of a cave in a hillside. A Scotchman who was in charge of public works at Bytown (Ottawa) in the late twenties, states that the Irish labourers often lived in mud cabins. Perhaps his nationality caused him to be somewhat prejudiced against the Irish, but there would seem to be considerable truth in his description. He says: "At Bytown on the Ottawa they burrow into the sand hills; smoke is seen to issue out of holes which are opened to answer the purpose of chimneys."[27]

The "common", or unimproved log house was seldom, if ever, comfortable, though it was often made to last the longer because it was exempt from the taxation imposed upon the more advanced types. As late as 1834 the assessors classed almost twenty-three *per cent.* of the homes in Upper Canada as log cabins, though two years earlier Mrs. Traill observed that there were very few houses of this type in the settlements along the St. Lawrence and on the main road north from Cobourg towards Peterborough,[28] though a large part of the latter district had been settled less than ten years. In fact a traveller who was particularly familiar with the settlements in the vicinity of Perth noticed as early as 1821 that clap-board homes were "the mode now most prevalent, both in town and country."[29]

Some log houses, even those built as first homes, showed interesting variations in architecture usually lacking in homes of the type. On the shores of Pigeon Lake, Peterborough County, a few English settlers of some wealth built log houses of various fancy shapes, but without much practical utility. Samuel Strickland, settled near Peterborough, describes a fine log home that he erected in 1826 as "of elm-logs, 36 feet long by 24 feet wide, which I divided

[26]*Ibid.*, p. 70.
[27]MacTaggart, *op. cit.*, Vol. II, p. 243.
[28]Traill, *op. cit.*, p. 80.
[29]John McDonald: *Narrative of a Voyage to Quebec, and Journey from thence to New Lanark, Upper Canada.* 1823. p. 21

into three rooms on the ground floor, besides an entrance-hall and staircase and three bedrooms upstairs."[30] He tells how he made by hand the pine shingles for its roof. When Strickland was living in Goderich (1829) as an employee of the Canada Company he constructed his house "with cherry-logs neatly counter-hewed both inside and out, the inter-stices between the logs being nicely painted with mortar."[31]

He was not a lover of log houses, however, in spite of the fact that those which he constructed were much superior to the usual home of the pioneer settler. Like his sisters, Mrs. Traill and Mrs. Moodie, he had been accustomed to a home of better type, and to this general objection were added other considerations which grew out of his experience:

"If I were commencing life again in the woods, I would not build anything of logs except a shanty or a pig-sty; for experience has plainly told me that log buildings are the dirtiest, most inconvenient, and the dearest when every-thing is taken into consideration. As soon as the settler is ready to build, let him put up a good frame, roughcast, or stone house, if he can possibly raise the means, as stone, timber and lime cost nothing but the labour of collecting and carrying the materials. When I say that they cost nothing I mean that no cash is required for these articles, as they can be prepared by the exertion of the family. Two or three years should be spent in preparing and collecting materials, so that your timber may be perfectly seasoned before you commence building. With the addition of from a hundred to a hundred and fifty pounds in money to the raw material a good substantial and comfortable dwelling can be completed."[32]

Homes of squared logs, clap-board, roughcast, stucco, stone or brick, many of them large and almost palatial, gradually replaced the more primitive type, and one may still see old log houses used as sheds, while the improved second home stands near by. Houses and barns of squared logs are still quite common in the outlying parts of Old Ontario, while many log houses of the more primitive type are now (1932) being erected in Northern Ontario by

[30]Strickland, *op. cit.*, Vol. I, p. 98.
[31]*Ibid.*, Vol. I, p. 263.   [32]*Ibid.*, Vol. I, pp. 170-1.

families aided by the government in a period of severe economic depression.

Colonel Thomas Talbot's first residence was a log hut. Mrs. Anna Jameson thus describes the fiery Colonel's second home at Port Talbot:

"It is a long wooden building, chiefly of rough logs, with a covered porch running along the south side. . . . The interior of the house contains several comfortable lodging-rooms, and one really handsome one, the dining-room. There is a large kitchen with a tremendously hospitable chimney, and underground are cellars for storing wine, milk and provisions. Around the house stand a vast variety of outbuildings of all imaginable shapes and sizes, and disposed without the slightest regard to order or symmetry. One of these is the very log hut which the Colonel erected for shelter when he 'sat down in the bush' four-and-thirty years ago, and which he is naturally unwilling to remove. Many of these outbuildings are to shelter the geese and poultry, of which he rears an innumerable quantity."[33]

Brick buildings were long a luxury in the province generally, though in certain districts where brick clay was readily available such homes became common when prosperity rewarded the toil of the pioneer. One of the first brick buildings in Upper Canada was the home erected in 1790 by Colonel James Bâby; around this mansion, long used as a fur-trading post, grew the village of Sandwich. The foundation of the building was of stone, and the wood used in its construction was of walnut. Another very early brick building was Captain Myers' house, erected on the brow of the hill at Myers' Creek (Belleville) about 1794; the bricks for this home were made in Sydney Township, five miles east of Trenton.

In the early eighteen-thirties travellers observed that the homes of Upper Canada were improving. Joseph Pickering, writing in 1832 from Port Talbot, refers to "new frame and brick houses and other buildings rising up everywhere".[34] Patrick Shirreff noticed "that the houses of the

[33]Anna Jameson: *Winter Studies and Summer Rambles in Canada*. 1838. Vol. II, pp. 195-6.
[34]Joseph Pickering to Effingham Wilson, March 21, 1832. See Joseph Pickering: *Inquiries of an Emigrant* 1831. Preface to the 4th Edition, 1832, p. x.

French along the banks of the Detroit River and Lake St. Clair were "generally brick, and occasionally frame, but seldom with the stone basement of the lower province. . . . On some parts of the River Detroit, Lake St. Clair, and on the Thames, many people reside literally amongst water, passing to and from their houses on planks."[35]   At the western end of Lake Erie and along the Thames, he found, however, that wood was almost the only building material: "The dwelling-houses and farm-offices are of the shabbiest kind, and only two brick houses were seen in a distance of twenty-seven miles, passing from Amherstburg round Lake Erie."[36]

Fortune frequently smiled upon the inhabitants of the towns somewhat earlier.   The Parliament Buildings of York, erected in 1796-7, were largely of brick, and by the eighteen-twenties many similar structures had been built.   Thomas Hamilton, a visitor to York in the early thirties, observed that brick was in common use, though the Government House was of wood, which he considered "a singular circumstance".[37]   Brockville had a number of brick buildings in 1821, and in several other towns, such as Cobourg and London, the same material was being used a few years later in building stores or homes; the brick farmhouse, however, was unusual until the fifties and sixties.   Many of the fine old mansions which may be seen throughout the rural districts of Old Ontario date from the era of prosperity ushered in by the Crimean War, a period of "good times" further intensified as a result of the Reciprocity Treaty and the American Civil War.

The erection of stone houses depended almost entirely upon the availability of the material.   One of the first stone homes in Upper Canada was erected by Colonel John Macdonell at Glengarry Point soon after the first Loyalist settlement along the shores of the St. Lawrence. The limestone buildings of Kingston and Bytown (Ottawa) resulted from a disposition to use readily available materials, and throughout the province many a "second" or

[35]Shirreff, *op. cit.*, pp. 209-10.   [36]*Ibid.*, p. 212.
[37]Thomas Hamilton: *Men and Manners in America.* 1833. Vol. II, p. 335.

"third" home was constructed of stones cleared from the fields.

The architectural design of the later houses and the appearance of their exterior and interior were almost as variable as their occupants. The influence of economic status, of taste, and of nationality predominated in the planning of the home. Dr. Dunlop describes the evolution of the house from the log-hovel to the brick mansion, and states that the history of any settlement could be read in the buildings and farmyard. This old-timer, always a hater of innovations, suggests that a well-built log house was good enough for him:

"The original shanty, or log-hovel, which sheltered the family when they first arrived on their wild lot, still remains, but has been degraded into a piggery; the more substantial log house, which held out the weather during the first years of their sojourn, has, with the increase of their wealth, become a chapel of ease to the stable or cow-house; and the glaring and staring bright-red brick house is brought forward close upon the road, that the frame dwelling, which at one time the proprietor looked upon as the very acme of his ambition, may at once serve as a kitchen to, and be concealed by its more aspiring and aristocratic successor."[38]

Most of the first settlers in "The Queen's Bush," as 2,000,000 acres of land near Lake Huron and Georgian Bay was commonly called, suffered hardships at the middle of the eighteenth century varying but little from those of the earlier periods. Mrs. Cook, who settled in the fifties in Bruce County, recalled that "the shanty to which we went had a bark roof, and this roof leaked so badly that when it rained my husband had to hold an umbrella over us when we were in bed".[39] The floors of this home were made of such lumber as drifted ashore from passing vessels. The first settlers in Beaver Valley, near Meaford, in the same period, erected houses of two stories, but they contained but one room on each floor, and the upper chamber was reached by a ladder.

---

[38]Dunlop, *op. cit.,* p. 109.
[39]Reminiscences of Mrs. Cook, quoted in W. L. Smith: *Pioneers of Old Ontario*, 1923. p. 261.

Although an orderly appearance certainly adds to any home, yet economic conditions in the early days were such that many a settler was too poor to spend much time or money improving his home. Those who judged by the exterior only, as travellers usually did, might have been agreeably surprised by the neatness of the interior. Home is, after all, more than logs or bricks: it is neat or slovenly in its appearance, pleasant or unpleasant in its atmosphere, in proportion to the effort of its inhabitants to make it so. The attractiveness of the interior of the home depends largely upon house furnishings, which are outside the scope of this chapter; but the appearance of the fireplace, as a permanent feature of most pioneer homes, is of interest here. Occasional American stoves were to be found in Upper Canada even before the War of 1812, but the open fireplace long remained the usual means of heating the home, although gradually superseded by outdoor bake-oven or by stove for cooking purposes.

The method of constructing the fireplace and chimney among the Loyalists has already been described; in later settlements there were variations. The pioneers of the Ottawa Valley proceeded as follows:

"If a stone could be found large enough to stand on the ground against the wall, it was set up; if not, a piece of thin wall was built with stones and blue clay mortar to keep the fire from the logs or wall of the building. Then two crooked cedars were got and the ends pointed or thinned to drive into the chinks between the logs on each side of the stone work. The other ends were pinned to the beam across the house, about four feet in from the end wall. Cedars were cut the length for these laths from one side to the other. The first lath was laid in a good bed of clay mortar on the stonework on the back. Then the cedars, flatted a little on their upper side, had a bed of mortar laid on, and laths cut laid on them across the lath on the back; some of them were nailed in the end to the crooked cedars, laid in plenty of mortar. When they reached to the level of the highest ends of these crooked cedars, with the three sides, or back and two sides, they laid a lath in mortar on the beam and formed the fourth side.

"So they built the chimney, which they called a fireplace till they got above the scoops. The substitute they made for hair in the mortar was cut straw or beaver-meadow hay, cut with the axe on a block, sometimes pounded to make it more pliable. The back was kept straight with the house wall, but the other three sides were drawn in so that from five or six feet wide at the bottom it would end in three by two feet at the top. The mortar was laid to give three-quarters of an inch on the inside of the laths, and made smooth to be safe. They often caught fire but a cup of water thrown against it generally extinguished it."[40]

In the later fireplaces brick or stone often replaced the clay-and-wood chimneys of earlier times, though where bricks were not available the old method had still to be used. Some distance up the chimney there was usually placed a cross-bar of iron or wood, and from this hung the chains to which were attached the pots and kettles used in cooking. "The hanging of the crane" was the sign of the establishment of a new home, and was sometimes the occasion of a celebration. The crane was fitted with hooks for the kettles and pots, which swung back and forth as required. Field stones were often used to place the wood upon, though in later days iron or fancy brass "dogs", sometimes known as andirons, were common. Among the implements, some of which were found in every fireplace, were the hand-bellows, tongs, a long-handled shovel, frying-pan and a variety of iron pots. Kettles of various sizes, but usually about two feet in diameter, were used for the baking of bread; these kettles had an iron lid, and coals were placed above and below while the bread was being baked.

Although its use in cooking came to an end with the introduction of stoves, yet the hearth has remained the symbol of home. The cheerful atmosphere of the open fire, enhanced, perhaps, by the chirp of the cricket, has made it the rallying-centre of the family. Many were the uses to which the fireplace was put: squashes were hung near it to prevent their being frozen, and guns to keep free from rust; in front, on poles suspended by cords from the ceiling, were placed chunks of beef or venison and

[40]J. L. Gourlay: *History of the Ottawa Valley.* 1896. pp. 47-8.

strings of apples; sometimes meat was hung to dry inside
the chimney, too far away from the fire to be roasted but
not so far up that it would be blackened by smoke. Mrs.
Catharine Traill's description of the second home of her
friend, Mrs. Thomas Stewart, one of the first settlers in
Douro Township, Peterborough County, shows us how delightful the fireplace and its surroundings might be made:

"Though so many years have elapsed since those days, I
can recall as a vivid picture the family group at Auburn in
the primitive log house. The father occupied one side of
the ample hearth from which the huge pile of blazing logs
cast broad lights and shadows on the walls and rafters
where all sorts of guns, pistols, fishing-rods, paddles and
models of canoes and small river craft were arranged, not
without taste for artistic effect. Indian bows and arrows,
and sundry skins of small, furred, native animals, claws of
bears, and wings and talons of eagles, hawks and herons
were fastened on the walls, while the head of a noble deer
with branching antlers supported other trophies of the
hunter's skill.

"The broad mantel-piece held curious fossils, specimens of rocks and crystals gathered from the limestone
boulders, with flint arrows and spear-heads and fragments of pottery of ancient Indian manufacture. By a
small work-table, relic of other days, might be seen the dear
mistress of the household with her three daughters, each
busily plying needle or knitting-pins; while on the warm
fur rugs, basking in idle enjoyment of the warmth, the
younger children and two noble dogs, one, that now rare
animal, an Irish grey-hound, a privileged personage; the
other a fine water-dog of good breed and appearance. Close
by, an Indian cradle held a sleeping infant. . . . Mr.
Stewart was then an honourable member of the Upper
House of Legislative Council; he lived to see much change
in the then densely-wooded township where his was almost
the first dwelling raised, and where he had heard the sound
of the chopper's axe awakening the echoes of those lonely,
forest-crowned banks of the rushing Otonabee."[41]

[41]Catharine Traill to Eleanor Dunlop, quoted in 2nd Edition, 1902,
pp. 144-5, of Frances Stewart: *Our Forest Home.* 1889.

THE REMAINS OF AN EARLY STONE FIREPLACE

FIREPLACE AND FURNISHINGS, 1813

AN OLD BREAD OVEN

KITCHEN UTENSILS IN 1813

CHAPTER II

FOODS AND COOKING

"Very merry at, before, and after dinner, and the more for that my dinner was great, and most neatly dressed by our own only maid. We had a fricasee of rabbits and chickens, a leg of mutton boiled, three carps in a dish, a great dish of a side of lamb, a dish of roasted pigeons, a dish of four lobsters, three tarts, a lamprey pie (a most rare pie!), a dish of anchovies, good wine of several sorts, and all things mighty noble and to my great content."

The Diary of Samuel Pepys, April 4, 1663.

SHAKESPEARE'S lines,

"Now good digestion wait on appetite,

And health on both,"

would hardly have been applicable to many foods in common use in pioneer days had it not been for the hard work which was essential in a new settlement. Certainly the foods were often of such coarse ingredients, and the meals so lacking in variety, "the spice of life", that they would seldom whet a modern appetite, much less be conducive to health. In considering the foods of other times it must be recognized, however, that, as in our day, nationality and economic status are the deciding factors in the meals of the various classes of people which make up a nation.

The first inhabitants of Upper Canada, apart from the Indians, were the garrisons at the forts, and the soldier's usual food of bully beef, pea soup and hard tack is too well-known to require much description here; there was, however, a considerable amount of salt pork eaten by the soldiers in Canada, and they varied their diet by netting large numbers of whitefish, salmon, sturgeon and other species then so plentiful in our lakes and rivers, and by shooting wild fowl such as ducks, turkeys and pigeons, and a large variety of game—deer, raccoons and rabbits, among others.

Governor Simcoe told a traveller that the commissariat had often to depend upon flour from London and salt meat from Ireland, for there was not much excess production of wheat or meat in Canada at that period.[1] That this was

[1]La Rochefoucauld-Liancourt quoted in William Canniff: *History of the Settlement of Upper Canada.* 1869. p. 204.

not always the case is shown by La Rochefoucauld-Lian-court's investigations in the summer of 1795; he learned that pork, peas and wheat were being exported in consider-able quantities from the vicinity of Kingston, and that some of the wheat was ground in Montreal and the flour sent back to Upper Canada.[2] Even fifty years later, how-ever, a traveller found that "quantities of salted provisions are still imported for the consumption of the soldiers."[3]

It was usual for the authorities to advertise in the *Gazette* in order to give local merchants a chance to fur-nish the supplies. On March 1, 1798, John McGill, govern-ment agent, advertised for "flour and peas, wanted at Fort George, for the supply of His Majesty's forces in Upper Canada". It was stipulated that the produce must be packed in casks, and "warranted to keep good and sound for twelve months after delivery".[4]

The food of the Indians, *voyageurs* and lumbermen in early times was much coarser than that of the first settlers. The Indians were accustomed to live largely on the fruits cf the chase, though some of them grew pumpkins, maize and tobacco. In later years contact with the white man added large quantities of rum, brandy and whisky to their diet, and made other changes. One of their main dishes in the early part of the nineteenth century was a sort of stew made up principally of lumps of venison and potatoes, but including anything else of an edible nature that they hap-pened to have. Another type of "Irish stew" common among the Indians was made up of rice, beaver and par-tridge, boiled with a little pounded corn.

The early Indian, French, and Scottish *voyageurs* of the North-West and Hudson's Bay Companies subsisted during their arduous expeditions into the Far West largely on bear grease and coarse cornmeal, with the addition of game and fish. Salt pork, peas and biscuits usually formed the main food of the "Goers and Comers" who covered the route from Montreal to the Grand Portage at Fort William; they were consequently called "Pork-eaters" by their much hardier

[2]Duc de la Rochefoucauld-Liancourt: *Travels through the United States of North America.* 1799. Vol 1, pp. 280-1.
[3]Anna Jameson: *Winter Sketches and Summer Rambles in Canada.* 1838. Vol. I, pp. 267-8.
[4]*Upper Canada Gazette*, March 1, 1798.

brethren in the interior. The French-Canadian bateaumen on the St. Lawrence and the lakes similarly ate raw pork and hard biscuit, which they appear to have enjoyed. Before setting out in the morning they would eat pea soup, and tobacco seemed almost a food to them, for they smoked a considerable part of every day. The food of the lumbermen varied but little from that of the settlers; but the manner of eating customary among them, as among *voyageurs*, bateaumen, and Indians, was uncouth, meals being considered as a necessity which should be completed as quickly and as easily as possible.

A notable exception to the coarse food which was the usual fare of the fur trader was the luxurious banquet sometimes provided on special occasions for high officials at the main posts. Many a grand dinner took place, for example, at the North-West Company's post at Fort William, where eastern and western traders met. Here, in an immense wooden building, was held the annual meeting. The partners from Montreal always eclipsed in importance their brethren from the interior posts, and the proceedings were conducted with a grandeur which recalls the days of feudalism.

It is recorded that "grave and weighty councils were alternated by huge feasts and revels, like some of the old feasts described in Highland castles. The tables in the great banqueting room groaned under the weight of game of all kinds; of venison from the woods and fish from the lakes, with hunters' delicacies, such as buffaloes' tongues and beavers' tails; and various luxuries from Montreal, all served up by experienced cooks brought for the purpose. There was no stint of generous wine, for it was a hard-drinking period, a time of loyal toasts and bacchanalian songs, and brimming bumpers.

"While the chiefs thus revelled in hall, and made the rafters resound with bursts of loyalty and old Scottish songs, chanted in voices cracked and sharpened by the northern blast, their merriment was echoed and prolonged by a mongrel legion of retainers, Canadian *voyageurs*, half-breeds, Indian hunters, and vagabond hangers-on, who feasted sumptuously without, on the crumbs that fell from their table, and made the welkin ring with old French ditties, mingled with Indian yelps and yellings".[5]

Upon their arrival in Upper Canada, the Loyalists, who, apart from a few hundred French on the Detroit, were the first permanent settlers of importance, were supplied by the government with rations, consisting of "flour, pork, and a limited quantity of beef, a very little butter, and as little salt".[6] The rations were continued for three years as a general rule; but, as their discontinuance unfortunately coincided with the bad harvests of 1788-9, it resulted that there was intense suffering among most of the inhabitants of Upper Canada, and especially among the settlers who had been unable to establish themselves firmly upon the land, and who were consequently ill-prepared for a period of scarcity. The hardships of "the famine year" and the straits to which the people were reduced, will be described separately,[7] but it may be said here that hundreds of families lived for months on such materials as soup from beef bones, bran, boiled green grain, and the herbs, roots, bark and berries to be found in the woods; many, particularly children, died from malnutrition. Game might have been more extensively used as food but for the fact that powder and arms were scarce at that time; while fish quickly became distasteful when eaten too frequently.

In ordinary times, however, the Loyalists had plenty to eat. Beef and mutton were long scarce since feed for farm animals was often unobtainable; but salt pork, relieved by fish and game, provided plenty of meat. In preparing pork the hams and shoulders of the carcass were usually smoked, and the rest preserved in strong brine. The smoke-house was generally used in April, when the best pieces of the meat were carefully washed and hung. A smudge of beach or maple sticks was then built upon the floor beneath, and the door tightly closed. After several days' smoking, the meat would keep for months, even through the heat of summer. In some localities a bee was held for butchering, and everything from the killing of the animals to the making of sausage was finished in one day.

[5] Washington Irving: *Astoria.* 18?. p. 25.
[6] Canniff, *op. cit.,* p. 184.
[7] See Section III, Chapter III.

To grind wheat into flour was a matter of great difficulty
in early times. Before the first mills were built by the government, and long after in the case of those settlers who
lived remote from them, a crude type of hand-mill, or a
hominy-block, supplied a very coarse wheat flour, sometimes
called "samp", from which an equally coarse bread was
made. As such flour contained all the bran it was, no
doubt, healthful; but it was not highly valued at the time if
the "precious stone flour" from the mill could be obtained.

The bread was usually baked in kettles in the fireplace,
though in after years a clay bake-oven was usually erected,
either in the wall near the fireplace or outside the home
under the same roof as the smoke-house. The kettles had
an iron lid, and hot coals were placed above and below
while the bread was being baked. An early settler said that
she had "never tasted better bread than some which was
baked in the old iron pots;"[8] but others with less experience
frequently found that a beautiful brown crust was merely
the "goodly outside" covering an interior of putty. Similar
kettles were used for the boiling of corn, and for cooking
pork and potatoes, which formed an important part of
each of the three meals of the day. A popular dish similarly
prepared was composed of game or fowl cut into small
pieces and baked in a deep dish, with a heavy crust.

The bake-kettle was superseded by the reflector, which
was "an oblong box of bright tin enclosed on all sides but
one. It was placed on the hearth with the open side next a
bed of glowing coals. In it were placed the tins of dough
raised a few inches from the bottom so the heat could
circulate freely about the loaves. The upper part of the
reflector was adjustable, to enable the housewife to inspect
the contents".[9]

The reflector was sometimes used for roasting, but a
roaster was kept where the family could afford it. This
utensil is described as "smaller than the reflector and constructed in a similar manner; and, running from end to
end through the centre, was a small iron bar, one end of

[8] Reminiscences of Mrs. Walter Riddell, in the *Farmer's Sun*, August
    4, 1898.
[9] W. S. Herrington: *Pioneer Life on the Bay of Quinté*. (In Lennox
    and Addington Historical Society, *Papers and Records*, Vol. VI,
    p. 12).

which terminated in a small handle or crank. This bar, called a spit, was run through the piece of meat, and, by turning the handle from time to time, the meat was revolved and every portion of the surface was in turn brought next the fire. The drippings from the meat were caught in a dripping-pan placed underneath for the purpose. These drippings were used for basting the roasting meat, and this was done with a long-handled basting spoon through an opening in the back, which could be closed at will".[10]

Cornmeal was extensively used among the pioneers, for corn was easier to grind than wheat. Porridge was made of the meal, and plenty of maple sugar eaten with it. For supper the hardened porridge was often cut in slices and fried; while cornmeal and buckwheat griddle cakes, eaten with wild honey, were frequently made, as was also Johnny cake, except in those ultra-loyal sections where an American dish was considered disloyal. Corn flour, sifted through a fine cloth, was made into a sweet, light bread, considered by many to be much superior to Johnny cake. Wild rice, highly prized by the Indians, is another grain which was considerably used by the Loyalists.

Tea was long too expensive to be a common drink, so a number of substitutes were used, such as hemlock, sassafras and a Canadian plant which now goes by the name of New Jersey tea. Many of the men preferred whisky or rum, which were for many years consumed in large quantities at meals and elsewhere. Maple sugar was in common use, though some of the wealthier settlers purchased the coarse, brown Muscovado sugar from merchants.

The restricted diet ordinarily available led many an inventive housewife to attempt special dishes. Some recipes were of British, others of French, German, American or Dutch origin. For example, "pumpkin loaf" consisted of boiled pumpkin and cornmeal baked into loaves and eaten hot with butter. Among other special dishes was the Dutch pot pie, often a popular dish at bees. Butter and milk were not always the common foods that one might suppose, for the scarcity of feed before turnips were grown, and the severity of the winters, prevented many a farmer from keeping cattle all the year round. In early times the

[10]*Ibid.*

use of butter, which was often of poor quality, was sometimes restricted to adults, while the children dipped their
bread into ham gravy.

Pies of wild fruits, and cakes of various kinds were
made when finer flour was available. Apples were not
commonly used in early times, but wild strawberries, raspberries, gooseberries, cranberries, blackberries, blueberries
and many other varieties grew in profusion near at hand and
were largely used. Greens from the woods supplied the general lack of vegetables, which were but little grown in the
early pioneer period. Until about the middle of the nineteenth century the tomato was considered poisonous, but its
beauty led to its being hung up in the house as a "love apple".
In general the Loyalists lived in plenty as far as food was
concerned; the reminiscences of early settlers are filled
with references to the huge quantities of game, fish, berries,
nuts, and other "natural blessings" that they found everywhere provided for their use by the bounty of Providence.

The only inhabitants of Upper Canada in Loyalist times
who were frequently able to enjoy the finer products of
the culinary art were the officers of the army, higher government officials, and occasional wealthy merchants. These
classes were located largely at Kingston, Niagara, Detroit
and, a few years later, at York. Governor Simcoe's wife
gives us in her diary a number of examples of the niceties
of cooking, and also describes several foods not generally
used by the less-privileged sections of the population. The
Simcoes had a cook-stove, at that time very rare in Canada,
and much less pork was used at their table, and more eggs,
veal, beef, fish and game. Racoon and porcupine meat,
boiled black squirrel, wild turkeys, ducks, and roasted
wild pigeons are among the variations in food referred
to in her diary.[11]

In summer, however, Mrs. Simcoe preferred to eat
chiefly vegetables and fruits, and she found that most people did the same, except that a little salt pork was usually
used in addition. In August and September large quantities
of boiled or roasted Indian corn provided the main part
of the dinner.[12] It is noted concerning the use of wild

[11]*Diary of Mrs. John Graves Simcoe*, March 10, 1793.
[12]*Ibid.*, August 31, 1795.

pigeons, then to be obtained in such profusion, that some of
the settlers in the Western District salted down the wings
and breasts in barrels for later use, "and at any time they
are good to eat after being soaked."[13]

The Simcoes were very fond of fish and a number of
varieties appeared on their table. Mrs. Simcoe describes the
Lake Ontario whitefish as "exquisitely good. We all think
them better than any other fresh or salt-water fish. They
are so rich that sauce is seldom eaten with them". As to
the method of cooking them she says: "They are usually
boiled, or set before the fire in a pan with a few spoonfuls
of water and an anchovy, which is a very good way of
dressing them".[14] Another fish sometimes used was the
sturgeon,[15] much coarser than whitefish, but better than
sea sturgeon. They were often as large as six feet in length,
and the manner of preparing them for the table is thus
described: "Cooks who know how to dress parts of them,
cutting away all that is oily and strong, make excellent
dishes from sturgeon, such as mock turtle soup, veal cutlets,
etc., and it is very good roasted with bread crumbs."[16]
Herrings were also used, Mrs. Simcoe noting that on a
bateau trip to Quebec she carried "tea, cold tongue and fowl,
and herrings".[17] At a ball at Niagara "some small tortoises,
cut up and dressed like oysters in scollop shells," were
served at supper, and were pronounced very good.[18]

Bread and cakes were, of course, commonly used by the
wealthier classes, and it is stated by Mrs. Simcoe that
American bakers made the best.[19] A Moravian woman
brought her a loaf of bread "so peculiarly good" that she
enquired the recipe, and learned that "it was made with
rennet and whey, without yeast or water, and baked in

---

[13]*Ibid.*
[14]*Ibid.*, November 4, 1792.
[15]Sturgeon Lake is thought to have received its name not because
    sturgeon were caught there, but from the fact that a tribe of
    Indians removed thither from Niagara, where they had been
    accustomed to engage in fishing. There are, however, early
    references to sturgeon as being found in the Trent Lakes.
    See, for example, the *Methodist Magazine*, 1828, p. 74. (Quoted
    supra, p. 61).
[16]Simcoe, *op. cit.*, November 4, 1792.
[17]*Ibid.*, September 21, 1794.
[18]*Ibid.*, April 23, 1793.
[19]*Ibid.*, August 6, 1793.

wicker or straw baskets. . . . The bread was as light as possible, and rich, like cake". [20]

The Governor's wife never tired of experimenting in the use of wild plants. The dried leaves of the tree known as the balm of Gilead were found to be "good in pea soup, or forced (*i.e.* ground) meat".[21] Wild asparagus was used, and a number of herbs as greens. Tea was commonly drunk at meals, as were also wines, which the richer classes were able to import. Wild grapes were sometimes made into wine, as well as into vinegar. Sometimes Mrs. Simcoe gathered the flowers of the sumach "and poured boiling water upon them, which tastes like lemonade; it has a very astringent, hard taste".[22] Coffee made of peas is referred to as used by some of the settlers nearby. Maple sugar was in common use, though imported sugar was available, and some was made from the sap of the black walnut.

Mrs. Simcoe was particularly interested in the variety of wild fruits which then grew in such profusion. The Indians were very fond of fruit and often brought fine samples to the Governor. On one occasion they gave him "cranberries as large as cherries, and as good", and stated that the best of them grew under water.[23] The Indians supplied the Simcoes with chestnuts also, "which they roast in a manner that makes them particularly good".[24] Thomas Talbot once brought Mrs. Simcoe "a cake of dried hurtleberries made by the Indians, which was like Irwin's patent black currant lozenges, but tastes of smoke".[25] May-apples, "a great luxury",[26] were sometimes preserved, and black whortleberries, larger than those of England, were found to make "as good puddings as Levant currants".[27]

The cultivation of peach and cherry trees had already been commenced at Niagara in 1793, and the Simcoes had "thirty large cherry trees behind the house, and three standard peach trees, which supplied us last autumn for tarts and desserts, besides the numbers the young men ate. My share was trifling compared to theirs, and I eat thirty in a day. They were very small and high-flavoured. When

[20]*Ibid.*, August 31, 1795.
[21]*Ibid.*, July 21, 1793.
[22]*Ibid.*, September 8, 1795.
[23]*Ibid.*, April 26, 1793.
[24]*Ibid.*
[25]*Ibid.*, November 4, 1792.
[26]*Ibid.*, August 31, 1795.
[27]*Ibid.*, August 7, 1794.

tired of eating them raw, Mr. Talbot roasted them, and they were very good".[28]   Among other fruits enjoyed by the Simcoes were wild strawberries, raspberries, plums, and water-melons, the cultivation of which had been introduced from the United States.   While the grapefruit was almost unknown in Canada until the end of the nineteenth century, and has come into common use only in recent years, Mrs. Simcoe notes in her diary that she "received some shaddocks, a species of orange, from the West Indies, which I considered excellent fruit."[29]

It may be assumed that foods similar to those described by Mrs. Simcoe were used by the official classes in Kingston, Niagara, Detroit and York, and by a few of the wealthier inhabitants in other settlements.   Duties of officials commonly ended about 2 p.m. and dinner was served at three.   An ordinary meal at York is described by Joseph Willcocks in his diary, under date of October 6, 1800: "We had for dinner a salmon, a fillet of veal, a pair of roast fowl and a bread pudding."[30]   On another occasion he ate "roast pork, sassauges, black Puddings, soup, corned beef and pancakes."[31]   On Christmas Day, 1800, he enjoyed a heavy repast of "soup, roast beef, boiled pork, a turkey, plum pudding and mince pies". [32]

Other inhabitants of the few villages scattered over Upper Canada at the opening of the century ate meals as variable in quality and variety as the economic and social status of families.   It is noticeable, however, that the English custom of serving a variety of meats, together with rich batter puddings and pies for dessert, was followed by the residents of both urban and rural districts insofar as their means enabled them to do so.   In the rural settlements, however, the time of meals varied with the circumstances of the various seasons; in summer it was customary to work an hour or so after daybreak, and then have breakfast; while dinner generally occurred at noon, and supper at dark.   Needless to say there was no comparison in table

[28]*Ibid.*, July 2, 1793.
[29]*Ibid.*, August 6, 1792.   The original name of the fruit was given in honour of a sea captain who was among the first Europeans to observe it growing and obtain samples.
[30]*Diary of Joseph Willcocks*, October 6, 1800.
[31]*Ibid.*, February 11, 1802.
[32]*Ibid.*, December 25, 1800.

J. Henry Sandham, R.C.A.

HUNTERS RETURNING WITH THEIR SPOIL

George Catlin

INDIAN STALKING DEER

Public Archives of Canada   J. Gillespie

Dundas, Canada West, in 1848

From Bigsby's *The Shoe and Canoe*, 1850   J. J. Bigsby

Andrew's Tavern, above Brockville

manners and ways of eating between the inhabitants of the rural districts and those of the official class in the towns, where dinner and supper were frequently served and eaten in style. At Niagara the Simcoes followed the custom among British governors of having a regimental band play during meals, though it may be said that the bands of that day bear little comparison in the matter of size or musical ability with those of to-day.

Prices of tea, sugar and other luxuries were very high at the commencement of the century. Pierce & Co.'s general store in York advertised tea in 1799 at from 8s. to 19s. per lb.; loaf sugar 3s. 9d. per lb.; and raisins and figs 3s. per lb.[33] In 1802 Quetton St. George & Co. offered for sale nutmegs, cinnamon, cloves and mace, butter, cheese, chestnuts, hickory and black walnuts and cranberries.[34] The excessive cost of transport by bateau and schooner kept the prices of all imported goods at such a height that the average citizen was precluded from purchasing them.

The meals at inns and wayside taverns were as variable as the establishments and their proprietors. In the very early period of settlement one was lucky to get a good meal at any tavern. Carey's Inn, near Gananoque, was well-known in the seventeen-nineties, but it was accessible only by open boat. Joel Stone, founder of Gananoque, lived with Carey for some time. The food which was provided was obtained with difficulty, for we learn that "no bread could be obtained except hard biscuits. For Mr. Stone and for travellers they kept a kind called King's biscuit, while for the others they provided navy biscuit. They kept two cows and exchanged the milk with the bateaumen for biscuit, and exchanged the latter again with the Indians for fish, venison, game and wild fruit."[35]

British travellers in Upper Canada usually expected much more than they were served at inns. In 1816 Lieutenant Francis Hall stopped at a tavern near Dundas and called loudly for veal or pork chops, but all the pork had been salted and no other meat was available, so bread with

[33]*Upper Canada Gazette*, July 13, 1799.
[34]*Ibid.*, December 11, 1802.
[35]Judge McDonald of Brockville quoted in J. Ross Robertson (Ed):
    The Diary of Mrs. John Graves Simcoe. 1911. p. 106.

cheese or butter was the menu.[36] In 1826 Joseph Pickering paid 1s 6d., New York Currency (about 19 cents), for breakfast at Umstead's Tavern, Talbot Street, and states that the meal was, "as usual, fried beef or pork, pickles and preserves, tea-cakes and butter".[37] Beer, cider and whisky were common drinks in taverns as well as homes, but cider would not keep long enough to be used all the year round.

In 1827 Captain Basil Hall and his wife came unexpectedly upon an inn some miles east of the Grand River; but the innkeeper was unaccustomed to visitors and had to forage for some time before an old hen was killed and some bacon, eggs and bread discovered for the entertainment of the guests.[38] Samuel Strickland stopped in 1828 at a German tavern, Sebach's, on the Huron Road; but the best he could get for supper was "a piece of dirty-looking Indian meal-bread, and a large cake of beef tallow, and, to wash down this elegant repast, a dish of crust coffee without either milk or sugar".[39]

In 1833, when Patrick Shirreff crossed into Upper Canada at Niagara after travelling in the United States, he was struck with the comparative crudeness of conditions on this side of the line. While he was one of those travellers who found more to find fault with than to praise, yet his opinions are certainly the same as almost anyone would express today if he were transplanted into the conditions which obtained in pioneer Upper Canada. Shirreff found the taverns objectionable because of the vulgar company as well as the poor food. He observed that "the bar-rooms of the hotels were filled with swearing, tipsy people," and that the butter served at meals, "instead of being, as in the States, hardened by means of ice, was an unclean liquid".[40]

At Richmond Hill Shirreff was served a dinner "of roast beef alone, so tough that my friend remarked that the animal must have died in the yoke from distress. Human

[36]Francis Hall: *Travels in Canada and the United States in 1816-17.* 1818. p. 211.
[37]Joseph Pickering: *Inquiries of an Emigrant.* 1831. November 3, 1826.
[38]Basil Hall: *Travels in America in 1827 and 1828.* 1829. Vol. I, p. 239.
[39]Samuel Strickland: *Twenty-seven Years in Canada West.* 1853. Vol I, p. 251.
[40]Patrick Shirreff: *A Tour through North America.* 1835. p. 94.

teeth could make little impression upon it, and I satisfied
hunger with bad bread and water."[41]   At the best hotel in
Goderich he was fortunate (?) enough to participate in a
"family dinner", the principal part of which was "a tureen
full of Scotch broth, with a tea-cup for a divider, and, from
the shortness of the handle, the fingers of the server were
immersed in stirring up the liquid.   The entertainment
was poor enough, and cost the moderate sum of sixpence
sterling".[42]   Between Amherstburg and Sandwich he had
breakfast at a small inn with a French sign; the fare consisted of "poor green tea, bad butter and worse bread".[43]

Mrs. Anna Jameson was similarly impressed by tavern
meals.   At an inn at Beamsville she was served a breakfast
of bad tea, "buttered toast, *i.e.*, fried bread steeped in
melted butter, and fruit preserved in molasses—to all which
I shall get used in time—I must try, at least".   The supper
meal at the same tavern is described as "the travellers' fare
in Canada", and consisted of "venison-steaks, and fried fish,
coffee, hot cakes, cheese, and whisky punch".[44]   Another
traveller noted that it was advisable to carry one's own provisions when visiting remote districts, for "split fowl and
leathery ham" was the usual fare at out-of-the-way inns.[45]

The standard of deportment at tavern meals was based
upon the rush and bustle of the American rather than the
stolid placidity and formality of the Englishman.   At most
pretentious inns a loud bell or horn was sounded a half
hour before, and at meal times, whereupon everyone rushed
into the dining-room and spent ten minutes or so eating his
food as rapidly as he could, without style or ceremony but
with great noise.   The fact that everyone sat at the same
table, irrespective of social position, was a source of great
annoyance to most English travellers; while to be surrounded by rustic labourers who used their knives as spoons
was not conducive to the enjoyment of meals.   In those
days it was customary to lay most of the blame for such
conduct upon the democratic Americans, who were considered by the average Englishman to be the source of all
evil.

[41]*Ibid.*, p. 106.   [42]*Ibid.*, p. 173.   [43]*Ibid.*, p. 198.
[44]Jameson, *op. cit.*, Vol. I, p.77.
[45]J. J. Bigsby: *The Shoe and Canoe, or Pictures of Travel in the
      Canadas.* 1850. Vol. II, p. 72.

Thomas Need, an Oxford graduate who lived for some years in the wilds of Verulam Township, Victoria County, and was the founder of the village of Bobcaygeon, gives an excellent description of tavern meals in Cobourg in 1832. The breakfast bell was sounded at 7.30 and repeated at 8 o'clock, whereupon there was "a general rush from all parts of the house and the neighbouring stores. . . . Instantly the work of destruction commenced—plates rattled—cups and saucers flew about, and knives and forks found their way indifferently into their owners' mouths or the various dishes on the table. There was little talking and less ceremony,— 'I say Miss' (to the lady in waiting) 'please some tea'—or, 'I say Mister', (to me) 'some steak, I guess I likes it pretty rawish', being the extent of both .

"The meal was composed of tea, coffee, toast, and bread, and the never-failing buckwheat cakes, with a variety of sweetmeats, crowned with a *pièce de résistance* in the shape of a huge greasy dish of beef steaks and onions. . . . The company was of a motley description, Yankees and emigrants, washed and unwashed, storekeepers, travellers, and farmers. . . . Ten minutes sufficed for the dispatch of the meal; after which, each and all retired in silence and haste as they had entered, stopping, however, as they passed the bar, for the never-failing dram and cigar, which concludes the business".

At dinner the host of the inn occupied the head of the table and "dealt out a 'Benjamin's mess' to each hungry expectant: puddings and creams succeeded the substantials, which were conveyed to the mouths of the different guests with frightful rapidity on the blades of sharp, dirty knives. I ventured to ask for a spoon, a request which only drew from 'Miss' a disdainful toss of the head, accompanied by the exclamation of 'My! If the man be'ent wanting a spoon now!' There was no conversation; and as soon as nature was satisfied the dinner-bolters severally rose from the table and quitted the room".[46]

In addition to the general faults everyone had his own pet objection to tavern meals: "Tiger" Dunlop, for example, disliked "everything deluged with grease and butter", as he found customary in the taverns in and

[46]Thomas Need: *Six Years in the Bush.* 1838. pp. 34-5.

near London. He blamed such methods of cooking upon the Dutch, and the type of meal led him to write humorous recipes, of which the following is a delicious sample:

"To dress beef steak:—Cut the steak about ¼ inch thick, wash it well in a tub of water, wringing it from time to time after the manner of a dish-clout; put a pound of fresh butter in a frying pan, (hog's lard will do, but butter is more esteemed), and when it boils put in the steak, turning and peppering it for about a quarter of an hour; then put it into a deep dish, and pour the oil over it till it floats, and so serve it."[47]

These examples of tavern meals must be taken as the worst that might be expected, rather than necessarily the usual fare; for people tend to emphasize their unfortunate experiences, and perhaps occasionally to mention the best, rather than to describe the commonplace. The average tavern meal was somewhere between these extremes, varying, as it does at the present day, with the efforts of the cooks and proprietors to provide good service. But it is quite evident that those who had to patronize taverns, either for meals or lodging, were subjected to many annoyances of which the food was often one of the least.

For grand events, however, the innkeeper or caterer in the towns could rise nobly to the occasion and provide a sumptuous repast. When the inaugural train ran over the Cobourg and Peterborough Railroad on December 29, 1854, a grand banquet was served in the town hall of Peterborough. The viands provided by Perkins, the caterer, are described as "of the most *recherché* description, comprising fresh cod from Boston, venison from the backwoods, and in fact all the substantials and delicacies of the season. As to the wines they were of the best and costliest kinds. In a word the entertainment was got up in the most artistic style—regardless of expense, and reflected great credit on the liberality of the Peterborough gentlemen".[48]

The period of pioneer life in the vast regions at the rear of the early Loyalist settlements lasted from about 1800 to the middle of the century, and well beyond in the case of the northerly sections of Old Ontario. The back

[47]William Dunlop: *Statistical Sketches of Upper Canada*. 1832. p. 56.
[48]*Cobourg Star*, January 10, 1855.

townships of the earliest-settled counties along the St. Lawrence, the Bay of Quinté, Lake Ontario, the Niagara River and Lake Erie, were gradually filled up, often by the children of the first settlers; while further north, "the backwoods" or "the bush" received an ever-increasing number of immigrants. In living conditions these new settlements differed but little from those of Loyalist days; though hardships were sometimes less intense, they were usually very great. While the foods and the methods of cooking were in some respects similar to those of the earlier period yet there were many variations; a complete account will, therefore, be of value, even though at the risk of some repetition.

There was always great difficulty, except in winter, in transporting supplies and provisions from "the front". Pork and flour in barrels were easiest carried, and consequently remained the staple foods. A 200-pound barrel of pork was usually worth about $20, and a barrel of flour of 186 pounds varied in price from $7 to $12. In many districts food was frequently scarce, and the threat of famine was always real. In 1835 and 1836 the harvests were particularly bad, prices were as much as five times the usual level, provisions were hard to obtain even for cash, and many people experienced want comparable to the "hungry year" of Loyalist days; but even in ordinary years the pioneer farmer often found it hard to supply his family with food.

A settler in the vicinity of Peterborough in the early twenties describes the scarcity of provisions during the first year of settlement; he states that it often happened that there were not sufficient provisions to supply his family and workmen for the next day. "I have gone out", he says, "with my ox-team and a man to forage, and after travelling an entire day returned with a couple of sheep that had not a pound of fat on them, a little pork and a few fowls."[49] When flour was not available, cakes were made out of plain bran, and Indian corn was boiled, and these foods, with salt pork and pease soup, made up the meals for both adults and children. The Stewarts used wild plants as

---

[49]Thomas Stewart to Basil Hall, April 21, 1828; quoted in Basil Hall, *op. cit.*, Vol. I, p. 317.

greens, while hemlock "tea" and burned Indian corn "coffee" were the substitutes for the real articles, which were too expensive. No milk was available during the first winter, as cattle could not be kept over because of the scarcity of winter feed; the lack of this important food was particularly hard upon the young children of the family, who could not readily accustom themselves to coarse meals.

The importance of a knowledge of foods and methods of cooking among immigrants may be gauged from the fact that almost all "Guides to Emigrants", though written largely by men, include considerable advice and a number of recipes for their information. Many of these booklets on emigration are more idealistic than practical, and their suggestion of the bounty of nature and the extreme kindness of neighbours called forth the indignation of such settlers as Mrs. Traill and Mrs. Moodie, who did not misrepresent the truth in their accounts of pioneer life.

The general foundation of settlers' meals was made up of pork, flour, potatoes and corn. Those who had not plenty of bread and potatoes were unfortunate, for starchy foods enabled one to eat quantities of salt pork. In summer a considerable amount of beef and other meats could be substituted by the more prosperous settlers; but many ate pork all the year round, attempting to vary it by making pork pies or other dishes.

When it became possible to keep cattle over the winter, buttermilk and cheese were common foods, and the abundance of game and fish made them readily available for the table whenever the settler had time to engage in sport. Some young men, like those referred to by Mrs. Moodie, "considered hunting and fishing as the sole aim and object of life";[50] but other settlers, who were too busy to hunt, traded pork or flour to the Indians in return for venison, fish, ducks, partridges, and other small game.

In new settlements, even after the middle of the nineteenth century, wheat had sometimes to be ground in a coffee- or pepper-mill, or by an improvised grindstone mill. The first settlers in Smith Township, Peterborough County, in 1818, roasted or boiled wheat to make it easier to grind,

[50]Susanna Moodie: *Roughing It in the Bush*. 1852. Edition of 1923, p. 305.

while some parents even chewed the grain in order to make it soft enough for their children to eat.

Bread was generally made from wheat flour, but corn, rye and buckwheat were sometimes used. After a settler had become fairly well established, he might buy a cook-stove, or at least build a bake-oven. This was commonly erected on a large stump, and consisted of brick, stone or clay, with a roof of bark logs or slabs to protect it from the rain and wind. A fire was built in the oven, and when it was hot the ashes were removed and the loaves put in to bake. There was no way for moisture to escape and consequently bread made in bake-kettles or ovens was frequently partially steamed. Some early settlers in Peterborough County kneaded the dough and baked the bread in a rather remarkable manner:

"A portion of a trunk of a basswood tree about three feet long and two feet in diameter was split in two halves through the centre. One of these was hollowed out as smoothly as possible, to be used as a kneading-trough. About three pounds of flour, with enough water to wet it thoroughly, was put into this and well kneaded. It was then flattened out and placed in a round long-handled pan, the front of which was held before the fire by means of a string attached to the end of the handle, while live coals were placed beneath and behind it."[51]

When wet weather set in it was found preferable "to roll up the wet flour in lumps about the size of a potato. These were put in holes scraped in the hot ashes, and covered also with hot ashes and then coals, so as to cause them to bake without being burned. This was found more palatable than that baked in the pan, and, in the absence of better, was highly esteemed".[52]

When the wheat had to be ground in a coffee-mill, the flour seldom made good bread, but usually "coarse and black".[53] Most settlers, however, managed to get fairly good milled flour, even if they tramped thirty miles for it. Women often mixed boiled potatoes, or cornmeal, with the wheat flour, partly to improve the flavour of the bread,

[51]Thomas Poole: *Early Settlement of Peterborough and Peterborough County*. 1867. p. 173.
[52]*Ibid.*
[53]Frances Stewart: *Our Forest Home*. 1889. 2nd Edition, 1902, p. 86.

but largely to save flour. The usual yeast was made from boiled hops, but "barm" composed of salt, flour and warm water, or milk, fermented, was employed in some districts; while if nothing better was available "bran leavings" was used to save those who ate the bread from indigestion.

Among other home-made products besides yeast were molasses, vinegar, gelatine, cider, beer, and sometimes whisky, though it was more usual to purchase the whisky from local distilleries, of which there were always plenty. Baking soda was not infrequently made from the lye of burnt corn-cobs, though settlers who lived near towns were able to buy such ingredients from merchants, some of whom manufactured for sale a good quality of yeast, vinegar, and other products of the kind.

Pumpkins were put to many uses as food, as well as providing excellent feed for cattle. They made good pies when boiled and mixed with eggs, milk and spices, sugar not usually being added. Some housewives sliced pumpkins and dried them for winter use, while many also made molasses from them, the recipe which Mrs. Stewart used being as follows: "It is cut into pieces, boiled till pulpy, then the juice is pressed out and boiled till it is thick and dark-coloured like treacle; it tastes rather acid and rather sweet; I think it very bad."[54] This type of molasses was sometimes called "punkin sass" by Americans. Pumpkin soup was another variation of this valuable food, which was the more used since other fruits and vegetables were not common among the rural inhabitants, for most of them had not time to spend in the care of gardens, even if the seeds had been readily available.

In later years apples replaced pumpkin in pies to a considerable extent. A paring bee produced large numbers of strings of dried apples, and these were suspended from the ceiling of kitchen or attic. After they were perfectly dry they might be packed in boxes or paper bags, and when needed for pies, puddings or tarts they were boiled with sugar. Samuel Strickland describes a similar method of preserving other fruits at small cost in a day when glass jars and even stone crocks were scarce:

"Plums, raspberries and strawberries are boiled with a

[54]*Ibid.*, p. 61.

small quantity of sugar, and spread about half an inch thick on sheets of paper, to dry in the sun. This will be accomplished in a few days; after which the papers are rolled up, tied, and hung up in a dry place for use. When wanted for tarts these dried fruits are taken from the paper and boiled with a little more sugar, which restores the fruit to its former size and shape. Our ladies make jams and jellies after the orthodox European fashion."[55]

With reference to the pickling of vegetables Mrs. Traill wrote:

"The great want of spring vegetables renders pickles a valuable addition to the table at the season when potatoes have become unfit and distasteful. If you have been fortunate in your maple-vinegar, a store of pickled cucumbers, beans, cabbages, etc., may be made during the latter part of the summer; but if the vinegar should not be fit at that time, there are two expedients: one is to make a good brine of boiled salt and water, into which throw your cucumbers, etc. . . . Another plan, and I have heard it much commended, is putting the cucumbers into a mixture of whisky and water, which in time turns to a fine vinegar, and preserves the colour and crispness of the vegetable; while the vinegar is apt to make them soft, especially if poured on boiling hot, as is the usual practice".[56]

Turnips, a luxury in early days, were grown quite extensively by some of the more progressive settlers in the thirties and forties, but their introduction had been recent, and few knew how to cultivate them properly. The Hon. Asa Burnham, an early settler near Cobourg, stated that in 1842 he and a few others first raised them in that neighbourhood: "I thought hoeing and cultivating them would rip them all up, but they turned out a fine crop. I stored them, but covered them up too warmly, so that they all rotted. I soon learned by experience how they should be treated".[57]

The experience of Mr. Burnham, who was one of the most progressive farmers in the province, is typical of that

[55]Strickland, op. cit., Vol. II, pp. 296-7.
[56]Catharine Traill: The Backwoods of Canada. 1836. Edition of 1929, pp. 355-6.
[57]Speech at St. Andrew's Society Dinner, November 30, 1864. Cobourg Sentinel, December 10, 1864.

of many a settler who attempted to introduce the cultivation of fruits and vegetables. For many years they were little grown except in the Niagara District, "the Garden of Canada", and along the Detroit River, where the French settlers had orchards in the early seventeen-nineties which supplied even Niagara with apples and cider. In both of these districts melons, peaches, cherries and apples were being cultivated before the commencement of the nineteenth century, while vegetables such as onions, cucumbers, celery and cabbage were soon afterwards commonly grown.

In other districts progressive settlers, like Thomas Need in Victoria County, and the Traills and Stewarts in Peterborough County, grew melons, lettuce and cabbage, and various root crops, which they were able to keep through the winter. Those whose means made possible the hiring of servants, often spent considerable time in horticulture, which enabled them to revive pleasant memmories of their gardens in Britain. In July, 1833, Thomas Need noted in his journal that he was occupied chiefly "in the garden, in which I sowed the seeds of cucumber, melon, lettuce, parsley, endive, mustard and turnip. I also planted potatoes for seed next year, and picked out cabbages and broccoli".[53]

Gooseberries, raspberries, strawberries and currants were grown from plants imported from England, but they were seldom as good as those grown in the Old Country. Most settlers, of course, were satisfied to gather the wild fruits, of which the grape was, perhaps, most extensively used. In the early sixties the cultivation of the grape was being investigated by the government with a view to its development, and the vineyards of the Niagara district were the result. Many settlers who had orchards paid but little attention to them, sometimes leaving the fruit to the pigs; but a few men made a name for themselves and conferred a benefit upon humanity by their care of the wild fruit trees. John McIntosh, an early settler in Dundas County, transplanted a number of wild apple trees in 1796, and one of them lived to allow grafts to be distributed throughout the province, the McIntosh Red earning the reputation of being one of the best apples.

[53]Need, *op. cit.*, p. 66.

Drinks varied with the locality, and the preference of individuals. Whisky, beer, cider, buttermilk, tea and coffee were commonly used at meals; while among special beverages was spruce beer, a popular summer drink in York during the early years of the town's history. Coffee was harder to obtain than tea, and burnt corn sometimes provided a substitute. Tea, chiefly green, was widely used, but, though it cost on an average about $1 a pound, it was frequently neither of good quality, nor well made; one traveller considered that some she was served at a tavern tasted "for all the world like musty hay".[59] Maple sugar sweetened it, if any sugar at all was used, and some people added whisky or brandy to make "bush tea" more palatable.

The duty on tea led to a great deal of smuggling. Merchants not infrequently imported one or two chests from Great Britain, with the custom-house mark on them, and then kept filling them up with smuggled American tea. A traveller was told in 1824 that "of every fifteen pounds sold, thirteen were smuggled"; and that one merchant in Niagara was known to have annually smuggled 500 to 1,000 chests of tea into the province.[60]

Those who were unable to purchase the real thing used hemlock, peppermint, "New Jersey tea", sweet balm and other herbs to make a beverage often quite palatable. A traveller familiar with the settlements in the vicinity of New Lanark and Perth in the early eighteen-twenties gives a somewhat detailed account of these substitutes:

"Different kinds of herbs are produced in the woods, which are gathered and used as substitutes for tea. One of these species is denominated velvet tea and abounds in marshy situations. Its leaves are green on the one side and yellow on the other. There is another species called sanspareil, or unequalled. Another kind is called maiden hair. The inner bark of the maple is likewise used in place of tea. A species of evergreen is denominated winter-green tea."[61]

Meals among the farmers of the thirties and forties varied with the age of the settlement and the prosperity

[59]Jameson, *op. cit.*, Vol. I, p. 97.
[60][W. N. Blane]: *An Excursion through the United States and Canada during 1822-23.* 1824. p. 395.
[61]John McDonald: *Narrative of a Voyage to Quebec, and Journey from thence to New Lanark, Upper Canada.* 1823. p. 18.

COBOURG IN 1840

SMITH'S FALLS IN THE EIGHTEEN-THIRTIES
The village was first known as Wardsville

BROCKVILLE FROM UMBRELLA ISLAND, 1828

of the family. There were many who lived on very plain
fare. In 1833 Surveyor Baird and party called for dinner
at a farmhouse near Rice Lake. A large pot of potatoes was
boiled and emptied on the table, and some salt placed near
by. The charge for the meal, as suggested by the very
discriminating host, was "seven pence ha'penny for the
officers and saxpence for the men".[62]

Joseph Pickering, who travelled through many newly-
settled districts in 1826, found that the typical meal he
could get at a farmhouse was "bread or cake, and butter
and potatoes, or 'mush-and-milk', if for supper". The latter
dish he describes as "ground Indian corn boiled in water
to the consistence of hasty pudding, then eaten with cold
milk. It is the favorite dish, and most people are fond of it
from its wholesomeness and lightness as a supper meal".
These meals he found usual for the first year or two after
settlement, but sometimes Johnny cake and meat were
added.[63] The cornmeal "mush" referred to by Pickering
was sometimes called "supporne" by Americans, and was
the only porridge until the late forties, when oatmeal came
into common use.

In the homes of the more prosperous settlers the food
was better. When Patrick Shirreff visited a friend in
Windsor (Whitby) "the dinner consisted of fried pork,
the standard dish of the country, eggs, new potatoes and
pancakes"; this he considered an excellent repast.[64] Mrs.
Jameson was similarly pleased with the food at a clergyman's home in Erindale: "I found breakfast laid in the
verandah: excellent tea and coffee, rich cream, delicious
hot cakes, new-laid eggs—a banquet for a king."[65]

John Langton, whose letters describe pioneer life in the
early thirties on the shores of Sturgeon Lake, refers to
barrelled beef, and turnips, as luxuries "which I reserve
for chance guests or such great occasions as Christmas or
New Year's days". He used fish, ducks and venison for variety in the summer, but from November to April inclusive,
"salt pork is the standing dish for breakfast, dinner and
tea, and a most expensive one it is, each member of my
establishment consuming at the rate of one and a quarter

[62]Poole, op. cit., p. 29.   [63]Pickering, op. cit., September 9, 1826.
[64]Shirreff, op. cit., p. 120.   [65]Jameson, op. cit., Vol I, p. 304.

pounds per day at 6d. per pound". To make the pork go farther he used many soups, of which "potato soup is the favourite and is so much relished by my men that it has become the ordinary dish at breakfast". This soup was made by boiling a lump of pork, an onion and a dozen or so potatoes "until it has acquired the desired consistency". The pea soup was not as good, consisting of "hard, black pease floating about in weak greasy broth".

Langton tried to make a plum pudding for Christmas, but "currants and suet were scarce, the eggs entirely wanting, and flour by much the preponderating ingredient", so it was a decided failure, although it was eaten. Sugar and milk were very scarce, so tea was usually drunk clear and strong; after the first months of settlement a goat was bought to supply milk. Bread was usually baked "in a frying pan before the fire". In one letter Langton wrote that his men broke out in boils because of the unbalanced pork diet, and he asks for recipes for preserving some of the wild fruits which grew in such abundance; he stated that he hoped to be able to domesticate some of the swarms of honey bees to be found in the woods.

Among the game which Langton occasionally used for food was the porcupine, which "upon the second trial I pronounce very good eating; there is a peculiar smell and taste about the meat which I judged it prudent to mitigate by parboiling, but after that he made a most excellent stew". A method of salting down fish in winter is described: two dozen potatoes were boiled, peeled and mashed in the bottom of a barrel, adding plenty of salt and pepper; then a maskinonge was boiled, and "at a certain stage if you take him up by the tail and give him a gentle shake over the barrel all the flesh will fall off"; salt and pepper is again added in considerable quantity, and the whole process repeated until the barrel is full, whereupon it is headed up and frozen. "It will keep in a cool place good until the beginning of June, and when any is wanted for use take out a sufficient quantity and fry it in little round cakes".[66]

In connection with Langton's cooking it must be re-

[66]John Langton: *Early Days in Upper Canada, Letters of John Langton*. 1926. References to food are found particularly on pp. 35, 38, 57-60 and 83.

membered that his was a bachelor's establishment of lumbermen, though on a comparatively small scale. Samuel Strickland refers to the food in large lumber camps as "fat barrelled pork, and beef pea-soup, and plenty of good bread, potatoes, and turnips. Tea, sugar, onions, or other luxuries, must be provided at their own expense".[67] In later years lumbermen were supplied with strong tea, though seldom with milk or sugar, for which molasses was substituted. Copious supplies of beans became customary with the pork, while pies and cakes in large quantities were made by the shanty cook.

The examples of foods and meals in the rural districts may seem to represent largely the conditions of the earliest and most difficult times. Usually it was only a few years before scarcity was changed to plenty, and often to abundance. As an example of an average meal in the Huron Tract, after the first years of hardship were over, may be taken the breakfast of "green tea and fried pork, honey-comb and salted salmon, pound cake and pickled cucumbers, stewed chicken and apple tart, ginger bread and *sauerkraut*";[68] and dinner and supper were merely a repetition of breakfast. Besides cabbage in the form of *sauerkraut,* other dainties enjoyed by German and Dutch settlers included *kohl* salad and *schmier kase;* these foods were particularly popular among the German settlers who entered Waterloo County in 1800 and succeeding years, and among those of the same nationality who settled in Lincoln, Welland and Haldimand Counties in the eighteen-thirties.

There was often a similar profusion in other parts of the province. Mrs. Stewart describes the food at a picnic in Peterborough County in 1838 as "cold fowl, ham, bread and butter, then melons, apples, wine and water";[69] while at a raising bee in 1841 was served "a roast pig and a boiled leg of mutton, a dish of fish, a large, cold mutton pie, cold ham and cold roast mutton, mashed potatoes and beans and carrots, a large rice pudding, a large bread-and-butter pudding, and currant and gooseberry tarts"[70]—a banquet which would have called forth praises from that lover of

[67]Strickland, *op. cit.*, Vol. II, p. 286.
[68]R. and K. Lizars: *In the Days of the Canada Company*. 1896. p. 55.
[69]Stewart, *op. cit.*, p. 158.
[70]*Ibid.*, pp. 174-6.

good meals, Samuel Pepys. Upon a similar occasion in the Ottawa Valley "the fatted calf or sheep was killed, or the best beef procurable was well roasted with well-boiled potatoes, the best of bread, buns, cakes, crackers, also puddings and pastries, whilst tea, coffee and whisky flowed in equal streams".[71]

The farther one went into "the bush", the more fish and game he found used as food. When Thomas Need (a bachelor) was visited by four travellers from Peterborough in 1833, he got them all to help in the preparation of the meal,—"one baked, another attended to the roast, while a third prepared the vegetables. In due time, I set before them a repast of the usual forest fare—fish, fowl, and venison—which my guests pronounced sumptuous, and enjoyed not the less on account of its novelty".[72] When Lieutenant-Governor Sir John Colborne honoured the infant settlement with a visit during a tour of inspection of improvements in the backwoods of the Newcastle District, Need rose to the occasion with a much more pretentious dinner-party:

"There was a noble maskalongy, supported by the choice parts of a couple of bucks; then for *entremets,* we had beaver tails (a rare delicacy), partridges, wild fowl and squirrels. My garden supplied the dessert, which consisted of melons, raised from English seed, but far exceeding their parent stock in size and flavour, plums, strawberries and apples; there were grapes too, rich in hue and beautiful in appearance, but unhappily tasteless to the palate as the fabled fruit of the Dead Sea shore. The high-bush cranberry, by far the most delicate and admired of all our native fruits, was not yet ripe, but his Excellency was pleased highly to extol the entertainment".[73]

The little village was then christened Rokeby by the Lieutenant-Governor; but as the rapids were called Bob Cajwin, or the Bob, the place ultimately took the name Bobcaygeon.

At Young's Point, Peterborough County, Mrs. Susanna Moodie was entertained by the Youngs in 1835, just before setting out upon an expedition to Stoney Lake. She describes the feast as consisting of "venison, pork, chickens,

[71]J. L. Gourlay: *History of the Ottawa Valley.* 1896. p. 11.
[72]Need, *op. cit.*, p. 71.
[73]*Ibid.*, p. 99.

ducks and fish of several kinds, cooked in a variety of ways; pumpkin, raspberry, cherry, and currant pies, with fresh butter and green cheese (as the new cream cheese is called), maple molasses, preserves and pickled cucumbers, tea and coffee",[74]—an excellent example of that hospitality for which the inhabitants of the rural districts have always been noted. Wedding suppers or Christmas dinners could not surpass the banquets which were often the meals of the pioneer settlers of but a few years previous.

As a general rule fresh meat was obtainable in the towns, but there were times even in Toronto in the late thirties when it was difficult to procure anything but salt pork; it may be assumed, however, that this condition was caused almost entirely by difficulties of transportation in the spring season, when the roads were breaking up, and navigation had not commenced. Mrs. Jameson refers to a comparative scarcity of this kind in Toronto in April, 1837. She was living in the fashionable western suburbs of the city of that day—in the vicinity of Spadina and Palace (Front) Streets— and the remoteness of the Toronto market necessitated management and forethought to keep the larder full.

"Our table, however, is pretty well supplied. Beef is tolerable, but lean; mutton bad, scarce, and dearer than beef; pork excellent and delicate, being fattened principally on Indian corn. The fish is of many various kinds, and delicious. During the whole winter we had black bass and whitefish, caught in holes in the ice, and brought down by the Indians. Venison, game and wild fowl are always to be had; the quails, which are caught in immense numbers near Toronto, are most delicate eating; I lived on them when I could eat nothing else. What they call partridge here is a small species of pheasant, also very good; and now we are promised snipes and woodcocks in abundance. The wild goose is also excellent eating when well cooked. . . . The higher class of people are supplied with provisions from their own lands and farms, or by certain persons they know and employ . . . Those who have farms near the city, or a country establishment of their own, raise poultry and vegetables for their own table. As yet I have seen no

[74]Moodie, *op. cit.*, p. 327.

vegetables whatever but potatoes; even in the best seasons they are not readily to be procured in the market".[75]

In the towns more luxuries were, of course, available. Those who could afford imported foods were usually able to buy them, though some luxuries—oysters, for example— had often to be purchased in large quantities. In the *Upper Canada Gazette,* published at York, occurs the advertisement of James F. Smith, a merchant at the corner of Church and Palace (Front) Streets, and in his announcement, dated March 25, 1830, he states that he "daily expects Oysters (in shell). Lobsters, Mackerel, North Shore Herring and Salmon pickled and smoked". He also advertises for sale a large variety of imported wines and liquors, "Sugar-Double, Single Refined, and moist; Tea of every description; Sauces, Pickles, East India preserves; Candied Lemons, Citron and Orange Peel; Anchovy Paste and Fresh Curry; Codfish of various kinds; Digby and Lockfine Herrings; English Cheese—Dolphin, King's Arms, Berkley, Pine Apple, Truckle and Double Gloucester; Tobacco, Snuff, Havanna Cigars and Pipes."[76] Thirty years earlier much of the tobacco brought into Upper Canada was smuggled from the United States, often hidden in barrels of salt.

The larger towns were provided with confections which might have been presumed to belong only to a later day. Previous to 1800 York had a bakery which supplied bread and cakes; and some of the other towns or large villages had similar establishments after the War of 1812. Even the "backwoods" village of Perth had two bakeries in 1821, though they were engaged chiefly in supplying incoming immigrants with bread. In the early thirties even ice cream, then usually called ices, was sold in York. Thomas Hamilton states that in passing through the streets he was "rather surprised to observe an *affiche* intimating that ice creams were to be had within. The weather being hot, I entered, and found the master of the establishment to be an Italian. I never ate better ices at Grange's".[77]

Some other luxuries available in York a century ago were sent by a friend to Mrs. Thomas Stewart of Peter-

[75]Jameson, *op cit.,* Vol. I, pp. 267-9.
[76]*Upper Canada Gazette,* March 25, 1830.
[77]Thomas Hamilton: *Men and Manners in America.* 1833. Vol. II, p. 335.

borough County, during an illness. The delicacies are described as "sago, tapioca, groats, ginger, and all the niceties
for an invalid".[78] It was many years later, however, before
imported fruits and nuts became common in the towns;
even in the sixties they were curiosities. At a conversazione
of Victoria College, Cobourg, on May 11, 1864, the refreshments included oranges, almonds, raisins, candies and
"cupid's messengers"; and it is stated that a soda fountain
was liberally patronized. The description of these delectable
dainties by the editor of the *Cobourg Sentinel* assures us
that such refreshments were quite unique.[79]

The meals in the towns varied according to the means
of the inhabitants. Most people had food similar to that
of the dwellers in the rural districts; but the wealthier
classes ate meals much like those of the Simcoes and Joseph
Willcocks, thirty or forty years earlier. Luxuries could be
purchased from the merchants, and delicacies prepared and
served in style by expert cooks; but it may be doubted that
any town meals ever surpassed in richness and variety
some of the banquets of the settlers in the backwoods.

Special events brought forth the same effort to provide
a good meal, whether people lived in the urban or rural
districts. Ann Macaulay of Kingston writes to her son in
Toronto that there was to be a grand christening, and "some
turkeys and three roasting pigs" were to be served to the
guests.[80] To roast animals whole was a favourite method
of cooking meat in "the good old days": on Queen Victoria's
wedding day, April 2nd, 1840, an ox was thus roasted in
the streets of Toronto, and everyone invited to come and
slice off a piece for himself![81]

With reference to meals in general it may be said with
certainty that most immigrants fared better in Canada
than they had in the Old Land. This fact was well expressed
by a Scotsman who entered into conversation with Patrick
Shirreff while they were chafing at the delay in the stage-
coach scheduled to carry them from Niagara Falls to the
town. The Scotsman volunteered the information that "the

[78]Stewart, *op. cit.*, p. 79.
[79]*Cobourg Sentinel*, May 14, 1864.
[80]Macaulay Papers. Ann Macaulay to John Macaulay, November 28,
    1837. (Archives of Ontario).
[81]Toronto *Mirror*, April 3, 1840.

beef of Canada was so tough that teeth could not chew it;
. . . . but when in the Old Country he got beef only once a
week, on Sunday, here he had it three times a day".[82]

John Howison found the same comparative profusion of
food in Upper Canada. He advised the intending emigrant
that he "must not expect to live very comfortably at first.
Pork, bread, and what vegetables he may raise, will form
the chief part of his diet for perhaps two years"; but while
travelling through the province and living for several
months among the people, he noticed that most settlers were
soon able to vary their diet with venison, poultry, vegetables, milk and various types of bread and cakes. Howison
was of the opinion that "in Upper Canada the people live
much better than persons of a similar class in Britain;
and to have proof of this, it is only necessary to visit
almost any hut in the backwoods. The interior of it seldom
fails to display many substantial comforts, such as immense
loaves of beautiful bread, entire pigs hanging round the
chimney, dried venison, trenchers of milk, and bags of
Indian corn".[83]

E. A. Talbot, who lived in Canada for five years, came
to the same conclusion, but he expresses it in his own peculiarly snobbish style. He usually disliked everything and
everybody, and he considered it humorous that "Irish moun-
taineers or Scotch Highlanders,—who, in their native country had seldom, except 'on some high festival of once a
year', sat down to a more luxurious meal than 'murphies'
and buttermilk, or to an oaten cake and porridge,—surrounded a table in Canada which groaned beneath the
weight of a profusion of sweetmeats and fine fruits, and
'did the honours' with all the politeness of newly-elected
Aldermen".[84]

After the middle of the century there were many
changes in foods, due largely to improvements in transportation and developments in manufacturing. Almost all canning and preserving of fruits and vegetables was done in
the home in earlier times, but canned goods became in-

[82]Shirreff, op. cit., p. 93.
[83]John Howison: Sketches of Upper Canada. 1821. 3rd Edition,
     1825, p. 270.
[84]E. A. Talbot: Five Years' Residence in the Canadas. 1824. Vol. II,
     p. 11.

creasingly important in the sixties. The introduction of packaged cereals took place some years later. The general use of maple sugar declined with the increasing importation of cane sugar, which was gradually refined from a dark brown, wet, raw sugar, so tightly packed in huge hogsheads that a boy was hired to climb in and hack it out with a hatchet, perhaps finding an occasional piece of cane as a reward for his labours. Tropical fruits, vegetables and nuts were at first a curiosity even in the towns, and some of them, such as the banana, have been introduced in comparatively recent times. Later still came the grapefruit, at first so bitter that one lady, who had purchased some to be in style, told her grocer that when she wanted more quinine she would order it from her druggist! Apple pie, long the standard dessert in town and country, has given place to many an innovation. Artificial refrigeration has not only changed the status of ice cream to a food, but has enabled the introduction of a large variety of frozen desserts, and made possible the extensive importation of fruits and vegetables, now available out of season in a profusion which would have astonished our pioneers.

CHAPTER III

THE "HUNGRY YEAR"

"The century's last decade came with signs
Foreboding evil to the forest land.
The sun and moon alternate rose and set,
Red, dry, and fiery, in a rainless sky;
And month succeeded month of parching drouth,
That ushered in the gaunt and hungry year,—
The hungry year whose name still haunts the land
With memories of famine and of death!"

WILLIAM KIRBY.[1]

AT the close of the American Revolution the British Government determined to do all in its power to assist Loyalist refugees and disbanded soldiers to establish a home in Canada. For three years they were to be provided with such rations as were allowed daily to the private soldier; and at the expiration of this period it was presumed that they would be able to provide for themselves. The requisite supplies were transported by bateau to each township, and depots were established where provisions were dealt out regularly to each family according to the number of children. They were also provided with spring wheat, peas, corn and potatoes for seed, and government grist-mills were constructed at Kingston, Niagara and Napanee for their use; but at the end of three years there were still many unprepared to support themselves, and, as a season of drought and poor crops coincided with the end of the rationing system, a period of unparalleled hardship was the result.

The year of famine,[2] known to some as "the scarce year", "the hard summer", or "the starved year", was 1788,

[1] William Kirby: *The Hungry Year*. 1878. p. 5.
[2] For an account of this unfortunate event we are almost entirely dependent upon the reminiscences of Loyalists who experienced the famine, for there is but little reference to it in official documents or in contemporary publications. Seventy-five years ago, when Dr. William Canniff was collecting the material for his *History of the Settlement of Upper Canada*, many people could remember the "hungry year", and he obtained valuable reminiscences of the event from men upon whose memory had been made a permanent impression of the extreme suffering occasioned by the scarcity. The chief other sources of material relating to the subject are referred to in the accompanying notes, numbers 1, 4, 5, 6, 7, 10 and 11.

though the distress commenced in some districts the year
previous and lasted until 1789. While crops were undoubtedly poor in almost every part of Upper Canada, Dr. William
Canniff does not emphasise any general failure, but suggests rather that neglect on the part of some, and inability
on the part of others, made it impossible for them to supply
themselves adequately with the necessities of life when
the government suddenly discontinued the distribution of
rations. Some settlers had come but recently to Upper
Canada and soon used up the supplies they had brought with
them; while others relied on the rumour that the King would
continue the distribution of food a year or so longer.

Canniff considered[3] that the Commissary Department of
the Army might have alleviated the suffering by bringing
up larger quantities of stores from Lower Canada, where
the scarcity was less acute. It appears remarkable that the
system of rationing was not immediately recommenced
when the scarcity became so great; but such reports as are
available indicate that there was great difficulty in obtaining food in large quantities, even in the United States, while
the slow means of transport of that day greatly delayed the
distribution of such food as was to be had. Even officials
engaged in the public service did not receive the rations
upon which they were entirely dependent.

It would appear that the scarcity, commencing with a
poor harvest in 1787, developed very gradually and surprised officials and settlers alike in its intensity; and as
the severe winter wore away, the spring of 1788 found the
inhabitants almost devoid of food and seed. Towards the
end of the famine Lord Dorchester allowed free importation of provisions from the United States *viâ* Lake Champlain, as his dispatch to Lord Sydney, under date of February 14, 1789, states.[4] Had the duties on such imports been
removed a year earlier much of the suffering might have
been avoided.

The French settlements along the Detroit River, and
such Loyalists as had arrived in Essex County did not
escape the severity of the famine year. Their communication with the rest of Upper Canada, and with Lower

[3]See William Canniff: *History of the Settlement of Upper Canada.*
    1869. pp. 195-201.
[4]Dorchester to Sydney, February 14, 1789.

Canada, was infrequent, and they were not dependent upon supplies from Montreal and Quebec. The main settled districts most remote from Lower Canada, the base of supplies, were those at Niagara and the Bay of Quinté, and there the distress seems to have been most intense; but there was also a very considerable scarcity of food all along the shores of the St. Lawrence.

The authorities seem to have distributed generously such supplies as were available at the garrison towns. The rations of the soldiers were reduced to a biscuit a day at Kingston to relieve the suffering of settlers; while at Niagara the "King's stores" were distributed among the people who lived close enough to come for them. Food was everywhere in great demand. Settlers are reported to have traded 200 acres of land for a few pounds of flour, a cow for eight bushels of potatoes, and a fine three-year old horse for fifty pounds of flour; and half-starved children on the shores of the St. Lawrence were known to beg sea-biscuits from passing boatmen and traders.[5]

In the Niagara district the drought and heat dried up wells and springs, and water was unobtainable at a distance from lake or river. Crops withered, cattle died, and game and wild birds practically disappeared, while frequent forest fires added to the trials of the inhabitants. Colonel John Clark of Niagara refers in his reminiscences[6] to the use as food of roots and greens from the woods, and states that a kind of tea was made from sassafras and hemlock. Captain James Dittrick of St. Catharines recalled many details: "We noticed what roots the pigs ate, and by that means avoided anything that had any poisonous qualities." He considered that the officers of the army did all in their power to mitigate distress, but the supplies were so limited that "only a small pittance was dealt out to each petitioner". He further states that dogs were killed to allay the pangs of hunger, "the very idea bringing sickness to some, but others devoured the flesh quite ravenously and soon became

[5]See T. W. H. Leavitt: *History of Leeds and Grenville.* 1879. pp. 22-3; and W. S. Herrington: *The History of Lennox and Addington.* 1913. pp. 39-40.

[6]Reminiscences of Colonel John Clark, Coventry Papers, Public Archives of Canada. (Most of the material is printed in Ontario Historical Society, *Papers and Records*, Vol. VII).

habituated to the taste". His family had also to kill a horse which could ill be spared from farm work; but there was nothing else to eat, and the horse "lasted a long time and proved very profitable eating".[7]

In reminiscences written for Egerton Ryerson, Thomas Merritt of St. Catharines states that many families had no food left when the harvest was still three months away; and that leaves, ground nuts, herbs and fish were the common foods; but that "in the middle of June moss became so thick in the river that they could not see to fish". Some settlers who had a cow lived on milk for all meals until the wheat had headed sufficiently, whereupon it was boiled for food.[8]

William Kirby's poem, *The Hungry Year*, emphasises the devastation wrought by drought and forest fire, and gives the Indian explanation of the catastrophe.

"Corn failed, and fruit and herb. The tender grass
Fell into dust. Trees died like sentient things,
And stood wrapped in their shrouds of withered leaves,
That rustled weirdly round them sear and dead.
From springs and brooks no morning mist arose;
The water vanished; and a brazen sky
Glowed hot and sullen through the pall of smoke
That rose from burning forests, far and near.

Slowly the months rolled round on fiery wheels;
The savage year relented not, nor shut
Its glaring eye, till all things perished,—food
For present, seed for future use were gone.
'All swallowed up', the starving Indians said,
'By the great serpent of the Chenonda
That underlies the ground and sucks it dry'."[9]

The reminiscences of settlers in the Bay of Quinté district give some additional details of conditions during the famine. In an address delivered at Picton in 1859 Canniff Haight said:

"Men willingly offered pretty much all they possessed

[7]Reminiscences of Captain James Dittrick, Coventry Papers.
[8]Reminiscences of Thomas Merritt, Coventry Papers.
[9]Kirby, *op. cit.*, p. 5.

for food. I could show you one of the finest farms in Hay Bay that was offered to my grandfather for a half hundred of flour and refused. A very respectable old lady . . . . was wont in those days to wander away early in the spring to the woods, and gather and eat the buds of the basswood and then bring an apron or basketful home to the children. Glad they were to pluck the rye and barley heads for food as soon as the kernel had formed; and not many miles from Picton a beef's bone was passed from house to house and was boiled again and again in order to extract some nutriment."[10]

During the winter, fishing was almost impossible, for the extreme cold froze up lake and river to a depth of two feet. Powder and shot were scarce or more game might have been obtained. Some of the inhabitants were so hungry that they did not wait even to dress the game they caught by snares, but roasted it as it was; others ate so many fish in the spring that they became ill. Children were sent to the woods to discover the storehouses of squirrels and remove the nuts. Catherine White stated that "bullfrogs were eaten when provisions were scant, and potatoes which had been planted were dug up to eat".[11] Some families had nothing to eat for weeks at a time but baked bran cakes, while millet seed was frequently a substitute for wheat flour. References are found to the use as food of such plants as wild rice, pigweed, lamb's quarter, ground nut and Indian cabbage; while the bark of trees and the leaves and buds of the maple, beech and basswood were found edible in some degree when boiled.

Henry Ruttan, whose parents had settled near Adolphustown among the first Loyalists, stated that the severe winter caused the deer to fall easy prey to the wolves, "who fattened on their destruction whilst men were perishing from want". His uncle had a little money which he had obtained from the sale of his captain's commission, and he used this to send two men two hundred miles to Albany, the journey being a hazardous one, for there were no roads and the route was largely by trail through the forests. In

[10]Quoted in Herrington, op. cit., pp. 39-40.
[11]Reminiscences of Catherine Chrysler White, Coventry Papers. (Printed in Ontario Historical Society, Papers and Records, Vol. VII).

many districts the snow was so deep that progress was almost impossible, but the men finally returned with four bushels of Indian corn. The Ruttans had also a cow, without which "all would have perished in the year of scarcity". The family of eight lived until the next harvest on this small amount of grain and the milk from the cow. By pounding the corn in a hollowed stump or hominy-block it was made into meal which was baked into bread and cakes. Roots, nuts and wild berries supplied additional food for the family.[12]

The famine affected life in all its aspects. There is a record of a "raising bee" where, instead of the copious supplies of food usually found at such gatherings, a pailful of eggs which had been saved for the occasion provided the food. They were beaten up with milk and rum, and the mixture was served as the only refreshment available.[13]

The commissariat officers at Niagara attempted to collect payment in later years for food distributed to settlers during the scarcity. When Prince Edward visited Niagara in 1791 some of the inhabitants approached him for relief from such treatment, and he ordered the officers to cancel all such debts and withdraw any lawsuits which had been instituted. "My father is not a merchant to deal in bread and ask payment for food granted for the relief of his loyal subjects", said the Duke of Kent in his reply to the petition. We have no record of any attempt to charge settlers in other sections of the province for such aid as they received during the famine.

A number of people died of starvation during the period of scarcity, while others met death as a result of eating poisonous roots, or from diseases induced by malnutrition. Henry Ruttan said that five of the inhabitants in the vicinity of Hay Bay were found dead, "including one poor woman with a live infant at her breast".[14]

Miraculous events are related as accompaniments of the famine. It is said that while one settler went on a journey in search of food, his wife and family were saved from starvation by being supplied with a rabbit every day by

[12]See Henry Ruttan: *Autobiography*. (In *Transactions* of the United Empire Loyalist Association of Ontario, 1899, pp. 77-8).
[13]Canniff, *op. cit.*, p. 201.   [14]Ruttan, *op. cit.*, p. 77.

the family cat, which had never been known to catch a rabbit previously, nor did it ever do so again after the father had returned eight days later with a little food. An old couple were reported to have been saved by wild pigeons who flew to the house and allowed themselves to be killed.[15] Such remarkable accounts may have been largely the product of over-wrought imaginations; but, in the absence of more exact historical material which it is possible to verify, these reminiscences enable us to picture some of the circumstances of a deplorable situation which for a time threatened the extinction of the infant Loyalist settlements.

The following year, 1789, brought relief to most of the inhabitants. A series of excellent crops rewarded those whose industry enabled them to sow a quantity of grain and potatoes, and the "hungry year" passed into memory as the most distressing period in the annals of pioneer life in Canada.

[15]See Leavitt, *op. cit.*, p. 23.

CHAPTER IV

GRINDING GRAIN INTO FLOUR

THE RELIGIOUS MILL

"The religious mill was the Shantz Mill at Port Elgin, operated by a man named Leader. The miller refused to run a minute after twelve o'clock on Saturday night. On one occasion, during a period of special pressure, a helper in the mill proposed to run right through the last night in the week in order to catch up. A man who happened to be present at the time, for a joke on the helper put some wet grain in the hopper as the clock was nearing the midnight hour. Exactly on the stroke of twelve the wet grain struck the stones and the mill stopped dead. 'I told you,' said the joker, 'that this was a religious mill and would not, under any circumstances, run on Sunday.' "[1]

WHEN the Loyalist settlers came to Upper Canada, they were for three years supplied with food by a grateful government; but one of the greatest difficulties with which these pioneers were beset was to get the grain which had been given to them ground into flour. Many of those who settled in Glengarry County, and in other districts along the St. Lawrence, were provided with portable mills, consisting of revolving steel plates; these mills were turned by hand like a coffee- or pepper-mill, but do not appear to have been popular, owing to the difficulty of their operation. No such utensils seem to have been distributed in the Bay of Quinté settlement or farther west, and the settlers in these regions had to get their grain crushed as best they could.

Various modes of milling flour at home were adopted, but in all of them the work was done by hand. The Indians were known to have used a hollowed-out stump for the purpose, or to have employed stones to crush grain into meal in finely-woven reed or wooden baskets; similar means were therefore adopted by the early settlers. Sometimes the grain was crushed with an axe upon a flat stone, but a more satisfactory method was the hominy-block or plumping-mill; this was a mortar made in the stump of a tree, or in a section of the trunk. A hardwood stump, often ironwood, was chosen, and it was hollowed out by building

[1]Reminiscences of Patrick Cummings of Bruce County, quoted in W. L. Smith: *Pioneers of Old Ontario*. 1923. p. 259.

215

a fire in the centre and keeping the outside wet, or by the use of a red-hot cannon-ball or other piece of iron. The hole was then cleaned out with axes and knives.

The size of these mills varied; sometimes the mortar contained only a few quarts, but frequently it held a bushel or more of grain. A pestle or pounder, of the hardest wood, was used to crush the grain; this pestle was six or eight feet long, about eight inches in diameter at the lower end, and at the top sufficiently small to be spanned by the hand. At first hand-power alone was used for grinding, but later a sweep-pole, sometimes attached to the bough of a tree, was added, and this made the work somewhat easier. Canniff describes it as "similar to a well-pole; and, a hard weighty substance being attached to the pole, much less strength was required to crush the grain, and at the same time a larger quantity could be done".[2]

Two men usually worked together at the plumping-mill. It was comparatively easy to make meal out of Indian corn or wild rice by this crude means, but the grinding of wheat was very difficult, and a great deal of labour was necessary to obtain even a coarse, brown flour. Captain James Dittrick of St. Catharines gives a few additional particulars of the hominy-block in his reminiscences of Loyalist days:

"The mills of rude workmanship were thinly scattered about the country, so that we had to content ourselves with a hollow stump to pound our grain in, which was done with a cannon-ball, fastened to a cord or bark of a tree, and affixed to a long pole which served as a lever. The bread or cakes thus made were not particularly white, but were eaten with a good appetite and proved wholesome."[3]

Early settlers occasionally boiled Indian corn in strong lye made from wood ashes, until the grains burst open; whereupon, after being well washed in clear water and allowed to dry thoroughly, it was easily ground in the plumping-mill.

The grinding of grain by these primitive means did not result in a very refined product. The bran was sometimes

[2]William Canniff: *History of the Settlement of Upper Canada.* 1869. p. 194.
[3]Reminiscences of Captain James Dittrick. (Coventry Papers, Public Archives of Canada.)

MILL ON THE APPANEE RIVER, 1795

The location of this early government mill was the left bank of the
river, in Fredericksburg Township

W. H. Bartlett

MILL AND BRIDGE ON THE RIDEAU RIVER, NEAR BYTOWN, 1840

A scene typical of almost any mill-stream in pioneer days

OLD KIRBY MILL, BRANTFORD

THE FLOOD GATE

separated from the flour by a horse-hair sieve, one of which often served a whole community; other settlers used a thin cloth for the same purpose, or winnowed the meal by sifting it in the wind. The entire work of making flour was quite frequently done by women, and the use of the hominy-block continued for many years, particularly in districts where grist-mills were remote. Early settlers describe long trips by canoe or bateau to obtain the precious "stone" flour which only the mills could produce. The white flour thus procured was often reserved for special occasions; though even milled flour was sometimes "black and bad",[4] owing to defective apparatus for cleaning the wheat.

The obtaining of satisfactory flour by any of the domestic methods was so difficult that the government ordered a grist-mill to be built near Kingston for the convenience of settlers along the St. Lawrence, in the Bay of Quinté district, and along the shores of Lake Ontario. This mill was erected in 1782-3 on the Cataraqui River, seven miles north of the fort, a location chosen as a central point to which the Loyalist settlers, who were about to be brought in, might most conveniently come from east and west. Robert Clark, a millwright, was employed by the government to take charge of the construction of the mill, and soldiers of the garrison at Kingston were detailed to do some of the rougher preparatory work in 1782. The mill and mill-house were constructed at a "raising bee" in 1783 by the united efforts of the first Loyalist soldier settlers to arrive in the district.

For four years no other mill was available to the inhabitants of this part of Canada, and grain was hauled to Cataraqui from such remote districts as Cornwall in the east, and Ontario and Durham Counties in the west. Many a settler carried his grain a long distance on his back or by hand-sleigh in winter, or in canoe, bateau or raft in summer. Roger Bates, for example, used to make the trip in the early seventeen-nineties from Darlington Township, Durham County; the journey took five or six weeks to accomplish by bateau, and at night the boat was pulled up on shore and used for shelter. In winter the lack of roads

[4]Frances Stewart: *Our Forest Home*. 1889. 2nd Edition, 1902, pp. 76-7.

forced some to tramp through deep snow many a dismal
mile, following an Indian trail or the windings of the lake
shore. No charge was made for grinding grain at the
Cataraqui Mill, but the congestion was frequently so great
that a man had to wait several days before his turn came.
The original mill remained standing until 1836.

In 1783 the government constructed a similar mill in
the Niagara district, near the mouth of 4-Mile Creek. After
a few months as a government mill it was operated by
Captain Daniel Servos. Early settlers at the head of Lake
Ontario had to make a two-day journey to this grist-mill,
which was for two years the only one in the western district. In 1784 it was planned to erect a church and a mill
at the Mohawk Village, near Brantford, but though the
church was erected in 1785 it was several years before the
mill was built.

In 1785 another mill in the Bay of Quinté district was
commenced by the government, and it was located on the
Apanee, or Napanee, River. The name is said to be Indian
for "flour", but the falls was called by that name before the
building was constructed. Not until 1787 was the mill
ready to commence operations, some of the machinery not
being installed until late in 1786. A bill of expenses gives
the cost of the materials and work, a considerable part
of the expenditure consisting of the purchase of rum for
those who aided in the raising.[5] In 1792 this mill seems to
have been rebuilt.

Though there was no charge at the Kingston mill, a
small toll was collected at Napanee; but the convenience of
getting their grain ground nearer home and without so
much delay was of great value to the Bay of Quinté settlers,
and the mill was long the best in the province. The third
grist-mill in this district was Van Alstine's, erected about
1796 at Lake-on-the-Mountain. In all of Upper Canada's
early mills more corn than wheat was ground at first, but,
as the clearing of the land increased, wheat-growing became more widespread.

Farther eastward, on the St. Lawrence, the Loyalist
settlers established a number of mills before the close of

[5]Account book of Robert Clark, millwright, quoted in Canniff, op. cit.,
    pp. 207-8.

the eighteenth century. At New Johnstown (Cornwall) water-mills were found to be impracticable owing to the shoving of the ice, so two windmills were early constructed there. In 1788 the first grist-mill in Dundas County was erected by Messrs. Coons and Shaver; this was a small structure in Matilda Township, one mile above the village of Iroquois, and it had one run of stone capable of grinding 100 bushels of grain per day. Soon afterwards John Munroe of Matilda built a larger mill with three run of stone. As early as 1791-2 Joel Stone, Loyalist founder of Gananoque, had a small grist-mill in operation at the mouth of the Gananoque River. As an example of average development in the front townships of the St. Lawrence after the War of 1812 may be taken Charlottenburgh Township, in Glengarry; here in 1816 there were "four grist-mills, with two additional pairs of stones, one of which additional pairs is for hulling barley and oats".[6]

On November 7, 1792, a "Statement of the Mills in the District of Nassau, specifying by whom erected, by what authority and what year, etc.", was issued by D. W. Smith, Surveyor-General, and Augustus Jones, government surveyor. The district of Nassau included the entire region from the Trent River to Long Point, but all of the mills were then located in what may be termed the Niagara district—between the head of Lake Ontario and Port Colborne. Of nineteen mills mentioned, four are both saw and grist, five are grist only, seven saw only, all of which had been built; and one grist- and two saw-mills were in process of erection. The report is worth quoting in full, but the saw-mills will be omitted as outside the scope of the present work. The details of location and ownership make possible the location of the exact sites of many of these very early enterprises; while other occasional details show that permission had to be obtained from the government before the mill was commenced, and give other interesting sidelights upon the subject. The list of grist-mills follows:

1. "A saw- and grist-mill near the Falls of Niagara, on the west shore of the River St. Lawrence, in the town-

[6]Robert Gourlay: *A Statistical Account of Upper Canada*. 1822. Vol. I, p. 559.

ship of No. 2, on lot No. 174, by John Burch, Esq., in the
year 1785 by permission of Major Campbell, the commandant at Niagara.

2. "A saw- and grist-mill on a creek called the Twelve-
Mile Creek, township No. 3, and lot No. 23 in the 10th
concession, by Duncan Murray, Esq., in the year 1786;
but he dying before they were completed, they were transferred to Robert Hamilton, Esq., who finished them in the
year following.

3. "A grist-mill on a creek called the Four-Mile Creek,
township No. 1, lot 2, 4th concession, in the year 1787, by
Peter Secord, senior, on the verbal promise made him by
Lord Dorchester at the house of the late Major Tice in
presence of Mr. Burch and others.

4. "A grist-mill on a creek called the Forty-Mile Creek,
lot No. 10, 1st concession, in the year 1789, by John Green.

5. "A saw- and grist-mill on Thirty-Mile Creek, township No. 5, Lot No. 22, 4th concession, in 1790, by William
Kitchen.

6. "A grist-mill on a branch of Twelve-Mile Creek, in
township No. 10, lot No. 5, 4th concession, in the year 1791,
by David Secord.

7. "A grist-mill on Four-Mile Creek, near the King's
Mills, in the year 1791, by David Servos, on ungranted lands.

8. "A grist-mill on a creek near the Sugar Loaf Hills,
Lake Erie, by Christian Savitz—unsurveyed.

9. "A saw- and grist-mill on a creek that empties into
the head of Burlington Bay, by Bargely and Wilson, in 1791.

10. "A grist-mill now erecting near Fort Erie, on the
west shore of the River St. Lawrence, at the Rapids, (on
a lot of John Gardiner's) by Mr. Dunbar."[7]

This report is concerned only with privately-owned mills,
the King's Mills at Four-Mile Creek being only incidentally
mentioned in number 7, above. The mill "near the Sugar
Loaf Hills, Lake Erie", (Number 8, above), was in the
vicinity of the present Port Colborne. Green's Mill,
(Number 4, above), was located on the Stoney Creek Road,
five miles east of the site of Hamilton. At one time this
mill ground all the flour for the garrisons of Upper Canada.

[7]Quoted in John Lynch: *Directory of the County of Peel.* 1874. pp.
9-10.

In 1794 there were about 100 settlers at the Forty (Grimsby), where Green's Mill was situated.

The development of milling facilities along the shores of Lake Erie followed the arrival at Long Point of Loyalists who removed thither from the Maritimes. Towards the close of the eighteenth century Captain Samuel Ryerse built the first mill on Long Point, and it was for many years the only one within seventy miles. In 1805 a grist-mill was erected at Turkey Point, and there were soon others at various locations along the Lake Erie shore. The first mill in the Talbot Settlement was erected at Port Talbot in 1807. When it was destroyed by American raiders in 1814 Colonel Talbot did not rebuild it, and for some years the settlers had to make a journey of several weeks in open boats—or with hand-sleighs upon the ice in winter— to the nearest mill at Long Point. Jonathan Doan's Mill at Sparta, South Yarmouth, was the second mill in the Talbot Settlement, and enabled many people to avoid the laborious journey to Long Point.

In 1819 two of the inhabitants of the district invented a type of hand-mill called a "bragh", and before the end of the year there was one in almost every house in the Talbot Settlement. It was made of granite stones fitted into a framework, the smaller stone being on top, and a massive bolt passing through the centre of both to fasten them together. By means of a large eye at the top of the bolt the mill was made portable, for a handspike could be inserted in the eye. One of the inventors of this hand-mill was Peter McKellar, and by his ingenuity he also erected a water-mill on the Sixteen-Mile Creek. He himself made all the wheels and gearing for his establishment, the irons were from Colonel Talbot's old mill, and the neighbours helped to construct a raceway. The water was sufficient to provide power from March to June, and for a time McKellar ran the mill all alone, day and night, from 2 am. Monday until 9 p.m. Saturday. Most of the settlers immediately gave up the use of their hand-mills, and men and women might be seen trudging over the roads with bags of grain, and home again from McKellar's with their meal.

To the westward of the Talbot Settlement in the valley of the Thames River, there were grist-mills before the close of the eighteenth century. Smith's *Gazetteer* of 1799 refers to the "good mills" in Delaware Township,[8] and to a mill at Chatham;[9] while still further west the milling facilities antedated by half a century the establishment of the province. The first settlements in Upper Canada were those made during the latter part of the French period along the Detroit River. Between 1734 and 1756 a considerable number of French settlers, many of them former soldiers, were allotted land in this locality under feudal tenure. One of the conditions of settlement was the erection of grist-mills, so windmill forts, combining utility with protection, became common; when there was a good wind one of these mills would grind one hundred bushels of wheat within twenty-four hours. The Montreuil Windmill at Sandwich was a noted landmark of the district until 1875, when it was demolished.

There were other methods of grinding grain in this locality in later days. Patrick Shirreff, an English farmer who visited the district in 1833, noted the grist-mills driven by the wind, and also "several propelled by oxen walking on an inclined plane, and they are very poor machines". In addition to these he saw some driven "by oxen and horses attached to a large wheel, moving horizontally a few inches from the ground". While he was at Sandwich he heard that a steam-power grist-mill was about to be erected there.[10] Besides the windmills in this district there were others at various points in Upper Canada where water power was not convenient or could not be used to advantage. They were early constructed, for example, at Cornwall, Prescott, York, Niagara and Fort Erie, and remained noted landmarks many years after their use was discontinued.

Flour-milling developed eastward from the head of Lake Ontario in much the same manner as it had elsewhere along "the front"; energetic inhabitants, not infrequently Americans, soon established grist-mills at strategic centres of settlement along the Lake Ontario shore. The first grist-mill in York County was erected by William Berczy,

[8] D. W. Smith: *A Short Topographical Description of His Majesty's Province of Upper Canada* . . . . 1799. p. 41.
[9] *Ibid.*, p. 39.
[10] Patrick Shirreff: *A Tour through North America*. 1835. p. 213.

William Gooderham's Windmill at York (Toronto), 1833

THE BURNING OF THE GOODERHAM MILL, TORONTO,
OCTOBER 26, 1869

THE "OLD MILL" ON THE HUMBER

A wooden mill was erected on the site in 1833-4, and a stone mill in
1837; the walls of the latter still stand

founder of the first settlement in Markham Township. He brought in his German-American settlers in 1794, and in the same year constructed both saw- and flour-mills on the Rouge River, his establishment being commonly called "the German Mills". The grist-mill was described as having "a pair of French burs and complete machinery bolting superfine flour",[11] and as it was the only mill between the head of the lake and Belleville, settlers brought grain to it from all directions, many of them following the shore of Lake Ontario and continuing up the Rouge.

Soon after were erected the first saw- and grist-mills on the Don River, commenced in the autumn of 1794; these were located on lot 13, East York Township, along the east bank of the stream, just below Todmorden. As they were operated by Timothy Skinner they were known as Skinner's Mills, but they were built through the initiative of Parshall Terry and a few other inhabitants of York. The approach to them by land was over the old Don Mills Road, a continuation of Broadview Avenue. The wife of the first Lieutenant-Governor of the province visited the mills in winter, driving on the ice of the Don "a mile beyond the Castle Frank, which looked beautiful from the river. The ice became bad from the rapidity of the river near the mill".[12]

A saw-mill was operated on the Humber by the government as early as May, 1794, but there was no grist-mill there at that early date. The saw-mill was located near the site of the present "Old Mill' and was not used after the War of 1812. A location for a grist-mill was reserved by the government and leased to John Wilson in 1798, but the lease expired without his having made any progress. A grist-mill was in operation on the Humber after the War, and settlers as far west as Peel County carried their grain to it to be ground.

The history of the site of the present "Old Mill" is of interest. In 1833-4 a wooden grist-mill was built there by Thomas Fisher, and replaced in 1837 by a stone mill erected by William Gamble. An English officer visited the establishment in May, 1840, and describes it as "conducted

[11]Advertisement of sale in the *Upper Canada Gazette*, April 27, 1805.
[12]*Diary of Mrs. John Graves Simcoe*, February 3, 1796.

on a very large scale. About one hundred people derive employment from it. It is supplied with corn for the most part from the United States. It is driven by two large breast wheels".[13] The stone walls of this mill still remain, though the structure was destroyed by fire in 1847, and another built in 1848. For some years longer it remained a centre of trade and business, but the coming of the railways in the fifties diverted the trade, and the establishment was closed in 1858. Previous to this date several other mills were being operated on the upper reaches of the Humber.

The first grist-mill along the Lake Ontario shore between the Rouge River and the Bay of Quinté was that erected in 1794 by Colonel Myers on Myers' Creek (also known as the Moira River), on the present site of Belleville. The earliest settlers at Smith's Creek (Port Hope) made a trip to this mill with their first grain in the winter of 1794-5, "the grain being dragged through the pathless woods on rough sleds".[14]

The Statement of Mills in the District of Nassau, quoted above, notes that a mill-site had been chosen "on a creek called Smith's Creek, north side of Lake Ontario, in the Township of Hope, lot No. 6 in front, at the head of a small pond".[15] Peter Smith had established a trading-post at that point in 1778, near the Indian village Cochingomink (or Pemiscutiank), and in 1790 he was succeeded in the Indian trade by one Herchimere. In 1793 the first settlers arrived, and in the following year the government offered a Loyalist, Elias Smith, a large grant of land on the shores of the creek if he would agree to build saw- and grist-mills. Work was commenced upon them in the spring of 1795, and the flour-mill was completed during that year under the direction of Captain John Burns; but the mill-race was unfinished, and the following spring the frost caused the banks to give way, resulting in a failure of the whole enterprise. Finally, in 1798, the mill was moved down the creek by an American millwright for $1,000, and saw- and grist-mills were in operation on the east bank of the

[13]Quoted in K. M. Lizars: *The Valley of the Humber*. 1913. p. 78.
[14]W. A. Craick: *Port Hope Historical Sketches*. 1901. p. 10.
[15]Lynch, *op. cit.*, p. 10.

creek a few months later. The excellence of the Smith's Creek mills resulted in their being patronised by settlers from far and near. About 1801 White's grist-mill was established seven miles to the east, near Amherst (Cobourg), and gradually others were erected on the main creeks and rivers along the north shore of Lake Ontario.

Some of the proprietors of early mills overcharged the settlers for grinding their grain, and consequently an Act was passed by the first parliament of the province to regulate the tariff. This law, which well exemplifies the practical utility of the acts of Simcoe's *régime*, forbade millers to take more than one-twelfth of the grist as payment for their work. The story is told that one-tenth was being considered, but one miller said this was not enough and suggested one-twelfth, which was thereupon made the legal rate![16]

It is, of course, not possible, nor would it be desirable, to refer to the development of milling facilities in every section of Upper Canada; but, the general course of events along the St. Lawrence and the Lakes having been described, some account of flour-milling in the rear of the earliest settlements will show the characteristic trend.

One of the first settlements back from the Lakes was that of Oxford County. Blenheim Township was surveyed for these settlers, of whom Thomas Horner was the first, by Augustus Jones in 1793, when the closest white inhabitants were near the Mohawk Village eastward and at Chatham in the west. The first mills in the county, both saw and grist, were erected by Horner in the vicinity of Princeton, on the Governor's Road. He had a saw-mill ready for use by 1798. The grist-mill was first operated in 1802, but in 1809 it was burned down and was never rebuilt. The second grist-mill in Oxford County was erected by James Burdick at Centreville in 1806-7. Both of these early enterprises were conducted in buildings only sixteen feet square.

When the first German settlers emigrated from Pennsylvania to Waterloo County in 1800-2 the nearest grist-

[16]A variation of this story, (which appears to have been current in early times), is given in Joseph Pickering: *Inquiries of an Emigrant*. 1831. April 2, 1826.

mill was at Dundas. To reach it an almost impassable road through the Beverly Swamp had to be traversed, and the great inconvenience and hardship of such a journey led to the erection of a small mill where the village of Shade's Mills (Galt) later developed. John Miller of Niagara erected the building, and one Maas was the first miller. The structure was of one and one-half storeys and measured twenty-four by twenty-eight feet. In later years many settlers far away in the "Huron Tract" carried their grain to be ground at the Galt mill, the trip being frequently made from North Easthope Township in the days before a mill was erected at Stratford.

As settlement proceeded in the various sections of the country a mill was almost the first consideration. The American settlers in Hull Township, on the Ottawa, were provided between 1802 and 1804 with a grist-mill, a saw-mill, a hemp-mill and a tannery by their leader, Philemon Wright, after whom the main settlement was appropriately named Wright's Mills (Hull). Across the river, in Upper Canada, the first soldier settlers began to arrive in Carleton County after the close of the War of 1812. The earliest arrivals patronised Wright's establishment, but in 1818-19 the government provided the first mills in the county at Richmond. Hamnet Pinhey erected saw- and grist-mills for the settlers of March Township, and other enterprising inhabitants of the county similarly benefitted their community as settlement proceeded.

In the valley of the Rideau the development was similar. When the settlement of the district was commenced in 1816, Perth, the central depot for the distribution of the soldier settlers, was soon provided with a grist-mill; while farther eastward in Lanark, Smith's Falls had mills operated in the early twenties by A. R. Ward, after whom the settlement received its first name, Wardsville.

It might have been presumed that the difficulties of grinding grain experienced by the earliest settlers in Upper Canada were not present in the later pioneer periods; but the hardships of settlement were often just as severe, and the methods just as primitive as in earlier times. This is well illustrated by the experiences of the first inhabitants of Peterborough County. In 1818 a few families moved into

Smith Township, far in "the backwoods". In the first years of settlement they had to carry their grain thirty or forty miles over a blazed trail to the mill at Port Hope, or afterwards to a small establishment on Galloway's Creek, in Cavan Township. In 1821 Adam Scott built small grist- and saw-mills on the Otonabee River, and around them grew the small settlement of Scott's Mills (Peterborough); but this grist-mill often broke down, and was insufficient to meet the needs of even the few settlers then in the district.

Many people in Smith went for weeks without bread, and Jacob Bromwell stated to Sir Peregrine Maitland in 1826 that he had had to resort to the expedient of making a miniature mill of himself, and had actually chewed corn until it became soft enough to bake into bread for his children. The Lieutenant-Governor was impressed with the lack of proper milling facilities, and in 1827 the government provided a good mill to replace Scott's. It was purchased soon after by John Hall and Moore Lee and operated successfully by them for some time. A few years later it was closer for some settlers in the district to travel to Purdy's Mills (the nucleus of Lindsay), where William Purdy, an American, erected a grist-mill in 1830, aided by his sons Jesse and Hasard.

The difficulties were the same in other districts. When the first settlers pushed northward from Uxbridge into Eldon Township in 1829, some of them were forced to grind their first grain "between two grindstones that were made to revolve with a crank turned by hand. The wheat was poured by hand through a hole in the upper stone. Between dark and bed-time enough would be ground to provide for the next day's needs. Later on we thought we were well off when we got a coffee-mill to do the grinding".[17]

Coffee-mills were also in use among many of the settlers in the district colonised by the Canada Company, and in the still larger territories to the north of the Huron Tract known as "the Queen's Bush", comprehending Dufferin, Grey, Bruce and Wellington Counties. An early settler at Belfountain, near Georgian Bay, stated that the work of grinding grain by the hand-mill was so laborious that men

[17]Reminiscences of Colin McFadyen, Eldon Township, quoted in W. L. Smith, *op. cit.*, pp. 140-1.

would rather "chop all day in the bush than grind a half bushel of wheat in the old coffee-mill".[18]   In the forties there was a grist-mill in operation at Belfountain, and early settlers from the vicinity of Meaford and Owen Sound brought their grists in home-made sleighs called jumpers, which were hauled by oxen; in summer the same crude sleds were often hauled over the trails, (which were seldom passable for ox-carts), or the grain was carried by men on their backs.

Where water transport was available it was much easier to carry grain to the mill by canoe or bateau. Roswell Matthews, the first white settler in the vicinity of Elora, took his first grain to market at Shade's Mills (Galt). With the help of his sons he had hollowed out a pine log thirty feet long.

"Eagerly launching this dug-out a mile and a half below the Falls, they embarked with sixteen bags of wheat, and paddling down to Galt they found a purchaser in Absalom Shade, who paid them fifty cents a bushel in cash. The dug-out was sold for two dollars and a half, and they returned home afoot, blithe as any birds of the forest."[19]

On some occasions when it was impossible to get grain ground Matthews was forced to boil wheat when it was in the milk. A few years after his arrival he attempted to establish a mill near the spot where he had first launched his canoe; but ice-packs destroyed two mill-dams in quick succession, and this, coupled with the fact that an Englishman was commencing a mill two miles below, discouraged further attempts. There was no mill in the vicinity until after the arrival of Captain William Gilkison, who founded Elora in 1832, moving westward from Prescott, of which also he had been the founder in 1811.

In other sections of Upper Canada the first mills were similarly a boon to the settlers for many miles around. The old "Red Mill" at Holland Landing served all the farmers in the vicinity of Crown Hill and Barrie; another early mill in this region was that at Newmarket, and it was followed in 1833 by one operated by the government at Coldwater.

In Peel County a number of mills were early established

18Reminiscences of Robert Brock, quoted in W. L. Smith, *op. cit.*, p. 184.
19G. M. Grant (Ed.) : *Picturesque Canada.* 1879. Vol. II, p. 482.

on the Credit River, one of the finest mill-streams in the province. Among the first was Timothy Street's Mill at Streetsville, erected soon after he had surveyed the district in 1819. The Etobicoke was in general a poor milling stream, but John Scott of Brampton erected a small structure for grinding or chopping grain for his distillery. His establishment attracted considerable attention because he had his mill-stones move vertically instead of horizontally, as was the usual practice, and some considered Scott's idea a decided improvement.

In a similar manner might be traced the first mills in each county in Ontario; but while it gradually became true that every settlement where there was sufficient water-power to turn the wheels had at least one mill, yet it was long not unusual for men, and even women, to have to carry grain many miles on their backs, and return home the following day with their flour. One of the Scotch fishermen from the Isle of Lewis who settled about the middle of the century in Huron and Bruce Counties once carried in a barrel on his back 100 pounds of flour for fourteen miles, and when asked how he felt he replied that he was not tired, "but she'll be a little pit sore apoot the back".[20]

Along the shores of Lake Huron the first settlers were served by a few mills erected by enterprising inhabitants. Brewster's Mill, on the lake shore of McGillivray Township, was used in the eighteen-forties by people many miles away in all directions. In the fifties the Harris Mill was the rendezvous of all inhabitants of Kincardine Township and the surrounding district, the farmers putting up at a log tavern near by while their grain was being ground. Those who lived farther inland, in the vicinity of Durham and Orangeville, carried their grists fifty miles or more to the mill at Guelph.

In many districts distilleries were early established in connection with grist-mills. In this manner the poorer grades of grain, such as wheat which had been frosted or rusted, as well as the surplus of the better grades used in the grist-mill, were utilised in the manufacture of whisky. As examples of distilleries operated with flour-

[20]Reminiscences of John S. McDonald, quoted in W. L. Smith, *op. cit.*, p. 258.

mills may be mentioned that of Adam Scott at Scott's Mills (Peterborough), and the York Windmill, erected in 1831-2 at the mouth of the Don by William Gooderham and James Worts; this building was first used as a grist-mill, and in 1837 was enlarged to include a distilling plant. In early days distilleries and breweries were almost as common as grist- and saw-mills.

The cost of mills varied from £180 to £600 ($2,400), according to the size of the dam and the way of finishing the establishment. A "common grist-mill" with one run of stones usually cost from £200 to £250, while a "good merchant's mill" was valued at from £800 to £1,000, the York Windmill costing the latter sum to construct. The capacity varied similarly, the small mill usually grinding from 4,000 to 15,000 bushels of grain *per annum*, while the better ones sometimes ground 40,000 bushels. Almost all of them could, if the necessity arose, increase their production by one-third by speeding up the process and working in the evenings and on Sundays, as many of them did in busy seasons.

The mill operated by water-power had one great drawback in the forced suspension of milling, often for long periods, in times of low water; the windmill, too, was obviously useless when there was no wind. In 1836 there were about 600 grist-mills in Upper Canada, a number which remained quite stationary, for in 1854 there were 610. Steam mills began to be fairly common at the middle of the century, though for many years the water-mills continued to form a large majority of the total number: in Oxford County, for example, there were in 1851 seventeen establishments, only three of which were worked by steam.

Flour-milling enjoyed its palmiest days in the forties, just previous to the discontinuance of the Canadian preference in the British market as a result of the abolition of the Corn Laws in 1849. Flour-millers in Montreal led in the annexation movement of that day, but the agitation soon died down, and the condition against which it was a protest was remedied temporarily by Lord Elgin's Reciprocity Treaty with the United States, 1854-1866. During the existence of this treaty, and particularly in the late fifties, railway and wagon, schooner and steamboat were busily employed in the carriage of grain and flour. Men still living in the town of Cobourg, for example, remember double lines of wagons extending half a mile from the harbour, awaiting their turn to unload. The American Civil War still further increased the grain and flour trade in many parts of Upper Canada, though certain localities experienced a depression.

Coincident with developments in transportation and changes in economic conditions was the passing of the small mill, the ruins of many of which are to be seen on river and creek throughout rural Ontario. In the sixties the iron turbine wheel was introduced and proved much more satisfactory than the old type. Most of the wheat is now sent to large mills which supply flour to retail merchants, who, in turn, distribute it to the consumer. With greatly improved machinery and methods much finer grades of flour are produced. The harder wheat grown in the Canadian West supplies the people of Ontario with most of their best flour, a development accelerated after the completion of the Canadian Pacific Railway in 1885 by a gradual change in Ontario from grain-growing to mixed farming, owing to the predominance of the Prairie Provinces as grain producers. The Ontario farmer, who used to haul his grain laboriously to the mill and return home with his flour, now buys it through his own United Farmers' Co-operative Society, or from a chain store, if indeed he needs much flour in a day when his wife buys her bread from the baker.

CHAPTER V

LUMBERING

"Let us recall the brave days of sail, with the great timber rafts dropping down to the coves, and the French-Canadian rivermen singing *En roulant ma boule*, or some such *chanson*: sun-bronzed, red-shirted men, with calks in the soles of their heavy boots, and surprisingly agile in leaping from log to log around the booms; hard brawny fellows, who scanned the Irish timber-stowers for the sight of some opponent in past waterfront fracas to seek or avoid."

F. W. WALLACE.[1]

No phase of pioneer life was more picturesque or more typically Canadian than the lumber industry. Long before the settler pushed his way into the backwoods the lumberman had slashed a bush road through many a remote forest and hauled timber to market. As settlement progressed, every farmer was for some years chiefly a lumberman, though he burned the timber instead of using it. Only enough logs for a primitive home were saved, for it was usually impossible in the early years of settlement to attempt to market lumber. Thousands of beautiful and irreplaceable trees of butternut, walnut, bird's-eye maple and many other varieties common at the time were piled in huge heaps and burned; timber was something to be got rid of as quickly as possible.

Our "second-growth" timber gives us but a poor idea of the extensive forests and huge trees of former times. Fortunately, however, early artists have provided a few representations which recall the days when the trees were towering giants. Pioneers tell of white pine trees sold for masts, over one hundred feet in length and three feet in diameter one-third the way up from the butt-end. Among hardwood trees the oak often attained a remarkable size. Samuel Strickland describes a notable tree which was long a landmark in the territory controlled by the Canada Company. It was located "near Bliss's Tavern, in the Township of Beverly", a short distance from Galt, and was called the Beverly-oak. Concerning its size Colonel Strickland says: "I measured it as accurately as I could about six

[1] F. W. Wallace: *Wooden Ships and Iron Men.* 1924. p. 101.

Public Archives of Canada   Lieutenant Philip Bainbrigge

A BUTTONWOOD TREE NEAR CHATHAM

W. H. Bartlett

A TIMBER RAFT IN A SQUALL ON LAKE ST. PETER, 1840

MODERN TIMBER RAFTS ARE TOWED BY STEAM TUGS

TIMBER COVES AT QUEBEC

feet from the ground, and found the diameter to be as
nearly eleven feet as possible, the trunk rising like a
majestic column, towering upwards for sixty or seventy
feet before branching off its mighty head".[2] Another oak
felled by lightning was found to have a diameter of five
feet three inches twenty-four feet from the ground.[3] Even
black cherry trees, now usually of small size, were to be
found ten or eleven feet in circumference seven feet from
the ground.[4] The magnificient appearance of these primeval
veterans of the forest seldom prevented their destruction,
however, though occasional trees remained to give later
generations some conception of the original grandeur.

In the French period an export trade in ship-building
material, masts and spars had developed with the West
Indies previous to 1700. Some oak planks and pine masts
had also been exported to France, but they were entirely for
government use. In later years shipbuilding, begun in a
small way under Intendant Talon, became an important industry along the St. Lawrence River; ten vessels of from
forty to one hundred tons were built in Canada in 1752.
Saw-mills were to be found in considerable numbers towards
the close of the French period, fifty-two being operated in
Quebec east of the Ottawa River in 1734. The exports of
lumber at the end of the French period do not appear extensive from the modern point of view, amounting in 1759
to a value of only $31,250.

General Murray, the first Governor after the British
conquest of Canada, was instructed in 1763 to set aside
as a reserve for naval purposes a certain section of each
township if suitable timber was to be found there; there
were other suggestions of the kind from time to time, but
no reserves were established other than those for religious
and educational purposes, which hampered settlement to
such an extent that public opinion would probably not have
tolerated any other unused land in the settled districts.

At the commencement of the British period the first important transatlantic trade in lumber developed. The
British bounties and tariff preferences were not large

[2]Samuel Strickland: *Twenty-seven Years in Canada West*. 1853. Vol.
        I, pp. 253-4.
    [3]*Ibid.*, Vol. I, pp. 256-7.   [4]*Ibid.*, Vol. I, p. 253.

enough, however, to allow successful competition by the inhabitants of British America with the Baltic timber. At this time, and for about half a century longer, the activities of the world were largely centred on wood, but in later years iron usurped the position of primary importance.

A considerable amount of "Quebec yellow-pine" found its way to the London market before 1800, but the great development in Canadian lumbering occurred when Napoleon's Continental System was operating in full force in 1808. In that year the imports from the Baltic countries fell away to one-eighth of their total in 1806, a reduction due to the success of the French in preventing the trade. To obtain the lumber necessary for the British navy the colonial timber industry was thereupon encouraged in 1809 by a preference, and within a year British North America was supplying Britain with 50,000 shiploads of lumber annually, of which total the Canadian exports were valued at about $400,000.

The trade increased rapidly in succeeding years, the duties reaching their crest in 1813 and being retained until 1842, except for a slight reduction in 1821. Though the Baltic lumber soon became available again, a considerable amount of apprehension remained in Britain, and this, with the desire to trade within the empire, continued the Canadian commerce. By the end of the Napoleonic War the value of the British timber imports from Canada was greater than those from the Baltic, and so remained until the early sixties.

In the French period the Richelieu River system had provided most of the lumber; but as settlement was extended westward and northward after the American Revolution the shores of the St. Lawrence and Ottawa Rivers and their tributaries, and the Bay of Quinté district, were extensive sources of supply. The demand was chiefly for squared timber of pine and oak, although a considerable number of masts were also exported, and there was a good market at Montreal and Quebec for planks, and staves for casks. The squared timber trade necessitated considerable waste in the rough squaring of the logs with the axe, but the process enabled easier packing on ocean ships, and, in addition, was desired for the British market.

Many Loyalist settlers along the St. Lawrence and the Bay of Quinté found the lumber industry more profitable than agriculture. The first timber raft from the Bay of Quinté was taken to Quebec by Samuel Sherwood in 1790; it was made up of masts cut three miles east of Trenton, and as there were then no cattle in that district he used tackle to haul the logs to the water.

Philemon Wright's American settlers on the Ottawa, near Hull, were early engaged in lumbering, which was soon the paramount industry in that district. In 1806 Wright examined the rapids along the Ottawa in preparation for driving down his first timber raft. This notable event took place the following spring, and the journey to Quebec from the banks of the Gatineau took thirty-five days. "But," Wright says, "having from experience learnt the manner of coming down, we can now (1823) oftentimes come down them in twenty-four hours."[5] Wright was also the first to run a raft through the Long Sault and the Chute au Blondeau on the St. Lawrence.

In 1823 over 300 rafts of timber, often loaded with other produce, made the trip down the Ottawa to Quebec, and by 1835 the lumbermen had penetrated to Lake Timiskaming —400 miles up the Ottawa. The characteristics of the lumber industry in this district are well described by John MacTaggart:

"The shantymen live in hordes of from thirty to forty together; throughout the day they cut down the pine trees, and square them in the 'pineries', or the oaks in the groves, and afterwards draw the logs to what is termed the bank, with oxen. When spring draws on, they form the lumber into small rafts, called cribs, and drop away down the rapids to market. When they come to any extensive sheets of still-water, the cribs are brought into one grand flotilla; masts, white flags and sails are sported; while with long rude oars they contrive to glide slowly along. Thus they will come from Lake Allumette, on the Ottawa, to Wolfe's Cove, Quebec, a distance of nearly 800 miles, in about six weeks.

[5]Philemon Wright: *An Account of the First Settlement of the Township of Hull.* 1823. (Appendix to Andrew Picken: *The Canadas.* 1832. p. xxviii.)

"On these rafts they have a fire for cooking, burning on a sandy hearth; and places to sleep in, formed of broad strips of bark, resembling the half of a cylinder, the arch about four feet high, and in length about eight. To these beds or 'lairs', 'trams' or handles are attached, so that they can be moved about from crib to crib, or from crib to the shore, as circumstances render it necessary. When they are passing a 'breaking-up' rapid they live ashore in these lairs, until the raft is new-withed, and fixed on the still-water below."[6]

In 1828 Philemon Wright's son, Ruggles Wright, erected a timber slide at Hull to avoid the Chaudière Falls. This was the first to be constructed, but soon afterwards these timber chutes, of crib-work construction with sluice gates to admit water, were common at the worst rapids of the rivers where lumbering was extensively carried on. Along the larger streams many of the slides were constructed by the government and a small charge was made for their use; in 1861, for example, the "slide dues" collected in Canada amounted to $55,546. Sometimes these chutes were narrow raceways which would carry only one log at a time; but for rafts they were about twenty-five feet wide, and a crib containing forty tons of timber, with the cookhouse and lumbermen on board, was easily carried over them to the quiet waters often fifty feet below. The Prince of Wales (later Edward VII) made a trip over a timber slide at Ottawa during his visit to Canada in 1860. His experience was, no doubt, similar to G. M. Grant's:

"We embark on board a crib above the slide-gates at the Falls of the Calumet. The raftsmen bid us take firm hold of one of the strong poles which are driven between the lower timbers of the crib. Above the slide the waters of the Ottawa are still and deep; at the left side, through the intervening woods, we can hear the roar of the cataract. The slide-gates are thrown open; the water surges over the smooth inclined channel; our crib, carefully steered through the gateway, slowly moves its forward end over the entrance; it advances, sways for a moment, then, with a sudden plunge and splash of water, rushes faster and faster between the narrow walls. The reflow of the torrent

[6]John MacTaggart: *Three Years in Canada.* 1829. Vol. I, pp. 241-2.

RAFTSMEN IN THE CALUMET RAPIDS, OTTAWA RIVER

Arthur Heming, O.S.A.

W. H. Bartlett

TIMBER SLIDE AT LES CHATS, 1840
The location is Fitzroy Harbour, twenty-five miles above Ottawa

A TIMBER CHUTE

streams over the crib from the front; jets of water spurt up everywhere between the timbers under our feet; then, dipping heavily as it leaves the slide, our crib is in the calm water beneath."[7]

At some timber chutes, notably that at the Cedars on the St. Lawrence, rafts and men were sometimes temporarily submerged during their progress. The turbulent Lachine Rapids were avoided by the use of the Back River, north of Montreal. Oak and pine, the two woods in demand at Quebec, were generally rafted together to help the oak keep afloat. Cash could usually be obtained at Quebec for lumber, almost all of which was exported to England for use in the navy, the ships of which were constructed of thick oak planks, while the masts were usually of pine. As much as $200 was paid at Quebec for a good mast. In a day when long-term credit and barter were the usual means of carrying on business, many a settler "drove" timber to Quebec, pitching camp on his raft, and sometimes taking produce to market both for himself and his neighbours.

After 1800, timber rafts were extensively used by merchants and traders in conveying the produce of Upper Canada to the lower province. Eight hundred barrels of flour, pork, ashes, or other produce were sometimes transported on one raft, which usually carried a large number of square sails to aid the oarsmen in moving it along with the current, a method of transport long a characteristic sight on our main river systems. It was sometimes attempted to move timber rafts on Lakes Erie and Ontario and other large bodies of water, but it was found to be both costly and dangerous owing to sudden storms. An early newspaper describes the loss of a valuable raft in 1826:

"We are sorry to learn that on Monday last, in attempting to tow across Lake Ontario, by the steamboat *Canada*, from the River Humber to the Welland Canal harbour, a large raft, consisting of 15,000 feet of choice timber, belonging to the Lock Company, a strong south-west gale arose, when about twelve miles out, and continued with such violence as to separate in pieces, in spite of every exertion by those concerned to prevent it, which scattered in

[7] G. M. Grant (Ed.): *Picturesque Canada.* 1879. Vol. I, pp. 229-30.

different directions, and floated off entirely at the mercy of the waves. It is probable, when we consider that westerly winds generally prevail at this season of the year, that this timber will drift ashore towards the lower end of the lake, and should this be the case it is earnestly hoped that all those who may observe or fall in with any of this valuable lot of lumber will take measures to secure the same, and immediately give information to Mr. Oliver Phelps, the Company's agent at St. Catharines, U.C., either by mail or otherwise as may be most convenient."[8]

Before the building of railroads the only districts in Upper Canada from which timber could be profitably exported were those near the waterways. By 1820 the western section of Lake Ontario was providing square timber for the trade at Quebec, while by 1830 Lake Erie, and, twenty years later, Lake St. Clair and even lower Lake Huron were sending their quota of the product. In the early forties the "back lakes" almost as far west as Lake Simcoe were being utilized to float square timber by way of the Trent system of lakes and rivers to Lake Ontario, and on down to Quebec. One of the noted timber slides erected in the Kawartha Lakes to prevent damage to the logs was "the Big Chute" at Burleigh Falls, Stoney Lake.

John Langton, an early settler on Sturgeon Lake, drove timber to Quebec over this route, the journey taking several months and costing about £2 15s. per piece of timber; but as the price obtainable at Quebec was £5 or more per piece, according to quality, the business was profitable in good years.[9] The largest mast ever shipped to Quebec is thought to have come from a township in the Lake Simcoe region, for Innisfill once sent one out of a length of 116 feet.

The life of the lumberjack was a hard one, but it attracted many young Canadians who wished a carefree and adventurous existence. Few who had experienced the excitable, if laborious life of the lumberman ever gave it up for the tamer pursuits of farming. Many an early settler hired out as a chopper for a farmer along "the front", or worked at a saw-mill in the summer or a lumber camp in

[8] York U. E. Loyalist, October 14, 1826.
[9] See John Langton: Early Days in Upper Canada, Letters of John Langton. 1926. pp. 201-9.

the winter in order to add to the meagre earnings produced by farming his own land. A contemporary writer
observed that "the lumber trade is of the utmost value to
the poorer inhabitants by furnishing their only means of
support during the severity of a long winter, particularly
after seasons of bad crops, and by enabling young men and
new settlers more readily to establish themselves on the
waste land".[10] Many settlers along the St. Lawrence
neglected their farms to engage in lumbering, which was
at times more profitable than agriculture; but in the "bad
years", when the Quebec market was glutted, many a
lumberman lost all he had ever made in the business.

Lumberjacks are the pioneers of civilisation, the first
to open up wild lands and make them available for settlement. To "make timber" the lumberman had first to secure
a "limit" from the government, though many dispensed
with this formality and merely trespassed on Crown lands.
After 1826 the government attempted a better system of
regulation, but there was no definite forest policy until the
middle of the century. Neither was the system of issuing
licenses well-defined: any one could get a "timber berth"
by sending to the Crown Timber Office an application accompanied by a surveyor's plan and a year's ground rent of $1
per square mile.

Timber limits varied in size from ten to one hundred
square miles or more, and they provided considerable
revenue, the rents or dues for lumbering rights on Crown
lands amounting in 1861 to $327,503. The first men to enter
the limit compose the exploring party of five or six experienced woodsmen, who look over and estimate the timber by
climbing some of the tall trees; they also pick out the site
for the camps and shanty, and lay out the course of the
roads to the most convenient watercourse or "drivable"
creek, where the "roll-way" is to be located.

The "head-swamper" and his gang then cleared a bush
road from the interior to the roll-way. A line of small ever-
greens was the method of marking the track to the depot
whence supplies for man and beast had to be drawn to the
camp. During the winter the men worked in gangs, felling

[10]Quoted in Herbert Heaton: *History of Trade and Commerce*. 1928.
      p. 227.

the trees, clearing away the branches and cutting the trunks into lengths; cant-hooks were used to roll them into position, the logs were squared if square timber was desired, and they were transported by oxen or horses over the road to the roll-way.

As many as fifteen teams of oxen were used to haul sleigh-loads of huge logs, or one 100-foot mast, to the river bank. To get all the oxen to move at the same time, and to keep them in steady motion, was no easy matter, and the shouting of the half-breed drivers as the great loads were hauled through the woods increased the excitement of the work. On each log was imprinted the "bush-mark" of the company, important for purposes of identification when more than one group of men are driving logs on one river. Some lumbermen not only cut down timber but also cleared the land and cultivated farms to provide provender for stock, and food for the men; and many added to their profits by developing by-products such as potash, wood-oils and medicinal bark.

The lumber-shanty was a large structure with a huge stone fireplace in the centre, and bunks built in tiers on the walls. There was seldom a chimney, but a large opening in the roof let the smoke out and ensured good ventilation. A great fire was necessary to keep the shanty warm under such conditions. The long winter evenings were passed by many in gambling and card-playing, or in singing and dancing to the fiddle; others were employed in drying and mending their clothes or sharpening their axes, while, perhaps, a comrade entertained them with *chansons de bois* depicting the hardship and adventure of the wild and free life in the Indian Territories.

French, Indians, half-breeds and Scotch Highlanders were the predominant nationalities found in pioneer lumber camps. In general the men were, "like sailors, very loose in their habits, and careless of their own souls. . . . It is hard to make any provision to reach their moral and spiritual wants".[11] On rare occasions, however, the visit of a Roman Catholic priest provided an opportunity for many to confess, and mass was said in the woods amid surroundings

[11]W. Fraser: *The Emigrant's Guide, or Sketches of Canada.* 1867. p. 48.

hardly less primitive than those under which, over two centuries earlier, Father Le Caron had sung the first masses in Champlain's bark lodge, surrounded by Huron warriors.

Plenty of food, similar to that of the average settler, was prepared by the lumber camp's cook. Salt pork, pea soup, bread and potatoes were the foundation of all meals, which were served in basins and washed down with copious draughts of strong tea, in early times provided only at individual expense. Whisky was forbidden at lumber camps, a regulation of great advantage in the woods, but which led to excesses when the gangs returned to civilisation. In later years molasses, beans and turnips were added to the menu of the lumberman, and pies and cakes became characteristic of their diet, the severe nature of their work enabling them to eat large quantities of rich and greasy food.

The typical costume of the early lumberman,—gray cloth trousers, flannel shirt, blanket coat fastened round the waist with a red or tri-coloured sash, cow-hide boots with heavy spikes, and a *bonnet rouge* for the head,—formed a picturesque *ensemble,* long familiar on our main river systems in summer, and in the vicinity of most settlements in winter.

When spring arrived the timber was released from its position on the shore; this was usually effected by moving the "key-log", located in such a position that it held all the others in place. Then commenced the long journey to market. In a good current the logs needed little attention except in shallow rapids, where dangerous lumber jams often occurred. Many a man risked his life in breaking up these blockades with the handspike by skilfully extracting the key-piece of the jam; for more serious jams a block-and-tackle was used, or the logs were blown up with gunpowder. Such work necessitates quick thinking and as speedy execution.

To keep the timber in motion it was often imperative to jump from log to log, even amid rapids, and a lumberjack required great nerve and dexterity, and a constitution which was not affected by the necessity of walking for many hours at a time in cold water. Cribs and rafts were formed in the larger bodies of quiet water, over which they were moved by long oars or sweeps, frequently of red pine, seven or eight men working at each sweep. When the wind was favourable large numbers of sails were hoisted, and where the current was strong the great rafts moved along at a good rate.

Withes, or twisted saplings, were often employed to link up the cribs into rafts, but a more convenient method was by the use of planks into which auger holes had been bored; these were placed over upright posts. Ninety or one hundred cribs were frequently joined to form a raft of an area of 30,000 or 40,000 square feet and a value of $15,000 to $25,000.

On the St. Lawrence the transport of timber was based not on the crib but upon the dram; this was a huge raft of many layers and frequently drew six feet of water. It took fifteen men a month to build the average dram, in which withes of birch and hazel fastened the traverses above to the timbers below; no nails or spikes were ever used in timber rafts, and only in the later period did chains and cables become customary as small steam-tugs replaced sweep and sail. Wooden houses took the place of the bark lairs of the early lumbermen, and the men were not infrequently accompanied by their families.

It could hardly be expected that lumberjacks would be among the quietest citizens when they returned to civilisation, though Colonel Samuel Strickland of Peterborough County wrote that he found the bad accounts of the lumbermen greatly exaggerated. He states that, "although large bodies of them have been lumbering close around me for the last four or five years, I have received nothing but civility at their hands; nor has a single application for a summons or warrant against them been made to me in my magisterial capacity".[12]

In other districts the same could not generally be said, however. Richmond and Bytown (Ottawa) were noted for extreme lawlessness in the early days, caused chiefly by fights among lumbermen, Irish labourers and ex-soldier farmers; for Bytown was often the first stopping-place on the way to Quebec:

[12]Strickland, *op. cit.*, Vol. II, p. 285.

"A Bytown c'est une jolie place
Ou il s'ramass' ben d'la crasse;
Où ya des jolies filles
Et aussi des jolis garçons.
Dans les chantiers nous hivernerons."[13]

The lumbermen, as the more transient class of the population, were probably in large measure to blame for the
quarrels which were the usual result of their arrival in any
settled district. All along their route to Quebec they were
a disturbing element, and fights and brawls with the inhabitants on the shores were a common occurrence. When
they had disposed of their timber the lumberjacks often
remained in city or town during the summer, or until their
money had all been spent on "the fiddle, the female or the
fire-water."[14] Then in the early winter they were off
to the woods to start the wild and adventurous round anew.

During the predominance of the squared timber trade,
which was at its height between 1840 and 1858, Wolfe's
Cove, near Quebec, was the great *entrepôt* of the lumber
industry. At Quebec were established the representatives
of British firms which had moved to British America from
the Baltic, where they had long engaged in the trade. The
Canadian connections of these firms were frequently maintained by the younger sons of families whose names were
a byword in the industry. Charles Poulett Thompson's interest in the Baltic timber trade was the chief reason for
the great objections emanating from Quebec and St. John
against his appointment as Governor-General in 1839.

The trade was early of a most speculative nature—often
a mere gamble in which money was tied up for two years
or more. At first firms obtained timber by contract, but in
later years there was a free market at Quebec. Dry rot and
fungus spoiled much timber, while the variability of freight
rates made it difficult to be sure of a fair price even for the
best. At Wolfe's Cove were located the "cullers", who
graded the timber according to quality, the refuse wood, or
culls, bringing an inferior price. MacTaggart, who wrote
in the late twenties, states that "there is a good deal of cor-

[13]Quoted in Grant, *op. cit.*, Vol. I, p. 179.
[14]Sir Richard Bonnycastle: *Canada and the Canadians*. 1846. Vol. I,
    p. 70.

ruption and bribery going on in this business, and many rafts of timber get a worse character than they deserve".[15] At that time nearly two-thirds of the timber brought to Quebec was white pine, "which generally brings five-pence, currency per cubic foot at Quebec, red pine eight-pence, and oak ten-pence".[16]

Timber-making was from the first an amateur work, and many settlers were ruined financially in the business. There was no concerted policy on the part of producers, and an excessive output, which commonly followed a prosperous year, glutted the market and caused heavy losses and hard times. In 1845, for example, 27,704,304 feet of squared timber was brought to market, but great over-production depressed the trade to a ruinous extent during the next three years.

The heavy work of loading the vessels was the last phase of the trade. As many as 300 boats might be seen shipping square timber at one time. The sailing-ships used to carry the wood to England had bow and stern port-holes for taking in the huge timbers, which were manipulated by tackle and windlass with man-power and horse-power. The intense activity is well described by F. W. Wallace:

"Engaged in this work were expert gangs of timber-stowers, mostly Irish, and rough, powerful men who could work like horses throughout the heat of a Canadian summer, and drink and fight with equal ability. These men were variously classed as timber-swingers, hookers-on, holders, porters, and winchers.

"When the rafts of timber were floated alongside the ship, members of the stowing gangs took their stations on the squared logs in the water and deftly extricated the individual timbers from the mass and pike-poled them into position for loading. On the ship's fo'c'sle-head, other men superintended the manipulation of the tackles for raising the timber up into the open port and swinging it inside the ship. In the hold, other members of the gang sweated with cant-hooks and hand-spikes, stowing the wet and heavy cargo.

"The tackles used to be operated by muscle-power in the

[15]MacTaggart, *op. cit.*, Vol. I, p. 245.
[16]*Ibid.*

Picturesque Canada. 1879

A LUMBER SHANTY

Picturesque Canada. 1879

MASS IN A LUMBER SHANTY

Picturesque Canada. 1879

THE ROLL-WAY

John Ross Robertson Collection   From a drawing on stone by Josh. Harwood

THE TIMBER-DROGHER COLUMBUS, 1824
A ship constructed of square timber to avoid the British Timber Duty

early days, with men tramping around the ship's capstan or turning a crab-winch, but later the portable donkey-boiler and steam winch were used. The scene around the coves was one of tremendous animation. Ships, as far as the eye could see, were being loaded, towed in or out, or departing, sometimes under sail or with a tug-boat pulling them to a fair wind or open water."[17]

In 1824 an unique type of ship was built at Quebec. The Scotch designer of the *Columbus*, Charles Wood, conceived the idea that he could evade the British timber tax then in force on oak and squared pine if he built the ship of such timber and broke it up on arrival in England. The *Columbus* was specially constructed to make this possible without damage to the timber, and the boat, known as a "timber-drogher", was launched on July 28, 1824, in view of 5000 people, a band being hired to provide suitable accompaniment.

The *Columbus*, 294 feet long and flat-bottomed, was packed solid with timber, and, rigged as a four-masted barque, successfully made the trip to London, but there was eighteen feet of water in her hold on arrival. The owners then decided not to break her up, and sent her back to Canada for another load; but on this voyage she foundered. Another ship of the same type, the *Baron of Renfrew*, a somewhat larger boat of 5294 tons, was launched in 1825 and sailed to England, but grounded near Dover and eventually broke up on the French coast. It was reported that insurance amounting to the huge sum of $5,389,040 was paid to cover the loss of the two boats.[18]

The Canadian preference in the British timber market came to an end during the forties and fifties, when Britain gradually changed from Protection to Free Trade. The administration of Sir Robert Peel greatly reduced the preference in 1842, and by 1846 it had suffered a further reduction along with the duties on grain and West Indian sugar. The trade in square timber received its last impetus in the early fifties with the outbreak of the Crimean War; this was followed by a depression in 1857, after which business revived to a considerable extent. The last vestige of protection vanished in 1860, and a few years thereafter the

[17]Wallace, *op. cit.*, p. 99.   [18]See *ibid.*, appendix, pp. 14-17.

square timber trade declined, a movement accelerated by the ever-increasing use of iron steamships in place of wooden sailing-ships.

In 1862 about 25,000 persons were directly engaged in lumbering in the Canadas, and there was no appreciable diminution in later years, for coincident with the decline of the squared timber trade there was fortunately a great increase in the export of sawn lumber to the United States and Great Britain. Much of the new trade was in deals—planks at least three inches thick—and there was some measure of protection accorded this trade at first. It developed more slowly than had that in square timber, because machinery and skilled labour were necessary; but it did not fall away to the same extent when the protection was removed.

The trade in square timber gradually became less and less, and almost disappeared during the early years of the present century. In 1910 there appears to have been none of it carried on, but there are occasional revivals from time to time. Only two years ago (1930) the old Booth firm of lumbermen were cutting square timber in Algonquin Park for the British market; but such survivals serve only to recall a famous trade whose greatness lies in the past.

The lack of saw-mills in early Loyalist days led to a considerable importation of sawn lumber from the New England states; but after the first few years of settlement saw-mills began to be erected at about the same rate, and often on the same sites as grist-mills. The first Canadian mills were on the shores of the St. Lawrence in Quebec, and, as settlement proceeded along the upper part of the river and on the Bay of Quinté, saw-mills to provide lumber for local purposes became common.

The earliest west of the Bay of Quinté, excepting the Detroit settlements, were those in the Niagara district. A report made by Surveyor-General D. W. Smith and Augustus Jones on November 7, 1792, mentions thirteen saw-mills in the Nassau District, which extended from the mouth of the Trent River to Long Point, Lake Erie. These were built between 1785 and 1792 in the following locations, the mills being given in the order of their erection: (1) near Niagara; (2) on 12-Mile Creek; (3) on 40-Mile Creek;

(4) on 15-Mile Creek; (5) on 30-Mile Creek; (6) on Black
Creek, seven miles in the rear of Fort Erie; (7 and 8) on
4-Mile Creek; (9) on Small Creek, called the Muddy Run,
near the Whirlpool; (10) on a creek emptying into Burlington Bay; (11) on a branch of 12-Mile Creek; (12) one being
erected on 12-Mile Creek; (13) one being erected on 40-Mile
Creek.[19] These mills were the source of supply of sawn
lumber for all settlers in the district. It will be noticed
that they are all in the Niagara region, which contained at
that time almost all of the settlers in the central part of
Upper Canada.

In later years the saw-mill, like the grist-mill, usually
followed close upon settlement in any district, their number,
size and equipment increasing greatly after the War of
1812. Thomas Need, in the eighteen-thirties the owner of a
saw-mill around which grew the village of Bobcaygeon,
states that "the erection of a saw-mill is always the first
marked event in the formation of a settlement in the Bush.
. . . This induces many to come into the neighbourhood, from
the facility it offers for building. Then, as the settlement
increases, some bold man is persuaded to erect a grist- or
flour-mill, which again serves as an attraction; a growing
population requires the necessaries of life at hand; stores
are opened, a tavern licensed, and in a few years a thriving
village, or, as in the case of Peterborough, an important
town, springs up in the heart of the forest".[20]

Need's establishment, which may be taken as typical of
the smaller mills, sawed 2000 feet of planks a day from
about six logs costing 15s. After paying a sawyer 5s. and
a labourer 2s. per day he found that he had a profit of
£1 2s. 6d. a day, the lumber selling readily at 30s. per 1000
board feet. Concerning the activities of his mill he says
further: "Having little else to do at this season, I took
my turn at the mill regularly, until the yard was cleared
out and all the logs of the neighbours sawn up. The principal demand was for deals, though several oak, elm, and
cedar logs were cut up for furniture and other domestic
purposes." Need states that a considerable amount of

---

[19]The report is quoted in John Lynch: *Directory of the County of
Peel*. 1874. pp. 9-10.
[20]Thomas Need: *Six Years in the Bush*. 1838. pp. 106-7.

timber was brought to him by neighbours, especially in the early years of the mill's existence; and that, "according to the practice of the country they leave half their planks in return for the use of the mill".[21]

Saw-mills operating on a large scale were to be found in Upper Canada soon after the commencement of the nineteenth century. In 1816 the best in the province was located in Hawkesbury Township, on the Ottawa River. Some eighty men were employed at this establishment, which was first owned by one Mears of Hawkesbury, and later by an Irishman named Hamilton. From the first work of providing a few neighbouring settlers with boards for doors and sashes for windows, the saw-mills had developed into manufactories of large quantities of all kinds of sawn lumber, which could be purchased in the eighteen-twenties for $5 per thousand board feet. At that time the wood supply in the eastern United States was becoming exhausted, and sawn lumber exports from Canada were soon of great importance.

As time passed the trade became increasingly extensive, and in 1854 there were 1,618 saw-mills in Upper Canada, with a production of nearly 400,000,000 board feet of lumber; of these mills 1,449 were water-wheels. In 1861 the Canadian lumber exports were valued at $8,693,638. The sawn lumber trade with the United States reached the peak during the course of the Reciprocity Treaty, 1854 to 1866, which, with the American Civil War in the early sixties, created a period of great prosperity for Canadian lumbermen.

With the decline of the squared timber trade and the rise of that in sawn lumber the process of lumbering underwent some changes. The squaring of the logs, which often wasted nearly one-quarter of the wood, and always left the forests in a dangerous condition because of the debris, was no longer necessary, and the timber was merely run down to the nearest saw-mill; this was not infrequently, however, a distance of 200 miles. In difficult and dangerous rivers no driving was attempted, but the logs were merely thrown in from the roll-way, and such as reached the mill without being dashed to pieces were sawn up into lumber.

[21]*Ibid.*, p. 103.

On lakes and less turbulent rivers, or where locks had been
built making possible the avoidance of the worst rapids,
the lumbermen often carried a shanty along with them on
a crib. The drives of logs, kept together by large boom-logs
chained to one another, moved slowly along lake and river
with the aid of the current, horse-power or steam tugs. At
rapids the booms were released and the logs were guided
by the pike-poles of the men among the rocks or through
the chutes, to be collected again in the quiet water below.

The type of lumber varied with the locality. The Credit
River district was early noted for oak, and staves were
floated down to its mouth during the days of the squared
timber trade, and afterwards to the mills along its banks.
Many a log of fine walnut was sent down the Thames River
from Dorchester and vicinity, and brought 75c. each at
Detroit. A typical mill at the middle of the century was
that at Nassau, near Peterborough, early the centre of a
large lumber trade from the back lakes. This establishment,
one of the best in the province for some years, was erected
in 1854 by Charles Perry, and was situated three miles north
of the town. It is described as having "two 'Yankee Gangs',
a 'Slabber', 'Stock Gang', and an 'English Gate', containing
in all 130 saws, besides circulars for butting, cutting laths,
etc. It has also a very ingenious machine for grinding slabs.
This mill has cut 90,000 feet in twelve hours".[22] In 1866
the mills of Peterborough County sawed 50,650,000 feet of
lumber for export, most of it being shipped over the Midland Railway to Port Hope, and thence to the United States
by schooner.

In the seventies the export of forest products from
Canada amounted to over $20,000,000 annually. The Can-
adian lumber exports to Great Britain were first exceeded
by those to the United States during the years of the Civil
War; and thereafter the American trade gradually superseded the British, in spite of the fact that the United States
Government placed a tariff on milled lumber, though admitt-
ing saw-logs free of duty. During the last twenty-five
years the Canadian lumber exports have remained practically stationary, averaging about two billion board feet
valued at over $60,000,000 *per annum;* of the total the

[22]*Peterborough Directory.* 1858. p. 65.

United States receives nearly 85 *per cent.* and Great Britain less than ten *per cent.* In recent years the possibility of developing an extensive export of lumber to the Orient *viâ* the Panama Canal has become prominent. Lumber is not, however, the all-important feature of our export trade that it was in the pioneer period: in 1830 nearly eighty *per cent.* of the total exports were of wood, while in 1904 only about sixteen *per cent.* could be placed in that category. Saw-mills, too, have decreased in number, as there are at present only about 1,000 in the province.

From early days the lumber industry in Ontario has moved through a series of zones from the St. Lawrence and its tributaries to the Ottawa and the lower lakes, and thence to Georgian Bay, and beyond to Lake Superior and the Hudson's Bay slope. Soon after 1860 the lumbermen ascending the tributaries of the Ottawa were meeting those working inward along the rivers flowing into Lake Huron.

Since the eighteen-sixties the outstanding development in lumbering has been the pulp and paper industry, which has become increasingly important with the passing of the years. Soft woods, such as hemlock, spruce, balsam, jack pine and poplar, of comparatively small value as sawn lumber, are now extensively used in the manufacture of paper, particularly newsprint. Another important change has made the timber supply of the future more secure, for the various provinces of the Dominion have all established policies of forest conservation and reforestation, the principles of which were almost unknown in pioneer days.

The industry has followed the capitalistic trend of the times in that larger and larger companies, many of them directed by forestry experts, control most of the trade. With the exception, however, of the use of small railways in place of ox-teams for transport, and the introduction of improved machinery in mills, the lumberman's life has not materially changed since the old days when the turbulent rivermen floated their mighty timber rafts down the Ottawa, singing

"Oh, when we get down to Quebec town, the girls they dance for joy.
Says one unto another one, 'Here comes a shanty-boy!'

G. H. Andrews

From the *Illustrated London News*, January 3, 1863

BREAKING A TIMBER JAM

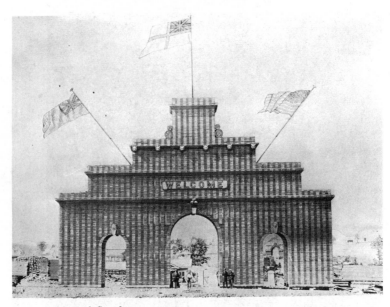

LUMBER ARCH, UNION SQUARE, OTTAWA, 1860

150,000 board feet without a nail; erected to welcome H.R.H. the Prince of Wales

From the *Illustrated London News*, October 20, 1860

THE PRINCE OF WALES DESCENDING A TIMBER SLIDE AT OTTAWA, 1860

One will treat us to a bottle, and another to a dram,
While the toast goes round the table for the jolly shanty-
    man.

I had not been in Quebec for weeks 'twas scarcely three,
When the landlord's lovely daughter fell in love with me.
She told me that she loved me and she took me by the hand,
And shyly told her mamma that she loved a shanty-man.

'O daughter, dearest daughter, you grieve my heart full
    sore,
To fall in love with a shanty-man you never saw before.'
'Well, mother, I don't care for that, so do the best you can,
For I'm bound to go to Ottawa with my roving shanty-
    man.' "[23]

[23]*Ye Maidens of Ontario.* The words and music may be found in
    Franz Rickaby: *Ballads and Songs of the Shantyboy.* 1926.
    pp. 79-81.

CHAPTER VI

MAPLE SUGAR MAKING

"Whan that Aprille with his shoures sote
The droghte of Marche hath perced to the rote,
And bathed every veyne in swich licour
Of which vertu engendred is the flour;
Whan Zephirus eek with his swete breeth
Inspired hath in every holt and heeth
The tendre croppes, and the yonge sonne
Hath in the Ram his halfe cours y-ronne,
And smale fowels maken melodye
That slepen al the night with open yë, ..."

GEOFFREY CHAUCER: Prologue to *The Canterbury Tales*. (1386).

AMONG the domestic manufactures of pioneer days few processes were more interesting or more important than the making of maple sugar. A comparatively small amount of coarse cane sugar was imported into Canada at the time, but it was obtainable only in the larger settlements and at high prices. While some settlers procured maple sugar from the Indians in trade, yet the scarcity of money prevented the purchase of things which could be made at home; so almost every farmer who had a sugar-bush spent a few weeks in the spring at sugar-making .

The art of making maple sugar, and the birch canoe, are among the few contributions of the American Indian to our civilisation. When the Jesuit missionaries began their work among the Indians shortly after 1600 they found them making sugar each spring in their primitive manner. In the Jesuit *Relations* there is reference to "a certain liquor that runs from the trees toward the end of Winter, and which is known as 'Maple Water'".[1] Father Paul LeJeune writes in 1634: "When they (the Indians) are pressed by famine they eat the shavings or bark of a certain tree, which they call *Micktan*, which they split in the Spring to get from it a juice, sweet as honey or as sugar. I have been told this by several, but they do not enjoy much of it, so scanty is the flow."[2] The only reference in the *Relations*

[1] R. G. Thwaites: *The Jesuit Relations and Allied Documents*. 1896-1901. Vol. LVI, p. 101.
[2] *Ibid.*, Vol. VI, p. 273.

252

to the process of manufacture is the following short account:

"There is no lack of sugar in these forests. In the Spring the maple trees contain a fluid somewhat resembling that which the canes of the islands contain. The women busy themselves in receiving it into vessels of bark when it trickles from these trees; they boil it, and obtain from it a fairly good sugar. The first which is obtained is always the best."[3]

The process of sugar-making among the early Indians was comparatively crude. They gashed the tree in a slanting direction with a tomahawk, and inserted a wooden chip or spout to carry the fluid drop by drop into birch bark receptacles resting on the ground. The Mohawk Indians commonly used a hollowed-out basswood log for a sap trough, the log being burned out as much as possible and then cleaned out with a stone adze.

Two methods of boiling the sap were in use. Earthenware pots were made by all but the Pacific coast Indians, and in these the sap was usually boiled; but when it was more convenient, red-hot stones were dropped into the sap trough, and, by removing these when cold and adding more hot stones, the sap was eventually boiled down, and the desired result achieved at the expense of a great deal of labour. Such primitive methods enabled the Indians to make only a comparatively small quantity of poor sugar, but it was highly prized as the only sugar available, and among some tribes it formed a considerable part of the food.

With the coming of the fur trader and settler, the Indians obtained iron kettles, and made sugar in a manner similar to, though somewhat cruder than that used by the early settlers. Thomas Need observed the Chippewas engaged in the work near Pigeon Lake in 1835, and wrote concerning the process:

"As soon as the sap begins to rise, which is early in April, the squaws betake themselves in families, or select parties, to the Maple Groves, or Sugar Bushes, as they are called; there they erect a camp, and prepare troughs and firewood, and collect all the kettles they can borrow or hire in the neighbourhood; this done, they begin to tap the trees

[3] *Ibid.*, Vol. LXVII, p. 95.

with a tomahawk, inserting a tube in each incision to receive the sap and conduct it into troughs underneath: each family or firm has its own bush, consisting generally of three or four hundred trees; these are visited in turn by two or more of the younger ladies, whose office it is to collect the sap and bring it to the fire.

"The most experienced among them is there placed to regulate the heat, which ought to be tolerably equal, and round her the rest of the party are busied in watching the process of boiling, and arranging the contents of the kettles; and finally, when by steady boiling the consistency of sugar is obtained, in delivering it over to others whose business it is to keep stirring the boiling mass as it gradually cools and settles. . . . There were several women and girls busily employed, while their lords and masters, as usual, were idling about or carelessly looking on. It is, however, but fair to state, that, as they do not assist in the labour, so neither do they share in the profits, which are sometimes considerable, and may always be looked upon as pretty pin-money for the ladies of the bush. . . .

"After the season was over, the party brought me a present of ten or twelve pounds of excellent sugar in return for the loan of my kettles." The sugar was weighed, and packed into neatly-sewn birch baskets by the Indians, and was then ready for the market. Need states that a camp produced between three and four hundred pounds in a favourable season.[4] Mrs. Simcoe notes in her diary that she purchased several baskets of maple sugar from the Indians, paying $3 for thirty pounds.[5]

Henry Schoolcraft, a noted authority on the Indians, describes the manufacture of maple sugar as "a sort of Indian carnival. The article is profusely eaten by all of every age, and a quantity is put up for sale in a species of boxes made from the white birch bark, which are called *mococks* or *mokuks*. . . . The boxes designed for sale are of all sizes; from twenty to seventy pounds weight. They are sold to merchants at six cents per pound, payable in merchandise. The number made in a single season by an industrious and strong-handed family is known to be from

[4]Thomas Need: *Six Years in the Bush.* 1838. pp. 104-6.
[5]*Diary of Mrs. John Graves Simcoe*, April 3, 1796.

thirty to forty, in addition to all the sugar that has been consumed".[6]

An early settler in Bruce County stated that a considerable amount of the maple sugar made in Canada by the Indians was sent to Montreal refineries, and eventually emerged as ordinary commercial brown sugar. He remembered seeing the northern Indians bringing their sugar to market: "A picturesque scene occurred in the spring of the year when the Indians came down from Manitoulin to sell their maple sugar. The journey was made in mackinaws,—open boats with a schooner rig; and the sugar was carried in mococks,—containers made of birch bark, each holding from twenty to thirty pounds."[7]

Early fur traders and *voyageurs* sometimes manufactured their own sugar, and during the process usually ate nothing but the product. Alexander Henry, one of the first British traders to enter the north-west after the British conquest, writes that "each man consumed a pound a day, desired no other food, and was visibly nourished by it".[8]

The method of sugar-making used by our pioneer settlers was capable of but little variation, and it is only in the last fifty years that there have been any appreciable changes in the process. The commencement of sugar-making depends upon the season: in some years the trees are tapped as early as February, in others as late as April; but as a general rule the work commences about the twentieth of March. The following description of the process is based largely upon the experiences of Colonel Samuel Strickland, a writer whose accounts of pioneer life are among the most authoritative.[9]

Before commencing actual operations it was necessary

---

[6]Henry Schoolcraft: *The Indian Tribes.* 1851-6. Vol. II, pp. 55-6.

[7]Reminiscences of John McNab, quoted in W. L. Smith: *Pioneers of Old Ontario.* 1923. p. 264.

[8]Alexander Henry: *Travels and Adventures in Canada and the Indian Territories, 1760-1776.* 1807. p. 218.

[9]See Samuel Strickland: *Twenty-seven Years in Canada West.* 1853. Vol. II, pp. 298-311. A detailed account of the maple industry from selecting the trees to making taffy may be found in W. M. Brown: *The Queen's Bush.* 1932, Chapter XXII. This is of special interest in that it describes a number of local variations in process as they applied to the Lake Huron and Georgian Bay counties, which were settled in the latter half of the nineteenth century.

to clear the sugar-bush of all underbrush, rotten logs and
fallen trees. The area was then usually fenced in so as to
prevent cattle from entering, for sometimes when this was
not done they would upset the troughs or drink so much
sap that they died from the effects. As near as possible to
the centre of the bush was located the boiling-place, and
from it roads radiated in all directions. These enabled an
ox-sled holding a barrel to be used in collecting the sap
from the buckets or troughs at the trees. A large store
trough, often a hollowed-out half-log, served to hold the sap
at the boiling-centre. This trough had frequently a capacity of over one hundred pails.

A round, wooden spout, hollow in the centre, and
variously known as a tap, spile or spigot, was inserted from
a half inch to an inch into the tree, the hole being best made
with an auger. A gash made by an axe was found to produce a better flow, but was hard on the tree, and the method
was therefore not generally used except when the trees
were soon to be cut down. The troughs, made of pine,
black ash, cherry, or butternut, were capable of holding
three or four gallons each, and were set exactly level immediately under the drip of the sap. In later days these
troughs were replaced by every variety of pail available on
the farm. The sap was found to run better on warm days
after frosty nights, and experience taught also that the tap
should be placed on the south side of the tree in the early
part of the season, but on the north side if it needed re-
newing towards the close of the run.

Iron or copper kettles were used in boiling the sap, and
care had to be taken to keep the fires burning day and
night. When the sap had been boiled down to a thin
molasses or syrup it was poured into a deep wooden vessel,
where it was allowed to settle; then the liquor was poured
into a copper boiler and clarified of earth and other impurities. Various clarifiers were used in pioneer days,
among them milk and eggs. Six eggs beaten up with about
a quart of syrup and poured into the sugar-boiler would
clarify fifty pounds of sugar. After the mixture was well
stirred the boiler was hung upon a crane over a slow fire,
and when the liquid began to simmer, the beaten eggs and
the impurities would rise to the surface. The moment the

boiling-point was reached the crane was swung off the fire, and the surface carefully skimmed; if this was properly done the molasses was bright and clear. It had still to be boiled down to sugar, and great care was necessary to prevent its boiling over. Various tests were applied to find when the syrup was sufficiently boiled down, one of the more common being to drop a little of the syrup into the snow, and if it hardened it was ready to remove from the fire. The syrup was then poured into pans and moulds, often of fancy shapes, and the cakes of maple sugar worth from 4d. to 7d. a pound were the result.

The first run was found to be best for sugar, so the more acid sap obtained towards the close of the season was often made into vinegar. The process was to boil down three pails of sap to one, adding a little yeast while the liquid was still warm. The barrel was then set in a sunny place to ferment. Some of the settlers discovered that maple sap would also make good beer, especially if essence of spruce or ginger was added to it. The juice from the yellow birch was similarly used by some settlers to make vinegar and beer. Occasionally, too, the sap of the black walnut was made into sugar, for Mrs. Simcoe in describing the refreshments served at Adam Green's house, near the head of Lake Ontario, states that "the sugar was made from black walnut trees, which looks darker than that from the maple, but I think it is sweeter".[10]

Samuel Strickland estimated that in a good season from eight to twelve hundred pounds of sugar and syrup might be made from a sugar-bush containing five hundred trees.[11] Bouchette's estimate of five and a quarter pounds per tree[12] may have applied occasionally in Quebec, but appears to be too high for an average yield in Upper Canada. In the pioneer period comparatively little syrup was made, almost all of the sap being boiled down into sugar. Robert Gourlay, writing a few years after the close of the War of 1812, found the sugar maple common in every settled district. He states that the sap was particularly useful "to the inhabitants in the early stages of their settlement; and

[10]Simcoe, *op. cit.*, June 12, 1796.
[11]Strickland, *op. cit.*, Vol. II, p. 300.
[12]J. Bouchette: *The British Dominions in North America*, 1831. Vol. I, p. 372.

might be rendered of more extensive and permanent use by proper attention to the preservation of the trees, the manner of tapping them, and some practical improvements in the process of reducing the sap to sugar".[13]

It was estimated that the amount of maple sugar made annually in the thirties and forties reached an average of 100 pounds per family;[14] but many settlers are known to have made from 1,000 to 3,000 pounds in a good season. As an example of maple sugar production at the middle of the century may be taken that of Oxford County, which in 1850 produced 477,320 pounds. In 1851 the production in Upper Canada totalled 3,669,874 pounds, and ten years later it was nearly double that amount.

After the middle of the century, however, the average farmer did not make maple sugar to the same extent as he had done earlier, the increase in total production being explained rather by the advance in population, and by the gradual development of maple sugaries where the manufacture of sugar was the main business of the farm. A contemporary writer states that the farmer soon found, after his land was mostly cleared, that his time could be spent more profitably on the cleared land than in the sugarbush; and "the moment he thinks he can earn on his cleared land in ten days as much as will purchase a larger quantity of sugar than he can make in ten days in the bush, he abandons sugar-making".[15] The increasing cheapness of imported cane sugar had, of course, an important influence on the Canadian maple sugar industry in that it obviated the necessity of domestic manufacture.

Sugar-making is referred to by a pioneer who engaged in it as "one of the most laborious processes which the early settler had to undertake".[16] It was one, too, in which accidents frequently occurred, resulting in considerable loss. Another writer, who was an observer rather than a participant, considered that the work was not usually laborious, but that "the sugar season is rather deemed one of festivity than toil".[17] There is no doubt, however, that sugar-

[13]Robert Gourlay: *A Statistical Account of Upper Canada*, 1822. Vol. I, pp. 151-2.
[14]Strickland, *op. cit.*, Vol. II, p. 298.
[15]Thomas Shenston: *The Oxford Gazetteer*. 1852. p. 64.
[16]Strickland, *op. cit.*, Vol. II, p. 304.
[17]Bouchette, *op. cit.*, Vol.I, p. 371.

From Henry Schoolcraft's *The Indian Tribes*

AN INDIAN SUGAR CAMP

From Carlile and Martindale's *Recollections of Canada.* 1873

A MAPLE SUGARY

Lieutenant Philip Bainbrigge

A BUSH ROAD IN UPPER CANADA, 1842

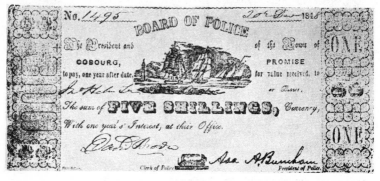

PAPER MONEY ISSUED BY THE VILLAGE OF COBOURG, 1848

making was usually a merry time among the young people,
for the approaching spring lent romance to the occasion.

"Soon the blue-birds and the bees
    O'er the stubble will be winging;
So 'tis time to tap the trees
    And to set the axe a-ringing;

Time to set the hut to rights,
    Where the girls and boys together
Tend the furnace fire o'nights
    In the rough and rainy weather;

Time to hew and shape the trough,
    And to punch the spile so hollow,
For the snow is thawing off
    And the sugar-thaw must follow.

Oh, the gladdest time of year
    Is the merry sugar-making,
When the swallows first appear
    And the sleepy buds are waking!"[18]

It is said that children seldom appeared in the sugar-
bush during the early stages of the process, but came in
large numbers, well-armed with spoons and ladles, when the
sugar or syrup was being made. The boiling-centre was a
favourite location for "sugar-eating bees" and other picnic
parties, but the depredations of the younger set were
usually regarded good-naturedly, for, after all, was not this
season one of the compensations for the many hardships of
pioneer life? Thomas Conant recommended the "sugaring-
off" as one of the greatest of life's pleasures:

"Reader, if you have not already tried it, don't fail to
make an effort to get to a sugaring-off, and my word for it
you will never regret it. . . . The wax is so sweet, so pure
and pleasant, and it's all so jolly, that such experiences are
always red-letter days in one's life calendar."[19]

During the past half century there has been an advance

[18]Quoted in William Canniff: *History of the Settlement of Upper
    Canada.* 1869. p. 203.
[19]Thomas Conant: *Life in Canada.* 1903. p. 128.

in maple sugar manufacture similar to that in other branches of agriculture. It is now a highly-organized commercial industry in which co-operative methods and labour-saving devices have been introduced; while at the same time much of the waste resulting from pioneer methods has been eliminated, and markets have been expanded. In early days the syrup made was often dark in colour and strong in taste, while now the best producers are exceedingly careful to maintain a reputation for fine quality, for the 50,000 Canadian manufacturers of maple products are in the business not to supply their own needs, as in pioneer days, but to sell in a competitive market in which only the highest grade commands adequate remuneration.

Some 8,000,000 trees are tapped annually in Eastern Canada, and produce on the average about two and a half pounds of sugar per tree. It is estimated by the Department of the Interior that there are approximately 60,000,000 sugar maples in Eastern Canada, so that the industry has by no means reached its maximum development. While in pioneer days comparatively little syrup was made, two-thirds of the total production is now in that form. The maple sugar output varies in direct ratio with the market price of cane sugar, the greatest production of maple sugar being in 1921 when cane sugar was very scarce. The industry is confined to the four eastern provinces, with Quebec the banner province, producing nine-tenths of the sugar and three-fourths of the syrup. Ontario comes second in production, Nova Scotia third and New Brunswick fourth.

A report on maple sugar production during 1931 is contained in a recent issue of the official monthly Dominion Government bulletin on agricultural statistics.[20] According to this report the production of maple sugar in Canada during the spring of that year was 5,484,100 pounds valued at $930,000, while that of maple syrup is placed at 1,314,700 gallons with a value of $2,606,900. The value of sugar and syrup was the lowest for some time, the highest point reached in the last six years being in 1929 when the total value of the output was $6,118,656.

Of the total production of sugar in 1931 Quebec supplied 4,726,000 pounds, Ontario 636,000 pounds, Nova

[20]Dominion Government *Bulletin on Agricultural Statistics*, June, 1931, pp. 184-5.

Scotia 63,000 pounds, and New Brunswick 58,500 pounds. Quebec's primacy is not so marked in the maple syrup branch, for that province produced 737,000 gallons, Ontario 572,400 gallons, and Nova Scotia and New Brunswick approximately three and two thousand gallons, respectively. The best remaining opportunities for the extension of the industry are to be found within the extensive Crown forest reserves in Eastern Canada, and in addition to legislation, and encouragement by its agencies, the government issues permits for the operation of sugaries on Crown lands.

The chief export market for Canadian maple products is the United States. In the calendar year 1930, out of 116,705 gallons of syrup exported, 114,202 gallons went to the United States, while of exports of maple sugar totalling 5,997,436 pounds, all but about 40,000 pounds went to the same market; most of these exports are used in the curing and manufacture of tobacco.

Discoveries of great practical value have recently been made by L. Skazin of the National Research Laboratories at Ottawa, and it is expected that they will enable the greater use of maple products as food, and in ice cream and confectionery manufacture. It will now be possible to prevent cakes of maple sugar from deteriorating into a hard and mottled condition; and, by a process of intensification, syrup can be made fifteen to twenty times stronger in maple flavour than heretofore.

It is quite apparent that, while the pioneer made the product almost entirely for his own consumption, the industry now relies to a large extent on the United States' market. But there are still many farmers who manufacture maple sugar in much the same manner as their forefathers did, and for them the season retains much of the *joie de vivre* of the "merry sugar-making" of pioneer days, so well described by Mrs. Susanna Moodie:

> "When the snows of winter are melting fast,
>   And the sap begins to rise,
> And the biting breath of the frozen blast
>   Yields to the Spring's soft sighs,
>   Then away to the wood,
>   For the maple, good,

Shall unlock its honied store;
And boys and girls,
With their sunny curls,
Bring their vessels brimming o'er
With the luscious flood
Of the brave tree's blood,
Into cauldrons deep to pour.

The blaze from the sugar-bush gleams red;
Far down in the forest dark,
A ruddy glow on the tree is shed,
That lights up the rugged bark;
And with merry shout,
The busy rout
Watch the sap as it bubbles high;
And they talk of the cheer
Of the coming year,
And the jest and the song pass by;
And brave tales of old
Round the fire are told,
That kindle youth's beaming eye."[21]

[21]Susanna Moodie: *The Maple Tree: A Canadian Song.* See 1923
Edition of *Roughing It in the Bush,* pp. 504-6.

CHAPTER VII

FISHING

"No life, my honest Scholar, no life so happy and so pleasant, as the life of a well-governed Angler; for when the Lawyer is swallowed up with business, and the Statesman is preventing or contriving plots, then we sit on Cowslip-banks, hear the birds sing, and possess ourselves in as much quietness as these silent silver streams, which we now see glide so quietly by us. Indeed, my good Scholar, we may say of Angling, as Dr. Boteler said of Strawberries. 'Doubtless God could have made a better berry, but doubtless God never did'; and so, if I might be Judge, 'God never did make a more calm, quiet, innocent recreation than Angling.' "

IZAAK WALTON: *The Compleat Angler.* (1653.)

EVEN before John Cabot returned from America in 1497 with the news that the shoals of fish off the Grand Banks were so great that they "stayed his ship", Basque fishermen are thought to have visited the fishing-grounds off Newfoundland. The first explorers of the interior of Canada found the fish in the same profusion. When Champlain passed through Lake Simcoe in 1615 he observed that the Indians carried on fishing "by means of a large number of stakes which almost close the strait, only some little opening being left where they place nets in which the fish are caught".[1] Because of the hurdles or stakes used in the construction of these fish-traps in the shallow water, the lake was sometimes known to the French as Lac aux Claies. The fishing industry was of similar importance along the St. Lawrence River in the latter part of the French period, and for a time fish were used in some localities as a type of money, in which the value of other commodities was measured.

When Alexander Henry, the famous fur trader, visited Cadot (Sault Ste. Marie) in 1762 he saw the Indians catching whitefish in the rapids with a long-handled net. He states that a skilful fisheman could sometimes catch as many as five hundred in two hours, some of them weighing from ten to fifteen pounds.[2] Another type of net, made from

[1] Samuel de Champlain: *Voyages.* (The Prince Society, Vol. III, p. 124.)

[2] Alexander Henry: *Travels and Adventures in Canada and the Indian Territories, 1760-76.* 1807. p. 59.

263

the bark of trees, was frequently used in the Straits of Mackinaw. In the days before the coming of the white man, and to a lesser extent afterwards, the Indians are known to have shot fish with arrows; but the spearing or netting of fish in summer, and in winter through holes in the ice, became common in the latter part of the French period, and only natives who had no contact with the white trader continued to use the more primitive bow and arrow.

It was customary for the Indians to come to the St. Lawrence and the Great Lakes on fishing expeditions twice a year; their wigwams were raised on the banks, and their encampments, with both men and women busily engaged in fishing or in curing, were an interesting sight to early travellers. In 1789, when Anne Powell was journeying from Montreal to Detroit, she observed the Indians fishing on the St. Lawrence:

"I walked out to enjoy a very fine evening. The bank of the River was very high and woody, the Moon shone bright through the trees; some Indians were on the river taking Fish with Harpoons, a mode of fishing I had never seen before. They make large fires in their Canoes which attract the fish to the surface of the water, when they can see by the light of the fire to strike them. The number of fires moving on the water had a pretty and singular effect."[3]

Methods which Indian and early trader used on the Humber River are typical of fishing during the last half of the eighteenth century. A traveller noted in 1760 "the extraordinary method of catching fish; one person holds a lighted torch, while the second strikes the fish with a spear. September is the season in which the salmon spawn in these parts, contrary to what they do in any other place I ever knew them before."[4]

Salmon-spearing was an occupation of intense enjoyment to the Indian, and one in which he would exert himself in body and mind for many hours at a stretch. There were two types of spears used,—the javelin, and the three-pronged fork, with an ash handle often twelve feet long. Night fishing was carried on by the Indians in canoes, by the use of a torch of birch bark at the end of a long pole; some-

[3]See W. R. Riddell: *Old Province Tales, Upper Canada.* 1920. p. 73.
[4]Quoted in K. M. Lizars: *The Valley of the Humber.* 1913. p. 113.

Royal Ontario Museum   Paul Kane

Spearing Salmon by Torchlight

From *Picturesque Canada*. 1879   H. Hamilton

A Trout Pool

FISHING SCENE AT WELLINGTON, LAKE ONTARIO, 1840

THE FISH MARKET, TORONTO, 1840

The site of the St. Lawrence Market. At the rear right is Weller's
Stage Office, at the junction of Front, Wellington and Church Streets

times, however, they attracted the fish by lighting a fire on
the bank of the river. Early traders and settlers improved
upon the Indian method by using a jack-light in the bow of
canoe or bateau. The socket in which the light was placed
was a circular iron grate on pivots that kept the fire upright, and pieces of pitch-pine, about eight inches long and
one and a half thick, would make a flare three feet high.

An adaptation of the Indian fire on the shore was a stage
erected in the river and supplied with a torch-light; from
this platform, or from a boat close by, men speared the
fish as they went up stream. If shoals of fish appeared,
two men sometimes killed enough during one night to fill
eight or ten barrels holding 200 pounds each.

During the day fish could frequently be speared from a
boat if the sun was bright. A more common method of
fishing by day, however, was to fell a tree at the water's
edge, and spear them from it; quiet and careful fishermen
could catch forty or fifty in a few hours in this manner.
A spearman had to learn to strike nearer than the fish appeared, or he almost invariably missed his object. Eels
were sometimes speared, but were more often caught on
night-lines.

In the eighteen-forties Paul Kane, the artist, saw the
Indians of the Middle West engaged in the spearing of fish,
and the sight recalled his boyhood days at York:

"We saw some Indians spearing salmon; by night this
has a very picturesque appearance, the strong red glare of
the blazing pine knots and roots in the iron frame, or light-
jack, at the bow of the canoe, throwing the naked figures of
the Indians into wild relief upon the dark water and sombre
woods. . . . As the light is intense, and being above the head
of the spearsman, it enables him to see the fish distinctly at
a great depth, and at the same time it apparently either
dazzles or attracts the fish. In my boyish days I have seen
as many as 100 light-jacks gliding about the Bay of Toronto,
and have joined in the sport."[5]

A method of fishing through the ice is described by
Samuel Hearne, the noted explorer of the Canadian north-
land:

"Angling for fish under the ice in winter requires no

[5]Paul Kane: *Wanderings of an Artist among the Indians of North
America*. 1859. pp. 30-2 .

other process than cutting round holes in the ice from one to two feet in diameter, and letting down a baited hook, which is always kept in motion, not only to prevent the water from freezing so soon as it would do if suffered to remain quite still, but because it is found at the same time to be a great means of alluring the fish to the hole."[6]

Mrs. Simcoe fished in a similar manner for red trout through the ice of the Don and Humber Rivers: "At the mouth of the Don I fished from my carriole, but the fish are not to be caught, as they were last winter, several dozen in an hour. It is said that the noise occasioned by our driving constantly over this ice frightens away the fish, which seems probable, for they are still in abundance in the Humber, where we do not drive. Fifteen dozen were caught there a few days ago."[7]

Thomas Need noticed that the Chippawa Indians exercised great patience in the spearing of fish in Pigeon Lake a century ago:

"We observed some forty or fifty or them in picturesque gipsy-like tents, watching for fish. They will stand many hours together over a hole in the ice, darkened by blankets, with a fish-spear in one hand, and a wooden decoy fish, attached to a line, in the other, waiting for a maskelongy or pike, which they strike with almost unerring certainty the moment the bait is seized. In this way a skilful fisherman will sometimes catch 150 or 200 lbs. weight of fish in a day; though, of course, very frequently they are a long time unsuccessful."[8]

One calm night in April, Need took his birch canoe, "fetched a spear and torch, and sallied forth amongst the floating ice, with so much success that in two hours I had captured nearly a hundred weight of fish. . . . As I was slowly moving along, a huge fish made a stroke at the gaily-painted paddle: he took me so entirely by surprise that I lost my equilibrium, and nearly upset the boat; and instead of spearing him, which I might easily have done, I was only thankful when he discovered his error and released his hold".[9]

[6]Samuel Hearne: *A Journey from Hudson's Bay to the Northern Ocean in the Years 1769-1772.* 1795. Journal, March 9, 1770.
[7]*Diary of Mrs. John Graves Simcoe,* February 3, 1796.
[8]Thomas Need: *Six Years in the Bush.* 1838. pp. 44-5.
[9]*Ibid.,* p. 104.

Until about a century ago sea salmon used to run up the
St. Lawrence River into Lake Ontario, where they were
caught in large quantities in the streams which flow into the
lake. Isaac Weld, who travelled in Canada in 1796, wrote:
"Lake Ontario, and all the rivers which fall into it, abound
with excellent salmon and many different kinds of sea fish
which come up the St. Lawrence."[10] For some unexplained
reason they stopped running up, and have never been seen
since. As their disappearance coincided rather closely with
the extensive use of steamboats, it has been suggested that
this was the cause of it; but there were other reasons of
more importance. The lack of salmon-leaps in streams
caused serious injuries to many fish, while thousands were
slaughtered or taken in gill nets at the foot of falls or mill-
dams which they could not surmount. Travellers noted
that huge numbers of fish were caught below Niagara Falls,
which blocked their further passage up the river. A very
early visitor, who estimated the height of Niagara at from
700 to 800 feet, stated that "the Beasts and Fish that are
thus killed by the prodigious Fall serve for food to fifty
Iroquese, who are settled about two Leagues off, and take
'em out of the water with their Canows".[11]

In addition to these hazards, and the reckless slaughter
of the salmon, the sawdust from mills was injurious to all
types of fish and helped to deplete the fisheries. As early
as 1806 an effort was made to conserve salmon, when an
Act was passed forbidding the netting of these fish in the
creeks of the Home and Newcastle Districts; in general,
however, effective measures were not taken until it was too
late to save the fisheries.

Reports from a variety of sources testify to the abundance of fish in Upper Canada during the pioneer period.[12]
The garrisons at the forts varied their food, and at the same
time amused themselves, by netting large numbers of whitefish and sturgeon, some of the latter caught at Niagara
being six feet long; while along the Detroit River the

[10]Isaac Weld: *Travels through the States of North America.* 1799.
    p. 295.
[11]Louis Lahontan: *Nouveaux Voyages dans L'Amérique Septentrion-
    ale.* 1703. Thwaites Edition, Vol. I, p. 137.
[12]See Vol. I, Chapter XV, of Robert Gourlay: *A Statistical Account
    of Upper Canada,* 1822, for a full description of the fish found
    in Upper Canada in the early pioneer period.

soldiers sometimes speared large sturgeon with their swords. The reminiscences of early inhabitants contain many allusions to the numbers and size of fish in the lakes and rivers of Upper Canada, and the ease with which they could be caught. Referring to the early years of the nineteenth century, one settler states that "a crotched pole would procure salmon in any of the creeks which flow into Lake Ontario";[13] another recalls that an old man speared seventy salmon in one afternoon.[14] Fishing was often left to the boys, because men were too busy in pioneer days to spare the time for such an occupation; and it is said that "the fish were so plentiful that the boys often waded in and threw them out with their bare hands. Few people had time for angling in those days so a pitchfork was used to catch all the fish you needed. By the use of a jack-light of fat pine it was no trouble for a few boys to throw out a wagon-load of fish in an evening".[15]

For many years pike were very plentiful in early spring in the creeks flowing into the Great Lakes; while whitefish and herring were caught in large numbers in the lakes in summer, and in November with seines in the creeks. Thomas Conant writes that schools of fish used to be so numerous along the shore near Oshawa that at times they prevented canoes from making any progress.[16] A century ago the harbour of Goderich "appeared to swarm with fish. When the sun shone brightly you could see hundreds lying near the surface. There was no difficulty in catching them, for the moment you threw in your bait you had a fish on your hook".[17]

The following description, which has reference to Wilmot's Creek, a stream flowing through Clarke Township into Lake Ontario, is quoted from a report prepared in 1869 by Messrs. Whitcher and Venning of the Federal Department of Fisheries, and may be taken as typical of the remarkable fishing to be found everywhere:

"In early times it was famous for salmon, great num-

[13]Reminiscences of Roger Bates, Coventry Papers. (Public Archives of Canada.)
[14]Reminiscences of Catharine Chrysler White, Coventry Papers.
[15]Letter of Dr. William Herriman to the *Cobourg World*, November 26, 1920.
[16]Thomas Conant: *Life in Canada*. 1903. p. 30.
[17]Samuel Strickland: *Twenty-seven Years in Canada West*. 1853. Vol. I, p. 270.

bers of which frequented it every autumn for the purpose of spawning. They were so plentiful forty years ago that men killed them with clubs and pitchforks, women seined them with flannel petticoats, and settlers bought and paid for farms and built houses from the sale of salmon. Later they were taken by nets and spears, over a thousand often being caught in the course of one night."[18]

Those who had no time to engage in the sport had no need to go without, for fish were traded to settlers by the Indians at a very low price. Mrs. Traill obtained a twenty-pound maskinonge from a Mississaga Indian for a loaf of bread; on the Humber River a salmon of ten to twenty pounds brought "one shilling, a gill of whisky, a cake of bread, or the like trifle";[19] while Samuel Strickland writes that "the Indians on Lake Huron traded fresh salmon trout for whisky and apples. One of our passengers purchased the largest I ever saw for a quart of whisky: it weighed no less than seventy-two pounds".[20]

Though stories are common of the great number of huge fish to be caught in pioneer days, the imagination of the people does not appear to have run to accounts of sea-serpents. Yet they were not without their fish stories. Among the notable tales related as truth was the statement that seals were to be found in both Lake Ontario and Rice Lake, (perhaps this is the origin of the present "Rice Lake Hudson seal" coats!); while the appearance of a Lake Superior mermaid, seen in 1782, was described and sworn to before the Court of King's Bench in Montreal. In Mrs. Simcoe's diary there is an interesting fish story which sh describes as follows, under date of February 18, 1796: "I heard an anecdote of black bass, which, if true, renders it probable they remain in a torpid state during the winter. An old hollow tree, which lay on the margin of the lake (Simcoe), half under water, being stopped and taken out, thirty black bass were taken out of it."[21]

In the "back" lakes and rivers trout were to be found in large quantities, as well as bass, maskinonge, whitefish, and

[18]The report is quoted in E. T. D. Chambers: *The Fisheries of Ontario*. (In *Canada and its Provinces*, Vol. XVIII, p. 604.)
[19]Lizars, *op. cit.*, p. 115.
[20]Strickland, *op. cit.*, Vol. II, pp. 132-3.
[21]Simcoe, *op. cit.*, February 18, 1796.

many other varieties, and they formed no small part of the menu of settlers. As the intensive work of settlement in the woods gradually decreased, men found time occasionally for sport, and great sport it must have been. John Langton, who settled on Sturgeon Lake in 1833, writes: "The bass is our staple commodity, and a most excellent one it is; if you are on the lake, tie a line, baited with a piece of red cloth, round your wrist, and proceed on your journey, and it is ten to one that before you have proceeded a quarter of a mile you will feel your prize." Langton states that maskinonge and eel were generally speared; and he considered whitefish, salted in barrels, almost as good food as herrings.[22]

Samuel Strickland, early settled near Peterborough, refers to the excellent fishing in Stoney Lake, at the foot of Burleigh Falls. In October, 1849, he camped there, and "one morning between breakfast and dinner my two eldest sons and myself caught with our trolling-lines thirty-five salmon trout, eight maskinonge, and several large lake bass, the total weight of which amounted to 473 pounds."[23] Twenty years earlier Colonel Strickland had been an employee of the Canada Company, which was organized to establish settlers in Upper Canada, particularly on the "Huron Tract". While in that district he often engaged in trout fishing on the Speed River, which he found "without exception the best for that species of fish I ever saw. I have frequently caught a pailful of these delicious trout in the space of two or three hours".[24]

It was not necessary in early times for Great Lakes fishermen to go far from shore to lay their nets. The *Cobourg Star* of June 28, 1831, describes "a very animating scene witnessed by us with much delight on Friday last, on the beach immediately in front of our town". A large net had been placed between the two piers then being constructed to form a harbour. Shortly afterwards the net was pulled in amid intense excitement, for most of the inhabitants of the village had come down to see the result. A haul of over twelve hundred fish was made, and the net

[22]John Langton: *Early Days in Upper Canada, Letters of John Langton*. 1926. pp. 34-5.
[23]Strickland, *op. cit.*, Vol. II, p. 238.
[24]*Ibid.*, Vol. I, p. 218.

set out again with almost equal success. "So", the *Star* says, "a sufficient supply being obtained, the whole were distributed with impartial and praiseworthy liberality among all present, every man, woman and child being loaded with large portions of this wholesome and nutritious food."[25]

Almost every settlement along the main lakes and rivers had its quota of fishermen. York's earliest fish market is described in an interesting manner by Dr. Scadding:

"In the interval between the points where now Princess Street and Caroline Street descend to the water's edge was a favourite landing-place for the small craft of the bay—a wide and clean gravelly beach, with a convenient ascent to the cliff above. Here, on fine mornings at the proper season, skiffs and canoes, log and birch bark, were to be seen putting in, weighed heavily down with fish, speared or otherwise taken during the preceding night in the lake, bay or neighbouring river. Occasionally a huge sturgeon would be landed, one struggle of which might suffice to upset a small boat. Here were to be purchased in quantities, salmon, pickerel, masquelonge, whitefish and herrings; with the smaller fry of perch, bass and sunfish. Here, too, would be displayed unsightly catfish, suckers, lampreys, and other eels; and sometimes lizards, young alligators for size. Specimens, also, of the curious steel-clad, inflexible, vicious-looking pipe-fish were not uncommon."[26]

The preserving of fish by salting them in barrels was early practised by the settlers in Upper Canada. A supply of food for future use was thereby obtained, and in addition there soon developed a trade, both local and with the United States, in barrelled fish. Salted salmon was worth from 30s. to 35s. a barrel of 200 pounds, while Lake Erie white-fish, caught in seines, sold at from 27s. to 32s. per barrel.

Fishing gradually assumed a position of prime importance. In the period just previous to the War of 1812 hauls of whitefish of one thousand or more were commonly taken at Niagara, and at almost any village on the shores of the Great Lakes. In later years, when fishing developed on a large scale, the hauls were much greater. A resident of Barrie recalled that he "once helped haul in a net near

[25]*Cobourg Star*, June 28, 1831.
[26]Henry Scadding: *Toronto of Old*, 1873. p. 31.

Willard's Beach, in Prince Edward County, that contained 14,000 fish".[27] In some parts of Lakes Erie and Ontario single hauls of 90,000 whitefish were not unusual. In the Detroit River fish used to be driven into pens where they were captured and dried by hundreds of thousands, to be used later as fertilizer; similarly, Lake Ontario whitefish were sold to farmers in the eighteen-sixties and used for manuring the land.

In addition to the eventual depletion of the fisheries, another result of the wasteful methods of netting fish was a demoralised market. People still living remember when fisherwomen carried large baskets through the streets and sold choice fish for five cents each. The slaughter continued, however, in spite of low prices, and it was not long before the waters were comparatively barren. Only in recent times has commercial fishing recovered through restocking from government hatcheries; and there are now several thousand men engaged in the industry in Ontario.

Commercial fishing first became important in the thirties and forties, and groups of hardy fishermen carried on the industry at almost every port, where their nets, drying in the sun, were long a characteristic sight. Towards the middle of the century the coastal fisheries had become depleted, and nets were of necessity laid at a considerable distance from shore. To row or sail small boats far out into the lake was dangerous, for sudden storms often arose. On April 1, 1875, a harrowing lake tragedy occurred off Cobourg. Four boats had gone out several miles from shore to inspect their nets, but an unexpected storm alarmed them and they attempted to return to the harbour. Two of the boats finally reached Cobourg with their crews in a state of complete exhaustion; but the other two never returned. Six men and three young boys lost their lives on this occasion, long remembered as one of the greatest tragedies among Great Lakes fishermen.

[27]Reminiscences of Henry Smith, in W. L. Smith: *Pioneers of Old Ontario*. 1923. p. 88.

CHAPTER VIII

PIONEER CO-OPERATION—"BEES"

"Many and sundry are the means which Philosophers and Physicians have prescribed to exhilarate a sorrowful heart, to divert those fixed and intent cares and meditations; but, in my judgment, none so present, none so powerful, none so apposite, as a cup of strong drink, mirth, musick and merry company".

ROBERT BURTON: *The Anatomy of Melancholy*. (1652.)

"After the specific duties of the bee were ended, the young men indulged in trials of strength, while their elders discussed the crops, prices, local politics and the prospects of the ensuing year. The elderly women extended the circulation of the personal gossip of the neighbourhood, while the younger ones, after disposing of the rude accompaniments of the feast, were ready for the dance, the round of country games and the repartee of flirtation."

ADAM SHORTT.[1]

ONE of the most notable characteristics of pioneer life in Canada was the spirit of co-operation. Remarkable generosity both in time and money is exemplified by the rebuilding of settlers' homes when destroyed by fire, the loss usually being entirely made up by the voluntary work and subscription of neighbours. One example out of many that might be quoted is noted in the *Cobourg Star* of January 25, 1831, where a fire is described which destroyed the cedar log home of one of the citizens. The account continues: "The loss of Mr. Hart, including upwards of $60 in cash, must at least amount to £150. We cannot express in too strong language the praiseworthy liberality that has been evinced by the inhabitants of our village upon this occasion. A subscription already amounting to upwards of £70 has been raised, and we have no doubt the entire loss of Mr. Hart will be made up to him."[2]

Such generosity is the more commendable when it is remembered that money was exceedingly scarce a century ago, and most people found it difficult to pay their taxes in cash, barter or long-term credit being usual in other business transactions. An example of praiseworthy co-operation is

[1] Adam Shortt: *The Life of a Settler in Western Canada before the War of 1812*. (Queen's University *Bulletins of History*, Vol. XII, p. 10.)

[2] *Cobourg Star*, January 25, 1831.

afforded by the action of the early settlers in a township where religious feeling ran high. The "Cavan Blazers", ardent Orangemen of the northern part of Durham County, had many a "run-in" with the Irish Roman Catholics of Peterborough County; but when the only Roman Catholic settler in Cavan took sick at harvest-time, the Blazers came secretly and prevented loss by harvesting his crop.

In many another way was pioneer life made bearable through co-operation. Roads were built by the subscription and labour of those who lived in the district through which they were to pass; settlers took turns in getting mail and supplies for their neighbours; but the most notable means of aiding one another was the "bee", or gathering of neighbours to help with farm work, a form of co-operation prevalent throughout the pioneer period and which still survives in barn-raisings and harvesting bees.

All bees provided entertainment and social intercourse as well as hard work. On that account they were usually called "frolics" in New Brunswick and the United States. Besides large quantities of food and drink, it was customary to provide a dance or "hoe-down" as the main amusement, while those who chose not to dance engaged in sports, games, and conversation. In pioneer days almost every activity was the occasion of a bee. Mrs. Moodie observed that "people in the woods have a craze for giving and going to bees, and run to them with as much eagerness as a peasant runs to a race-course or a fair; plenty of strong drink and excitement making the chief attraction of the bee".[3]

When new settlers arrived in a district it was quite usual for those already located to help construct the first shanties for the newcomers. The next work was the clearing of a piece of land, an almost endless task if one worked alone. A good workman might clear an acre of land in a week, but he could not burn it all. A half dozen men working together sometimes chopped and burned an acre in a day, but as a general rule a settler was fortunate if he could clear ten acres per year. There were various methods of clearing the land for cultivation: "slashing" was the

[3]Susanna Moodie: *Roughing It in the Bush.* 1852. Edition of 1923, p. 305.

felling of the trees with the intention of leaving them where they fell, and burning them later when they were dry; "windrow felling" was the same procedure except that the trees were so cut that they fell in rows; while "girdling" or "ringing" consisted of the clearing away of underbrush, and then cutting a ring in the bark of the larger trees and allowing them to stand until dead, a method which saved time but was not advantageous in producing good crops.

The devastation which resulted from this means of killing trees is well described by Mrs. Anna Jameson, who saw, on the main road between Hamilton and Brantford, "a space of about three miles, bordered entirely on each side by dead trees, which had been artificially blasted by fire, or by girdling. It was a ghastly forest of tall white spectres, strangely contrasting with the glowing luxurious foliage all around. . . . Without exactly believing the assertion of the old philosopher, that a tree feels the first stroke of the axe, I know I never witness nor hear that first stroke without a shudder; and as yet I cannot look on with indifference, far less share the Canadian's exultation, when these huge oaks, these umbrageous elms and stately pines, are lying prostrate, lopped of all their honours, and piled in heaps with the brushwood, to be fired,—or burned down to a charred and blackened fragment,—or standing leafless, sapless, seared, ghastly, having been 'girdled' and left to perish".[4]

Settlers of means frequently hired "American choppers", Irish immigrants, half-breeds, or other inhabitants anxious to earn extra money, to clear their land at a price varying from $10 to $20 an acre; but whatever means was chosen it was usual for chopping and burning to continue all the first summer, and thereafter during the winter. When oxen were not available the laborious "hand-log" method had to be used to remove the timber. In some low-lying districts, such as Lambton County and the front of Glengarry, logging was complicated by the superabundance of water. When the land was but little above the level of lake or river the soil was often of such gluey nature that oxen and logs sank in sloughs of mud.

[4]Anna Jameson: *Winter Studies and Summer Rambles in Canada.* 1838. Vol. II, pp. 102-3.

In general, however, logging was not beset with such difficulties. At the middle of the nineteenth century much of Huron County was in process of settlement, and one settler in McGillivray Township describes how he chopped eight acres the first winter, "and next spring my wife and I logged most of it by hand. I cut the logs in short lengths so that they would be easier to handle, and cut the trees off close to the ground so that the stumps would not be in the way of cultivation. It was certainly no light winter's work to cut up the trees, many two and three feet through, growing on eight acres".[5] John McDonald, who settled in 1855 in Kincardine Township, Bruce County, did what thousands of pioneers had done from Loyalist times down through the years: "For four successive years I spent the winters in chopping, the springs in burning and seeding, and the summers in working for other farmers at 'the front' ".[6]

It was so difficult to do this work alone that the logging bee was early the most typical example of pioneer co-operation. All the settlers living within a radius of fifteen or twenty miles were invited to the bee, and always brought oxen and implements with them. Sometimes a "butler" or "boss" was placed in charge to give the necessary directions, and after underbrushing the piece of land the workers proceeded with logging.

The trees were usually chopped down in such a manner that they would fall in heaps as far as possible. Several large piles were formed on each acre of land and all the logs were dragged thither by oxen, while men with handspikes built up the heaps until they were about eight feet high. When the region had been entirely cleared, the piles were fired with the help of underbrush and branches.

There was no thought of saving any of the timber: it had to be got rid of as quickly as possible. As the wood was green it often required several burnings to dispose of the piles of logs. The collecting and burning of the half-burnt wood was sometimes called "the branding". Charred logs and rotten wood were gathered by three or four men and a yoke of oxen dragging a single chain between them; a

[5] Reminiscenses of Linwood Craven, quoted in W. L. Smith: *Pioneers of Old Ontario*. 1923. p. 239.
[6] Reminiscences of John McDonald, quoted in Smith, *op. cit.*, p. 256.

James Weston

A Logging Bee in Muskoka

From F. G. Weir's *Scugog and its Environs*

OLD SQUARE LOG SCHOOLHOUSE ON SCUGOG ISLAND

Robert Harris, C.M.G., R.C.A.
Reproduced by Permission of the National Gallery of Canada

A MEETING OF SCHOOL TRUSTEES

"yoke and bow" was used when the larger logs were dragged
away, while men picked up the smaller pieces. Walter
Riddell, an early settler near Cobourg, describes a day in
the branding-field as one long to be remembered: "With
a blazing sun overhead and ashes heated like unto a fiery
furnace underneath, the men looked like a lot of chimney-
sweeps after a day at branding."[7] Women still living recall
the noisy shouting at the oxen as the men laboured all day
at this work, and the preparation of meals "for thirty
blackened men" at the close of the bee.[8] In new settlements
during July the whole countryside was illuminated by the
burning of log heaps. To see a hundred of these fires
blazing at once on a dark night was a spectacle not soon
forgotten.

To save the work of chopping the trees into lengths
which could be readily handled, small fires, in some districts
called "niggers", were occasionally used. These were placed
on top of the logs at intervals of twenty or thirty feet, and
kept burning until the logs were burned through. A settler
in Zorra Township, Oxford County, sent back word to his
friends in Scotland that he had one hundred niggers working for him; whereupon "the whole parish was agog with
excitement over the Zorra man's wonderful wealth in con-
trolling the services of no less than one hundred negroes".[9]

In later years when the farmer had more leisure the
best ashes were usually collected, and either made into potash or sold to a potashery in the nearest village. There was
a ready market for pot and pearl ashes in the early days,
the product being usually shipped to Montreal in large barrels. The ashes from ten acres of forest would make about
five barrels (2500 pounds) of potash, for which a price of
from 9s. to 25s. or more per cwt. was obtained, the price
depending upon the condition of the market and the grade
of the product. Samuel Strickland considered that a settler
should receive at least 25s. per cwt. to recompense him for
his work.[10]

The ashes were usually stored and kept dry in small log

[7] Reminiscences of Walter Riddell, Hamilton Township, in the
    Farmer's Sun, August 4, 1898.
[8] Reminiscences of Mrs. (Dr.) Richard Jones, Cobourg. (Unpublished.)
[9] W. A. Mackay: *Pioneer Life in Zorra*. 1899. pp. 167-8.
[10] Samuel Strickland: *Twenty-seven Years in Canada West*. 1853.
    Vol. I, p. 169 fn.

houses built for the purpose, and those settlers who wished to avoid the difficult process of potash-making, sold the ashes for about 4d. a bushel, or took a little whisky or other goods in exchange. One writer advised intending immigrants that "when potash brings a good price, and the land to be cleared has those sorts of timber growing on it the most proper for the purpose, the ashes will often pay for clearing the land. If not preserved at all, land can be hired to be chopped, logged, burned, and fenced at from 45s. to 52s. per acre".[11] Advances in chemistry had seriously affected the ash trade by the late thirties, and eventually put an end to it altogether; but many farmers long continued to make lye from ashes, and, by the addition of grease, to manufacture their own soft soap.

Lime-burning was a process often connected with the logging bee. Large quantities of lime were necessary for filling cracks in the walls, and building chimneys for the log house. It could be purchased at from 6d. to 1s. 3d. per bushel, but many settlers burned their own. The timber from at least half an acre of land was formed into an immense pile, on the top of which was constructed a frame in which to place the limestone. Some twenty ox-cart loads of the stone were then drawn and thrown on top of the heap, after being broken into small pieces by a sledge hammer. The pile was then fired and would be consumed over night, though the red coals remained hot for a week, when the white lime could be collected and covered. Colonel Strickland held such a lime-burning in 1826 at his farm in Douro Township, Peterborough County, and wrote that about one hundred bushels of lime were obtained, sufficient for all purposes for a house thirty-six feet by twenty-four feet.[12]

Enterprising settlers sometimes obtained charcoal from their timber, though charcoal-burning was never practised in Canada on so extensive a scale as was long characteristic of England. John Thomson, who was located near Lake Simcoe, noted in his diary on several occasions that his men were engaged in the work; in October, 1834, for example, he writes that "five hands commenced cutting basswood

11Joseph Pickering: *Inquiries of an Emigrant.* 1831. 4th Edition, 1832, p. 107 fn.
12Strickland, *op. cit.*, Vol. I, pp. 97-8.

logs and splitting them to make a charcoal heap."[13]   A
settler's first logging, however, almost always resulted in
the burning of all the timber. In later years it was customary to save some of the best pieces for building purposes, and to split logs for rail fences, but it long remained
usual to burn up the greater part of the wood cleared from
the land, and often none whatever was saved.

The free use of liquor at logging bees was characteristic.
In some districts it was customary to provide whisky for
the men in the proportion of one gallon to each yoke of
oxen; while in others a copious supply, without limit, was
available. What was not consumed during the bee lasted
through the night. Sometimes the workers at a logging
were divided into gangs, and each had a certain proportion
of the fallow to clear. Whisky played no small part in keeping up the excitement of the contest, and in urging all to
work at the highest pitch, but it also led to occasional cheat-
ing and considerable fighting. J. W. Dunbar Moodie's short
parody well describes the usual events at a logging:

"There was a man in our town,
In our town, in our town—
There was a man in our town,
He made a logging bee;
And he bought lots of whisky,
To make the loggers frisky—
To make the loggers frisky,
At his logging bee.

The Devil sat on a log heap,
A log heap, a log heap—
A red-hot burning log heap—
A-grinning at the bee;
And there was lots of swearing,
Of boasting and of daring,
Of fighting and of tearing,
At that logging bee."[14]

It is no wonder that the better-class settlers, and especially women bred in homes of refinement, evinced a pronounced aversion to bees of all kinds, and particularly to

[13]Diary of John Thomson, October 14, 1834. (Archives of Ontario.)
[14]Quoted in Moodie, op. cit., p. 304.

those at which excesses were the rule. Mrs. Moodie presents the case very strongly, and shows that the amount of work accomplished at a bee was often less than expected:

"A logging bee followed the burning of the fallow as a matter of course. In the bush, where hands are few and labour commands an enormous rate of wages, these gatherings are considered indispensable, and much has been written in their praise; but to me they present the most disgusting picture of a bush life. They are noisy, riotous, drunken meetings, often terminating in violent quarrels, sometimes even in bloodshed. Accidents of the most serious nature often occur, and very little work is done when we consider the number of hands employed, and the great consumption of food and liquor. I am certain, in our case, had we hired with the money expended in providing for the bee, two or three industrious, hard-working men, we should have got through twice as much work, and have had it done well, and have been the gainers in the end. . . . We had to endure a second and a third repetition of this odious scene before sixteen acres of land were rendered fit for the reception of our fall crop of wheat."

The logging bee from which Mrs. Moodie drew her conclusions was held on a hot July day in 1834, and consisted of thirty-two men. Mistress and maid were busy for two days previous preparing vast quantities of food. The men, a typical aggregation, included half-pay officers and various types and nationalities of settlers of lower rank: "the four gay, reckless, idle sons of ——, famous at any spree, but incapable of the least mental or physical exertion; . . . the two R—s, who came to work and to make others work; my good brother-in-law, who had volunteered to be the Grog Boss; . . . the Youngs, the hunters, with their round, black, curly heads and rich Irish brogue; . . . the ruffian squatter P—, from Clear Lake,—the dread of all honest men; the brutal M—, who treated oxen as if they had been logs, by beating them with handspikes; and there was 'Old Wittals' . . ., the largest eater I ever chanced to know; . . . . there was John—, from Smith-town the most notorious swearer in the district; . . . there was a whole group of Dummer Pines . . . , all good men and true."

At dinner time all sat down to "the best fare that could

be procured in the bush: pea soup, legs of pork, venison, eel, and raspberry pies, garnished with plenty of potatoes, and whisky to wash them down, besides a large iron kettle of tea. . . . My brother and his friends, who were all temperance men, and consequently the best workers in the field, kept me and the maid actively employed in replenishing their cups". While some of the men "were pretty far gone" by that time, there was nothing particularly objectionable until supper, when "those who remained sober ate the meal in peace, and quietly returned to their homes, while the vicious and the drunken stayed to brawl and fight. . . . Unfortunately we could hear all the wickedness and profanity going on in the next room. . . . The house rang with the sound of unhallowed revelry, profane songs, and blasphemous swearing. It would have been no hard task to have imagined these miserable, degraded beings, fiends instead of men. How glad I was when they at last broke up and we were once more left in peace to collect the broken glasses and cups, and the scattered fragments of that hateful feast".[15]

Similar conclusions as to the inefficacy of bees were reached by the Rev. William Proudfoot, who lived in the London District. Some ninety men, though not all at one time, were busy for three days in raising his log house. Owing to his profession, and to the fact that most of his helpers were members of his own congregation, the Rev. Proudfoot was not required to follow the almost invariable custom of providing food and drink; these requisites were supplied by the workers themselves, and the clergyman considered that he was most fortunate in that respect, for he wrote in his diary: "Had I to give them their victuals and drink the raising would have cost an outlay more than a frame house. Many of the people came for the sole purpose of drinking, and never once assisted in lifting a log."[16].

One of the heaviest and most difficult pieces of work was "stumping", or removing the stumps from land which had

---

[15]Moodie, *op. cit.*, pp. 305-314. The "Pines" were the Paynes, whose descendants are still prominent inhabitants of Peterborough County. The identity of most of the other participants in this bee is best, for obvious reasons, left undisclosed.

[16]*Diary of William Proudfoot*, June 12, 1833.

been logged. The first crops were usually sown among the stumps, which occupied about one-eighth of the field. Apart from the waste of that much of the land, their presence was not a very great disadvantage in a day of primitive agricultural methods. Stumps of many softwood trees rotted away in a year or two, but those of hardwood lasted eight or ten years, and resinous stumps, like the pine, much longer. In early York stumps were prominent in the streets, from which they were removed by the operation of the Stump Act. Any person found intoxicated might be sentenced to the task of eradicating a certain number of stumps, and, after his "community service", the culprit was usually very sober and very tired, and did not repeat his offence. This law was so beneficial to York that other localities imitated it, as may be seen from an item in the Niagara *Canada Constellation* under the heading "Stump Loyalty".

"The Stump Law, although framed for the particular benefit of York, meets with such universal approbation that it is expected considerable exertion will be made to extend it through the province. Its beneficial influence has been proven at Chippawa, even during the late extremely frosty days, where it has been enforced on several without mercy, and in every instance on those whose law knowledge was too circumscribed, or who found it in vain to plead the jurisdiction or limitations of the act, and, submitting to the hard sentence, dug through the frozen earth singing

'Come all you joyful topers
Come follow, follow me' ".[17]

A more general method of accomplishing this necessary work was a stumping bee. Various methods were used in the work: some of the stumps were chopped out, others were dragged out by oxen after chains had been fastened around the chief roots; many, especially pine stumps too solid to move, were burned out, or removed by blasting. In some districts a stumping-machine, composed of a screw fastened to a framework, was used; this operation consisted in elevating the machine and the root by using oxen or horses to provide power. The stump fences which are still

[17] Niagara *Canada Constellation*, January 4, 1800.

a characteristic feature of the rural landscape recall many an old-time stumping bee.

Philemon Wright, the founder of Hull, describes stumping activities at his settlement fifteen years after its commencement:

"In 1815 I employed some men in taking out the small stumps and roots, and levelling of the roughest places, as the roots began to decay according to the size of the stumps. Beech and rock maple stumps are much more easily taken out after the seventh year; pine, elm, basswood, and hemlock are less liable to rot, and therefore require about fifteen years before they can be taken out, especially those of the largest size. Every season I set apart a certain number of days, and take from two to six pair of oxen, harnessed with strong chains, which are fastened round the stumps and drawn up, collected together into piles, and burnt upon the ground."[18]

The raising bee is one which has survived to the present. There was but little variation in types of buildings in the pioneer period: house, church, store, barn and mill were usually much alike except in size, and a raising bee was the ordinary means of their erection. The first grist-mills in Upper Canada, near Kingston, Niagara and Napanee, were the result of bees, and a considerable part of their cost appears, from the accounts, to have been expended in rum for the entertainment of the Loyalist soldier-settlers who raised the structures.

In 1834 the saw-mill of Thomas Need, founder of Bobcaygeon, Victoria County, was similarly raised by the united efforts of the inhabitants of the district. Need wrote in his journal on July 3rd:

"They assembled in great force and all worked together in great harmony and good will, notwithstanding their different stations in life. When the last rafter was fixed, a bottle of whisky was broken on the top, and, sundry others having been distributed among the humbler members of the hive, the party separated, well satisfied with their day's work. The completion of the saw-mill was an event of vast interest to all the inhabitants of the settlement, who looked

[18]Philemon Wright: *An Account of the First Settlement of the Township of Hull.* 1823. (In Andrew Picken: *The Canadas.* 1832. Appendix, pp. XXXII and XXXIII.)

to exchange their rude shanties in a little time for neat frame houses."[19]

"An emigrant farmer of twenty years' experience" describes a raising bee as "a general rising throughout the settlement . . . One small party was in the woods cutting down the timber, followed by a couple of hands to line it out; then came the scorers and hewers, and at their heels again the teamsters, with oxen and horses to haul it to the place, where five men put it up as fast as it was brought to them, and after a day spent apparently more in fun and frolic than in hard labour, the out-shell of a capital log house, with the exception of a roof, was put up."

On the following day some of the neighbours returned to complete the house, (the work was being done in this instance for a shoemaker whose home had been destroyed by fire) ; the rafters were put up, the house boarded, spaces for doors and windows cut out, and everything completed. Some of the neighbours "furnished boards, others shingles, a carpenter the door and sashes, and the storekeeper the glass, putty, nails, etc., all of which the man paid for in work at his trade in the course of the following six months."[20]

One hundred men often gathered to raise the framework of a large barn, teams of oxen being used to haul the largest logs. The process varied with the type of building, but the framework was usually constructed on the ground and then raised into position by the men, who used long pikepoles for the purpose. Sometimes a race was held by the two teams of men at work on the opposite sides of a barn, a competition which enlivened the proceedings but resulted in their taking dangerous risks which occasionally ended in fatal accidents. Mrs. Moodie refers to the raisings in the Peterborough district as "generally conducted in a more orderly manner than those for logging. Fewer hands are required, and they are generally under the control of the carpenter who puts up the frame, and if they get drunk during the raising they are liable to meet with very serious accidents."[21]

Another early settler in the same county, in describing

[19]Thomas Need: *Six Years in the Bush.* 1838. p. 96.
[20][J. Abbott]: *The Emigrant to North America.* 1844. pp. 44-5.
[21]Moodie, *op. cit.,* p. 305.

the raising of her new home in 1841, writes of the huge preparations which had to be made, for he who "called the bee" was expected to provide a "spree", as well as to return the work day for day when similarly called. The young ladies came to help with the baking of the huge quantities of pies and cakes which were served for dinner, in addition to "a roast pig and a boiled leg of mutton, a dish of fish, a large cold mutton pie, cold ham and cold roast mutton, mashed potatoes and beans and carrots, a large rice pudding, a large bread-and-butter pudding and currant and gooseberry tarts". This meal was eaten at noon, and afterwards the raising continued.

Later on it began to pour rain, so the men went into the old house and drank punch and smoked cigars, while "the young people chatted or flirted as they fancied". A substantial tea was served soon after, whereupon dancing commenced to the fiddling of one of the men, and this continued until eleven. A supper almost as substantial as the dinner was then brought forth, after which dancing was resumed and continued until one. As no one could venture out because of the rain, the whole eighteen were somehow accommodated for the night. "And I hear", says Mrs. Stewart, "that they laughed almost all night instead of sleeping". In the morning all were busy before breakfast, and by noon the structure was raised, and the hostess considered that they should be glad that nothing but the rain had interrupted the work, "for often dreadful accidents happen at these raising bees".[22]

The food served at bees was not always of such quality and in such abundance. During the "hungry year" of Loyalist days many a gathering received but scant refreshment; at one raising during that period of famine the only food served was a mixture of eggs beaten up with milk and rum. In later years, too, workers were not always luxuriously treated, the exigencies of the times often permitting to be served only such coarse foods as bran cakes, boiled Indian corn, salt pork, pea soup, and the usual whisky. In fact such was the generosity and good nature of one's neighbours, (so we are told in one Emigrants' Guide), that,

[22]Frances Stewart: *Our Forest Home.* 1889. 2nd Edition, 1902, pp. 174-6.

if they knew that a settler's circumstances made it impossible for him to provide meals for the crowd, "some whisky and the evening frolic are sufficient inducements for the attendance of your neighbours".[23]

One of the most interesting accounts of a raising bee is that given by John Thomson, a retired naval officer who located in 1832 in Medonte Township, Simcoe County. Owing to unfavourable weather this raising lasted three days, the third of which was largely spent in an inquest over an Indian who was killed in what is termed "a half-playful wrestling scuffle". There is so much of interest in Thomson's account that it is worth giving in full just as he recorded the events in his diary.

"*Saturday, April 19, 1834*:—Sent off two hands to raise the country to come on Tuesday to get up the frame of the barn . . . .

"*Monday, 21st*:—Very rainy. Poor prospects for tomorrow's work; two hands at the village bringing over a supply of whisky, etc., the other two making the pike poles for raising the frame, cleaning and preparing the shanty for the accommodation of the people coming from a distance. . . .

"*Tuesday, 22nd*:—A bad rainy morning; however, as people came forward we commenced towards 9 o'clock to put the bents of the building together. . . . It was with difficulty we got them persuaded to stay and persevere tomorrow; however, I sent for a fiddler and cajoled and flattered them as well as I could, with the assistance of Mr. Kinsopp, Majors Darlings and Rowes, these being gentlemen and messed in the dining room, while the others, landed proprietors but no gentlemen, lived in the kitchen; (this) caused some envious feeling among certain Yankiefied personages of the latter class, and consequently we mixed among them and did all we could to do away with any bad impression, and pleased them wonderfully well.

"*Wednesday, 23rd*:—Began to put up the frame with thirty men or thereabouts; found the bents so heavy that at first we feared a failure, but, after everyone got themselves fairly put to their mettle, it went up and so did all the others before night. . . . In the afternoon several men

[23]William Hickey: *Hints on Emigration to Upper Canada.* 1834. p. 46.

who had come from Oro, perhaps ten or twelve miles off, went away, and made our party still weaker. We also got the wall plates up to the beams ready for putting into their places in the morning. While the men were at supper this evening a half-playful wrestling scuffle occurred. . . . Joseph St. German was thrown down in the kitchen, and, melancholy to tell, he received some mortal injury, and in the course of seven or eight minutes expired, to the horror and regret of everyone. . . .

"*Thursday, 24th*:—Sent a warrant to the constable to call a jury by daylight; they assembled about half-past 11 o'clock and proceeded to investigate the unhappy occurrence of last night, and found a verdict of manslaughter against Ronald McDonald. . . Very cold day: the people could hardly stand upon the top of the barn to get the plates on; indeed, had it not been for the detention as witnesses on the inquest, I believe they would all have decamped by daylight; no great wonder if they had, as I am sure they must all be sick enough of the job. The inquest was over by half-past three, and all hands got away by five o'clock. They have used a barrel of pork and one of flour with fifteen gallons of whisky, besides tea and sugar, etc. One of the hands made a coffin for St. German, and he was removed immediately after the inquest by his friends".[24].

This is by no means the only death resulting from fights at bees. Magistrates who did not relish being continually engaged in settling disputes avoided trouble by making themselves hard to find. "When I became a magistrate", said Squire George Munro, "I used to go away to the woods when I heard there was a fight at a bee, and keep away till the blood cooled down, and that generally ended the matter".[25]

Colonel Strickland, a magistrate for many years, considered that bees in general were "a continual round of dissipation—if not of something worse. I have known several cases of manslaughter arising out of quarrels produced by intoxication at these every-day gatherings".[26]

There were often local variations in the conduct of raising bees. In some communities it was customary to

[24]Diary of John Thomson, April 19-24, 1834. (Archives of Ontario.)
[25]Quoted in C. O. Ermatinger: *The Talbot Regime*. 1904. p. 102.
[26]Strickland, *op. cit.*, Vol. I, p. 37.

"christen" buildings with whisky, like ships at launching. Benjamin Waldbrook, who lived near Oakville, remembered barn-raisings where this ceremony was performed.

"Once, at a raising near Ancaster, I saw a man, bottle in hand, run up the peak where two rafters joined. There, balancing on one foot, he sang out:

> 'It is a good framing
> And shall get a good naming.
> What shall the naming be?'

When the prearranged name was shouted back the man on the rafters so declared it as he cast the bottle to the ground. Was the bottle broken? No, indeed! As it contained the best liquor supplied at the raising, care was taken to see that it fell on soft ground, and the moment it fell it was surrounded by a crowd of men, still thirsty despite the liberal libations already supplied."[27]

David Dobie, who lived in Ekfrid Township, on the banks of the Thames, recalled a case of human life destroyed by wild beasts. This unfortunate incident, perhaps unique in pioneer annals, happened as a result of drunkenness at a raising:

"One night after a raising, a party of helpers were on their way home, and one, who had imbibed more freely than the others, refused to go further. He was accordingly left in a fence-corner to sleep off the effects of the liquor. Next morning, on his failure to return home, some men started out to look for him. They found the place where he had slept, but there was scarcely a shred of body or even of clothing left. Wolves had found him helpless, torn him limb from limb, and feasted on the mangled carcass."[28]

The amount of whisky distributed at bees by the "whisky-boys", "grogmen" or "grog-bosses" was so great that there are records of as much as eighty gallons consumed at one bee.[29] "One man had charge of the bottle, and

---

[27] Reminiscences of Benjamin D. Waldbrook, near Oakville, quoted in Smith, *op. cit.*, p. 176. Spirited accounts of a logging bee and a raising, with local variations as they applied to the later-settled counties between Lake Huron and Georgian Bay, may be found in W. M. Brown: *The Queen's Bush*. 1932. Chapters XVIII and XIX.

[28] Reminiscences of David Dobie, quoted in Smith, *op. cit.*, pp. 223-4.

[29] Patrick Shirreff: *A Tour through North America*. 1835. p. 125.

AN OLD TIME BARN-RAISING NEAR BRANTFORD

Ontario Motion Picture Bureau

A MODERN BARN-RAISING AT WOODBRIDGE, ONTARIO

THE QUILTING BEE

MINUETS OF THE CANADIANS

A dance was the inevitable end of every bee

if he was judicious the people went home sober";[30] if he was not, fighting and other disorders were the inevitable consequence. The whisky habit was so deep-rooted that, until Temperance Societies began to gather headway in the forties and fifties, it was difficult to get men to come to a bee under any other conditions. We find that in 1832 a citizen of Wentworth County accomplished the remarkable feat of getting his saw-mill erected without whisky; but it was evidently a most unpopular move on his part, for when he tried to arrange a barn-raising under the same conditions he had to send to the Methodist Indian mission on the Credit before he could obtain men.[31]

Another instance of the same kind occurred in Cobourg in the forties. A builder named Bradbeer, who had "signed the pledge", found that his usual helpers refused to come to raise a barn when they heard that no liquor was to be served. The cause of temperance was vindicated, however, for with the aid of the town clerk a large number of "temperance people" were obtained to help with the raising, and they enjoyed tea and coffee as refreshment.[32]

Here and there other men with strength of character fought against the abuses of the whisky habit and strengthened the temperance movement. Among the first to abolish liquor at bees were Quakers and Methodists. John Gunn, early settled near Beaverton, put an end to liquor at loggings on his farm after a fight had occurred; similarly Abner Chase of Yarmouth Township succeeded in getting a barn raised without the aid of whisky. The example of these and other men exerted a good influence which spread far beyond the confines of the communities in which they lived.

After the rise of Temperance and Total Abstinence societies an ever-increasing number of men were found on the side of common sense and law and order at bees, and whisky-drinking gradually declined. Among other "temperance settlements" was that of Flos Township, near Georgian Bay. The first settlers in this district were mainly the sons of Oro Township pioneers. One of them states that "no whisky was even seen at raising or bee in this section. . . .

[30]J. L. Gourlay: *History of the Ottawa Valley.* 1896. p. 11.
[31]Cited in Emily Weaver: *The Story of the Counties of Ontario.* 1913. p. 165.
[32]Letter of James H. Bradbeer in the *Cobourg Sentinel-Star*, June 3, 1920.

To that fact is largely due the prosperity of the settlement".[33] Many of the inhabitants of rural Ontario were pioneers in the temperance movement just as they were pioneers in settlement, and they formed the nucleus of the campaign for temperance legislation, which reached its culmination in Canada during the Great War.

Bees were very democratic institutions, even in a day when social distinctions were rigidly drawn. In the Adelaide military settlement in the London District occurred a logging bee in which a man later Chief Justice of Upper Canada, another a county judge, a third afterwards a rector, and an old colonel, participated. There were times, however, when some of the more aristocratic "gentlemen" did not at first appreciate the full force of democratic sentiment, and had to be compelled to eat with the mob instead of separately, as they intended. This attitude on the part of refined people is not to be wondered at when we consider the low level of manners and the excesses which were characteristic of the gatherings.

There were numerous other occasions when settlers assembled from far and near to help with farm work—and at the same time to "let off steam", for bees provided a social outlet for the emotions. There were hauling bees, ploughing bees, bees at hay-cutting and harvest-time, bees to build stone or rail fences. A British magazine quotes a traveller to Upper Canada in 1819 as of the opinion that the English "are more offended with the fences than anything else they see in this new country". But the ease with which they could be made at a bee, one log often providing eighty rails, soon reconciled them to rail or stump fences, particularly since stone walls could be erected only at great expense of labour and money, and the hedges of England were unsuitable and inconvenient in a new country "on account of harbouring vermin".[34]

Samuel Strickland attended a mowing and cradling bee in Darlington Township in 1825, and found thirty-five men cutting hay and rye, and ten cradlers. So well did they work that by evening the whole of these crops had been harvested, and there was time for gymnastics, trials of

[33]Reminiscences of Noah Cotton, quoted in Smith, *op. cit.*, p. 301.
[34]James Strachan quoted in the *Farmer's Magazine*, August, 1820, p. 331.

strength, running and jumping, and other popular pastimes such as throwing the hammer and putting the stone. During the day the "grog-boss" dealt out plenty of refreshment from a pail, while a couple of meals were served, consisting of "roast lamb and green peas, roast sucking-pig, shoulder of mutton, apple-sauce, and pies, puddings and preserves in abundance, with plenty of beer and Canadian whisky".[35]

Butchering day, or "the killing" was a busy time, when six or eight pigs, and perhaps some cattle as well, were slaughtered and dressed, the whole work—even to making sausages—being of necessity done in one day. Among the women there were paring bees, preserving bees, quilting bees,—where each woman worked on one section of a patchwork quilt,—fulling, and linen-spinning bees. Colonel John Clark, a Loyalist settler near Niagara, remembered linen bees where the young people spun from flax as much as sixty yards of fine linen, the only payment being a supper and a dance.[36] Logging and quilting were sometimes combined into a "double bee", and in the same manner the quilting in the afternoon often preceded the husking in the evening, in which the men participated. As W. S. Herrington neatly puts it: "The afternoon tea now serves its purpose very well, but modern society has yet to discover the equal of the quilting bee as a clearing-house for gossip."[37]

Perhaps the husking bee provided most pleasure to the participants. Piles of corn were arranged in the barn, which was illuminated by candles placed in tin lanterns. Walter Riddell gives an excellent description of the course of events: "At these bees lads and lassies occupied alternate seats, and when one of the former found a big red ear of corn he had the privilege of kissing the girl next him. And it is surprising what a lot of big red ears were found." The husking was followed "by a dance, and refreshments in the form of cake, home-made cheese and punch".[38]

[35]Strickland, op. cit., Vol. I, pp. 35-37.
[36]Reminiscences of Colonel John Clark, Niagara. (Coventry Papers, Public Archives of Canada.)
[37]W. S. Herrington: Pioneer Life on the Bay of Quinté. (In Lennox and Addington Historical Society, Papers and Records, Vol. VI, p. 17.)
[38]Reminiscences of Walter Riddell, Hamilton Township, in the Farmer's Sun, August 4, 1898.

Pumpkins were early an important food, used in a variety of ways. A settler near Kirby, Clarke Township, recalled that "the pumpkin bee was a social function, and lads and lassies gathered from miles around to peel and string pumpkins for drying, just as those of a later generation had their apple-paring bees. And what delicious pies those dried pumpkins did make."[39]

The later paring bees were interesting events, at least in Dundas County, where "each of the boys, accompanied by his peculiar home-made paring machine, would bring his best girl. . . . The boys tossed the peeled apples from the machines, which were caught by the girls, who quickly completed the work".[40] A common type of paring machine re-resembled a two-pronged fork, upon which the apple was placed; there was generally an attachment which enabled the coring of the apple. It was usual to slice the apples and place them to dry on racks above the fireplace or kitchen stove. Perhaps the following account is typical of the proceedings at the average apple-paring bee:

"The young folks make a grand night of it when the bee comes off. The laughing and frolic is unbounded; some are busy with their sweethearts; some, of a grosser mind, are no less busy with the apples, devouring a large proportion of what they pare; and the whole proceedings, in many cases, wind up with a dance on the barn floor."[41]

In addition to the bees which had as their main purpose the accomplishment of work, there were "house-warmings", spelling bees, maple sugar-eating bees, and other frolics where no work was done. Perhaps the best description of this type of gathering is that written by a young Scotch traveller who played a most important part in what might be called, in the vernacular of the day, a "sparking bee", or —in more modern terms—a "petting party". When he arrived at the home to which he had been invited, David Wilkie found "a goodly cluster of misses with smooth, smiling faces, beaming beneath a load of clear and glistening tresses, that seemed to have cost them a deal of extra trouble for the occasion. . . . I was introduced to the good old squire himself, with whom I was soon knee-deep in a

[39]Reminiscences of H. L. Powers, quoted in Smith, *op. cit.*, p. 312.
[40]J. S. Carter: *The Story of Dundas County.* 1905. p. 49.
[41]C. Geikie: *Life in the Woods.* 1873. p. 326.

sea of humdrum prosification of and concerning the state of the foreign markets, sour cider, and the price of pork. We were regaled with refreshments, small cakes, currant tarts, and similar puffery. . . . As the room became more obscure, the masters and misses drew closer together. . . . The moon, (for luckily there was one), smiled beautifully in upon them".

Soon the squire slipped away and the visitor was invited to join "this round-robin of honest men and bonnie lassies. Being naturally endowed with Scotch caution, I intended, whatever might chance, to keep a sharp look-out after my heart!" Wilkie soon found, indeed, that this was no place for him! A large bone button was passed from hand to hand, and he was asked to guess where it was, in which he was not correct; he was, therefore, sentenced to place himself "between the two young squiresses on the window-seat. They were quite in the shade, for the moonbeams merely glanced along the outlines of their flowing curls and snowy necks. . . .

"The fair one on my right hand . . . complied with the sentence which followed by placing herself on one of my knees, to which I kindly assisted her, to render the penance as light as possible. The lady on my left . . . . was consigned to the precious support of my vacant limb. . . . The lock-up house was my knee, and the chains that bound them were my arms. Not content with the extent of the penal duties I was already made to perform, the master of ceremonies, with more refined wickedness, brought me once more beneath the lash of the law, and awarded the additional penance that I do forthwith salute the two culprits in the condemned cell. Time had got so far ahead that we had now to think of home; and I was obliged, however reluctantly, to resign my romantic post and dive into the woods, leaving all the alluring fascinations of the magical button behind, which, I doubt not, has often before the occurrence of this busy bee caused many a heart to ache, and many a head toss over a sleepless pillow".[42]

Except among families where dancing was considered sinful, and the fiddle an instrument of the devil, the invariable end of every bee was a dance in the house, the barn,

[42]David Wilkie: *Sketches of a Summer Trip to New York and the Canadas.* 1837. pp. 182-6.

or the "ballroom" of a tavern. Quadrilles, reels and jigs, waxing fast and furious as the fiddler struck his stride, and the aching muscles of even the old men were limbered up, alternated with rustic plays and "kissing games" until the small hours of the morning, when every laddie saw his lassie home, perhaps with the help of a flambeau of dry cedar bark.

Such were the bees of the pioneer period. In a day of severe and unremitting toil, of privation and hardship, they provided social intercourse and diversion as important to the life of the people as the work accomplished.

CHAPTER IX

AMUSEMENT AND SOCIAL LIFE IN THE RURAL DISTRICTS

"After dinner we fell to dancing, and continued, only with intermission for a good supper, till two in the morning, the musick being Greeting and another most excellent violin, the best in town. And so with mighty mirth and pleased with their dancing of jigs afterwards several of them, and among others Betty Turner, who did it mighty prettily, and then to a country dance again, and so broke up with extraordinary pleasure as being one of the days and nights of my life spent with the greatest content, and that which I can but hope to repeat again a few times in my whole life."

The Diary of Samuel Pepys, March 2, 1669.

THE life of the pioneer settlers in Canada was one of hardship, but the difficulties under which they lived were to some extent relieved by co-operation, not only in work but in play. The "bees" which were so characteristic of early life in Upper Canada supplied that social intercourse which is essential to a well-balanced life. Judged by modern standards some pioneer amusements were crude, leading occasionally to regrettable excesses; but there was a wholesomeness among the vast majority of the people which pervaded their social life, and frowned upon any variation from the spirit of honest fun.

In considering the pleasures of the pioneers it must first be understood that "it takes all kinds of people to make a world"; what is one person's pleasure is another's aversion. There were many who considered all worldly amusement sinful, and to be avoided at any cost. Prominent among these were the Friends or Quakers, who often took disciplinary action against members of their societies guilty of backsliding; we find, for example, that the disfavour of their co-religionists fell upon some who "had attended a noisy, unruly and unlawful assembly called a chivaree"; and likewise upon three Quakers on Yonge Street who were "guilty of assisting in tarring and carrying a woman on a rail".[1] In addition to the more serious breaches of conduct—swearing, drinking, fighting, gambl-

[1]A. G. Dorland: *A History of the Society of Friends in Canada*. 1927. p. 10.

ing, immorality and horse-racing—other less harmful diversions, such as card-playing, music and dancing in one's home, were deprecated, and persons persisting in such practices were expelled from the society.

Though social life in a Quaker community was greatly restricted, yet most Quakers had the same sense of humour to be found among other sections of the population, even though it was usually hidden by a solemn face and quaint garb. In later days they sometimes had debating societies, while at all times "their Yearly, Quarterly and Monthly meetings filled a social as well as religious need in a pioneer state of society which was very simple and had few outlets for demands of this kind. Members would travel great distances to attend these gatherings which were the occasion of lavish hospitality. Indeed these were notable social events which had a large place in the life of the early Quaker community".[2]

The early Methodists were similarly opposed to amusements of a worldly nature; in the days of the first class-meetings the violin was forbidden as a sinful musical instrument (if such a thing is possible!), chiefly because it was commonly used to supply the music for dancing. This prohibition of the one common source of music left them without any, for the accordeon and concertina were not invented until 1829, while melodeons and "pianofortes" were not common in Canada until many years later.

The scarcity of musical instruments led to greater stress being laid upon singing in the home and the church. Singing-schools were organised each winter in many neighbourhoods and provided a means of social intercourse, though the unfortunate singing-master often found it difficult to keep order among those who did not come to sing. The Methodists were particularly noted for singing in unison at their religious services, the congregational singing at the York Conference of 1831 being described as "most delightful and heavenly".[3] The Jesuit missionaries had a small organ in Quebec as early as 1661, but organs were uncommon a century ago in the churches of Upper Canada. One method of obtaining the key in which the congregation

[2] *Ibid.*
[3] Anson Green: *Life and Times.* 1877. p. 153.

THE RED MEETING-HOUSE, STAMFORD, 1800-40

CELEBRATION OF THE ROYAL WEDDING DAY, BURLINGTON
BAY, 1863

From Conant's *Upper Canada Sketches*   E. S. Shrapnel

A METHODIST CAMP-MEETING

Reproduced by Courtesy of the Maple Leaf Gardens, Inc.

18,000 PEOPLE AT DENTON MASSEY'S YORK BIBLE CLASS, MAPLE LEAF GARDENS, DECEMBER 13, 1931

Probably the largest indoor assembly in the history of Canada

sang consisted in the striking of a tuning-fork by the leader.

While not pleasures in the usual sense of the word, the class-meeting and the camp-meeting of the Methodists often provided a "love-feast" which, despite occasional emotional excesses, may be considered as a form of higher spiritual pleasure. The services of the other denominations, while more orthodox and impersonal, were equally important in the social life of the community. Church services were early held in courthouses or other government buildings, in taverns, stores or private homes, until it was possible to erect a church building by the subscription and labour of the members.

In most denominations the service was most informal, though a sense of decorum was apparent in the custom of men and women sitting in separate sections of the room. Sometimes the men removed their coats in warm weather, and people frequently walked in and out during the course of the service; while often the week's mail was distributed at the church door at the close. There were Sunday schools for the children in connection with most churches, and in some cases they had a few books to be distributed among those whose education was sufficient to enable them to read. In fact the social life of the pioneer community centred in the church and the school, the clergyman and the teacher being not infrequently the same person. Social intercourse was extended, and education as well as amusement supplied by tea-meetings and socials, singing-schools and spelling-matches, literary and debating societies, though such organised activities were seldom found during the first years of settlement.

Many of the inhabitants of Upper Canada were not as scrupulous with regard to their pleasures as were the Quakers and early Methodists. There were many, too, who were forced by the manners and customs of the times to join upon some occasions in questionable activities which they would ordinarily have avoided. One of the worst of these customs, and the most far-reaching in its effects, was the excessive drinking of spirituous liquors, a habit which, though by no means universal, pervaded social life in all parts of the country, and was as prominent in the backwoods as in the towns. Whisky was early considered an antidote to the hardships and misfortunes of pioneer life, and a means temporarily to forget care and trouble. At almost every gathering liquor was served in abundance, and it was considered in the thirties that he was "a moderate man who does not exceed four glasses in the day".[4] Many people attended bees, weddings, auction sales, and other social assemblies merely for the purpose of drinking; liquor was frequently taken to revival camp-meetings and consumed by those who came to scoff but did not remain to pray. Even funeral wakes were not exempt from strong drink, and on at least one occasion "so hilarious did the participants become that the corpse was offered a share of the beverage".[5] The poor quality of the drink often made its effects much worse: one writer compares the usual liquor to fire and brimstone, "made of frosty potatoes, hemlock, pumpkins and black mouldy rye".[6]

The number of inns and taverns that existed in Upper Canada in former times would surprise the present generation. Every crossroad had one or more, and the main highways supported many dozens of them. The small city of Toronto had in 1850 a total of 152 taverns and 206 beer shops to supply a population of about 30,000 and such farmers as brought their produce thither to market. Distilleries were among the first establishments in most settlements, and provided large quantities of cheap liquor, usually obtainable at 25c. a gallon, or even less; and almost all taverns were maintained largely by the sale of strong drink. A traveller refers to "taverns and low drinking-houses" as the chief places of public amusement in Upper Canada;[7] while another writer found "every inn, tavern and beer shop filled at all hours with drunken, brawling fellows; and the quantity of ardent spirits consumed by

---

[4]Letter of William Hutton in the *British Farmer's Magazine*, April, 1835, p. 114.
[5]M. A. Garland and J. J. Talman: *Pioneer Drinking Habits, and the Rise of the Temperance Agitation in Upper Canada.* (Ontario Historical Society, *Papers and Records*, Vol. XXVII, p. 345).
[6]John MacTaggart: *Three Years in Canada.* 1829. Vol. I, p. 199.
[7]Anna Jameson: *Winter Studies and Summer Rambles in Canada.* 1838. Vol. I, p. 293.
[8]"An Ex-Settler": *Canada in the Years 1832, 1833 and 1834.* 1835. p. 25.

them will truly astonish you". Men went from tavern to tavern treating one another all round, and the amount of liquor consumed often led to fatal accidents. Of the sudden deaths investigated by coroner's juries, excessive whisky-drinking was found to be by far the most frequent cause.

The temperance movement originated in the United States, and spread into Canada at the commencement of the second quarter of the nineteenth century. Montreal was long the temperance centre of Canada, and there the first Temperance Society was formed in 1828. A few months later a number of township societies had been formed in Upper Canada, and by 1832 there were 10,000 members of such organisations in the province. The early societies usually restricted their warfare against intoxicants to whisky, rum and brandy, and emphasised temperance rather than prohibition; but in later years beer and wine were added to the proscribed list, and in 1835 the first of a large number of Total Abstinence societies was organised in St. Catharines. The reaction against the drinking habits of the times gathered headway down through the years, though the societies were opposed by many as a "Yankee" institution, which reason, and his own personal appetite, led Colonel Talbot to dub them "damned cold water drinking societies".[9]

Apart from the excessive use of intoxicants there were among the pioneers no very harmful habits which are not present to at least as great an extent now. The use of snuff was comparatively harmless, and both men and women were more or less fond of it in the earlier periods of settlement. The tobacco habit, while by no means universal, was quite general among all classes of the male population. Women were not usually addicted either to tobacco or intoxicants; some of the old ladies did enjoy smoking an old, blackened clay pipe, but cigarettes had not been invented, and smoking by young women in general is a very recent innovation.

Some of the girls of a century ago were not, however,

[9]Speech at St. Thomas, April 23, 1832. See the *Talbot Papers*, Section II, pp. 124-6. (*Transactions* of the Royal Society of Canada, 1909).

averse to appearing sophisticated and *risqué* upon occasion. Joseph Pickering notes in his journal in 1826 that while he was stopping at Loder's Tavern on Talbot Street "some smart lasses came in during the evening, who live just by, most of whom took a smoke with the landlord and the landlady, passing the short black pipe from one to another! Disgusting as this practice is, it is not so much so as one in common use in the eastern part of Maryland, of girls taking a "rubber" of snuff—that is, taking as much snuff as will lie on the end of the forefinger out of a box, and rubbing it round the inside of the mouth"![10]

There were many evils traceable in a large measure to the excessive drinking habits. Drunkenness, "the vice and curse of the country",[11] was generally accompanied by profanity, immorality, lawlessness and crime. Boisterous activities and cruel habits were considered amusing by people of low or degenerate mentality. Murder and robbery were common, and while some men stole sheep, horses and cattle, others repaid a grudge or satisfied a depraved desire by maiming them. Burning barns, breaking windows, smashing store signs, and other types of horseplay and vandalism, were of frequent occurrence, and even in modern times such activities are occasionally carried on where the vigilance of the police and magistrates is insufficient to prevent them. In the first years of villages and towns there was frequently a similar disregard for the rights of property, and early newspapers contain notices of the following type:

"Two Dollars Reward.—Whereas on Friday night last some evil-disposed person fired a gun at the house of the subscriber, ... whereby upwards of twenty squares of glass were broken, and the premises otherwise injured, the above reward will be paid on the conviction of the offenders."[12]

Similarly in York twenty dollars reward was offered for the apprehension of the man "who is so depraved and lost to every sense of social duty as to cut with an axe or knife the withes which bound some of the fence round the

---

[10]Joseph Pickering: *Inquiries of an Emigrant.* 1831. November 2, 1826.
[11]Jameson, *op. cit.*, Vol. I, p. 76.
[12]*Cobourg Star*, January 18, 1831.

late Chief Justice's farm on Yonge Street, and to throw down the said fence".[13]

On many occasions the public conscience was aroused by flagrant disregard for the principles of law and order. Mob justice was not infrequent in some parts of Upper Canada, particularly where the regular course of law enforcement was tardy, and in instances where a moral but not a legal crime had been committed. Prominent in this connection was the "Old Sorrel", a species of summary justice dealt out to those who had offended the sense of morality of the neighbourhood. This punishment consisted in tarring and feathering the culprit, with the addition, at times, of "riding the fence rail"; anyone treated in this manner was expected to leave the district immediately. Altercations arising from such types of mob rule were usually ignored as far as possible by the authorities, even where deaths resulted, though as civilisation advanced such occurrences could not be tolerated and have fortunately become infrequent.

A few men of low, if not perverted tastes took a savage delight in the sufferings of animals, and were to be found—as they occasionally are at the present day—carrying on such sports (?) as bull- or bear-baiting, dog-fighting and cock-fighting. Two centuries earlier these crude activities had been quite common in England, especially during the period of reaction which followed the Puritan repression of Commonwealth days; but even at that time John Evelyn considered them "butcherly sports, or, rather, barbarous cruelties, ... a rude and dirty pastime";[14] while Samuel Pepys, whose interests were universal, and who was by no means fussy in his amusements, found cock-fighting "no great sport", and soon "had enough of it" and its accompaniments—"swearing, cursing and betting".[15] In Canada these so-called old English sports so offended the public sense of fair play and decency that they have been prohibited by law in modern times.

Wrestling and fighting were long popular public amusements. Gourlay stated that "the vulgar practice of pugil-

[13]*Upper Canada Gazette*, July 23, 1803.
[14]John Evelyn: *Diary*, June 16, 1670.
[15]Samuel Pepys: *Diary*, December 21, 1663, and April 6, 1668.

ism, a relic of the savage state", was declining in 1817,[16]
but it by no means died out. It was commonly considered
that the best man was he who could knock his opponent
senseless, and seldom did the rules of the Marquis of
Queensbury apply to any such pugilistic encounters. Feats
of strength and skill were deservedly popular at bees and
other public gatherings; in fact the supremacy of a township frequently rested upon the ability of its representatives to dispose of all comers in some athletic competition.
Races were less popular than wrestling or fighting for
public spectacles of this kind. On one occasion the "Fifth-
towners", as the inhabitants of the Township of Marysburgh were called, considered that the "Fourth-towners",
across the Bay of Quinté in Adolphustown, were "too smart
and stuck-up"; so they challenged them to pick out three
of their best wrestlers to settle the relative "smartness"
of the townships. Needless to say they were not to be
"stumped", and sent Samuel Dorland, Samuel Casey and
Paul Trumpour to uphold the reputation of Adolphustown
against the chosen men of Marysburgh, whose names have
not come down to us, perhaps because they were worsted in
the encounter.

"The hour was fixed, and a nearby field was selected
where hundreds were on hand 'to see fair play' and help
decide which township had the best men. These were all
noted athletes, and they were then young and in their
prime. Samuel Dorland, afterwards a colonel in the militia
and a leading official in the Methodist Church, was an expert wrestler, and used to boast, even in his old days, that
he seldom if ever met a man who could lay him on his back.
He soon had his man down. Samuel Casey, who afterwards
became a leading military officer and a prominent justice of
the peace, was one of the strongest men in the township,
but not an expert wrestler. He was so powerful in the legs
that his opponent, with all his skill, could not trip him
up, and at last got thrown down himself. Paul Trumpour,
who was the head of what is now the largest family in the
township, was not so skilled in athletics; but he was a
man of immense strength. He got his arms well fixed

[16]Robert Gourlay: *A Statistical Account of Upper Canada*. 1822. Vol.
I, pp. 252-4.

around his man and gave him such terrible 'bear-hugs' that the poor fellow soon cried out 'enough', to save his ribs from getting crushed in, and that settled it. The Fourth-town championship was not again disputed."[17]

There were among the pioneers many who delighted in the opportunities which Canada afforded for the field sports whch they had enjoyed in the Old Land. Dr. Dunlop fills up twenty-one pages in describing—for the benefit of immigrants!—the rare hunting, gaming, hawking and fishing available in Canada.[18] But while some had leisure in which they could enjoy such pastimes, most of the early settlers were too busy to enter into them unless necessity compelled them to obtain food in that manner. Field sports cannot be described in detail here, but it is sufficient to say that fish, birds and animals now almost extinct were obtainable a century ago in a profusion which would astonish the sportsman of today.

Among the activities of this type which were sometimes a necessity was raccoon-hunting. Many a boy and his dog amused themselves in the green-corn season driving the raccoons from the fields to the woods, from which, if no other artifice availed, they were forced by felling the trees. The hunting of deer many be taken as a typical Canadian field sport. A man who frequently engaged in such amusements during the pioneer period considered that deer-hunting was "a very exciting sport; but I prefer still-hunting, (or deer-stalking, as it is called in the Highlands of Scotland), to driving them into the lakes and rivers with hounds. The deer are not now (1853) nearly so numerous as they formerly were. . . . To give my readers some idea how plentiful these wild denizens of the forest were some years since, I need only mention that a trapper with whom I was acquainted, and four of his companions, passed my house on a small raft on which lay the carcasses of thirty-two deer—the trophies of a fortnight's chase near Stoney Lake. The greater number of these were fine bucks.

"I once had seventeen deer hanging up in my barn at

[17]Thomas W. Casey: *Old Time Records*. Quoted in W. S. Herrington: *The History of Lennox and Addington*. 1913. p. 137.
[18]William Dunlop: *Statistical Sketches of Upper Canada*. 1832. pp. 32-52

one time—the produce of three days' sport, out of which
I had the good fortune to kill seven. Parties are now made
yearly every October to Stoney Lake, Deer Bay, or the
River Trent. I do not know anything more pleasant than
these excursions, especially if you have agreeable companions, a warm camp, and plenty to eat and drink. . . .
This is one of the great charms of Canadian life, particularly to young sportsmen from the Mother Country, who
require here neither license nor qualification to enable them
to follow their game; but may rove in chase of deer or
other game at will".[19]

Bird life was found in similar profusion a century ago.
Joseph Pickering notes in his diary on April 8, 1826:
"Pigeons, in great flocks, going out daily northward; some
people with nets and decoy pigeons will catch several
hundred in a day, when they sometimes take only their
breasts and salt them down, and make beds of their
feathers".[20] In the late summer of the same year he observed that "pigeons again made their appearance in large
flocks, as also wild turkeys; partridges, larger than the
English breed, and quails, less than those of Europe, are
also numerous".[21] The wild turkeys sometimes weighed
fifteen pounds when dressed.

Fishing, which Izaak Walton so appropriately called
"the contemplative man's recreation",[22] has been a noted
amusement in Canada from the earliest times. Even the
Indian was inclined to look upon it as an exciting pleasure
rather than a means to obtain food. Many a pioneer
participated in the enjoyments of fishing in a day when even
a poor fisherman could well-nigh fill his canoe in a few
hours. In general the sport has changed, as the years have
passed, from spearing to angling; but even if no fish are
caught, the unsuccessful angler's consolation is the same as
it was three centuries ago when Robert Burton wrote:

"Fishing is still and quiet: and if so be the Angler
catch no Fish, yet he hath a wholesome walk to the Brook-

[19]Samuel Strickland: *Twenty-seven Years in Canada West.* 1853.
    Vol. I, pp. 78-9.
[20]Pickering, *op. cit.*, April 8, 1826.
[21]*Ibid.*, August 26, 1826.
[22]See the title-page of the First Edition, 1653, of Izaak Walton: *The
    Compleat Angler.*

Reproduced by Courtesy of Miss Caddy   Edward Caddy, D.L.S.

STONEY LAKE IN THE FIFTIES

PROWSE'S HOTEL, BEAUMARIS, MUSKOKA LAKES, IN THE EIGHTIES
Note the emphasis placed upon the Billiard Room

Public Archives of Canada   Ensign James Peachey

CATARAQUI (KINGSTON) IN AUGUST, 1783

From Heriot's *Travels through the Canadas.* 1807   George Heriot

FALL OF MONTMORENCIE IN WINTER
The joys of carrioling are here apparent

side, pleasant shade by the sweet silver streams; he hath
good air, and sweet smells of fine fresh meadow flowers;
he hears the melodious harmony of Birds."[23]

A sporting event early characteristic of the Canadian
summer was the regatta. Canoe races in which Indian and
voyageur vied with settler aroused the greatest interest
among those who lived near the waterways. John Mac-
Taggart, writing in the eighteen-twenties, considered that
there were "few finer scenes than a Canadian Regatta:
fifty canoes on the smooth broad lake, *voyageurs* fancifully
adorned, the song up in full chorus, blades of the paddles
flashing in the sun as they rapidly lift and·dip, while the
watery foam-bells hurry into the hollow of the wakes".[24]
The first regattas were on the St. Lawrence or the Ottawa,
but as early as 1838 there were similar aquatic competitions
at Fenelon Falls, and at other settlements in the "back
lakes" region of the old Newcastle District, which was to
become in later years so popular a summer resort.

Just as characteristic of Canada were the sports of
winter. Snow-shoe and dog-sled had long been necessary
for winter travel over Indian trail and along frozen lake
and river, and they were supplemented in the days of
settlement by sledge and carriole. Travel by carriole was
just as pleasurable in winter as the canoe was in summer,
and it was a time when travelling was but seldom pleasant.
The settler's sleigh was usually home-made and its body
ran very close to the ice; while that of the "gentlemen"
in the towns had runners, and was often a very elaborate
affair. The carriole had no covering, so travellers were well
bundled up in furs. Sleighing-parties have remained a
characteristic Canadian winter pleasure though the motor-
car is gradually replacing horse-drawn vehicles.

Tobogganing, or, as sometimes spelled, "traboggining",
was another winter sport early enjoyed by the young people.
Skating, which originated in Holland, was also a favourite
amusement, though it was frequently considered improper
for girls to participtate in such a form of pleasurable exercise. Curling commenced in Canada towards the close of

[23]Robert Burton: *The Anatomy of Melancholy.* 1652. Dell Edition,
1927, p. 478.
[24]MacTaggart, *op. cit.*, Vol. I, p. 308.

the eighteenth century, when some of the officers of the garrison at Quebec became interested in the game as a means of relieving a monotonous life. In Upper Canada the game was first played at Kingston about 1820, and on the Don River at York nine years later; soon afterwards it was popular in many another settlement, particularly where the Scotch predominated. In this sport, as in many another activity, the rural settler frequently walked many miles to join his brethren in the nearest village, and all gathered at a favourite stretch of ice on river or lake.

Visiting has always been a popular diversion among all classes of people. Formal calls were made by the social set in the towns, and very informal visits in the rural districts. Births, marriages and deaths provided an excellent opportunity for the exchange of civilities, and it was usual to provide guests with food, and frequently with lodging as well; it is said that farmers thought it "nothing extraordinary to make an excursion of six or seven hundred miles in the winter in their sleighs to see their friends".[25] Sunday was the great day for local visiting, and it was generally considered that no time was so appropriate for "sparking" (courting) as Sunday evening. The improvement of roads and the invention of the motor-car have greatly facilitated travel, and might be presumed to have increased visiting; that this is not the case is the fault of the great amusement of "listening-in", not only to the radio, but also of an older variety,—that major sport of many communities—listening in over the party telephone line!

Surprise parties, where ten or twelve families suddenly descended upon the home—and sometimes the larder—of mutual friends, were a popular form of visiting in the rural districts, and have survived to the present. The women obtained a considerable proportion of their pleasure in visits, for their activities were more restricted than those of the men. Many pioneer women seldom went anywhere beyond a neighbour's, the market, or the general store; their lives were often monotonous, for it was usually considered improper for females to enter into the men's ac-

[25]D'Arcy Boulton: *Sketch of His Majesty's Province of Upper Canada.* 1805. p. 11.

tivities, and there were in the country few libraries and fewer readable books. The men, on the other hand, frequently had occasion to visit the town, and their contact with the official, the merchant and the tradesman was not only diverting, but affected, even if unconsciously, their attitude towards life, and lessened the monotony of their existence. They also engaged from time to time in hunting and fishing, visited taverns, attended bees, fairs, horse-races, militia training, circuses, and elections; some also entered into curling, bandyball, lacrosse, football, quoits and other sports.

Social intercourse among farmers was increased through the activities of Agricultural Societies and kindred organisations. There were a few societies in existence in Upper Canada before 1825, the first being at Niagara in 1793; but they did not become important throughout the province until the thirties and forties. With them came the local fairs and, later, the Provincial Exhibition, which were of value not only in developing agriculture but also in that they provided some contact with the outside world; horse-racing, ploughing-matches, and, in later years, amusements more or less commercialised, were prominent at all fairs, and soon became an attraction of outstanding importance to the average citizen.

Associations among farmers' wives were not formed as early as the Agricultural Societies among the men, but in later years the Women's Institutes became increasingly important in developing social life. The Temperance Societies which became so common in rural Ontario in the forties and fifties provided many people with opportunities for advancement and pleasure similar to those afforded by the agricultural organisations, for in both cases papers were read and debates held upon subjects of popular interest.

The early settlers were too busy to indulge in amusement very often, so it was customary to crowd a great deal into one "spree", as a social gathering was often called. A bee, a wedding, or an auction sale was not always over in one day, for the participants frequently extended the jollification several days longer. This was particularly true of a wedding, which was a notable community event in the early days. A wedding procession of lumber-wagons was often a feature, and "each gallant was supposed to support his partner upon his knee, and thus economise room".[26]

While fighting was common enough at bees and other gatherings, nothing of the kind was allowed at a wedding celebration, where it was considered that everyone should be good-natured. A dance was the inevitable concomitant of a wedding; in fact to dance until daylight during several succeeding nights was not uncommon. The older people seldom attended the wedding celebration, probably feeling that their absence would be appreciated; but they usually joined in the dances.

A species of amusement once very common, and still to be found in some parts of Ontario, was the charivari or chivaree; this was, in early times, particularly connected with second marriages, or when the parties were unequal in age, or unpopular. The custom was to be found in parts of England, and in Canada it originated among the French in Quebec. Gourlay wrote early in the pioneer period concerning the usual reasons which led to the chivaree:

"I have observed no essential peculiarity in the funerals or weddings of this country; but there is a singular custom of 'chereverreeing', as it is called, a newly-married couple, where the match is thought to be unequal or unseasonable; as between an old man and a young girl, or within a short period after the death of a former husband or wife. Sometimes it is in consequence of the offence so frequently caused by a neglect of invitation to the wedding."[27]

The chivaree party would steal up to the home of the newly-wedded, usually after midnight, and suddenly music (?) from tin horns, horse-bells, "bull-roarers", "horse-fiddles", tin pans, and copper kettles would burst upon the ears of those within the house. If the bridegroom did not come forth and meet the demands for refreshments, or money (to be spent at the tavern), the discordant uproar would continue the rest of the night, and often on succeeding nights. Where the marriage was considered particularly objectionable the charivari was much more serious

[26]"An old lady in Ameliasburgh" quoted in William Canniff: *History of the Settlement of Upper Canada.* 1869. p. 239.
[27]Gourlay, *op. cit.,* Vol. I, p. 254.

than a serenade. The roysterers have been known to climb
to the roof of the house and close up the opening of the
chimney with the intention of smoking the wedding party
out; fighting, and occasionally death, resulted from such
proceedings. Gourlay noted that the chivaree was sometimes a subject of prosecution, but that it was generally
considered best to regard it "with good humour, as a joke
unworthy of serious notice".[28]

Bees were, perhaps, the most noted occasions of amusement in the rural districts in pioneer days. An early
settler in the Bay of Quinté district refers to them as
"great institutions in those days. Every settler was
licensed to make two or three each year, provided he furnished a good 'pot pie', and plenty of grog, and never made
any objections to his guests fighting".[29] Races, gymnastics,
wrestling matches, feats of strength such as putting the
stone and hurling the hammer, axemanship, and skill in
handling recalcitrant oxen or horses provided amusement
for many of the younger people at bees. They spent the
evening in dancing, while the older men and women who did
not care to dance concluded the day's work by conversation
about their common interests—the crops, prices, local politics, and such news as had come from the Old Land.

Paring, quilting and the other domestic bees supplied
the women with an opportunity to become acquainted; here
were discussed family affairs, house furnishings, recipes,
new arrivals in the neighbourhood, and the usual run of
petty scandal. It has been said that these bees have never
been equalled as "a clearing-house for gossip";[30] but the
men learned just as much news at the tavern, the blacksmith shop, the general store and, in later days, at the
barber shop, though the last-named sanctuary disappeared
when bobbed hair became the fashion!

The dances or "hops" which almost invariably closed
every bee were frequently held in the barn. Games and
"forfeits" alternated with dancing, and were frequently
accompanied by much flirtation. Such "kissing bees", like

[28]*Ibid.*
[29]"An old settler in Ameliasburgh" quoted in Canniff, *op. cit.*, p. 628.
[30]W. S. Herrington: *Pioneer Life on the Bay of Quinté.* (Lennox and
    Addington Historical Society, *Papers and Records*, Vol. VI,
    p. 17).

all other evils, are stated by some writers to have originated in the United States; though it may be said that in general these amusements were then considered quite innocent, whatever opinion might be held by later generations.

Of all the amusements of early times dancing was the most universal and appears to have given the greatest pleasure to the greatest number. The rhythmic beats of the war dance of the savage have been varied through the centuries into other types of sound, until many consider the jazz of today a reversion to type. The music supplied at dances was not, however, the all-important matter in pioneer days: where a fiddler or a bag-piper was not obtainable the young people whistled, sang, or made music with a comb. In much of the dancing in the rural districts more exercise than grace was apparent. Waltzing was not generally popular, the square dance being most in vogue. In the towns, dancing-schools taught various fancy minuets and quadrilles, but the backwoods settlers were quite satisfied with the usual country dances. Scotch and Irish reels, four-hand and eight-hand reels, jigs and hornpipes varied in popularity with the nationality of the participants.

Above the noise of the dancing could be heard the scraping sound of the fiddle, and the voice of the caller-off as he shouted "Salute your Partners", "Promenade All", or "Grand Chain". Some rustic dances called for equally rustic directions from the caller-off, whose shouts "Balance to the next and all swing out", "Gents hook up, ladies bounce back", "Down the centre and chaw hay", usually exhibited more ingenuity than gentility. Among the popular dance music of pioneer days were prominent *The Soldiers' Joy, Money Musk, Old Dan Tucker* and *Pop Goes the Weasel*. The enthusiasm of the dancers usually in-.creased as the night passed:

"The dancers hop and reel round, toes up and heels down, and turn to the right and left with one foot, and clap their hands and snap their fingers, and whoop, with ever-increasing heartiness. The fiddler gets inspired, plays faster and faster, his foot keeping time on the big chest, making a loud hollow sound. The boys get around him, and every time he rises from the chair they move it a little nearer the edge of the chest. At last the excitement is at its height; up goes a whoop, and down comes the chair, fiddler and all, landing on Farmer M's head, and the heads of two or three others, bringing them to the floor in a heap. Soon order is restored, the fiddle starts again, and the fun goes fast and furious."[31]

While the barn was good enough for most rural dances, it became customary in some localities to hold dances in the dining-room,—or in the "ball-room" over the driving-shed,— of the country tavern. Guests at inns had frequently to vacate their rooms when a large dance was being held. The young men usually took up a collection among themselves to pay the expenses, while the girls brought the refreshments. An old soldier, a negro, or someone else in the neighbourhood who had a reputation as a fiddler, usually provided the music.

A man who frequently officiated as fiddler at dances states that almost anyone was allowed to join in the fun, even if he was a stranger in the community. Once while he and his brother were travelling westward from Port Hope along the Kingston Road, they came to an inn where a dance was in progress, and, upon the invitation of the landlord, joined the party. Scarcely had they entered the room "when two girls came up and invited us to be their partners. (We did not wait for introductions in those days). The dance was the 'opera reel', with girls on one side and boys on the other in parallel lines. It was while holding opposite lines that the fancy steps were put in. My brother was one of the best fancy dancers I have ever seen, and after the girls saw how he could 'step it off' we had no lack of partners for the rest of the evening. I sometimes served as fiddler at local dances, and even yet I can see the bright-eyed girls, clad in homespun, as they swing in the arms of the swains of long ago."[32]

In the "Huron Tract" there were in the thirties, when it was in process of settlement, dances in taverns which were by no means cheap: while the ladies paid nothing, a gentleman's subscription was about $5, for which sum, however, he was entitled to bring with him a partner and a

[31]W. A. Mackay: *Pioneer Life in Zorra.* 1899. pp. 180-1.
[32]Reminiscences of H. L. Powers, Clarke Township, in W. L. Smith: *Pioneers of Old Ontario.* 1923. pp. 312-13.

servant, and "to be supplied with wine and other liquors, with tea and supper for himself and them". On producing a ticket anyone was admitted, whether strangers or not, and without any introduction. Before the dance commenced, "a solemn silence reigns, the gentlemen sitting on one side, the ladies on the other"; but once the dancing was under way all formalities were at an end, and the party seldom broke up before daylight.[33]

Rural balls were frequently the most attractive of amusements available to pioneer settlers. People would travel many miles through the bush to participate in the fun. It is said that a certain log schoolhouse in Guelph Township was erected "more for the purpose of holding a yearly dance than for educational purposes". The Paisley Block Ball was inaugurated in 1832 and soon became famous, "waxing beyond the concessions; and ultimately died after a long and brilliant career, through its sheer popularity".[34] Youth, beauty and music—a sugar-kettle outside for the preparation of whisky toddy—a huge currant loaf carried by several men—home-made cheese and home-made biscuits—a song composed for the occasion and sung to the air of *The Wearin' of the Green*—these combined to render the allurements of the Paisley Block Ball high in the public estimation. And even if many of the participants found it difficult to carry on farm work when the rising sun put an end to the festivities, all looked forward with keen anticipation to the next October and a renewal of the event.

In many ways, though often indirectly, were the rural inhabitants influenced by the more highly-developed social life of the towns. In spite of the difficulties of transportation and communication there was not usually that separation between urban and rural dweller which might have been expected. During the early years of all settlements hamlet and village were part of the township, and even the rather dry work of governing the municipality supplied diversion and interest to many a farmer. Until 1842 the township meeting provided the usual means of carrying

[33]R. and K. Lizars: *In the Days of the Canada Company*. 1896. p. 57.
[34]Thomas Laidlaw quoted in Fred Williams: *Do You Know?*, in the Toronto *Mail and Empire*, October 7, 1932.

on such local affairs as were within the powers of municipalities. The District Councils Act of 1841 instituted county councils, which enabled men to establish a greater contact with, and interest in their fellow-settlers in other parts of the county. Town and village councils frequently drew some of their most public-spirited members from the rural inhabitants dwelling near by, for anyone living within two miles of a settlement might be elected to its municipal council. People took their politics very seriously in pioneer days, and debate and argument frequently gave way to personalities and fisticuffs, all of which added to the spice of life even if it created hostility and enmity between families.

Among the first commercialised amusements to become available to all except the most remote settlers was the circus. Such organisations were almost exclusively of American origin and their advertisements were always greatly exaggerated. Appearing first in the towns, they were soon visiting every settled part of the province, stopping usually at well-known taverns and putting on their performance under canvas. It was unusual for them to attempt any programme, the show consisting of a menagerie, some of the animals of which could perform. From press advertisements a historian has been able to follow the itineraries of several of these circuses, and to show how generally accessible they were, though, of course, remote or "backwoods" settlers had sometimes to walk thirty miles or more to see them:

"In 1828 one organisation, with a typical itinerary, stopped at Ancaster on June 16th and 17th, Jones' Inn, Dundas, the 18th, Summers' Inn, Nelson, the 19th, and Smith's Inn, Trafalgar, on the 20th. . . . Another circus, in 1836, after travelling through the Bathurst District, stopped at Kingston, Bath and Belleville. On reaching Toronto it remained three days, then went to Markham, Crew's Tavern at Thornhill, Newmarket, and French's Tavern on Yonge Street. It next proceeded west to Munro's Inn and the Nelson Hotel. Thus in the Home District alone there were nine performances within forty miles. These examples are ample evidence that the public well patronised these entertainments, and problems of communication did not make them inaccessible, except to the most isolated settlers."[35]

Many of these travelling shows were American in sentiment to an extent that is so frequently apparent in modern times in the motion pictures of Hollywood; but perhaps it was stretching the point a little to exhibit at a tavern near Ancaster a show including "the glorious victory over the British at New Orleans". No wonder a traveller considered it "a public insult".[36]

Theatrical entertainments, exhibitions and concerts of either local or itinerant talent, and somewhat more ambitious than those attempted at rural taverns, became increasingly common in the towns as the years passed, and they were patronised not only by the townspeople but by many inhabitants of the neighbouring districts. The lodges and other social organisations of the urban centres had also an influence on rural life. The National Societies of St. George, St. Patrick and St. Andrew, though organised in the towns, usually drew many members from the surrounding country; while Agricultural and Horticultural Societies often contained more rural than urban members, though the meetings were commonly held in a tavern at or near the town. The Public Exhibitions of schools and colleges, resembling in some respects the modern "commencement", attracted proud parents from all parts of the country, but they must have been rather monotonous affairs to the vast majority of the audience.

The rural inhabitants also took a prominent part in the militia parades, usually held on the King's birthday, and in such other holiday festivities as took place in the towns. Parade-day, which was held at convenient points in the rural districts as well as in the towns, consisted in a small amount of rather ludicrous drill followed by horse-races and other sporting activities, and frequently ending in fighting engendered by excessive drinking. Mrs. Jameson's description of parade-day in 1837 at Springfield (Erindale),

[35]J. J. Talman: *Social Life in Upper Canada, 1815-1840.* p. 134. (Unpublished). The paging is of the typewritten MS.
[36]Pickering, *op. cit.*, November 5, 1826.

GRAND MENAGERIE
By Permission of the Police.

Zebra.

Camel.

THIS Grand Collection of BEASTS, late of N. Y. City Zoological Institute, will be exhibited at COBOURG, on Friday, the 3d day of September FOR ONE DAY ONLY, from 1 to 5 in the Day.

This collection comprises the largest and most general variety perhaps now travelling. The splendid preservation of the Giraffe or Camel-Leopard, is beautiful beyond description. Shortly after shipping it died, the proprietor sustaining a loss of some $20,000, but the animal being so extraordinarily fine and full grown, it was thought proper it should be preserved in the most natural and perfect way, which renders this grand display of Natural Curiosities still more attractive and complete.

The Keeper Mr. Shaffer, will enter the den of the Lions, Tigers, &c. and fondle and handle them with seeming ease; the perfectly cool and collected manner in which he enters and maintains throughout is perhaps unequalled in the known world, not excepting the celebrated Van Amburg, who has astonished all Europe in this most daring and unaccountable manner.

The Proprietors would say to the Public that this Exhibition is under the strictest discipline in all its departments, and so entirely foreign in its nature from all Circus or Mountebank Shows, that it meets with most cordial and general approbation even in the most refined and religious communities—from the fact that it serves rather to instruct than traduce the nobler qualities of the mind.

ADMITTANCE 1s. 3d. Children Half Price.
Cobourg, Sept. 18th, 1840. 2w48

From the *Cobourg Star*, August 20, 1840

MENAGERIE ADVERTISEMENT, 1840
The typical travelling circus of a century ago is here described in characteristic language

GRAND MILITARY STEEPLECHASE, AT LONDON, C.W.,
MAY 9, 1843

A "TURN-OUT" OF THE 43RD LIGHT INFANTRY AT THE FALLS
OF NIAGARA, 1839

The various officers may be identified from the original print

in the County of Peel, may be considered typical of the 4th
of June celebration in the rural districts:

"On a rising ground above the river which ran gurgling
and sparkling through the green ravine beneath, the motley
troops, about three or four hundred men, were marshalled
—no, not marshalled, but scattered in a far more picturesque fashion hither and thither: a few log houses and
a saw-mill on the river bank, and a little wooden church
crowning the opposite height, formed the chief features of
the scene. The boundless forest spread all around us.

"A few men, well mounted and dressed as lancers, in
uniforms which were, however, anything but uniform,
flourished backwards on the green sward, to the manifest
peril of the spectators; themselves and their horses,
equally wild, disorderly, spirited, undisciplined: but this
was perfection compared with the infantry. Here there was
no uniformity attempted of dress, of appearance, of movement; a few had coats, others jackets; a greater number
had neither coats nor jackets, but appeared in their shirt-
sleeves, white or checked, or clean or dirty, in edifying
variety. Some wore hats, others caps, others their own
shaggy heads of hair. Some had firelocks; some had old
swords, suspended in belts, or stuck in their waistbands;
but the greater number shouldered sticks or umbrellas. Mrs.
M. told us that on a former parade-day she had heard
the word of command given thus—'Gentlemen with the
umbrellas, take ground to the right! Gentlemen with the
walking-sticks take ground to the left!'

"Now they ran after each other, elbowed and kicked each
other, straddled, stooped, chattered; and if the commanding
officer turned his back for a moment, very coolly sat down on
the bank to rest. Not to laugh was impossible, and defied
all power of face. Charles M. made himself hoarse with
shouting out orders which no one obeyed, except, perhaps,
two or three men in the front; and James, with his horsemen, flourished their lances, and galloped and capered and
curveted to admiration. . . .

"The parade-day ended in a drunken bout and a riot,
in which, as I was afterwards informed, the colonel had
been knocked down, and one or two serious and even fatal
accidents had occurred; but it was all taken so very lightly,

so very much as a thing of course in this half-civilised community that I soon ceased to think about the matter."[37]

Contemporary accounts of holiday celebrations show that excesses were expected, and that the authorities were surprised and quite obviously pleased when the day passed off without "bloody battles", fatal accidents, or other untoward incidents. In the rear concessions, particularly where the lumbering industry was prominent, serious trouble was frequently the result of holidays, fairs, or other occasions where rival elements in the population came together. Bytown and Richmond on the Ottawa were the scene of several such riots, and on many occasions clashes were very narrowly averted.

Elections, held both in the towns and at rural taverns or other convenient locations, usually lasted a week, and were often productive of riotous conditions, for men's political feelings and animosities were easily aroused at a time when life was hard, and kept inflamed by the incitements of the electoral practices of the times—open voting, intimidation and bribery, and, what was even worse, the intoxicants freely distributed at the expense of the candidates. An excellent description of a typical election week is given by Walter S. Herrington:

"Parliamentary elections today are very tame affairs compared with those of a century ago. The open vote afforded opportunities for exciting scenes that the rising generations know not of. The closing of the bars on election day has robbed the occasion of a good deal of romance. The actual voting contest is now limited to eight hours, from nine to five, and one might rest peacefully in a room adjoining a polling booth and not be aware that an election was in progress. It was all very different even fifty years ago. Whisky and the open vote were two very potent factors in keeping up the excitement. Instead of having several booths scattered throughout each township there was only one in the electoral district.

"The principal village in the district was generally selected, but sometimes the only booth was set up in a country tavern, especially if it was in a central location and the proprietor could pull enough political strings. A platform

[37]Jameson, *op. cit.*, Vol. I, pp. 300-303.

would be constructed out of rough boards and protected
from the weather by a slanting roof. On Monday morning
of election week the candidates and their henchmen would
assemble in the vicinity of the platform, which was known
as the husting. The electors would come pouring in from all
parts of the electoral district. Each party would have its
headquarters at a tavern or tent, or both, where the workers would lay their plans. The forenoon would be spent in
listening to the orators of the day, and at one o'clock the
polling would begin.

"It is easy to imagine what would happen to the doubtful
voter when he arrived at the village. As the poll was kept
open every day until Saturday night it is not quite so easy
to picture the scene during the last day or two of a hot
contest. Couriers with foaming horses were going and coming. Heated discussions frequently terminated in a rough-
and-tumble fight in which a score or more participated.
Drunken men reeled about the streets until carefully stowed
away by their friends in a tent or stall in the tavern stable.

"If the inebriate had not yet polled his vote, his whilom
friends would be more solicitous in the attention bestowed
upon him. It not infrequently happened that the indifferent
voter would purposely play into the hands of both parties.
It was a golden opportunity for free lunches and whisky,
and the longer he deferred the fateful hour when he was
to announce to the returning officer the candidate of his
choice the more difficult it was for him to choose. In his
dilemma he would seek his solace in a little more whisky,
and, in the end, perhaps vote for the wrong man. If unhappily he did make such a mistake, his political guardians
never failed to call his attention to the error in a manner
not likely to be soon forgotten. Such incidents were thereafter associated in the mind of the offended with the unpleasant recollections of the village pump or the nearest
creek."[38]

Public holidays were infrequent in pioneer days, but
there were more occasions when both townsmen and farmers would call it a day and hold a celebration in honour of

[38]Herrington: *Pioneer Life on the Bay of Quinté* (Lennox and Ad-
    dington Historical Society, *Papers and Records*, Vol. VI, pp.
    20-21).

some notable event. Among the most usual opportunities in war time for such festivities were the reports of victories over the enemy,—even if the news did arrive three or four months after the event!

Even in "the backwoods" any excuse for a celebration was promptly seized. Samuel Strickland describes an impromptu holiday in 1830 among the employees of the Canada Company near Goderich, then "far in the bush". The occasion was about two months after the death of George IV and the accession of William IV, a newspaper having just been received from the Old Country with the news. The squire read the proclamation to the assemblage, which included "everyone within ten miles"; then nine British cheers were given, the National Anthem was sung, "accompanied by the Goderich band composed of two fiddles and a tambourine", and everyone drank his Majesty's health from a pail of whisky with a tea-cup floating on the surface, "even the fair sex, on this propitious occasion, not disdaining to moisten their pretty lips with the beverage".

After the party had eaten and drunk everything in sight the band struck up *The Wind Shakes the Barley*, and country dances, French fours, and Scotch reels alternated on the level meadow; while those who did not dance amused themselves in ball-playing, pitch-and-hustle, and a variety of old English games. Even the "Yankee" millwright waxed enthusiastic: "I do declare", said he, "if this don't almost put me in mind of the 4th of July. Well, I vow if I don't feel quite loyal. Come, let us drink the old gentleman's health agin. I guess I feel as dry as a sand-bank after so much hollerin' ".[39]

Picnic parties, often combined with berrying or fishing, were more frequent when the hardships incident to the first years of settlement in the wilds were past. The experience of the Hon. William Hamilton Merritt, who, when a youth of sixteen, "went strawberrying with a nice party, lots of fine young girls, very delightful",[40] is typical of such activities. The "merry maple sugar making" was similarly an occasion of happiness among the young people, and

[39]Strickland, *op. cit.*, Vol. I, pp. 289-91.
[40]Journal of William Hamilton Merritt, July 8, 1809. (Coventry Papers, Public Archives of Canada.)

"sugar-eating bees" and other parties of a pleasant character welcomed the first signs of spring. In later years tea-meetings, fowl or oyster suppers, garden parties and strawberry festivals, usually in connection with church or school, were prominent events in every locality, and their popularity has remained undiminished to the present.

The pleasures of home life are, perhaps, better imagined than described. The evenings spent around the open fire, reading and sewing, cracking nuts or popping corn with the children, provided most satisfaction and enjoyment to those whose training and inclination enabled them to appreciate the better things of life. Among such people pleasures and amusements were undoubtedly most refined and of greatest permanence. A settler of education frequently spent most of his spare time writing letters to "the old folks at home", —letters which have so greatly enriched the annals of pioneer life in Canada. Many examples might also be given of the pleasure derived from the beautiful scenery, the luxuriant wild flowers, and the birds and animals, all so characteristic of the country. One settler was very enthusiastic about Canadian sunsets, and wrote in his diary:

"June 6, 1843,—Sunday—I witnessed on this evening a splendid and gorgeous sunset, far surpassing anything of the kind I had ever seen at home. Even a sunset in Italy, as a commissariat officer settled on a farm near me (who had served in that country) declared, could not be compared to it".[41]

Among those in whom the love of nature was a source of infinite pleasure none rank higher in their contribution to the literature of pioneer life than the Strickland sisters, Mrs. Catharine Traill and Mrs. Susanna Moodie. Settled near Lakefield at the foot of Katchawanoonk Lake, they were in the beautiful Kawartha Lakes district. Mrs. Moodie describes a long-anticipated trip northward to Stoney Lake in the summer of 1835. They started out early one beautiful morning and paddled up the Katchawanoonk to Young's Point, where dwelt the first Youngs, hunters and millers. Two of the sons were to conduct the Moodies through Clear Lake to Stoney Lake, long the jealously-guarded paradise of Handsome Jack and his Indian tribe.

[41]Quoted in *Letters from Canada*, 10th Edition, 1862, p. 26.

After a banquet at the Youngs, which for variety of game, fish and pies would have done credit to the famous epicure, Samuel Pepys, the party of six set out. Two beautiful new birch bark canoes had just been purchased from the Indians, and in these the expedition was soon approaching Sandy Point, then a ridge extending half way across Clear Lake. A stop was made here to pick some of the beautiful flowers which grew in profusion; then the canoes rounded the point and entered Stoney Lake, the first sight of which called forth exclamations of delight from Mrs. Moodie:

"Oh! what a magnificent scene of wild and lonely grandeur burst upon us as we swept round the little peninsula, and the whole majesty of Stoney Lake broke upon us at once, another Lake of the Thousand Isles in miniature, and in the heart of the wilderness! Imagine a large sheet of water, some twenty-five miles in length, taken up by islands of every size and shape, from the lofty naked rock of red granite to the rounded hill covered with oak trees to its summit, while others were level with the waters, and of a rich emerald green, only fringed with a growth of aquatic shrubs and flowers. Never did my eye rest on a more lovely or beautiful scene. Not a vestige of man or his works was there. The setting sun that cast such a gorgeous flood of light upon this exquisite panorama, bringing out some of these lofty islands in strong relief, and casting others into intense shade, shed no cheery beam upon church spire or cottage. We beheld the landscape, savage and grand in its primeval beauty".[42]

[42]Susanna Moodie: *Roughing It in the Bush*. 1852. Edition of 1923, pp. 320-337.

CHAPTER X

AMUSEMENT AND SOCIAL LIFE IN THE TOWNS

"Had I but plenty of money, money enough and to spare,
The house for me no doubt, were a house in the city-square;
Ah, such a life, such a life, as one leads at the window there!

Something to see by Bacchus, something to hear, at least!
There, the whole day long, one's life is a perfect feast;
While up at a villa one lives, I maintain it, no more than a beast.

Ere you open your eyes in the city, the blessed church bells begin:
No sooner the bells leave off than the diligence rattles in:
You get the pick of the news, and it costs you never a pin.

Bang-whang-whang goes the drum, *tootle-te-tootle* the fife.
Oh, a day in the city-square, there is no such pleasure in life!"
ROBERT BROWNING: *Up at a Villa—Down in the City.*

WITH the exception of the settlements along the Detroit,
where the French predominated, and a few "backwoods"
villages where American influence early made itself felt,
the social life of the towns of Upper Canada during the first
half century after the creation of the province was pat-
terned after that of English towns of the same period.
This was largely a result of the influence of the official
class and the military, for the first towns, if they can be
dignified by that appellation, were primarily garrison towns.
Before entering upon a description of the social life of
these first centres of population it is essential to describe
their birth and early development.

When the Province of Upper Canada was established
in 1791 the chief inhabitants were a few thousand United
Empire Loyalists who had settled, during the preceding
seven years, along the shores of the St. Lawrence, the
Bay of Quinté, the head of Lake Ontario, and the Niagara
and Detroit Rivers. The settlement at Detroit had at that
time about 2,000 inhabitants, mostly French, and it was
the largest town in the province. When it was surrendered
to the United States in 1796 its population decreased from
2,200 to 500 owing to the exodus of British and French
Loyalists to the other side of the Detroit, where they could
remain under British rule. Fort Malden (Amherstburg)

was thereupon established to replace Detroit for military purposes, while Sandwich was laid out to accommodate many of the civilians.

Kingston, Niagara and York had each a share in the early administration of the government of Upper Canada, and each was a garrison town. While, however, Kingston and Niagara had been military and naval posts for many years, the town of York was not founded until 1793. In 1794 Kingston had a population of 345, while a lesser number of people lived at Niagara and York, the garrison comprising most of the inhabitants in every case. The growth of these settlements was very slow for many years, York increasing from 336 in 1801 to 577 in 1809, and having a population of only 1,240 in 1820.

By 1823 the population of Upper Canada had increased to about 130,000, but the largest town was Kingston with 2,336 inhabitants. At the end of the first quarter of the century the chief towns and villages of Upper Canada were Cornwall, Prescott, Brockville and Gananoque on the St. Lawrence; Perth and Richmond in the Ottawa Valley; Kingston, Bath, Napanee and Hallowell (Picton) in the Bay of Quinté district; Belleville, Cobourg, Port Hope and York along the shores of Lake Ontario; Hamilton, Dundas and Ancaster at the head of the lake; Grimsby, St. Catharines, Niagara, Queenston, Chippawa and Fort Erie in the Niagara district; St. Thomas, Vittoria, Burford, Woodstock and Shade's Mills (Galt) in the inland districts northward from Lake Erie; and Chatham, Sandwich and Amherstburg in the west. Many of these settlements were very small "backwoods" villages, but they were centres of trade for large areas surrounding them, and in most cases had post offices to add to their importance. The present large cities of Ottawa and London, and many a smaller one, had not even been founded in 1825.

The turning-point in the growth of population occurred in the late twenties, when immigration on a large scale resulted in a great development of the towns. York, for example, comprised only 1,817 people in 1827, but by 1833 it had a population of 6,094, and was to become the city of Toronto in the following year. In 1837 Cobourg had a population of 1,653, while thirteen years earlier it had num-

W. H. Bartlett

THE CITY HALL AT BROADWAY AND PARK ROW, NEW YORK
CITY, 1837
The New York bus of a century ago may be seen in the foreground

From *London Interiors.* 1842

THE STOCK EXCHANGE, LONDON, ENGLAND, IN 1840
These reproductions of steel engravings illustrate contemporary
conditions in New York and London

From the *Illustrated London News*, April 4, 1868

MR. AND MRS. DISRAELI'S ASSEMBLY AT THE NEW FOREIGN
OFFICE, LONDON, 1868

Reproduced by Courtesy of Miss Ivy Romain, who appears at the lower right.

FANCY DRESS BALL IN AID OF THE PROTESTANT ORPHANS'
HOME, TORONTO

The old Music Hall, Adelaide and Church Streets, April 19, 1870

bered only about 100; Brockville had 1,130 inhabitants in
1830, and Brantford was surveyed into village lots during
the same year. St. Thomas, London and Bytown (Ottawa)
were rapidly becoming thriving towns. An exception to
the general development was provided by the slow growth
of the western villages, Chatham, Amherstburg, Sandwich
and Richmond (Windsor), none of which had a population
of more than a few hundred until the late forties.

In describing the social life of the towns, York will
serve as an example of the development of the official and
garrison towns, of which Kingston and Niagara were the
chief others; and Cobourg will provide an illustration of the
growth of social life in settlements of lesser rank. What
was taking place in York and Cobourg may be presumed to
have been characteristic, with local variations, of the other
towns along "the front"; while social life in the later-
settled "backwoods" villages was similar, due allowance
being made for their remoteness and comparative inac-
cessibility. Many other towns will, however, be mentioned
from time to time.

At Kingston, Niagara and York, and to a lesser extent
at Amherstburg, the presence of government officials,
officers of the army and navy, and other "gentlemen", gave
a higher tone to social life than was usually to be found
elsewhere during the early period of settlement. The
amusements of that day depended largely upon individual
effort, or upon arrangements made by small groups of social
equals. Both women and men were fond of visiting their
friends and associates, and such calls, especially on New
Year's Day, were of a much more formal nature than visits
in the rural districts, where the elements of spontaneity
and surprise predominated in the interchange of civilities.

Class distinctions were very rigid in early days, and
the fashionable society of these first towns was restricted
to a comparatively small section of the population. The
military and civilians alike were fond of horse-racing and
field sports, fishing and sailing, football and cricket in
summer, and of skating and carrioling in winter; while
at all seasons dancing, chess, whist, wine and conversation
served to while away the time.

Mrs. Simcoe gives some account of these activities in

her diary. While at Niagara she wrote: "We play at whist every evening. Colonel Simcoe is so occupied during the day with business that it is a relaxation. I have not lost one rubber since the 28th of November. We usually play four every evening."[1] Two weeks later she notes: "Mrs. Macaulay gave me an account of a subscription ball she was at, which is to be held in the town of Niagara every fortnight during the winter. There were fourteen couples, a great display of gauze, feathers and velvét, the room lighted by wax candles, and there was a supper as well as tea."[2] In 1796 she refers to a ball at her house where "we danced eighteen couple and sat down to supper seventy-six".[3] Military bands supplied the music at these official social functions, and at all fashionable balls or "assemblies" in the garrison towns full evening or military dress was worn.

The first notice with reference to public dances in York occurs in the *Gazette* of December 8, 1798, where it is announced that a meeting of "the gentlemen of the town and the garrison" will be held at Miles' Hotel to arrange for the York assemblies.[4] The earliest of these events of which we have an intimate account took place at Frank's Hotel in 1814. The original manuscript of the arrangements informs us that "at a meeting of the gentlemen of York, subscribers to the assemblies, Stephen Jarvis and George Ridout, Esquires, were appointed managers for the season, the sum to be paid by each subscriber to be three pounds, Halifax currency. . . . First dance on St. Andrew's night, dancing to begin at half-past eight o'clock. The dresses worn by the ladies are called "chaste and elegant"; while a private letter gives us the interesting information that "one lady of great loveliness" wore black lace over an underskirt of crimson, with an artificial rose in her waist and hair.[5] A few prominent merchants usually joined the government officials and the officers of the garrison in these dances.

A notable ball took place at Niagara in 1807, on the

[1]*Diary of Mrs. John Graves Simcoe,* December 31, 1792.
[2]*Ibid.,* January 15, 1793.   [3]*Ibid.,* June 4, 1796.
[4]York *Upper Canada Gazette,* December 8, 1798.
[5]See John Ross Robertson: *Landmarks of Toronto.* 1894-1914. Vol. I,
    p. 498.

evening of the King's Birthday, June 4th. It provided a fitting climax to the annual militia parade-day, and appears to have been arranged on a grander scale than any held previously in Upper Canada. The *Gazette* contained a full account of it:

"His Excellency Lieut.-Governor Gore, having previously announced his intention of celebrating his Majesty's birthday at this place, arrived with Mrs. Gore and suite early on Tuesday morning.

"On Wednesday, the 3rd, a numerous and splendid assemblage of ladies from various and distant parts of the district were presented to Mrs. Gore, who received them with all that ease and politeness which inspires confidence, and for which she is so universally distinguished and admired.

"The ball commenced at 8 o'clock in the Council House, which was fitted up and lighted in an elegant manner, with an orchestra of the charming band of the 41st Regiment. A temporary building was also erected, eighty feet in length and of sufficient width for two sets of tables to accommodate 200 persons at supper, and the building was connected with the dancing-room by a covered way.

"Mrs. Gore and the Honourable Robert Hamilton led off the first dance, and about fifty couple of spirited dancers occupied the floor till one o'clock, when they retired into the supper-room where a most sumptuous entertainment, served up with true English elegance, was provided. Everything rare and good was found on the hospitable board, and the wines of Champagne and Burgundy served to recruit the exhausted spirits and called for a renewal of the dance, which was kept up till after daylight, when the company separated, highly satisfied with their princely entertainment.

"On the whole the birthday was celebrated with a splendour and magnificence hitherto unknown in this country."[6]

People frequently travelled long distances to be present at the social gatherings of the *élite*. Mrs. Anna Jameson wrote on May 20, 1837: "Last night a ball at the government-house, to which people came from a distance of fifty— a hundred—two hundred miles—which is nothing to signify

[6]*York Gazette*, June 13, 1807.

here. There were very pretty girls, and very nice dancing". The wealthier classes usually insisted on the best of music at their assemblies, and if the Paul Whiteman or Vincent Lopez of the day was not available the deficiency was quickly noticed; Mrs. Jameson, for example, referring to the same ball, observed that "we had all too much reason to lament the loss of the band of the 66th Regiment, which left us a few weeks ago—to my sorrow".[7]

It was not easy to be up-to-the-minute in dance steps when square and fancy dancing was in vogue. Quadrilles and schottisches were usual at the fashionable balls at Government House on such occasions as the opening of legislature; while dancing schools endeavoured in addition to insure proficiency in "Zodiac's New Pantomime, Scotch Sling, Children's Hornpipes, the 6th and 4th Hanoverian Waltzes, De la Cour Minuet walked in six corners, and Country Dances".[8]

In some localities the character of the inhabitants, apart altogether from the influence of the officers of the garrison or the officials of the government, was the factor which led to the development of a gay and refined social life. In Cobourg, for example, sleighing parties, afternoon teas and informal dances were prominent in the early twenties among a number of aristocratic families of half-pay officers and other "genteel" settlers. A few years later the gentlemen settlers in the Newcastle District were holding "Bachelor's Balls" in Cobourg and Peterborough, and the select society in which they moved was said to be "the most brilliant and polished in Canada".[9]

Even backwoodsmen like John Langton and Thomas Need arrayed themselves in full dress and drove thirty or forty miles to attend these dances. In 1833 Need travelled from Peterborough to Cobourg by sleigh to attend a ball,

[7]Anna Jameson: *Winter Studies and Summer Rambles in Canada.* 1838. Vol. I, p. 292. One of the most celebrated fancy-dress balls in the early days of York was one held in 1827 in the assembly room of Frank's Hotel; this was given jointly by John Galt, Commissioner of the the Canada Company, and Lady Mary Willis, wife of Mr. Justice Willis. A full description of the event may be found in Henry Scadding: *Toronto of Old.* 1873. pp. 111-12.

[8]Kingston *Upper Canada Herald,* August 2, 1825.

[9]Patrick Shirreff: *A Tour through North America.* 1835. p. 123.

and was "amply repaid for the trouble by a lively dance, good music, and excellent supper. The ladies of Upper Canada, like their sisters of the Northern States, are strikingly handsome in early youth, and pleasing and natural in their manners: about thirty couple of dancers assembled, who kept up the ball until nearly daylight".[10] In February, 1836, he wrote in his journal: "On the 29th, (being leap year), I mounted my sleigh and drove along the new road, to assist at a ball given by the bachelors of the district at Peterborough. 'A ball in the Bush!' I think I hear my fair partners of former days exclaim; but let me assure them that the bachelors of our district are not at all to be despised, and that the 'rank and fashion' of the neighbourhood comprised nearly 200 persons."[11]

A similar social life flourished at other points where aristocratic settlers were to be found in sufficient numbers. Near Woodstock Mrs. Jameson found the society "particularly good; several gentlemen of family, superior education, and large capital, (among whom is the brother of an English and the son of an Irish peer, a colonel and a major in the army), have made very extensive purchases of land and their estates are in flourishing progress".[12] She observed, however, an unfortunate lack of social intercourse in many other parts of Upper Canada, a condition which bore most heavily upon the women. Referring to London she noted that "here, as everywhere else, I find the women of the better class lamenting over the want of all society, except of the lowest grade in manners and morals. For those who have recently emigrated, and are settled more in the interior, there is absolutely no social intercourse whatever".[13]

The wayside tavern and the town inn were centres of the social life of the community to an extent which is hard to realise in modern times. The inn, like the mill, formed the nucleus around which developed many a village; and not infrequently the tavern-keeper was the best-known and most popular man in the district. The first church services and circuses were held at taverns, as well as dances, ban-

[10]Thomas Need: *Six Years in the Bush*. 1838. p. 47.
[11]*Ibid.*, p. 116.
[12]Jameson, *op. cit.*, Vol. II, p. 124.
[13]*Ibid.*, Vol. II, pp. 146-8.

quets, and the meetings of Agricultural Societies, lodges and other social organisations. Those who, like Sir John Falstaff, enjoyed taking their ease at their inn had plenty of choice in a day of taverns. In addition to the usual pleasures of eating, drinking and smoking, there was evident a spirit of conviviality in many a hostelry. The roaring logs of the winter fireplace added zest to the discussion of clergy reserves, bad roads, and European news three months old.

A type of amusement in which many an early traveller participated was the pleasure created in stage-coach hostelries when the guests gathered around the open fire in the living-room and related their experiences of travel and adventure. Mine host of the inn was always ready to develop any subject of interest, for the hotel-keeper was in close touch with everything that affected the life of the community, and was first informed of the news from distant parts. Much of this sociability and entertainment disappeared when coaching days came to an end, and the importance of the inn was still further diminished by the speedy travel made possible by the motor-car; but, though the growth of centres of population has removed the intimate touch between host and guest, the hotel remains much more than "a house of public entertainment",[14] for it is the meeting-place of conventions, clubs and banquets, and the social centre for balls, bridges and receptions.

Lodges and fraternal societies played a very important part in early social life, especially after settlements had grown into thriving communities. The first Masonic Lodge in Canada was formed among the members of the garrison at Halifax in 1749, and the first in Upper Canada at Niagara in 1793. Among other fraternal organisations were the Saints and the Orangemen, a celebration of the latter association being recorded in the press of York in 1822.[15]

The National Societies of St. Patrick, St. George and St.

[14] A "house of entertainment" was an inn without a tavern license. The difference was more imaginary than real, however, for Joseph Pickering observed (*Inquiries of an Emigrant*, November 4, 1826) that one was served whisky with his meals, but the law was superficially observed by charging only for the food, though the price was always made high enough to include the drink!

[15] *York Gazette*, July 18, 1822.

Andrew were long important in the social life of the towns. These organisations date from the early years of the province, for they were prominent in Niagara in the seventeen-nineties. A St. Andrew's Dinner, for example, was held there on November 30, 1799, the Hon. Robert Hamilton entertaining thirty Scotchmen and a few of other nationalities on that occasion. A report of the event says that it was considered that "no dinner on any occasion has been given in the Canadas equal to Mr. Hamilton's".[16] In some instances the Societies were early established but were intermittent in their activities, so that it is not always easy to trace their inauguration. After the first quarter of the nineteenth century the organisations were more common. In the early twenties there was a St. George's Society in York, while in the thirties and forties some or all of the national societies were to be found in Cobourg, By-town, Kingston, and numerous other towns. At first all meetings were held in taverns, but in later days many societies had club-rooms of their own.

It was natural that such organisations should be formed at a time when many of the inhabitants of the province had come but recently from the Old Land. The feeling of nationality was strong, and the memories of former days amid very different surroundings were fondly treasured. The English, Irish and Scottish societies were at the height of their popularity in the late fifties and early sixties, when many of the first settlers of importance were still living, and before the growth of national feeling in Canada had received a strong impetus as a result of the Fenian Raids and the Confederation movement. A description of the activities of the societies in Cobourg during this period may be assumed to be characteristic of the organisations.

On April 23, 1864, the members of the St. George's Society combined the celebration of St. George's Day with that of the 300th anniversary of the birth of Shakespeare. An outdoor demonstration during the day was prevented by heavy rains, but at 7 p.m. about 150 men, including representatives of the other national societies, sat down to a dinner of which it is said in the press that "the Roast Beef of Old England occupied prominent places on the table,

[16]Niagara *Canada Constellation*, December 7, 1799.

which was loaded with all that the eye could fancy or the palate suggest". No less than twelve toasts were proposed by the chairman and each was responded to by one or more speakers. Between toasts many a good old song was sung, among them *The Fine Old English Gentleman, When I a-Courting Went, Old King Cole,* and *The Laird o' Cockpen.* As midnight approached, the proceedings waxed Shakespearian when the Principal of the Grammar School gave an excellent characterisation of Sir John Falstaff, choosing the ever-popular humorous scenes from the second act of the first part of Shakespeare's greatest historical play, *King Henry the Fourth.* The meeting was thus concluded in great merriment, and the happy company departed for their homes with reluctance.[17]

The St. Andrew's Society similarly celebrated the anniversary of its patron saint on November the 30th of each year. In 1862 a grand dinner was held in Cobourg, and the speech-making and singing thereafter occupied several hours, among the most popular songs being *The Scottish Thistle, Wha wad na fecht for Charlie, The Miller of Fife, Scotland Yet,* and the inevitable *Laird o'Cockpen.* After the last regular toast the President left the chair, and the party continued the round of toast, speech, song and chorus until the wee sma' hours o' morn.[18]

A particularly elaborate procession was characteristic of the St. Patrick's Day celebration. Headed by the Chief Marshall, the Union Jack and a brass band, the members, adorned with their gay regalia, paraded the streets of the town on March 17, 1862, carrying the insignia of the order, flags, battle-axes and wands. They proceeded to church, where the priest delivered an address on the life of St. Patrick; whereupon the members paraded back to the Globe Hotel and listened to speeches by the officials of the Society, after which the proceedings came to a close with cheers for Auld Ireland, Canada, and the Queen. The *Cobourg Sentinel* comments upon "the respectable and orderly manner" in which the celebration was conducted: "Nothing but good feeling, sobriety, order and decorum reigned throughout the whole day's proceedings, and Irishmen in this

17See the *Cobourg Sentinel*, April 30, 1864.
18*Ibid.*, December 6, 1862.

neighbourhood may long remember and feel proud of the manner in which St Patrick's Day was celebrated in Cobourg in 1862."[19]

It was usual for inhabitants of the rural districts to join their brethren in the towns in the activities of the national societies. Meetings were usually held once a month, and on special occasions balls and picnics were arranged which added not a little to the social life of the community. While the feeling of nationality remained very strong it was not unusual for fights and brawls to result from these activities, though such regrettable occurrences were more characteristic of events of a more partisan nature, such as Orangemen's "walks". In the seventies and eighties, however, so cordial were their relations that it was customary in Cobourg for the members of the three national societies to join in honouring each patron saint in turn by marching in a body to the church named by the Society directly concerned in the anniversary.

The national societies have continued to the present in some towns, the St. George's Society of Toronto, for example, having celebrated the anniversary in 1932 by holding the 98th annual dinner. But the survivals, if the same in name, are more in the nature of a "high festival of once a year", and have retained but little of the spirit of their predecessors of the later pioneer period; for the sense of original nationality decreased after the passing of the first generations, and there gradually developed a national feeling distinctly Canadian. There was, too, another circumstance which, though much less important, influenced in varying degrees all organisations in which banquets formed a prominent part: this was the changing attitude towards the free use of wines and liquors. As drinking in public came to be considered a vice rather than an accepted custom some men lost interest in such gatherings; for, whatever may be one's opinion concerning the use of intoxicants, there is no doubt that their effect at such meetings was to induce conviviality and create merriment, even if it was somewhat artificial, and, if judged by modern standards, not infrequently lacking in refinement.

Perhaps the most important mutual-benefit organisation

[19]*Ibid.*, March 22, 1862.

was that of the fire-fighters. At first everyone in the community was expected to join in such activities,—in fact it was his own interest to do so in a day when wooden buildings predominated, and when many a settlement was almost obliterated by fire. As fire brigades were soon to become prominent in the life of the town, some account of their development will not be out of place here. A regulation was in force in York in 1800 requiring that each householder must have a ladder leading from the ground to the roof of his house, and another placed on the roof as an approach to the chimney.[20]   In December, 1802, Governor Russell presented a fire engine to the town, and as an expression of their gratitude the citizens built a firehall by subscription.   In the eighteen-twenties it was the law in York that each householder must keep two leathern buckets hanging in a conspicuous place in front of his home. The only bell in the town was in St. James' Church, and upon an alarm of fire a double row of citizens was formed from the burning building to the Bay, or the nearest cistern or pump, and along one line passed buckets of water, while the empties returned along the other.   Among regulations adopted in York was one stating that fire wardens should have "a white handkerchief on the left arm, above the elbow, as a distinguishing badge of authority", and anyone who did not obey their orders might be fined from twenty to forty shillings.[21]

In 1826 the first fire department was organised in York, and among the members of this purely voluntary association were "some of the most respectable merchants and tradesmen of the town".   There were Fire-engine and Hook-and-Ladder companies, each with a full quota of officers.[22]   In a similar manner fire-fighters' organisations developed in other localities, and in many instances remained entirely voluntary societies until almost the end of the century. The members carried out their duties without remuneration, the social activities of the company being the chief attraction, though in some towns fire-fighters were exempt from poll tax, from militia duty in peace time,

[20]Ladders may be seen on the roofs of the houses of the garrison
      at York in the illustration facing page 105.
[21]York *U. E. Loyalist*, January 26, 1827.
[22][W. L. Mackenzie's] *New Almanac for the Canadian True Blues.*
      1834. p. 11.

ENGINE OF THE TORONTO FIRE BRIGADE, 1837

Effectively used in December, 1837, when Peter Matthews' rebels set
fire to the Don Bridge

ROSSIN HOUSE FIRE, TORONTO, NOVEMBER, 1862

A centre of social life for a century; 1833—British Coffee House;
1855-7—Rossin House, rebuilt in 1863; 1909—Prince George Hotel

FIREMEN'S ARCH IN COBOURG IN THE SEVENTIES

A Fire-Fighters' Meet—Rochester, Port Hope, Belleville and Oshawa

COBOURG FIREMEN AND PARADE MACHINE IN THE SEVENTIES

Volunteer fire brigades long played an important part in social life.
In the rear is Victoria Hall, opened in 1860 by the Prince of Wales

and from serving in the capacity of constable, juryman, or in any other office.

There was a spirit of camaraderie in the firemen's organisations that led to much wholesome rivalry between the companies of a brigade, and to competitions sometimes even international in scope. The Cobourg firemen, for example, frequently travelled to Kingston, Peterborough, Brantford and Rochester to engage in meets with other brigades, and to enjoy a social "good time" with them. In one town at least a certain spirit of bravado developed within the firemen's organisations, for it is more than hinted that some of the many incendiary fires in Cobourg in the sixties and seventies were started by firemen to provide excitement and to enable one company, which knew of the certainty of the fire before it occurred, to arrive upon the scene before its rivals.[23] It appears, however, that such activities were restricted to old, unused buildings; nor does the questionable conduct of individuals in any way detract from the public spirit and self-sacrifice which was characteristic of fire-fighters in Cobourg as elsewhere.

There was an annual festival and parade-day for the firemen of Cobourg, when the entire brigade of some 250 men marched in full uniform, and each company was inspected by the municipal council and received the cheers of its admiring friends. Fire engines and other equipment were polished to perfection for the occasion, and companies sometimes even had parade machines valued at $1500 or more, and without practical utility apart from the admiration which their display engendered! A grand supper and ball concluded the festival, and it was for many citizens the social event of the season. Among other activities of firemen's organisations were smaller dances, social evenings, picnics, and friendly calls upon the fire-fighters of neighbouring towns; there were occasions, too, when a minstrel show or some other theatrical venture would be undertaken by the members of the brigade.

The amusement and social intercourse based upon firemen's organisations came to an end with changing con-

[23]See E. C. Guillet: *Cobourg*, in the *Cobourg Sentinel-Star*, August 14, 1930. For many valuable reminiscences with reference to the history of Cobourg the writer is indebted to Postmaster Andrew Hewson.

ditions. As fire-fighting apparatus developed in efficiency, and centres of population increased in size, a more permanently-reliable force of firemen became necessary. In most towns and villages the fire department now receives some remuneration, and has lost most of its voluntary character; while in the cities fire-fighting has become a full-time occupation second to none in importance among civic employees.

Upper Canada had many citizens of the calibre of John Evelyn, the English diarist of the seventeenth century, who wrote on December 2, 1673, after a day of benevolent and charitable activities: "It was one of the best daies I ever spent in my life." Among associations of a philanthropic nature was the Stranger's Friend Society, established in York in 1822 for the reception and relief of immigrants. Citizens of Cobourg, Kingston and other ports frequently welcomed new arrivals, and provided supplies, paid hospital expenses, and in many other ways brightened what was often a very sad time. Of a similar nature were religious organisations such as the Society for Promoting Christian Knowledge, and the British and Foreign Bible Society, which had numerous branches in Upper Canada. A little over a century ago the first Temperance Societies began to be a strong force for good, and in the eighteen-thirties there was a parent organisation in Toronto called the Upper Canada Temperance Society.

Prominent among associations which aimed at mutual improvement was the Mechanics' Institute. Joseph Bates, who had had experience in such societies in London, England, appears to have established the first in Upper Canada at York in 1831. Four years later this organisation was granted £200 by the government to aid in the establishment of a library and the conduct of educational classes and weekly lectures. In York a membership fee of 5s. per year was charged, and many men of importance gave their time to provide an opportunity for improvement among "the middle classes, working men and intelligent mechanics",[24] who, in a day of social exclusiveness, had little chance to develop intellectually and culturally.

It was frequently difficult to maintain interest in the Institutes. When Mrs. Jameson visited Toronto in 1837 she

[24]*Cobourg Sentinel*, January 17, 1863.

found that there was a commercial news-room, but that this was "absolutely the only place of assembly or amusement, except the taverns and low drinking-houses. An attempt has been made to found a Mechanics' Institute and a literary club; but as yet they create little interest, and are very ill supported".[25] In later years, however, the Institute in Toronto was more successful, and, in addition to its regular activities, there were occasional exhibitions of fine and decorative arts, designing, fancywork, and other crafts. In 1883 the Toronto Mechanics' Institute came to an end, its building on Church Street becoming a public library.

Mechanics' Institutes became very numerous in Upper Canada in the fifties and sixties, even small villages frequently having organisations. It was found in many localities that the societies languished from the lack of support of those whom they were formed to benefit; but upon the whole they were for half a century a very valuable contribution towards the provision of a broader life for tradesmen and labourers. They were conducted under the direction of officers chosen from among those in the community —frequently the leaders in business and professional life— who interested themselves in the organisation. The Institutes were eventually supplanted in their library facilities through the operation of the Free Libraries Act of 1882; while their social and recreational activities were undertaken by the Canadian Institute, and, later, by the Young Men's Christian Association.

Many of the public libraries of the province have consequently grown out of the library of the local Mechanics' Institute. There were a few, however, of earlier origin. The first in Upper Canada was established at Niagara in 1800, and was supported by private subscription. A few of the wealthier early inhabitants had private libraries, and frequently allowed their books to pass around among their friends. In the early thirties there were good public libraries at Niagara, York, Kingston and Cobourg.

Among other associations of an educational nature were literary, debating and oratorical societies. One of the earliest of these organisations was formed in 1831 at York by Archdeacon Strachan; a few years later similar societies

25Jameson, op. cit., Vol. I, pp. 273-4.

were in operation in many other towns. All such associations provided social intercourse and relieved the monotony of life, as well as developing the individual; they were, too, a means of creating a democratic feeling of social and political equality.

At the time of the opening of the War of 1812, when feeling against the United States was running high, the Loyal and Patriotic Society was formed in York, and grants of money were made to many whose services merited reward. Medals were struck in London to be given out to those worthy of them, but so difficult was the task of selection that the Society came to an end before any were distributed, and the medals were all destroyed! The British Constitutional Society was another ephemeral organisation of early times, as was also the Upper Canada Agricultural and Commercial Society, which held meetings in York previous to 1808 when it was dissolved from lack of support. Thirty-three years later Sir Richard Bonnycastle visited Toronto and learned that there had been "various attempts to get up respectable races, to establish a theatre, and a winter assembly for dancing", but without much success; he also states that a national Literary and Philosophical Society was organised with difficulty, but lasted only about a year.[26]

While learned societies received but scant support, the advancement of music was no greater. In 1837 Mrs. Jameson found that Archdeacon Strachan was collecting subscriptions to provide a £1000 organ for St. James' Church in Toronto, and that "an intelligent musician" had trained a good choir; but she learned that the conductor had received so little encouragement "that he is at this moment preparing to go to the United States".[27]

In the thirties and forties the first brass bands began to be organised among the citizens of some of the more progressive towns. These developed in imitation of the regimental bands in the garrison towns, and provided an important outlet for musical ability. The National Societies, and other organisations which frequently held parades, usually aided in the financial support of the town band. As

[26]Sir Richard Bonnycastle: *The Canadas in 1841*. 1842. Vol. I, p. 168.
[27]Jameson, *op. cit.*, Vol. I, p. 274.

time passed, interest in higher types of music increased, and concerts in which famous musicians supplied the entertainment were occasionally held in the larger towns.

There were many progressive citizens interested in agriculture and horticulture. Under the auspices of Agricultural Societies local exhibitions were early held in almost every settled part of Upper Canada. Queenston had a fair previous to 1800, and there were others during the first quarter of the new century, especially after the War of 1812. The legislation of 1820 aiding the societies financially proved a great impetus to the establishment of fairs and exhibitions, and they were held twice a year, during the early twenties or before, at York, Cobourg and Port Hope. Horse-races and ploughing matches were early characteristic of the fairs, of which that in the autumn was the more important because the crops were then ready for exhibition. In some cases the fair of the county society was held alternately in the chief villages, and there were also others sponsored by township or village agricultural societies.

In 1846 the Agricultural Association of Upper Canada was formed, and the first Provincial Exhibition was held in Toronto the same year. During the next twelve years the fair alternated among the chief towns of the province, being held on two occasions in Hamilton, Cobourg, Toronto and Kingston, while Niagara, Brockville, London and Brantford were the locale of the exhibition once each. The attendance of the Lieutenant-Governor added social prestige to the Provincial Exhibition, and he was the *raison d'être* of numerous fashionable events, which usually included a levee after a triumphal procession through the streets in the carriages of the aristocracy.

At the middle of the century and afterwards, Horticultural Societies were formed in many towns, and the exhibitions which they held provided an incentive to the introduction and proper culture of flowers and fruit. In Cobourg it was customary to close the exhibition with a reception and promenade in Victoria Hall. In later years Horticultural Societies usually co-operated with the agricultural organisations in holding a combined fall fair, an event which still thrives in many centres of population throughout the province.

Private schools and colleges were an important factor in elevating and broadening the social life of some towns. Upper Canada College in York, and Upper Canada Academy, later Victoria College, in Cobourg, are examples of schools which developed with the towns in which they were established. Through the agency of public lectures, receptions, conversaziones and balls they permeated the intellectual and social life of the district.

A prominent feature in such schools was the Annual Examination and Exhibition, an event in some measure similar to the modern Commencement which has recently become usual in public as well as private schools. The Public Examination of the Upper Canada Academy in April, 1840, occupied three days, and attracted some spectators from a distance, though many who would have attended were unable to do so because of the bad roads. The attendance was largest in the evenings, and particularly on the last evening. The examination of each day opened with prayer and sacred music, and "the exercises were agreeably and judiciously interspersed and diversified with music, vocal and instrumental, by the Preceptress and some of the young ladies, and with declamation and dialogues by some of the male students". During the day, classes were examined in the subjects of study; while essays and speeches somewhat more generally interesting filled the evening session. Among the "original compositions" read by young ladies was one considered very appropriate at the time, "The Pernicious Effects of Novel Reading", which, no doubt, induced many in the audience to read novels.

The third day of the Examination was known as the Annual Exhibition, and "before the hour of commencement the chapel was crowded to excess, and great difficulty was experienced in conducting the young ladies from the entrance to the seats assigned to them. Nothing was to be seen but a mass of moving heads, and fears were entertained that order could not be preserved, which, however, was happily not the case". During this session there were no less than twenty addresses, dialogues, declamations or orations on subjects of every type and variety; some spoke in English, while others showed their ability in Latin, Greek, French or Hebrew. A Valedictory Address by a clever student, and a concluding speech by the Principal, formed a fitting climax to such a display of erudition.[28]

It may be assumed that few people attended the Exhibitions of schools unless they were directly interested in students in attendance; and, even though family pride was gratified by their evident progress in education, yet the lengthy and learned examination must have been, upon the whole, a monotonous proceeding to a large majority of the audience.

Lectures, dramatic readings and the display of oratorical ability were popular forms of entertainment in many localities. Such events were frequently arranged under the auspices of churches, literary societies or colleges. The Literary Association of Victoria College sponsored the appearance in Cobourg in 1864 of Vandenhoff, advertised as "the celebrated dramatic reader and entertainer". Tickets for this "rare treat" were only 25 cents, and the front seats were reserved "for ladies and the gentlemen accompanying them".[29] In 1863 J. H. Siddons, professor of elocution, and his daughter, Fanny Kemble Siddons, were brought to Cobourg by the Mechanics' Institute, and gave two performances consisting of readings, songs and music. Such was the popularity of this well-known theatrical family that some of the citizens organised a complimentary concert and reception in their honour.

Among college activities of a non-academic nature were public receptions or *soirées*, attended chiefly by the intellectually and socially *élite*. Accompanying the Annual Convocation of Victoria College in 1863 was an event new to Cobourg—a conversazione. This proved very popular, and it was consequently repeated in 1864 and succeeding years. A press account of the event says that it was "not very much like the model evening parties with which we are acquainted, for it apparently partakes of them all to some extent, and makes up in the variety of the scene what is wanting in life and enthusiasm". The Quadrille Band was

[28]See Letter of the Rev. John Manly in the *Christian Guardian*, April 29, 1840; or Nathanael Burwash: *History of Victoria College*. 1927. pp. 48-53. In Henry Scadding: *Toronto of Old*. 1873. pp. 157-9, may be found the details of similar proceedings at the 1819 examinations of the York Grammar School.
[29]*Cobourg World*, November 25, 1864.

in attendance and "performed some beautiful pieces, including polkas, waltzes, galops and orchestral selections, very agreeable to listen to. . . . The ladies turned out in all the gay plumage this season affords, their gorgeous opera cloaks and brilliant flowing costumes lending an elfin charm to the scene, which became more varied and intensified as they glided along the spacious avenues allotted for promenading. The beauty, fashion and intelligence of our locality were better represented than ever we remember to have witnessed before".

Those who had been accustomed to the dance found the promenade a little aggravating. The editor of the *Cobourg Sentinel* noted that "when we glanced along the extended lines of beaming countenances and sparkling eyes which filled Victoria Hall on Wednesday evening we were reminded of the remark of a traveller, 'that Cobourg could boast of more beautiful women than any town he had visited in Canada' "; but while the music was found to be "enlivening to march to when a blooming nymph is safely leaning on each arm", yet it was "most decidedly tantalising to those who are accustomed to use the swelling melodies for livelier purposes". Delectable refreshments, including oranges, a luxury at that period, and almonds, raisins, candies and "cupid's messengers", were served to the guests, and a soda fountain was liberally patronised. The evening's entertainment closed with songs and recitations, and the whole affair was considered "one of the richest and one of the pleasantest that it has been our fortune in many years to witness".[30]

One of the first sports to be developed in Upper Canada was horse-racing, which, with sailing and fishing, formed the chief diversion of the garrisons at Kingston, Niagara, Detroit, Amherstburg and York during the first years of the existence of the province. The first race-track was probably that opened at Niagara in the early seventeen-nineties, and "the Sport of Kings" quickly spread everywhere. The following announcement of a meet at Niagara in 1797 illustrates the chief characteristics of town races:

[30]*Cobourg Sentinel*, May 14, 1864. This interesting account and several others quoted from the *Sentinel* were written by Daniel McAllister.

"Niagara Races—Will be run over the new course on the plains of Newark (West Niagara) on the 6th day of July next, a purse of twenty guineas; on the 7th one of ten guineas, and on the 8th the entrance money, be it more or less. The best of three heats, twice round to a heat, making one mile, more or less. Free for any mare, horse or gelding, carrying not less than 150 lbs., which shall be entered with either of the stewards on or before Monday, the 3rd of July, together with the dress of riders, as no one will be permittted to ride unless dressed in a short round jacket; caps not being to be had, a black handkerchief must be worn as a substitute.

"No person will be allowed to enter horse, mare or gelding without first becoming a subscriber, and the sum of four dollars, being the entrance money, must at the time of entering be paid in hand.

"The races will begin at 11 o'clock a.m. of each day, and it is requested that no dogs be brought on to the course."[31]

One of the earliest race-courses at York was laid out before the War of 1812, at the commencement of the peninsula leading to what is now the island. This was a straight track, and its location was chosen largely because the peninsula was a popular resort for those who enjoyed the pleasures of walking, riding and driving; particularly did the military engage in these pursuits so characteristic of English watering-places. The importance attached both to the race-course and the other facilities for pleasure on the peninsula may be seen from the attempt to build by private subscription in 1822-23 two bridges over the Great and Little Don. Though these causeways were partially constructed, there was not money enough to complete them until 1835, and then only with the aid of a subsidy from the military chest, made available through the interest of the Lieutenant-Governor, Sir John Colborne. Their opening was an occasion of gratulation no less than that in modern Ontario when a stretch of paved highway is officially inaugurated; but in this instance the old-world pomp and ceremonial was reminiscent of a lord mayor's installation.

In towns like Kingston, Cobourg, York and Niagara the "gentlemen" of the district formed steeplechase and other

[31]Niagara *Upper Canada Gazette*, June 28, 1797.

racing clubs of a semi-private nature. Cobourg, for example, had three race-courses during the predominance of the turf. Many of the members of these clubs followed the way of life of English gentlemen, having fine estates and large stables of horses specially bred for the hunt and the race-track. Some men, like the Hon. George S. Boulton of Cobourg, had private driveways constructed through their extensive estates, and there the members of the family drove in their carriages or rode horseback in no less style than the nobility in London's exclusive Rotten Row.

Tandem and carriole clubs were other organisations dependent upon horses, the membership of these societies being largely restricted to officers. The Toronto Tandem Club was organised in the winter of 1839-40, and the activities included weekly drives in sleighs and cutters to the Peacock Inn or some other favourite resort, where gay dinners not infrequently drew forth poetical effusions from the more gifted members.[32]

In the so-called backwoods settlements, like Richmond, Perth and Bytown, horse-races were much less aristocratic events, and commonly resulted in fights and brawls; while in all parts of the province gambling and drunkenness were characteristic of such sporting activities. There were races of all varieties and conditions, but they were usually restricted to native horses, which the meets aided greatly in developing. In the pioneer period the gambling element, which has always been pre-eminent in horse-racing, was productive of a great deal of evil; men had then little actual cash to wager, but bets of 10,000 feet of lumber, barrels of pork or flour, and even of land grants and homes, were quite usual.

During the winter months horse-racing on the ice was early a popular sport in all parts of the province. A man still living recalls his participation in many a race on the Bay of Quinté, at Trenton and Belleville, on Lakes Scugog and Simcoe, and in the vicinity of Port Hope and Peterborough. Valuable purses were awarded at these meets, long characteristic of the Canadian winter season.[33]

[32]See Robertson, *op. cit.*, Vol. II, pp. 1040-48.
[33]See the reminiscences of Monroe Lawson, Brighton, in E. C. Guillet: *Cobourg*, in the *Cobourg Sentinel-Star*, June 25, 1931.

W. H. Bartlett

COBOURG, 1840

The building flying a flag is the Customs House. In the background
old Victoria College stands out prominently; and at the right is the
first Anglican Church

From the *Illustrated London News*, May 9, 1868

FUNERAL PROCESSION OF THE HON. D'ARCY MCGEE, MONTREAL, 1868

CRICKET MATCH AT TORONTO, SEPTEMBER 2ND AND 3RD, 1872

The Cricket Grounds were situated just south of College Street, west of University Avenue. This match was between "twelve of the Gentlemen of England and twenty-two of the Toronto Club"

"THE FASTEST IN THE WORLD"

PROFESSIONAL HOCKEY—CHICAGO BLACK HAWKS VS. TORONTO MAPLE LEAFS

13,500 fans at the Maple Leaf Gardens, Toronto, November 12, 1931. Similar ceremonies are usual at the opening of the baseball season.

Among the earliest outdoor games to be played in Upper Canada were lacrosse, bandyball, football, cricket and curling. Lacrosse originated among the Indians, but it was not prominent in the days of early settlement. Bandyball had some of the charactertistics of both tennis and hockey. Football and bandyball were commonly played by those who did not aspire to social heights, while cricket was particularly the game of the English middle and upper classes, and curling that of Scottish settlers. Some of the first clubs were formed among officers resident in the older towns. In the late thirties there were cricket clubs in Toronto, Hamilton, Ancaster, Brantford, Woodstock, Guelph, Cobourg and Kingston, and probably in other towns. Curling soon ceased to be a monopoly of the Scotch, and there were clubs during the same period in Toronto, Fergus, Galt, Guelph, Niagara and Kingston, as well as in certain townships. Cricket gradually decreased in importance and is now played in Canada chiefly at preparatory schools where the cultivation of an English attitude is considered desirable.

Inter-club games, particularly in cricket and curling, were sometimes played in the thirties and forties, though the difficulties of transportation placed such competitions in the category of a half week's holiday. It took three days, for example, for the curlers of Toronto to engage in a competition with the Hamilton club; and when the Cobourg Cricket Club visited Bowmanville in 1846 to play a friendly game it was most convenient to travel the day before on the steamboat *America*, though the distance was only twenty-five miles.

Football, bandyball and tennis were usually played more informally, and seldom resulted in the formation of clubs in the early period. In later days Association football (soccer) was an organised sport in urban centres, as well as in most townships; but, except among "Old Countrymen" in the towns, the game has been largely replaced by baseball or by rugby football. Quoits and other hurling games were early popular, especially in the rural districts, but golf and lawn bowling had not been introduced, much less such ephemeral sports as miniature golf and box lacrosse. Baseball was first played in Canada in the sixties, when it was introduced from the United States. The rules of this sport differed in some respects from the baseball of today. It was a real "he-man's" game at its inception, for no gloves were used; but, (possibly because men become more effeminate as life grows easier), the old game is being to some extent replaced by softball, in which our "emancipated" women join—though often with more enthusiasm than grace.

Toronto and Kingston were among the earliest towns to have Yacht Clubs, and during the early sixties Cobourg and other ports joined in the competitions, which were notable sporting events. The regattas frequently lasted two days or longer, and a few enterprising citizens who invested money in yachting were responsible for the sailing races, which attracted entries from many Lake Ontario ports. A ball usually provided an enjoyable culmination to the races, which were very fashionable occasions, quite different from the canoe regattas which, from the days of early settlement, had been held along the Ottawa and at some of the "back lakes" settlements.

Among indoor games whist, chess and billiards had their devotees. Some hotels in the towns had billiard tables, and matches for cash prizes were occasionally held. Chess clubs frequently competed against one another, one match between Cobourg and Port Hope in 1864 being carried on by telegraph, then only seventeen years old and still something of a novelty.

Special occasions which provided amusement for both urban and rural population—for people came from far and near to be present—were elections, militia parades and public holidays. Elections usually lasted a week unless one candidate retired before the time was up. William Lyon Mackenzie describes an election at Niagara Falls as attracting people of all nationalities, plus "poetical as well as most prosaical phizes, horsemen and footmen, fiddlers and dancers, honourables and reverends, captains and colonels, beaux and belles, wagons and tilburies, coaches and chaises, gigs and carts; in short, Europe, Asia, Africa and America had there each its representative among the loyal subjects and servants of our good King George, the

fourth of that name".[34] The opening and closing days drew
particularly large crowds, most people coming to receive
free liquor and to enjoy themselves, rather than for the
purpose of voting. Drunken brawls frequently occurred,
and at the end of the voting an outburst of enthusiasm led
to parades, horse-play of one type or another, and fighting
between the partisans of the victor and the vanquished.

In later years such celebrations gradually became somewhat more genteel, though no less enthusiastic. In 1861
the news of victory in a provincial election led to a
celebration in Cobourg which included a torchlight procession led by the town band. A newspaper states that
"conspicuous in the front ranks of the procession was a
coffin borne by four individuals and supposed to contain
the remains of the defeated leader of the opposition party,
on either side of which, in large letters, appeared the inscription, 'Brown Politically Dead'. Finally the procession
arrived at a point below the town, where preparations had
been made for a bonfire. The coffin was placed upon the pile,
the match was struck, and the town soon became illuminated by the flame. During the night large quantities of
fireworks were sent hissing through the air." The editor
is pleased to say in closing, however, that "all passed off
without any serious disturbance, much to the credit of the
party in honour of the defeat of the great political leader
of which the demonstration was got up".[35]

The militia parades provided a holiday usually observed
in the rural districts as in the towns. All men from sixteen
to sixty-five years of age were enrolled in the militia and
many of them took part in the proceedings on parade-day,
which consisted of a little drill and a good deal of horse-
racing and drinking. June the 4th, the birthday of George
III, was celebrated in this manner long after his death,
and in later years Victoria's birthday, May 24th, superseded it. In the larger towns where there was a garrison of
regulars it was usual to have a review of them also; but
in every case the military manoeuvres ended in a *feu de joie*.

The militia parade grew out of the establishment of

[34]W. L. Mackenzie: *Sketches of Canada and the United States.* 1833.
    p. 89.
[35]*Cobourg Sentinel*, July 13, 1861.

the Upper Canadian militia, for it was obviously necessary that some pretence at the training of the citizens should be made. There appears, for example, in the *Niagara Herald* of May 23, 1801, a notice inserted by Samuel Street, Deputy-Lieutenant of the County of Lincoln, that the militia will meet at Chippawa Bridge on June the 4th, and that "all quakers, menonists or tunkers" must attend, bring certificates of exemption and pay the exemption fee, "or expect to be proceeded against as the law in such case directs". In the same issue the *Herald* announces that "it is intended to make the 4th of June a day of rejoicing in this county, as well for the added years as for the recovered health of His Majesty. It is said that after the review at Queenston, there will be premiums on the best shots among the armed companies; that there will be a horse-race in the afternoon, and that other plans are in forwardness for promoting the amusements of the day".[36]

In most cases the militia parades were ludicrous in appearance and more or less useless in accomplishment. Some men came to them in partial uniform and with some sort of arms, but the general effect led to such descriptions as "a parti-coloured and curiously-equipped regiment", and "a laughter-stirring spectacle".[37] Joseph Pickering describes in his journal "training-day" as the occasion "when the militia meet at appointed stations, near home, throughout the province, to be trained, some with guns and some without. I need not say that they learn but little when the reader is informed this is the only day in the year they meet, and then not half of them perhaps, and nearly one-half of the officers know as little of military exercises as themselves; it is merely a frolic for the youngsters".[38] Another writer emphasises the ludicrous appearance of the militia:

"One might have imagined that each man of them kept his own tailor. . . . As far as we could discern, not one garment was kin to another, they were as distinct as the countenances of the wearers; and the *chapeaux* that defended their craniums from the sun, too, of every discordant

[36]*Niagara Herald*, May 23, 1801.
[37]Need, *op. cit.*, p. 12.
[38]Joseph Pickering: *Inquiries of an Emigrant.* 1831. June 4, 1826.

variety. Lastly, the weapons that dangled from the fists of the doughty heroes would have been still more difficult to classify: guns, whips, bludgeons, hoes, umbrellas, canes, sticks."[39]

Most of the participants came not to drill but for the day's outing, and they were usually impatient for the commencement of the horse-races and other holiday activities. In the larger towns a ball provided a fitting close to the day's festivities. In the capital the presence of the governor and the garrison added interest and dignity to the celebration of the King's birthday. At York in 1799 "the Queen's Rangers fired three volleys, the militia assembled on the beach, and a Royal Salute of 21 guns was fired by the Royal Artillery. At night the Government Buildings were superbly illuminated, at which place his Honour the President gave a splendid ball and supper".[40]

The events of parade-day at Niagara in 1807 included a reception by Lieutenant-Governor Gore:

"On the morning of the birthday the militia began to make their appearance at an early hour, and about 12 o'clock 1,000 formed in a line on the plains for the review of his Excellency, who expressed the highest satisfaction at their conduct and appearance.

"Previously to seeing the militia, his Excellency on horseback, attended by his aide-de-camp, Lieut. Loring of the 49th Regiment, appeared on the garrison parade during the royal salute in honour of the day, and at two o'clock held a levee at the commanding officers' quarters, where the officers of the militia and other gentlemen from distant parts of the district, not before introduced, were presented."[41]

After the middle of the century the militia was frequently important in social life all the year round. The celebration of the Queen's birthday, May 24th, was often carried out in more style than had been usual on earlier parade-days. In 1861, for example, the streets of Cobourg "presented a very military appearance as the cavalry and rifles, with their red and green uniforms, passed through

[39]David Wilkie: *Sketches of a Summer Trip to New York and the Canadas*. 1837. pp. 158-9.
[40]York *Upper Canada Gazette* June 8, 1799.
[41]*York Gazette*, June 13, 1807.

to join their comrades at the several stations assigned for their meeting. . . . At eleven o'clock the town was enlivened by the soul-stirring strains of Professor Chalaupka's unrivalled Cobourg Brass Band, which marched from their band-room to the armoury of the rifles, and escorted them to Perry's Common, where they were joined by the cavalry under the command of Colonel Boulton, and both joined in a grand *feu de joie* in honour of Her Majesty's birthday".[42]

It was usual on such occasions to close the day's festivities with a ball. Among other activities connected with the militia were picnics, and rifle matches with units in neighbouring towns; while the young ladies of seventy years ago were not as mid-Victorian as one might have presumed, for in Cobourg a number of them actually took a course of twenty-four lessons in military manoeuvres, and are said to have performed the various evolutions with credit.

An interesting holiday celebration occurred in Toronto on April 2, 1840, in honour of Queen Victoria's marriage. A peculiar account of the event says that "one ox roasted whole . . . was brought into the centre of the Market Square in Procession. . . . Every person, Man, Woman and Child who intended to partake of this banquet was requested to come cleanly attired, each with a 'Knife, Fork and Plate'. The City was beautifully illuminated from 8 o'clock to 11. There was also a display of Fire Works and Balloons".[43]

Whenever royalty or the highest officials of the country honoured communities with a visit, the occasion was always a memorable one. The progress through Canada in 1860 of the Prince of Wales, later Edward VII, was punctuated by a series of enthusiastic receptions and balls wherever he went, marred only by a few partisan demonstrations arising out of the strong religious prejudices of the times. Triumphal arches were everywhere erected, and the inhabitants lost no opportunity to show the popular prince everything of interest along his route. The celebrated Blondin performed in his presence unparalleled feats on a tight-rope at Niagara Falls; at Ottawa they ran a special

[42]*Cobourg Sentinel*, May 25, 1861.
[43]Toronto *Mirror*, April 3, 1840.

G. H. Andrews

GRAND CANOE RECEPTION ON THE ST. LAWRENCE TO THE PRINCE OF WALES

Given by Sir George Simpson of the Hudson's Bay Company when the Prince visited Dorval, August 29, 1860

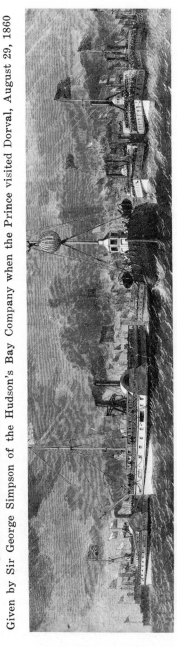

G. H. Andrews

From the *Illustrated London News*, October 13, 1860

HIS ROYAL HIGHNESS ESCORTED TO MONTREAL BY A FLEET OF LAKE AND UP-RIVER STEAMERS

KING AND JORDAN STREETS, TORONTO, 1818-1933

The magnificent 33-storey Canadian Bank of Commerce Head Office, the highest building in the British Empire, stands on the site of the first Methodist Church in Toronto, a primitive frame meeting-house which in 1834 became (*horribile dictu!*) the Theatre Royal.

excursion for him down a timber slide; while at Cobourg
he must needs be given a trip on the pet enterprise of the
citizens—the Cobourg and Peterborough Railway—though
the trestle bridge over Rice Lake was too unsafe to allow
His Royal Highness to cross by that means. Ballroom
dancing received a great impetus by the visit of this de-
votee of Terpsichore, and many of the social belles of
Canada West were thrilled by a dance with the future
king.

An occasion which sometimes assumed the characteristics of a holiday and resulted in a large gathering of people
was a public execution,—fortunately comparatively rare.
Many people were then of the opinion of Dr. Samuel Johnson: "Sir, executions are intended to draw spectators. If
they do not draw spectators they don't answer their purpose. . . . The age is running mad after innovation. . . .
The old method was most satisfactory to all parties; the
public was gratified by a procession; the criminal was supported by it. Why is all this to be swept away?"[44]

When Dr. W. H. King was hanged at Cobourg in June,
1859, many people travelled all night to be present, and
10,000 persons, including some 500 women, saw the murderer pay the penalty; even schools were closed because of
the general exodus towards the place of execution. Such an
event was always expected to produce a speech from the
murderer, warning his hearers to avoid the pitfalls which
had brought him to the gallows; and this execution ran
true to form, for the Doctor, though insisting upon his in-
nocence up to the last day, finally confessed his guilt and
admitted that his punishment was deserved. The huge
crowd which witnessed the "sad spectacle" are said to have
"preserved the utmost good order during the whole time.
. . . . All dispersed quietly and went to their respective
homes, and the unfortunate Dr., I hope, went home to
heaven".[45] Interest in the morbid has, of course, always
been a prominent characteristic of human nature. The dead
man's spiritual adviser, the Rev. Vanderburg, had a congregation of 1,500 to hear him preach on the following Sun-

[44]James Boswell: *Life of Dr. Samuel Johnson.* 1791. Everyman's
Library, Vol. II, p. 447.
[45][Alexander Stewart]: *The Life and Trial of William H. King,
M.D., for Poisoning His Wife at Brighton.* 1859. p. 53.

day in his small rural church at Codrington; and no less than three books were published concerning the life and death of Dr. King.

In particular instances the exploitation of natural attractions as amusement centres was early evident. The vicinity of Niagara Falls was commercialised by the establishment not only of hotels and mills but refreshment booths and a variety of amusements of the type usually associated with beaches and pleasure resorts. The tavern-keepers and concession-owners arranged spectacles from time to time to attract crowds. In 1827 and 1829 old schooners, with animals as enforced passengers, were sent down the river to amuse large crowds of the curious who had assembled, though the boats broke up before they reached the Falls; and in later years many people attained notoriety or death by daring attempts to go over the Falls, swim the rapids, or cross the river on a tight-rope. Barnet's Museum of stuffed birds and animals, and the Camera Obscura, which beautifully reflected the Falls, were among the amusements of nearly a century ago which were worthy of a visit.

The development of commercialised picnic-grounds began in York over one hundred years ago. The Island was early noted as a pleasure resort, and was approached by canoe or horse-boat. A notice in Mackenzie's *Almanac* for 1834 refers to an hotel there for the convenience of picnic parties:

"Horse-boat to the Island. A boat propelled by four horses runs every day from the Steamboat Wharves to the Starch Factory on the peninsula or island across the Bay— her trips regulated to suit public convenience. Fare to and from the island, 7½d. A hotel has been opened on the island to accommodate sportsmen, parties of pleasure, etc."[46]

By 1850 the Island had developed greatly as a pleasure resort, and contained some of the amusements which have long characterised the beaches and other public playgrounds. Under the head "Cheap Pleasure", L. J. Privat advertises his horse-boat service across the Bay. The

[46][W. L. Mackenzie's] *New Almanack for the Canadian True Blues.* 1834. p. 15.

steam ferry *Victoria* succeeded its more primitive forerunner in 1851, but the reference in the advertisement to
pasturage for horses and cattle shows how close to rural
life Toronto was at that period:

"That Safe and Convenient Horse-Boat, the *Peninsula
Packet* will leave Mr. Maitland's Wharf, foot of Church
Street, every day at ten o'clock a.m., 12, 2, 4, and 6 p.m.,
for the Peninsula Hotel. Returning at 11 a.m., 1, 3, 5 and
7 p.m. precisely. Fare to and from, 7½d. Family Season
Tickets $4 each. Swings and Merry-go-round, etc., for the
amusement of Children. Dinners, Lunches, Teas, etc., to be
had at the shortest notice. Good pasture for Horses and
other cattle, which can be conveyed over by the first boat
—not later."[47]

In many towns where there was no such beauty-spot to
be developed as a centre of recreation, picnics and similar
gatherings were commonly held in pleasant groves. The
first park in many a town grew out of the "common" where
it had long been customary to hold the militia parades,
cricket and football matches, and other similar activities
of town life.

It was nearly half a century after the arrival of the
first settlers before commercialised theatrical exhibitions
were to be found in Upper Canada. Writing just previous
to 1820 Robert Gourlay found that "the country is too
young for regular theatric entertainments and those delicacies and refinements of luxury which are the usual attendants of wealth. Dissipation, with her fascinating train
of expenses 'and vices, has made but little progress on the
shores of the lakes".[48] Among the earliest dramatic efforts
were occasional plays produced by the officers of the garrisons at York, Kingston and Niagara; in these the female
parts were usually taken by men. As a general rule only
comedies were attempted, Goldsmith's *She Stoops to Conquer* being among the number. The first theatrical performances by professionals were introduced by American
companies in the eighteen-twenties. Two plays were
usually produced for one evening's entertainment, a rather

---

[47]Advertisement quoted in Robertson, *op. cit.*, Vol. II, p. 884.
[48]Robert Gourlay: *A Statistical Account of Upper Canada.* 1822.
      Vol. I, p. 250.

serious play being followed by a boisterous comedy, with
perhaps a little vaudeville during the intermission.

The course of development of theatres in York may be
taken as typical of that in the other towns of Upper Canada.
The first theatre in the town was the ballroom of Frank's
Hotel; there, in the early twenties, travelling companies
presented such plays as *Pizzaro; Barbarossa, or the Siege of
Algiers; Ali Baba, or the Forty Thieves; The Lady of the
Lake;* and *The Miller and His Men.* A small stage, few
dramatic effects, and little or no scenery were characteristic of this as of all other early theatres in Upper Canada.
In 1824 a local club, the Canadian Amateurs, was giving
occasional dramatic performances in the Little Theatre,
located in the rear of Frank's Hotel. After its use for religious purposes was discontinued in the early thirties, the
Wesleyan Chapel on King Street was used as a theatre. In
1834 it was given the name Theatre Royal and the first
entertainment was *A Panorama of the Burning of Moscow.*
The early theatres of York usually charged half a crown
for good seats, and 1s. 3d. for those in the rear.

It is, of course, impossible to gauge the value of any
entertainment from the producers' announcements; nor
can a press report of it always be accepted as unbiased
criticism. The fact that most of the players "hailed from"
the United States prejudiced the chances of a fair reception at the hands of a considerable number of people, among
whom the editor of the *British Colonist* appears to have
been one of the most pronounced in his views. With obvious dislike he records a visit to the Theatre Royal in 1839,
when "a party of strolling players from Yankee-land" were
performing. He says that "the performance commenced
with what was styled in the bills 'The much-admired farce
of Nature and Philosophy', on the youth who never saw
a woman. . . . Both the farce and the actors of it are
altogether too contemptible for criticism". A Scotch song
was "brutally murdered" by Mrs. Lennox. This was followed "by an attempt to act the opera of *The Maid of Cash-
mere,* and it was but an attempt. Miss Ince danced tolerably well, and that is all that can be said in favour of the
performance. By this time our patience was quite exhausted; we left, and immediately set to write this notice,

lest by delay we might so far forget what we had witnessed as to do injustice afterwards to any of the company by detracting from their just merits as players. . . . There is no reason why such a miserable catchpenny as that at present in operation should be tolerated. The municipal authorities should interfere and abate the nuisance".[49]

In spite of such scathing criticism, however, it is probable that this company was no worse than the average of the day; and it is likely that many unprejudiced patrons enjoyed the entertainment provided. The spread of the drama into other parts of Upper Canada depended largely upon the growth of communities, and their accessibility; amateur productions were frequently to be found first, and performances of travelling companies later.

Several organisations of minstrels were playing in Canada West in the early sixties, among them being Christy's and Sharpley's; a similar performance was given by Kelly's Theatrical Troupe. Some minstrel shows had a repertoire of "stock" plays, particularly of the more emotional and humorous types, and many of them had brass bands. With its light program of vaudeville and burlesque, broad comedy and sentimental melodrama, the minstrel show is a type of entertainment which has retained its popularity with the average amusement-seeker, for it does not require the same capabilities and attention that are necessary for the proper appreciation of the higher operatic and dramatic performances.

In addition to the minstrel shows there were circuses and various types of travelling exhibitions to interest those who found dramatic performances and educational lectures not to their liking. Some of these shows, notably the circuses, not only travelled from town to town, but were also presented at or near rural taverns, the proprietors of which usually acted as agents of the organisations insofar as the advance sale of tickets was concerned. The circus, usually of American origin, was among the first commercialised amusements to tour Upper Canada. As early as the eighteen-twenties travelling menageries found their way into all but the most remote sections of the province, and

[49]Toronto *British Colonist*, September 4, 1839.

were consequently almost as well-known to the farmer as
to the dweller in the towns.

In the fifties and sixties Van Amburgh's "collection of
the animal kingdom" was among the most popular of the
organisations which travelled the province. When circus
performances were given they frequently offended the sen-
sibilities of the more refined, so Van Amburgh advertised
that, as there was no such entertainment accompanying
his show, "it will afford an opportunity to the most religious
of gratifying their curiosity in seeing with their eyes some
of the wonders of the animal creation". The admission
charged for afternoon and evening exhibitions was 25 cents
for adults and 15 cents for children, and it is announced
that the show "will form a feast to the naturalist, and an
opportunity to the Christian philosopher to contemplate
the Wisdom and Power of the Supreme Being in the creation of animated nature".[50]

As early as 1827 York had a resident circus under the
management of Besnard and Black. This was held in the
barn of Dr. Forest's Hotel on King Street, east of Sher-
bourne. There was no menagerie connected with it, the
entertainment consisting of "riding and feats of horseman-
ship, trapeze and horizontal bar performances, and tricks
of juggling". Mrs. Besnard was the favourite of the circus-
goers of that early period, and her "tossing of balls and
knives was one of the principal features of the show".[51]

The regular amusements available in Toronto in the
late fifties were closely associated with saloons, two of the
more pretentious of which were the Terrapin, (formerly
the St. Nicholas, and situated on King Street near the site
of the present King Edward Hotel), and the Apollo Saloon
and Concert Room on the same street. In describing the
attractions of these places of entertainment a contemporary
publication introduces the subject by noting that "we believe there is no city of its size on the continent which is
pestered with so many saloons and taverns; and, if the
morals and habits of our people were to be judged by this
criterion, the stranger would form a very unfavourable
and unjust opinion".

[50]*Cobourg Sentinel*, July 6, 1861.
[51]Robertson, *op. cit.*, Vol. I, p. 479.

The Apollo Saloon appears to have staged nightly a show which may be called the forerunner of the night club, though it was available upon much more reasonable terms. The price of admission was only twelve and one-half cents, and from his modest investment the patron was entitled to "a smoke or a drink", as well as to witness a "performance of negro minstrelsy, comic and sentimental singing, etc". The actors, Mr. Burgess and Mr. Den Thompson, are described as "inimitable in their way, ... the one as a negro performer, and the other as a 'broth of a boy' from the Emerald Isle". Visitors to the Provincial Exhibition of 1858 are assured that "the place is well worthy of a visit".

The same authority describes for us Toronto's theatre of that period—the Royal Lyceum—which, "although small, and, since the hard times commenced, has not met with the encouragement its management merited, is an exceedingly pleasant resort". The manager, Mr. Nickinson, was himself "a first-rate actor", and he was ably assisted by others "equally good in their line", notably Mr. Petrie, Mr. Marlowe, Mr. Lee, Mrs. Marlowe and Miss Frost. The "general run of pieces" were well presented by this stock company, and we are glad to learn that "the performances are always characterised by morality and good breeding".[52]

Shows featuring midgets and monstrosities were not in early days confined to fall fairs and exhibitions. The 1863 variety of Tom Thumb visited Cobourg, accompanied by "his beautiful little wife, the fascinating Queen of Beauty, and Commodore Nutt, the $30,000 Nutt, (so called because he received that amount from P. T. Barnum for three years' service), and Elfin Minnie Warren, the smallest lady of her age ever seen—all four weighing but 100 pounds". As an extra attraction it is announced that Tom Thumb's wife "will wear the identical wedding costume as worn at Grace Church on February 10, 1863, when $60 was offered for a ticket to the wedding; here the same thing can be seen for a trifle". Before the show commenced there was—as has

[52]These Toronto amusements of 1858 are described in the *Descriptive Catalogue of the Provincial Exhibition, 1858.* Second Edition, 1858, p. 79.

long been customary with circuses and minstrel shows—a
street parade.[53]

Previous to the days of motion pictures there were
numerous attempts to give graphical representations of
popular subjects, usually with an accompanying lecture, or
with music on the tambourine or some sort of "musical
machine". There were figures in wax as well as illustrations of other kinds. Large numbers of pictures illustra-
tive of Bunyan's *Pilgrim's Progress* comprised one entertainment, while others consisted of panoramas of Biblical
themes, the Holy Land, and kindred subjects. On one
occasion in the early sixties a panorama of the *Bible* was
exhibited for six nights in Cobourg, and may be presumed
to have visited all parts of the province.

Another performance, "sure to inculcate a high moral
tendency and to warn every young man, and older one, too,
who has commenced to tamper with the intoxicating glass",
was Verey's Zographicon, consisting of a lecture, accompanied by 150 views from *The Pilgrim's Progress,* and
Arthur's *Ten Nights in a Bar Room.* The allegorical representations and striking scenes were given with "full and
very often touching and vivid explanations", and were of
a character "calculated to give an elevated tone to the
morals of the community".[54]

It was early considered—and it still holds true—that
concerts, lectures and shows were more attractive to
patrons if they were advertised as from London or New
York. Friend's Panorama of the British Isles was heralded
as "direct from St. James' Hall, London, England", and the
art work is described as "a moving panorama painted by
Mr. Friend himself on over 50,000 feet of canvas". The
exhibitor is referred to as "the celebrated artist, vocalist,
musician and entertainer", who "will sing melodies, accompanying himself on different instruments, including a
Grand Euphonium Piano".[55] Performances and lectures of
this kind may be assumed to have been neither better nor
worse than those of today; the best of them must have

[53]*Cobourg Sentinel,* October 17, 1863.
[54]*Cobourg World,* November 25, 1864.
[55]*Cobourg Sentinel,* May 14, 1864 .

contributed greatly to the education and enjoyment of those who attended.

It has always been characteristic of showmanship to advertise productions in a most bombastic and exaggerated manner. To this was added in the pioneer period, and later, an evident intention of attracting people to performances by announcing them in huge, almost unpronounceable words; possibly this was a recommendation in a day when education was not so generally diffused. We find, for example, the Papyrotamia, or gallery of paper cuttings, which was shown in Meighan's Ball Room, York, in 1827; and in later years a magician advertised his show as "The Grand Thaumaturgic Psychomanteum", and himself as "the celebrated artist and arch-magician, Professor Anderson, known throughout the civilised Globe as the Wizard of the North, and an Illusionist, Physicist, Thaumatist and Traveller", whose "Soirés de Prestidigitation constitute the most marvellous entertainment in which, at any time, the attempt has been made to blend the highest science with the most genial amusement".[56]

The same high-sounding names were still further developed in the advertisements of circuses and menageries of the sixties. J. B. Lent's travelling show visited Cobourg in 1862 under the name "Hippozoonamadon", which was described as "the largest exhibition in the world", a combination of three circuses, a hippopotamus and elephant exhibition, and an aquarium. A word large enough to frighten the most learned savant is used to describe a part of the Hippozoonamadon—the Athleolympimantheum—in which Mlle. Ariane Felecia from Paris formed the main attraction, for she is described as "the most beautiful, graceful, daring and dashing equestrienne in the world". Numerous other features, including the Grand Opera Band, were offered as a part of the Hippozoonamadon—and all for twenty-five cents![57]

In the folowing year J. B. Lent came around again, probably with the same show; but he had been able to invent for it a new name—Equescurriculum. In addition to the "unparalleled combination of three circuses" there was "a troop of acting bears, the educated sacred Indian bull, leap-

[56]*Ibid.*, October 11, 1862.   [57]*Ibid.*, July 5, 1862.

ing buffaloes and performing dogs and monkeys". The whole formed "a magnificent phalanx of exhibitions—perfection in every detail"; and, as before,—all for twenty-five cents.[58]

Times have changed, however. We still have magicians and circuses, vaudeville and burlesque, comedies and tragedies, romances and melodramas; we have revived the comic opera of Gay, and Gilbert and Sullivan, and developed the typically American musical comedy and girl-and-music show; and in addition to all these we have the radio and the talking motion picture. But something has gone out of town life: Hippozoonamadons, Equescurriculums, Thaumaturgic Psychomanteums and Athleolympimantheums have departed from our midst forever!

[58]*Ibid.*, July 25, 1863.

CHAPTER XI

PIONEER SPORTS—CURLING

> "When Winter muffles up his cloak,
> And binds the mire like a rock,
> Then to the loch the Curlers flock
> Wi' gleesome speed."
>
> BOBERT BURNS.[1]

THE ancient Scottish sport of curling, or channel-stane as it was long called, is very closely connected with pioneer life in Canada. In the history of the early settlement of our country there is but little reference to organised sport, but among the first games played in both urban and rural districts was curling.

An authority on the development of the game in Scotland writes that "the early history of curling is involved in such obscurity that the time even of antiquarians might be better employed in eating beef and greens, or in playing the game, than in endeavouring to discover its origin." The game is certainly of great antiquity, for references to curling (and to golf as well) are found in a book published in 1638; while in the 1695 edition of Camden's *Britannia* the Isle of Copinsha, in the Orkney group, is described as containing "in great plenty excellent stones for the game called curling".[2] The stones that were early used were irregular in size and shape. Some of these have been recovered from the bottom of "lochs" and mill-dams; one is dated 1551, and is eleven inches long, ten inches broad and five inches thick.

The game should be considered the national sport of Scotland if the enthusiasm of the players is any criterion. We find many a sentiment written in the following strain:

> "I've played at quoitin' mony a day,
> And maybe I may da'et again,
> But still unto myself I say
> *This* is no the channel-stane.

[1] Robert Burns: *Tam Samson's Elegy.*
[2] See John Kerr: *The History of Curling.* 1890. p. 88.

Oh for a channel-stane!
The fell guid game the channel-stane;
There's no game that e'er I saw
Can match auld Scotland's channel-stane."[3]

The Scottish curler always finds it difficult to appreciate the Englishman's enthusiasm for cricket:

"Old England may her cricket boast,
    Her wickets, bats, and a' that;
And proudly her Eleven toast,
    Wi' right good will and a' that.
For a' that, and a' that,
    It's but bairns' play for a' that;
The channel-stane on icy plain
    Is king o' games for a' that."

In the last stanza of the same poem the writer strikes a philosophical note in referring to death as the last curling match:

"And when the score o' life is made,
    As made it will for a' that;
When hin-han death's last shot is played,
    And time's a hog, and a' that,
For a' that, and a' that,
    Our besom friends for a' that,
We hope to meet, each rink complete,
    Round Higher Tee for a' that."[4]

The first *Annual* of the Ontario branch of the Royal Caledonian Curling Club, issued in 1876, contains a long account of the "Great Gathering" of the Grand Caledonian Curling Club at Kilmarnock, Scotland, on October 22, 1841, when over 150 "brithers a'" met under the presidency of Lord Eglinton. The dinner in the town hall was laid out in unusual splendour. Speech followed toast for several hours, and songs of a lively nature were interspersed to add zest and induce merriment. One man was present who had curled as early as 1784; while another notability was

[3] James Hogg ("the Ettrick Shepherd"), quoted in John Macnair: *The Channel-Stane, or Sweepings frae the Rinks.* 1883-5. Vol. I, p. 52.
[4] H. Shanks: *Curling Song.* See Macnair, *op. cit.*, Vol. III, pp. 75-7.

Thomas Samson, the son of the Tam Samson whom the beloved Rabbie Burns complimented as a curler in the lines

"He was the king o' a' the core
To gaird, or draw, or wick a bore,
Or up the rink like Jehu roar
In time o' need;
But noo he lags on death's hog-score—
Tam Samson's deid!"[5]

Throughout the centuries that the game has been played in Scotland it has always been noted for its democratic tendencies. An early encyclopaedia states that "peers, peasants, clergymen, farmers, country gentlemen, tradesmen and artisans all meet hilariously and familiarly for the occasion".[6] In Canada, too, "the spruce tailor, the burly stonemason, the active weaver, the quiet-thinking minister, the humble voter, and the M. P. are all on a level. The grand test is who curls best."[7] The sense of good sportsmanship, alike in victory and defeat, has been equally prominent wherever curling has been played, for, in the words of the poet,

"It's a slippery game for a' that;
We're ne'er afraid to meet on ice
The best o' folks for a' that."[8]

Curling began in Canada at Quebec in the last years of the eighteenth century, though the first organised club was instituted in Montreal in 1807. Among the earliest curlers were Scotch officers of the garrisons, who relieved the monotony of military life by engaging in the game. Matches were played on the St. Lawrence River, and there is record of a game in 1807, on the river below Montreal, as late as April 11th. Among the rules of the first club, which contained twenty members, was that it should meet "at Gillis's on Wednesday every fortnight at 4 o'clock to dine on salt beef and greens; . . . . and the club dinner and wines shall

[5] Robert Burns: *Tam Samson's Elegy*.
[6] *Chambers' Encyclopaedia*. 1860-68. Vol. III, p. 368.
[7] William Roper: *A Canadian Plea for Curling*. Reprinted from the Guelph *Mercury* in the 1876 *Annual* of the Ontario Curling Association, p. 82.
[8] Shanks, *ibid.*

not exceed 7s. 6d. a head".[9]　During the War of 1812 the members of the club did not meet as frequently as before.

In later years matches occurred between the curlers of Montreal and Quebec, half of the players of each club proceeding to the other and playing the match the same day, so that no news which might affect the result could be obtained at either city,—for these mighty tussles were of great importance to the participants.

In 1835 a notable match between the two cities (perhaps the first inter-club match in Canada) was played on neutral ice at Three Rivers. The Montreal players left the city on January 7th and 8th, some in the stage and some in their own conveyances, the first of them arriving at Three Rivers about noon on the 9th. The roads were very bad as there had been a heavy snow. At Three Rivers there was difficulty in finding ice, and the curlers had to make use of a very uneven piece at the mouth of the Black River. Two rinks a side engaged in the match, and when it was over the score stood: Quebec 31, Montreal 23.

At the grand dinner afterwards there was no haggis, nor was there "good, nor even tolerable whisky to be had at Three Rivers";[10] but these deficiencies were in some degree made up by nine roast turkeys and excellent champagne, though the latter appeared to some to be very much out of place at a Scotchmen's dinner. The eight Montrealers, who had been defeated, paid £3 2s. 6d. each for the dinner and about the same amount for transportation, so it is no wonder that victory in these matches was so desirable!

The records of the Montreal Club state that in 1837-38 "there was no club dinner because of the insurrection"; but in spite of the Rebellion there was considerable curling "on a new artificial rink made of wood and put up under cover in the St. Ann suburb, near the Lachine Canal".[11] This was probably the first closed rink in Canada.

French-Canadians did not know what to think of these activities of the Scotchmen upon the ice. One of them, a farmer near Quebec who had just seen the game for the first time, related excitedly to his neighbour: "Today I saw a band of Scotchmen, who were throwing large balls of iron

[9]Quoted in Kerr, op. cit., p. 324.
[10]Colonel Dyde quoted in Macnair, op. cit., Vol. IV, p. 80.
[11]Macnair, op. cit., Vol. IV, p. 81.

SKATING IN THE RINK

Though undoubtedly a little *risqué*, the ladies are enjoying the sport

THE TORONTO RED JACKETS ON TORONTO BAY, 1873

T. McGaw is at the "hack", having just delivered his stone. J. Grey and D. Walker are the sweepers, the former with his broom in the air. Captain Perry is the skip with one knee on the ice. It is a good "end", for all the stones are "in the house".

CURLING ON THE DON RIVER, 1860

CURLING IN HIGH PARK, TORONTO, 1860

These companion sketches were made by the same artist, whose name
is unknown. The Rennies were the leaders of a group who enjoyed
the "roarin' game" on Grenadier Pond.

like tea-kettles on the ice, after which they cried 'Soop! soop!', and then laughed like fools. I really believe they ARE fools."[12]

The introduction of curling into Upper Canada followed closely upon the settlement of Scotchmen in the various parts of the province, though it was not long before teams of non-Scotch, sometimes referred to as "Barbarians", were enthusiastically engaged in the game. The first club in the province was probably that formed at Kingston in 1820. As early as 1829 curling was enjoyed on the Don River, though the first Toronto club was not organised until the winter of 1836-37. The Humber River, Grenadier Pond in High Park, and the Bay were also used by Toronto curlers in later years.

Several of the pioneer clubs of the province were formed in the "Huron Tract", which was being settled by the Canada Company in the eighteen-thirties. The earliest of these clubs was at Fergus, Wellington County, in 1834, the gloom of the first winter being dispelled by the introduction of the game. The Hon. Adam Fergusson was the founder of this Scottish settlement in the Township of Nicholl, and he was the organiser and first President of the Fergus Club. Similar associations were instituted at Galt and Guelph in 1838, but there had been curling on Altrieve Lake, near Galt, a year or two earlier. Among other early clubs in Upper Canada were those at Perth, West Flamborough, Niagara, Scarborough, Newmarket, Dundas and Milton.

In playing the game various substitutes have been made for the granite stones always used in Scotland, and now invariably in use in Ontario. In the early days of curling at Fergus, Galt and Guelph, blocks of hardwood, usually maple or beech, were employed; at Fergus they were sometimes loaded with lead in order that they might be approximately equal in weight. Iron handles were inserted into these blocks.

In Quebec and Montreal bell-shaped irons weighing from sixty-five to eighty pounds were commonly used, and this tended to lessen the intercourse between the curlers of Canada East and Canada West. The origin of the use of

[12]*Ibid.*, Vol. I, pp. 73-4.

irons is said to have been the metal-rimmed hubs of the gun-carriages, into which handles were inserted. These primitive "stones" were used by the officers of the garrison, who soon had a blacksmith imitate them. It was found that the intense cold sometimes cracked granite stones, so the use of irons was continued; but at present both types are found in Quebec. The use of irons was general also among the early curlers at the village of Dundas in Upper Canada.

When the game was introduced in Niagara, in 1836, one gentleman was generous enough to import from Scotland sufficient granite stones for the use of all the members of the club. In Toronto and vicinity stones were always used, some being imported from Scotland, while others "were made by the stone-cutter to the club, from blocks of excellent quality picked up by him on the land in the vicinity".[13] At the Oshawa Curling Club may still be seen a number of these roughly-hewn curling stones, a curiosity reminiscent of other times.

To keep the ice free from dirt and snow during the game brooms are used. In Scotland they were made of the Scotch broom as a general rule, though occasionally birch twigs or heather were substituted. In Canada corn brooms were in common use, but the early curlers near Scarborough, who had emigrated from Lanarkshire, imported stocks of genuine Scotch broom, which under their cultivation soon became popular.

The rules of curling have changed but little through the centuries, the important matter being to get one's stone nearest the "tee", and to keep it there until the "end" has been played. The length of games has changed considerably, however. In Scotland, where the continuance of the curling season was very precarious, it was customary to play all day, a lunch of bread, cheese and whisky being taken to the loch to stave off the pangs of hunger. In Canada, too, many an early curler is said to have set out the night before and travelled all night on "Shank's mare", curled all the next day, and returned home thereafter. Some clubs played three-hour matches, while in the early Toronto Club (now Toronto Victorias) a certain number of shots, as 7, 13, 21, or more usually 31, signified the end of a game. The "points game", consisting of a series of difficult shots, was long popular, and the individuals making the best scores were awarded Caledonian medals by the Canadian branch of the Grand Caledonian Curling Club.

It is interesting to know that the Rebellion of 1837 had its effect upon curling. It was usual among Toronto curlers at that time to have the players "fall in" in the order in which they were to play, and "number off" from right to left. In those trying days, "when military terms and ideas were infused into every department of life", it was considered that a man who played in the wrong order was fit neither for a soldier nor a curler![14]

Owing partly to the customs of the times, and partly to the country in which the game originated, whisky-drinking during matches was early prominent and long persisted. In fact a writer observed in 1875 that "many people are under the impression that whisky and curling go hand in hand. This was the case at one time, but I rejoice to say that bottles of whisky at the head of each rink during play is now the exception and not the rule."[15] An interesting example in picture form of this change in sentiment is found in the first *Annuals* of the Ontario Curling Association. In the 1876 *Annual,* and for a year or two following, appeared an engraving of the famous Red Jackets playing a match on Toronto Bay. The game is being contested with much spirit, some of which, however, was obtained from time to time from a basket of bottles which are in plain view at one end of the rink. As temperance sentiment grew stronger the presence of the whisky evidently caused uneasiness in the minds of many, for in the 1879 *Annual* the same engraving appears, but with the addition of a black cloth which has been discreetly drawn over the bottles, giving the basket a most innocent appearance!

Difficulties of transportation made inter-club matches infrequent during the first half of the century. When the Toronto Club arranged to play a match with the Hamilton Thistles in the early fifties it took three days to do so,— one to travel the forty miles by sleigh, another to play the match, and a third for the return home. In spite of these

[14]*Ibid.,* p. 21 fn. [15]Roper, *op. cit.,* p. 82.

difficulties it was customary to hold an annual "bonspiel", the word being derived from the Danish *bondespil,* meaning "a rustic game". On February 12, 1839, a bonspiel was held on the Don River, Toronto, and twenty-four curlers from outside points measured their skill against a similar number from the city. The governors of Canada have usually taken an active interest in the game, and at this match the spectators included the Governor-General, Lord Sydenham, and the Lieutenant-Governor of Upper Canada, Sir George Arthur.

The completion of the Grand Trunk Railway from Montreal to Toronto in 1856, and the building of the Great Western Railway in the Lake Erie region, made possible the largely-attended annual bonspiels which are still so popular among curlers. In 1858 Burlington Bay was the location of the event, while the following year East played West on the Don River.

Another interesting occasion in the fifties was a tussle at Quebec between Scottish and "Barbarians". An account of the match describes "the host of ladies and gentlemen, and many gay equipages", the "bursts of merriment", and the "snatches of broad Scotch" as the curlers coaxed on an important stone with honied expressions, as though their lives depended on the issue of the game. In the background arose the fortress of old Stadacona, where the target practice of the artillery "seemed as if it were a royal salute to the curlers". Many "fair admirers" witnessed the match in spite of a biting north-west wind.[16]

It was quite usual in the early days to play under severe weather conditions, perhaps exposed to a heavy snow drift, and with the thermometer below zero. On January 8, 1864, four curlers had their ears frozen during a match at Port Hope with the curlers of Cobourg. A contemporary account of the event says: "The game commenced at noon, with an interruption of twenty minutes for lunch; the time set was 4.15 p.m., and although the day turned out one of the most severe that we have had this winter, the 'roarin' game' was kept up with much spirit, notwithstanding four of the players suffered severely from Jack Frost playing tricks with their ears."[17]

[16]See Kerr, *op. cit.,* p. 326.
[17]*Cobourg Sentinel,* January 15, 1864.

On February 10th the Port Hope curlers played a return match at Cobourg, on the ice of the Victoria Skating Rink at the Factory Creek.   Play commenced at noon and continued until 5 p.m.; but at two o'clock John Butler called the players from the ice and served refreshments, "which we can speak of with much credit to his good lady, for the excellent cup of coffee and other good things which we received at her hands." At the end of the match the participants were served a sumptuous dinner at the North American Hotel; after which President Ward of the Port Hope Club presented the "Broom", with colours attached, to the Cobourg curlers, as a token of victory.[18] This trophy, like the modern silver cup or tankard, was retained as long as the holders could successfully defend it on the ice.

Just as the tiresome but necessary "shovel exercise" had been one of the main reasons for the formation of clubs, in order that "the time which was formerly wasted in preparations that may be performed by labourers is now spent in the game,"[19] so, in the same way, the uncertain weather conditions led, in the early seventies, to the building of closed rinks, which soon became common throughout the province.   One of the last and most notable of open-air bonspiels was held on Burlington Bay in 1875.   No less than 360 curlers were present for the East *versus* West match, and the only prize awarded was a gold medal to the Chatham Club for having the highest average score.   This bonspiel followed almost immediately upon the organisation of the Ontario branch of the Royal Caledonian Club, formed chiefly because the eastern Canadian clubs were so far away and used irons in place of stones.   A description of this bonspiel in the first Ontario Curling Association *Annual* (1876) notes that: "the Bay presented a most lively and festive appearance.   Crowds of spectators, including many of the fair sex, on foot and in sleighs, covered the Bay during the contest."[20]

A famous Canadian team in the sixties and seventies was the "Red Jackets" of the Toronto Club.   The team obtained its name at the International Bonspiel at Buffalo in 1865, when twenty-three rinks of Canadians defeated the American curlers by 658 shots to 478.   At the height

[18]*Ibid.*, February 13, 1864.   [19]Bicket, *op. cit.*, pp. 36-7.
[20]A full account of the event is found in the 1876 *Annual*, pp. 86-95.

of their effectiveness the Red Jackets consisted of T. Mc-Gaw, lead; Major Gray, second; D. Walker, third; and Captain Charles Perry, skip. The Ontario Curling Association *Annual* for 1886 says: "They continued to play together in the same positions for about ten years (1868-1878), during which time they travelled many thousands of miles on curling excursions, and played against select rinks from many of the strongest clubs in Canada and the United States, and won seventy-five matches in succession before they met their first defeat; a record, we may well believe, without a parallel."[21] During the heyday of this team there was another, the "Callants" of Montreal, which was almost as famous for the skill of its members. A remarkable feature in connection with this team was that the combined ages of the four members amounted to 287 years. These veterans of the besom and the stane challenged any club to a friendly game. The challenge was accepted nine times and on each occasion the Callants were victorious.

An interesting event in the annals of Canadian curling occurred on December 11, 1876, when the first curling match in the province of Manitoba took place in Winnipeg. In this match the old Scottish custom of playing for oatmeal to be distributed among the poor of the parish was imitated. After the game the prize, a barrel of meal, was presented to the Winnipeg General Hospital. In more recent years Manitoba curlers have repeatedly proven themselves the best in the Dominion in many a competition open to the outstanding teams of the various provinces.

All of the winters of earlier times were not "old-fashioned", for we find that the winter of 1875-76 was as mild as that of 1931-32, and drew forth a

CURLER'S LAMENT ABOUT THE WINTER OF 1876

Oh! Canada, adopted mither!
You've kept us in a dreary-swither,
Have ye forgot us a'thegither?
   Ye're sair to blame
For sendin' sic saft southern weather
   For curlers' game.

[21]Obituary notice of Captain Charles Perry, 1886 *Annual*, pp. 97-8.

December cam and ga'ed awa',
And scarcely brought a frost ava;
January's been a'e continued thaw
      Just much the same,—
Contrary quite to Nature's law,
      With scarce a game.

                *   *   *   *

Oh! cheerful frost, we'd welcome thee,—
Each curler's voice shouts loud with glee.
We'd gladly gather round the tee
      And ne'er gang hame;
We'd play as long as we could see,
      Grand roarin' game![22]

To keep abreast of the times an increasing number of
modern curling clubs use artificial ice, which provides
facilities for the game during five or six months of the year,
irrespective of weather conditions. But many an old club
—like the Toronto Victorias—has proud memories of the
days of open-air curling, and the old times are recalled
whenever we hear George S. Lyon sing *My Wild Irish
Rose*, or Henry Wright thunder out—with the help of his
fellow-curlers—*Jock McGraw*. Such joviality represents
the good-comradeship inspired by the game; for in earlier
times the devotees of the sport met at the festive board after
the match and dined on the proverbial curler's fare; whereupon all joined in the

CURLERS' SONG AFTER THE BEEF AND GREENS
(Air—*Willie Brewed a Peck o' Maut.*)

Now, brothers in the roaring game,
      Come, join a curling stave with me,
As if your soul were in the stane,
      And heaven itself were near the tee.

Chorus:- Then soop, soop, soop! soop, soop, soop!
      And draw the creepin' stane a wee;
The ice may thaw, the day may snaw,
      But aye we're merry round the tee.

[22]1877 *Annual*, pp. 105-6. The poem was signed "W. (Toronto)".

Then hand around the neeshin' horn
The wintry evenings quickly fa';
Wha lose today may win the morn—
Thou roarin' game, hip hip hurrah![23]

[23]1876 *Annual*, pp. 109-110.

SECTION IV
TRAVEL AND TRANSPORTATION

CHAPTER I

INDIAN TRAILS, LOYALIST ROUTES AND CHANNELS OF TRADE

"The next day was calm, and we arrived at the entrance of the navigation which leads to Lake aux Claies[1]. We presently passed two short carrying-places, at each of which were several lodges of Indians containing only women and children, the men being gone to the council at Niagara. . . . On the 18th of June we crossed Lake aux Claies, which appeared to be upward of twenty miles in length. At its further end we came to the carrying-place of Toronto. Here the Indians obliged me to carry a burden of more than a hundred pounds' weight. The day was very hot, and the woods and marshes abounded with mosquitoes; but the Indians walked at a quick pace, and I could by no means see myself left behind. The whole country was a thick forest, through which our only road was a foot-path, or such as, in America, is exclusively termed an Indian path. Next morning at ten o'clock we reached the shore of Lake Ontario. Here we were employed two days in making canoes out of the bark of the elm tree, in which we were to transport ourselves to Niagara. . . . On the 21st we embarked at Toronto, and encamped, in the evening, four miles short of Fort Niagara, which the Indians would not approach till morning."

ALEXANDER HENRY (1764)[2]

BEFORE the arrival of Europeans in America the native Indians had well-defined routes of travel which they used in hunting trips and on the war-path. In these long journeys they followed the waterways wherever it was possible to do so, and used portage paths to avoid rapids. Well-travelled trails, often worn from six inches to a foot into the ground, were followed through the woods from one body of water to another; and these paths were observed and used by the earliest French explorers and traders. The Indians found canoe travel on the Great Lakes impracticable except close to shore or among islands. They also avoided dangerous rapids, such as those on the St. Lawrence, whenever it was possible to accomplish their purpose by an easier route. The routes by which the Indians crossed Lake Ontario at the eastern end are thus described by William Canniff:

"There is evidence that the Mohawks, upon the southern shore of Lake Ontario, were accustomed to pass across the

[1]The "entrance of the navigation" was the Bay of Matchitashk, or Matchedash. Lac aux Claies was an early French name for Lake Simcoe, having reference to the stakes used by the Indians of Champlain's day in fishing in the shallow parts of the lake.

[2]Alexander Henry: *Travels and Adventures in Canada and the Indian Territories, 1760-76.* 1807. pp. 179-80.

waters to the northern shores by different routes. Thus one was from Cape Vincent to Wolfe Island, and thence along its shore to the west end, and then either to Cataraqui, or up the Bay of Quinté, or perhaps across to Amherst Island, where, it seems, generally resided a chief of considerable importance. A second route followed by them in their frail bark canoes was from a point of land somewhat east of Oswego, called in later days Henderson's Point, taking in their way Stony Island, the Jallup Island, and stretching across to Yorkshire Island and Duck Island, then to the Drake Islands, and finally to Point Traverse. Following the shore around this point, Wappoose Island was also reached; or, on the contrary, proceeding along the shore westward they reached East Lake. From the northernmost point of this lake they directed their steps, with canoes on their heads, across the carrying-place to the head of Picton Bay, a distance of a little over four miles."[3]

There were several routes by which the Indians travelled northward and westward. By the long chain of lakes and rivers now known as the Trent system, and early called the Toronto Lakes, they penetrated to Lake Simcoe, and on by Lake Couchiching and the Severn to Georgian Bay and the upper lakes. This was the route over which in 1615 the Hurons led Champlain from Georgian Bay to Lake Ontario, and it was long considered the most direct way; over two centuries later the same belief prompted the construction of the Trent Valley Canal.

Other routes which were followed northward by the Indians as approaches to the headwaters of the Trent system were the rivers emptying into Lake Ontario, such as the Cataraqui (Rideau), the Napanee, the Moira, the Ganeraské, Duffin's Creek, the Rouge, Don, Humber and Credit. In addition to the Jesuit mission stations earlier inaugurated in Huronia there were Sulpician missions at or near the mouths of some of these rivers. One was established in 1668 in the Cayuga Indian village of Kenté on the south side of Prince Edward County, either on West Lake or Weller's Bay; another, Ganneious, was located not far from the mouth of the Napanee River; a third, Ganeraské, on the

[3]William Canniff: *History of the Settlement of Upper Canada*. 1869. p. 133.

LES CHATS FALLS, UPPER OTTAWA RIVER, 1840
A romantic beauty-spot in early times

LAC DES ALLUMETTES IN 1840
Where Champlain's Voyage of 1613 ended

FORT WILLIAM IN 1856

W. H. Bartlett

PORT HOPE, 1840

The site of the Ganeraské Mission of the French period; the Indian
Village Pemiscutiank or Cochingomink ("the commencement of the
portage"); in the days of the fur trade (1778-1819) called Smith's
Creek; and for a short time known as Toronto post office

site of Port Hope; a fourth, Gandalskiagon or Gandaseteiagon, at Frenchman's Bay, the port of Whitby; and a fifth at Teieiagon, between the Humber and Credit. A mission was also located on the St. Lawrence opposite Prescott, at the mouth of the Oswegatchie River; this post, situated on the present site of Ogdensburg, was commenced in 1749.

The importance of these locations led to the establishment of trading-posts at most of them before or during the days of early settlement. Three of these antedated settlement, the post at Pemiscutiank or Cochingomink ("the commencement of the portage"), later called Smith's Creek (Port Hope), established about 1778; Fort Rouillé, near the mouth of the Humber, erected by the French in 1750; and the Oswegatchie trading-post, which was by 1753 important in the French trade with the Onondaga, Oneida and Cayuga Indians.

The Humber trail was by far the most important of the routes to the Trent system and Lake Simcoe. As early as 1615 the Huron Indians led Etienne Brûlé across this portage from Lake Simcoe to Lake Ontario, and probably proceeded southwards as far as the Niagara district, for from the mouth of the Humber a Mississaga trail was well beaten where the present Lake Shore Road runs, and the path continued to the Falls of Niagara and beyond. The entire Niagara region was intersected by well-known trails from Indian days down through the French and early British periods. In 1640 Brébeuf and Chaumonot travelled from a Huron mission in the present Township of Medonte, near Penetanguishene, to the Indian village Onguiara, near Queenston, their route following an Indian trail which is thought to have run through the present towns of Beeton, Orangeville, Georgetown, Hamilton and St. Catharines.

Indian paths from the head of Lake Ontario towards the river systems to the westward are described as follows:

"From Burlington Bay the Indians used a portage into the Upper Thames, and another from the forks of that river into Lake Erie at Point aux Pins. Three well-defined trails led from different points on the Grand River to Lake Ontario, and there was also a portage less than five miles in length from that stream into the Chippawa. The carrying-place at Niagara Falls lay on the eastern bank of the river and was about nine miles long."[4]

Along Lake Erie there were forest paths well-known to the Indians, but in later years the traders did not penetrate the northern shores of this lake as they did those of Lake Ontario; they merely coasted the shore until Detroit was reached, stopping only occasionally for shelter. This district was long inhabited by the Neutrals, referred to in 1616 by Champlain as a powerful nation holding a large extent of country and numbering 4,000 warriors.[5] The Neutrals appear to have been a settled tribe, living in villages and cultivating such grains and vegetables as they were familiar with, chiefly maize, tobacco and pumpkins. From 1650 to 1653 the Iroquois made several expeditions against the Neutrals and exterminated them as a separate tribe, and for nearly 150 years the northern shore of Lake Erie was known only as an Iroquois hunting-ground. Dr. James H. Coyne gives the main Indian paths in this region as five in number, chiefly portages from one river to another. One or two of them were referred to above, but are more minutely described by Dr. Coyne:

"One led from the site of Dundas to a point on the Grand River near Cainsville; another from the latter stream to the Thames River near Woodstock, and a third from the upper waters of the Thames to Lake Huron. Besides these there was a trail from the Huntly farm, in Southwold Township on the River Thames, to the mouth of Kettle Creek; and a fifth from the Rondeau to McGregor's Creek near Chatham. These were thoroughfares of travel and of such rude commerce as was carried on by the savages with their French and English neighbours."[6]

While forts, trading-posts and mission stations were early established along the St. Lawrence, Lake Ontario and the Detroit, none was to be found anywhere along the north shore of Lake Erie. But when the Talbot Road was blazed in 1809-11 it followed the general course of an Indian path.

[4] E. A. Cruikshank: *Early Traders and Trade Routes in Ontario and the West, 1760-83.* (In *Transactions* of the Canadian Institute, Series 4, Vol. III, part 2, pp. 256-7.)

[5] Samuel de Champlain: *Voyages.* (The Prince Society. 1878-82. Vol. II, p. 148.)

[6] J. H. Coyne: *The Country of the Neutrals.* (In *Historical Sketches of the County of Elgin.* 1895. pp. 20-21.)

The earliest explorers of the lower lakes were Champlain, Brûlé, Joliet, Dollier, Galinée, Hennepin, La Motte and La Salle, most of whom wrote interesting descriptions of the regions through which they passed. Several of these explorers penetrated to the upper lakes, and from their accounts, and that of Nicolet, we obtain our first knowledge of Western Ontario. Excepting those of Champlain and Brûlé, these explorations were carried on almost entirely by the water routes, supplemented by portages around waterfalls or from one body of water to another.

In his notable expedition from Quebec through Ontario in 1615, Champlain ascended the Ottawa to the tributary waters of the Mattawan, whence the Indians led him to Lake Nipissing by a land trail beginning about forty miles up the Mattawan river. From Lake Nipissing Champlain continued his journey by way of the French River and the coast of Georgian Bay to a point just west of Penetanguishene. Following the course of the Severn River, Sparrow Lake and Lake Couchiching the Hurons led him to their villages near Lake Simcoe. A few weeks later Champlain and a war party of Hurons proceeded eastward by water about fourteen miles, after which they followed a portage trail of twenty-five miles and reached what was presumably Sturgeon Lake. They continued by lake and river through the Trent system, probably avoiding Stoney Lake and neighbouring waters by travelling over the well-known five-mile Indian trail from Chemong Lake to the Otonabee River, a short-cut which would eliminate many tiresome portages. The journey continued down the Otonabee and through Rice Lake, the Trent, and the Bay of Quinté to "the great lake of the Entouhonorons",[7] which was crossed by a protected route among the islands.

A few weeks later the unsuccessful war party returned from the Iroquois country south of Lake Ontario, and probably ascended the Cataraqui (Rideau) River. They proceeded in a leisurely manner in a north-westerly direction, stopping for a while to hunt. The return journey to the Huron villages was made in early winter over ice and snow, and along a route some distance north of the Trent system. They reached their destination on December 23, 1615, and

[7]Champlain, *op. cit.*, Vol. III, p. 125.

Champlain spent the winter among the Hurons, finally returning to Quebec on July 11, 1616, after a forty-day trip.

When the Loyalists trekked northward to Canada at the close of the American Revolutionary War they followed six main routes. Many thousands used the easiest of these—the ocean voyage—by sailing from New York and other ports in British ships which were sent to take them away; some proceeded to the Maritime Provinces, while others ascended the St. Lawrence to Quebec and continued up the river by bateau. The other five routes were more difficult, but had long been used in the fur trade by Indian and *voyageur* as approaches to the British posts.

The Hudson route to Lake Ontario is called by Canniff "by far the most commonly-travelled way taken by those who came into Canada after the close of the War".[8] The general route over which these Loyalists passed followed the Hudson River to a point ten miles beyond Albany, where the river divides; thence by the western branch, called the Mohawk River, and by Wood Creek to Oneida Lake, which was reached by a portage; or by a branch of Wood Creek which led towards Lake Champlain. Those who reached Oneida Lake followed the Oswego River to Lake Ontario, and coasted east or west along its shores or crossed the lake by schooner. Most of the Loyalists who approached Canada by this route proceeded westward to the Niagara River and entered Upper Canada at the point which was soon to become the capital of the newly-created province.

A considerable number of Loyalists reached Lake Erie by following the Potomac River and French Creek, and crossed the lake by schooner. Many proceeded to Detroit, crossing the Detroit River into Essex County at once, or after Detroit was surrendered to the United States in 1796. Another approach to Lake Erie and the Detroit was by way of the Mississippi, concerning which route an early writer said: "It is worthy of notice that a person may go from Quebec to New Orleans by water all the way except about a mile from the source of the Illinois River."[9] Only occasional portages were necessary in following these routes, and it is unlikely that in any one of them the carrying-

[8]Canniff, *op. cit.*, p. 131 .   [9]Quoted in Canniff, *op. cit.*, p. 131.

places totalled more than thirty miles, though the distance travelled was often many hundreds of miles.

The fifth and sixth Loyalist routes were to the south of the St. Lawrence, one of them being given by Canniff as "by Long Lake which feeds Racket River, that empties into the St. Lawrence at St. Regis, opposite Cornwall";[10] while the other was the military route, so often used before and after that time by French, British or American armies, *i.e.*, by Lake Champlain and the Richelieu River to Sorel. Many of the Loyalists walked the entire distance; others travelled by ox-cart, canvas-covered wagon, bateau or Schenectady boat; while in winter some made their way on snow-shoes or by trains of sleighs arranged after the fashion of the "French train"—a long, narrow sleigh, pulled by one or more horses driven tandem style to allow easier passage through the forests.

Many of the Loyalists were met by military boats on Lake Champlain and helped over the remaining part of the journey; but not a few were forced to cross "what was then called the Willsbury wilderness, and Chataguee woods", where, before 1800, "there was but one tavern through all that vast forest, and this of the poorest character. Indeed it is said that while provision might be procured for the horses, none could be had for man".[11] Those who entered Canada by this route in winter had to remain at Sorel or New Johnstown (Cornwall) until spring, when, by the use of bateaux, (to borrow which the men had often to walk to the Bay of Quinté during the winter), the women and children and their few possessions could be transported farther up the St. Lawrence to what was soon to be named Upper Canada. Some of those who travelled by land carried their baggage fastened to their saddles, and in the same manner their children were placed in panniers on either side of the horse.

The development of military and commercial posts west of the St. Lawrence did not commence until the latter part of the seventeenth century. The first French fort on Lake Ontario was established in 1673 by the Count de Frontenac at Cataraqui, a strategic position at the junction of the St. Lawrence, Lake Ontario, the Bay of Quinté and the Rideau

[10]*Ibid.*, p. 132.   [11]*Ibid.*, p. 143.

system; the fort which was built was named Frontenac, and the Chevalier de La Salle was placed in charge of it. In 1679 La Salle set out to explore the centre of the continent, and erected a stockade *en route,* at the mouth of the Niagara River. By 1725 this post had become quite a solid fortress, and greatly facilitated trade between Michilimackinac and Montreal. The first British military post on Lake Ontario developed in 1728 from the small trading-post called Chouéguen, established six years earlier at the mouth of the Oswego River. Under the protection of these forts, French and British merchants competed for the Indian trade.

The French routes of travel from the St. Lawrence to the upper lakes were chiefly two: the first was Champlain's route by way of the Ottawa River, Lake Nipissing and the French River to Georgian Bay, and thence to Michilimackinac and the Kaministiquia River, and by the Grand Portage to the Far West; the second followed the Bay of Quinté and the Trent system to Georgian Bay, a route plainly marked on early French maps, but which was not always available after the Huron nation had been wiped out by the Iroquois between 1648 and 1650. Occasionally French *voyageurs* made the longer and more difficult trip along the north shores of Lakes Ontario and Erie, and reached the upper lakes by way of the Detroit.

Towards the end of the French period we find the Humber and Credit Rivers, supplemented by well-established trails, used as approaches to Lake Taranto (Simcoe), from which the fur traders' route continued by either the Severn or the Nottawasaga to Georgian Bay, the Severn being used in very early times, and the Nottawasaga more usually followed in later days. The Ganeraské portage, between the streams later called Smith's Creek and Sackville's Creek, was similarly used to reach Rice Lake. Each of these routes cut off a considerable section of what must have been at best a tedious journey.

It must be remembered in connection with the use of these rivers, and of others even smaller, that the streams of today have much less water than they had in the days of the fur trade and early settlement. The clearing of the forests from the face of the land has led to the quick evaporation or drainage of the surface water, and many a noble river has shrunk to a mere creek, with insufficient depth to float a boat except in the season of spring floods. It was quite usual, however, for Indian and trader to ignore small stretches of navigable waters, and to save time by portaging the entire distance. This was the case, for example, over the Humber-Holland portage, even in Indian days. Such a policy not only gained the time wasted by frequent portages, but also obviated in some cases the carriage of boats, for the Indians were accustomed to make new elm bark canoes at several stages of a long journey.[12] The trader, however, had to portage his canoe, and consequently followed whichever method he found most convenient.

During the latter part of the French period Toronto and Frontenac were known as "King's Posts". Ninety canoes were annually permitted to go to the southern and western posts—Niagara, Toronto, Frontenac, La Presentation, Detroit, Ouias, Miamis, Michilimackinac, La Baye, St. Joseph and Illinois, together with their dependencies; most of these were on the American shore of the lakes, though even as late as 1816 many of them were still considered (at least by the few inhabitants) to be in British territory. Twenty-eight canoes were sent each year to the northern posts, which were Temiscamingue, Chagouamigon, Nipigon, Gamanistigouia, Michipicoton, Mer du Ouest, Rivière des Kikipoux, Lake Huron, and Belle Rivière. The average value of each canoe-load was 7,000 livres. There were a number of smaller posts which ranked as dependencies, and also several on the Ottawa-Lake Nipissing route, four of which were abandoned just previous to the Seven Years' War.

Towards the close of the French period a trade route which had been only occasionally used came into considerable prominence. The French found that much of the Indian trade was passing from the upper lakes through the Detroit River and Lake Erie to the British post at Fort Orange (Albany); consequently it was decided to establish a French post along the route to intercept the trade, and Fort Pontchartrain (Detroit) was built by Cadillac in

[12]See the description of Alexander Henry's experiences, at the beginning of this chapter.

1701. During the continuance of the fur trade this route was considerably used, though most traders found the Humber-Holland portage a shorter and cheaper approach to the upper lakes.

Some of the names along these early channels of commerce recall the days of the fur trade. The Montreal River, flowing into Lake Superior, was so called because it was one of the canoe routes on the return voyage from the West to Montreal; Matchedash Bay is named on old French maps Baie de Toronto, because it penetrated inland towards Lake Taranto (Simcoe); and Canada Creek, flowing into the Mohawk River, along the Hudson route, was so named because it was part of the traders' trail to Canada.

The Humber-Holland[13] portage route was a well-known Indian trail long before the white man was first led across it; but when the Iroquois exterminated the Hurons in 1648-50, and the Neutrals in the Lake Erie region during the next three years, the route became almost exclusively an Iroquois path. When Father Hennepin passed along the north shore of Lake Ontario in 1678, an Indian village, Taiaiagon[14] (a "portage" or "landing-place"), was located a few miles west of the Humber, called by early writers the River Tau-a-hon-ate. A French map, dated at least as early as 1679, has the Humber portage marked on it with a description stating that it is "the road by which the Iroquois go from the country of the Ottawas to trade with New Holland". The writing on the map also implies that the Trent system and the Bay of Quinté had formerly been used by the Iroquois until Fort Frontenac was erected by the French, which prevented further use of that route.[15] The British trading-post in New Holland which was their destination was Chouéguen (Oswego); here the Iroquois traded with their traditional friends, and obtained a larger amount of cheap English rum in trade than the French could afford to give of the more expensive brandy. Towards the middle of the next century French traders were sent

[13]The Holland River was named after Surveyor-General Major S. Holland.

[14]Indian names were never consistently spelled, and in many instances it is more of a virtue than a vice to vary the orthography, for it was customary to spell them phonetically. Toronto, Teieiagon and many other names have numerous variants.

[15]See p. 171 fn. of the Bain Edition of Alexander Henry's *Travels*.

Mrs. Edward Hopkins

CANOE TRIP OF THE ARTIST AND HER HUSBAND IN A HUDSON'S BAY CANOE

A canot du maître, showing typical arrangement of passengers and goods.

A LINK IN THE CARRYING-PLACE OF TORONTO

THE RIVER TAU-A-HON-ATE OF INDIAN DAYS; KNOWN TO THE
FRENCH AS THE TORONTO RIVER; LATER CALLED
ST. JOHN'S CREEK; NOW THE HUMBER

to intercept this trade at the village Taiaiagon between the Humber and Credit; and in 1750 Fort Rouillé, more generally called Fort Toronto, was erected for the same purpose. This post, two miles east of the Humber, was the terminus of the Holland-Humber trade route until 1759, when it was destroyed by the French to prevent its capture.

In the early years of the British period the trading-posts and routes in the vicinity of Lake Ontario decreased greatly in importance. In 1750 forty or fifty traders were established at Oswego, but by 1779 only one, named Parlow, remained, and a party of Indians and revolutionists pillaged his post. He took shelter in a small fort on Carleton Island; other merchants followed him there, and a fair trade was carried on with the neighbouring Indians for some years. The Oswegatchie fort farther east had never been a favourite resort for traders, except, perhaps, in the first years of its existence.

Along the north shore of Lake Ontario there were traders between 1770 and 1780 at Pinewood Creek and at Piminis-cotyan Landing (Pemiscutiank, at the mouth of the Gan-eraské), and probably also near the mouth of Duffin's Creek, at Gandalskiagon. Sometimes one would winter at the Mississauga village on the shores of Rice Lake. Farther west the trade at the mouth of the Humber was continued in the British period when St. Jean Baptiste Rousseau, usually known as St. John, received a license in 1770 to establish a trading-post, which he seems to have previously erected on the east bank of the Humber, near the mouth. It may be assumed that he was active in the trade in that vicinity many years before, for at least as early as 1756 the river was known as St. John's Creek, and retained that name until Governor Simcoe's day, when most of the old names gave way to new. Several other men, notably one Knaggs, were also engaged in the nefarious rum trade at Toronto.

The old trade routes were not, however, being used to the same extent as in the French period. Benjamin Frobisher said in 1785:

"I have seen several persons who have gone from hence (Montreal) to Lake Huron by the carrying-place of Toronto, but have met with only one who set out from the Bay of Kentie (Quinté), and that so far back as the year 1761, and the knowledge he seems to have of the country he travelled through I consider very imperfect."[16]

The Humber-Holland trail extended from the mouth of the Humber to the eastern branch of the Holland River, at a point where that stream ceased to be navigable. In 1792, when Augustus Jones was surveying in this district, he came upon the trail, which he described as "an Indian foot-path leading to lake La Clie (Simcoe), near a pond of St. John's".[17] On September 25, 1793, Governor Simcoe set out from York to visit Lake Huron. The party included four officers, a dozen soldiers and some Indians, and this well-known trail was the route followed to Lake Simcoe. Among the members of the expedition was Lieutenant Pilkington, who made sketches and maps during the course of the trip. Mrs. Simcoe states in her diary that the party "rode thirty miles to the Miciaguean (Mississaga) Creek, then passed a terrible bog of liquid mud. The Indians with some difficulty pushed the canoe the Governor was in through it. . . . They proceeded about thirty miles across Lac aux Claies, now named Simcoe, in which are many islands, which Colonel Simcoe named after his father's friends and those gentlemen who accompanied him. The river (Severn) from thence to Matchedash Bay afforded the most picturesque scenery, from the number of falls and rapids in it. Some of them were avoided by carrying the canoes on the shores; others they risked going down".[18] At Matchedash there was located a permanent trader as early as 1778.

During the return trip of the Governor and his party, an Indian who carried most of the supplies decamped and "reduced the stock so much that the Governor set out with only two days' provisions and the expectation of five days' march to bring them to York. The Indians lost their way, and when they had provisions for one day only they knew not where they were. The Governor had recourse to a compass, and at the close of the day they came on a

[16]Quoted in Cruikshank, *op. cit.*, p. 274 .

[17]Surveyor Jones' notes, quoted in K. M. Lizars: *The Valley of the Humber*. 1913. p. 40.

[18]*Diary of Mrs. John Graves Simcoe*, October 25, 1793. See also Alexander Macdonnell: *Diary of Governor Simcoe's Journey from Humber Bay to Matchetache Bay, 1793*. (The date of publication is unknown, but the pamphlet was an extract from the *Transactions* of the Canadian Institute, 1890.)

surveyor's line, and the next morning saw Lake Ontario. Its first appearance, Colonel Simcoe says, was the most delightful sight at a time when they were in danger of starving, and about three miles from York they breakfasted on the remaining provisions."[19]

All traces of this old portage route have long been obliterated, with the possible exception of the remains of a corduroy road in the swamp near Holland Landing, on Lake Simcoe. The carrying-place was known by the name Toronto at both ends and followed the present course of Yonge Street in some parts. The length of the portage for canoes was only twenty-four miles from the Humber to the Upper Holland Landing—the old Indian landing-place for canoes. The Lower Landing, one and one-half miles down the stream, had to be used by boats of deeper draught, and at that point the River Holland was about twenty-five yards wide.

When settlement north of York commenced in 1794 the old trail was in part widened into a blazed path or bush road to which was given the name Yonge Street. Further work was done upon this road by the Queen's Rangers in 1796, when it was pushed through to Lake Simcoe. These improvements were an incentive to commerce, for the traders of the North-West Company soon after discontinued their canoe route up the Ottawa, and travelled in bateaux along the shore of Lake Ontario to York. At the Carrying Place between the Bay of Quinté and Picton Bay, Asa Weller took their boats on wheels over a four-mile portage. At York they crossed the peninsula (now the island) at the foot of the present Woodbine Avenue, and proceeded up the Don to the Don Mills; from this point they portaged their bateaux on wheels by Yonge Street to Lake Simcoe, sometimes employing a windlass to help haul the boats up the steepest hills.

The Holland River, Lake Simcoe and the Severn River were considered one stream by the Indians. The North-West Company's traders, however, followed a slightly different route, proceeding from Holland Landing across Lake Simcoe to the present site of Barrie, and thence by a nine-mile portage to Willow Creek, which was followed to the Not-

[19]*Ibid.*

tawasaga; this river was navigable to its mouth on the east shore of Iroquois (Georgian) Bay. Smith's *Gazetteer* of 1799 describes more minutely the route from the vicinity of the Narrows, Lake Simcoe: "From the bay west of Francis Island there is a good path, and a short portage into a small lake; this is the nearest way to Lake Huron, the river which falls from Lake Simcoe into Matchedash Bay, called the Matchedash or Severn River, making a more circuitous passage to the northward and westward."[20]

From Georgian Bay the trade route to Michilimackinac and the Grand Portage skirted the shores of Lakes Huron and Superior. Sometimes a two weeks' journey from York to Penetanguishene was made overland, the route following a trail around the west side of Lake Simcoe to Kempenfeldt Bay, and by a similar path of over thirty miles to Penetang'. The Indians frequently followed these trails when they made their annual journeys to York to receive treaty payments and presents. Before the War of 1812 the North-West Company urged the government to construct a roadway from Lake Simcoe to Penetang' in order to improve the trade route, but nothing was done at the time. When the American fleet on Lake Erie won the battle of Put-in Bay in 1813, the fur trader's route was threatened and Michilimackinac became less secure from attack; so instructions were received from England to establish a naval depot at Matchedash, at the mouth of the Severn River, but Sir George Prevost, the Governor, considered Penetanguishene a better location and had the post constructed there. A corduroy road was built by the soldiers as a military measure, while a naval detachment proceeded to Penetanguishene.

Before the close of the eighteenth century, however, the North-West Company and other traders had been using the route extensively, and on several occasions the Company contributed large sums of money towards the improvement of Yonge Street. Smith's *Gazetteer* states that the cost of transporting goods to Michilimackinac was from £10 to £15 per ton less than it had been over the former Ottawa route, and that the Yonge Street approach was also much more

[20]D. W. Smith: *A Short Topographical Description of His Majesty's Province of Upper Canada* . . . . 1799. p. 25. The "good path" was a well-known trail *via* Coldwater.

satisfactory than that *via* the Niagara River, Lake Erie and Detroit River to the upper lakes.[21] Twenty years later, however, traders were still debating as to which of the last two routes was better: Robert Gourlay wrote that "the question of preference is still agitated by the respective partisans of these different routes, and seems not yet decided by satisfactory experiment".[22]

The diversion of the western trade from the Mississippi to the Great Lakes led to many plans for the development of the lake route in both direct and indirect connections. In spite of the building of the Welland Canal it was believed, especially before the great period of railway construction had commenced, that some short-cut between Lake Huron and the St. Lawrence or Lake Ontario would be of great advantage in accelerating trade. There was, however, a notable difference of opinion, even among experts, as to the best course which such a canal should take. There were five main competing routes, each of which was estimated to require an expenditure of from $20,000,000 upwards: (1) the Scugog route from Lake Simcoe to Lake Ontario through Ontario County; (2) by way of the valleys of the Holland and Nen (Rouge) Rivers; (3) by way of the Holland-Humber route; (4) by the Trent River system; and (5) *via* Lake Nipissing and the Ottawa River to the St. Lawrence. That which eventually received the approval of the government was the Trent route.

Though this river system was early developed in some small sections, there was long a bitter controversy over the advisability of following it *in toto*. Soon after the War of 1812 Robert Gourlay wrote that "in the course of time it may become an object of importance to connect Rice Lake by a canal with Lake Ontario direct, instead of following the present canoe route by its natural outlet into the Bay of Quinté".[23] About 1820 the Trent Canal was proposed by the Imperial Government as a colonisation and military route, and surveyors were sent out to make plans; but some residents of the Niagara peninsula influenced the Canadian

[21]*Ibid.*, p. 154.
[22]Robert Gourlay: *A Statistical Account of Upper Canada.* 1822. Vol. I, p. 94.
[23]See W. A. Craick: *Port Hope Historical Sketches.* 1901. p. 36.

Government to divert the work from the Trent Valley, and to commence operations upon the Welland Canal instead.

In the early thirties, however, the Trent development was revived and the Government of Upper Canada commenced work upon a canal from Lake Simcoe to Lake Ontario, and as a part of the plan the Port Hope and Rice Lake Canal Company began digging at the Rice Lake end; but this scheme was soon abandoned, like many another early promotion. Some progress was made, however at Bobcaygeon and other points, and in 1835 a surveyor estimated the length of the route from Rice Lake to Lake Simcoe to be 110 miles, the number of dams and locks at thirteen and thirty-seven, respectively, and the cost of construction, including stone locks 134 feet by 33 feet, at slightly more than $1,000,000.

From time to time sporadic efforts were made to go on with the work, but the scheme developed very slowly. In the early sixties a noted engineer, T. C. Keefer, was surveying the possibilities of the construction of a canal from Mud (Chemong) Lake to Lake Ontario *viâ* the Beaver River and Lake Scugog, as well as such other connecting links as would be necessary to complete the route to Lake Simcoe. Following the receipt of his report in 1863 a Select Committee of Parliament was appointed to consider the matter. In 1864 this body reported that, if any canal were to be built from Georgian Bay to Lake Ontario *viâ* the Simcoe Valley, "the Scugog route should be preferred to any other".[24]

At the same time promoters were advocating a canal over the Talbot Portage, from Lake Simcoe *viâ* the Talbot River and across country to Balsam Lake; while others were partisans of the Ganeraské or Trent canals. At one time or another the Provincial and Dominion Governments have spent many millions of dollars on the improvement of the Trent Valley Canal, but its use has been restricted to pleasure boats and a small local trade in lumber; in fact the development of railways and highways has altered whatever importance the route may have had in the eyes of promoters, while the cost to enlarge the present canal to

²⁴See William Kingsford: *The Canadian Canals*. 1865. p. 101.

From a Mural in the Chateau Laurier, Ottawa.   C. W. Jefferys, R.C.A.

NORTH-WEST COMPANY VOYAGEURS, AND RAFTSMEN ON THE OTTAWA, .1820

Samuel Hearne

From Hearne's *Journey from Hudson's Bay to the Northern Ocean*

FORT PRINCE OF WALES, HUDSON'S BAY, 1777.

From Bigsby's *The Shoe and Canoe.* 1850   J. J. Bigsby

INDIAN RENDEZVOUS, DRUMMOND ISLE

From Bigsby's *The Shoe and Canoe.* 1850   J. J. Bigsby

THE RAT PORTAGE

enable its navigation by large vessels appears to be prohibitive.

It was not until nearly a quarter of the nineteenth
century had passed that land transport was extensive, except
in winter. Pack-horses had carried loads over bridle-paths,
oxen had hauled sledges in summer over blazed trails, and
in some districts a light ox-cart could be successfully used
for short distances; but the stage-wagon or coach adopted
for some years the inevitable policy of discontinuing service
at the end of the winter season, and it was general to use
the water routes where at all possible. Schooner and steamship provided long-distance transport on the Great Lakes
during the navigation season, and were to be found in the
more remote lakes and rivers wherever settlers of initiative
had taken up land. Bateau and canoe carried on local
traffic along the shores of the waterways, and it was usually
preferable to use a circuitous water route even where there
was a roadway direct. Long after Yonge Street had been
opened, for example, the settlers in Markham Township
found it more convenient to travel to and from York by
way of the Nen (Rouge) River and the shore of Lake
Ontario; and in the same way most summer traffic between
York and Niagara was carried on either in large vessels, or
in small craft which skirted the head of the lake, some men
making a business of renting bateaux for the purpose.

In 1823 John Bigsby accompanied a surveying party of
the Boundary Commission from Kingston to the Lake of
the Woods. As the trip was made by canoe over the old
fur trader's route, Bigsby's account of it is of great interest;
and, since it describes important points *en route* as they
appeared at almost the close of the trading era, extensive
quotations will be made from the narrative.

The expedition coasted along the Bay of Quinté and
crossed the portage at the Carrying Place. They kept close
to shore all the way up Lake Ontario, camping at night in
a small tent, usually "in some glen near the Lake. Perhaps
there was occasionally a tavern within half a mile of us,
but as we were well-provided we did not go in quest. Our
last camp was pitched on Gibraltar Point, on the outer side
of Toronto Harbour—a mere swamp, a breeding-ground for
ague. If we had passed the night in town all our men would

have been intoxicated, with the recklessness of soldiers and sailors going long voyages. We never saw a human being from Presqu'île to Toronto, 100 miles (save at Coburgh), very few houses, and those miserable ones, partly because we were always under the shadow of alluvial cliffs, or beneath a fringe of woods, left perhaps for shelter. Once or twice we caught sight of the smoke of a distant steamer, or heard in the early morning the loud complaint of the loon, a large and beautiful fowl, as it floated a mile or two out on the quiet waters".[25]

From York, boat and baggage were taken on stout wagons thirty-seven miles to Holland's Landing, "then scarcely more than a single public-house in a marshy country on the River Holland, seven miles from Lake Simcoe".[26] Among the inns passed *en route* are mentioned Montgomery's Tavern, four miles north of York, Fleck's Inn, fourteen miles farther north, and Gamble's, eleven miles beyond Fleck's. Crossing Lake Simcoe they stayed at Johnson's Inn (Barrie), which Bigsby describes as "a clap-boarded house, square in shape, and rather large, standing upon a gravelly bank, close to the lake. It contained a good kitchen, three or four sleeping-rooms (partly in the roof), two good parlours, and a bed-chamber for guests of quality. I have had worse at the best hotel in Washington".[27]

The party portaged nine miles to Willow Creek, and "worked cautiously among fallen trees and loosened masses of earth for eight miles along the perpetual doublings of the creek, among inundated woods of alder, maple, willow, and a few elm and ash."[28] Then they proceeded along the Nottawasaga, with "many sharp turns and long reaches, amid spots of exquisite woodland beauty".[29] After running a rapid some nine miles long, the party entered the wider river, and passed through Sunnidale Township to its mouth, where, on the left bank, was the small trading-post of Mr. Robinson. They proceeded through Georgian Bay to Parry's Sound, "two long, low barn-like huts, among sand-hills, mounds and dwarf cedars",[30] and thence twenty miles north-west to the fur-trading post of La Ronde, near the

[25]J. J. Bigsby: *The Shoe and Canoe, or Pictures of Travel in the Canadas*. 1850. Vol. II, pp. 61-2.
[26]*Ibid.*, p. 64.   [27]*Ibid.*, p. 71.   [28]*Ibid.*, p. 78.
[29]*Ibid.*, p. 79.   [30]*Ibid.*, p. 98.

Shamenega River; this consisted of "a melancholy-looking log house, with a cluster of out-houses, sunk for protection behind some sand-heaps and rocks".[31]

Crossing the mouth of the French River the expedition followed the north coast of Lake Huron to the Sault, the Canadian village then consisting of a "straggling line of fifteen log-huts on marshy ground, with, at its lower end, the comfortable dwelling of Mr. Ermatinger. . . . The North-West Company of fur traders have an important post near the head of this village, close to the rapids, on the broad tongue of low land full of little water-courses, which is the British portage. This post consists of a good resident's house, large storehouse, stables, labourers' dwellings, garden, fields, and a jetty for their schooner. The cattle were in a remarkably good condition.

"The American village is but small: it has, however, two or three houses of a better class, and is on higher ground, with a few Indian wigwams interspersed. The Americans have a stout barrack here, called Fort Brady, and two companies of infantry. Mr. Johnson, a much respected Indian trader, lives here most hospitably in a house whose neatness is in striking contrast with the careless dilapidation reigning around. . . . Mr. Ermatinger built a windmill, in a vain attempt to induce the people to grow wheat. The white and red inhabitants of St. Mary's live chiefly on whitefish caught in hand-nets at the foot of the rapids, and they are salted in very large quantities".[32]

The canoe was hauled by oxen across the British portage, and the party coasted in it along the north shore of Lake Superior as far as the Grand Portage (Fort William), a distance of 445 miles. Here, on the Kaministiquia ("River of the Isles") were still some remnants of the palmy days when the famous North-West Company post received the rich bales of furs from the Great West. Bigsby had his meals in the Company's great hall, where everyone was seated from the head of the table down, according to rank. From Fort William they proceeded during the last days of June up the Kaministiquia and on over the Grand Portage to Rainy Lake and the Lake of the Woods. It was not many

[31]*Ibid.*, p. 99.   [32]*Ibid.*, pp. 123-5.

years before such journeys from one end of Upper Canada
to the other were merely a memory of the past.

Far in the northland were the Hudson's Bay Company's
posts. The original policy of the members had been to
remain at the forts on Hudson's Bay and receive the peltries
from the Indians, who came long distances to barter for
supplies. Towards the close of the eighteenth century, however, several of the factors of the Company had worked their
way far into the north and west on exploring expeditions.
Their great rival, the North-West Company, had been
formed, and had taken for its policy the aggressive plan of
pushing farther and farther into the Great West and inter-
cepting the trade to Hudson's Bay; consequently the English
traders were forced to enter into the rivalry of westward
expansion if their success in the trade was to continue.

The original routes of travel westward from the Bay
forts were over the Nelson and Churchill Rivers, but they
were eventually abandoned because of the heavy current
and difficult rapids. The usual route thereafter was up
the Hayes River, and then by the Main, Steel and Hill Rivers
to a point 141 miles from York Factory. It was necessary to
employ the tow-line over almost all this section, but during
the next 192 miles thence to the Saskatchewan paddles could
be used most of the way over the numerous lakes and rivers
which formed the traders' route. From Norway House, near
the Jack River, the fur trader continued his arduous journey
to Fort Chipewyan and beyond. After the union of the two
great trading companies in 1821 this northerly approach
to the West superseded almost entirely the Great Lakes
routes which had long been used by the North-West Company. In winter the dog-sled train was the mode of travel.

West of the Rockies pack-horse and scow often replaced
canoe in the fur traders' expeditions to the Pacific coast.
One of the most vivid pageants of pioneer days in Canada
was the passing of the fur brigade of the Hudson's Bay
Company. Each year an impressive cavalcade, led by the
Chief Factor in beaver hat, frilled linen and blue coat with
metal buttons, journeyed southward with the twelve months'
accumulation of valuable furs. As the expedition passed
from New Caledonia down the Fraser River from Fort St.
James to Fort Alexandria, and on to Kamloops, it was

Charles F. Comfort, O.S.A.
Reproduced by Courtesy of the Governor and Committee of the Hudson's Bay Company
LAST DOG TRAIN LEAVING LOWER FORT GARRY, 1909

John Ross Robertson Collection   James Hamilton
DUNDAS STREET AT LONDON, C.W., IN 1840
View looking west from Wellington to Ridout Streets. The left foreground is now the location of the Municipal Buildings, Federal Square

H.B.C. YORK BOATS AT NORWAY HOUSE, 1867

The York Boat was first constructed in 1826, and the last were built in 1923

BRIGADE OF YORK BOATS IN A STORM ON THE SASKATCHEWAN

saluted at every post by the roar of three guns. From Kamloops the costly merchandise was transported by horses overland to the Columbia River, whence scows conveyed it to the world's markets.

Some of the old channels followed by the Loyalists in entering Canada continued to be the main routes of trade and travel for many years. Thomas Horner, for example, followed the Hudson route when he travelled from Albany to Oxford County in 1796:

"He packed his goods in two small roughly-made boats which he launched on the River Hudson, near Albany, proceeded up the Hudson to the River Mohawk, and up said river about 100 miles; then carried their goods and boats across the Norvel Creek, thence down the Norvel Creek to Lake Oneida, across the lake to the Oswego River; thence into Lake Ontario and along the southern coast of that lake to the Burlington Bay beach; drew their boats through a small outlet of the Bay, and then proceeded across the Bay and landed, all safe, near where Sir Allan MacNab's castle now stands. The boats were then made fast for future use, and the goods drawn by oxen, on roughly-made sledges, to their destination in Blenheim".[33]

By similar routes many Americans, (sometimes called late Loyalists), attracted by Governor Simcoe's land-settlement policy, entered Upper Canada during the seventeen-nineties and travelled along the shores of the lakes until they reached the lands allotted them. The approaches to the St. Lawrence also continued in use for some time. In the first quarter of the nineteenth century, before the State of New York completed its canal system, exports from northern Vermont and New York passed northwards to Quebec and Montreal. They were transported *via* Lake Champlain and the Richelieu, or over other rivers which flow into the southern side of the St. Lawrence, much of the trade being carried on in large dug-out canoes. Until 1822 American lumber, grain and other produce was admitted free of duty and re-exported, particularly to the British West Indies. This trade ended with the completion of the canal system of New York State in 1824, together with the imposition of duties on such exports into Canada.

[33]Thomas Shenston: *The Oxford Gazetteer*. 1852. p. 30.

Until after the end of the eighteenth century the mail service between the lower province and Upper Canada had been only occasional. Mail and dispatches were taken, at intervals of many weeks, to Kingston by courier, and on to Niagara and Detroit by the King's sailing-ships. In the period when navigation was impossible there was usually one "winter express", made up of one or two white men and an Indian. They travelled with dog-teams or on snow-shoes, and the trip was generally made by way of Oswego and the south shore of Lake Ontario to Niagara, and thence by the north shore of Lake Erie to Detroit, the return journey following the same route. As settlement proceeded, however, many winding trails or more regular concession allowances were blazed into roads, either by government surveyors, by statute labour, or as subscription roads through the initiative of the settlers along the route.

Soon after the War of 1812 arteries of land communication pierced from east to west, and they were followed by colonisation roads northward as settlement proceeded. Ox-cart and stage-coach began to supersede bateau and horseback courier, though for many years the roads retained most of the characteristics of foot-path and bridle-path; they were of value as winter roads, but could be travelled upon at other seasons only with the greatest difficulty. On the St. Lawrence the old means of transport survived until the building of the canals, and in the remote parts of the province the canoe long held its pre-eminent position on the trade routes; but by the commencement of the second quarter of the century the old time-honoured trade routes were rapidly passing out of use. Occasional expeditions by canoe or bateau passed through Old Ontario, but the sight was regarded as a curiosity and a relic of the past. With the march of time, schooners and steamship monopolised the river systems; while the roads—many of them still trails in all but name—were gradually supplanted in land transport by the Iron Horse.

CHAPTER II

THE CANOE

"As *voyageurs*, or ramblers of any kind, they find much delight, so that a number of them be together. They will endure privations with great patience; will live on peas and Indian corn for years together. They are seldom troubled with melancholy; suicides are very rare amongst them; and madmen and lunatics as much so. They are good at composing easy, extemporaneous songs, somewhat smutty, but never intolerant. Many of their canoe-songs are exquisite; more particularly the air they give them. . . . We must be in a canoe with a dozen hearty paddlers, the lake pure, the weather fine, and the rapids past, before their influence can be powerfully felt. Music and song I have revelled in all my days, and must own that the *chanson de voyageur* has delighted me above all others, excepting those of Scotland."

JOHN MACTAGGART (1829).[1]

WHEN the European first approached the shores of America he found the Indians using canoes as their only means of travel by water. The name of the boat originated with the natives of the West Indies, who told Christopher Columbus what it was called. In early times canoes were of four main types: the skin, the dug-out or log, the elm bark and the birch bark; and of these the birch canoe was the most commonly used in Canada, for its lightness made possible a good rate of speed, as well as easy portaging around rapids or across country.

Though the skin canoe was occasionally found among the Indians the boat was most typical of the land of the Eskimos, where its use was universal. Of the two varieties of skin canoe found among these inhabitants of the Arctic snows the *kayak* was in most common use. The construction and characteristics of the *kayak* are described as follows:

"This is a shuttle-shaped craft, about fifteen feet long and just wide enough to let its single paddler sit flat on the bottom. It differs from the Indian canoe in being entirely decked over. The skin of the grey seal, when that best of canoe skins can be found, is carefully sewn, so as to be quite waterproof, and then stretched as tightly as a drumhead all over the frame, except for the little 'well' where

[1]John MacTaggart: *Three Years in Canada*. 1829. Vol. I, pp. 254-5.

the Eskimo sits with his double-bladed paddle. As he tucks himself in so closely that water cannot enter he does not fear to be capsized, for he can right himself with a sweep of his paddle. *Kayaks* are very light and handy, as the frame is made either of whalebone or spruce. The *oomiak* is the Eskimo's family boat and cargo carrier, flat-bottomed, not decked in, and sometimes big enough for twenty people with their gear. It is made of much the same materials."[2]

The dug-out or log canoe was used by the Indians for hunting, and for other short trips where it was an advantage to create as little noise as possible; for the wild rice and rushes would make a great rustling against the sides of the birch canoe. The dug-out was also in general use among our early settlers for fishing and hunting, and in the carriage of small loads of produce short distances. Numerous references are found to their use as ferry-boats, as, for example, on the Detroit River, where two log canoes were once used in the carriage of passengers and freight between Windsor and Detroit.

Pine, black walnut, butternut and basswood were the chief woods used in the construction of the log canoe, the two last being the lightest and not as easily split by the heat of the sun. In making the boat a half log of the desired length was hollowed out, and if the work was well done the log canoe could easily be portaged by one man. Some of those built by the Indians showed rude attempts at carving on bow and stern. Occasionally large dug-out canoes were employed in unloading schooners. Samuel Strickland, while an employee of the Canada Company, saw one of these, and describes it as follows:

"The largest I ever saw of this kind was made out of a pine tree, and was twenty-six feet long and three feet nine inches beam. I assisted to unload a schooner with her on Lake Huron. She would easily carry nine barrels of pork and four or five men to paddle her."[3]

Joseph Tyler, a picturesque hermit-squatter on the banks of the Don, built a log canoe which was more than locally famous. It is described as consisting of "two large pine

[2]William Wood: *All Afloat.* 1920. pp. 24-5.
[3]Samuel Strickland: *Twenty-seven Years in Canada West.* 1853. Vol. II, pp. 48-9.

logs, each about forty feet long, well shaped and deftly hollowed out, fastened together by cross dovetail pieces let in at regular distances along the interior of its bottom. While in process of construction in the pine woods through which the Mill Road passes, on the high bank eastward of the river, it was a wonderment to all the inquisitive youth of the neighbourhood, and was accordingly often visited and inspected by them. In this craft he used to pole himself down the windings of the stream all the way round into the bay, and on to the landing-place at the foot of Caroline Street, bringing with him the produce of his garden, and neat stacks of pine knots, ready split for fishermen's light-jacks. "He would also on occasion undertake the office of ferryman. On being hailed for the purpose he would put across the river persons anxious to make a short cut into the town (York) from the eastward. Just opposite his den there was for a time a rude causeway over the marsh. At the season of the year when the roads through the woods were impracticable, Tyler's famous canoe was employed by the Messrs. Helliwell for conveying into town, from a point high up the stream, the beer manufactured at their breweries on the Don. We are informed by Mr. William Helliwell of Highland Creek that twenty-two barrels at a time could be placed in it, in two rows of eleven each laid lengthwise side by side, still leaving room for Tyler and an assistant to navigate the boat."[4]

The most notable use of the dug-out was in the trade between the St. Lawrence and Hudson Rivers in the days before the steamship and the railway. These boats were twenty feet or more long and usually of white pine, red or white cedar, or the tulip tree. If well tarred and painted they would last for ten or twelve years' continual use. Canoes of this kind are still occasionally employed in the Atlantic coast fisheries, but otherwise such boats are now as rare as the birch canoe.

In the Hudson trade the log canoes were paddled, or were poled along by the crew standing. Sometimes oars were used to propel the boat, a means which enabled one man to send it through the water at a good rate of speed. As a type, however, the dug-out was vastly inferior to the lighter

[4]Henry Scadding: *Toronto of Old.* 1873. p. 229.

canoes, being more liable to upset and harder to repair; it likewise drew more water, cracked in the sun, and rotted quickly if the best care were not taken of it.

The elm bark canoe was used by many tribes of Indians for more temporary purposes than were served by the dugout or birch canoe. It was quite usual to abandon them after they had served to cross a lake or to descend from the headwaters of rapid streams which would injure the more fragile bark canoe. They were still being employed by the Chippawa Indians a century ago, when the "Huron Tract" was in process of colonisation through the efforts of the Canada Company.

These boats were of rude construction, being made out of an entire roll of the bark of the swamp elm. This was sewed up at both ends and the seams gummed. Two thwarts were fastened across the upper edges of the canoe to keep the bark expanded to a width of about three and one-half feet at the centre, and to provide a place for the occupants to sit. The roots of tamarack or cedar were used to sew the seams and fix the thwarts; but before being used the roots were scraped, split, and soaked in water. A preparation of cedar or pine gum mixed with pitch or resin prevented the seams from leaking.

Samuel Strickland saw many elm bark canoes, which had been constructed by the Indians at the end of the spring hunt and maple sugar season, descending the Maitland River near Goderich, laden with baskets of sugar and their traps and game.[5] This type of canoe, which seldom lasted for a whole season, was commonly used where speed of manufacture was an important consideration. On June 19, 1764, Alexander Henry, the noted Scottish trader, reached the mouth of the Humber from Lake Simcoe, a captive of the Indians whom he accompanied. He writes:

"Here we were employed two days in making canoes out of the bark of the elm tree, in which we were to transport ourselves to Niagara. For this purpose the Indians first cut down a tree; then stripped off the bark in one entire sheet of about eighteen feet in length, the incision being lengthwise. The canoe was now complete as to its top, bottom and sides. Its ends were next closed by sewing the

[5]Strickland, op. cit., Vol. II, pp. 49-50.

bark together, and, a few ribs and bars being introduced, the architecture was finished."[6]

In this manner they made two canoes, and the seventeen members of the party paddled between sunrise and sunset from Toronto to within four miles of Fort Niagara.

The birch bark canoe was of much greater importance than the other types; in fact for many years after the arrival of the Europeans in America it was the only means of long-distance travel by water. The birch canoe was first extensively employed by Champlain in his explorations, and in later times its use by explorers, missionaries, traders and soldiers was almost universal. The Hudson's Bay Company and its great rival, the North-West Company, long used large *voyageur* canoes to penetrate far into the interior of the country, carrying heavy cargoes of supplies to western post and returning to civilisation laden with bales of furs; but it is doubtful if any examples of these beautiful boats have been preserved.

Only a knife was needed in making a birch canoe. The Indians commonly constructed them in the early summer when the sap made the bark easy to work, but if dry or frozen bark had to be used hot water was applied to soften it; occasionally trees were found large enough to enable the building of a twenty-foot canoe of one piece without seams. After peeling off the bark in large rolls the Indian proceeded in the following manner:

"A frame, which is called *gabarie* by the Canadian French, is then suspended by four stout posts. This indicates the inner form and length of the vessel. Gunwales are then constructed of cedar wood, which sustain ribs of the same material that are closely arranged from its bow to its stern. The next process is to sheathe the ribs with thin, flat and flexible pieces of cedar placed longitudinally. The sheathing of bark is then adjusted, and sewed together by means of a square-bladed awl and thread composed of the fibrous roots of the cedar, called *watab*, which are soaked in hot water. The seams are then pitched with boiled and prepared gum from the pitch pine, which is payed on with a small swab. The bow and stern, which are

[6]Alexander Henry: *Travels and Adventures in Canada and the Indian Territories, 1760-76*. 1807. pp. 179-80.

recurved, are usually decorated with figures of animals or other pictographic devices."[7]

Among some tribes the decorations on the canoe were totem signs, the designs of serpents, beavers, etc., often being beautifully executed by the use of dyed porcupine quills. The gunwale of the birch canoe was very important as it held the ribs together; there was often a second gunwale, called by the French the *faux maître*, on top of the birch skin to hold it on the ribs. Bottom-boards were inserted to protect the bark base and ends of the canoe, and the boat was often reinforced inside by a bulkhead at the bow, sometimes rising above the gunwale and carved like a figurehead. The Indian canoe varied in size from one of twelve feet holding two persons to the war canoe, thirty-six feet long and propelled by fourteen paddles.

In the heyday of the fur trade Three Rivers was the principal centre of canoe-building on the St. Lawrence. As a general rule *voyageur* canoes were from twenty to thirty feet long and four or five in breadth. There was no distinction between bow and stern, both ends rising to a sharp point well above the gunwale. The process of manufacture varied but little from the Indian method. The ribs or laths were usually of cedar or pine and were bent like an ox-bow, terminating in the gunwales which, with the bow and stern posts, were also of white cedar, the lightest and most durable wood afforded by the Canadian forests. The bars or thwarts which held the gunwales in position were of maple, elm or ash, and were attached, through holes bored in their ends, by a seizing of young roots, a method of fastening which enabled their easy replacement; for though much stronger than cedar these hardwood thwarts were far more perishable.

The sheathing of white birch bark was cut into strips about one-eighth of an inch in thickness and they were sewed together and lashed to the gunwale with the fine, tough and durable filaments obtained by boiling the young roots of the spruce, the cedar, or the leatherwood tree. Strips of bark were also applied to the inside of the seams if such reinforcement was considered necessary. An early writer states that "birch bark of a yellowish colour, without

[7]Henry Schoolcraft: *The Indian Tribes.* 1851-6. Vol. II, p. 513.

W. H. Bartlett

CANOE-BUILDING AT PAPPER'S ISLAND, UPPER OTTAWA, 1840

W. H. Bartlett. 1840

THE BURIAL PLACE OF THE VOYAGEURS
A romantic spot on the Upper Ottawa

W. H. Bartlett

WORKING A CANOE UP A RAPID

The scene depicted by this noted English artist was long familiar near the Cedars Rapids, below Coteau Junction

wrinkles, is generally considered the best, and will last the longest: this bark is found in the remote woods, and the canoes from the inland territories of the north are always preferred."[8]

The joints were made watertight by the use of the raw gum of the pine or tamarack, or with a prepared pitch compound of resin and tallow, either of which gums adhered firmly and became very hard. The boat was thus completed without the use of nails or any other metal materials. The weight of a large canoe was only 500 pounds, a lighter boat for its tonnage than any other craft of equal strength. As a general rule the life of the canoe was six or seven years. Since birch bark is very elastic the boats stood a great deal of rubbing on water-worn rocks; but if damaged they could be repaired very quickly by patching:

"When they spring a leak they run them instantly ashore, pull them from the waters, and turn the bottom up; a fire is then kindled, and a burning cleft faggot is taken and run along the seams, while the *voyageur* blows through the cleft; this melts the gum, which is then pressed down by the thumb, and so the cure is effected. If a hole has been punched in the bark, the piece is extracted and a new piece inserted. When done she is soon in the water and away again on the voyage."[9]

The birch tree was almost indispensable to the Indian and *voyageur*, for in addition to its universal use for canoes it "forms the covering for the wigwam or hunter's camp— gives utensils in which flour is kneaded and water boiled— is the papyrus on which the Indian pioneer sketches, with native plumbago, hieroglyphics (which are left in cleft sticks at the portage landing) for the guidance of his following tribe—and makes the resinous torch for lighting the portage, the camp, or the night fisher's spear; while the green wood from which it is stripped burns as readily on the camp-fire as the dry wood of any other tree."[10]

The manufacture of canoes was not an expensive process, for all the materials were readily obtainable. The large fur trader's canoe usually sold for about 300 livres, an

[8]MacTaggart, *op. cit.*, Vol. I, p. 305.
[9]*Ibid.*, Vol. I, p. 307.
[10]T. C. Keefer: *Travel and Transportation.* In John Lovell (Ed.): *80 Years' Progress in British North America.* 1863. p. 133.

amount equal to $50. A small canoe might be purchased from the Indians for a small sum of money, or in barter for whisky or some other article of trade. Thomas Need bought a fourteen-foot canoe from a native, and wrote in his diary concerning his purchase: "Having observed a little fleet of canoes on the lake, I went out and bargained with an Indian for one for a couple of dollars. . . . Its buoyancy was so great that I have crossed the lake on a stormy day with the carcasses of a couple of deer in it."[11]

A canoe of average size carried a load of three tons, but the largest canoes could transport as many as sixty men or fifty barrels of flour, and drew two feet of water as they were paddled along with the gunwales almost at the water's edge. These boats were called by the French *canots du maître* and were frequently as large as forty feet long, six feet wide and two deep. At the other extreme was the very small canoe, nine feet long, used to carry a single *voyageur* and his supplies.

Occasionally sails were employed on canoes, though in general their use was considered dangerous in boats without a keel—and no true canoe ever had a keel. Samuel Strickland refers to seeing a very large canoe carrying both mainsail and topsails, "with an ingenious contrivance, which enabled them to hoist both at the same time, and lower them instantaneously; a good precaution in squally weather." He at first mistook the boat for a small schooner. It crossed Lake Huron from Saginaw Bay with twenty-five Indians and several bales of fur.[12]

A canoe of special construction was used a century ago by the garrison at Penetanguishene. It was built of Russian sheet iron and was curved up at each end like a birch canoe. An Indian made the pattern for this boat, which was about twenty-four feet long, and capable of holding twenty barrels of flour or six passengers and their attendants, fourteen paddlers, and provisions and supplies requisite for passengers and crew. This canoe was once portaged from Holland Landing to Toronto, being hauled along Yonge Street on rollers by teams of horses. Lewis Solomon, a French Canadian *voyageur*, in recounting his experiences in the iron

[11]Thomas Need: *Six Years in the Bush*. 1838. p. 61.
[12]Strickland, *op. cit.*, Vol. II, p. 51.

boat, stated that he "made several excursions up Lake Huron in it. It was rigged for sailing but was no good in a storm, as it cut through the waves and was in danger of filling, while the bark canoe bounded over them."[13]

The Indians and French-Canadian *voyageurs* who took such a prominent part in the fur trade were a hardy race. It was quite usual to paddle eighteen hours a day, and the canoeman became accustomed to only four or five hours' sleep. At times 100 miles of paddling and six portages were accomplished within twenty-four hours; but in spite of the laborious nature of the work the *voyageurs* were "always ready and cheerily jump up to their work" long before daylight.[14] In the northern latitudes 2 a.m. was the customary hour to start out each day, and camp was pitched between eight and ten at night.

In some rapid-flowing rivers a tow-line was used to haul the canoes along the shore. At portages where the boats were unloaded the baggage was carried on the backs of the men. The regulation portage load was 150 pounds, but many a *voyageur* could carry 200 to 400 pounds on his back by means of a leather sling or strap passing across the forehead. They often transported such a load across a ten-mile portage and were back to get their boat within six hours. At some portages the canoe and its cargo was carried across as it was, without unloading. Sir Alexander Mackenzie refers to the use of this method over "the first Portage de Chaudière"; that carrying-place is described as 643 paces along, and "the rock is so steep and difficult of access that it requires twelve men to take the canoe out of water: it is then carried by six men, two at each end on the same side, and two under the opposite gunwale in the middle."[15]

The usual cargo of one canoe was, in addition to eight or ten men's personal baggage, "sixty-five packages of goods, six hundred weight of biscuit, two hundred weight of pork, three bushels of pease, for the men's provision; two oilcloths to cover the goods, a sail, etc., an axe, a towing-line, a

[13]Reminiscences of Lewis Solomon, in A. C. Osborne: *The Migration of Voyageurs from Drummond Island to Penetanguishene.* (In Ontario Historical Society, *Papers and Records,* Vol. III, pp. 133 and 135.)

[14]Archibald McDonald: *Peace River. A Canoe Voyage from Hudson's Bay to the Pacific.* 1872. Note 6, p. 44.

[15]Sir Alexander Mackenzie: *General History of the Fur Trade.* 1801. pp. 38-9.

kettle, and a sponge to bail out the water, with a quantity
of gum, bark and watape to repair the vessel. An European, on seeing one of these slender vessels thus laden,
heaped up, and sunk with her gunwale within six inches
of the water, would think his fate inevitable in such a boat,
when he reflected on the nature of her voyage; but the
Canadians are so expert that few accidents happen".[16]

About one-third of the *voyageurs* of the North-West
Company wintered in the far west, where they engaged in
the chase, at double the regular wages; these men were
known as North Men or Winterers. The other two-thirds
remained at the Company's posts scattered throughout the
West, and attached to them were some seven hundred
Indian women and children, maintained at the expense of
the Company. The men and their helpers were occupied
chiefly in scraping and cleaning the skins, and in making
up and arranging the bales of furs. In summer these
voyageurs were the "Goers and Comers" between Lake
Superior and Montreal, and their wages varied from £85
sterling *per annum* for guides and interpreters down to £18
for paddlers or "middlemen in the canoes". The foremen
at the bow held positions of more importance, for their
skill was needed to help the steersmen guide the boat
among the rocks, iron-shod poles often being used for the
purpose in a rapid stream; these men consequently received about £50 wages. In every case employees were provided with clothing and maintenance. At the close of the
eighteenth century there were about 1280 men, exclusive
of Indians, in the pay of the North-West Company. The
traders were often Scotch, while the *voyageurs* were French-
Canadians, half-breeds or Indians. About fifty clerks were
included among the Company's employees, the clerk receiving only about £100 for from five to seven years' ap-
prenticeship; but thereafter he was paid from £100 to
£300 *per annum*, or given a share in the Company.

During the season of navigation the canoes proceeded
back and forth between Montreal and the West. They generally travelled in brigades so that the crews might help
one another over the many portages on their long and
hazardous voyage. The usual route to the west in the early

[16]*Ibid.*, p. 35.

period was up the Ottawa to its headwaters, and thence *viâ* Lake Nipissing and the French River to Georgian Bay; the canoes then continued along the north shores of Lakes Huron and Superior to the Kaministiquia River. The fort on the banks of this river, where Fort William is now situated, was for nearly two centuries a noted meeting-place in the fur trade; here the Winterers of the North-West Company met the Goers and Comers, and at this post was held the annual meeting of the Company. In the Council Chamber of the fort representatives of the two great rival fur companies met in 1821 and joined forces, most of the trade thereafter following the Hudson's Bay route.

Thirty miles from the mouth of the Kaministiquia the traders commenced the Grand Portage to the western lakes and rivers of the Indian Territories. The 900-mile journey from Lachine to the Grand Portage included thirty-six portages and occupied from twelve to twenty days. The Goers and Comers were frequently derisively called *Mangeurs du Lard*, or Pork-Eaters, by "the old hands in the interior, to whom they are unequal in encountering the difficulties incident to a voyage from Lachine to the mouth of the Columbia, whither some of them are sent and become almost skeletons by the time they reach their destination, through the unavoidable privations and hardships they have to undergo".[17]

The canoemen's fondness for music led to such names for carrying-places as Portage Premier Musique. They were, too, quite frequently religious, and were careful to make offerings at the shrine of St. Anne, dedicated to the tutelar saint of *voyageurs*. The village of St. Anne long contained the last church on the island of Montreal, and the journey to the Grand Portage was considered to commence there; in fact both village and church owed their existence to the pious contributions of the Canadian boatmen. In a house near the rapid of St. Anne was written Thomas Moore's *Canadian Boat Song*,[18] during his visit to America in 1804. The poem is based upon the *chanson*

[17]Paul Kane: *Wanderings of an Artist among the Indians of North America.* 1859. pp. 50-1. In the *Montreal Herald* of August 26, 1820, it is noted that two of the partners of the N.-W. Company had reached Montreal after travelling 1,800 miles in ten days.
[18]The poem is quoted at the commencement of the next chapter.

supposed to be sung by those *voyageurs* who are on the point
of leaving civilisation for the Grand Portage.

The most notable Nor'Wester was Alexander Mackenzie,
and his explorations to the Arctic and to the Pacific stand
out among the remarkable achievements of Canadians. In
the summer of 1789 he was making his way to the Mackenzie River, which he was soon to follow to the Arctic Ocean.[19]
A typical day's travel by canoe is recorded in his diary in
language characteristic of explorers:

"We embarked at half-past two in the morning, and
steered north-west by north twenty-one miles, north-west
by west five miles, west north-west four miles, west six
miles, doubled a point north-north-east one mile, east five
miles, north two miles, north-west by north one mile and
an half, west-north-west three miles, north-east by east
two miles; doubled a point one mile and an half, west
by north nine miles, north-west by west six miles, north-
north-west five miles; here we landed at six o'clock in the
evening, unloaded and encamped."[20]

This day's travel of seventy-two miles by canoe is an
eloquent example of the hardihood of his Indian *voyageurs,*
for they fought against a head wind almost all day, and it
was so cold that they had to use their mittens.

In 1793 Mackenzie was the first white man to reach the
Pacific Ocean by the overland route. He describes as follows
the canoe in which he made the voyage, and his cargo and
companions:

"Her dimensions were twenty-five feet long within, exclusive of the curves of stern and stem—twenty-six inch
hold and four foot nine inch beam. At the same time she
was so light that two men could carry her on a good road
three or four miles without resting. In this slender vessel
we shipped provisions, goods for presents, arms, ammunition and baggage to the weight of three thousand pounds,
and an equipage of ten people, namely, Alexander Mackay,
Joseph Landry, Charles Ducette, François Beaulieu,

[19]Recent historical research suggests that Peter Pond deserves a
greater share of credit for the exploration of the Great West;
and that he and not Mackenzie discovered the Mackenzie River.
See H. A. Innis: *Peter Pond, Fur Trader and Adventurer.*
1932.
[20]Sir Alexander Mackenzie: *Voyage from Montreal through North
America.* 1801. June 6, 1789.

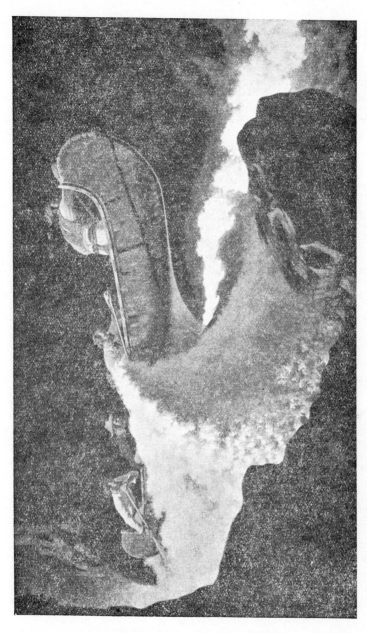

Arthur Heming, O.S.A.

SIR ALEXANDER MACKENZIE CROSSING THE ROCKIES, 1793

SIR ALEXANDER MACKENZIE

Baptist Bisson, François Courtois, and Jacques Beauchamp, with two Indians as hunters and interpreters."[21]

One of Mackenzie's *voyageurs*, François Beaulieux, lived until 1872, forming a remarkable connection with the era of exploration in Canada.

The organisation of the Hudson's Bay Company was similar to that of its great rival, but the first posts of the Company, and its base of operations, were on Hudson's Bay, and consequently only in the Far West did the traders of the two companies ordinarily meet. The "Merchant Adventurers to Hudson's Bay" originally travelled westward by the Nelson and Churchill River routes to Norway House on Lake Winnipeg, and thence by the Saskatchewan River to the prairies; but the Hayes River route was later substituted for the Nelson and Churchill as they were so difficult of navigation owing to the strong current.

The Company used two main types of canoes, the "North Canoe" of light weight and specially constructed for speedy travel; and the *canot du maître* similar to that used by the North-West Company between Lachine and Fort William. The former boat employed a crew of eight or nine men, and the latter from sixteen to eighteen. Malcolm McLeod, a well-known member of the Company, said of the *canot du maître*: "I never heard of such a canoe being wrecked or upset or swamped; they swam like ducks."[22] With a storm deck formed of a red canvas oilcloth thrown over the goods, these canoes could withstand even the heavy seas of Huron and Superior.

A notable canoe trip occurred in 1828, when the Governor of the Hudson's Bay Company, Sir George Simpson, travelled from York Factory, Hudson Bay, to the Pacific. Archibald McDonald, Chief Factor, kept a journal of the voyage. On July 12th at 1 a.m. a start was made, "with three cheers, under a salute of seven guns from the Garrison, and against a strong tide, we were soon round the first point by the free use of the paddle and one of its accompanying *voyageur* airs".[23] The tow-line had to be employed against the strong current on the Hayes, Main,

[21]*Ibid.*, May 9, 1793.
[22]Quoted in McDonald, *op. cit.*, Note 2, pp. 41-2.
[23]*Journal of Sir George Simpson*, July 12, 1828, quoted in McDonald, *op. cit.*

Steel and Hill Rivers, a total of 141 miles, and then paddles were used 192 miles by river and lake to the Saskatchewan. One month after leaving York Factory the expedition arrived at Fort Chipewyan and was accorded a distinguished reception after the 1,200-mile trip.

A few days later the journey to the Pacific was continued. Governor Simpson always had the best *voyageurs* procurable for his canoe, and his Iroquois paddlers, who often kept up a rate of sixty strokes to the minute, were accompanied only by such Canadians as could equal them. Six miles per hour was made in quiet water, and ninety miles a day down stream was the average. One of the most noted feats in the history of navigation occurred during the last stage of this voyage when the canoes shot Simpson's Falls, under the overhanging cliffs of the narrowest gorge of Fraser's Canyon. Early in the morning of Saturday, October 11th, the three months' expedition came to an end at Fort Langley on the Pacific coast.

Apart from its use in the fur trade the birch canoe provided an indispensable means of transportation in pioneer days. The first settlers on the Ottawa used to travel by canoe to Montreal for supplies, one man sometimes making the laborious trip alone. Canoe transport, like that by bateau, was expensive, however. A bushel of corn worth two or three shillings in the east cost 20s. when it had been carried to the Kaministiquia River; but in the absence of other means of carriage the canoe had to be extensively used by all classes of inhabitants.

The first Lieutenant-Governor of Upper Canada, John Graves Simcoe, used canoes on several of his expeditions into the interior of his new province between 1793 and 1796, as well as for pleasure journeys. Mrs. Simcoe wrote in her diary on October 30, 1793: "We have received from Montreal a birch bark canoe. . . . It requires ten men to paddle, is large enough to contain four or five passengers to sit very commodiously in the centre under an awning. An Indian woman came today with pitch, which is made by the Indians from fir trees, to gum the canoe if any part of it is worn off by bringing it hither."[24] After her first trip in the new boat she "was delighted with the swift and easy

²⁴*Diary of Mrs. John Graves Simcoe*, October 30, 1793.

motion of the canoe, and with its appearance." A table was placed in the water to make it easier for her to enter and leave the boat.[25]

The birch canoe was used during the white man's wars just as in the battles of Indian days. During the War of 1812 many soldiers travelled by canoe or bateau to reach the field of battle. This was particularly true during 1813, when schooners could not be used on Lake Ontario because the enemy's naval forces controlled the lake. The first British success in the war occurred on July 17, 1812, when a small expedition of Regulars and Canadian *voyageurs* captured Michilimackinac. Nearly sixty years later Colonel Garnet Wolseley kept in touch with the various sections of his expedition to the Red River by using a large bark canoe paddled by experienced boatmen.

Birch canoes were long extensively used in the carriage of mail, passengers and freight across the St. Lawrence, even in winter. In February, 1839, sixteen passengers perished when a canoe was upset among pieces of floating ice while making the trip from Levis to Quebec. That the journey at this season was a hazardous one may be seen from a traveller's account of his voyage:

"The last time I ever had occasion to cross the St. Lawrence the thermometer stood at 26° below zero. A dense fog shrouded the river, which, as we stood upon the bank, became condensed, and fell in a thick shower of hoarfrost. We got into the canoe upon the wharf, stretched ourselves at the bottom thereof, were muffled up to the eyes in furs, and as our friends crowded round the long narrow receptacle I felt excessively as if I was already in my coffin, and was only waiting to be let down.

"Presently we *are* let down with a vengeance; there is a rush down the steep bank, followed by a grating over the rough ice, then a plunge into the river, and we are so wrapt in fog that we can see nothing a yard from the canoe. The boatmen are fine muscular men, in shaggy beards and coats, who sing the old songs of the Canadian *voyageurs*, except when they are too much occupied in groping their way through the mist.

"At last it partially clears, and we find ourselves sur-

[25]*Ibid.*, November 9, 1793.

rounded by floes of ice. Huge masses are jammed and squeezed up into fantastic shapes to a height of ten or fifteen feet. We edge our way through the narrow lanes of water between the ice-fields, following a devious course, sometimes breaking through a thin crust of ice, until our onward progress is altogether arrested; then the *voyageurs* jump out, and pull the canoe upon the ice,—while we remain resigned at the bottom of the boat,—and rattle us over the jagged surface of the floe until we reach open water, when we are again launched, and at last, to our great gratification, find ourselves pulled up under the steep bank at Point Levis.

"If the tide be running down, it often happens that canoes are carried many miles below Quebec, and the unfortunate passengers not infrequently spend the whole night struggling amid floating ice."[26]

In August, 1827, an English traveller, Captain Basil Hall, was in Montreal, where he was fortunate enough to meet Captain John Franklin, already famous as an Arctic explorer, who had just returned from the two-year expedition into northern Canada for which he was soon to be awarded a knighthood. Franklin had not yet discharged the fourteen *voyageurs* who had brought him in a large Hudson's Bay canoe from Fort William *viâ* the upper lakes and the Ottawa River to Montreal, a distance of 1400 miles; so he invited Hall to take a morning's excursion with him on the St. Lawrence and Ottawa Rivers.

Captain Hall had often seen the smaller canoes paddled by a couple of Indians, "but it was a very different thing to feel oneself flying along in this grand barge, as it might be called, nearly forty feet long by upwards of five in width. She was urged forward at the rate of nearly six miles per hour by fourteen first-rate and well-practised Canadian *voyageurs*. . . . Each *voyageur* wields a short, light paddle with which he strikes the water about once a second, keeping strict time with a song from one of the crew, in which all the others join in chorus. At every stroke of the fourteen paddles, which in fact resembles one blow, such is the correctness of their ear, the canoe is thrown or jerked forward so sharply that it is by no means easy to sit

[26]Lawrence Oliphant: *Minnesota and the Far West*. 1855. pp. 28-30.

upright on the cloaks and cushions spread nearly in its centre".[27]

Samuel Thompson considered himself similarly fortunate when he was ascending the St. Lawrence in 1833, for he saw Sir George Simpson, Governor of the Hudson's Bay Company, leaving Lachine for the west.

"The party was escorted by six or eight Nor'-West canoes —each thirty or forty feet long and manned by some twenty-four Indians in the full glory of war-paint, feathers and most dazzling costumes. To see these stately boats, and their no less stately crews, gliding with measured stroke in gallant procession, on their way to the vast wilderness of the Hudson's Bay territory, with the British flag displayed at each prow, was a sight never to be forgotten. And as they paddled, the woods echoed far and wide to the strange weird sounds of their favourite boat-song:

> À la claire fontaine,
> M'en allant promener,
> J'ai trouvé l'eau si belle,
> Que je m'y suis baigné.
> Il y a longtemps que je t'aime,
> Jamais je ne t'oublirai.' "[28]

Among the most romantic descriptions of a canoe voyage is that given by Mrs. Anna Jameson,[29] wife of the Vice-Chancellor of Upper Canada, and an authoress of some note. In 1837 she visited Sault Ste. Marie, then little more than an Indian mission. On August 6th she was at Manitoulin, "the abode of the Great Spirit", which had early been appropriated to the use of scattered Indians without any fixed place of residence, and others from the United States who wished to remain British.

The most direct route from Manitoulin to civilisation was by canoe to Penetanguishene, and thence *via* Lake Simcoe and Yonge Street to Toronto. The party with which Mrs. Jameson travelled consisted of two canoes twenty-

[27]Basil Hall: *Travels in America in 1827 and 1828.* 1829. Vol. I, pp. 381-2.
[28]Samuel Thompson: *Reminiscences of a Canadian Pioneer.* 1884. pp. 36-7.
[29]Anna Jameson: *Winter Studies and Summer Rambles in Canada.* 1838. Vol. III, pp. 313-338.

five feet long and four feet wide. In addition to baggage, each boat contained three or four passengers, seven French-Canadian canoemen, and, in the stern, an Indian steersman with a very long paddle. A handkerchief twisted about the head, or a cap with a tassel, a gaudy shirt and a pair of trousers, with a gay L'Assomption sash and lurid garters, formed the picturesque costume of the *voyageur*.

At the departure the Indians on the shore uttered wild cries and discharged their rifles, for nearly one hundred canoes were on their homeward journey to the Lake Superior region after a fur-trading trip. The route to be followed to Penetanguishene was through the islands of Lake Huron and Georgian Bay, and a very picturesque voyage it must have been. At sunset each day the party camped on a suitable island, enjoying a supper of excellent trout and whitefish which were then so plentiful in Ontario waters. Next morning they were off again at break of day.

"The *voyageurs* measure the distance by pipes. At the end of a certain time there is a pause, and they light their pipes and smoke for five minutes; and then the paddles go off merrily again at the rate of about fifty strokes a minute, and we absolutely seem to fly over the water. *Trois pipes* is about twelve miles. We breakfasted this morning on a little island of exceeding beauty, . . . abounding with beautiful shrubs, flowers, green mosses, and scarlet lichens. . . .

"This day we had a most delightful run among hundreds of islands, sometimes darting through rocky channels so narrow that I could not see the water on either side of the canoe; and then emerging, we glided through vast fields of white water-lilies; it was perpetual variety, perpetual beauty, perpetual delight and enchantment from hour to hour. The men sang their gay French songs, the other canoe joining in the chorus. . . . They all sing in unison, raising their voices and marking the time with their paddles. One always led, but in these there was a diversity of taste and skill. If I wished to hear *En roulant ma boule, roulette,* I applied to Le Duc. Jacques excelled in *La belle rose blanche.* Louis was great in *Trois canards s'en vont baignant*".[30]

Next day the party landed on the Island of Skulls, an

[30]*Ibid.,* pp. 319-21.

Arthur Heming, O.S.A.

THE PIONEERS

Reproduced by Courtesy of the Artist

Mrs. Edward Hopkins

THE ARTIST AND HER HUSBAND IN A HUDSON'S BAY CANOE RUNNING RAPIDS

ancient sepulchre of the Hurons. Skulls and bones were still scattered about with the rough stones which had once been heaped over them. The canoes passed within a few miles of the mouth of the Rivière des Français, which formed the chief line of communication with Montreal by way of Lake Nipissing and the Ottawa River. Ever since Champlain had followed this route in 1615 it had been the trail of fur trader and Indian to civilisation.

Among the birds seen on the way Mrs. Jameson mentions wild pigeons, then to be found in great flocks in Canada but now almost extinct. A few miles beyond the Island of Skulls they passed the Bear Islands, "where an Indian had shot nine bears in a single day. We found three bears' heads stuck upon the boughs of a dead pine— probably as an offering to the souls of the slaughtered animals, or to the Great Spirit, both being usual".[31]

Next day they passed Isle des Chrétiens, where there was formerly a large settlement of Jesuit missionaries. The same evening, after a trip of four days, the *voyageurs* reached the bay of Penetanguishene, "so-called from a high sand-bank at the entrance, which is continually falling away. The expressive Indian name signifies 'Look! It is falling sand.'"[32] In Penetanguishene there had been an elaborate and extensive dockyard and naval depot during the War of 1812, but in 1837 only the stone fort remained, serving as barracks for a few soldiers from the garrison at Toronto.

The general use of canoes in the Canadian fur trade came to an end two years after the union of the Hudson's Bay and North-West Companies. In 1823 Sir George Simpson found that canoe transport was too expensive, and ordered that the York or Hudson Bay boat, (which, though not flat-bottomed, was a variation of the bateau), should be used over all the main trade routes of the Hudson's Bay Company. Other characteristics of the fur trade have passed away with the march of time, though conditions approaching "the old days" still obtain in remote Labrador.

Modern canoes are made of canvas, wood or metal. In Northern Ontario the Indians use small "Peterborough" canoes for quick trips, while the flatter-bottomed sixteen-

[31]*Ibid.*, p. 335.   [32]*Ibid.*, p. 338.

foot "chestnut" type provides a family boat somewhat safer, and capable of holding three-quarters of a ton of freight. Both boats are light and canvas-covered. Dug-outs of cedar are still found among the Indians of British Columbia, though they are making an ever-increasing use of motor-boats, in which they themselves install the engines. The birch canoe is now a curiosity even in the Canadian north-land. Paddles of almost every shape and size and of all kinds of wood have been employed in canoes in the past, but most of them have been similar to the type now in use, though many of the *voyageurs* showed their characteristic love of bright colours by staining them a vivid vermillion.

Canada remains the centre of canoe manufacture, and many of the very waters where the *voyageur* was wont to travel in a day that is gone are now plied by the pleasure craft of the summer resident. Among the most popular canoes in use today is the "cedar strip", a boat with some resemblance to the birch canoe in its foundation ribs. In the centre of a famous summer resort district is the town which was the terminus of Mrs. Jameson's delightful canoe trip in 1837. Penetanguishene was long closely connected with the life of the *voyageurs,* and in 1828 it was the scene of an extensive immigration of these hardy and daring men, who removed thence from Drummond Island. Fortunately a lover of history obtained the reminiscences[33] of many of the picturesque pioneers who for centuries were so charac-teristic of Canadian life.

[33]See Osborne, *op. cit.*

CHAPTER III

BATEAU AND DURHAM BOAT

A CANADIAN BOAT SONG

Faintly as tolls the evening chime
Our voices keep tune and our oars keep time.
Soon as the woods on shore look dim,
We'll sing at St. Ann's our parting hymn.
Row, brothers, row, the stream runs fast,
The Rapids are near and the daylight's past.

Why should we yet our sail unfurl?
There is not a breath the blue wave to curl;
But, when the wind blows off the shore,
Oh! sweetly we'll rest our weary oar.
Blow, breezes, blow, the stream runs fast
The Rapids are near and the daylight's past.

Utawas' tide! this trembling moon
Shall see us float o'er thy surges soon.
Saint of the green isle! hear our prayers,
Oh, grant us cool heavens and favouring airs.
Blow, breezes, blow, the stream runs fast,
The Rapids are near and the daylight's past.

THOMAS MOORE (1804).

THE first boat on the St. Lawrence River was the bark canoe, universally used by Indian, explorer and fur trader. But the difficulties of the route were such that the St. Lawrence was generally avoided in the western fur trade, the Ottawa being used in its stead. Previous to the coming of the Loyalists the chief travellers to Upper Canada were the soldiers for the garrisons at Forts Cataraqui, Oswego, Niagara, Detroit and Michilimackinac, and these used bateaux or canoes, more usually the former, because they were suitable not only for the rough passage up the river but also for travel on the lower lakes. With the coming of the Loyalist refugees in 1783 and succeeding years, the use of bateaux on the St. Lawrence greatly increased, for traffic up and down the river was then for the first time continually necessary in the carriage of passengers and freight.

The name *bateau*, (spelled by most early writers *batteau*), was used in the pioneer period to denote a variety of wooden vessels, ranging in size from a small skiff to a barge almost as large as the Durham boat. The word,

415

originally French, but later commonly used in English, has really no exact meaning with regards to the kind of craft, but was intended merely to signify all boats smaller than barques or schooners, exclusive of canoes. Though a name of such wide application, there was nevertheless a general type, but the size varied. The typical French-Canadian bateau, as used on the St. Lawrence, was flat-bottomed, from thirty to forty feet long, and from five to eight feet wide at the centre; the sides were about four feet high and nearly perpendicular, and both bow and stern usually came to a sharp point about a foot higher than the rest of the boat. Lachine was early a centre of bateau-building, and there was a drydock at the village, owned by one Grant in early times. White oak was found to be the most satisfactory wood for the construction of the bottom, and light fir for the sides. Four or more benches or seats were laid across the boat for the convenience of the oarsmen and their passengers.

In other waters the size of the bateau varied with the conditions. Below Montreal, and occasionally in open parts of the river above, the larger boats had sometimes a "hurricane-house", a small cabin constructed of a light framework covered with canvas, in which a table and half a dozen chairs would be the height of luxury for travellers. The boats were of great importance at the ports of Montreal and Quebec for discharging ballast and loading vessels. They were to be seen at all hours of the day and night looking for employment, and "hooking-on" to every passing sailing-ship in order to bargain with the masters for the work. Large bateaux were also the rule on the Ottawa, many of them being seventy-five feet long, ten or twelve feet wide, five feet deep, and partly decked. The use of boats of this size on the Ottawa route was aided by the building of a bateau lock by a private company at Vaudreuil in 1832. These large vessels commonly carried three tiers of barrels above deck. On Lakes Ontario and Erie boats of a similar type were used, many of them capable of carrying 100 barrels of produce.

The great merit of the bateau consisted in its entire adaptation to all conditions along a most difficult route. Early travellers usually referred to it, however, in terms of qualified praise,—"tolerable sailers and not difficult to row", and "clumsy-looking but efficient",[1] being typical descriptions. It was almost impossible to capsize it, even in the rapids; and, since it was flat-bottomed, it drew only about twenty inches of water even when fully loaded with forty barrels of flour. It could thus creep slowly along a shallow shore without being seriously damaged by the water-worn rocks.

It was heavy work to bring bateaux up the St. Lawrence, and the crews rested frequently during their strenuous exertions; a distance of about three-fourths of a mile on an average, but varying from half a mile to four miles or more according to the conditions of travel, was called *une pipe*, and a short period of smoking refreshed the French-Canadian *voyageurs* at these intervals before they recommenced their difficult work. They were accustomed, also, to sing as they rowed or poled the boats along. One of their favourite boat songs commenced:

"Dans mon chemin j'ai rencontré
Deux cavaliers très bien montés;"

and every verse had the refrain

"À l'ombre d'un bois je m'en vais jouer,
À l'ombre d'un bois je m'en vais danser."

The poet Moore composed his *Canadian Boat Song* in 1804 in imitation of the spirit of the *voyageur chansons,* of which he wrote that when sung at sunset on the beautiful St. Lawrence they had given him greater pleasure than "the finest compositions of the first masters".[2]

A lug-sail with about fifteen feet of hoist was part of the equipment of the bateau, and was used on the open sections of the river, particularly Lakes St. Louis and St. Francis, and above Prescott; this sail was set upon a mast consisting of a rough pole, sometimes with a spare oar lashed to the upper end to make it stronger, the foot of the sail being raised about five feet above the boat so that the steersman could see under it. The boats sailed well before the wind,

[1]Basil Hall: *Travels in America in 1827 and 1828.* 1829. Vol. I, p. 361.
[2]Thomas Moore: *Poems.* Oxford Edition, 1915, p. 124 fn. His *Canadian Boat Song* is quoted at the head of this chapter.

but the defective rigging, and the lack of a keel and a weather helm, made sailing into the wind a difficult matter, and but little headway could be made with sails alone. The usual rate of travel in calm weather was about three miles per hour; but even with a good wind behind them the bateaux seldom accomplished more than thirty miles a day owing to the unusual difficulties along the route.

The equipment of a St. Lawrence bateau was, in addition to oars and sails, six setting poles about nine feet long, iron-shod and pointed, grappling irons, an anchor, and the necessary cooking apparatus. On the Ottawa the Indian crews frequently had small cook-stoves, but otherwise the equipment was much the same.

The Durham boat was introduced into the St. Lawrence waters in 1809 by Americans who had used it on the Mohawk River. This type of vessel had carried on trade between Albany and the Mohawk River region and the lower lakes. Canniff states that Mr. Duncan, of Augusta, was one of the earliest to engage in this commerce, and "introduced the trade between the Mohawk and Buffalo which led to the construction of the Erie Canal".[3]   On the St. Lawrence route the boat was at first manned entirely by the men who had been accustomed to its use, but in later years it was adopted to a considerable extent by Canadians, though the crews were generally English-speaking. About 1824 the first regular line of Durham boats on the Ottawa River was inaugurated by Judge Macdonell, an old Nor'wester; they made scheduled trips between Point Fortune and Montreal, with little opposition for the trade except Cushing and Russell's tri-weekly stage from St. Andrews.

The Durham boat was a flat-bottomed barge with a slip keel and centre-board, rounded bow and square stern, and a long rudder. Sometimes the bottom of the boat was shod with iron to prevent damage from the rocks. The usual length was from eighty to ninety feet, and the vessel was of nine or ten feet beam, with a capacity about ten times that of the early bateau. The load down stream was about 350 barrels, or thirty-five tons; while some eight tons was the usual cargo up stream, though more might have been

[3] William Canniff: *History of the Settlement of Upper Canada*. 1869. p. 141.

carried up the rapids if there had been a greater trade in that direction.

As the vessel was constructed primarily for use as a freight-carrier, but little consideration was given to the accommodation of passengers or crew. The sleeping-quarters were located wherever a little space was to be found, perhaps on the forward deck, or under tarpaulins anywhere. The only one whose quarters were better was the skipper, who frequently had a small place aft which was dignified by the name of cabin. A very small cook-stove stood on the deck in the open, wherever it was least in the way, and no other equipment for the convenience of those on board was to be found.

A writer, in describing the sailing arrangements of the Durham boat, refers to the vessel as "a species of sloop having one rather tall mast with a curiously-devised joint about four feet above the deck, so that the mast could be lowered at any time in going through the canals or passing bridges without displacing the cargo. As this mast was well forward, it admitted of a long boom, so that a large sheet of canvas could be used. Well aft there was sometimes a portable jurymast, easily handled, which was used only when hoisting the main mast. There was a large hatchway for half the length of the boat in the center of the vessel. Aft, towards the bow, and on both sides of the hatchway, was the deck. There was no railing or bulwark other than a covering board about three inches in thickness".[4]

When adverse winds or heavy currents prevented the use of sails, the Durham boat was poled or "set" up the river. Slats were attached to the deck along the course of the long narrow gangway on either side of the hatchway, and they prevented the crew from slipping as they poled the boat along. The poles were made "of the best white ash or hickory, about twenty feet in length, with a steel-pointed socket in order that they might not slip upon the rocky bottom. On the other end was a neatly-turned hardwood button, similar to that upon a carpenter's brace, which fitted nicely to the shoulder".[5] In using the pole each crewman commenced at the bow of the boat, and, facing the

[4]H. R. Morgan: *Steam Navigation on the Ottawa River.* (Ontario Historical Society, *Papers and Records*, Vol. XXIII, p. 371.)
[5]*Ibid.*

stern, bent low as he placed the button to his shoulder and walked along the gangway, shoving the vessel its own length on each trip; for hours at a time several men on each side of the boat would work laboriously at this monotonous method of navigation.

Some of the Loyalist refugees, and later travellers to Upper Canada, used the Schenectady boat, a variation of the bateau; it was flat-bottomed, usually small, and rigged with an ungainly sail. The name originated from the fact that most of these boats were built at Schenectady, in New York State. There were never a great many of them in use in this province, but a number were built by families on setting out for Canada, and were to be occasionally seen in later years on the Bay of Quinté. The rate of speed of the Schenectady boat varied with the conditions along the route; but a traveller, writing in 1835, stated that "the line of boats which start from Albany to Schenectady on their way to Upper Canada go two and one-half miles an hour, taking in stoppages, charging one and a half cents per mile, including board. This mode of travelling is preferred by large families and prudent settlers".[6]

Schenectady boats appear to have been employed in the early official mail service between Kingston, York and Niagara, two of them having been purchased by the government in the summer of 1794 for that purpose. One boat left Kingston every Monday during the season of navigation and proceeded to "the Presqu'Isle at Quinté" (later named the Carrying Place), where it was met by the boat from York; dispatches and passengers were interchanged, and the vessels returned to their respective headquarters.

The crews of the bateau, Schenectady boat and Durham boat were variable. On the St. Lawrence they carried from five men to ten or more, according to the difficulties of the trip. Two oarsmen on each side, and a steersman, were sufficient for the descent of the St. Lawrence, but double the number often comprised the crew in the ascent. The method by which bateaux and Durham boats were propelled depended upon the conditions. In quiet waters the oars were used, the crew alternately sitting and rising from the thwarts and pulling in unison to their quaint songs and

[6]Quoted in Canniff, *op. cit.*, p. 142.

From *Picturesque Canada.* 1879

LOADING A BATEAU AT LOW TIDE

Canada Steamship Lines' Marine Historical Collection   George A. Cuthbertson

WHALEBOATS USED IN BRADSTREET'S EXPEDITION WHICH
CAPTURED FORT FRONTENAC, 1758

From Heriot's *Travels through the Canadas.* 1807　　　　George Heriot

CASCADES OF THE ST. LAWRENCE

W. H. Bartlett

VIEW FROM THE CITADEL AT KINGSTON, 1840

chants. Lieutenant Hall found this method of propulsion very tedious:

"It cost us fifteen hours to row from Coteau-du-Lac to Cornwall, with but one incident during the voyage; this was a purchase, or rather barter, of biscuit for dried eels, with a party of half-naked Indians whom we found idly occupied under a clump of trees on the shore in curing the produce of their fishery".[7]

Where the current was strong most of the members of the crew would go ashore, and with loops or bridles over each trackman's shoulder they would walk in the water or along the edge and tow the boats, while a picked crewman steered with a long sweep. A traveller observed that the bateaumen were "compelled, almost every hour, when actually melting with heat and fainting through fatigue, to jump into the water, frequently up to their arm-pits, and to remain in it towing the boats until they are completely chilled. They then have recourse to the aid of ardent spirits, of which on all occasions they freely partake, and in a few minutes are once more bathed in perspiration".[8]

In other rapids it was possible for some of the crew to remain on board and use their iron-shod poles to guide the boat among the rocks. Sometimes these poles were crossed at short intervals with small bars of wood like the feet of a ladder; the boatmen would thrust their poles into the channel, and grasping successively the wooden bars, worked their way from bow to stern of the boat. This method was of greatest value in the larger bateaux and in the Durham boats, while in the smaller craft the poles were usually used by boatmen in a stationary position.

On the St. Lawrence the boats often travelled in brigades of from five to twelve, with a conductor in charge of each brigade; this enabled the crews to aid one another in portaging freight, and in other ways decreased the difficulties of what was at best a laborious trip. Frequently bateaux were tied together when towing was necessary, and by the united strength of all crewmen a much easier ascent was made. Man-power had sometimes to be supple-

[7] Francis Hall: *Travels in Canada and the United States in 1816-17.* 1818. p. 155.
[8] E. A. Talbot: *Five Years' Residence in the Canadas.* 1824. Vol. I, p. 86.

mented by windlasses where the rapids were very strong, while horses and oxen were in demand at such places as Pine Tree Point and Point Iroquois. Many farmers in the vicinity of these rapids earned more than $4 a day at this work, and there was often considerable rivalry in obtaining employment, and in currying favour with the captains or conductors in charge of regular bateau lines.

At times, when the banks were too steep for "tracking" the boats, they were dragged over the rocks on a skidway of small rolling logs. Long before any system of continuous canals was planned, small locks for bateaux had been constructed by the French at the Cascades, the Coteau, and the Long Sault Rapids; but these were only partial in extent, and in no case did they overcome the whole of any rapid. The first bateau lock to be built was that cut through limestone at Coteau du Lac in 1780-81. Others were constructed at the time of the Loyalist immigration into Upper Canada. The locks were considerably improved and enlarged in 1804 by the Royal Engineers as military works. The first canal on the St. Lawrence, at Lachine, was not opened until 1824, though it had been commenced by the French as early as 1700.

The bateau and the Durham boat had each its peculiar advantages, but in general it may be said that while the bateau was smaller, yet it was preferable in case of a sudden severe squall. Isaac Weld, while finding the bateau to be "a very heavy, awkward sort of vessel either for rowing or sailing", considered it much safer for navigation on the St. Lawrence than a keel-boat, such as schooner or Durham boat. He describes an experience in a storm as proof of the value of his preference:

"We had reached a wide part of the river and were sailing along with a favourable wind, when suddenly the horizon grew very dark and a dreadful storm arose, accompanied with loud peals of thunder and torrents of rain. Before the sail could be taken in, the ropes which held it were snapped in pieces, and the waves began to dash over the sides of the bateau, though the water had been quite smooth five minutes before.

"It was impossible now to counteract the force of the wind with oars, and the bateau was consequently driven on shore; but the bottom of it being quite flat it was carried smoothly upon the beach without sustaining any injury, and the men, leaping out, drew it up on dry land, where we remained out of all danger till the storm was over. A keel-boat, however, of the same size, could not have approached nearer to the shore than thirty feet, and there it would have stuck fast in the sand, and probably have been filled with water."[9]

Captain Basil Hall was similarly caught in a storm while travelling by bateau, and on this occasion the yard-arm of the sail was smashed by the force of the wind. The boat was blown sideways towards an island, upon the lee side of which the crew finally effected a landing, but not before all of them had become greatly excited, and, usurping the captain's prerogative, had taken a hand at bawling orders at one another; even Captain Hall almost took command of the proceedings![10]

A typical trip up the river with merchandise during the early years of the nineteenth century took twelve days. The goods were carted from Montreal to Lachine, where bateaux and Durham boats took their departure westward. They sailed through Lake St. Louis, and at the Cascades were locked past the first rapids, one-fourth of the cargo remaining in the boats while the rest was carted to the head of the Cedars. To reach this point they had to be dragged up the Split Rock and Cedars Rapids; here the boats were reloaded and passed the Coteau by a lock into Lake St. Francis. Above Cornwall there were two locks in the Long Sault, one of them having been built privately as a speculation. Between Milles Roches and the head of the Long Sault, lighterage was again necessary, the whole cargo frequently having to be removed from the boats and hauled around the rapids in wagons. From Prescott the boats were sailed, rowed or poled into Lake Ontario without difficulty.

When steamships began to navigate the upper St. Lawrence in 1818 it became quite usual for them to tow bateaux and Durham boats over that section of the route, but the

[9]Isaac Weld: *Travels through the States of North America.* 1799. pp. 190-1.
[10]Basil Hall, *op. cit.*, Vol. I, pp. 374-9.

difficulties of the remainder of the voyage varied but little until the canal system was complete about thirty years later. Those boats which locked through at the Cascades and the Coteau Rapids paid toll, which amounted in the case of a Durham boat to £2 10s. for the two locks. In 1818 a total of 315 Durham boats and 679 bateaux paid toll at the Coteau locks, while six years later the numbers were 268 and 596, respectively, the diminution being caused partly by a failure in the harvest of 1823 and partly by the operations of the Imperial Trade Act of 1822. About one-half of the Durham boats and a smaller proportion of the bateaux in use in 1824 were American. To the boats which used the locks must be added about twelve *per cent.* which avoided toll by laboriously working their way up or around the rapids by more difficult means. Between 1818 and 1825 the trade up the St. Lawrence averaged about 5,000 tons annually, but by 1832 it had increased to 21,000 tons. In 1833 the revenue over and above expenses of the locks at the Cascades, Split Rock and Coteau du Lac amounted to £876; and during that year 863 bateaux and 612 Durham boats paid toll at these points.

The expenses of a freight trip up the St. Lawrence from Lachine to Kingston were quite heavy; toll, towing, land carriage and wages for one Durham boat loaded with about eight tons cargo totalled £30 7s. ($121.40). The rivermen received in wages 3s. 6d. per day and the average trip lasted twelve days. The chief articles of commerce at that time were barrels of flour, peas, pork, salt, potash and rum, and bales of furs. The average cargo of a bateau on the St. Lawrence was from three to four and one-half tons, and a cask of rum was the standard in estimating the freight charges, the cost of carrying a barrel from Lachine to Kingston being from $3 to $3.50. It was sometimes observed that casks of wines and liquors were noticeably lighter at the end of a trip! Salt was transported at the lowest rates, the charge being only 3s. 9d. per cwt. in 1825.

Upon the whole, however, bateau transport was exceedingly costly. At the time of the War of 1812 the government had to pay nearly £200 to have a 24-pound cannon transported from Montreal to Kingston, and £676 for the carriage of an anchor of 76 cwt. over the same route; while it was stated in the British Parliament that "when the Imperial Government sent out two vessels in frames, one of them, a brig, cost the country in carriage, the short distance between these two cities, the enormous sum of £30,000 sterling".[11]   To carry a barrel of flour from St. Catharines to Niagara the charge was about one-third of its value; and the excessive cost of transport to the Talbot Settlement about 1817 resulted in such high prices that a bushel of wheat would buy no more than a yard of cotton, and eighteen bushels had to be given in exchange for a barrel of salt.

The transport of goods down the St. Lawrence was comparatively easy and therefore much speedier.   At first furs were the only export, but potash, grain and other products were sent down in ever-increasing quantities after the settlement of Upper Canada commenced in 1783-4.   Before 1800 most of the produce made the trip on timber rafts, or in scows or "arks", which were broken up and sold as lumber in Montreal.   There were some bateaux in operation, however, and they frequently carried almost equal loads in both directions, bringing up provisions from below for the new settlers, and taking down peltries and such other exports as they could obtain as cargo.

Soon after 1800 the bateau, and later the Durham boat, began to supersede the raft and scow in St. Lawrence transport, the average bateau carrying thirty or forty barrels down stream, while the Durham boat could take 350 barrels. The usual passage from Kingston to Lachine lasted only four days and the expense involved was restricted to the wages of the crew and pilotage at the worst rapids, which totalled about £6 1s. 6d. ($24.30) for a boat with a crew of six men. The downward trade between 1818 and 1825 averaged from 150,000 to 175,000 barrels *per annum,* or roughly 15,000 tons, about three times as great as the trade up the river. By 1832 it had so increased that some 800 Durham boats and from 1,200 to 1,500 bateaux were employed in it, the down trade totalling aout 66,000 tons annually.

The rates charged for the downward trip were, of course,

[11]Speech of Sir J. Murray in the British House of Commons, September 6, 1828, cited in Tackabury's *Atlas of the Dominion of Canada,* 1875, p. 36.

much less than those necessary to meet the difficulties of transport up the river. An advertisement published at Kingston in February, 1819, gives freight rates in detail. The charge for carrying a barrel of flour *viâ* this line of Durham boats from Niagara, Queenston or York to Montreal was 5s. 6d. ($1.10); from Kingston to Montreal the freight was 1s. less. Potash was packed in barrels of 500 lbs., and consequently the charge was larger, being 10s. from Kingston to Montreal, and 12s. 6d. from ports near the head of Lake Ontario. Barrels of pork were charged an intermediate rate of 8s. 3d. from Queenston, Niagara and York, and 6s. 9d. from Kingston; other merchandise travelling from Lachine to Kingston paid 5s. per cwt.

That a special effort was made to cater to passengers may be seen from the following item in the same advertisement: "An elegant Passage Boat will also leave Kingston every tenth day for Montreal, which will be fitted up in the most commodious manner and prevent any delay to passengers leaving the upper part of the lake in the Steam Boat *Frontenac,* it having been built for the purpose of leaving this place immediately after her arrival".[12] The owners of this line were Thomas Markland, Peter Smith, Lawrence Herkimer, John Kerby and William Mitchell. It may be presumed that the rates by bateau varied but little from these quotations, for all types of boats competed for the same trade.

The first use of bateaux on the Lakes was for war purposes. In 1687 Governor Denonville had 198 of them, as well as three larger vessels and 142 canoes, engaged in transport service on Lake Ontario. During the last years of the French period both French and British relied upon them for the carriage of troops and supplies, and they were frequently used for long trips, though each nation had a few sloops-of-war on Lake Ontario. During the Seven Years' War the small boats used by the British were called whaleboats, though they were merely a variation of the bateau and were similarly propelled.

Bateaux once proved of great value to the French as a means of quick communication between Fort Niagara and Fort Rouillé (Toronto). In 1757 word was received at the

[12]Quoted in Canniff, *op. cit.,* pp. 145-6.

former fort of an Indian plot to pillage the trading-post near the mouth of the Humber, and it was frustrated by Captain Pouchot, who sent two boats armed with swivel guns which soon intimidated the Mississaga Indians encamped near the fort.

That the perils of navigating the Great Lakes in small schooners and bateaux were not restricted to the danger of shipwreck and drowning is apparent from the following ghastly tale, reminiscent of Coleridge's *Ancient Mariner*:

"Letters from Detroit by Monday's New York mail inform us that several boats with goods had been seventy days in crossing Lake Erie, in which time the distress of the people was so great that they had been obliged to keep two human bodies which they found unburied on the shore, in order to collect and kill the ravens and eagles which came to feed on them, for their subsistence. Many other boats have been frozen up within forty miles of Detroit, and several traders' small boats with goods had been lost."[13]

During the War of 1812 canoes and bateaux were extensively used in the carriage of supplies and men from Quebec and Montreal to Kingston, York, Niagara and Amherstburg. An expedition to Michilimackinac led to a British victory in the first engagement of the conflict; while bateaux were used by the Americans to effect a crossing at Queenston in 1812, and a landing west of York in 1813. The boats were of special importance to the British on Lake Ontario during 1813, when the enemy was temporarily in control of the lake and prevented much use of schooners. During the course of the war numerous settlers joined the bateau service along the north shores of Erie and Ontario, soldiers and supplies being transported up and down, and prisoners who had not been paroled being sent eastward to Kingston or Quebec. In 1814 British reinforcements were sent to Michilimackinac *via* Yonge Street and Lake Simcoe, travelling in bateaux on Willow Creek and the Nottawasaga River to Georgian Bay, and on to the western fort.

Over half a century later, in the notable military expedition to the Red River in 1870, the Hudson's Bay Com-

[13]Quoted from the *Annual Register* for 1770 in E. A. Cruikshank: *Early Traders and Trade Routes in Ontario and the West, 1760-83*. (*Transactions* of the Canadian Institute, Series 4, Vol. IV, p. 309.)

pany's "York" boats provided the chief means of transport; these, though not flat-bottomed, were otherwise similar to the bateau, and weighed from 700 to 900 pounds, 126 of them being used to carry the force and its supplies. The York boat had largely replaced the canoe in the noted fur Company's trading expeditions after 1823, due to the orders of Sir George Simpson, Governor of the Company, who found that the canoe was much more expensive to operate.

The commercial use of bateaux on Lake Ontario preceded the creation of the province. When Governor Simcoe removed from Niagara to Toronto in the summer of 1793 bateaux were being run once a week from Kingston, carrying passengers and goods. The route was *viâ* the Bay of Quinté, and at the Carrying Place the boats were hauled upon low wheels or trucks drawn by oxen owned by Asa Weller, a tavern-keeper; thence they continued along the shore of the lake. Besides this regular service there were other boats owned by small merchants and pedlars who carried on local trade. During the Loyalist period Captain Myers, for example, operated bateaux on the Bay of Quinté to transport his own freight, and for the accommodation of settlers in the carriage of produce down the bay and river, and supplies back. Myers' usual route was to Kingston and back, but on one occasion he went to Montreal. His system was to charge for freight on the trip down, and give the owner of the freight a free passage back. It is said that the Captain made the journey as pleasant as possible for his passengers: "He always kept his grog in his 'caboose', and would deal it out to all. There was no doubt much of jollity and pleasant yarn-spinning during the long passages upon the tranquil waters of the Bay".[14]

An interesting development in the use of bateaux followed upon the opening of Yonge Street in 1796 by Augustus Jones, at the order of Governor Simcoe. The North-West Company had formerly sent brigades of canoes up the Ottawa, and thence by way of Champlain's old route to Georgian Bay and westward; but at the end of the century they commenced to send fleets of bateaux up the St. Lawrence and the Bay of Quinté to the Carrying Place,

[14]Quoted in Canniff, *op. cit.*, pp. 144-5.

where they were portaged to Lake Ontario and followed the shore to York. They crossed the peninsula at the foot of the present Woodbine Avenue, (where, in 1858, Toronto Island was created during a storm), and, proceeding up the Don River to York Mills, continued northward overland by Yonge Street. The hill above Yorkville was a difficult ascent to overcome on wheels, and a rude windlass or capstan had to be installed at the top to haul up the bateaux.

When Lake Simcoe was reached the boats proceeded by the Severn River to Georgian Bay. To aid in their passage into Lake Superior the first canal at Sault Ste. Marie was constructed by the Company in 1797-8; this had but one small lock, thirty-eight feet long, with a lift of nine feet. Canoes continued to be used over the Grand Portage from the Kaministiquia River to the far west, the bateaux being of greatest value on the more open Great Lakes.

It was found that supplies could be carried to Michilimackinac by this route at a saving of from £10 to £15 per ton, and consequently the Company made contributions of several thousand pounds to aid in improving Yonge Street. Supplies for even the far-distant Spanish settlements on the Mississippi travelled over this route, for it took only ten or twelve days to cover the distance from Montreal to Lake Ontario—the most difficult section of the trade route to the west—while it required four months to pole a keel-boat up the Mississippi from New Orleans to St. Louis.

Bateaux were similarly used on Lake Erie and were obtainable at Chippawa and Fort Erie, though some were carried on wagons from Lake Ontario over the Niagara portage road at a cost of £10 and upwards each, a capstan being used to ascend the hill. In the *Canada Constellation* of December 7, 1799, occurs an interesting item with reference to the carriage of freight on the Niagara River:

"The transportation by water from the Chippawa to Fort Erie has hitherto been expensive and slow, being performed by bateaux of five men each, and carrying 100 barrels. Twenty-seven were usually employed. Mr. Marcus Hulings Jr., from Pittsburgh, with Mr. Charles Craig, boatbuilder, this fall built a boat on the construction of those used in the Susquehannah and other rapid rivers, that carries 100 barrels, and plied by seven men, that performs the trip with also a great saving of time. For this laudable and advantageous improvement Judge Hamilton has presented them with £30. We understand that they intend to add another boat in the spring. They have it in contemplation to view the river from Kingston towards Montreal, and if boats can be constructed for those waters they will next year have a sufficient number there (to supply the needs of) our commerce."[15]

The carriage of passengers by bateau was not effected without great inconvenience. The Loyalists ascended the St. Lawrence in these boats under the most adverse conditions; there was no regular service and the men had sometimes to paddle up in a canoe and arrange at the Bay of Quinté for bateaux to come down and get their families. John Ferguson wrote in 1788 from the Bay of Quinté district: "I arrived here after a most tedious and fatiguing journey—nineteen days on the way—sometimes for whole days up to the waist in water or mire."[16] Many a traveller had a long wait before an opportunity occurred to proceed up the river, and then he probably had to work his passage by taking a hand at the oars.

The journey up the St. Lawrence and through Lakes Ontario and Erie was accomplished in early days only by the use of various means of transport. In 1789 William Dummer Powell, first Judge of the District of Hesse, (comprising the territory from Long Point westward), travelled from Montreal to Detroit, accompanied by his wife, six children, and a sister, Anne. Anne Powell wished to keep a journal of her experience, but, finding that impossible under the conditions of travel, she wrote an account of the trip from memory. On May 11th the party left Montreal, and Miss Powell gives this description of the first part of the journey:

"We now went to our Boats; one was fitted up with an awning to protect us from the weather, and held the family and bedding. It was well-filled, eighteen persons in all, so you may suppose we had not much room. . . . The next day we reached a part of the River where the boats are obliged to be unloaded and taken through a Lock, the rapids

---

[15]Niagara *Canada Constellation*, December 7, 1799.
[16]Quoted in Canniff, *op. cit.*, p. 139.

TIMBER RAFT AND DURHAM BOAT AT CAP SANTÉ ON THE
ST. LAWRENCE, 1840

VILLAGE OF CEDARS, RIVER ST. LAWRENCE, 1840

LACHINE RAPIDS

W. H. Bartlett

THREE RIVERS, 1840

Voyageur canoes for the western trade were constructed chiefly at
Three Rivers

being too strong to pass. . . . . We breakfasted at the house of a man who keeps the Lock."

They proceeded on land by a variety of equipages, "a Calash for the Ladies, a saddle horse for Mr. P., and a waggon for the children and servants. In the evening we went on ten miles further to a public-house where we were tormented with Fleas and Dirt". The journey continued the next morning, the boats being sailed at times. The party reached Kingston on the tenth day of travel, and proceeded by schooner to Niagara, where they arrived four days later. From Niagara to Fort Schlosser they travelled by "calash" (*calèche*), on horseback, or on foot, visited the Falls of Niagara, and continued by bateau from Fort Schlosser to Fort Erie, whence a schooner conveyed them to Detroit.[17]

Travellers' accounts show that the bateau trip up the St. Lawrence long continued to be replete with hardships. There was little shelter for passengers by day or night unless tents were carried; the crews bivouacked on the shore, while any passengers who could afford to pay for accommodation sought it in such scattered inns or farmhouses as were willing and able to provide it. Most travellers, however, slept and ate on the shore with the crew, for even in 1817 the average farmhouse along the route could furnish no beds; though a writer notes that he was permitted to bring his bed from the boat and spread it on the floor, "where we enjoyed a refreshing sleep". As to food he says: "We had bread along with us, and got plenty of milk from our host at two-pence a pint, this being the only article of provision he could furnish".[18]

Another traveller states that he was refused accommodation at a farmhouse, and even driven out of the barn, so that he had to be content to sleep on the shore. Justice constrained him to state, however, (and this particular man was very seldom bothered by any such scruples!), that "the people who live on the shores of the St. Lawrence have so frequently been imposed upon, plundered, and otherwise maltreated by various evil-disposed immigrants in their pro-

[17]See William R. Riddell: *Old Province Tales, Upper Canada.* 1920. pp. 64-92.
[18]William Bell: *Hints to Emigrants.* 1824. pp. 49-50.

gress to the Upper Province, that, if we had experienced even worse treatment than this which I have related, it ought not, under such provoking circumstances, excite much astonishment."[19]

In general it was true that the most primitive conditions of travel were found in the earliest period, though in some respects there was little improvement even half a century later. When Isaac Weld journeyed up the St. Lawrence in 1796 he found it necessary to make elaborate preparations before undertaking the trip. In addition to a tent, and buffalo skins to sleep on, provisions for several weeks had to be carried. He notes that the passengers either helped the crew work the boats up the rapids, or tramped through the woods to the next stretch of navigable water.[20]

The journey in 1792 of Lieutenant-Governor and Mrs. Simcoe to the newly-created province of Upper Canada well illustrates the difficulties of the trip, even under circumstances which would tend to make the voyage as pleasant as possible. On June 8th the Governor's party embarked in three bateaux at Quebec, and reached Cap Santé the same night. During succeeding days the Simcoes proceeded in a leisurely manner, although a start was usually made at six or earlier each morning. On June 11th they reached Three Rivers, "where we paid a great price for a bad breakfast at an inn kept by an Englishman", writes Mrs. Simcoe in her diary.[21] Two days later the party arrived at Montreal, and remained ten days at Chateau de Ramezay, the Government House.

When the journey was recommenced it was necessary, because of the Lachine Rapids, to portage by carriage over a very rough road. The Simcoes then re-embarked in bateaux, but at times they had to walk along the shore when the rapids were too strong. Mrs. Simcoe refers to an early tragedy in the navigation of the St. Lawrence: "We went on shore at the Cascades, and walked a mile through a wood and saw the boats pass some tremendous rapids near this place, where General Amherst lost eighty

[19]Talbot, *op. cit.*, Vol. I, pp. 87-92.
[20]See Weld, *op. cit.*, pp. 257-276.
[21]*Diary of Mrs. John Graves Simcoe*, June 11, 1792.

men during the last war by coming down without con-ductors in the boats."[22] This disaster occurred at the Cedars Rapids, and sixty-four boats were lost in addition to the drowning of eighty-eight men. Amherst's force was two months and seventeen days travelling from Schenectady to Montreal, a remarkable instance of the slowness of trans-portation in early times.[23]

When the Governor's party approached the village of Cedars the passengers travelled by *calèche,* and wagons were used to transport the baggage; while at Coteau du Lac the passage was made less arduous by the use of locks. When they reached Glengarry they were welcomed by Highlanders in their national dress; and further up the river another reception awaited them, for Mrs. Simcoe notes: "The Governor went to the Isle St. Regis to visit the Indians at their village, where they received him with dancing in a fierce style, as if they wished to inspire the spectators with terror and respect for their ferocious appearance."[24]

As the trip by boat up the Long Sault Rapids was dangerous and tedious, the Simcoes rode horseback and be-came acquainted with the dangers of corduroy bridges, "composed of trunks of trees unhewn, of unequal sizes, and laid across pieces of timber placed lengthways".[25] On June 30th they passed the River Gananowui (Gananoque), and half a mile beyond found Carey's Inn too dirty to provide pleasant accommodations, so a tent was pitched and they slept in it through incessant rain. Mrs. Simcoe rested well, but was "surprised to find how wet the bed clothes were in the tent when I rose, and yet I caught no cold, though these nights were the first in which I slept in a tent".[26] The Governor and his wife were impressed with the beauty of the Thousand Islands, through which they passed in large bateaux, reaching Kingston on July 1st.

Early in the nineteenth century travellers bound for Detroit or Sandwich sometimes made the long trip from

[22]*Ibid.,* June 23, 1792.
[23]The details of Amherst's expedition and the tragedy at the Cedars may be found in the *Annual Register* for 1760, p. 59; a part of this description is quoted in William Kingsford: *The Can-adian Canals.* 1865. p. 11 fn.
[24]Simcoe, *op. cit.,* June 25, 1792.
[25]*Ibid.,* June 26, 1792.   [26]*Ibid.,* June 30, 1792.

Quebec entirely by bateaux. While the voyage was certainly tedious, yet it was not without interest if one enjoyed a wild, carefree life. Dr. William Dunlop, better known to pioneers as "Tiger Dunlop", was one of these, and he found the mode of travel "far from unpleasant, for there is something of romance and adventure in it". All supplies were carried, and camp was pitched at night at the mouths of creeks, or at other sheltered and picturesque spots. The crew was made up of "seven stout, light-hearted, jolly, lively Canadians who sang their songs all the time they could spare from smoking their pipes. Often they sang and danced all night, for if the Frenchman has a fiddle sleep ceases to be a necessary of life for him".[27]

These characteristics of bateaumen are referred to by other writers, one of whom describes the boatmen drinking their grog and sleeping on the ground with one tarpaulin under and one over them—swearing and singing far into the night.[28] John Howison observed that at the end of the day's work some of the crew "reclined around the fire, talking barbarous French, and uttering the most horrid oaths; others sat in the boats and sang troubadour songs; and a third party was engaged in distributing the provisions. They resembled a band of freebooters. Most of them were very athletic, and had the sharp physiognomy and sparkling eyes of a Canadian. The red glare of the fire communicated additional animation to their rude features; and their bushy black beards and discordant voices rendered them rather a formidable-looking set of people".[29]

Howison appreciated "the pleasure of a respectable tavern" in Kingston after his bateau trip up the St. Lawrence, for he says: "For three days I had been disgusted with the dirtiness, noise and grossness of the Canadian boatmen, and, during as many nights, had been prevented from sleeping by the fumes of rum and tobacco, the bites of musquetoes, and the hardness of the planks which formed my bed."[30]

[27]William Dunlop: *Statistical Sketches of Upper Canada.* 1832. pp. 53-4.
[28]Bell, *op. cit.,* p. 58.
[29]John Howison: *Sketches of Upper Canada.* 1821. 3rd Edition, 1825, pp. 41-2.
[30]*Ibid.,* p. 57.

It would appear that the crews were sometimes as "tough" as they appeared to travellers. Samuel Strickland ascended the St. Lawrence in a Durham boat in 1825, and in his account of the journey he wrote: "We had hard work poling up the rapids. I found I had fallen in with a rough set of customers, and determined in my own mind to leave them as soon as possible, which I happily effected the next evening when we landed at Les Cèdres." Strickland walked to Prescott and waited there two or three days until the Durham boat (which had his baggage) caught up with him —an interesting example of the slowness of St. Lawrence navigation.[31]

Sir Richard Bonnycastle describes in some detail the pilfering to which one's goods were sometimes subjected: "Your *compagnons de voyage* on board a bateau or Durham boat, which is a *monstre* bateau, are French-Canadian *voyageurs*, always drunk and always gay, who pole you along up the rapids, or rush down them with what will be will be.

"These happy people have a knack of examining your goods and chattels which they are conveying, in the most admirable manner and with the utmost sang-froid; but still they are above stealing—they only tap the rum cask or the whisky barrel, and appropriate any cordage wherewith you bound your chests and packages. I never had a chest, box or bale sent up by bateau or Durham boat that escaped this rope mail."[32]

In 1818 E. A. Talbot made the trip up the river in a Durham boat. He found that "the accommodations which this boat afforded were so poor that our situation during the thirteen days of our voyage from Lachine to Prescott was in reality 'below the reach of envy'. To make room for my mother and the children in the wretched little hole of a cabin, my brother and I were frequently obliged to sleep on the shore in the open air". Between the 18th of August and the 1st of September the journey of 120 miles was completed, but "I think I may say, without any danger of hyperbole, that during this short period each of us en-

[31]Samuel Strickland: *Twenty-seven Years in Canada West*. 1853. Vol. I, pp. 11-13.
[32]Sir Richard Bonnycastle: *Canada and the Canadians*. 1846. Vol. I, p. 93.

countered greater difficulties, endured more privations, and submitted to stronger proofs of our fortitude than had been our lot in all the preceding years of our lives. We were obliged by day, in consequence of the great weight of our luggage, to assist the sailors in towing the boat up the rapids, often up to our armpits in water; and by night to rest our enervated and shivering limbs on the inhospitable shores of this river of cataracts."

When, for the sake of variety, Talbot and some others struck into the woods to tramp for a mile or two they wandered into an impassable swamp, and did not join the boat again until the following day, after a very miserable experience. They had, however, fortunately chanced late at night upon a log house, and had been allowed to sleep on the kitchen floor; but the Durham boat continued on its journey without the slightest interest in their whereabouts, or whether they ever appeared again.[33]

It is probable that most travellers who were not too fatigued to have any feelings would agree with Lieutenant Francis Hall, whose reaction to the ascent of the river consisted largely of boredom:

" 'Tis a sad waste of life to ascend the St. Lawrence in a bateau. After admiring the exertions with which the Canadian boatmen force their long flat-bottomed barks against the rapids, there is nothing left but to gaze listlessly on the descending current, and its low wooded shores; while the monotony of the oar-stroke is scarcely broken by the occasional rustling of a wild duck through the sedge, or the cry of the American kingfisher as he darts from some hanging bough on his scaly prey."[34]

Mrs. Thomas Stewart, an early settler in Peterborough County, journeyed up the St. Lawrence in 1822, and gives us many interesting details of the life of passengers and crew. The intense heat of August was unpleasant, but the crew objected to the carrying of umbrellas, so the passengers had to sit in the glare of the sun. The food of the boatmen was "raw pork and hard biscuit which they enjoy much; they eat often, and drink quantities of the lake water. In the morning before setting out they always have hot pea-soup".

[33]Talbot, *op. cit.*, Vol. I. pp. 87-92.   [34]Francis Hall, *op. cit.*, p. 154.

The Stewarts spent one night at an inn, "but between the heat and visitations of troublesome insects we could not sleep". To replenish their supplies they were occasionally able to buy bread and milk from farmers; the beds in these homes they found excellent. Once they slept on the hay in a barn, while Mr. Stewart sometimes lay down in the grass on the riverside, though when he awoke his clothes were soaked by the morning dew. Summing up the nine-day trip, however, Mrs. Stewart, much braver than Edward Talbot, wrote: "We met with no hardships and but few difficulties."[35] What would in modern times pass for extreme hardship was cheerily faced by our pioneer settlers. The Stewarts were fortunate in having money, with which crude accommodation might be purchased; but that most immigrants suffered intensely during the voyage up the river the following pathetic description by Patrick Shirreff shows beyond a doubt:

"At Coteau-du-Lac our steamer took seven bateaux in tow, in one of which I counted 110 immigrants of all ages, who were doomed to pass the night on board. Men, women and children were huddled together as close as captives in a slave-trader, exposed to the sun's rays by day, and river-damp by night, without protection. It was impossible to look upon such a group of human beings without emotion. The day had been so intensely hot that the stoutest amongst them looked fatigued, while the females seemed ready to expire with exhaustion. Conversation was carried on in whispers, and a heaviness of heart seemed to pervade the whole assemblage. Never shall I forget the countenance of a young mother, ever anxiously looking at twin infants slumbering on her knee, and covering them from the vapour rising from the river, and which strongly depicted the feelings of maternal affection and pious resignation. Night soon veiled the picture, and, I fear, brought no relief to the anxious mother."[36]

Immigrants had frequently to jump into the water and work with the crews in hauling the boats against the strong current. The lack of changes of clothes, together with the

[35]Frances Stewart: *Our Forest Home*. 1889. 2nd Edition, 1902, pp. 11-14.
[36]Patrick Shirreff: *A Tour through North America*. 1835. p. 143.

intense heat, dampness and exposure at night, and the drinking of too much river water, all combined to cause much sickness and frequent deaths. An average of twenty miles a day was sometimes maintained throughout the ascent of the St. Lawrence; but the best accommodations at night were limited to the floor of farmhouse or inn, and one was usually considered fortunate if he was allowed such protection as might be gained in a barn or haystack. At Prescott the bateau transport of immigrants sometimes ended, and there was frequently a congestion of a thousand or more sick and weary travellers near the town. Delays of weeks during which tents or barns formed the living quarters of the incoming settlers were not at all unusual, and fever and ague took a heavy toll.

Some immigrations, as, for example, those conducted by the Hon. Peter Robinson in 1823-25 to Lanark and Peterborough Counties, were provided with necessaries at the expense of the government; but most emigrants paid their own way from Europe to the new land. The lowest cost of transit into Upper Canada was by Durham boat, in which one might travel from Montreal to Prescott for about $1, without board. Although the cost varied, the expenses of travel between Montreal and York by Durham boat usually amounted to about £3 15s. ($15) per family, including provisions. After the steamships became common they frequently entered into cut-throat competition for business, and immigrants might make a faster, more convenient, and not infrequently a cheaper trip over some sections of the journey than was possible by the more primitive bateau.

One's experiences when travelling down stream were much more pleasant. Some excellent description is contained in Mrs. Simcoe's record of her impressions on the downward trip in 1796. The Governor was a "good sport" and insisted on shooting all rapids, though his wife was not so enthusiastic. While passing the "terrifying" Gallops Rapid, seven miles above Iroquois, Mrs. Simcoe saw merchants' bateaux working up the rapid "with the greatest labour, exertion and difficulty, and the velocity with which a boat appeared flying downwards with great rapidity formed a contrast well worth seeing".[37] The descent of the Long

[37]Simcoe, *op. cit.*, July 27, 1796.

Sault was made "in an hour without sailing, and seldom rowing, though near particular currents they rowed with great exertion. The most agitated part is towards the end of the rapids, where the river becomes wider; here I had an opportunity of seeing the boats which followed us; they appeared to fly. I compared them to race-horses trying to outrun each other. The velocity was extreme; sometimes the whirlpool turned them round; at others the head of one and the stern of another boat appeared buried under the waves".[38]

On the following day the Simcoes approached the Cedars Rapids, where a portage of four miles by *calèche* was usually made; but the Governor wished to experience all the thrills, so preparations were accordingly completed to continue by water. Mrs. Simcoe considered the Cedars "much more frightful than the Long Sault. I cannot describe how terrifying the extent of furious, dashing white waves appeared, and how the boat rose and plunged among them, the waves sometimes washing into the boat. There is a place called 'the run' near the locks, which is like going down the stream of an overshot mill, and I really thought we never should have risen out of it. The men rowed with all their might, and in passing it called out '*Vive le Roi!*' "[39]

Finally the Governor's party shot the Lachine Rapids, considered most dangerous of all because the water is so shallow. Colonel Simcoe wished his wife to sketch the rapids, though she believed it was his way of attempting to keep her mind off the great danger of the passage, of which the pilot, "to make himself brave, was perpetually reminding us. . . . I was more disposed to have cried than to have talked". But, though they passed a timber raft stuck on the rocks, the Simcoes successfully navigated the rapids and arrived safe and sound at Montreal.[40]

A traveller's account of a trip from Kingston to Montreal by bateau and Durham boat in 1811 illustrates the hardship and inconvenience which might be met with even on the downward trip: "I left Kingston on the 6th of April, 1811, but, as the travelling then was not as it is now, I did not arrive in Montreal till the 15th. . . . Durham boats

[38]*Ibid.*, July 28, 1796.   [39]*Ibid.*, July 29, 1796.
[40]*Ibid.*, July 30, 1796.

were scarce on the Canada side at that time, but it was thought if I could get to the American shore I would find one on its way to Montreal. Well, I found a man in Kingston, just from Grindstone Island, who had brought up some shingles and tar to sell, and he told me if I could get to Briton's Point, several miles down the river from Cape Vincent, and to which place he would take me, that he thought I would find a Durham boat there." The following are excerpts from the Rev. Miles' diary of the journey:

"Left Kingston in an open skiff—head wind—rowed hard till about eight in the evening, when, having blistered both hands, and being very much fatigued, we drew our skiff on shore, and camped on the shore of Long Island, about five miles from Grindstone Island. Wind strong from the north—very cold and without victuals or fire—feet wet—slept some, walked some, and by daybreak was somewhat chilled.

"The wind abated and we stuck to our oars until about eleven o'clock, when we made Grindstone Island, weary and very hungry—ate a hearty dish of *sapon* and milk—rested about an hour—set off for Briton's Tavern on the American shore, where we were only ten minutes, as good luck would have it, before we engaged a passage for Cornwall in a Durham boat; and, a breeze coming up directly from the south, our American boats immediately hoisted sail and proceeded about thirty miles, when the wind changed, and we put into a bay on Grenadier Island about nine in the evening. Ate some supper at a house owned by Mr. Baxter —spread a sail upon the floor, and seven boatmen and four passengers camped before the fire.

"April 9th—Still a head wind. At 7 p.m. hoisted sail— at 1 a.m. arrived at a house on the Canada shore, and slept on the floor till daylight. April 10th—Left for Ogdensburg, where we arrived at 3 p.m. April 12th—Still a head wind. April 13th—Left Ogdensburg and arrived at Cornwall. April 14th—Left Cornwall and arrived at McGee's, Lake St. Francis. April 15th—Left McGee's and arrived at Montreal about 8 p.m. Travelling expenses from Kingston to Montreal, $9.75."[41]

In later years a trip eastward on the St. Lawrence was

[41]The diary of the Rev. Miles, quoted in Canniff, *op. cit.*, pp. 140-1.

not usually unpleasant, though a journey from York to Montreal took about two weeks. As one writer says, a man undertaking such a voyage "made his will and arranged his affairs, solemnly bade farewell to his family with far more feeling than a traveller in modern days would leave Quebec for Liverpool".[42] The·bateau trip from Kingston to Prescott was frequently pleasurable, the boats skimming merrily along among the Thousand Islands. The remainder of the descent to Montreal required more skill on the part of the boatmen, but very seldom was there any loss of cargo during the running of the rapids.

The downward trip took only from two to four days and was quite inexpensive, the charge for a passenger in 1828 being only 4s. 6d. between Prescott and Montreal, while the 140-mile trip by steamship and stage, though taking only one day, cost 31s. 6d. The voyage by bateau is described by a traveller as "enchanting and entertaining, cheap and expeditious. Distance is forgotten amidst the hilarity and music of these watermen".[43]

At each rapid it was usual for the bateaumen, and especially the conductor of a brigade, to perform some "slight and quick acts of ceremonial devotion"[44] to aid in avoiding the dangers in running the rapid; that there was great risk may be seen from the fact that the nine-mile Long Sault was sometimes run in fifteen minutes. John Ogden refers to the boatmen's "scrupulous demeanour as they passed the churches and monuments of religion", and states that churches were visited at the hours of devotion.[45]

Thomas Hamilton made the downward trip under very favourable conditions in 1833. He accompanied several officers, and the party were provided with seats beneath an awning. Hamilton wrote concerning the descent under the care of the French rivermen:

"A merrier set of beings it is scarcely possible to imagine. The buoyancy of their spirits was continually finding vent in song or laughter. . . . On approaching any formidable rapid, all is silent on board. The conductor is at

[42]Kingsford, op. cit., p. 11.
[43]John Ogden: A Tour through Upper and Lower Canada. 1799. p. 58.
[44]Joseph Pickering: Inquiries of an Emigrant. 1831. August 30, 1829.
[45]Ogden, op. cit., p. 45.

the helm, and each of the crew at his post. All eyes are steadfastly fixed on the countenance of the helmsman, whose commands seldom require to be expressed in words. Every look is understood and obeyed with the promptitude of men who know their peril. Accidents rarely occur, and in truth the danger is just imminent enough to create a pleasant degree of excitement in the *voyageur*. . . .

"We slept at a poor village, the name of which I forget. Our boatmen, who had all day been pulling at the oars, like true Canadians instead of going to bed got up a dance with the village girls, and the ball was only stopped by the re-embarkation of the party on the following morning. The whole crew were drunk, with the exception of the conductor, but the appearance of the first rapid sobered them in an instant."[46]   In fact so accustomed were the bateaumen to the navigation of their craft that a traveller observed that "with empty boats the man who steers is often the only one awake".[47]

The more extensive use of schooners on the lakes after the close of the War of 1812, and the introduction of steam navigation with the launching of the *Frontenac* and the *Ontario* in 1816-17, gradually put an end to the use of bateaux on Lakes Ontario and Erie. They remained for some years in local trade along the shores, and as ferryboats to load and unload steamships and schooners, which would anchor at some distance from land. In calm weather ships would sometimes approach close to shore or sand-bar, and passengers and goods could then be carried to land on the backs of the sailors. The construction of harbours ended this crude procedure, and also the use of bateaux in discharging and loading. The *Cobourg Star* of March 22, 1831, states that the "great inconvenience and risk of loading and unloading vessels in bateaux has been surmounted, and we had last summer the gratification of beholding steamboats of large burthen lying beside the Harbour Company's wharf".[48]

The last regular bateau service between Belleville and Montreal was that conducted by Messrs. Fanning and

[46]Thomas Hamilton: *Men and Manners in America*. 1833. Vol. II, pp. 338-342.
[47]Simcoe, *op. cit.*, September 17, 1794.
[48]*Cobourg Star*, March 22, 1831.

Covert. This line of boats continued in operation many years after the first steamship appeared on the Bay of Quinté; the service commenced in the spring as soon as the ice was out of the Bay, on one occasion (in 1830) as early as the end of March.

On the rapid section of the St. Lawrence the bateaux remained in use longer. In the late twenties a "steamship-and-stage" line of conveyances was extensively used on the American side of the St. Lawrence, and in the early thirties a similar service was available on the Canadian side. By this means the inconvenience of bateau travel was avoided by those who could afford to pay the higher rates. It was not until the early fifties that both bateaux and Durham boats were largely displaced by steamships, the use of which became possible over the entire Montreal-Prescott route only when the St. Lawrence canals were completed; for many years longer, however, the old boats remained in use among the inhabitants along the river, and in local trade.

Just as the first settlers on the lower lakes used bateaux to coast along the shore, carrying their grain to the mill and their produce to market, so the same boats were plied in later years on Lake Simcoe between Holland Landing and Barrie; and, as settlement spread northward towards Lake Huron in the forties and fifties, bateau and raft were invaluable to the first inhabitants. Many of the pioneers of Bruce County travelled by schooner up the lakes to Southampton, and then used bateaux or canoes to ascend the Saugeen River to the interior. Some of them proceeded fifteen miles in this manner, as far as Paisley, the boat often having to be towed against the strong current by one man while another kept it off shore with a pole. Other settlers made their way to Walkerton, and then built rafts which carried them and their supplies twenty miles or more down stream with the current.

But the march of time had put an end to the general use of the bateau. It was replaced by what an old-timer called "the ugliest species of craft that ever diversified a marine landscape",[49] though, of course, he saw it in the days when the large paddle-wheels which propelled it could be kept going only at the cost of filling the atmosphere with

[49]Dunlop, *op. cit.*, p. 54.

dense clouds of black smoke belched forth from two huge funnels. For nearly a century, however, bateau and Durham boat were indispensable to the inhabitants of Canada, and the craft furnish an excellent illustration of the ingenuity of man in surmounting the most difficult conditions of water transport which long characterised the navigation of the St. Lawrence River system.

CHAPTER IV

THE SAILING-SHIP

THE LOSS OF THE SPEEDY

"A more distressing and melancholy event has not occurred to
this place for many years,—nor does it often happen that such a
number of persons of respectability are collected in the same vessel.
Not less than nine widows, and we know not how many children,
have to lament the loss of their husbands and fathers. It is somewhat remarkable that it is the third or fourth accident of a similar
nature within these few years—the cause of which appears worthy
of the attention and investigation of persons conversant in the art
of shipbuilding."[1]

THERE has always been something romantic and intriguing
about "going down to the sea in ships". Whether it be
fishing smack or emigrant trader, Spanish galleon or East
India merchantman, the life of the sailor has always been
the loadstone tempting many a lad to run away to sea; and
it mattered not that the hardships were severe, the toil
unremitting, and the dangers ever-present, for was there
not that glorious independence of sailing before the mast
to "strands afar remote", of visiting regions very different from hum-drum civilisation,—perhaps even the opportunity to achieve fame and fortune?

The earliest sailing-ships built in Canada were two very
small vessels constructed by Pontgravé at Port Royal in
1606. In 1663 a *galiote,* or brigantine, was launched at
Quebec; and two years later Jean Talon, the "Great Intendant", arrived in Canada, and almost immediately commenced the building, at his own cost, of a vessel of 120 tons.
The following year a similar ship was launched, and the
construction of sailing-vessels soon became a well-established industry in French Canada.

The first sea-going vessels were known as *barques,* and
they were chiefly used to carry goods and furs between
Montreal and Quebec. In 1752 ten ships of from 40 to 100
tons were built in Canada, but the materials employed were
poor and the cost high. The Lake Champlain region furnished most of the timber used during the French period in
the construction of vessels and in trade. After the British

[1]*Upper Canada Gazette,* November 3, 1804.

conquest, and particularly in the early seventeen-seventies, shipping developed rapidly in Canada. The number of vessels engaged in fishing or trade increased from eighteen in 1769 to ninety-seven in 1775.

The general development in sailing-ships on 'the Great Lakes was from vessels of the brig, brigantine and barque types to the schooner of two masts, and in later days of three, four and five masts. The brig had two square-rigged masts, while the brigantine had the foremast square-rigged and the mainmast fore-and-aft rigged, like a schooner. A barque carried three masts, two being square-rigged, and the mizen schooner-rigged. The gradual change to the schooner occurred because it was more economical to operate, for less sailors were needed than were necessary to handle square-rigged ships.

The first sailing-vessels to navigate the waters of the Great Lakes were small craft called by the French *brigantines,* and they were used by early explorers in pursuing their discoveries and carrying on the fur trade. These boats were semi-open vessels, and not of the same type as the variant of the brig. Examples of this boat are described in the accounts of the explorations of such men as La Salle, La Motte and Hennepin. In 1678, just before winter set in, Hennepin left Fort Frontenac in a small brigantine of ten tons. The stormy weather forced the party to keep close to the north shore of Lake Ontario, and they were at times driven into the mouths of rivers for shelter; but after encountering many difficulties they reached Niagara early in December.

In 1679 La Salle built what is generally conceded to be the first sailing-ship to navigate Lake Erie and the upper lakes. This vessel, the *Griffon,* was of sixty tons, and was built at the mouth of Cayuga Creek, six miles above Niagara Falls. With the aid of sails and two tow-lines the Niagara River was ascended, and the *Griffon* launched upon an adventurous career on Lakes Erie, Huron and Michigan. Her sails and her seven guns made a great impression upon the Indians; but on the return trip from Green Bay, laden with furs, she was lost in a storm on Lake Huron with all on board.

As early as 1687 the French had three small vessels

Canada Steamship Lines' Marine Historical Collection   George A. Cuthbertson
THE BUILDING OF THE GRIFFIN, 1679
The blacksmith's forge may be seen at the rear left

W. H. Bartlett
THE LIGHT TOWER, NEAR COBOURG, 1840
Gull Light is about half way between Cobourg and Port Hope

H.M. SCHOONER ONONDAGA

A typical King's Ship of the seventeen-nineties. The Simcoes sailed
to Niagara in the *Onondaga* in 1792.

NAVY HALL, NIAGARA, 1792

engaged in transport on Lake Ontario, in addition to 198 bateaux and 142 canoes. In 1726 they built two small schooners and placed them in service between Fort Frontenac and Fort Niagara, and by 1741 there were four vessels on the lake. The first British warship, inaugurating a naval force on Lake Ontario which lasted almost a century, was a schooner forty feet long launched at Oswego in 1755. This boat was armed with twelve swivel guns, and fourteen oars were used to propel her when there was no wind. Both nations had sloops-of-war on the lake during the Seven Years' War, though the capture of Oswego by a French fleet in 1756 gave France complete control for about two years. In August, 1758, however, Colonel John Bradstreet put an end to French domination of Lake Ontario by sailing from Oswego to Kingston with a fleet and destroying the fort and the stores; nine French armed sloops were burned or captured during the raid.

The growth of shipping on the lower lakes was quite rapid after the British conquest. On May 29, 1767, the *Register* notes that "there are now four brigs, from forty to seventy tons, and sixteen armed deck-cutters on Lake Ontario". An official return dated July 30, 1778, gives a list of the vessels built on the lakes since 1759. All on the lower lakes were King's ships and, excepting one constructed at Michilimackinac in 1777, they were built at Oswego, Oswegatchie, Niagara, Navy Island or Detroit. On Lake Ontario had been launched five schooners, three sloops and four scows; on Lake Erie, seven schooners and six sloops; and one sloop each on Lakes Huron and Michigan, both of these being owned by merchants. Of the total it is noted that eleven were cast away or burned, four were "in service till decayed", and twelve were still in service: these were the sloop *Caldwell* and two scows on Lake Ontario; the schooners *Gage, Hope, Faith* and *Dunmore*, and the sloops *Angelica, Felicity* and *Adventure* on Lake Erie; the sloop *Welcome* on Lake Huron; and the sloop *Archangel* on Lake Michigan. In 1782 there were in use on Lake Ontario five schooners or sloops and four scows, and on Lake Erie eleven vessels.[2]

Upon the outbreak of the American Revolution all ships

[2]See E. A. Cruikshank: *Early Traders and Trade Routes in Ontario and the West, 1760-83.* (In *Transactions* of the Canadian Institute, Series 4, Vol. IV, pp. 310-13.)

and crews on Lake Ontario were impressed for the public service, and nothing larger than an open boat was allowed to be constructed for private use during the war years. This control of shipping by the government lasted until after the War of 1812, and most trade was carried on during this period by armed merchantmen and warships. There were continual complaints concerning the unsatisfactory manner in which the trade was conducted by the government ships.

During the course of the Revolutionary War the British Government built for use as transports a few warships at Niagara, and on Carleton Island, at the east end of Lake Ontario. One of the largest of these armed ships was the *Ontario*, a vessel of the snow type carrying twenty-two guns. In October, 1780, this boat left Niagara for Oswego, carrying a detachment of the King's Own Regiment. Nothing was ever heard of her after she left port, and the only relic of the wreck was a drum which was washed up on shore at the eastern end of Lake Ontario. One hundred and seventy-two men lost their lives in this marine tragedy, and it "produced a melancholy effect which long remained in the minds of those acquainted with the circumstances".[3] It was considered by one expert at the time of its construction that the *Ontario* was being built "too flat-bottomed, and that she would overset".[4]

More intimate details of the shipping on the lakes during the last ten or fifteen years of the century are available owing to the researches of Dr. William Canniff, the diary of Mrs. John Graves Simcoe, and the accounts of travel in Canada published by Isaac Weld and the Duc de la Rochefoucauld-Liancourt. From these sources may be obtained not only the size and general characteristics of the ships, but also valuable information concerning the crews and their wages, the regulations under which the boats carried passengers and freight, and many minor details of great interest.

In 1783 the first Loyalist settlers began to arrive in the vicinity of Kingston, and soon afterwards ships were being

[3]Reminiscences of Colonel John Clark, Niagara. (Coventry Papers, Public Archives of Canada.)
[4]Quoted in Cruikshank, *op. cit.*, p. 312. The same man (Glennie) states that 133 perished in the disaster.

built there for the British naval force on Lake Ontario. The first vessels were constructed "at Murney's Point and at Navy Point",⁵ presumably the old names for Point Frederick and Point Henry, respectively. In 1787 there were three vessels sailing Lake Ontario, and two others being built. Surveyor Collins proposed Carleton Island as affording the best shelter for a dockyard, but his recommendation was rejected, and in 1788, when Kingston was selected as the principal military and naval station on Lake Ontario, the dockyard and storehouses were established at Haldimand Cove.

On July 1, 1792, Lieutenant-Governor Simcoe and his wife arrived at Kingston *en route* to Niagara, and the following day they visited the shipyard across the bay. Concerning the Provincial Marine on Lake Ontario Mrs. Simcoe wrote:

"There are two gunboats lately built on a very bad construction. Col. Simcoe calls them the *Bear* and the *Buffalo* as they are so unscientifically built, and intends they shall aid in carrying provisions to Niagara. The present establishment of vessels on this lake consists of the *Onondaga* and *Mississaga,* named after the Indian tribes, top-sailed schooners of about 80 tons, and the *Caldwell,* named after Col. Caldwell, which is a sloop. They transport all the troops and provisions from hence for the garrison of Niagara, Forts Erie and Detroit."⁶

When La Rochefoucauld visited Canada in 1795 he found that the Royal Navy on Lake Ontario consisted of "six vessels, two of which are small gunboats stationed at York". The *Mohawk* had just been built, and was similar to the *Onondaga,* which carried twelve guns. He states that the ships never lasted longer than six or eight years, for they "are built of timber fresh cut down, and not seasoned". He found also that a large amount of labour and expense was necessary to keep them in running order, "the timbers of the *Mississaga,* which was built three years ago, being almost all rotten".⁷ Isaac Weld also observed that vessels

⁵William Canniff: *History of the Settlement of Upper Canada.* 1869. p. 149.
⁶*Diary of Mrs. John Graves Simcoe,* July 2, 1792.
⁷Duc de la Rochefoucauld-Liancourt: *Travels through the United States of North America.* 1799. See particularly Vol. I, pp. 271-6 and 289-90.

wore out quickly, but he said it was "owing to the fresh water".[8]

The season of navigation was usually about seven months. On November 5, 1792, while at Niagara, Mrs. Simcoe notes in her diary that "the ships sail for Kingston this week, and remain there closed up by the ice in that harbour until April".[9] The length of a voyage by sailing-ship depended entirely upon the wind. The Simcoes were three days on the *Onondaga* in travelling from Kingston to Niagara in July, 1792; but on another occasion the voyage was made in twenty-two hours. The sloop *Sophia* made a record trip of eighteen hours between Kingston and Queenston in 1795. Similarly the passage from Niagara to York might take a day or more; but the *Mississaga* once made it in four hours.

The ships were operated under considerable difficulties, for sailors were not easily obtained in early Upper Canada. Some were brought from the Atlantic coast, but Isaac Weld observed in 1796 that men "from the seaports cannot be got except at high wages, and have to be kept over the winter".[10] La Rochefoucauld learned that seamen's wages were from eight to ten dollars a month, the officers being paid at a higher rate, up to $2 a day for captains.[11] Mrs. Simcoe noticed when travelling on the *Onondaga*, in charge of Commodore Beaton, that "the men who navigate the ships on this lake have little nautical knowledge, and never keep a log-book. This afternoon we were near aground".[12]

In the almost entire absence of merchant vessels, the King's ships carried most of the freight that passed up and down the lake between Kingston, York and Queenston. The greater part of the traffic consisted of merchandise to Queenston, and furs back to Kingston; and the usual rate was 36s. per ton, almost as much as for the Atlantic crossing. In 1795 La Rochefoucauld noticed that of the four gunboats on Lake Ontario, "two are constantly employed in transporting merchandise". He was informed that it was the Governor's intention to build ten smaller gunboats on

---

[8]Isaac Weld: *Travels through the States of North America.* 1799. See Chapter XXX, especially pp. 284-8.
[9]Simcoe, *op. cit.*, November 5, 1792.
[10]Weld, *ibid.*
[11]La Rochefoucauld-Liancourt, *ibid.*
[12]Simcoe, *op. cit.*, July 23, 1792.

Lake Ontario, and ten on Lake Erie.[13] In 1796 Weld found
that there were three King's ships of about 200 tons, carrying eight to twelve guns; and also several gunboats, which
were at that time out of commission. He describes as follows the method by which the government schooners carried
on trade: "The naval officers of these vessels, if they be
not otherwise engaged, are allowed to carry a cargo of
merchandise when they sail from one port to another, the
freight of which is their perquisite. They likewise have the
liberty and are constantly in the practice of carrying
passengers across the lake at an established price."[14]

The first carriage of passengers by the King's ships occurred in 1791, and the fare was two guineas, wines included, a moderate charge when it is considered that a
voyage from Kingston to Niagara might last a week in unfavourable weather. The steerage passage cost one guinea.
In 1796 Weld found the accommodation on board ship quite
pleasant, and "the cabin table well-served, including port
and sherry wine".[15] A few details of interest concerning
travel on these ships are found in Mrs. Simcoe's diary.
Concerning her first trip to Toronto she wrote: "We embarked on board the *Mississaga,* the band playing in the
ship. It was dark, so I went to bed and slept until eight
o'clock the next morning, when I found myself in the
harbour of Toronto."[16] In December, 1793, she notes that
the *Onondaga* "ran aground on the west side of Gibraltar
Point"[17] (now Hanlan's) ; but, after being first abandoned,
it was finally hauled off the sandbar.

Special signals were used in York when the King's ships
were ordered to sail. They were to be flown from the
mast-head of the vessels, and repeated at the blockhouse
near the Don, as the following announcement issued from
the Lieutenant-Governor's office shows:

"Notice is hereby given that when the King's Vessels
have received their orders to proceed from hence to Niagara
or to Kingston the following signal will be hoisted at the
Foretop Gallant Mast Head, and repeated from the Block-

[13]La Rochefoucauld-Liancourt, *ibid.*
[14]Weld, *ibid.*   [15]*Ibid.*
[16]Simcoe, *op. cit.,* May 29, 1793.
[17]*Ibid.,* December 8, 1793.

452 EARLY LIFE IN UPPER CANADA

house in town, viz.: To Niagara, a White Flag; to Kingston, a Blue Flag."[18]

The usual method of announcing to intending travellers that a vessel was about to leave port was to blow repeated blasts on a long tin horn, which was sounded at intervals previous to their casting loose and at the moment of departure. A King's ship long prominent on the lake, and one which was frequently used by Lieutenant-Governors Hunter and Gore, was the *Toronto* (or *Toronto Yacht*), built in 1799 by a Loyalist, Joseph Dennis. Just previous to the opening of the War of 1812 she ran aground near Gibraltar Point and had to be abandoned. Her hull was for many years a conspicuous object and attracted many visitors. An authority describes as follows the accommodations which early travellers found aboard these ships of the Provincial Marine:

"First-class passenger and military officers were accommodated aft in tiny two- and three-berth cabins which opened off a main saloon. Those who could not pay for cabins were forced to make themselves as comfortable as circumstances permitted. The cabins were badly lighted and ill-ventilated. Lighting came from windows or a skylight by day. Candles were used at night for illumination. Furnishings were simple and all passengers carried their own bedding. . . . The berths, or bunks, were springless affairs that depended for all comfort on the mattresses. On some of the better vessels these were filled with feathers".[19]

While the government retained control of all shipping on Lake Ontario, yet it appears that they did not restrict the building of merchantmen except during war years. After 1790 a few of these ships began to appear, the first Canadian vessel being (according to Canniff) the *York*, built

[18]*Upper Canada Gazette*, June 5, 1802. A large amount of information
    with reference to sailing-ships on Lake Ontario may be found in
    Henry Scadding: *Toronto of Old*. 1873. pp. 508-576. Most of
    the descriptions and advertisements therein contained are from
    the *Gazette* and other contemporary newspapers, but in some
    instances the files from which Dr. Scadding quotes have since
    been lost or burned.
[19]George A. Cuthbertson: *The Good Old Days*, in *C. S. L. Chart*,
    (published by the Canada Steamship Lines), Volume 17, No. 3.
    Cuthbertson's *Freshwater: a History and a Narrative of the Great
    Lakes* (1931) is a valuable and handsomely produced account
    of Canadian navigation, particularly by sail and steam.

at the mouth of the Niagara River in 1792.[20] In the following year the *Simcoe* was constructed on Simcoe Island for the North-West Company, and it was commanded by Henry Murney. Another merchantman, the *Lady Dorchester*, was also sailing Lake Ontario in 1793. In the same year Joel Stone, the Loyalist founder of Gananoque, launched the *Leeds Trader*, one of the earliest ships to sail the upper St. Lawrence. In 1793 twenty-six sailings from Kingston harbour were recorded, but most, if not all of the vessels concerned were King's ships. By 1795, however, at least three merchant vessels were sailing Lake Ontario; their size was from sixty to one hundred tons, and they made eleven voyages in that year. In 1796 Isaac Weld learned during his travels on the lake that "several decked merchant vessels, schooners and sloops of from fifty to two hundred tons, and also numberless large bateaux, are kept employed on Lake Ontario. There are no United States' boats except bateaux".[21]

Previous to 1800 several other merchant ships were launched. The *Mohawk*, owned by the North-West Company, was engaging in trade before the close of the century. In 1798 Henry Murney built the *Prince Edward* at the Stone Mills in Marysburgh Township, Bay of Quinté. This notable ship was long in use on Lake Ontario, and was built entirely of red cedar, an exceedingly durable wood then common along the Bay. She was large enough to allow 700 barrels of flour to be stowed beneath her hatches. During the War of 1812 the *Prince Edward* was used by the government as an armed vessel.

During the last years of the eighteenth and early years of the nineteenth century such mail and dispatches as arrived irregularly at Kingston from Montreal were carried on the government ships to Niagara, and on to Detroit by privately-owned schooners engaged in the fur trade. Goods were portaged from Niagara to Fort Chippawa, three miles above the Falls, and then carried by bateau to Fort Erie. Fifty or sixty wagons passed daily in the carriage of freight over the portage road around Niagara Falls.

Early travellers seldom sailed Lake Erie, and conse-

[20]William Canniff: *Canadian Steam Navigation.* (Tackabury's *Atlas of the Dominion of Canada.* 1875. p. 69.)
[21]Weld, *ibid.*

quently our knowledge of shipping in that region is less complete. Merchant ships were on the lake much earlier than they were employed on Lake Ontario, but there were not usually as many King's ships in commission. An early issue of the Detroit *Tribune* stated that four vessels plied on Lake Erie and the Detroit River in 1766. These were the *Gladwin, Lady Charlotte, Victory* and *Boston;* another early boat was the *Beaver.* The vessels engaged in the carriage of troops, provisions and furs between Fort Erie and Detroit, the voyage taking from six to nine days. All of these ships, with the exception of the *Beaver,* were launched in 1763-4. In 1767 the *Brunswick* was built, and the *Enterprise* was constructed at Detroit in 1769. In 1780 there was a large dockyard at Detroit and nine vessels there, while in 1796 twelve merchant vessels were owned in the town, which passed from British to American control in that year.[22]

The chief King's ships on Lake Erie in the late seventeen-nineties were the *Ottawa* and the *Chippawa.* On May 3, 1796, Mrs. Simcoe noted in her diary that the former ship left Detroit during a snow storm on April 27th, and made the trip to Fort Erie in thirty-six hours.[23] During the spring of 1796 the *Francis* was launched on Lake Erie by the government and named after Governor Simcoe's son. In 1797 the schooner *Washington* was built near Erie, Pennsylvania, but after a year's service on Lake Erie it was brought on wheels around Niagara to Lake Ontario.

When Isaac Weld visited the Detroit River during his travels in Canada in 1796 he found it "crowded with Indian canoes, bateaux, sailing-ships, and several pleasure boats of officers of the garrison of the new fort Malden".[24] At that time sailing was almost the only amusement of the officers at the ports. When the Simcoes were in Kingston in 1792 Mrs. Simcoe wrote in her diary: "We sailed half a league this evening in a pretty boat of Mr. Clark's, attended by music, to Garden Island, opposite Kingston."[25]

When the new century opened, shipbuilding on Lake Ontario was largely in control of the government, and was

[22]Most of this information is quoted from an issue of the Detroit *Tribune* by Canniff in his *History of Upper Canada*, pp. 147-8.
[23]Simcoe, *op. cit.*, May 3, 1796.
[24]Weld, *op. cit.*, p. 343.   [25]Simcoe, *op. cit.*, July 16, 1792.

chiefly of small vessels thirty to sixty feet long. As settlement increased, the vessels gradually became larger. The
King's ships were augmented at this time by the launching
of the schooners *Duke of Kent* and *Speedy,* the latter of
which was soon to figure in a notable marine tragedy. In
October, 1804, this vessel, under Captain Paxton, was proceeding from York to Newcastle, the proposed capital of
the Newcastle District, on Presqu'île Point. On board were
Mr. Justice Cochrane and various other officials, several
witnesses, and an Indian prisoner charged with murder.
The trial was to take place on the arrival of the ship at
Newcastle, but, though the vessel was sighted off the Point
on the evening of October 8th, before she could gain shelter
she was overwhelmed by a hurricane and snow storm, and
all on board, numbering thirty or forty persons, were lost.
Pieces of the wreck were afterwards picked up on the
opposite shore.

The inconvenience and loss which was characteristic of
travel by sailing-ship is further illustrated by three items
of news from one issue of a contemporary publication:

"On Thursday night last a boat arrived here from
Schenectady, which place she left on the 22nd ult. She
passed the York, sticking on a rock off the Devil's Nose; no
prospects of getting her off."

"A small deck-boat lately sprang a leak twelve miles distant from Oswego. The people on board, many of whom
were passengers, were taken off by a vessel passing, when
she instantly sank; cargo and all lost."

"A vessel supposed to be the *Genesee* schooner has been
two days endeavouring to come in. It is a singular misfortune that this vessel sailed more than a month ago from
Oswego laden for this place, and has been several times
in sight, and been driven back by heavy winds."[26]

In October, 1796, Isaac Weld experienced a stormy
trip in a Lake Erie schooner. With a number of other passengers he embarked at Malden (Amherstburg) in a vessel
of seventy tons. The only difference between cabin and
steerage passage was the side of the boat upon which the
accommodations were situated, though the cabin passengers
had to pay extra for the services which they did not receive.

[26]Niagara *Canada Constellation,* December 7, 1799.

A heavy wind arose, and almost all of the twenty-six passengers which crowded the ship were sea-sick; but the captain refused the entreaties to turn back, until the storm waxed so furious that he had no choice. A shelter was finally obtained between the Bass Islands, Put-in Bay; but, at four o'clock the next morning the anchor gave way, forcing the ship to put to sea, or be driven on the rocky shore. Unfortunately, however, the sailors hoisted the mainsail when they were ordered to raise only the jib, and their error led to the boat's being whirled towards the rocks, from which it was kept only by casting anchor; though only a stone's throw from the shore, and held by an anchor that might any minute give way, Weld and his companions ate their breakfast "regardless of the impending danger, and afterwards sat down to a game of cards".

Scarcely had they been an hour at the game when the vessel began to drift, and the cry "All hands aloft" was heard. Just as Weld reached the deck the ship struck, and this was soon repeated with every wave: the women in the hold shrieked (as well they might), while axes were raised to cut down the masts.

A passenger with experience in the navy advised the captain not to prevent all escape by such a course of action, though he considered that the yards and topmasts should be cut away. His advice was taken, and for four hours they expected the boat to be dashed to pieces any minute. The passengers began to gather their valuables and write their wills as the waves dashed over the ship, (one man being so heavy with dollars that he must have sunk immediately!); but after a night of suspense the wind moderated, and then changed, so that the vessel was able to put to sea again, and, in an almost disabled condition, reached Fort Erie four days later, "after a most disagreeable passage."[27]

In order to help defray the cost of lighthouses on Lake Ontario the legislature passed an Act in 1803 imposing a "lighthouse duty" of 3d. per ton of each vessel entering the ports of Kingston, York and Niagara. This tax did not fall with undue heaviness upon any type of sailing craft, but when the steamships came upon the lake there was a protest at the amount they had to pay. The owners of the

[27] Weld, *op. cit.*, pp. 417-24.

Frontenac (launched in 1816) were partially relieved of the tax after presenting petitions to parliament.

During the War of 1812 both Great Britain and the United States had fleets of warships on the lower lakes. In 1813 Sir James Yeo's British fleet on Lake Ontario consisted of the frigate *Wolfe*, and the smaller vessels *Royal George, Prince Regent, Earl of Moira, Simcoe, Duke of Gloucester* and *Seneca*. The American fleet under Commodore Chauncey held control of the lake during most of 1813, the chief ships being the *President Madison*, the *Oneida*, the *General Pike*, and five single-gun schooners, all of which took part in the first attack upon York on April 27th. Four additional schooners accompanied the same fleet on a second raid upon the capital on July 31st of the same year. Two of the American schooners, the *Hamilton* and the *Scourge*, capsized in a storm on August 8th, and two others, the *Growler* and the *Julia*, were captured on the 10th by the British fleet.

In 1814 the British launched, among others, the *Princess Charlotte* and the *St. Lawrence*, the latter being 190 feet long with 102 guns, the largest fresh-water warship ever built. These vessels put an end to the American control of Lake Ontario, the additions to the United States fleet during 1814 consisting only of the *Superior* and the *Mohawk*.

The British fleet on Lake Erie in 1813 was made up of the brigs *Detroit, Queen Charlotte, General Hunter* and *Lord Prevost*, and two schooners, the *Chippawa* and *Little Belt*. The Americans had a still smaller fleet in the early part of the year, but quickly built additional ships at Erie, Pennsylvania. Under the command of Commodore Perry the American fleet was made up of the *Lawrence*, the *Niagara*, the schooners *Scorpion* and *Ariel*, and the gunboats *Somers, Porcupine, Tigress* and *Trippe*. The guns of the British fleet out-ranged those of the American ships, but many of them were unworkable through faulty equipment. The Americans, on the other hand, outnumbered the *British* in ships, guns and men, and by ordering his fleet to close up at short range as quickly as possible Perry defeated the British under Commander Barclay, on September 10, 1813, with the result that for a year no British ship sailed Lake

Erie.   By 1814 the Americans had added a number of schooners to their fleet, among them the *Caledonia* and the *Ohio*.

On the upper lakes there were in 1814 no vessels except two small North-West Company boats, the *Mink* on Lake Huron, and the *Perseverance* on Lake Superior, and one British schooner, the *Nancy*, which had been converted into a warship.   A large American expedition set out from Detroit to capture Michilimackinac and drive these ships from the lakes.   The American fleet consisted of the *Lawrence*, the *Niagara*, the *Scorpion*, the *Tigress*, the *Caledonia*, and the *General Hunter* and, though unsuccessful in the attack on Michilimackinac, they destroyed the two small ships of the North-West Company, and then proceeded to seek out the *Nancy*.

This deservedly famous schooner was launched at Detroit in 1789.   She was described as "a perfect masterpiece of workmanship and beauty", and had a figurehead of "a lady dressed in the present fashion, with a hat and feather".[28]   The *Nancy* made many voyages from Fort Erie with cargoes for the Grand Portage at Fort William.   In later years she was similarly employed by the North-West Company on Lakes Erie, Huron and Michigan, and had the reputation of being the fastest and most reliable boat sailing the lakes.   Upon the outbreak of war she entered the government service, and for two years was active in the upper lakes.   At the time of the American attack on Michilimackinac the *Nancy* was sailing Lake Huron.   Three American ships attacked her, and though she put up a gallant resistance, the odds were too great, and the ship had to be burned in the Nottawasaga River.   One hundred and eleven years later the stern of the sunken schooner was discovered protruding out of the water, and the vessel has since been raised and preserved as a memorial of her distinguished services in 1813-14.

As settlement proceeded in Upper Canada after the War of 1812 the number of schooners rapidly increased.   They

28Quoted in E. A. Cruikshank: *An Episode in the War of 1812*. (In Ontario Historical Society, *Papers and Records*, Vol. IX, p. 75.) For a full account of the career of the *Nancy*, see C. H. J. Snider: *The Story of the Nancy and other Eighteen-twelvers*. 1926.

were the grain carriers, and a large trade in lumber, potash and other products soon developed with the United States, as well as local commerce between lake ports on the Canadian side; consequently the nickname "wooden wagons" came to be very appropriately used for sailing craft. When George Heriot visited Kingston he found "the number of vessels in the employ of merchants considerable", and he noticed that they were usually built of red cedar or oak;[29] but the former valuable wood soon became too scarce for such general use. When the first steamship began to operate on Lake Ontario in 1816 there were more than sixty schooners engaged in passenger or freight service; on Lake Erie, however, the total tonnage at that time was only 2,067.

In later years Port Burwell was one of the most noted centres of shipbuilding on Lake Erie. Between 1834 and 1875 some forty-two vessels were constructed there. Long after steamships became common, small sloops and schooners were frequently depended upon for the transit of both passengers and freight, particularly for local trade on the Canadian side. Owners of sailing-vessels also competed successfully in the commerce between the Canadian shore and Ohio ports.

For many years there was very inferior harbour or even wharf accommodation at the ports along the Canadian shores of the lakes, and ships had often to anchor at a distance from shore while bateaux carried passengers and goods to and from the vessel. Very few schooners were constructed for any other purpose than the carriage of freight, and accommodations for passengers were usually very unsatisfactory; while storms or adverse winds frequently delayed the ships and prevented their stopping at ports where (as was usually the case in early times) no harbours had been constructed. Mrs. Frances Stewart, an early settler near Peterborough, made a trip by schooner from York to Cobourg in 1822, and found the experience very unpleasant. The captain proved to be "a rough, surly, vulgar wretch", who took every opportunity to annoy his passengers; but when he was told his conduct would be reported he became as cringing as he had formerly been unbearable. Towards evening a storm arose and prevented an approach to

[29]George Heriot: *Travels through the Canadas.* 1807. pp. 131-2.

Cobourg, where there was merely a landing-wharf. The ship was driven back towards York during the night; but the next day the weather moderated and a landing was made at Cobourg.[30]

An example of rates and conditions of passage in a vessel which attempted to adhere to a schedule is provided by an early advertisement, which announces that the *Duke of Richmond*, a sloop of 100 tons built at York in 1820, was scheduled to leave York for Niagara "Monday, Wednesday and Friday at 9 a.m. Leave Niagara on Tuesday, Thursday and Saturday at 10 a.m., between July and September"; and after that, "according to notice". The commander, Edward Oates, stated his rates of passage as follows: "After cabin, ten shillings; fore cabin, 6s. 6d.; sixty lbs. of baggage allowed for each passenger, but over that, 9d. per cwt., or 2s. per barrel bulk".[31]

While many a sailing-ship provided a satisfactory passenger service under favourable weather conditions, it may be assumed that the voyage of the Rev. Isaac Fidler in 1831 was characteristic of travel by lake schooner:

"On our arrival at Oswego I proceeded to the harbour in quest of a trading vessel bound for York, in Canada, and had the good fortune to find one that would sail in an hour. I agreed with the captain for $9 for myself, family and baggage, and he on his part assured me he would land me safe in twenty-four hours. Our provision was included in the fare. Instead of reaching York in one day we were five days on the lake. . . . The cabin of the vessel served for the sitting, eating and sleeping room of passengers, captain and crew. . . . The food generally placed before us for dinner was salt pork, potatoes, bread, water and salt; tea, bread and butter, and sometimes salt pork,—for breakfast and tea; no supper."[32]

A number of sailing-ships were converted into steamers when steam navigation began to assume importance. One

[30]Frances Stewart: *Our Forest Home*. 1889. 2nd Edition, 1902, pp. 17-18.
[31]Quoted in Barlow Cumberland: *Canoe, Sail and Steam*. (*Canadian Magazine*, Vol. XLII, p. 88.)
[32]Isaac Fidler: *Observations on the Professions, Literature, Manners and Emigration in the United States and Canada*. 1833. pp. 253-6. A passage of six days between Prescott and York, and one of two and one-half days from Niagara to York, are described in Henry Scadding: *Toronto of Old*. 1873. p. 541.

of these was the *Niagara*, "an old schooner into which an engine had been placed". The Rev. Anson Green travelled in this boat in 1828 and found it anything but pleasant: "The lake was rough, and I was fearfully sick, constantly wishing that I was on my saddle again."[33] His experience was typical of the misfortunes of many a traveller, but land transport was no better, for the stage-coach was just as unpleasant in its own way.

Among those who had a fleet of schooners engaged in the Lake Ontario trade in the thirties was Daniel Conant, who lived near Oshawa. One of his ships, the *Industry*, was lost in an ice floe in December, 1837, while taking Rebellion refugees across the lake to Oswego. Those on board narrowly escaped death, but after great difficulties reached the American shore.[34]

Other remarkably adventurous voyages took place from time to time. In the early twenties Captain Samuel Ward, an American residing on the St. Clair River, took his schooner, the *St. Clair*, to New York City *viâ* the Erie Canal, then under construction. He had to unship the masts at Buffalo and reset them in his schooner on the Hudson. Soon after the building of the St. Lawrence canals a number of Great Lakes schooners made notable voyages to the ocean. In 1847 the *New Brunswick* of St. Catharines sailed with grain for Liverpool, and was the first lake craft to cross the Atlantic. Several other ships had made the same voyage by the middle of the century. In 1849 the American barquentine *Eureka* sailed with passengers from Cleveland to the Atlantic, and continued around Cape Horn to California. In 1856 the *Madeira Pet* was the first English ship to reach Chicago from Liverpool.

The first American vessel to sail across the Atlantic and return with a cargo was the barque *J. C. Kershaw*. On July 22, 1857, she left Detroit with a cargo of lumber, and returned from Liverpool in the autumn, laden with iron and crockery; but as the canals were closed for the winter she

---

[33] Anson Green: *Life and Times*. 1877. p. 123.
[34] See *infra*, Section V, Chapter V. Winter voyages by sailing-ships were not uncommon. In the *Niagara Herald* of January 29, 1829, appears an advertisement announcing that "during the continuance of the present open season . . . . the fast-sailing schooner *George Canning*, commanded by Capt. J. Whitney, ... will ply as a Packet between York and Niagara."

did not reach Detroit until navigation opened in 1858.
During 1858 and 1859 twenty-seven other sailing-vessels
made the trip from the Great Lakes to Europe.

Before the building of the first canal lock of commercial
importance at the American Sault, some shipowners had
portaged their schooners around the rapids at Sault Ste.
Marie. Most traffic, however, was trans-shipped between
Lakes Huron and Superior until a canal over a mile in
length was constructed in 1855 by the State of Michigan
at a cost of about $1,000,000; this achievement ranks in
importance with the construction of the St. Lawrence
canals.

The large three-, four-, and five-masted schooners were
in use chiefly after the introduction of steamships. John
Howison, who travelled in Canada just after the first steamers had begun operations on the lakes, stated that "the
steamboat now monopolizes almost all the carrying business,
to the great detriment and annoyance of the owners of
(sailing) vessels";[35] but the wish must have been father to
the thought, for such a generalisation was premature.
While many may have feared that the heyday of the sailing-
ship was past, yet for sixty years the schooner was able to
compete successfully with the steamship in the carriage of
freight. Marine engines and boilers long remained expensive, and the coal necessary to supply the power occupied
space which the sailing-ship could utilise for cargo; consequently many a sailing-vessel was financially successful,
while some of the smaller steamers were run at a loss.

The palmiest days of the lake schooners were between
1845 and 1862. There were sailing-ships of every type, built
by professionals and amateurs; wood was cheap, and many
a schooner was a floating lumber yard of squared timbers
of pine or oak. Not a few farmers lumbered their forest
land in the winter and turned their hand to ship-carpentry
in the spring, building their own boats for the lake
trade, which was frequently quite remunerative. In the
fifties all lake ports were similar to Cobourg, which included
among its citizens a large quota of captains, sailors, fishermen and shipwrights; its harbour was a sea of masts, its

35John Howison: *Sketches of Upper Canada*. 1821. 3rd Edition, 1825,
    p. 74.

wharves hummed with activity, and the song of the jolly tar filled the air. All along the shores of Ontario and Erie, ports flourished which are now not even names. Many a schooner would "land" anywhere if a cargo were promised, but lack of shelter often forced a hasty retreat if the wind changed. Ports of call included mouths of creeks and other mere anchorages:

"Between Hamilton, at the head of the lake, and Cobourg, half way towards its foot, were two dozen or so, Wellington Square, Port Nelson, Bronté, Oakville, the Anchorage Farm, Port Credit, Ducks Bay, the Etobicoke mouth, the Dutchman's Bar, Mimico Creek, the Humber mouth, and the Humber Mills, Toronto, Highland Creek, Port Union, Dunbarton, Frenchman's Bay and Fairport—these last three in one—Duffin's Creek, Port Whitby, Darlington, Bond Head Harbour, Port Hope, and possibly others. I have skipped, for example, the mouth of the Rouge, where small vessels loaded, and one three-master was built. Some of these places had not even a wharf; schooners 'anchored off', and their cargoes were floated out to them".[36]

In 1863 schooners to the number of 1,040 sailed the Great Lakes, and there were 337 other craft—barques, brigs, sloops and barges— which brought the total of sailing-ships to 1,377. At that time 136 side-wheel steamers and 258 propellers and tugs made up the steam craft. In the late sixties, however, the railway began to compete successfully for the freight traffic, and the steamboat had long since monopolized the lake passenger service. In the eighties the schooners began to dwindle rapidly in numbers and importance, though a few remained until the present century as "stone-hookers", or in the transport of coal across the lakes into Canada. One of the last coal schooners in regular service was the *Charlie Marshall* of Cobourg. This boat was to be seen until the early years of the Great War, but, like the few others left on the Lakes, went eastward down the St. Lawrence, where war-time prices were commanded by these old-timers.

It took about one hundred years for the steamship to replace the sailing-ship on the ocean. Until the forties the

[36]C. H. J. Snider: *Wooden Wagons and Iron Rails.* (In *Canadian National Railways Magazine*, October, 1931, p. 8.)

Canadian mails crossed the Atlantic by sailing-vessel, but by that time the steamship had proved its worth, and by transferring the mails to it the average time for a letter to cross was only one-third of what it had been. But in 1854 the port of Montreal was visited by 174 sailing-ships and only six ocean steamers, and even in 1880 the sailing-ships entering that harbour slightly outnumbered the steamships.

In the last forty years, however, the decrease in sailing-vessels on both ocean and lake has been very rapid. In 1890 there were more than five times as many steamships, while in 1907, out of 742 vessels which called at Montreal, only eighteen were schooners. During the same period the change in material from wood to metal, and the great development in steam power, have caused a decline in shipbuilding in Canada which amounts almost to the extinction of the industry. In 1875 about 500 vessels of all types were constructed in Canada, while in 1900 only twenty-nine were built.

The sailing-ship is fast becoming a curiosity on the Great Lakes. Until the Great War an odd vessel using sails might be seen engaged in fishing, but motor-boats and steam tugs are now used exclusively in that industry. As recently as 1929 a large schooner, the *Our Son*, was still engaged in trade in the upper lakes;[37] but this ship, the last of its kind, was lost in a storm on Lake Michigan in that year. Such sailing craft as still remain above water will evidently not be long among us. On two occasions a century ago old schooners came to an ignoble end by being sent over Niagara Falls in order to provide a spectacle for the curious and attract trade to the taverns; just as, in the present day, an occasional old ship which long withstood the ravages of time ends its existence in flames at Sunnyside Beach to fill the cash-registers of an amusement park. In this age of speed and power, racing yachts are almost the sole survivals of the vessels which for centuries provided the only means of long-distance travel by water.

[37]While an occasional reference has been made to sailing-ships on the upper lakes it has not been attempted to cover these waters in this essay; to do so adequately will require a separate chapter.

CHAPTER V

THE STEAMSHIP

"But your march of improvement is a sore destroyer of the romantic and picturesque. A gentleman about to take such a journey nowadays orders his servant to pack his portmanteau and put it on board the *John Molson* or any of his family, . . . and away you go smoking and splashing and wallopping along at the rate of ten knots an hour in the ugliest species of craft that ever diversified a marine landscape."

"TIGER" DUNLOP (1832).[1]

THE true forerunner of the steamboat was the horse-boat, a vessel adapted to provide ferryage where the route was short and sheltered. Paddle-wheels were used on horse-boats, but the power was not only vastly inferior to that generated by steam, but there was also a difference in the arrangement by which the power was transferred to the wheels. The steam-engine had been efficiently used for more than a quarter of a century on land, and the wheels for many years on the horse-boat, before the two were combined in the steamboat. As early as 1793 horse-boats worked by four horses were in operation on the Niagara River at Niagara, Queenstown and Fort Erie. Some years later a similar means of transport was in use on Lake St. Francis, where the low, swampy land in the front of Glengarry made land transport difficult, if not impossible.

In later years the horse-boat was commonly employed as a ferry in most parts of Upper Canada, succeeding the canoe and bateau for that purpose, and being succeeded in turn by the steam ferry. As late as 1850 a horse-boat was in use in the harbour of Toronto. This was the *Peninsula Packet*, advertised as a "safe and convenient" means of reaching what is now Toronto Island, a popular pleasure resort.[2] The *Packet* was operated by five horses, and it was taken off the route only in 1850, when it was succeeded as a ferry-boat by the small steamer *Victoria*.

The method of operation of horse-boats is described in John Ross Robertson's *Landmarks of Toronto*, with refer-

[1]William Dunlop: *Statistical Sketches of Upper Canada*. 1832. p. 54.
[2]See John Ross Robertson: *Landmarks of Toronto*. 1894-1914. Vol. II, p. 884.

ence to the *Peninsula Packet* and its predecessors. The paddles which propelled the boat were "set in motion by two horses who trod on a circular table set flush with the deck in its centre. This table as it revolved worked upon rollers, which, being connected with the shaft, set the paddles in motion. The horses were stationary; the table on which they trod was furnished with ridges of wood radiating like spokes from the centre, which the horses caught with their feet, thus setting the table in motion. For some time the boat was worked by only two horses, but after about two years an alteration was effected in the arrangements, and in the vessel as well: instead of two horses, five were introduced, and they walked round and round the deck exactly as horses do when employed in working a threshing-machine, and the vessel was set in motion precisely as such a machine is".[3]

The atmospheric steam-engine was first invented by the Marquis of Worcester in 1663. As early as the reign of Queen Anne wasteful and clumsy engines were being used to pump water in the mines of Cornwall, England; and, though these crude machines were somewhat improved by Newcomen and Smeaton, they were still very imperfect when James Watt began his experiments in the construction of steam-engines. In 1769 Watt perfected the existing engine to such an extent that he is considered its inventor.

It was over thirty years, however, before a satisfactory application of the principle of steam power was made to propel boats, though as early as 1543 a Spaniard had made an unsuccessful attempt to operate a steamship in the harbour of Barcelona. The first satisfactory steamship was Symington's *Charlotte Dundas,* which towed vessels on the Forth and Clyde Canal in 1803. This boat was quite successful, but, as its waves were found to wash away the banks of the canal, it was forced to discontinue operations.

British manufacturers were early as famous for steam-engines as they have been in modern times for powerful gasoline motors; and among those who examined Symington's boat and engine was an American, Robert Fulton, who used a British engine in the *Clermont,* which he successfully operated on the Hudson River in 1807-8. The second steam-

[3]*Ibid.*, Vol. II, p. 763.

THE HORSE-BOAT PENINSULA PACKET

A "safe and convenient" means of reaching Toronto Island in 1850. "Good pasture for horses and other cattle, which can be conveyed over by the first boat".

THE ACCOMMODATION, 1809

This steamship, built at Montreal by John Molson, was the first in Canada

Canada Steamship Lines' Marine Historical Collection

THE STEAMSHIP WALK-IN-THE-WATER, 1818

John Ross Robertson Collection   C. H. J. Snider

THE STEAMSHIP GREAT BRITAIN, 1830-42
One of the most popular of early steamships

boat in America was the *Accommodation*, built by the Hon.
John Molson of Montreal in 1809. The engine for this boat
was made at the ancient iron works at Three Rivers, which
was at one time the source of Canada's supply of iron goods.

The *Accommodation* measured seventy-two feet in length
of keel, had an engine of six horsepower and was equipped
with two paddle-wheels. Her two funnels belched forth
great clouds of black smoke as she began her maiden trip on
Wednesday, November 1, 1809. She left Montreal at 2.30
p.m. and reached Quebec on Saturday at 8.30 a.m.; but
of the sixty-six hours thirty were spent at anchor, for the
boat had no lights to enable it to travel at night. The maximum speed was not much more than four miles per hour
down the river, but the return journey took more than a
week. The fare down stream was $8 per passenger, and up
stream $9, including meals and berth. Only ten passengers
risked their lives on the first trip, though there was accommodation for twenty. The boat's engine was not strong
enough to propel it through the St. Mary's Current, below
Montreal, during the return trip, so ox-teams were called
into service and gave effective aid by towing.

Although Molson suffered a considerable financial loss
on this venture he ordered a better engine, and launched the
Swiftsure, twice as large as the *Accommodation*, in 1811.
This boat, though more sure than swift, was in operation
during the War of 1812 and proved of great service to the
government. In 1818 Molson's St. Lawrence Steamboat
Company had six additional steamers in operation, chiefly
between Montreal and Quebec. In the early twenties the
use of steam tow-boats or tugs was developed on the lower
St. Lawrence, the first of them being the *Hercules*.

The first steamship on the Great Lakes was the Canadian
vessel *Frontenac*, built at Ernesttown, Bay of Quinté, and
launched on September 7, 1816. The smaller American
steamer *Ontario* was being constructed at the same time
at Sackett's Harbour, but was not launched until April,
1817. The *Frontenac*, like almost all early steamships, was a
schooner-rigged vessel, and had one funnel. A contemporary
newspaper in describing the launching of the boat said that
"she descended with majestic grandeur into her proper
element, the admiration of a great number of spectators. . . .

Good judges have pronounced her to be the best piece of naval architecture yet produced in America".[4]

The *Frontenac* was much larger than her American rival, having a length over all of 170 feet, and two paddle-wheels forty feet in circumference. The total cost of the boat was nearly $100,000, a very large sum in pioneer days. The original route was from Prescott to Niagara, but on the first trip to Prescott the boat touched, (it is said not un-willingly), a rock in the river; so her owners, who were interested in maintaining trans-shipment at Kingston, henceforth restricted her operations to Lake Ontario. An exact schedule was, of course, difficult to follow, but the round trip took about nine days, and the fare for cabin passengers from Kingston to York was $12, baggage over sixty pounds being charged extra. Steerage passengers paid $3 and provided their own food; gentlemen's servants were similarly accommodated, for they were not permitted to travel cabin class.

This boat of 740 tons was considered a floating palace by the travellers of the day. A Scotchman, John Howison, sailed from Kingston to York on the *Frontenac* in 1819, and thoroughly enjoyed himself after the tedious trip up the St. Lawrence by bateau: "I could not but invoke a thousand blessings on the inventors and improvers of the steamboat for the delightful mode of conveyance with which their labours have been the means of furnishing mankind. It required some recollections to perceive that I was not in the Kingston Hotel."[5]

The *Frontenac*, which had a speed of about ten and one-half miles per hour, was built by Messrs. Trebout and Chapman as a result of the initiative of a number of Kingston merchants, and her captain throughout her existence was James Mackenzie. The same Company built the *Queen Charlotte*, which was in operation in 1818 along the Bay of

---

[4]*Kingston Gazette*, quoted in William Canniff: *History of the Settlement of Upper Canada.* 1869. pp. 600-4.

The present account of steam navigation is restricted almost entirely to the lower lakes and rivers, and is not intended to cover the development of the steamship on Lakes Huron, Michigan and Superior, which is a story in itself.

[5]John Howison: *Sketches of Upper Canada.* 1821. 3rd Edition, 1825, p. 62. The advertisement of the *Frontenac* in the *Kingston Chronicle* of April 30, 1819, gives many additional details of the service provided by this famous ship.

Quinté and on the St. Lawrence as far east as Prescott; the builder of this boat was Henry Gildersleeve, and she was the first river steamer in Upper Canada. The *Kingston Gazette* was rather doubtful of the financial success of steamships, but considered that they were "an interesting experiment", and should be of great advantage to the public.[6] The two boats had a monopoly of the Canadian traffic on lake and river for some time, but it is significant that in 1825 the *Frontenac* sold at auction for $6,200. The buyer was the Hon. John Hamilton, of Kingston, a man who spent most of his life in the development of steam navigation on the St. Lawrence and Lake Ontario.

Another famous early steamship on Lake Ontario was the *Canada*, built at the mouth of the Rouge River in the winter of 1825-26. The *U. E. Loyalist* refers to the first appearance of the *Canada* in the harbour of York: "The new steamboat *Canada* was towed into port this week by the *Toronto* from the mouth of the River Rouge, where she was built during the last winter. . . . Six steamers now navigate the St. Lawrence and Lake Ontario in this province, besides the *Canada* and a boat nearly ready for launching in Brockville."[7] The seven ships on the lake were valued at £39,500.

The *Canada* was the first regular Canadian mail steamer on Lake Ontario, and made the trip between York and Niagara in the fast time of a little over four hours. Among other early steamships on the York-Niagara route were the *Martha Ogden*, an American vessel which began to run in 1826, and the *Alciope*, whose maiden trip occurred in 1828. The traffic on Lake Ontario was soon to increase greatly owing to the opening of the Welland Canal in 1829, and the Rideau Canal in 1832.

The first steamship on Lake Erie was christened *Walk-in-the-Water*. She was built at Black Rock, near Buffalo, and was launched on May 28, 1818. The *Walk-in-the-Water*

---

[6] See E. A. Cruikshank: *Notes on Shipbuilding and Navigation.* (Ontario Historical Society, *Papers and Records*, Vol. XXIII, pp. 40-41.)

[7] York *U. E. Loyalist*, June 3, 1826. A large amount of interesting information concerning Lake Ontario steamships is quoted from contemporary newspapers (some of the files of which have since been lost or burned) by Dr. Henry Scadding in his *Toronto of Old*, 1873, pp. 538-576.

was named in honour of a well-known Indian Chief. She was 135 feet long, and her boiler and engine are described as follows: "The boiler, twenty feet long and nine feet in diameter, was placed forward of the main shaft, and the engine was aft of it. The engine was of the vertical type with a cylinder thirty-six inches in diameter and a four-foot stroke".[8]

The *Walk-in-the-Water* left Buffalo on her maiden voyage at 1 p.m. on August 23rd, having twenty-nine passengers on board. The first intentional stop was made off Dunkirk. Sails were used to help out the engines, and by the following morning she had reached Erie, where a large supply of cordwood was taken on. Upon reaching Cleveland she remained seven hours in the harbour to allow time for sufficient admiration, and then proceeded at ten miles per hour on her journey to Detroit, a stop being made at Sandusky *en route*. The 290-mile trip from Buffalo to Detroit was completed in 44 hours, 10 minutes.

Captain Job Fish, who had had experience on the Atlantic, had been imported to take charge of the *Walk-in-the-Water*, and he was fully cognizant of the importance of his position. At each port he "would mount one of the paddle-boxes and issue commands to the engineer through a speaking-trumpet in his best deep-sea voice, and in the intervals he would exchange greetings with people in the surrounding boats, and give meticulous care to the assistance of the ladies over the side into the boats".[9] The fare from Buffalo to Detroit was $18 for first class, and $7 for steerage. Steam whistles were not in common use at that time, for there was no steam to waste in making a noise; so in place of a whistle a four-pound cannon was securely lashed on the forward deck, and when the steamer was nearing a town the cannon came into action to announce to all and sundry that they might expect her approach.

The power of the engine in the *Walk-in-the-Water* was not sufficient to enable her to proceed up the Niagara River against the current, so she was regularly towed up by "a horned breeze" consisting of twenty yoke of oxen. This early steamship was the pride of the American ports and

[8]G. B. Catlin: *The Story of Detroit.* 1923. pp. 233-4.
[9]*Ibid.*, p. 236.

was also popular among the inhabitants of Chatham, Sandwich and Richmond (Windsor). When the French along the Detroit saw smoke belching forth from her stack thirty feet above the deck they called her a floating saw-mill!

That steamboats were much more than a nine days' wonder is quite apparent from contemporary opinions. The *Upper Canada Gazette* carried in 1818 the following news item: "The swift steamboat *Walk-in-the-Water* is intended to make a voyage early in the summer from Buffalo, on Lake Erie, to Mackinaw, on Lake Huron, for the conveyance of company. The trip has so near a resemblance to the famous Argonautic expedition in the heroic that expectation is quite alive on the subject."[10]   Such a voyage was also made in 1822 by a steamship, which created quite a stir as it progressed into the wilds:

"During the summer of 1822 a very large and splendid steamer, (I have seen none equal to it in Europe, 1849), made her appearance in the Huron waters—the first vessel of the kind that had been seen there. Red men and white flocked to see her from great distances. . . . The steamship arrived at the appointed day crowded with fashionables from the Atlantic shores of the United States, eager to penetrate so safely and agreeably into the far Indian solitudes".[11]

The *Walk-in-the-Water* was wrecked near Buffalo during a gale on November 1, 1821. She was replaced by the *Superior* in the following year. The earliest Canadian steamers on Lake Erie were the *Chippawa* and the *Emerald*. In the late twenties appeared the *Pioneer,* of Buffalo, the first high-pressure steamer on the Lakes. Another notable event occurred in 1836, when the first cargo of grain to be transported from Lake Michigan to Buffalo was carried by steamship, the load consisting of 3000 bushels of wheat. Among well-known steamboats on Lake Erie in the thirties were the *Cynthia McGregor,* the *Western,* and the *Thames.* The last-named was burned by the so-called Patriots at Windsor during the raid upon that village on December 4, 1838.

[10]*Upper Canada Gazette,* 1818. (The date of the issue is not available.)
[11]J. J. Bigsby: *The Shoe and Canoe, or Pictures of Travel in the Canadas.* 1850. Vol II, p. 152.

Steam navigation on the Ottawa River commenced in 1819, when the first steamship sailed from Grenville to Hull. This was the inauguration of a service between the two settlements due to the initiative of Philemon Wright. In 1822 the *Union* was built at Hawkesbury, and is described as "in construction and appearance crude, in speed slow, and in accommodations decidedly limited".[12] The first steamboats were, however, hailed enthusiastically by the settlers along the river, for previously they had had only the canoe, the bateau and the timber raft for all travel and transportation by water. In 1830 there were two more steamships, one of which, the former scow *Pumper*, (renamed the *Rideau*), was the first steamer to pass through the Rideau Canal, which she accomplished in the late spring of 1832, to be followed shortly after by the *Union*.

Soon after the opening of the Rideau Canal an immigrant family had an uncommonly tedious and, at the same time, eventful voyage upon it. The diary of John Treffry, who settled in Oxford County in 1834, is the basis of the following account of his canal trip in that year on the small steamer *Enterprise*, plying from Bytown to Kingston:

"The first adventure occurred when the steamer sprang a leak and it became necessary to borrow a pump from a barge in tow to keep the water under control. Two days later the engine broke down and the captain took two of the Durham boats, which the steamer was also towing, and started for Kingston to secure assistance. Meantime those on board the steamer ran short of provisions and had to make good the deficiency by fishing. They even tried to capture a deer which appeared on the bank, but failed in the attempt. The situation was not made brighter when the cook mutinied. Finally the captain returned with help and provisions, and the *Enterprise* was able to reach Kingston by the thirteenth of May, seven days after leaving Bytown".[13]

While this was a most unusual voyage, yet it shows the difficulties travellers might be required to face on the canal steamships. Ten years later the service on the Rideau

[12]H. R. Morgan: *Steam Navigation on the Ottawa River.* (Ontario Historical Society, *Papers and Records*, Vol. XXIII, p. 370.)
[13]John Treffry's diary, quoted in W. L. Smith: *Pioneers of Old Ontario.* 1923. pp. 195-6.

was still unsatisfactory. Before the St. Lawrence Canals
were completed the usual route for travellers who wished
to avoid the bateau trip between Montreal and Kingston
was by the roundabout way up the Ottawa to Bytown and
then down the canal to Kingston. A traveller in 1845 refers
to his voyage in "the small steamer *Quebec*" to Bytown, and
"the dirty little canal steamer" on the Rideau; but there
was a great difference when he reached Kingston and travelled on Lake Ontario in "the clean and commodious
Sovereign".[14]

Developments in navigation on the Ottawa River were
at first limited to improvements to aid the passage of
bateaux. The Ottawa route commences at Lachine, and the
river is navigable to St. Anne's, near the entrance to the
Lake of Two Mountains. At high water the rapid at that
point could be passed, while on the opposite side, at
Vaudreuil, it was always navigable, though the passage was
more circuitous than that at St. Anne's. In 1832 a bateau
lock was constructed at Vaudreuil to aid navigation. In
1843 the Provincial Government completed the lock commenced four years earlier at St. Anne's, and, since this lock
was 200 feet long by forty-five wide, a large passenger
steamer could then be run a distance of forty-five miles from
Lachine to Carillon, at the foot of the Long Sault of the
Ottawa. The rapids in the twelve-mile section between
Carillon and Grenville were passed by three separate locks,
the first of which was commenced in 1819 by the Imperial
Government, and the others nearly ten years later. From
Grenville to Ottawa the river is navigable, and a large
passenger steamer operated in later years on this section,
though it was confined to it by being too large for the
locks of the Grenville and Rideau Canals; this steamship
connected with a portage railway between Grenville and
Carillon, a steamer between Carillon and Lachine, and the
railway thence to Montreal. In the sixties, therefore, two
railways and two steamboats were necessary to convey a
passenger from Montreal to Ottawa.

Above Ottawa a number of improvements had been
made. For several miles navigation was obstructed by the
rapids and falls of the Chaudière, but a macadam road

[14]Reminiscences of the Rev. William Tomblin. (Unpublished.)

established connections with an iron steamer on Lake Chaudière. At the Chats an abortive attempt had been made to connect the Chaudière and Chats Lakes, which were three miles apart and had a difference in level of fifty feet; but in the early sixties the obstructions to navigation were surmounted by a horse railway connecting with the iron steamers operating on both lakes. Still higher up, two other steamships plied on short sections of navigable water separated by rapids around which transportation was accomplished over portage roads. By these various means was the navigation of the Ottawa effected from its mouth to the head of Deep River, or to the rapids of the Deux Joachims, a distance of about 300 miles. All navigation beyond these points was restricted by the swift current and numerous rapids to the bark canoe, the most primitive vessel for water transport, but undoubtedly the most pleasant and agreeable of them all as far as the passenger is concerned.

The navigation of Upper Canada's smaller rivers was extensively developed before the great era of railway construction in the late fifties. The Grand River, for example, was first improved when the Grand River Navigation Company commenced in 1833 the building of dams and locks. A considerable trade sprang up between Brantford and Lake Erie ports, 111 steamers arriving and departing from the former town in 1850. Millions of feet of lumber and much other produce was exported, while two passenger stern-wheelers, the *Red Jacket* and the *Queen*, were scheduled to ply between Brantford and Buffalo in twenty-four hours. The flourishing port soon gave way before the onslaught of the railway freight yard, for the Grand River trade collapsed when the Grand Trunk and Great Western Railways spread their tentacles through Canada West in the period 1854-60.

The development of steam navigation on the upper St. Lawrence was hindered by rapids. In 1826 the first steamers were operated on Lake St. Francis in front of Glengarry County, and on Lake St. Louis farther down the St. Lawrence, in order to connect with stages which were run over the rest of the distance between Montreal and Prescott; in 1828 the entire trip cost 31s. 6d. This collaboration between the land and water systems of transportation was early apparent. In 1819 an "elegant" Durham Boat (if such a thing ever existed!) carried passengers between Kingston and Montreal, meeting the *Frontenac* on her arrival at Kingston every tenth day; while in the summer of 1830 William Weller advertised that he had made arrangements which enabled the travelling public to go from York to Prescott conveniently, for his coaches left York twice a week and connected with the steamboat *Sir James Kempt* at the Carrying Place, thus providing "a pleasant and speedy conveyance between York and Prescott, the road being very much repaired, and the line fitted up with good horses, new carriages and careful drivers. Fare through from York to Prescott £2 10s., the same as the lake boats.[15]

For some time no steamer ventured farther down the river than Prescott, but in 1832 a stern-wheel steamship, the *Iroquois*, was built to overcome the rapids between Long Sault and Prescott. At first horses and oxen were needed to help at Rapide Plâtte; but experience and improved boilers later enabled the *Iroquois* to ascend by steam power alone, and thereafter the stages were discontinued except over the twelve-mile portage around the Long Sault between Dickinson's Landing and Cornwall. The Rev. Anson Green was in Prescott in 1832 and noted that "now the steamers begin to run down to Dickinson's Landing, at the head of the Long Sault; yet the most of the goods sold in this province are still towed up this river in Durham boats".[16]

A curious experiment in steamships was the *Rapid*, built about 1835 through the enterprise of some farmers living on the shores of the St. Lawrence in Dundas County. The hull consisted of two hollow cigar-shaped cylinders, between which a large wheel operated. Her first trip down the river was also her last.

During the eighteen-twenties steamboats were operated under considerable difficulties. Few harbours had yet been built, and it was therefore customary for the ship to anchor at some distance from shore while passengers and goods were transferred by bateaux or Durham boats. The wharf at York was approached by early steamships only with

[15]*Christian Guardian*, June 12, 1830.
[16]Anson Green: *Life and Times*. 1877. p. 167.

great difficulty, the vessel being brought to a standstill some way out in the harbour, and boats lowered from the fore and aft gangways; these craft carried hawsers, and when they had reached shore the ship was solemnly hauled to the wharf, the onlookers evincing surprise that the feat could be successfully accomplished.

The boats themselves were not altogether satisfactory: most of them required two boilers to supply sufficient energ to operate the two paddle-wheels; while it often happened that it was difficult to steer paddle-wheelers, especially in a heavy wind. Some of them, too, like the *Niagara* on Lake Ontario, had formerly been schooners, and had been converted into unsatisfactory steamships by removing the masts and rigging and installing an engine; while others, like the *St. George,* were schooner-rigged, and used both methods of propulsion. These deficiencies made sea-sickness a very common occurrence among passengers, and many travellers avoided lake travel on this account, preferring to take a chance on the stage from York to the Carrying Place, from which they could proceed eastward by steamer through the comparatively quiet Bay of Quinté and St. Lawrence.

In the early thirties steamships became common on the lakes and rivers of Upper Canada. A traveller noted in 1833 that they entered and departed from the harbour of York "almost hourly";[17] while even the back lakes of the Trent System had steamboats at that time. In 1832 was launched the first steamer on Lake Simcoe, a small boat of the same name. A few years later the steamships *Morning* and *Beaver* were operating on Lake Simcoe in connection with stage lines from Toronto. The machinery for the former vessel had to be hauled up Yonge Street from Toronto on rollers made from sections of tree trunks, several weeks being spent in the trip.

In 1833 Rice Lake had two "fire-ships", as the Indians called them, the *Pemedash* and the *Northumberland,* which were used to carry passengers and goods up the Otonabee to Peterborough. The original name of the former boat was *Pem-e-dash-cou-tay-ang* (Lake of the Burning Plains), the Indian appellation for Rice Lake. The steamship was

[17]Patrick Shirreff: *A Tour through North America.* 1835. p. 105.

launched on June 12, 1832, at 11 o'clock, and the *Cobourg Star* reported in language customary upon such occasions: "She glided safely and majestically into her destined element".[18] These steamers supplied a necessary and valuable service, even though the Rev. Anson Green found in 1840 that the crews had locked up their boats and departed for points south to see an execution; as a result of which neglect on their part the reverend gentleman nearly drowned himself while attempting to cross to the Indian Mission in a leaky skiff.[19]

John Langton refers in his letters to a trip on the first steamer on Mud (Chemong) Lake in 1833. She was "built like a scow,. . . .very much after the shape of a wash tub. . . . Unfortunately her steam is exhausted directly. . . . We stuck in the mud for an hour, during which we broke our pump and had therefore to stop every now and then, for nearly an hour, to pump the boilers full again by hand."[20] But this was, of course, far in the backwoods of the old Newcastle District.

In 1832 travellers on the Canadian side of the St. Lawrence made the voyage into Upper Canada either by bateau or a combination of stage and steamship. Mrs. Moodie proceeded westward by the latter service, and at Prescott boarded the *William IV*, which she describes as "a fine new steamer, crowded with Irish emigrants, proceeding to Cobourg and York."[21] During the voyage a heavy storm arose which greatly detracted from the pleasure of the trip. Mrs. Moodie describes the day as "too stormy to go upon deck— thunder and lightning, accompanied with torrents of rain. Amid the confusion of the elements I tried to get a peep at the Lake of the Thousand Isles; but the driving storm blended all objects into one, and I returned wet and disappointed to my berth. . . . The gale continued until daybreak, and noise and confusion prevailed all night, which was greatly increased by the uproarious conduct of a wild Irish emigrant who thought fit to make his bed upon the mat before the cabin door. . . . The following day was wet

[18]*Cobourg Star*, June 13, 1832. [19]Green, *op. cit.*, p. 233.
[20]John Langton: *Early Days in Upper Canada, Letters of John Langton.* 1926. p. 27.
[21]Susanna Moodie: *Roughing It in the Bush.* 1852. Edition of 1923, pp. 62-3.

and gloomy. The storm had protracted the length of our voyage several hours, and it was midnight when we landed at Cobourg".[22]

When Patrick Shirreff visited Canada in 1833 he chose to take the "American line of conveyances" up the St. Lawrence, in preference to the more tedious service on the Canadian side. He writes that he travelled "by stage to Lachine, from thence to Cascades by steam, from Cascades to Coteau du Lac by stage, and again by steam to Cornwall. On reaching Cornwall I immediately proceeded on board the American steamboat *Dalhousie* which conveyed us across the Hoogdensburgh. From thence we were conveyed to Ogdensburgh by land. At five in the morning the *United States* steamboat left Ogdensburgh for Brockville and Kingston".[23]

The same traveller gives us his impressions of the conditions on board the *Great Britain,* popular among immigrants in their voyage from Prescott to York:

"The night-scene on board the *Great Britain* formed a counterpart to that of the bateau on the St. Lawrence, almost every inch of surface being crowded with reposing individuals. . . . The aged and infirm sought shelter down below; the boys clustered round the chimney-stalks for heat, while the more hardy stretched themselves on the upper deck with almost no covering".[24]

Many of these immigrants had no money to pay their fare, so they pawned some of their goods, and quite often considerate friends came to the ship and redeemed them at the end of the journey. When they landed in small numbers at a port it was sometimes possible for them to get accommodation at an inn—if they could pay for it; but in Captain Hale's *Instructions to Emigrants* (1832), we find that "when a large party are together they commonly get housed in a barn, which is seldom charged for and may probably have offers of employment".[25] Most immigrants travelled steerage, the charge being only about one-half the regular rate. Although their hardships were frequently great on the lake ships of one hundred years ago, yet this section of the voyage was pleasant compared to the bateau

[22]*Ibid.,* pp. 64-5.   [23]Shirreff, *op. cit.,* p. 143.
[24]*Ibid.,* pp. 146-7.
[25]See *Emigration, Letters from Sussex Emigrants.* 1833. p. 80.

trip up the St. Lawrence, and to what was often a very rough passage of from two to four months across the Atlantic in a sailing-vessel.

A lake captain describes the steamship service on Lake Ontario in the early thirties as follows:

"In 1833, when I came to Canada, a steamer left Prescott every day for Toronto and Hamilton and Niagara. The names of the boats forming the line were the *Great Britain, William the Fourth, St. George, Cobourg, United Kingdom* and *Commodore Barry.* The American steamer *United States* left Prescott every Sunday for the head of the lake. The Canadian steamers were ahead of the requirements of the country at that time. The traffic and travel were not sufficient to make steamboat enterprise remunerative. There had been the year previous, 1832, a large immigration which had no doubt stimulated steamboat building."[26]

In the thirties a new type—the high-pressure steamship—began to appear on the lakes. Patrick Shirreff travelled in one of them, the *John By,* a ship which finally ended her career by running ashore near the mouth of the Credit. Shirreff did not enjoy his journey in her from York to Hamilton:

"The *John By* had been constructed to ply on the Rideau Canal, with paddle-wheels in the stern—the worst-sailing and most ill-constructed boat in Canada. The engine was high-pressure; and if a vessel was to be built for roasting passengers the *John By* might have furnished useful hints".[27]

Mrs. Jameson found in 1837 that most of the small steamboats on the lakes had high-pressure engines, "which make a horrible and perpetual snorting like the engine on a railroad".[28] She travelled on one of these ships on Lake St. Clair, though the boat had been built "to navigate the ports of Lake Huron from Penetanguishene to Goderich and St. Joseph's Island, but there it utterly failed". This steamer

[26]Reminiscences of Captain Twohy of Hamilton, quoted in William Canniff: *Canadian Steam Navigation.* (Tackabury's *Atlas of the Dominion of Canada.* 1875. p. 71.)

[27]Shirreff, *op cit.,* pp. 147-8.

[28]Anna Jameson: *Winter Studies and Summer Rambles in Canada.* 1838. Vol. II, p. 275 fn.

is described as "a wretched little boat, dirty and ill-con-trived. The upper deck, to which I have fled from the close, hot cabin, is an open platform, with no defence or railing around it; . . . . a gust of wind or a pitch of the vessel would inevitably send me sliding overboard".[29]

The amount of wood consumed by early steamboats may be gauged from Mrs. Jameson's statement that an American vessel sailing between Detroit and Fort Gratiot stopped at numerous "landings" *en route* for the purpose of taking on wood, at one of which, Palmer's Landing, "this process has already occupied two hours, and is to detain us two more, though there are fourteen men employed in flinging logs into the wood-hold".[30] Steamships, she observed, af-fected the phraseology of the Americans in characteristic fashion. When in Detroit Mrs. Jameson learned that "Will you take in wood?" signified "Will you take refreshment?"; "Is your steam up?" meant "Are you ready?"; while a witty friend wrote her not to be alarmed "at the political and social ferments in America, nor mistake the whizzing of the safety-valves for the bursting of the boilers".[31]

In 1840 there were fifty steamships on Lake Ontario, and in the forties and fifties both passenger and freight lines developed rapidly. There were many well-known passenger steamboats, among them the *Great Britain, Con-stitution, Traveller, Hamilton* and *Queenston*. On the lower St. Lawrence in 1836 the Torrance Line operated in opposi-tion to the Molson steamships; among the boats of the former line was the *Canada,* famous as the largest and fastest steamship in the New World at that time. On Lake Erie during the same period were such boats as the *Thames, Adelaide, Calula, Wave,* and *Dispatch,* all of which were of great importance in the service along the Canadian shore, as well as across the lake to American ports.

Keen competition soon led to the building of luxurious and more luxurious ships. In 1833 the first cabins were built on deck, and a few years later the equipment of the best steamships included thickly-carpeted dining salons with individual tables and revolving chairs, buffets and bars, paintings and mirrors, lounges and smoking-rooms,

[29]*Ibid.,* Vol. II, p. 276.   [30]*Ibid.,* Vol. III, pp. 6 and 7.
[31]*Ibid.,* Vol. III, p. 7.

and sumptuous menus and wine-lists. Many of these accoutrements were somewhat out of place in boats, and there was a reaction in later days which led to the present more sensibly furnished ships, though the costliest of them in the upper lakes service are much more luxurious than ever before.

Sir Richard Bonnycastle gives an excellent description of the characteristics of steam navigation in Canada in the forties. In 1841 he came up the St. Lawrence into Lake Ontario, travelling in a steamer from Lachine to Lake St. Louis. On this boat, "in a limited space close to the boiler we had a bad and very dear dinner, with no better beverage than warm water".[32] From the Cascades he travelled by wagon-coach, observing the canals in process of construction. At Prescott he embarked on the *Great Britain*, which he found "worked by very fine engines. It resembled a floating village in its extent, and was so remarkably easy in its motion that our night transit was scarcely perceptible".[33] This ship was capable of carrying nearly 1,000 passengers, but in a storm on Lake Ontario "nothing but the great power of the engines saved the vessel".[34]

The *Great Britain* appears to have merited the high praises of many a traveller. One calls it "a very noble steamer";[35] another states that it had "as many conveniences as a fashionable hotel. The cabins are long and broad and furnished in the most sumptuous manner—that appropriated to the use of the ladies has sofas, mirrors and every other luxury".[36] Bonnycastle describes steamships in general as well-conducted, except that the price of wine was exorbitant. On the Toronto-Niagara route the *Transit* was "fitted out with a service of plate and china. They very often have music on board, and in the ladies' cabin a piano. A respectable stewardess waits on the female cabin passengers, who are ushered to dinner by the captain and take the head of the table".[37] When he landed at Toronto, however, "on a narrow decaying pier", he was "jostled

[32]Sir Richard Bonnycastle: *The Canadas in 1841.* 1842. Vol. I, p. 86.
[33]*Ibid.*, Vol. I, p. 101.   [34]*Ibid.*, Vol. I, p. 133.
[35]Thomas Hamilton: *Men and Manners in America.* 1833. Vol. II, p. 335.
[36]Quoted in George V. Cousins: *Early Transportation in Canada.* (*University Magazine*, Vol. VIII, p. 617.)
[37]Bonnycastle, *op. cit.*, Vol. I, p. 138.

almost into the water by rude carters plying for hire on its narrow bounds, and pestered by crowds of equally rude pliers for hotel preferences".[38] The aristocratic Sir Richard found the same disagreeable conduct at all the other ports, and also noticed the inconvenience caused by the fact that all the boats, "for some unaccountable reason", preferred to start upon their voyages at night.[39]

Among the most popular steamships plying upon Lake Ontario in the forties was the *Chief Justice Robinson,* a boat of 400 tons built at Niagara in 1842. This ship carried the mail between Toronto, Hamilton and the Niagara ports, and long remained high in the public estimation. Sir Richard Bonnycastle found this boat, and others operating on Lake Ontario in 1846, even more luxurious than those upon which he had travelled five years earlier.

"You can have every convenience on board a Lake Ontario mail-packet, which is about as large as a small frigate and has the usual sea equipment of masts, sails and iron rigging. The fare is five dollars in the cabin, or about £1 sterling; and two dollars in the steerage. In the former you have tea and breakfast, in the latter nothing but what is bought at the bar. By paying a dollar extra you may have a stateroom on deck, or rather on the half-deck, where you find a good bed, a large looking-glass, washing-stand and towels, and a night-lamp, if required. The captains are generally part owners, and are kind, obliging, and communicative, sitting at the head of their table, where places for females and families are always reserved. The stewards and waiters are coloured people, clean, neat, and active; and you may give sevenpence-halfpenny or a quarter-dollar to the man who cleans your boots, or an attentive waiter, if you like; if not you can keep it, as they are well paid.

"The ladies' cabin has generally a large cheval glass and a piano, with a white lady to wait, who is always decked out in flounces and furbelows and usually good-looking. All you have to do on embarking or on disembarking is to see personally to your luggage; for leaving it to a servant unacquainted with the country will not do.

[38]*Ibid.,* Vol I, p. 146. The "narrow pier" was Maitland's Wharf.
[39]*Ibid.,* Vol. I, pp. 146-7.

W. H. Bartlett

Maitland's Wharf, Toronto, 1840

The location was the foot of Church Street. In the rear is the Ontario House (later the Wellington Hotel), the Royal York of the day.

A Grain Freighter on Lake Superior

In 1928 more than 424 million bushels of wheat arrived at Fort William and Port Arthur for shipment *viâ* the Sault Canals

NEW & IMPORTANT ARRANGEMENT.

ROYAL MAIL THROUGH LINE

FOR

KINGSTON, COBOURG, PORT HOPE, DARLINGTON, TORONTO AND HAMILTON.

 ☞ ONLY LINE without TRANSHIPMENT. ☜

THE FOLLOWING FIRST CLASS UPPER CABIN STEAMERS

COMPOSE THIS LINE, VIZ.:—

KINGSTON, (Iron) - - - - - -	Capt. KELLEY,
BANSHEE, - - - - - - -	" HOWARD,
PASSPORT, (Iron) - - - - -	" HARBOTTLE,
NEW ERA, - - - - - -	" MAXWELL,
CHAMPION, - - - - - -	" SINCLAIR,
MAGNET, (Iron) - - - - -	" TWOHY.

They were built expressly for LAKE and RIVER NAVIGATION—COMMODIOUS, STAUNCH and in every respect WELL FOUND with every requirement for SAFETY ; and fitted and furnished with EVERY MODERN CONVENIENCE and COMFORT.

ONE of these Steamers leaves the Canal Basin, Montreal, EVERY DAY (except Sundays) at 9 A. M. and LACHINE on the arrival of the NOON train from Montreal, for the above and intermediate Ports, DIRECT WITHOUT TRANSHIPMENT,

CONNECTING AS FOLLOWS:

At Hamilton, with the GREAT WESTERN RAILWAY for *London, Chatham, Windsor, Detroit, Chicago, Galena, St. Paul, Milwaukie, &c.*

At Toronto, with the NORTHERN RAILROAD for *Macinaw, Green Bay* and all Ports on Lake Michigan.

At Niagara, with the ERIE AND ONTARIO RAILROAD for *Niagara Falls, Buffalo, Cleveland, Toledo, Columbus, Cincinnati, &c.*

TO THE TOURIST OR PLEASURE SEEKER,

This Line affords a most desirable conveyance—comfortable, pleasant and expeditious, passing through the delightful scenery of the Lake of **THE THOUSAND ISLANDS** and all **THE RAPIDS OF THE ST. LAWRENCE BY DAYLIGHT.**

TO FAMILIES MOVING WEST THE ADVANTAGES ARE UNEQUALLED,

The Steamers running through WITHOUT TRANSHIPMENT, and DIRECT to the Railway DEPOT at TORONTO and HAMILTON, the ANNOYANCE and DAMAGE in the removal of Luggage (subject to Transhipping Lines,) is ENTIRELY AVOIDED.

☞ TICKETS, or further information can be procured from C. F. MUCKLE, at the Hotels; on board of the Steamers; or at the Office, 49 McGill Street.

ALEX. MILLOY, Agent.

Royal Mail Through Line Office,
49 McGill Street.

Montreal, October, 1857.

From Lovell's *Canada Directory*

STEAMSHIP ADVERTISEMENT, 1857

"The comfort of some of these boats, as they call them, but which ought to be called ships, is very great. There is a regular drawing-room on board one called the *Chief Justice*, where I saw, just after the horticultural show at Toronto, pots of the most rare and beautiful flowers, arranged very tastefully, with a piano, highly-coloured nautical paintings and portraits, and a *tout ensemble*, which, when the lamps were lit, and conversation going on between the ladies and gentlemen then and there assembled, made one quite forget we were at sea on Lake Ontario, the 'Beautiful Lake,' which, like other beautiful creations, can be very angry if vexed.

"The Americans have very fine steam vessels on their side of the lake, but they are flimsily constructed, painted glaringly white and green and yellow, without comfort or good attendance, and with a devil-may-care sort of captain who seems really scarcely to know or to care whether he has passengers or has not, a scrambling hurried meal, and divers other unmentionables."[40]

The stages by which the first steamboats developed into the luxurious vessels described by Bonnycastle are outlined by Judge Pringle:

"The steamboats of the old days were very different from those now in use. They had no saloons or cabins on deck for passengers. The gentlemen's and ladies' cabins were both below the deck, the latter being a small apartment at the stern of the boat. On each side of these cabins were built berths in tiers. The passengers' meals were served in the gentlemen's cabin. The deck, covered in warm weather with an awning, was a very pleasant place for lounging or walking on. After a while the ladies' cabin was placed on deck, and the deck which formed its roof was extended to the bow and formed a delightful promenade. As the number of travellers increased, more accommodation was required for them, and was got by building a saloon on the promenade deck, with a row of staterooms on each side. By these successive improvements the modern steamboat was evolved from the original one."[41]

[40]Bonnycastle: *Canada and the Canadians*. 1846. Vol. I, pp. 95-8.
[41]J. F. Pringle: *Lunenburgh, or the Old Eastern District*. 1890. pp. 107-8.

The individual ship, characteristic of the early period, had soon to give way before the line of steamships. Donald Bethune of Cobourg formed the Bethune Line, and in 1842 received the first contract for the carriage of mail from Dickinson's Landing, on the St. Lawrence, to Toronto, the route being covered in thirty-six hours. In 1837 a line of steamships was formed under the management of John Hamilton, and this became in the forties the Royal Mail Line, long famous for its service in the carriage of both passengers and the mails. Three ships, the *Princess Royal*, the *City of Toronto* and the *Sovereign*, were early engaged on the route between Kingston and Toronto, while the *Highlander*, the *Canada* and the *Gildersleeve* were on the St. Lawrence. One of the ships of this line, the *Passport* (later renamed the *Caspian*) sailed Lake Ontario until the early years of the present century. In 1855 was built the *Kingston*, which carried the Prince of Wales, later King Edward VII, when he visited Canada in 1860.

A few of the Royal Mail Line steamships were built of iron, which was soon to replace wood in the construction of ships. A contemporary advertisement (1857) describes the boats as "commodious, staunch, and fitted with every modern convenience and comfort". The ships of the Line at that date are given as "the *Kingston* (Iron), the *Banshee*, the *Passport* (Iron), the *New Era*, the *Champion* and the *Magnet* (Iron)".[42] The Royal Mail Line provided the only through service from Montreal to Hamilton without trans-shipment.

Until the completion in 1856 of the Grand Trunk Railway to Toronto, schooner and steamship had a monopoly of freight traffic during the navigation season; and it is only in comparatively recent years that they have been largely supplanted by the railways, which provide a quicker means of transport, though at higher rates. With the completion of the St. Lawrence canals it was at last possible, in 1850, for a vessel drawing nine feet of water to sail from Chicago to the Atlantic, and this had proved a great impetus to the development of navigation on the Great Lakes.

Following the invention, in 1839, of the screw propeller by Ericsson and Smith, the first vessels of a new type ap-

[42]John Lovell: *Canada Directory, 1857-8*. 1857. p. 1219.

peared on the scene. Most of them were small, narrow, high-pressure boats, commonly called "puffers". It is said that they were "remarkable for their volume of smoke and the noise of their steam-whistles. Their size enabled them to get anywhere. In the beginning the passengers were accommodated in the barges towed by the steamer, but later on the 'puffers' were enlarged to receive passengers".[43] These boats operated on parts of the St. Lawrence between Prescott and Montreal, and in 1847 the *Gildersleeve,* under Captain Hamilton and Pilot Rankin, was the first steamer to shoot the Long Sault Rapids.

The first propeller ship on Lake Ontario, the *Vandalia,* was launched at Oswego in 1841, and later sold to Canadians. In 1842 two ships were built in imitation of her at Buffalo, after she had passed through the Welland Canal. A year or two later magnificent upper-cabin steamers, such as the *Empire,* were plying between Buffalo and Chicago; these fine boats accommodated from 1,000 to 1,500 passengers in very luxurious quarters. It was not long before propeller steamships became common; one was even running below Niagara Falls, the first *Maid-of-the-Mist* being launched in 1846. But until early in the present century the old paddle-wheelers still continued to operate, especially on Lake Ontario; in fact several of them remain in effective use as ferry-boats between Toronto and the Island, and a few others may be found here and there in Canada.

In 1862 there were 1,200 sailing-vessels, American and Canadian, on the Great Lakes, while 363 steamships, of which 100 were tugs and 150 side-wheelers, were operating at that time. A contemporary authority wrote as follows concerning the failure of the large side-wheelers to run at a profit: "The mammoth side-wheel steamers cannot pay; they were the creation of rival railway routes as an attraction for passengers, were sustained as long as possible by railway capital or railway receipts, but now they are, with two exceptions, either rotting at the railway docks or have gone to sea."[44]

An important development in transport on Lake Ontario

[43]John Molson: *From the Canoe to the Railway.* 192?. p. 34.
[44]T. C. Keefer: *Travel and Transportation.* In John Lovell (Ed.): *Eighty Years' Progress in British North America.* 1863. p. 182.

occurred in 1907, when the *Ontario No. 1*, a steel car-ferry of 5,146 tons, began to operate between Cobourg and Charlotte, the port of Rochester. A large crowd assembled to see this boat turn around and back into its slip for the first time in the Cobourg harbour, the difficult task taking an hour; but practice enabled it to be accomplished in a few minutes on later occasions. The boat was built to carry twenty-eight cars of coal, and soon displaced the few schooners still engaged in that trade. In 1915 this ferry was joined by a sister ship, the *Ontario No. 2*, slightly larger, and both boats run winter and summer, many excursions to and from the United States patronising them in the latter season.

Similar ferries for the accommodation of railway cars and automobiles operate on Lake Erie and the Detroit River, where their introduction occurred much earlier. In 1854 the first railway ferry-boat ran between Windsor and Detroit, carrying both freight and passengers; but it was a slow and expensive business to break up trains, load the boats, and assemble the cars on the other side of the river. The first car-ferry service was inaugurated on January 1, 1867, by the Great Western Railway Company, the first ferry, the *Great Western*, being built in England at a cost of $190,000 and sent over in sections to Windsor, where it was assembled; it had a capacity of fourteen cars. Within the next few years five other car-ferries were installed by Michigan railway companies.

Marine tragedies have occurred on the Lakes from time to time. One of the lesser-known disasters took place on Lake Erie in the spring of 1851, when the steamship *Commerce* sank near Port Maitland with a loss of twenty-five lives. The details of the tragedy are told in an inscription on a tombstone in the cemetery of Christ Church, Port Maitland:

"The Officers, Non-commissioned Officers and Privates of the Reserve Battalion, 23rd Royal Welsh Fusiliers, have erected this Stone to mark the spot where lie the Remains of Assistant Surgeon Grantham and 24 men, women and children of that Regiment, who perished near this shore by the sinking of the Steamer *Commerce* on the night of the

6th of May, 1851, on their route from Montreal to London, C.W."[45]

The greatest tragedy in the history of the Great Lakes occurred nearly three-quarters of a century ago. The Canadian steamer *Lady Elgin* left Chicago on the evening of September 9, 1860, with an exceptionally large number of passengers, some 200 excursionists to Milwaukee augmenting the usual quota. As the ship went out into Lake Michigan a strong wind arose, and the difficulties of navigation were further increased by a heavy fog. During the early hours of the morning the *Lady Elgin* was rammed by the schooner *Augusta*, and 330 passengers perished when it was found that most of the lifeboats were defective; about thirty-five residents of Canada West were among the drowned.

Many who are still living will recall a notable marine disaster of fifty years ago. On September 14, 1882, the Canadian steamer *Asia* foundered in Lake Huron during a heavy storm. Among the 148 persons who lost their lives was William Henry, father of the present Prime Minister of Ontario, the Hon. George S. Henry. The fury of the storm smashed two lifeboats as they were being launched,and only seventeen people succeeded in embarking in a small metal craft equipped with air chambers. After being several times capsized, the lifeboat was finally washed ashore near Pointe-au-Baril; it contained at that time five bodies and two persons still alive—a man and a woman,—and these were the sole survivors of the disaster.

It took the steamship nearly a century entirely to displace the sailing-ship. In 1833 a Canadian-built boat, the *Royal William,* was the first vessel to cross the Atlantic using steam as the main motive power for the whole distance; but even in 1880 more sailing-vessels than steamships visited the port of Montreal. From that year onward, however, sailing-ships rapidly decreased in number. The lake marine followed much the same course. It was at its height just before the completion of the Grand Trunk Railway, and concerning the change a contemporary authority considered that "the decrease since 1857 in the Canadian

[45]Quoted in Fred Williams: *Do You Know?* (Toronto *Mail and Empire,* May 6, 1932.)

lake marine is owing to the insane efforts of the Grand Trunk Railway to rival the water route, the only result of which has been to ruin the boat-owners and exhaust the railroad".[46]

In the early sixties the lake marine revived to a considerable extent. In 1862 there were on the lakes 363 steamships of all types—paddles, propellers and tugs—with a tonnage of 132,327 and a value of $5,576,000; of this total 100 ships were Canadian. After 1870 the invention of the compound engine and improvements in condensers made possible cheaper transportation by water, though these advances were not utilised in lake ships as quickly as they were in the ocean service. But, with the development in the same period of cheap steel by Bessemer, a longer-life rail was made available to the railways, and this, with coincident advances in locomotive and car construction, in speed and organisation, made it increasingly difficult for the lake marine to compete successfully for freight and passenger traffic, and both schooners and steamships gradually decreased in numbers and importance. In recent years, however, steam navigation has recovered to a considerable extent, particularly in the passenger service and in long-distance transport of grain and other commodities from the upper lakes. The Canada Steamship Lines, for example, has fourteen large and palatial passenger ships and eighty-five freight steamers engaged along the 2,000-mile waterway between Duluth and the Saguenay River, a fleet which makes it the largest fresh water transportation company in the world.[47]

[46]Keefer, op. cit., p. 136.
[47]One of the most handsome and valuable of recent historical publications is George A. Cuthbertson's Freshwater; a History and a Narrative of the Great Lakes. (1931.) Though the treatment is somewhat technical, there is nothing which can approach this work as a history of lake shipping, and it contains many beautiful illustrations executed by its author.

CHAPTER VI

By Indian Trail and Blazed Path

"My path was a winding Indian trail where no wheel carriage had ever passed. I was obliged to jump my horse over logs, ride him through deep mud-holes and bridgeless streams, guided sometimes by marked trees. . . . . Our circuit embraces all the country between Bowmanville and the Carrying Place, the River Trent and Mud Lake. It requires a ride of 400 miles to get round it, which we performed winter and summer on horseback."

REV. ANSON GREEN (1824).[1]

THE speed of modern transportation is probably the most remarkable development among the many changes which have occurred during the past century. It used to be true in many parts of Upper Canada during all except the winter months that the quickest way to accomplish a journey was to walk; and for many decades travelling by land during three seasons out of the four was an ordeal to which one submitted only when it was unavoidable. At the close of the eighteenth century the province had no roads worthy of the name, and the shores of Lakes Ontario and Erie were often travelled in preference to the blazed trails which formed most of the roadways that had been opened. The winter season was the great period of transportation in pioneer days, for a sleigh might be driven almost anywhere with comparative ease. Conditions of travel during the Loyalist period are thus described by William Canniff:

"Travellers from Montreal to the west would come by a bateau or Durham boat to Kingston. Those who had business further west made the journey to Ernesttown, Bay of Quinté, on horseback. A white man conducted them to the River Trent. . . . At this place the traveller was furnished with a fresh horse and an Indian guide to conduct him through an unsettled country, the road being little better than a common Indian path, with all its windings. Sometimes the traveller continued his way around the head of the lake to Queenston. The road continued in this state until about the year 1798."[2]

[1] Anson Green: *Life and Times*. 1877. pp. 50-1.
[2] William Canniff: *History of the Settlement of Upper Canada*. 1869. p. 144.

Typical of the experiences of settlers along Lake Ontario at the close of the eighteenth century was that of Asa Burnham, a pioneer near Cobourg. He once took an ox-sleigh load of grain along the Lake shore to the grist-mill which had been built in the late seventeen-nineties at Smith's Creek, now Port Hope. Before he had commenced the return journey a sudden thaw removed the ice from the beach, so he had to return through the woods. The line of a future highway (the Danforth Road) had been blazed, and in places trees had been felled, but they remained where they had fallen, and the difficulty of guiding a vehicle along such a trail even in winter may be readily imagined.

The first Lieutenant-Governor of Upper Canada, John Graves Simcoe, made several expeditions of exploration and investigation into what were then the outlying sections of the province. On February 4, 1793, he left Newark (Niagara) to visit Detroit, which had not yet been surrendered by the British. Accompanying him were several officers, among them Lieutenant Thomas Talbot, later famous as the founder of the Talbot Settlement, and Major E. B. Littlehales, from whose diary[3] we obtain an interesting account of the trip. The description of the country through which the party passed will show how close to the primitive conditions of Indian days the whole region still was.

They commenced their journey in sleighs along "very indifferent" roads, but in the later stages of the trip they walked a great deal. During the first day they crossed 12-Mile Creek, and by evening had arrived at 20-Mile Creek, where they slept "in one of Colonel Butler's houses". The following day they reached 40-Mile Creek (Grimsby) where the arrival of an Indian "express" from Kingston detained the party a day; on the 6th they visited Nelles' house at the Grand River, and the following day, "Captain Brant's at the Mohawk Indian Village, going along the ice on the Grand River with great rapidity for a considerable way". Here the Indians fired a *feu de joie* in honour of the Governor, and the party attended divine service at the

[3]*Journal of E. B. Littlehales.* 1889. (Edited by the Rev. Henry Scadding.) See February 4 to March 10, 1793.

wooden church, where they were pleased with "the devout behaviour of the squaws, the melody of their voices, and the excellent time they kept in singing hymns".[4]

When they left the village on the 10th they were accompanied by Joseph Brant and twelve of his tribe who acted as guides and helped supply game over the long portage to Delaware. They passed over the Burford plains, "crossed two or three rivulets through a thick wood, and one a salt lick", and stopped in the afternoon to enable the Indians to construct elm bark wigwams, which they did with amazing celerity.

On February 12th they reached the Thames (then called the La Tranche), crossing the main branch of the river soon afterwards at the site of London. On February 15th the party arrived at the Delaware Indian village, noticing near by many examples of Indian carving of animals "and various figures of Indians returning from battle with scalps". The last stage of the journey to Delaware was accomplished by walking on the ice of the La Tranche. They spent a day at the council of the Six Nations, and then travelled "twelve or fourteen miles, part of the way through plains of white oak and ash", arriving at a Canadian trader's; and a little beyond, "in proceeding down the river, the Indians discovered a spring of an oily nature, which upon examination proved to be a kind of petroleum".

On the 17th they passed the Moravian Village,[5] which had been established only in the previous May; here four missionaries were in control of the Delaware Indians. The following day they crossed the Thames, and soon after "were agreeably surprised to meet twelve or fourteen carrioles coming to meet and conduct the Governor". At four o'clock they arrived at Dolsen's,[6] "a promising settlement", and from there proceeded to the mouth of the Thames, twelve miles farther, "and saw the remains of a considerable town of the Chippawas". As they approached, a detachment of Canadian militia on the east bank of the Detroit fired a *feu de joie,* and the Governor's party crossed the river in boats, amidst floating ice. A similar reception by the mil-

[4]*Diary of Mrs. John Graves Simcoe,* February 12, 1793.
[5]Near the present village of Bothwell.
[6]Now Chatham.

itary awaited Colonel Simcoe at Detroit, where the garrison fired a royal salute in his honour as he entered the town.

The return journey to Niagara was commenced on February 23rd, several Detroit officers accompanying the party as far as the point where the carrioles had met them on the 18th; then, "each taking his pack or knapsack on his back, we walked that night to the Moravian Village". The homeward trip was made more slowly, as the party did not always follow the beaten path but often turned aside to explore. The Governor took a special interest in the situation at the forks of the Thames (now London), and decided that it was "eminently calculated for the metropolis of Canada".

Proceeding eastward they once lost the track, "but were released from this dilemma by the Indians, who, making a cast, soon descried our old path to Detroit". On March 3rd they again saw Captain Brant, and on the fifth met the "annual winter express", the only means of carrying mail and dispatches between Lower Canada and the upper province during the season when navigation was impossible. On the sixth the Governor's party reached the Mohawk Village, the Indians having come out to meet them with horses at "the end of the plain, near the Salt Lick Creek". The Mohawks staged a great celebration for the Governor, including several "large meals and the customary dances"; and the members of the party, dressed in Indian clothes, were adopted as chiefs. The following day Colonel Simcoe reached Wilson's Mills (Ancaster), where a heavy snowstorm prevented progress for two days; but on the 8th they approached Burlington, and on March 10th the Governor arrived at Navy Hall, completing his first trip of exploration into the hinterland of Upper Canada.

There were two main streams of Loyalist and "late Loyalist" immigration into Upper Canada: the first was by way of the St. Lawrence and Lake Ontario, the second across the Niagara River. The experiences of Thomas Choate will serve as an example of the hardships of travel at that time. In 1796 Choate followed the second route and took up land in Wentworth County, near the present site of Glanford. During the next two years he made several trips to New Hampshire and back on foot, sowing seed in

George Romney

THAYENDANEGEA—CHIEF JOSEPH BRANT

Mrs. John Graves Simcoe, after Lieutenant Pilkington

THE MOHAWK VILLAGE, GRAND RIVER, 1793

Brant's House   Council House   Mohawk Church

William Cruikshank, R.C.A.

BREAKING A ROAD

the spring and returning to harvest his crops in the fall. In 1798 he brought three brothers and two cousins named Burnham with him, the party travelling with ox-sleighs, though the oxen had to proceed singly most of the way over the narrow Indian trails. The sleighs carried tools and other baggage while the men walked alongside, and each night they camped wherever they were when darkness came. For several weeks they were ill with smallpox, contracted when they called at a house to replenish their provisions. Upon reaching the Niagara River the men effected a crossing above the Falls by lashing a pole across an old flat-bottomed boat, fastening an ox's head to each end of the pole, and forcing the animals to swim across, thus propelling the scow and its passengers and baggage.

Of a similar nature was the experience of Peter Reesor, one of the first settlers in the vicinity of Stouffville. Shortly after 1800 he made a six weeks' journey on horseback from Pennsylvania to the Township of Markham, with a view to discovering a suitable location for a settlement. He was on the point of commencing the return journey to Pennsylvania when a stranger offered him 400 acres of land for his horse, bridle and saddle; he immediately closed the deal, and made the 500-mile return trip on foot. As a result of Reesor's investigations in Upper Canada Abraham Stouffer led a band of settlers to the new land in 1804, and the village of Stouffville was founded.

Many years later it was still common to walk long distances, because it was often the speediest, if not the only method of travelling by land. Many an early settler carried his grain on his back thirty miles to a mill, and returned during the night with the flour. Garrett Oakes, a pioneer in the Talbot Settlement, stated that during the War of 1812 the settlers had to go to the nearest store, at Port Ryerse on Long Point, for their salt, pay $12 a bushel for it, and carry it away on their backs. One man had walked two hundred miles when he finally got his salt back home. Oakes, who lived in Yarmouth Township, describes a similar journey which he had to make to obtain a few yards of cloth:

"In the year 1813 Colonel Talbot sent word to the few settlers that he had wool to be let out to be made into cloth on halves. I hired a horse and went and got fifty pounds. Here was forty miles travelled. I then hired a horse and took the wool to Port Dover and had it carded, for which I paid $6.25, and returned home, which made one hundred miles more. My wife spun the rolls, and I had made a loom for weaving, but we had no reed for flannel. I then went sixty miles on foot to a reed-maker's, but he had none that was suitable, and would not leave his work on the farm until I agreed to give him the price of two reeds, $6.50, and work a day in his place; this I did, and returned home with the reed. My wife wove the cloth, and I took my half to Dover to the fulling-mill. When finished I had eighteen yards, for which I had paid $34.75 and travelled 140 miles on horseback and 260 miles on foot, making four hundred miles, requiring in all about fifteen days' labour".[7]

Even in the eighteen-twenties and -thirties long walks were frequently a necessity. In 1826 Samuel Strickland tramped from the vicinity of Scott's Mills (Peterborough) to Darlington Mills, later named Bowmanville, the journey being necessary because of his wife's illness. He walked the entire distance, fifty-eight miles, in one day. When he had reached within five miles of his destination he went into an inn for some refreshment; here he heard some men talking about a funeral to be held the next day, and was informed that it was his wife whose death was the topic of conversation. One can imagine his feelings as, almost exhausted in body and mind, he trudged the remaining five miles.[8]

In 1823 Robert Reid, another early settler in Douro Township, walked forty miles to Cobourg, and continued to York on horseback. He returned in the same manner, but before reaching home he had the unpleasant experience of losing his way and walking many miles out of his course. This misfortune necessitated his spending the night under a tree, the more unpleasant as he had had no food since breakfast. Although it was cold weather and he had no coat he did not suffer any serious after-effects, and reached home at ten o'clock the next morning.

[7]Garrett Oakes: *Pioneer Sketches.* (*St. Thomas Weekly Home Journal,* 1876-7.)   See the Elgin County *Historical Atlas.* 1877. p. ix.
[8]See Samuel Strickland: *Twenty-seven Years in Canada West.* 1853. Vol. I, pp. 102-4.

In the winter of 1832-33 the Rev. Benjamin Cronyn, a clergyman near London, set out on foot with his friend Colonel Curran, carrying a quarter of beef on a pole for the relief of starving settlers near Adelaide. Night came on and the raw beef attracted wolves, then common in the district. To add to their troubles the travellers lost the trail in the dark, but finally came upon a chopper's shanty. Here they remained part of the night, making a fresh start with a lantern before daylight. When their light went out they lost the trail again, and the wolves were dangerously near when, fortunately, the two men were discovered by some of the settlers who had been on the look-out in expectation of their arrival with the anxiously anticipated supply of food.[9]

Civilisation is comparative. In pioneer days those who lived in the villages that skirted the St. Lawrence and the lower lakes considered the back townships to be in a state of semi-barbarism; for, though all of the earliest settlements were on the shores of lake and river, it was not long before enterprising families began to occupy the best sections of the interior. The Kingston Road and Dundas Street were bad enough one hundred years ago, but they were excellent highways in comparison with the blazed trails which were frequently the only means of communication with the back townships. Journeys of two or three days to travel thirty miles were quite usual. Whenever possible the waterways were used, because a much quicker trip could be made by water than by land. A Methodist circuit-rider describes the usual conditions of travel in newly-settled districts:

"The last of August we passed into the new settlements about thirty miles from York.[10] English, Irish and a few American families received us kindly. For horses there were neither roads nor feed. A pocket compass to guide us through forests of four to ten miles without a house, and a hatchet to fell trees for crossing the rivers, were part of our necessary outfit. But the houses were crowded. To

---

[9]See C. O. Ermatinger: *The Talbot Regime.* 1904. p. 142.

[10]The Townships of Toronto, Etobicoke, Chinguacousy, Erin, Esquesing and Trafalgar were at that time (1821) in process of settlement.

see the people coming from every direction with flaming torches was a sight to thrill our hearts."[11]

Among the first to take up land in the vicinity of Peterborough were the Reids and the Stewarts, who obtained grants of land in Douro Township in 1822. Reid went out in advance with workmen in order to build log houses in preparation for the arrival of the families. A few weeks later Stewart proceeded from Cobourg with supplies and additional workmen. An ox-cart took the party to Rice Lake, the road being rough all the way. At dark they reached the ferry-house at Tidy's Tavern. Next day they obtained a boat, crossed Rice Lake, and continued up the Otonabee River, having travelled fifteen miles by night. Discovering a few rough boards they built a shanty for shelter, and some Indians came and traded them venison for whisky. The following day they continued their journey to Scott's Mills, and thence two miles through the woods to the site of the log houses.[12]

The same trip by land was even more difficult. In February, 1823, Mrs. Stewart and her family made the journey by sleigh, the route passing through the townships of Hope, Cavan and Monaghan, at that time very thinly settled. Occasional clearings were seen the first day, and at night a stop was made at Page's Inn, where the present village of Centreville is located; here they slept on the floor of the sitting-room, for the only bedroom had no fireplace.

On the following day they proceeded along the blazed trail which was the only road northward. Concerning this part of the trip Mrs. Stewart wrote: "All our journey lay through thick woods. . . . The trail wound in and out between trees, which it was often difficult to pass. . . . Two or three times we had to stop that a pass might be cut for our sleighs where trees had fallen across the road. For nine miles we drove through the woods without seeing any habitation except some Indian huts."

Crossing the river on foot through deep snow the party was met by Mr. Stewart with an ox-sleigh. The difficulties of the last stage of the journey were even greater, for "late

[11]The Rev. Fitch Reed, quoted in J. E. Sanderson: *The First Century of Methodism in Canada*. 1910. Vol. I, p. 124.
[12]The journey is described in Frances Stewart: *Our Forest Home*. 1889. 2nd Edition, 1902, pp. 20-22.

in the night when we were in the dark forests it began to
snow again. The progress was much more difficult than I
ever expected; the sleigh being heavily loaded I was
obliged to walk. Our lantern, unfortunately, became filled
with snow, and the candle so wet that it could not be relit
with the tinder box". At last after five miles of difficult
travel the log house was reached.[13]

John Langton describes an interesting journey into "the
backwoods" by another route, ten years later. Proceeding
along the Kingston Road from York with a sleigh, he had
to walk eighteen miles in mud six inches deep. After staying the night at a tavern in Pickering he "struck back into
Uxbridge, having some tolerable sleighing after the first
ten miles from the Lake. The next day one of our sleigh
runners, being worn out by the bare roads, gave way and
detained us so long that we could only reach a miserable
farmhouse in Brock".

The following day the sleigh broke down again; but a
few miles farther on they purchased "a sort of vehicle
called a jumper, for the enormous sum of half a dollar. . . .
We drove in grand style to Purdy's Mill[14] that night".
Early in the morning they continued eastwards again, but
the manner in which they had amused themselves, by
"trusting too much to the jumping powers of our carriage",
caused the jumper to break down. Some repairs were made
with an axe and an auger, and they proceeded more carefully for a time, but the finish was not pleasant:

"We were obliged once more to take to our horses, leaving our luggage behind. Two or three and twenty miles on
bare backs, with the additional pleasure of harness, was
enough to teach us for the future not to jump too high;
and though I shall not cease to uphold the excellence of
jumpers, I will be content with exhibiting them on a level
road and not attempt to clear sawlogs again."

On arriving at Peterborough Langton found a Bachelors'
Ball in progress, so he danced all night, and then continued
in a hired sleigh to his log home on Sturgeon Lake.[15] Such
was travel in the backwoods in pioneer days!

[13]*Ibid.*, pp. 25-29.   [14]Now Lindsay.
[15]John Langton: *Early Days in Upper Canada, Letters of John
Langton.* 1926. pp. 80-82.

Farther westward, in a district part of which had been settled much longer, the conditions of land travel were frequently just as bad. In 1837 Mrs. Anna Jameson paid a visit to Colonel Talbot, and at the end of her stay a farmer's cart was the best vehicle available to take her westward from Port Talbot to Chatham. During the first part of the journey she sat on a seat slung on straps, and the roads were fairly good; but when it became necessary to leave Talbot Street and turn into a side road dividing Howard and Harwich Townships,—then the trouble commenced. Mosquitoes were thick in the forests through which the "town line" led, and they added greatly to the difficulties of the trip. Mrs. Jameson's account of the journey is quoted at length, for she gives an excellent description of the scenery, and most interesting impressions of the appearance of settlers' clearings:

"The road was scarcely passable; there were no longer cheerful farms and clearings, but the dark pine forest and the rank swamp, crossed by those terrific corduroy paths, (my bones ache at the mere recollection!), and deep holes and pools of rotted vegetable matter mixed with water, black, bottomless sloughs of despond! The very horses paused on the brink of some of these mud-gulfs, and trembled ere they made the plunge downwards. I set my teeth, screwed myself to my seat, and commended myself to Heaven—but I was well-nigh dislocated!

"At length I abandoned my seat altogether, and made an attempt to recline on the straw at the bottom of the cart, disposing my cloaks, carpet-bags, and pillow so as to afford some support—but all in vain; myself and all my well-contrived edifice of comfort were pitched hither and thither, and I expected at every moment to be thrown over headlong; while to walk or to escape by any means from my disagreeable situation was as impossible as if I had been in a ship's cabin in the midst of a rolling sea.

"But the worst was yet to come. At the entrance of a road through the woods,

'If road that might be called where road was none
Distinguishable,'

we stopped a short time to gain breath and courage, and

refresh the poor horses before plunging into a forest of about twenty miles in extent.

"The inn—the only one within a circuit of more than five-and-thirty miles—presented the usual aspect of these forest inns; that is, a rude log-hut, with one window and one room answering all purposes, a lodging or sleeping-place being divided off at one end by a few planks; outside, a shed of bark and boughs for the horses, and a hollow trunk of a tree disposed as a trough. Some of the trees around it were in full and luxuriant foliage; others, which had been girdled, stood bare and ghastly in the sunshine. To understand the full force of the scripture phrase, 'desolate as a lodge in the wilderness', you should come here!"

After a short stop at this backwoods inn the journey continued.

"Turning the horses' heads again westward we plunged at once into the deep forest, where there was absolutely no road, no path, except that which is called a blazed path, where the trees marked on either side are the only direction to the traveller. How savagely, how solemnly wild it was! So thick was the overhanging foliage, that it not only shut out the sunshine but almost the daylight; and we travelled on through a perpetual gloom of vaulted boughs and intermingled shade. There were no flowers here—no herbage. The earth beneath us was a black, rich vegetable mould, into which the cart-wheels sank a foot deep; a rank, reedy grass grew round the roots of the trees, and sheltered rattlesnakes and reptiles.

"The timber was all hard timber, walnut, beech, and basswood, and oak and maple of most luxuriant growth; here and there the lightning had struck and shivered one of the loftiest of these trees, riving the great trunk in two and flinging it horizontally upon its companions. There it lay in strangely picturesque fashion, clasping with its huge boughs their outstretched arms as if for support. Those which had been hewn to open a path lay where they fell, and over their stumps and roots the cart had to be lifted or dragged. Sometimes a swamp or morass lay in our road, partly filled up or laid over with trunks of fallen trees by way of bridge.

"As we neared the limits of the forest some new clearings broke in upon the solemn twilight monotony of our path: the aspect of these was almost uniform, presenting an opening of felled trees of about an acre or two; the commencement of a log house; a patch of ground surrounded by a snake-fence, enclosing the first crop of wheat, and perhaps a little Indian corn; great heaps of timber-trees and brushwood laid together and burning; a couple of oxen dragging along another enormous trunk to add to the pile. These were the general features of the picture, framed in, as it were, by the dark mysterious woods."

At length they emerged from the forest into the valley of the Thames, an enjoyable change, as may easily be imagined, from being "dragged along in a heavy cart, ... tormented by mosquitoes, shut in on every side from the light and free air of heaven. . . . The first view of the beautiful little town of Chatham made my sinking spirits bound like the sight of a friend".[16]

As the settlement of the province spread northwards new districts came into occasional contact with civilisation. The Rev. Anson Green, an early Methodist "travelling preacher", describes a trip from Barrie to Owen Sound in 1844 which illustrates the method of approach to newly-settled districts in "the bush". The party left Barrie early one morning in a wagon, carrying provisions and camp equipment, and after travelling eight miles they reached the head of Willow Creek, "one of the most unpleasant on which I ever rode— a deep, crooked, narrow stream, surrounded by an extensive swamp and overhung with bushes". They continued on horseback over an old corduroy road built by soldiers during the War of 1812. The timbers of this roadway were as decayed as the remains of an old fort which stood near by, and progress was slow and difficult. A rowboat was used on the creek, though paddles instead of oars had to be employed because the stream was so narrow. In the early afternoon a stop was made on the banks of the Nottawasaga River and a meal prepared, but swarms of mosquitoes diminished the enjoyment of the food. "Mr. Cathey's house and saw-mill, in Sunnydale", was reached soon afterwards,

---

[16]Anna Jameson: *Winter Studies and Summer Rambles in Canada.* 1838. Vol. II, pp. 223-32.

MRS. ANNA JAMESON ON THE LAKE SHORE ROAD, 1837

6TH STREET, CHATHAM, U.C., IN 1838

"The beautiful little town of Chatham. . . ."—Mrs. Anna Jameson

C. W. Jefferys, R.C.A.

WILLOW CREEK, AUGUST

"A deep, crooked, narrow stream, surrounded by an extensive swamp
and overhung with bushes."—The Rev. Anson Green

Captain W. H. Grubbe

BARRIE ON LAKE SIMCOE, C.W., 1853

following a stretch of thirty miles without a habitation in view; here the party remained all night.

The following morning Mr. Cathey "took his team and conveyed our craft over the portage to the Georgian Bay", thus saving about twelve miles' rowing. A new mill had just been erected where Collingwood now stands, and there were a few small clearings at the base of the hills. Forty miles of rowing on Georgian Bay brought the party to St. Vincent, thirty miles from Owen Sound by water and twenty by land. Early next morning they proceeded on horseback through the woods, without a sign of a road in some sections. Owen Sound was "in its infancy; scarcely a house seems to be finished; but its position, surrounded as it is by rich lands and flowing streams, indicates that it will one day be a large and prosperous city".[17]

Women, too, experienced the hardships of pioneer travel. In 1827-8 the Canada Company had cut a road through the forest between the newly-established settlements of Guelph and Goderich. Samuel Strickland was at that time an employee of the Company, and his wife had remained at Guelph while he was at work in Goderich. She determined to make the hazardous trip over the recently-cut road, then no more than a trail, so she hired a settler to transport herself, her child and a nursemaid.

For the first two days satisfactory progress was made in the ox-cart; but when they entered the section of roadway that had been most recently blazed their difficulties commenced, and in the next five miles the wagon was twice upset. The party had still over sixty miles to go, and they walked the entire distance. Each day they covered about fifteen miles, Mrs. Strickland carrying her child, for the servant was too young and too tired to be of much help. Two of the remaining four nights they camped out, and finally, after a most exhausting trip, reached Goderich on the morning of the sixth day.[18]

Conditions of travel in this district were much the same thirty years later. In 1854 John S. McDonald was at Ancaster, and left in the following year for Kincardine Township where he intended to settle. Ox-carts were still com-

[17]Green, *op. cit.*, pp. 279-82.
[18]See Strickland, *op. cit.*, Vol. I, pp. 266-70.

monly used on the Huron Road, though there was a stage which progressed slowly over part of the route. Mr. Mc-Donald travelled by wagon as far as he could, the trip to his new home taking eight days, and the route being by way of Galt, Stratford, Hunter's Corners (Seaforth), and Goderich. Mud and corduroy alternated over the entire road from Galt westward, and it was often difficult for Mrs. McDonald to keep her seat in the wagon. McDonald's description of the journey and of the first years of settlement in Kincardine Township assures us that the later pioneers endured hardships varying but little from those of earlier times:

"The country was fairly well-settled as far as Stratford; but from that place to Goderich the clearings were small, and the Townships of Kinloss, Ashfield, Huron and Kincardine, while mostly taken up, were still covered with forest. From Belfast to our new home, a distance of eighteen miles, there was no roadway whatever, the only guide to the lot being a blaze left by surveyors; and over the last twelve miles of that blazed trail Mrs. McDonald carried an infant in her arms.

"It was fall when we reached our home in the bush, and the first winter was spent in making a clearing. In spring, after burning the slash and putting in a crop, I tramped all the way back to Ancaster to earn enough to see the family through the following winter, Mrs. McDonald and the children meantime spending three weary months with the nearest neighbour. In the fall, with my cradle on my back, (there were no self-binders in those days), I tramped home to harvest our own little crop and prepare for winter. The purchase of groceries necessitated a walk of eight miles each way. The Harris Mill, twenty-two miles distant, was the nearest point at which we could obtain flour, and that meant two days in going and coming. . . . It was eight long years after our first winter in the bush before I was able to spend all my time on our farm".[19]

For many years longer the conditions of travel and transportation remained crude and difficult in Ontario, and even now one has only to visit outlying districts to find

[19]Reminiscences of John S. McDonald, quoted in W. L. Smith: *Pioneers of Old Ontario.* 1923. pp. 256-7.

people living in circumstances characteristic of pioneer life. All honour is due to the first inhabitants in all parts of our province, who made the best of such primitive means of communication as were available, and who toiled hard and long that their children might not have to undergo the same experiences and suffer the same privations.

CHAPTER VII

ROADS AND ROAD-BUILDERS

THE TRANSITION OF TRANSPORTATION

"When I picture the cart that the Patriarchs used,
That oxen drew patiently day after day,
It is not surprising that Joseph refused
To go for his brethren and bring them away.
The wheels they were hewn from the trunk of a tree,
The creaking I cannot describe with a pen,
And, picturing this, you will readily see
How thankful I am that I didn't live then.

When I think of the coaches of days long ago
The gentry made use of with joy and delight,
That often were stuck in the mud and the snow,
And held up by highwaymen night after night;
When I think of their springless condition, to me
A great satisfaction is mine once again,
And, joining with me, you will readily see
How thankful I am that I didn't live then.

When I think of the motor-car silent and swift,
In the dark sky of transport, so long overcast,
I see in my vision a limitless rift
That heralds the dawn of the best thing at last.
There is comfort and speed in the automobile
That none can deny, and no one gainsay;
Then I know that with me you will readily feel
How thankful I am that I'm living today."

PERCY H. PUNSHON (1911).[1]

THE chief means of transportation in pioneer Canada was by the use of the magnificent waterways; but as early as 1667 an Inspector of Roads was appointed in Quebec to superintend the ever-increasing need for a means of communication by land between settlements. Under the French *régime* the Royal Road was to be twenty-four feet wide, with a ditch on either side three feet wide and three feet deep. Progress was inevitably slow, but in 1733 the King's Highway from Quebec to Montreal was completed, and in subsequent years the work of road-building was extended to the district south of the St. Lawrence. Most travel occurred upon these roads in winter, and there were strict regulations by which farmers along the route were forced to

[1]The entire poem of five stanzas may be found in the centennial issue of the *Picton Gazette,* December 29, 1930.

aid in their maintenance. Small pine trees were to be planted twenty-four-feet apart so that the roadway would be marked in winter, any farmer ignoring this duty being subject to a fine of ten francs. It is interesting to know that a similar fine might be levied against anyone who violated the speed law by trotting or galloping his horse on Sundays in the vicinity of a church.

In Upper Canada an occasional Indian path or portage trail was all that was to be found at that time. During the Seven Years' War the French or British armies built short sections of road for military purposes, particularly in the neighbourhood of the main forts, Kingston and Niagara. At the time of the arrival of the first Loyalist settlers in Upper Canada there were not, however, any roads in the whole region which could justify the name. The earliest inhabitants along the St. Lawrence and the Bay of Quinté and in the Niagara district blazed trails through the woods near their settlements, except where the water transportation was good; but for many years, until the War of 1812 demonstrated otherwise, it was considered a waste of time and money to open a road where "slack-water" transportation had been made available by the bounty of nature. Bateaux and canoes on the St. Lawrence and Ottawa Rivers, with the addition of a few government schooners on Lakes Ontario and Erie, supplied the needs of explorer, fur trader, soldier and settler; while land travel, essential only in winter, was made comparatively easy at that season by snow and ice, which made the most remote points accessible by snow-shoe and dog-sled.

Such was the extent of the development of transportation in Upper Canada when the province was created in 1791. Once each winter an "express" for the convenience of the army and merchants travelled from Montreal to Detroit and back, carrying any mail that had accumulated since the close of navigation. The express usually consisted of a white man with one or two Indian guides, and they travelled on snow-shoes along the St. Lawrence to Kingston, then by Oswego and the south shore of Lake Ontario to Niagara, and thence by a well-known trail along the north side of Lake Erie to Detroit. No road was necessary for this type of travel, but axes were carried to aid in clearing away brush or travelling over ice. Some travellers to Niagara in winter came through the United States, and though this route was easier than that on the Canadian side it was a difficult trip at best.

Road construction and maintenance along the shores of the St. Lawrence and the Bay of Quinté was retarded by the facilities available by water; but, except for about fifty miles of the distance, a highway had been blazed from Montreal to Kingston within a few years of the arrival of the Loyalists in Upper Canada. At the time of the creation of the province, in 1791, this road appears to have been considered open for the purpose of postal services, but it was complete only from Montreal to Lake St. Francis and from Cornwall to Prescott. Ferries were employed to cross the Ottawa River at Isle Perrot, and there was a horse-boat in use on Lake St. Francis because the low land in Glengarry made road-building difficult, and in addition the water transportation was good. Isaac Weld, who travelled in Canada in 1796, refers to this partially completed road and says that "no one ever thinks of going thither by land, on account of the numerous inconveniences such a journey would be attended with".[2] With reference to the construction of the highway Canniff quotes an early Loyalist settler:

"I recollect when the King's highway was established from the provincial line to Kingston; the line was run by a surveyor named Ponair, with a surveyor under his direction by the name of Joseph Kilborne. The distance was 145 miles, and at the end of each mile was planted a red cedar post, marked on it the number of miles from the provincial line. This line of road was made some years after the first settlement, but I have forgotten the year."[3]

The road from Kingston to Burlington Bay was similarly incomplete because of the good navigation available on Lake Ontario: roads (mere bridle-paths) had been opened only in certain sections, and there was a general lack of bridges. In some districts the lake shore was the only road, and over it many a traveller walked from Kingston to York. The first section of roadway in this part of the province was un-

[2]Isaac Weld: *Travels through the States of North America.* 1799. p. 258.
[3]Henry Sherwood quoted in William Canniff: *History of the Settlement of Upper Canada.* 1869. p. 135.

doubtedly that constructed in early Loyalist days between
Kingston and Bath, and when the first mail road was
planned towards the close of the century it passed through
Bath. This great artery of communication was called the
Danforth Road after Asa Danforth (or Danford), an
American who contracted in 1798 to blaze a roadway forty
feet wide along the front of Lake Ontario at a price of
$90 a mile; this work was carried on during the next three
years.

The course of the Danforth Road followed the shore of
the Bay of Quinté from Kingston to Bath, and continued
through Adolphustown to Dorland's (later Young's) Point.
A ferry carried travellers from the Point to Lake-on-the-
Mountain, whence the road continued to the head of Picton
Bay. The route through Prince Edward County touched
Bloomfield, Wellington, Consecon and the Carrying Place,
and the road then followed the coast of Lake Ontario to
York, though at varying distances from the shore.

In the Bay of Quinté district, where the old road had
merely to be improved, Danforth's headquarters was at one
of the earliest taverns in Upper Canada, that of Henry
Finkle at Bath. Farther westward most of the roadway
had to be blazed, for but little had been previously opened.
On August 2, 1799, the Niagara *Canada Constellation* stated
that "forty miles of excellent road" had already been constructed through "the wilderness from York to the Bay of
Quinté".[4] Four months later the *Gazette* announced that
"the road from York to the Midland District is completed
as far as the Township of Hope, about sixty miles, so that
sleighs, wagons, etc., may travel it with safety. The report
which has been made to the government by the gentleman
appointed to inspect the work is highly favourable to Mr.
Danford, the undertaker, and less imperfections could not
be pointed out in so extensive a work. The remaining part
will be accomplished by the first of July next."[5]

In 1800 the Danforth Road was open from Kingston to
Ancaster. It soon fell into a bad state of disrepair in many
sections where there were no settlements, for the owners of
reserved and unoccupied lands were bound by no obligation
to perform statute labour upon it. The highway was conse-

[4]Niagara *Canada Constellation*, August 2, 1799.
[5]*Upper Canada Gazette*, December 14, 1799.

quently of little value as a route of long-distance travel, and even in its best sections was little better than a blazed trail. The state of the main post roads of Upper Canada at this period is best shown by the carriage of the mails. During the navigation season they always followed the water routes; while the infrequent winter postal service was, until after the War of 1812, conducted by sleigh or horseback courier to Dundas and Niagara, and on foot west of Dundas.

The portage road around Niagara Falls was merely an enlargement of the trail of Indian days, the existence of which was noted by the first French explorers. This roadway had been improved from time to time by soldiers and traders, and over it large wagons, laden with rum and other goods upward and furs downward, were hauled by four or five yoke of oxen from Queenston to Niagara and Chippawa, and sometimes on to Fort Erie. During the navigation season as many as fifty wagons a day are stated to have passed over this route at the close of the eighteenth century;[6] while stage-wagons carried passengers, and other travellers rode horseback or tramped across the portage, among the latter being many peddlers carrying packs. From Chippawa to Fort Erie bateaux were commonly used, and the Indian trade was continued by schooner to Detroit and Michilimackinac.

A road had been blazed as early as 1785 from Niagara as far inland as Ancaster by the Loyalist settlers, the cost of the work being met by private subscription. Before the end of the century there were other roads in this district. One was opened from Niagara to Burlington Inlet, following the lake shore closely all the way; another proceeded along the foot of the escarpment; and there were several short roadways. A contemporary opinion concerning the road development in this region is interesting. In 1796 Mrs. Simcoe, wife of the first Lieutenant-Governor, wrote in her diary that Mr. Green had lately, "at the Governor's request and expense", cut a road through the wood towards 40-Mile Creek, and that the Governor intended to open a road on the mountain from Niagara to the head of

[6]D. W. Smith: *A Short Topographical Description of His Majesty's Province of Upper Canada. . . .* 1799. p. 31.

COPP'S FERRY, NEAR GEORGEVILLE, L.C., 1840

THE FINKLE TAVERN, BATH

One of the first inns in Upper Canada

THE KING'S HEAD INN, BURLINGTON BAY, 1796

This noted government inn was located near the present Hamilton
Waterworks

BETWEEN COBOURG AND YORK, 1830

A scene typical of districts in process of settlement

the lake, instead of travelling upon "a most terrible road below, full of swamps, fallen trees, etc."[7]

The Simcoes once rode part of the way from Niagara to Burlington Bay, and Mrs. Simcoe describes a ride of five miles by moonlight over "that terrible kind of road where the horses' feet are entangled among the logs and water and swamp";[8] but she was so engaged with the beauty of the moonlight scene that she forgot the difficulties of travel and was soon at the King's Head Inn, at the southerly end of Burlington Bay; this hostelry was built by the government for the convenience of travellers from York to Niagara, and to facilitate communication between Niagara and the La Tranche River (later named the Thames), where Governor Simcoe at first intended to establish the seat of government.

As an example in this district of road-building by private subscription may be taken the Black Swamp Road in Lincoln County. An advertisement dated at Newark (Niagara), January 30, 1799, announces that at a meeting in Hind's Hotel of the subscribers to the road, overseers were appointed and it was resolved that subscription papers be opened at "Mr. Heron's in Newark, Mr. David Secord's Mills near Queenston, Mr. Clendenen's Mills at the 12-mile Creek, Mr. Robert Nelles' Mill at the 40-mile Creek, and at Mr. James Wilson's in Ancaster, where those gentlemen who are inclined to aid so necessary a work will have an opportunity of adding their donations".[9]

The road or causeway was nearly two-thirds completed by March 15th, when the trustees inserted an announcement in the *Gazette* informing the subscribers that "there are 387 rods causewayed and 240 only remain undone, which at one and a half dollars, will make 360 dollars. Thus that tremendous Black Swamp bridge that has been estimated at so many thousand dollars and calculated to take up so much time has been nearly two-thirds done in about one month, that too in a severe winter. Upper Canada cannot boast a work of the kind so far advanced in so short a time. Three hundred and sixty dollars more, gentlemen, and the work will be completed. The money

[7]*Diary of Mrs. John Graves Simcoe*, June 10, 1796.
[8]*Ibid.*
[9]*Upper Canada Gazette*, February 8, 1798.

that has been subscribed being all expended, the trustees hope the subscribers will be good enough to pay into the hands of either of them their respective donations; any further donation will be thankfully received and carefully expended".[10]

In spite of the efforts of public-spirited citizens, however, the average road was almost impossible to "navigate" in any season except winter.   A very disgruntled traveller wrote to the editor of the *Niagara Herald* concerning his experiences on roads near the head of Lake Ontario in 1801:

"I have lately had the misfortune to ride on the roads of this district, particularly through Barton and Saltfleet, and esteem my escape from broken neck, legs and arms more miraculous than that of the survivors of the memorable battle of the Devil's Hole.   Besides the pains I endured on my own account I had those of a feeling man towards distressed families in wagons breaking down, falling into deep gullies and bridgeless creeks from whence it seemed impossible to emerge—the women and children wading through these like Pharaoh's hosts, through the (not Red but) muddy sea.   These roads may be the best of any for the people of the townships in which they lay, but they are not so for others, and if the inhabitants have not public spirit enough to keep them passable the law ought to make them do it; and if there is no law existing to that end the law makers should be convened, and, like jurors in cases of life and death, be not suffered to part till they agreed on one."[11]

Soon after his arrival at York in 1793 Simcoe ordered Captain Smith and one hundred men to open Dundas Street westward from the head of Lake Ontario towards the La Tranche.   The name of the road commemorates Henry Dundas, Secretary of State of the Imperial Government. Simcoe's intention was that ultimately there should be a highway from the eastern to the western limits of the province; but the work was done in small sections, and not until many years after his death was there any such artery of communication.   At first the section westward from the important lake port, Dundas, towards the La Tranche was

[10]*Ibid.*, March 15, 1798.
[11]*Niagara Herald*, September 12, 1801.

commenced, and Mrs. Simcoe notes in her diary that Captain Smith had returned to York in October after a month's absence during which twenty miles of roadway was opened.[12] This road was needed to avoid the detour by Queenston and Fort Erie in westward travel to the Mohawk Village, near Brantford, and beyond.

A few roads east and west of Delaware, presumably parts of Dundas Street as planned by Simcoe, had been blazed before 1793. A survey map made in the spring of 1793 by Patrick McNiff shows a road leading "from the Delawares to the Moravian Village", another to the entrance of Kettle Creek on Lake Erie, and a third leading to the Mohawk Village on the Grand River.[13] It appears that these were well-known Indian trails and had been in part surveyed and blazed into roadways by Augustus Jones and other surveyors in 1791 and 1792. From the Mohawk Village there was, by 1794, Dundas Street to the present site of London, and, in some sections, farther westward; though from London there was good water transportation available along the Thames to Lake St. Clair, and this was very generally used.

The "Governor's Road", as Dundas Street was commonly called, was further developed by settlers, whose presence often prevented the highway from falling into disuse and disrepair. The section from Burlington Bay to York was not blazed as early as the remaining parts because water transport along Lake Ontario was good. In September, 1793, Mrs. Simcoe writes that there was a road over which one could walk three miles on either side of the camp at York;[14] but it was at least seven years before Dundas Street was open from York to Ancaster as part of the highway built by Asa Danforth. The roadway as eventually opened was blazed about three miles back from the lake in order to avoid the difficulty of bridging streams near their outlets, and for greater safety in transporting troops and supplies in time of war.

The old Mississaga trail along the lake shore from York

[12]See Mrs. Simcoe's *Diary*, September 23, 1793 and October 27, 1793.
[13]Quoted by J. H. Coyne in *Historical Sketches of the County of Elgin*, p. 42. (Published in 1895 by the Elgin Historical and Scientific Institute.)
[14]Simcoe, *op. cit.*, September 27, 1793.

to the head of the lake was not blazed into a road until many years later. The first official notice in connection with the Lake Shore Road appeared in the *Gazette* in 1804, when the government asked for tenders for roadwork and bridges from Peter Street in York to Burlington Bay. The road was to be a continuation of Lot (Queen) Street, and of a width of thirty-three feet;[15] but while part of the section from York to the Credit River may have been constructed at that time the remainder was not, for we find in the *Gazette* four years later a reference to the advisability of opening a lake shore road from the head of the lake to the Credit.[16] In the early years of the century Dundas Street and the Lake Shore Road were considerably confused, and it is often impossible to tell which is meant.

It is often difficult to differentiate between the opening of a new road and the repair of an old one that has become impassable. Dundas Street west of York, for example, followed the course blazed by Asa Danforth in 1798-1800; but in 1806 the bridges and a large part of the roadway had fallen into such a state of disrepair that tenders were asked by the road commissioners of the Home District for the opening of "the road called Dundas Street, leading through the Indian Reserve at the River Credit, and also to erect a bridge over the same river, and to bridge and causeway the road beyond as an aid to statute labour, which is not sufficient."[17]

Ferries were used in early times to effect a crossing of large rivers such as the Humber and the Credit. Surveyor-General Smith wrote in 1799 that there was "a small house of entertainment" at the mouth of the Credit,[18] and the inn-keeper was also in charge of the ferry. This was a government-owned inn and was kept by Thomas Ingersoll, one of the first white residents of Toronto Township, and, after his death, by his son Charles; and later when Charles moved westward and founded Ingersoll, the inn and ferry were kept by George Cutter. In 1803 Donald Cameron was ferryman at the Humber, where, a few years later, was established McLean's Inn, the only place of rest for travellers between the Credit and York. In later years Dundas

---

[15]*Upper Canada Gazette*, August 4, 1804.
[16]*Ibid.*, September 17, 1808.
[17]*Ibid.*, June 21, 1806.   [18]Smith, *op. cit.*, p. 26.

Street west of York again fell into disrepair and was not greatly used because of the deep ravines and, in many cases, bridgeless streams; in fact only recently have high viaduct bridges enabled general use of this old roadway.

Frequently the initiative of settlers was responsible for the building of long stretches of road. In the *Canada Constellation* of September 13, 1799, appears an account of the early settlement of Oxford County and the district westward to the mouth of the Thames, which commenced in 1794. With reference to road-building there the writer says:

"These settlers, being aware of the importance of roads in raising the value of property, early set about to open and extend them; and, notwithstanding the numerous discouragements and the immediate necessities of their families, they in one year, at the expense of Mr. Thomas Ingersoll, cut and bridged a road from Burford to Le Trenche, through a wilderness of 25 or 30 miles. Mr. Elisha Putnam of that Town (Oxford) by subscription has since continued the road from thence to Allen's, Delaware Township. The subscription being inadequate to completely finish the work it was left in an unfinished state, but passable for sleighs. He has been by no means discouraged, but issued a subscription to cut a road from Allen's to the Moravian grant, a further distance, as it must run, of fifty miles, to be ten feet wide, and the logs lying crosswise to be cut out twelve feet long.

"Without waiting the issue of the subscription, and relying on the patriotism of his neighbours and gentlemen in other parts of the province who hold lands upon that river, he began, and has already opened half the distance, and promises, if the liberality of his friends be equal to it, that he shall immediately complete the whole. The Moravians will extend it seven miles, when it will form a junction with the old road, from which there will be a good wagon road forty miles to the mouth of the river. Thus we shall have by the ensuing winter a land communication with Detroit, and not a day's ride without settlements; such is the enterprise of our western inhabitants that 150 miles of road is made without the least allowance from Government."[19]

[19]Niagara *Canada Constellation*, September 13, 1799.

At the commencement of the new century road development in Upper Canada was obviously very incomplete; from the eastern boundary to the Detroit River there was merely a series of portage roads to fill in the gaps where water transport was inconvenient, difficult or impossible. The navigation of the Thames to Lake St. Clair was supplemented in 1803 by the Baldoon Road, constructed by Lord Selkirk's Scottish settlers in that region. About the same time the government opened "the old Stage Road" along the shore of Lake St. Clair from the mouth of the Thames River to that of the River Pike; but the roadbed was hard to keep in repair, and in later years was submerged.

Simcoe's second great road project was Yonge Street, named after Sir George Yonge, Minister of War in the British Cabinet. A bush road was partially surveyed by Augustus Jones in 1793-94, but it was blazed only in part, and was improved chiefly by William Berczy's settlers in Markham Township. Towards the close of 1795 Governor Simcoe ordered Jones to open the road to Lake Simcoe, and operations were commenced on the 4th of January, 1796. The Queen's Rangers were engaged in the work, and the 33-mile road from York to Pine Fort Landing, Lake Simcoe, was blazed in about six weeks. On February 18, 1796, Mrs. Simcoe wrote in her diary that "the party who went to cut the road from hence to Lake Simcoe, called the Yonge Street, are returned after an absence of seven weeks. The distance is 33 miles and 56 chains."[20]

The road was long much like all others at that time,— full of stumps, pools of water and other obstructions; in fact each time it was improved it was usual to refer to the road as being "opened". In 1799, for example, the editor of the Niagara *Canada Constellation* announced that he had been informed that the North-West Company was thinking of establishing communication with the upper lakes *viâ* Yonge Street, and that the government "has actually begun to open that street for several miles, which example will undoubtedly be no small inducement to persons who possess property on that street and its vicinity to exert themselves to open and complete what may be justly

[20]Simcoe, *op. cit.*, February 18, 1796.

considered one of the primary objects of attention in a new country—a good road".[21]

It is quite evident that a great deal of work had to be done on Yonge Street before it could be used effectively, for we are told that "so rough was the track that when, in 1797, Balser Munshaw, one of the founders of the village of Richmond Hill, sought a wilderness home along this thoroughfare it was found necessary to take his canvas-top wagon apart, and drag the wheels and axles and other equipment up the steep hills by means of strong ropes".[22]

Between 1799 and the War of 1812 the North-West Company contributed many thousands of pounds towards the improvement of Yonge Street, which formed an important link in their main trade route to Michilimackinac and the Great West. The change from the old canoe trail up the Ottawa came just as the century closed, the York *Gazette* announcing on March 9, 1799: "We hear that the N. W. Company has given twelve thousand pounds towards making Yonge Street a good road, and that the N. W. commerce will be communicated through this place".[23] The Company's bateaux were soon following the shore of Lake Ontario to York and crossing on wheels over Yonge Street to Lake Simcoe, the highway having meanwhile been somewhat improved by the government and the Company, with the aid of the subscriptions of settlers along its course. In 1801, however, its condition was still very bad, a surveyor's report stating that there were unburned trees and brush in the roadway, and that the greater part of it was "not passable for any carriage whatever on account of logs which lie in the street".[24] In the late thirties Yonge Street was partially macadamized, though the type of soil prevented even the twelve miles so improved from remaining long in good condition.

The extension of the highway northward from Lake Simcoe was commenced twenty years after the first opening of Yonge Street. During the closing months of the War of 1812 a detachment of soldiers under William Dunlop

---

[21]Niagara *Canada Constellation*, August 23, 1799.
[22]J. Ross Robertson: *Landmarks of Toronto*. 1894-1914. Vol. V, p. 20.
[23]*Upper Canada Gazette*, March 9, 1799.
[24]Report of Surveyor Stegmann, York County *Historical Atlas*. 1878.
    p. x.

constructed a nine-mile portage road from the present site of Barrie, on Kempenfeldt Bay, to Willow Creek; the completion of this link in the winter of 1814-15 enabled speedier communication between York and Penetanguishene, a roadway over the entire distance being gradually blazed. Until 1847 the road northward from Lake Simcoe was of little value because of its poor condition; in that year, however, the continuation of Yonge Street to Penetanguishene was cleared out and made passable. This famous pioneer highway, originally extending only a few miles northward from York, is now 490 miles long if we include the Ferguson Highway extension from Severn Bridge to Cochrane; while a roadway constructed 140 miles farther north along the Timiskaming and Northern Ontario Railway would carry the route to Moosonee, on the shores of James Bay.

During, or immediately after the War of 1812 the missing links in the main east-to-west highways were completed, for their lack was seen to be a great disadvantage during that war. The Danforth Road had fallen into disrepair in many sections because of the entire lack of any effective system of road maintenance. In settled districts statute labour kept it generally passable, but where it traversed reserved lands, or regions unsettled because of absentee owners or for other reasons, it was no better than a trail. In 1815-16 another great highway, the Kingston Road, which followed the Danforth Road in some parts but was in general nearer the lake shore, was being opened, and late in 1816 it was complete from Montreal to Kingston. A contemporary writer thus describes the course of the Bay of Quinté section:

"The great road from Kingston to York divides at Ernest Town. One branch passes on the north side of the bay, crossing the Apanee on a bridge at the mills, and the Trent by a ferry near its mouth. The other continues on the lake shore, passing the bay by a ferry from Adolphus Town over the peninsula of Prince Edward. They unite a little west of the head of the bay".[25]

At the commencement of 1817 the Kingston or York Road was complete to York, and it was for the first time

[25]Robert Gourlay: *A Statistical Account of Upper Canada.* 1822. Vol. I, p. 97.

possible to carry on long-distance land transportation. Stage-sleighs operated over the route during the winter, but at other seasons this and most other roadways were little used except by travellers on horseback. The navigation of lake and river long remained preferable, except to those who sought to avoid sea-sickness. Such stage-wagons as dared to operate in summer had a difficult time of it, and a traveller refers to land journeys as "the roughest on either side of the Atlantic".[26] Concerning the state of the roads near the head of Lake Ontario in 1816 Lieutenant Hall writes: "It took us three hours to accomplish the five miles of road betwixt the head of the lake and the main road, called Dundas Street, which runs from York towards Lake Erie and Amherstburg".[27]

Another system of roadways, early important as the great thoroughfare through a well-settled district, was due to the colonisation efforts of Colonel Thomas Talbot. In the Talbot Settlement the roads were commenced in 1809 under the direction of Colonel Mahlon Burwell, and the first sections were completed in 1811. This highway was gradually extended, and eventually the two main branches were completed from Fort Erie to Sandwich, and from Port Talbot to London. Talbot Street was not greatly retarded by reserved lands and soon became known as the best road in the province; it was one of the first to be improved from the original corduroy to more advanced types of construction.

In 1827 there was a complete road connection between Halifax and Amherstburg, made up chiefly of the Kempt Road, the Kingston Road, Dundas Street, and the Baldoon Road. For many years, however, the state of the highways of Upper Canada remained a public disgrace. In 1832 Dr. William Dunlop advised intending settlers that there were "only two seasons when you can travel with any degree of comfort—midsummer and midwinter; the former by horseback or in a light wagon, the latter by sleigh."[28] But very often the roads were almost impassable even in midsum-

[26]Francis Hall: *Travels in Canada and the United States in 1816-17.* 1818. p. 152.
[27]*Ibid.*, p. 212.
[28]William Dunlop: *Statistical Sketches of Upper Canada.* 1832. pp. 54-5.

mer: in July, 1833, Patrick Shirreff found the Kingston Road east of York "worse than any yet travelled on", an average of from two to three miles per hour being the most that could be accomplished in the stage-wagon.[29] The road from York to Hamilton, and westward to the Grand River, was somewhat better in places, though a traveller refers to being "sadly knocked about" by riding over certain sections which were still largely corduroy.[30] The Talbot roads were, on the whole, in a comparatively good condition; but farther west, in Essex and Kent Counties, it was often difficult to travel even on horseback.

One of the earliest macadamised roads in Upper Canada was constructed over the portion of the Kingston Road between Kingston and Napanee. The province set aside $120,000 for this work, largely owing to the enterprise and influence of Judge J. S. Cartwright, and in 1837 the reconstruction of the roadway commenced. James Cull was the engineer in charge of the work, which was completed in 1839 at a cost of $12,000 more than had been anticipated. It was expected that toll-gates every five miles would soon repay the cost of the enterprise. This piece of road was for many years an excellent highway, and much the best section of the Kingston Road. In the thirties an effort was made by persons interested in the Danforth Road, (usually called Dundas Street at that time), to improve it east of York in place of what was sometimes called Cornell's Road (the Kingston Road), but the latter continued to be the main route of travel.

In outlying regions at a distance from the main east-to-west highways the development of roads accompanied or closely followed settlement. In 1799-1800 Messrs. Ward and Smith were slashing a roadway from Dundas to Waterloo County as an accommodation for the first German settlers then beginning to enter that district; the road passed through the notorious Beverly Swamp, and this section of it was long impassable, a circumstance which led to many travellers' stories of terrifying adventures.

The Ottawa River district was opened for settlement after the War of 1812. Philemon Wright and his American

[29] Patrick Shirreff: *A Tour through North America.* 1835. p. 119.
[30] *The Diary of William Proudfoot,* January 5, 1833.

James P. Cockburn

THE KINGSTON-YORK ROAD, 1830

Field

PERTH, LANARK COUNTY, CANADA WEST, IN 1853

UP-TO-THE-MINUTE IN 1905

This one-cylinder Cadillac of 1905 was a great advance over the "curved-dashed, tiller-steered motor carriages" of 1902. W. D. Wilson, Toronto, is the driver of the car, which was photographed in the grounds of Bishop Bethune College, Oshawa.

settlers had been located at Hull since 1800, but the district across the river was first settled in 1816. The Richmond Road—a blazed trail from Perth to Richmond—was opened by soldier settlers in 1818, and a road had also been pushed northwards from Brockville, though in 1820 two miles per hour was the usual rate of travel over it. The difficulties of transport over such bush roads are well described by John McDonald, who journeyed from Brockville to New Lanark and New Perth in 1821. His party consisted of a large number of immigrants, several wagon-loads of whom were upset frequently during the trip.

"One boy was killed on the spot, several were very much hurt; one man got his arm broken, and our own wagoner, in spite of all his care and skill, was baffled, his horse having laired in a miry part of the road where he stuck fast; and even after he was loosed from the yoke the poor animal strove so much to no purpose that he fell down in a state of complete exhaustion three times in the mire. The mire was so tenacious, being a tough clay, that we were compelled to disengage his feet from the clay with handspikes before we got him freed. . . . Fortunately a team of oxen came forward, which the owner loosed from the yoke and fastened to our wagon. With these and the horse together the wagon was at length pulled out. . . .

"Next morning, . . . when we came again to the road it appeared so very bad that it put us to a complete stand, seeing no way of getting through it. We at last concluded that the only alternative left us was to pull up the farmers' fences, which we did in two places, and thus got through and then closed them up again. This was a new mode of travelling to us, but the only one by which we could at all hope to get through. Every now and then we were compelled to cut down the fences, as it was wholly a region of woods through which we had to pass".[31]

The most important addition to the highways of the province in the late eighteen-twenties was the Huron Road, which made available a means of communication by land between Lake Ontario and Lake Huron. This roadway was blazed largely through the lands of the Canada Company

[31]John McDonald: *Narrative of a Voyage to Quebec, and Journey from thence to New Lanark, Upper Canada.* 1823. pp. 10-11.

in 1827, and was an exception among early roads in that it was opened prior to the arrival of settlers. From Galt to Guelph the work was under the direction of Absalom Shade, while from Guelph to Goderich the men in charge were Messrs. Campbell, Pryor and Dunlop of the Canada Company. In the thirties this road was still largely corduroy, with stumps two or three feet in height left standing, and it remained chiefly mud or corduroy until long after the middle of the century.

Among other early colonisation roads was Hurontario Street, running in a north-westerly direction from Port Credit through the centre of the Townships of Toronto, Chinguacousy and Caledon to the north-west part of the last-named township, near Orangeville, and thence to Collingwood on Georgian Bay. In 1837 was commenced the Garafraxa Road, or Rankin's Road, as it is often called after its surveyor, Charles Rankin; the route lay from Oakville to Owen Sound, but forty miles of the roadway—from Oakville through the Townships of Trafalgar, Esquesing, Erin and Garafraxa—had been built previously. In 1842 the Sydenham Road, from Arthur, in Wellington County, to Owen Sound, was blazed to make possible the colonisation of another section of the same district. Other regions in the "Queen's Bush" were opened for settlement by the building of the Durham, the Northern and other colonisation roads which were constructed from time to time. So great was the development in this period that in the early forties there were about 6,000 miles of post-roads in Upper Canada.

In the early sixties the government began several road-ways in both Upper and Lower Canada in order to encourage settlement in the "backwoods" districts. Those in Upper Canada were seven in number: (1) The Ottawa and Opeongo Road, 171 miles long, between the Ottawa River and Lake Huron. (2) The Addington Road, 61 miles long, running northward from the settled districts of Addington County to the Opeongo Road. (3) The Hastings Road, 68 miles in length, connecting Hastings County with the Opeongo Road, and nearly parallel to the Addington Road. (4) The Bobcaygeon Road from Bobcaygeon northwards through Victoria County;

it was intended that this roadway should eventually reach
Lake Nipissing. (5) The Frontenac and Madawaska Road.
(6) The Muskoka Road from Lake Couchiching to the
Grand Falls of Muskoka, to intersect "Peterson's Line"
which was intended to be linked up with the Ottawa and
Opeongo Road. (7) The Sault Ste. Marie Road, from the
Sault to Goulais Bay. As the roadways were blazed the
districts were opened for settlement, but for a long time
progress in both road and settlement was slow. Another
roadway which was pushed into the wild lands in the early
sixties was the Burleigh Road, north from Lakefield through
the remote sections of Peterborough County. For several
years the bridges along this road were annually burned
out, a misfortune quite commonly experienced in the backwoods districts.

In the year following Confederation the Dawson Road
westward from Prince Arthur's Landing (later named Port
Arthur) was commenced. In 1868-69 this highway had been
blazed forty-eight miles from Thunder Bay to Shebandowan
Lake. During the winter of 1869-70 bridges were constructed over the two largest rivers which the road crossed,
and in the spring the roadway was pushed six or seven miles
farther. This was the extent of its development when
Wolseley's expedition to the Red River was pushing
westward in 1870 to the scene of trouble; and of the small
section completed, parts had been washed away by floods
or burned over by forest fires.

During the rest of the nineteenth century the construction of roads preceded or immediately followed the development of new settlements in the various parts of the province,
both in Old and New Ontario. There was but little improvement in the general condition of highways, however,
and even at the close of the century it was true that there
were almost no roads which were good at all times of the
year; while in general the provincial roadways were almost
impassable during at least two months of each year at the
season of the spring floods. It was not until the advent of
the present century, and the motor-car, that there was any
attempt to make genuine macadamised roads on a large
scale, and their construction depended almost entirely upon
the progressiveness of counties. With the exception of

these improvements in the roadbed the appearance of the main highways changed but little until after the Great War, when, with the great increase in motor traffic, service station and gasoline tank began to replace blacksmith shop and watering-trough; while the old tavern days are recalled by the ever-increasing refreshment booths, tea-rooms and wayside road-houses which are now so characteristic of the King's highway.

As motor traffic increased, even these improved roads were found unsuitable, and our main highways are gradually being made "permanent" by the use of various types of concrete surface. One of the first asphalt motor roads in Canada was the Toronto-Hamilton Highway, commenced in 1914 to relieve unemployment, and formally opened on November 24, 1917. A commission under George H. Gooderham supervised the construction of this highway, which cost $1,250,000, or about $33,000 a mile,—much less than many a later road where natural difficulties were greater. The high cost of this type of roadway necessitated that such important work be done largely by the Provincial Government, under whose control the system of King's Highways is gradually being extended in all directions. Since 1917 a total of $113,880,538 has been spent upon these arteries of communication; but the more remote districts have not been neglected in the meantime, for the Department of Public Highways is continually engaged in the development of colonisation roads in the sparsely-settled townships of Southern Ontario, as well as trunk roads through the North. That Ontario is the banner province of the Dominion with regard to highways is quite evident when we learn that out of a total of 80,497 miles of surfaced roads throughout the Dominion 44,740 miles are in Ontario.

The latest great roadway to be undertaken by the government is the Ontario section of the Trans-Canada Highway. This road enters the province at Pembroke, and will pass through New Ontario to Kenora. The highway is either completed, under construction, or has been definitely planned from Pembroke to North Bay, and from Schreiber to Kenora *via* Nipigon, Port Arthur, Fort William, and Dryden; while the course of the roadway over the section between North Bay and Schreiber has not been definitely settled, but will pass through one or more of the towns Sudbury, Sault Ste. Marie, Cobalt, Cochrane and Hearst. The length of the Ontario section of this highway will be about 1,386 miles, and its cost when completed is estimated by the Minister of Lands and Forests at from $10,000 to $20,000 a mile.[32] A large grant by the Federal Government enabled some 40,000 men to be employed in road development in Northern Ontario during the fiscal year ending October 31, 1932, but it will not be possible during a period of economic depression for either the Federal or Provincial Governments to continue to finance the project at the same pace. Though it will be many years before this great highway across Canada is complete, the breadth and scope of the undertaking will do much to decrease the possibilities of secession from the Dominion; and when finished it will undoubtedly prove a most important factor in preserving the union of the provinces by facilitating intercourse between them.

[32]Speech of the Minister of Lands and Forests in the Legislative Assembly of Ontario, March 8, 1932.

CHAPTER VIII

THE DEVELOPMENT OF ROAD CONSTRUCTION

THE CORDUROY ROAD

"Half a log, half a log,
 Half a log onward,
Shaken and out of breath,
 Rode we and wondered.
Ours not to reason why,
 Ours but to clutch and cry
While onward we thundered."

CARRIE MUNSON HOOPLE.[1]

THE first roads in Upper Canada followed the course of Indian trails or lumbermen's and traders' portage routes. The development from a foot-path to a wagon road was usually very gradual; the settlers who used the trail found it to their advantage to make their path easier by breaking off overhanging branches or removing stumps, and it was general to avoid such obstacles as hills, rocks or swamps by going around them wherever it was possible.

In winter, snow and ice, "the great democratic elements in the physical constitution of Canada",[2] made it possible for early settlers, using their home-made sledges, to travel with ease where it was almost impossible to go by any method at other seasons. The usual farmer's sleigh was a "jumper",—merely a wooden box on runners often not even shod with iron; but there were various modifications of these sleds, including the elaborate *traineaux* and *carrioles* owned by the wealthy in the towns. Bundled up in buffalo robes and bearskins, the traveller made his way pleasantly and speedily across the country, and the farmer "visited all his friends and transacted all his exterior business".[3]

An early writer, in describing the importance of winter travel, states that almost every farmer had a team of horses and a sleigh or sledge, "which he employs usually, a part of the winter at least, in visiting his distant friends. Travelling here is so habitual that a farmer and his wife think

[1]Carrie Munson Hoople: *Along the Way*. 1909.
[2]T. C. Keefer: *Travel and Transportation*. In John Lovell (Ed.): *Eighty Years' Progress in British North America*. 1863. p. 117.
[3]Andrew Picken: *The Canadas*. 1832. p. 269.

524

it nothing extraordinary to make an excursion of six or seven hundred miles in the winter to see their friends; neither does such a trip incur much expense, for they usually carry with them in their sleigh provisions for their journey, as well as grain for the horses. This may be considered as a great amusement, affording the most lively satisfaction, and forming the mind with redoubled vigour to undertake the fatigues of the following year".[4]

The winter transportation that was possible over the snow roads or on the ice of lake and river was, in fact, one of the main sources of the rapid prosperity of the country: for during this season the farmer was able to take his produce to market and to obtain a year's supplies; while lumbermen commonly drew all their provisions to the camps and hauled their lumber to the water during this season. Even as late as 1825 it was estimated that at least two-thirds of the crops were transported in winter.

Travelling over the ice was not without its dangers, however, and many a sleigh broke through, occasionally with fatal results. On February 15, 1834, for example, the Rev. Matthew Millar, Presbyterian minister at Cobourg, was drowned in the Bay of Quinté when his cutter broke through the ice while he was on a return journey from Perth. Such accidents were, in fact, not infrequent, and in describing winter travel Mrs. Simcoe notes in her diary that "the people of the States are particularly expert in saving horses from drowning; they travel with ropes which they fasten round the horses' necks if they fall into the water; pulling it stops their breath, and then they float and can be pulled out; then they take off the rope as quickly as possible, and the horse travels on as well as before".[5]

It was a general policy in early days to use the roads only in winter and to depend on water transportation during the navigation season. The emphasis in road-building was therefore laid upon the portage roads, where water transportation was difficult or impossible. Until the War of 1812 showed the inconvenience resulting from such a policy, the construction of roads elsewhere was retarded. The main portage trails were those around the worst

[4]D'Arcy Boulton: *Sketch of His Majesty's Province of Upper Canada.* 1805. p. 11.
[5]*Diary of Mrs. John Graves Simcoe*, February 27, 1795.

rapids of the St. Lawrence and Ottawa Rivers, and between Queenston and Chippawa, avoiding the Falls and the rapid part of the Niagara River. The latter road, originating as an Indian trail, was early improved by the soldiers of the garrison and became an important artery of trade between Lakes Ontario and Erie; in 1795 some fifty wagons a day were carrying merchandise or furs over this highway, of which a considerable part is now under water.

There was a similar, though poorer and less-used road connecting the French *côtes* or settlements established along the Detroit River in the latter part of the French period. This roadway, like the old stage road constructed on the shore of Lake St. Clair by the government about 1803, entailed considerable expense to keep in a passable condition, for the course of both lay through low or swampy territory, and both have long been under water. The shores of Lake Erie and Lake Ontario were also frequently used by early travellers, particularly before the opening of the Talbot and Kingston Roads, as preferable to the existing trails which were often impassable.

For many years the opening of a road merely meant the blazing of a road allowance, the widening of a trail or footpath, or the development of what was at best merely a bridle-path in summer and an ox-sled road in winter. To convert these trails into summer roads the first thought was to use the vast quantities of timber which had to be removed from the face of the land, and which were commonly burned as almost valueless; consequently there developed the notorious corduroy type of road construction, the word originating in the ridged cloth which was in common use and noted for its wearing qualities.

An authority, in describing the construction of corduroy roads, says: "Whole hecatombs of trees are sacrificed to form a corrugated causeway of their round trunks, laid side by side, over which wagons can be slowly dragged or bumped, any attempt at speed being checked by immediate symptoms of approaching dissolution in the vehicle".[6] Another writer describes the logs used in the construction of a road as "from nine inches to two feet in diameter, not squared, flattened, nor even straight, and often far apart".[7]

[6]Keefer, *op. cit.*, p. 119.
[7]K. M. Lizars: *The Valley of the Humber.* 1913. p. 56.

In some districts, however, care was taken to make as good a road as possible. The best results were obtained by splitting the logs in half and placing the flat side downwards; and if the trouble were taken to place the largest logs in the swampy land, and to do the work as evenly as possible, a fairly satisfactory road was usually the result, especially if earth and stone were used to fill the inequalities; but if little was done to improve the roadway in after years, it soon tended to degenerate into abysses and holes, and called forth the most severe criticism of several generations of travellers.   References to the terrible corduroy roads, "more abominably jolty than anything a European imagination can conceive",[8] are found in almost every account of early travel in Canada. Captain Basil Hall describes the condition of the Kingston Road east of York in July, 1827, in terms which leave little to the imagination:

"The horrible corduroy roads again made their appearance in a more formidable shape by the addition of deep, inky holes, which almost swallowed up the fore-wheels of the wagon, and bathed its hinder axle-tree. The jogging and plunging to which we were now exposed, and the occasional bang when the vehicle reached the bottom of one of these abysses, were so new and remarkable in the history of our travels that we tried to make a good joke of them".[9]

A journey westward from Hamilton ten years later is similarly described:

"The roads were throughout so execrably bad that no words can give you an idea of them. We often sank in mudholes above the axle-tree; then over trunks of trees laid across swamps, called corduroy roads, where my poor bones dislocated. A wheel here and there, or a broken shaft lying by the roadside, told of former wrecks and disasters. In some places they had, in desperation, flung huge boughs of oak into the mud abyss, the rich green foliage projecting on either side. This sort of illusive contrivance would sometimes give way, and we were nearly precipitated into the midst.   When I arrived at Blandford my hands were swelled and blistered by continually grasping with all my strength an iron bar in the front of my vehicle to prevent myself from being flung out".

[8]Quoted in Lizars, *op. cit.*, p. 56.
[9]Basil Hall: *Travels in America in 1827 and 1828.* 1829. Vol. I, p. 267.

When Mrs. Jameson had reached her destination she found that the journey of twenty-five miles had taken nine hours, and that she was "dreadfully weary, fevered and bruised, and my limbs ached woefully. I never beheld or imagined such roads. It is clear that the people do not apply any—even the commonest—principles of road-making; no drains are cut, no attempt is made at levelling or preparing a foundation. . . . The statute labour does not appear to be duly enforced by the commissioners and magistrates, and there are no labourers and no spare money".[10]

During the same year Mrs. Jameson travelled from Oxford Township to London. For the first few miles the road plunged through the Pine Woods, and the difficulties along this section were very great.

"The driver had often to dismount and partly fill up some tremendous hole with boughs before we could pass— or drag or lift the wagon over trunks of trees—or we sometimes sank into abysses from which it is a wonder that we ever emerged. . . . These seven miles of pine forest we traversed in three hours and a half".[11]

Another traveller expressed the opinion that the corduroy road "should have been included by Dante as the proper highway to Pandemonium, for none can be more decidedly infernal".[12]

Such were the reactions of travellers to the notorious type of road which originally formed a large part of almost every highway in the province; but it was the best road possible under the conditions which existed during the early settlement of Upper Canada, and was particularly essential in forming a base for a roadway through swampy land, though the frost sometimes destroyed the roadbed in a single season by heaving the logs out of position.

Co-existent with corduroy roads were corduroy bridges. The Simcoes found them in common use when they were travelling into the newly-created province of Upper Canada in 1792. Mrs. Simcoe wrote in her diary during the trip:

"It is certainly necessary to have a horse of the country to pass the bridges we everywhere met with, whether

---

[10]Anna Jameson: *Winter Studies and Summer Rambles in Canada.* 1838. Vol. II, pp. 119-21.
[11]*Ibid.,* Vol. II, pp. 138-9.
[12]John MacTaggart: *Three Years in Canada.* 1829. Vol. II, p. 310.

From Warburton's *Hochelaga, or England in the New World.* 1846

FARMER'S JUMPER AND GENTLEMAN'S CARRIOLE

From Carlile and Martindale's *Recollections of Canada.* 1873

A CALÈCHE AND A BUCKBOARD ON A CORDUROY ROAD

THE GOAT ISLAND BRIDGE, NIAGARA FALLS, 1827

This bridge, located a short distance above the Falls, was a source of
wonder to early visitors

TIMBER SLIDE AND CORDUROY BRIDGE

A typical scene on the Ottawa River

across the creeks (very small rivers) or swamps. The bridges are composed of trunks of trees unhewn, of unequal sizes, and laid loosely across pieces of timber placed lengthways. Rotten trees sometimes give way and a horse's leg slips through, and is in danger of being broken. The horse I am now riding had once a fall through an old bridge. He now goes very carefully".[13]

Thirty years later the Rev. Anson Green found "these miserable log bridges"[14] common throughout the country; on one occasion a corduroy bridge proved useful to him, however, for his horse got away while he was giving it a rest, and he was able to overtake it on the bridge where the animal was afraid to break into a run! Many travellers were surprised that the bridges ever stood the weights to which they were subjected, for they were very lightly constructed, usually without the aid of engineering skill. Along with the roads, they merited the epithet "infernal", and were "universally described as exceedingly uneven, disagreeable, and shaking to the bones".[15]

After a journey along the St. Lawrence River in 1833 a traveller wrote his impressions of roads and road-building; he noticed that there was a general attitude of apathy with respect to the condition of highways:

"Our road was now every mile getting worse, and the wooden bridges across brooks and ravines appeared to my unpractised eye to be almost impassable. My fellow-travellers, however, (an amiable young lady included), testified neither surprise nor alarm, and, of course, it did not become me to complain. The planks of the bridges were frequently so loose, so rotten, and so crazy, that I am yet at a loss to conjecture how our bulky machine and the four high-mettled steeds escaped without falling through. A sufficient supply of stone for repairs lay along the roadside, generally, too, in heaps, as gathered from the land; while timber for the bridges was certainly not far to seek. The period of annual repair had not, however, yet come round, and even then no metal would be applied; the road would merely receive a sort of levelling, often, as I was

---

[13]Simcoe, *op. cit.*, June 26, 1792.
[14]Anson Green: *Life and Times*. 1877. p. 53.
[15]Picken, *op. cit.*, pp. 267-8.

assured, with the plough, and the mud-holes be in some temporary way filled up."[16]

With reference to the general condition of bridges in Upper Canada during the same period an acute observer wrote in 1832: "There is a great want of good bridges in almost every part of the province. There are a few good substantial wooden frame ones built of late; but there are numbers of logs, some of which are nuisances—it is at the risk of the neck to ride over them. A native will pass over these bridges, through practice, without noticing them, while an European just arrived would shudder".[17] Many an early bridge was covered, both to protect the wood from decay and to keep the passageway free from snowdrifts.

The procedure in opening a road was always much the same. An explorer went ahead, closely followed by two surveyors with compasses; blazers then notched trees intended to be the boundaries of the road, and woodmen chopped down those which were in the course of the roadway; gangs of men followed to clear away the trunks and brush, and wagons with provisions brought up the rear. Sometimes those engaged in road-building cut down the trees over the entire course, and then returned to clear away debris; this was the method adopted by the Canada Company in opening the Huron Road in 1827. It was quite usual to leave the stumps until they had rotted, and consequently the roadway was seldom absolutely straight even over small sections. Fevers and agues were common among road-builders, forty men being emaciated with ague at one time during the blazing of the Huron Road.

Some conception of the actual work of pioneer road construction may be gained from a letter written by Augustus Jones to the Surveyor-General, the Hon. D. W. Smith. In asking for a larger allowance for road development near the Humber River he wrote: "In opening the road I am now at I find it is actually necessary to have two yoke of oxen for hauling the timbers for the bridges, as men cannot move timber of a sufficient size. A plough will also be of great use in levelling off the small hills".[18] Similarly

[16]Adam Fergusson: *Practical Notes Made during a Tour*. 1834. pp. 86-7.
[17]Joseph Pickering: *Inquiries of an Emigrant*. 1831. Appendix to the 4th Edition, 1832, p. 189.
[18]Quoted in Lizars, *op. cit.*, p. 50.

Mahlon Burwell's journal shows the difficulties which he encountered in surveying the Talbot Road in 1809-11. Bad weather conditions delayed operations greatly, while it was almost impossible to secure supplies for man or beast; wheat had to be bought as it stood in the fields, threshed by the road-builders and then carried to the nearest mill, where they had also to do the milling.

Some of the main arteries through the province were opened by military, others by civilian labour. Simcoe's two great roads—Dundas Street and Yonge Street—were blazed largely by men of the Queen's Rangers; while Talbot Street, the Danforth Road and the Kingston Road were among the great highways opened by civilian workmen. Augustus Jones' first survey of Yonge Street in 1793 was only partial, and the road was little more than an opening through the woods, the improvement of which rested largely with Berczy's settlers in Markham Township. In 1795 Governor Simcoe directed Jones to survey and open a cart road from the harbour at York to Lake Simcoe, and he appears to have started the work on January 4, 1796, at a post that he had previously planted near Lake Ontario. On February 16th he reached Pine Fort Landing, Lake Simcoe, and a few days later was back in York to report to the Governor that his work was completed. The field notes of the surveyor[20] refer to the houses of early settlers at various points in the first twenty-two miles, and to numerous bridges which also had been built previous to this survey.

The original course of Yonge Street wound in and out to avoid the hills, but it was eventually straightened. It was at first difficult to travel over the road even on horseback, as Mrs. Simcoe notes in her diary on March 31, 1796, less than two months after it was opened: "Walked to Castle Frank and returned by Yonge Street, from whence we rode. The road is as yet very bad; there are pools of water among roots of trees and fallen logs in swampy spots, and these pools, being half frozen, are rendered still more disagreeable when the horses plunge into them".[21]

[19] See Middleton and Landon's *The Province of Ontario* , Vol. I, pp. 122-5, for a summary of Burwell's notes on the opening of Talbot Street.

[20] See York County *Historical Atlas*, 1878, pp. VI to XI; and John Lynch: *Directory of the County of Peel*, 1874, p. 12, for a summary of Jones' notes concerning his survey.

[21] Simcoe, *op. cit.*, March 31, 1796.

An example of road construction amid the rigours
of a Canadian winter is afforded by the military roadway
opened between Lake Simcoe and Penetanguishene during
the War of 1812. In the autumn of 1814 it was decided to
establish a dockyard at Penetanguishene, so a road had to be
cut to that point, a distance of about thirty miles. Dr.
William Dunlop volunteered to conduct the work, and went
northward in December by way of Yonge Street with a
company of Canadian Fencibles and the same number of
militia. Lake Simcoe was found to be insufficiently frozen
over to permit crossing on the ice, but two days later Dunlop
skated across it and found it satisfactory; just as the men
were about to commence the journey, however, there was a
noise like thunder, and the ice broke up all over the lake.

Instead of waiting for it to freeze over again it was
decided that, "having a coil of rope with us, it should be
stretched along, and each take hold of it and drag his hand-
sleigh on which was his knapsack and provisions, as
well as divers tools, implements, and stores requisite for the
expedition. In this guise we proceeded across the lake;
the disasters were numerous, but none of them serious.
A fellow in stepping on a fracture of ice in the shape of the
letter V would plunge in and then be dragged out again by
his comrades, amidst shouts of laughter. In this mode we
progressed for upwards of six hours until we reached
the opposite side, where a huge pile of logs was kindled,
a space swept clear of snow, and we sat down to a late
dinner".[22]

The militia, who were from the neighbourhood, had gone
ahead three weeks earlier and had blazed a roadway some
distance northward from Lake Simcoe; so the force under
Dunlop proceeded several miles in advance of the militia,
trudging through three feet of snow: "Six or seven men led
on snow-shoes in Indian file, taking care to tread down the
snow equally; then followed the column, also in Indian file.
At about every thirty yards the leader of the column stepped
aside and, letting the rest pass him, fell into the rear. By
this means, after the fatigue of first breaking the snow, he
could march on a beaten path, and thus, alternating labour
and rest, the thing was comparatively easy. By sunset we

[22]William Dunlop: *Recollections of the American War.* 1905. pp. 92-3.

had made about five miles beyond the militia camp, and it was counted, considering the road, a very fair day's journey".[23]

After shanties had been erected the work of road-building commenced. Snow, often six feet deep, prevented the use of horses or oxen, so that all "packing" (carrying provisions and supplies) had to be done by men, about one-half of the detachment being continually at this work. The cost of the road was very great, for thirty men could not haul logs with drag-ropes as easily as a yoke of oxen might have done had their use been possible. Dunlop says: "I would undertake tomorrow to cut a better road than we could possibly do, for forty pounds a mile, and make money by it, —give me timely warning and a proper season of the year; whereas I am convinced that £2500 or £3000 did not pay for the one we cut".[24]

With reference to the completion of the road Dunlop describes how officers and men, in building bridges, "had to stand for hours up to the middle in ice-cold water; ravines had to be bridged when the logs had to be dragged out of swamps through four feet of snow".[25] During the course of the arduous work there were no cases of accident or sickness, "except casualties such as cutting feet, (a very common accident even among experienced choppers), and bruises from falling trees".[26] Just as the road was finished, and the men were looking forward to a pleasant summer at Penetanguishene, word was received that the war was over, and all were ordered to return to York and their respective regiments.

The first laws in Upper Canada with reference to roads carried with them no financial aid from the Provincial Legislature. They were paid for by the Imperial Government as military works, or were built at the private expense of settlers or traders interested in the advantages which would accrue from their construction. The North-West Company, for example, contributed large sums of money towards improving Yonge Street, for they used it as a portage road to Lake Simcoe in their extensive trade to Michilimackinac and the Far West, a saving of £10 to £15

[23]*Ibid.*, pp. 93-4.   [24]*Ibid.*, p. 96.
[25]*Ibid.*, p. 100.   [26]*Ibid.*, p. 99.

per ton being effected by the use of this route instead of the Ottawa River.

A number of the earliest roads in Canada were constructed during wars by French, British or American armies, and it was customary for many years to employ the soldiers of the garrisons in building or repairing roadways in times of peace; but no road work was being done by the military at the time of the creation of the province, and the Government of Upper Canada had no surplus revenue to devote to roads until 1804, when a start was made with a vote of £1000. By 1816 the grants had reached £21,000, but after that very little was done until 1830. In the next decade a total of £228,000 was voted for road-building. Among other Acts of Parliament with relation to roads was one "To Prevent Damage to Travellers on Highways"; this act was always in the public eye, for it was continually being amended in a vain effort to improve conditions of travel. So bad was every road when first opened that it often made but little difference to the inhabitants it was supposed to serve, and people frequently preferred to ignore it and to follow bush roads to which they were accustomed.

The development of facilities for land transport thus devolved in large measure upon the inhabitants themselves. They were required as a condition of their land grants to open a road in front of their lots, and, by an Act of the first parliament, to share in the work of maintaining the highways. As an accommodation for themselves many early settlers combined to build "subscription" roads through their entire district without government aid. An early example of initiative of this kind was shown by the first Loyalist settlers in the Niagara district, who had blazed a road from Niagara to Ancaster, the limit of their settlement, by 1785. The following notice, inserted in the York *Gazette* by John Van Laute, pathmaster of that town, illustrates the same commendable spirit of co-operation:

"A number of public-spirited people collected on Saturday last to cut down the hill at Frank's Creek. His Excellency the Lieut.-Governor was informed of it and immediately dispatched a person with a present of fifty dollars to assist in improving the Yonge Street road. To His

Excellency for this liberal donation, and to the gentlemen who contributed, we return our warmest thanks".[27]

For many years the great hindrance to the development of roads in Upper Canada was the unoccupied land held in large blocks by the Crown or speculators, or set aside as clergy reserves. The absentee holders of these tracts were not bound by the obligation which lay upon resident owners to make and maintain highways. In some districts the road came to an end at the boundary of these unoccupied lands; in others it was built, but soon fell into disrepair where there were no residents interested in its upkeep. Even where there were no reserves or absentee owners it usually happened that the swampy land was not taken up for settlement, and consequently, since no one had the duty of blazing a highway through it, the road came to a sudden end, or was only partially blazed by those living in the vicinity.

Robert Gourlay, in his investigation of economic conditions in Upper Canada shortly after the War of 1812, found this state of affairs a great grievance and the main cause of the deplorable condition of the roads. He observed, however, that land travel was increasing, "and the roads are advancing towards a more perfect state by the annual application of statute labour, and the aids granted from time to time by the legislature out of the provincial funds". The settlers of Aldborough Township, in which there were no clergy reserves, informed Gourlay that while the public roads were tolerable, and gradually improving through the labour of those living near them, the great difficulty lay in the unsettled lands:

"The lands owned by non-residents in the concessions near the River Thames, and the reserve lots, seem to retard the growth of our township, as well as the province at large. A tax upon the lands of absentees might induce them to sell to persons who would become actual settlers, which would facilitate the improvement of our settlement; and if His Majesty's Government would dispose of the reserved lands throughout the province we are of opinion it would much contribute to improve the same".[28]

[27]*York Gazette*, November 11, 1807.
[28]Robert Gourlay: *A Statistical Account of Upper Canada.* 1822. Vol. I, pp. 350-1.

The maps of the early surveyors of Upper Canada show road allowances in straight lines, except along the waterfront, where they usually conformed to the course of river or lake. Concession lines were generally one mile and a quarter apart and as straight as possible. It will be asked why most of our present roads wind in and out instead of following straight courses. The answer is that many of these road allowances were entirely ignored; the original winding bush-paths and trails, avoiding swamps and hills where possible, continued to be followed, and were gradually improved and enlarged; while in many cases no roads were ever built in the spaces left for them by the government surveyors.

In the second session of the first parliament of Upper Canada, in 1793, the roads were placed under overseers called pathmasters, who were to be appointed by the rate-paying inhabitants at their annual township meetings. Everyone was required to bring tools and to work from three to twelve days on the highways, those who owned carts and teams having to labour at least six days. The regulations for statute labour as they applied in 1831 provided that every male not rated on the assessment roll was liable to two days' labour on the roads; those rated up to £25 had to do three days' roadwork, and property-owners assessed from £25 to £500 were required to work from three to twelve days, according to their assessment; while those rated above £500 were subject to a similar, though not proportionate increase in their labour.

The great difficulty in the system of statute labour was its enforcement. In many municipalities officials were very lax, even though aided by a provision for the commutation of the work into a money payment of 2s. 6d. (50 cents) per day, an amount later increased to a maximum of twice that sum.

Another provision in the early regulation of roads was that they should be not less than thirty nor more than ninety feet wide. The alteration of the course of roadways was provided for by the first parliament, which left the matter in the hands of Justices of the Peace. On the sworn certificate of a majority of twelve of the chief freeholders of a district a road might be changed; that many were deviated through the influence of landowners, thus making the road permanently crooked, there can be no doubt, for we find numerous cases where the convenience of one man must have been the main reason for the change.

The general development from the corduroy road hinged upon the clearing and drainage of the surrounding district. As the land was drained the logs were often left high and dry, but were frequently allowed to remain "because the laborious and plebeian occupation of digging is required to extract them".[29] As time passed, however, they rotted away, and the holes in the roads had to be filled with earth and stone. It was difficult to construct ditches in the early period because of the lack of tools and time, so little else but corduroy could have been used in pioneer road-making. As settlement advanced, however, and government aid became available, better roads gradually evolved. The "common" road was the first improvement over the corduroy, and though it had no artificial roadbed, yet the roadway was drained and bridged and the steep hills were reduced. This type of highway entailed considerable expense, for it was usually laid out in straight lines and surmounted obstacles rather than avoided them. Such a road could be made serviceable except for the heaviest traffic, but its condition depended entirely upon the amount of work which was done upon it.

During the period 1825-1850 the turnpike or toll road, in general use in England at that time, was introduced into Upper Canada. In 1826 the corduroy along Talbot Street was being taken up and the road turnpiked, and a traveller who saw it being done noticed that "four men and two yoke of oxen—one yoke and two men to plough, and the other to scrape—will do as much work in this way, where there are no obstructions, as fifteen or twenty men in the same time by the ordinary way of digging".[30] Besides the usual policy of ploughing and scraping the earth to the centre of the road, many highways were gravelled, and others planked. In the forties and fifties numerous plank roads were built in Upper Canada; the citizens of Cobourg, for example, built a number of them leading to the town

[29]Keefer, *op. cit.*, pp. 119-20.
[30]Pickering, *op. cit.*, November 1, 1826.

in order to encourage trade. The writer has before him an
agreement between The Cobourg and Rice Lake Plank
Road and Ferry Company and several owners of saw-mills,
who agreed to furnish 350,000 board feet of three-inch
planks at 25 shillings ($5) per thousand,—less than one-
tenth the cost of the same lumber to-day.[31] Some of the
main roads were similarly improved from time to time.
In 1853 an extraordinary rise of the waters of the Great
Lakes washed out a part of the Lake Shore Road west of
Toronto, and it was partially planked in that year.

A traveller describes as follows the method of building
the plank roads that he observed in process of construction
in 1842 "from London to Brantford, to Port Stanley, Sarnia,
Goderich", and in other localities:

"The whole breadth of the clearing through the forest is
sixty-four feet, the roadbed is thirty feet wide, the ditches
on each side are eight feet wide at the top, two feet at bottom, and three feet deep from the crown of the road. The
plank-way, on which is the travelling for rough-shod horses
only, is sixteen feet wide. There are five rows of sleepers
4 x 6 inches laid in the ground, the earth well rammed
down on each side of them. Three-inch plank, twelve inches
wide, is laid on the sleepers and secured to them by spikes
of iron six and a half inches long by three-eighths of an
inch square. The road is graded to an elevation not to
exceed two and a half degrees; all the material should
be of the best pine, and the expense averages £500 currency
per mile, or £400 sterling".[32]

At first plank roads were thought to be a great invention. A Scotch traveller considered that "the best thoroughfares of all are the plank roads, which I never heard of till
I reached Canada".[33] Sir Richard Bonnycastle was travelling along the shore of the St. Lawrence in 1845 and
traversed "a plank road as smooth as a billiard table".[34]
But, though satisfactory at first, the type was a failure

[31]For a more complete account of this venture in road construction,
    see E. C. Guillet: *Cobourg*. (In the *Cobourg Sentinel-Star*,
    June 12, 1930.)
[32]Sir James Alexander: *L'Acadie, or Seven Years' Explorations in
    British America*. 1849. Vol. I, p. 141.
[33]Quoted in Lizars, *op. cit.*, p. 64.
[34]Sir Richard Bonnycastle: *Canada and the Canadians*. 1846. Vol. I,
    p. 91.

except as a temporary expedient. It was valuable where the roadbed was of sand, or if there was no gravel in the vicinity; but variations in the grade of lumber and in the condition of the roadbed made constant and expensive repairs necessary, particularly after the heavy frosts of winter.

Turnpike or toll roads of gravel or plank construction were soon common throughout Upper Canada, and the road companies which controlled them were authorized to collect toll from the users of the road, in return for which right they agreed to keep the roadbed in repair. Pedestrians and animals were sometimes charged toll, as well as all vehicles using the road. In general, however, the joint-stock companies in charge of the highways kept them in a miserable condition; frequently they spent nothing on the road that could be avoided, but erected a toll-gate every four or five miles no matter how poor the roadway was. Some of them pretended to macadamise their roads, but the process was more imaginary than real. A contemporary writer considered that there was "no stronger instance of the patience and law-abiding disposition of the people than their toleration of so great an imposition as most of the toll roads of Upper Canada".[35] The following broadside[36] with its grim humour and thinly-veiled venom illustrates the general antipathy towards toll-gates, sharpened in this instance by local jealousy:

TENDERS WANTED

"Tenders will be received until the 20th inst. for the construction of 100 Mud Scows to run between Cobourg and Port Hope on the Macadamized (?) Road connecting the two places, which is owned by Cobourg Capitalists. The Company feel that the new mode of conveyance is necessary, as the loss of horses, wagons and valuable lives in the fathomless abyss of mud during court week was fearfully alarming. Until the completion of the said Mud Scows the Company will continue to exact toll from those who may be so fortunate as to escape alive through the gates. Though

[35]Quoted in George V. Cousins: *Early Transportation in Canada*. (In the *University Magazine*, Vol. VIII, December, 1909, p. 615.)
[36]Port Hope *Guide*, March 15, 1859.

the legality of such exaction may be open to question, they confidently expect that in view of the public spirit of the Company in providing the Scows aforesaid the public will submit to be victimized. Dated at Cobourg this 15th day of March, 1859.

SIMON GRUMPY,
Sec. Road Co."

In spite of continual criticism, however, toll roads, which many people considered "relics of barbarism", survived in some parts of the province until recent years. The town of Cobourg, for example, was surrounded by five toll-gates, on roads east, west and north, as late as the closing years of the Great War; while the last toll-gate in Ontario disappeared only in 1926. But the ever-increasing motor traffic rendered their use impracticable, and other means of maintaining highways had to be evolved.

Toll is still collected for the use of certain large bridges. Before the days of the turnpike road a charge was often made at such connecting links, or for ferryage. Many an early road lacked bridges, small streams being forded, while a ferry-boat, often operated by Indians, supplied a means of crossing the larger rivers. A surveyor noted in 1827 that "the only mode of crossing the River Trent is by scow in summer, and on the ice in winter". He considered that a toll bridge would have returned good dividends, and would have been much more satisfactory to those who had to use the Kingston Road.[37] Among other early ferries on the main highways were those by which travellers crossed the Rouge, Humber and Credit Rivers.

The principles of road construction evolved by the great English and Scotch road-builders of the period 1775-1825 were slow in coming into use in Canada. Many a good road had been built in Britain by Metcalf, Rennie, Telford and Macadam by the employment of better material for road surface, while in Canada the use of uncrushed gravel long continued; this resulted in most of the gravel remaining in the centre of the road or being scattered into the ditches, and in the formation of deep ruts which broke many a wheel. In the construction of most roads no effort

[37]Report of John Smith, quoted in Picken, *op. cit.*, pp. 153-4.

THE CHECK TOLL-GATE, DUNDAS AND ST. CLAIR, 1857

This was one of four toll-gates on Dundas Street near Toronto. Toll was collected until 1894, and this toll-gate disappeared in 1897

W. H. Bartlett

BRIDGE BETWEEN BYTOWN AND HULL, 1840

Considered by contemporaries a remarkable engineering achievement

THE BLOOR STREET VIADUCT OVER THE HUMBER RIVER
Typical of modern road-building

A "MADE IN CANADA" CAR, 1905

Advertised as having "power, good lines, is luxurious in finish, but best of all it can stand the rack and wear of Canadian Roads. Price $1,500". Canada's first automobile was an electric car resembling a large baby carriage, built in Toronto just forty years ago (1893) by F. B. Fetherstonhaugh. John Moodie of Hamilton imported the first gasoline automobile in 1898.

was made to prepare a firm roadbed, gravel being merely dumped on the surface. Joseph Pickering wrote in 1832 that the only piece of "gravelled hard-made road" he had noticed for some years was the main street of York.[38]

In the thirties the Talbot roads were, upon the whole, the best in the province. One of the first sections of the main east-west highway to be macadamised was that between Kingston and Napanee which was built in 1837-9 at a cost of $132,000; Canniff says that it was "for many long years the exception in an execrable road".[39] In the late thirties Yonge Street was macadamised for a distance of twelve miles northward from Toronto, and was consequently a good wagon road at some seasons of the year; the rest of the roadway is referred to by a traveller in 1845 as "mud and etceteras, too numerous to mention. . . . A Slough of Despond". He states that large sums of money had been expended upon the macadamised section, but that it was not permanently a good road because of the brick-clay soil and the many deep excavations and cuts and high embankments.[40] The worst part of this highway was the Blue Hill, where there was a very precipitous ascent and descent across the Rosedale ravine; this passage was often as terrifying to travellers as were those of the Rouge, the Credit, the Sixteen-Mile Creek, and many another deep watercourse on the Kingston Road and Dundas Street.

While some so-called macadamising was being done in various parts of Upper Canada the roads were in general unimproved. An officer who traversed the province in 1840 considered that there were no roads worthy of the name, but "the three best tracks through the forest" were Dundas, King and Yonge Streets".[41] As early as 1804 an attempt had been made to repair Dundas Street and improve it by erecting eighteen-foot causeways and bridges over that part of the road from York to Burlington Bay; and in 1836 grants from the legislature enabled the gravelling and macadamising of some sections of it; but an observant traveller, Mrs. Anna Jameson, wrote in 1837: "Dundas

[38]Pickering, *op. cit.* Appendix to the 4th Edition, p. 189.
[39]William Canniff: *History of the Settlement of Upper Canada.* 1869. p. 231.
[40]Bonnycastle, *op. cit.*, Vol. I, p. 111.
[41]Quoted in Lizars, *op. cit.*, p. 59.

Street is very rough for a carriage, but a most delightful ride. You are almost immediately in a pine forest, which extends with little interruption about fifty miles to Hamilton."[42] At some seasons of the year this road, in common with many others, contained gullies fifty or sixty feet deep worn away by swollen streams, and travel by coach or wagon was dangerous if not impossible; while progress upon many a highway, like that from Sandwich to Chatham, was difficult even on horseback, not only because of the poorness of the road but also owing to lack of accommodation for man or beast *en route*. The Huron Road from Galt to Goderich had been open only a few years when Patrick Shirreff travelled over it in 1833; he found it two-thirds corduroy, and worthy of the epithet "horrid", but he adds: "Without meaning to praise corduroy roads I must say they are by far the best and smoothest portions."[43] This highway was later improved, and came to be known as "the Stone Road"; but even in the fifties it was chiefly mud or corduroy, and a traveller stated that it was only with great difficulty that anyone could keep his seat in a wagon as it bumped over the roughly-laid logs.[44]

A number of colonisation roads were pushed northwards towards Lake Huron and Georgian Bay in the forties and fifties. The Government of Upper Canada constructed these arteries in a somewhat different manner from that employed in the earlier pioneer periods. The building of the Garafraxa Road, surveyed by Charles Rankin in 1837 and opened in succeeding years, may be taken as typical of the procedure. Contracts were let "in sections of ½, 1, 1½ and 2-mile stretches; where swamps were encountered the minimum length was given out; where good timber and high land occurred longer mileage was contracted for. The road was surveyed one chain (sixty feet) in width, and was cleared of timber; but all stumps, excepting those interfering with making the road passable, were allowed to stand. Causeways of logs were laid across swamps and streams to make the road passable for wheeled vehicles. . . .

"All trees eight inches in diameter and under were cut

---

[42]Jameson, *op. cit.*, Vol. II, p. 7.
[43]Patrick Shirreff: *A Tour through North America*. 1835. p. 181.
[44]Reminiscences of John S. McDonald, quoted in W. L. Smith: *Pioneers of Old Ontario*. 1923. p. 255.

close to the ground. The whole of the timber on the road allowance was cut into logging lengths—twelve to fourteen feet—and these, together with all brushwood and rubbish, were piled on each side of the road, that later, when dry, it might be burned. . . . In swamps and where causewaying was required, the whole of the timber had to be cut close to the ground for a width of twenty feet in the centre of the road. Causewaying was made of straight, sound logs, laid evenly and close together and at right angles to the roadway, and each log had to be sixteen feet long. All bridges of fifteen feet span and under were included under the head of causewaying. Contracts for chopping and logging the road varied from twenty-three pounds sterling to twenty-five pounds sterling per mile, and causewaying from 7s. 6d. to 10s. per rod."[45]

In 1841 there were about 6,000 miles of post-roads in Upper Canada, though their use was frequently difficult and sometimes impossible; even in 1850 there were still some settlements in the province inaccessible to any wheeled vehicle. In the early sixties the government of the Canadas commenced seven great lines of roadway in Upper Canada and five in Lower, and laid out for settlement the lands through which they passed. In Upper Canada these roads were chiefly in the "backwoods" districts of the Upper Ottawa, Muskoka and Lake Superior, and progress upon them was very slow; it not infrequently happened that bush fires burned out the bridges annually for many years. Meanwhile, even on the main roads, there was for thirty years or more little or no improvement in the methods of road construction.

In 1894 the Good Roads Association came into existence in Ontario, and succeeded in arousing considerable interest in improved methods of road construction. Four years later the appearance of the first automobiles (early called "motor carriages") drew forth an interesting prophecy from the Provincial Instructor in Road-making, who reported that "motor carriages may be seen on the streets of the larger cities, and present indications are that they will become an important means of travel and communication."

[45]W. M. Brown: *The Queen's Bush*. 1932. Chapter V.

The general state of the roads at that time may be gauged from the same report:

"It is doubtful if there is a mile of true Macadam road in Ontario outside a few towns or cities. There are miles of road which are covered with dirty gravel or rough, broken stone, and are popularly supposed to be macadamised. To-day the majority are little better than trails. From the middle of October until the end of December, and from the first of March to the end of May, a period of five months, by far the greatest part of the mileage of the province is mud, ruts and pitch-holes. There are at least two months when the roads are practically impassable."[46]

The advent of the motor-car soon made the improvement of the highways a national necessity. Genuine macadamised roads were gradually built, at first in small sections and in scattered districts. Good road machinery—stone crushers, graders and rollers—was soon to become a familiar sight as the old roadways were improved for the ever-increasing motor traffic.

In cities blocks of wood and bricks were used in early paving, but in modern times most pavements of this type have been superseded by concrete. Since the advent of the automobile such paving has been found necessary because motor-cars suck up the dust and destroy the surface of the road. Macadam's method of placing large rocks at the base, with smaller stones towards the surface, where crushed stone was used to enable it to mat together, is the method still employed in macadam roads, with the modern addition of tar or oil to make a hard surface and keep down the dust. The same foundation is used for the "tarmac", concrete or asphalt streets which have recently become common in the towns of the province.

After the Great War the great increase in motor traffic necessitated similar roadways throughout the province, and under the control of the Provincial Government these King's Highways are fast becoming a network of permanent roads. The motor-coach lines which now operate so extensively on these highways recall the old coaching days before the coming of the railways, but the contrast between the

[46]Report of A. W. Campbell, 1898.

two methods of road transportation is so great that it hardly admits of comparison.

About $25,000,000 is spent annually by Ontario on the construction and maintenance of highways. Motor-cars, of which there were 1,530 in 1907, were first taxed in 1914, and they now provide most of the revenue for road construction by means of a high gasoline tax and motor licenses; for it is rightly considered that those who use the highways most should pay most towards their upkeep. According to the latest statistics Ontario has 66,922 miles of roads, and of the total mileage nearly one-third is classed as "unimproved"; but 38,647 miles of roadway have been brought to grade and surfaced with gravel, while there are 6,193 miles of paved roads, and the mileage of "permanent" highways is continually increasing.

During the winter of 1931-32 the construction of the Ontario section of the Trans-Canada Highway was undertaken by the Provincial Government as a measure of unemployment relief in a period of depression; this roadway, the Ontario section of which is nearly 1,400 miles long, is being built in the most approved method of concrete construction to withstand the more extreme climatic conditions of New Ontario, for concrete roads suffer from frost almost as much as did the old corduroy type.

In modern road-building dangerous hills are avoided by the construction of great bridges and viaducts, improvements which are almost indispensable in a day when the province has nearly a million motor-cars. The increasing toll of casualties due to accidents on the highways has led to a recent change of policy in road construction. In 1930 experiments were conducted on a small section of roadway in Central Ontario, and in the following year were extended to a larger stretch of road between Lancaster and Ottawa. These preliminary trials have been so satisfactory that plans are now under way to eliminate all deep ditches, and to build all road shoulders to a width of ten feet instead of five, as has been the practice for years. Where the shallowing process renders drainage inadequate the Department of Highways will lay tile alongside the road to meet the situation, and motorists may eventually be able to drive off the roadway right up to the fence without any mishap.

The inauguration of this policy by the Minister of Highways is of great importance, for it will henceforth govern the construction of new highways, as well as being gradually applied to the alteration of the present roads to suit the new requirements.[47] But even with the great advances in road construction there are no permanent roadways, though it is quite possible that the world's scientists and inventors may yet revolutionise road-building by the discovery of some material upon which even the heaviest motor traffic will have no appreciable effect.

A summary of road development and expenditure in Ontario during 1931 is contained in the 1932 budget speech of the Provincial Treasurer:

"At the end of 1931 we had 2,977 miles of King's Highway in the Province, as compared with 2,738 miles at the end of last year. Of this mileage there was 1,055.89 miles of concrete surface, 207.52 of asphalt, 261.36 of bituminous penetration, 325.05 of macadam, 471.18 miles of mixed macadam and retread, and 658 miles of gravel.

"In the year 1931 there was expended on all road construction, including the King's Highways, colonisation roads, and roads in Northern Ontario, the sum of $28,741,118.45, capital and ordinary. Comparing current expenditure on highways with current revenue for highway purposes for the year 1931, the figures are as follows: maintenance, $6,621,440; interest, $8,253,787; debt retirement based on twenty years, $4,992,319; total, $19,867,546.

"The current revenue for the same year was: motor vehicles and gasoline tax, $16,561,088; county and suburban area repayment, $399,692; total, $16,960,780, or 85.3 *per cent.* of the current expenditure.

"Our King's Highways are maintained to a very high standard as to surface, grades and curves, and, in addition to the benefits of a high-class road system for the citizens of Ontario, our investment in highways indirectly is of very substantial benefit through the tourist traffic it creates for the Province as a whole."[48]

The "tourist industry", which in modern times depends largely upon the highways, has been continually in-

---

[47]The new policy was announced on November 10, 1932.
[48]Budget speech of the Provincial Treasurer in the Legislative Assembly of Ontario, March 11, 1932.

creasing in importance with the building of improved roads. During the five years ending in 1930 the immense sum of $1,303,491,000 was expended in Canada by tourists, most of whom were attracted by the comparatively easy access to the natural beauties of the country which motor roads have afforded.

CHAPTER IX

THE STAGE-COACH

"The arrival of the coach was the great event of the day at the inn. In a twinkling the stable-boys were unhitching the horses and driving them into their stalls. Perhaps a passenger got out, his carpet-bags and valises were thrown down from the roof or from the rack behind, and he went in to seek lodging. The driver, striking his great boots with his whip, strode into the tap-room to get a drink; the passengers who were going farther washed the dust from their throats with hot or cold drinks handed in through the window. In five minutes the fresh horses came prancing out, the great traces were caught up and fastened, the coachman mounted the box, he cracked his long whip over the backs of the team, the stable-boys jerked off their blankets, and they were off."

D. J. DICKIE.[1]

AN intermittent drizzling rain depressed the spirits of those whose business took them out of doors. The Rev. William Proudfoot was exceedingly unfortunate, for he was travelling westward from York by stage (an open wagon), over roads "indescribably bad", even worse than they usually were a century ago. A January thaw had made Dundas Street a veritable slough of mud—wherever it was not corduroy.

There was little he could do but contemplate the conditions of travel. The stage might easily have been made comfortable, he mused, by raising the seats three inches higher, covering them with painted canvas, and placing a strap behind to rest one's back, and some straw to keep it warm and clean; there was no doubt about it, the stages "are so constructed as if the comfort of the passengers were never once thought of".

In Toronto Township a stretch of corduroy was encountered, and "the jolting over the logs was exceedingly painful"; the rest of the day's journey was through mud, "very deep and as adhesive as glue", which converted the wagon (if it had not always been that way) into a vehicle "as dirty as mud could make it". One can picture the reverend gentleman protecting himself from streams of liquid dirt by the use of his umbrella, for whenever the horses

[1] D. J. Dickie: *In Pioneer Days*. 1926. p. 177.

A CALÈCHE

These were the first public conveyances in Canada

Public Archives of Canada   Artist Unknown

A WINTER STAGE-COACH

This stage is equipped with the unusual luxury of a stove

Sketch made with the Camera Lucida by Captain Basil Hall

AMERICAN STAGE-COACH, 1827

Coke Smyth

POSTING ON THE ST. LAWRENCE

Coke Smyth was drawing-master to Lord Durham's children during their sojourn in Canada, 1838-9

moved faster than a walk, the revolution of the wheel shot slugs of mud at him with unerring precision. And it was all so hopeless, for he learned that there was no opposition line of stages in prospect, the present proprietors having a 21-year contract with six years still to go! As the bedraggled clergyman approached Buck's Tavern, in Trafalgar, he roused his brain to greater activity and estimated that the thirty miles from York had been covered at an average rate of two and eight-elevenths miles per hour; and his day's "roadwork" is summed up in his diary by the statement: "I was sadly knocked about today."[2]

The first public vehicle to travel the roads of Canada was the *calèche*. In Quebec the European system of travelling by post was early in force, and several laws were passed between 1780 and 1819 to regulate the service. The sixty leagues between Quebec and Montreal, for example, was divided into twenty-four stages, and the *maîtres de poste* were obliged to keep four *calèches* and four *carrioles* ready at one quarter of an hour's notice to forward a passenger to the next stage. The *calèche* has been described as "a gig upon grasshopper springs with a seat for two passengers; the driver occupies the site of the dashboard, with his feet on the shafts and in close proximity to the horse, with which he maintains a confidential conversation throughout the journey, alternately complimenting and upbraiding him, and not failing to impress him with the many virtues of his master".[3] Another writer refers to "the high, creaking, shaking calashes of Lower Canada, invented in the sixteenth century".[4]

The traveller was usually received with much ceremony at each stage-house by the lady of the inn, and the courtesies which one received made such journeys quite pleasant. Until 1819 the *maîtres de poste* held exclusive privileges to conduct the service, and the rates varied from 20c. to 25c. a league, or $12 to $15 for the entire trip of three days from Quebec to Montreal. There was also a

[2]*The Diary of William Proudfoot*, January 5, 1833. See London and Middlesex Historical Society, *Transactions*, Part XI, pp. 26-27.
[3]T. C. Keefer: *Travel and Transportation*. In John Lovell (Ed.): *80 Years' Progress in British North America*. 1863. p. 111.
[4]J. J. Bigsby: *The Shoe and Canoe, or Pictures of Travel in the Canadas*. 1850. Vol. I, p. 173.

public mail-stage between St. Johns and Quebec towards the close of the eighteenth century, but most travel followed the water routes.

Mrs. Simcoe, wife of the first Lieutenant-Governor of Upper Canada, had the experience of posting on the St. Lawrence in the winter of 1795, and as the Deputy Post-master-General at Quebec had sent orders to all post-houses to keep horses in readiness there was not "the least trouble in waiting or paying. She considered the post-horses "very good; they drive tandem, and change every three leagues". On February 10th they travelled sixty-three miles on the ice of the St. Lawrence without changing horses. On Lake St. Francis, "my driver left the carriage and walked behind with the other drivers; every half mile he came and whipped the horses violently, and I saw no more of him till we had gone another half mile, the horses steadily pursuing a slight track on the snow; but had there been air-holes in the track they pursued, as sometimes happens on the ice, what would have become of us? It put me in mind of the reindeer, who travel self-conducted".[5]

Calèches were early available to travellers over the Niagara portage road, but they were hired as private conveyances by those who did not prefer to walk, or travel by wagon or other means. At the end of May, 1789, William Dummer Powell, first Judge of the District of Hesse, was journeying with his family to Detroit, and his sister Anne records in her account of the trip that the ladies travelled over the Niagara portage in "calashes" while the men went on foot or on horseback.[6]

The first public stage-coaches in Upper Canada were operated a few years later on the same road, which was the first highway in the province. According to his own statement J. Fanning of Chippawa was the first to establish a stage in Upper Canada; he does not give the date, but it must have been previous to 1798, when the first advertisement of public conveyances appears in the *Gazette*. Fanning stated that his stage-coach "is as easy as any in the province, and the goodness of the horses and carefulness of the driver are exceeded by none." He informed the public that they would not be overcrowded in his coach, for "generally four and not exceeding five passengers" would be admitted; while for the better accommodation of aristocratic customers he added that "way passengers will not be taken but by request of the passengers; by this limitation and rule the passengers will not be incommoded, and be the choosers of their own company, which is an inviting circumstance to ladies and gentlemen in particular, who may have a choice in this respect".[7]

Fanning's stage ran between Chippawa, Niagara (Newark) and Fort Erie, and there were several other stage proprietors in the district during the late seventeen-nineties. The first advertisement in the *Gazette* announcing public conveyances occurs on May 26, 1798, and was inserted by Fairbanks and Hind. It gives many details of the service:

"J. Fairbanks and Thomas Hind acquaint their friends and the public in general that their Stage will continue to run between Newark and Chippawa on Mondays, Wednesdays and Fridays, to start from Newark at 7 o'clock a.m. of each day, and return the same evening provided four passengers take seats by 4 o'clock in the afternoon; otherwise to start from Chippawa the following morning at 7 o'clock, and return the same evening. Each passenger is allowed 14 lb. baggage, and to pay one dollar; way passengers to be taken up at sixpence N.Y.C. per mile. Will stop at Queenston each way 20 minutes. Good horses and careful drivers are provided, and that attention and dispatch which are necessary to the ease, satisfaction and convenience of the passengers may always be expected. Letters 4d. each."[8]

During the winter of 1799-1800 Stephen Bates carried the mail between Niagara, Buffalo and Canandaigua, New York State, and announced that he would convey passengers in his sleigh "at the following rates:—from Niagara to Canandaigua, $6.00; from Buffalo to Canandaigua, $5.00, and other distances in proportion: way passengers admitted

[7] *Niagara Herald*, May 16, 1801.
[8] Niagara *Upper Canada Gazette*, May 26, 1798. "N.Y.C." refers to New York Currency, in which the "York shilling" was 12½ cents and the £=$2.50; while in "Quebec", "Halifax" or "Provincial" Currency the shilling was 20 cents and the £=$4.00.

to a seat on reasonable terms".[9]   Though this service was
purely American, most of the Canadian mail and almost all
travellers eastward availed themselves of it, for there was
but one "winter express" in the Canadian service, and even
that commonly travelled *via* the south shore of Lake Ontario.

In the summer of 1801 James Macklem and Markle &
Hamilton advertised the "Niagara and Chippawa Stages".
The fare was 4s. from Niagara to Queenston, or from
Chippawa to Queenston.   The charge for 150 pounds of
baggage was the same as that for one passenger, but any
traveller might carry fourteen pounds gratis.   The owners
had made arrangements for the stages to start "for the
Hotel in Niagara and Mr. Macklem's at Chippawa at 8
o'clock in the morning—meet at Mr. Fairbanks' at Queenston, exchange passengers and return. The proprietors have
at great expense procured easy carriages, good horses and
careful drivers".[10]   The public coaches carried the mail
until August 1, 1801, when "postmasters' stages" were inaugurated to conduct the mail service between Niagara,
Queenston and Chippawa, where post offices had but recently been established.

In other parts of Upper Canada, land travel was not a
necessity, for water transportation was convenient even if
not always easy.   But as early as 1808 stages operated
irregularly over parts of the route between Montreal and
Kingston.   On January 1, 1816, Barnabas Dickinson's stage
line commenced a regular service over this territory;
covered sleighs left Samuel Hedge's, St. Paul Street, Montreal, and Robert Walker's Hotel, Kingston, on Mondays
and Thursdays, and arrived at their destination Wednesdays and Saturdays.   In summer a stage-wagon ran from
Montreal to Prescott and carried the mail, which was taken
the rest of the way to Kingston on horseback.   This stage
must have had great difficulty in negotiating at least eight
miles of the journey between Montreal and Kingston, for
the last three miles in Upper Canada of the main road and
the first five miles in Lower Canada were incomplete at that
time.

[9]Niagara *Canada Constellation*, December 14, 1799.
[10]*Niagara Herald*, April 25, 1801.

The Danforth Road was completed between Kingston and York in 1800, but owing to clergy reserves and absentee landowners it was not kept in a state of repair over the entire distance, and could not be used throughout by vehicles. In the latter part of 1816, however, the Kingston Road was open, in part following the Danforth Road and in other sections being nearer the lake shore. In January, 1817, Samuel Purdy inaugurated the first stage line over the road, leaving Daniel Brown's Inn, Kingston, every Monday, and York every Thursday. The half-way house on this three-day trip was Spaulding's Inn, Grafton, and the fare was $18, with baggage limited to twenty-eight pounds per passenger; the following winter Purdy reduced the fare to $10. At the opening of navigation this service was discontinued.

Among other proprietors of stage lines during the first years of the Kingston Road were Messrs. Jonathan Ogden, Hicks, and J. Powers. Ogden had carried the mail once a week on horseback between Trenton and York before the road was opened. Powers lived in Darlington, and in 1823 inserted the following notice in the *York Gazette*:

"Stage Notice—J. Powers respectfully informs the public in general that he will run a stage on the road between York and Kingston during the sleighing season, and that no exertion shall be wanting on his part to give satisfaction to those who may please to honor him with their commands."[11]

Coach lines did not come into regular operation west and north of York as early as the eastern lines along the Kingston Road; it was long customary to hire a wagon if one desired transportation westward. The first stage between York and Niagara ran in 1816 and charged $5 for a passage. In 1825 Chauncey Beadle petitioned for exclusive rights to run a stage line over this route, which required at least seventeen hours to cover. For many years the decayed bridges and swollen streams both east and west of York led to the capital of Upper Canada being referred to as "holding an impregnable and unapproachable position", but coaches made their way as best they could.

After 1817 the Talbot Road was greatly extended, and was soon known as the best in Upper Canada. There were

[11]*York Gazette*, January 9, 1823.

two main branches of the highway, one from London to St. Thomas, Port Stanley and Port Talbot, and the other westward from Fort Erie to Sandwich, and thence north to Sarnia over the road built by the government in 1803. In the twenties the first stages in this territory were operating on the Talbot roads. In 1827, after two years' effort, a public-spirited physician of St. Catharines obtained the exclusive right to run a stage for twenty-one years from Ancaster through Brantford, Burford, "the Long Woods" and Delaware to the Detroit River. He did this to induce other parties to provide the much-needed accommodation. Under this stimulus a line of four-horse coaches began to run in 1828, but this did not pay, so the service was reduced to an uncovered wagon; this, too, was abandoned after a short time, and for several years there was no through line of stages between Lake Ontario and the Detroit River. The line which was opened in 1828 continued operations as far as London, however, the passage from Hamilton to London costing $4.50; to travel from York to London at this time took two days. In 1835 coaches were again in operation through to the Detroit River.

The period of stage development which has been outlined—roughly the first thirty years of the century—was one in which the characteristic "coach" was seldom better than an open wagon or sleigh. Travellers' accounts of experiences in these vehicles are comparatively rare, because few visitors to Upper Canada at that time did more than call at the chief ports as they sailed through Lakes Ontario and Erie in schooner or steamship. Lieutenant Francis Hall, who was in Canada in the summer of 1816, writes that he "took the stage-wagon at Cornwall, and can answer for its being one of the roughest conveyances on either side the Atlantic".[12]

Ten years later Thomas Stewart travelled in the winter stage from Cobourg to York on a night when the thermometer registered 22° below zero. The sleigh is described as having "a sort of oilcloth cover or head". Mrs. Stewart wrote concerning the trip: "The occupants of the coach were almost frozen when they reached York at three o'clock

[12]Francis Hall: *Travels in Canada and the United States in 1816-17*, 1818. p. 155.

the next morning. My husband made his way to an hotel, took a hot drink and went to bed; he felt no bad effects after the journey and exposure."[13]

In summer the journey by stage-wagon was just as arduous owing to bad roads. In July, 1827, Captain Basil Hall was travelling by stage eastward from York, and in his account of the trip he refers to "the horrible corduroy roads", filled with "deep, inky holes which almost swallowed up the forewheels of the wagon"; at times the stage was "forging, like a ship in a head-sea, right into a hole half a yard deep". These difficulties along the most important highway in Upper Canada were bad enough; but when the travellers arrived at the River Rouge they found there was no bridge. A boy with a canoe provided the only means of crossing, so the passengers were ferried over, the horse yanked across, and the carriage hauled over by the passengers with the help of some chains and the horse. No wonder Captain Hall wrote: "We reached our sleeping-place fatigued to the last gasp".

The next day the party proceeded forty-three miles to Cobourg, a journey which was accomplished at the cost of "thirteen hours of as rough travelling as ever was performed by wheeled carriage".[14] It is not remarkable that early settlers are known to have walked from York to Kingston and to have arrived a day ahead of the stage-coach. Even as late as 1831 the mail-courier on horseback had to be substituted for the stage, because the roads were absolutely impassable for wheeled vehicles.

The stage-wagon was not the usual vehicle of public conveyance on the main highways after 1830; but as it long remained characteristic of travel in the more remote districts, and even on the main highways frequently replaced the better coaches when the roads were worse than usual, some further description of this type of transportation will be of interest. In 1837 Mrs. Anna Jameson hired "a light wagon, a sort of gig perched in the middle of a wooden tray, wherein my baggage was stowed"; in this she was conveyed from Hamilton to Brantford at a cost of five

[13]Frances Stewart: *Our Forest Home.* 1889. 2nd Edition, 1902, p. 87.
[14]Basil Hall: *Travels in America in 1827 and 1828.* 1829. Vol. I, pp. 267-72.

dollars.[15] To travel westward thirty miles from Blandford Township to London, "the best and only vehicle which could be procured"[16] was a baker's cart, and the charge was $7.

A few weeks later, when Mrs. Jameson was leaving Port Talbot for Chatham after visiting the founder of the Talbot Settlement, "the best vehicle which the hospitality and influence of Colonel Talbot could provide was a farmer's cart with two stout horses. The bottom of the cart was well filled with clean soft straw, on which my luggage was deposited. A seat was slung for me on straps, and another in front for the driver, who had been selected from among the most respectable settlers in the neighbourhood as a fit guide and protector for a lone woman. The charge for the two days' journey was to be twelve dollars".[17]

Wagons, roads, and a typical Irish driver are described in an interesting manner by Sir Richard Bonnycastle, who was taking a side trip from Yonge Street into Gwillimbury Township in 1846:

"The four wheels, of a narrow tire, are attached without any springs to a long body formed of straight boards, like a paino-case only more clumsy; in which, resting on inside rims or battens, are two seats with or without backs, generally without, on which, perhaps, a hay-cushion or a buffalo-skin, or both, are placed. Two horses, good, bad, or indifferent, as the case may be, the positive and comparative degrees being the commonest, drag you along with a clever driver who can turn his hand to chopping, carpentering, wheelwright's work, playing the fiddle, drinking, or any other sort of thing, and is usually an Irishman or an Irishman's son. For two dollars and a half a day he will drive you to Melville Island, or Parry's Sound, if you will only stick by him; and he jogs along, smoking his dudeen, over corduroy roads, through mud-holes that would astonish a cockney, and over sand and swamp, rocks and rough places enough to dislocate every joint in your body, all his own being anchylosed or used to it, which is the same thing in the dictionary.

"He will keep you *au courant* at the same time, tell the

---

[15]Anna Jameson: *Winter Studies and Summer Rambles in Canada.* 1838. Vol. II, p. 101.
[16]*Ibid.,* Vol. II, p. 131.　　[17]*Ibid.,* Vol. II, pp. 207-8.

name of every settler and settlement, and some good stories to boot. He is a capital fellow is 'Paddy the driver', generally a small farmer, and always has a contract with the commissariat."[18]

When the settlement of Upper Canada became more rapid in the eighteen-thirties and -forties, staging increased greatly in importance; and, though the roads were seldom much better, the type of stage in use was sometimes an improvement over the wagon. William Weller, one of the most famous of Canadian stage-owners, first appears on the scene in the late twenties. In the summer of 1830 he operated coaches twice a week between York and the Carrying Place, where connection was made with a steamship to Prescott. In an advertisement he emphasises that the road has been repaired, and his stage line "fitted up with good horses, new carriages and careful drivers".[19] It is significant, however, that stages accepted baggage only at the owner's risk.

The following winter the number of stages on the Kingston Road was increased to five a week, as the following announcement shows: "Montreal, Kingston and York Mail Stages, five times a week. Leaves Montreal, Kingston and York every day except Saturdays and Sundays at 4 o'clock a.m., and arrives the following days. All baggage at the owner's risk.—H. Dickinson, Montreal; H. Morton & Co., Kingston; W. Weller, York."[20] William Weller's office in York in 1834 was in the east end of the old Coffin Block, at the corner of Front and Market (Wellington) Streets. The usual fare from Kingston to York at this period was $6, while $3\frac{1}{2}$d. per mile was charged for short distances. Thirty pounds of baggage was usually carried free of charge, while two hundred pounds cost the owner the same as his own passage.

Even on the main highways the stages were not run as extensively during the navigation season as in the winter, and many of the horses were turned into the pasture for the summer; but there was always some local traffic, and a few coaches had to be kept in operation for those who

[18]Sir Richard Bonnycastle: *Canada and the Canadians.* 1846. Vol. I, pp. 114-16.
[19]York *Upper Canada Gazette,* January 14, 1830.
[20]*Cobourg Star,* January 11, 1831.

wished to avoid sea-sickness by travelling over the land route eastward from Toronto at least as far as the Bay of Quinté. As a general rule open stage-wagons, hauled by two or four horses, were used on back lines, "the covered coaches kept in the vicinity of the larger towns where the roads were better, and where it was worth an effort to 'take in' the unwary".[21] It was possible for travellers on the main roads to hire an "extra" or postchaise for their own use, but they were often surprised that others would avail themselves, without the slightest hesitation, of private as of public coaches. Judge Pringle gives an interesting description of a winter journey westward from Cornwall on the Kingston Road in the early thirties:

"The author has still a vivid recollection of his first journey from Cornwall to York. He started from Chesley's Inn, then the Cornwall stage-house, about nine in the evening of the last Friday of January, 1833, in a stage-wagon. There was no snow on the ground, but, the road being hard-frozen and smooth, good time was made, and he arrived at Kingston stage-house between nine and ten on Saturday night, where he remained until about seven in the morning of the following Monday, when he started on the drive to York, this time in a comfortable sleigh. He passed through Napanee, Belleville, Trenton, Cobourg, Port Hope and other small towns, travelling continuously day and night until he got to Bett's Inn, then the York stage-house, on Wednesday evening. The journey, not including the delay of at least thirty-four hours at Kingston, took about eighty-six hours. How would the present generation (1889), who think twelve hours between Cornwall and Toronto rather slow, like to go back to the travelling of the 'good old days'."[22]

In July of the same year Patrick Shirreff journeyed eastward from York, and found conditions of travel almost intolerable: an average of only three miles per hour was made by the mail-stage, which was an open wagon driven by one team of horses. He remarked that "the roads were worse than any yet travelled on, and the driver stopped two

[21]Keefer, *op. cit.*, p. 114.
[22]J. F. Pringle: *Lunenburgh, or the Old Eastern District.* 1890. pp. 109-110.

WILLIAM WELLER.
(1799-1863.)
The king of stage-coach
proprietors was for three
years Mayor of Cobourg

HENRY BURT WILLIAMS.
(1813-64.)
Toronto cabinet-maker and
the originator of omnibuses
on Yonge Street

John Ross Robertson Collection   J. W. Cotton

A WELLER STAGE ON THE KINGSTON ROAD

1841.

SUMMER ARRANGEMENT

BETWEEN

KINGSTON & TORONTO

BY THE

BAY OF QUINTE,

Six times a week each way?

FROM the 1st of May next and during the summer months, the Mail Stage will leave Belleville for Toronto immediately after the arrival of the Bay Steamers, passing through Port Trent, Brighton, Colborne, Grafton, Cobourg, Port Hope, Clarke, Darlington, Whitby and Pickering.

GOOD FOUR HORSE COACHES

(Entirely new,) with steady experienced drivers, going through from Belleville to Toronto in twenty four hours, and from Cobourg to Toronto by day light.

REDUCED FARES.

Belleville to Toronto,	- -	120 miles.	- - £1 0 0
Cobourg to Toronto,	- -	72 do.	- - 0 10 0
Port Hope to Toronto,	- -	65 do.	- - 0 10 0

The above line of Stages will leave the General Stage Office, Toronto, for Belleville, every Sunday at 10 o'clock, A. M. and every Monday, Tuesday, Wednesday, Thursday, and Friday at 5 o'clock, P. M. after the arrival of the Steam Boats from Niagara and Hamilton.

Strangers will find a great advantage in taking this route; by leaving Kingston (the Capital) in a Steam Boat, they have a fine view of the country forming the Bay of Quinte, fast rising into importance since the late alteration of the Seat of Government, and taking the Stage at Belleville, will pass through the above named townships, which for fertility of soil and density of population will yield to none in the Province, thus reaching the city of Toronto at 8 o'clock P. M.

WM. WELLER,

Proprietor,

Cobourg, April 28, 1841. tf36

N. B.—A Steam Boat leaves Kingston going up, and Belleville going down the Bay, every morning, (Sundays excepted.)

From the *Cobourg Star*, August 11, 1841
WELLER'S STAGE ADVERTISEMENT

William Weller's signature as President of the Cobourg and Rice Lake Plank Road and Ferry Company, 1847

hours at a hotel notwithstanding our anxiety to get him away".[23]

The spring of the year was the most difficult season for the operations of stages. In 1839 the Rev. Anson Green and the Rev. Matthew Richey, Principal of Upper Canada Academy, Cobourg, travelled seventy miles by coach to Toronto. The trip was very unpleasant:

"The Rev. Mr. Richey and I had a most wearisome journey to the Capital (Toronto) on the 5th of April to attend the Missionary Anniversary. The frost was out of the ground, and our stage stuck fast several times, and the poor horses were jaded almost to exhaustion. We frequently walked along by the fences, leaving our poor horses to drag the empty coach through the mud as best they could. We were nearly two days and a night getting from Cobourg to Toronto."[24]

When the roads were at their worst it was not infrequently necessary to resort to some ingenious expedient in order to ascend a steep hill. Heavy ropes secured to a stout tree on a hilltop were occasionally used by the driver and his passengers to assist the horses in hauling the stage up a steep incline where the roadway was all but washed out; while on other occasions horses and men combined to raise the front wheels out of a pitch-hole, and then went around to the rear to push or pry the back out in a similar manner, fence rails and logs being employed to form a causeway across the hole.

With the introduction of steamships on parts of the upper St. Lawrence in the late twenties came better stage services at the portages; four-horse covered coaches ran between Montreal and Lachine, and stages from the Cascades to Coteau Landing and from Cornwall to Prescott. In 1828 the steam-and-stage trip between Prescott and Montreal could be made in one day along the American side, though the cost of passage was expensive; a few years later, in the early thirties, a similar service was available by a Canadian line.

In 1832 Mrs. Susanna Moodie travelled up the St. Lawrence by the stage-and-steam line. Between Cornwall and

[23]Patrick Shirreff: *A Tour through North America*. 1835. p. 119.
[24]Anson Green: *Life and Times*. 1877. p. 227.

Prescott "nine passengers were closely packed into our narrow vehicle, but the sides being of canvas, and the open space allowed for windows unglazed, I shivered with cold, which amounted to a state of suffering, when the day broke and we approached the little village of Matilda. It was unanimously voted by all hands that we should stop and breakfast at a small inn by the roadside, and warm ourselves before proceeding to Prescott".[25] Mrs. Catharine Traill travelled over the same route on an excessively hot day and "was dreadfully fatigued . . . , being literally bruised black and blue".[26] She considered, however, that the steam-and-stage line was operated "with as little trouble to the passenger as possible".[27] In 1832 a steamer service overcame the rapids between Long Sault and Prescott, and thereafter stages were unnecessary except for the twelve-mile portage between Dickinson's Landing and Cornwall.

In 1837 the stage service from Niagara to York *via* Queenston, St. Catharines, Ancaster and Hamilton operated three days a week each way. The scheduled time from Ancaster to York was eleven hours, but needless to say it was seldom possible to adhere to any schedule, even in winter, the Canadian coaches, like those of England, always operating under the proviso "If God wills". In 1835 William Weller, owner of the Telegraph Line of stages, commenced a daylight service between Toronto and Hamilton during the winter season, and followed the Dundas Street route. The half-way house on this highway during staging days was Emerson Taylor's Tavern at Credit or Springfield, (later named Erindale).

The roads west of Toronto were just as bad as the Kingston Road. An excellent example of the misery which might at any time be experienced by stage travellers is afforded by an account given by Canniff Haight of a trip in November, 1846, from Hamilton to Niagara. The stage was a lumber-wagon with a canvas covering, and in the four seats were its driver and seven passengers, including a young child who cried most of the way. The luggage was all tied

---

[25]Susanna Moodie: *Roughing It in the Bush.* 1852. Edition of 1923, pp. 60-61.
[26]Catharine Traill: *The Backwoods of Canada.* 1836. Edition of 1929, p. 74.
[27]*Ibid.*, p. 66.

on behind, and the "coach" set off from Hamilton at 6 p.m.
The night was very dark and it rained at frequent intervals, but the journey continued all night. The roads were
so bad that the passengers had on several occasions to get
out and walk in the mud. The weary travellers had no
alternative except to seek lodging for the night in a tavern
or farmhouse, and they chose to continue. Finally, when
all were nearly exhausted, the stage entered Niagara just
as the sun was rising.[28]

William Weller's Royal Mail Line of four-horse coaches,
brightly-coloured vehicles with the King's coat-of-arms emblazoned on the side, was the most famous line of stages
during the coaching period. It was no small business to
organise a regular service from Hamilton to Montreal, with
branches from Dundas to Niagara, up Yonge Street, and
in many other directions. Relays of horses had to be provided at intervals of about fifteen miles, together with
stables and stable-keepers. To signify his approach the
driver would sound his horn as he drew near each village,
for the coming of the coach was an event of importance in
those days: the bustle of the hostlers changing the horses,
and the general excitement attendant upon the arrival of
passengers and mail formed a welcome variation in the
quiet life of village and town.

After some delay while the mail was sorted, the stage-
driver resumed his seat upon the box, and with a crack of
the whip the journey was resumed. Inns and taverns at
frequent intervals provided meals and refreshment and a
place to sleep, if, indeed, the coach did not travel all night.
Among the best-known taverns along the Kingston Road
was Farewell's, one mile east of Skae's Corners (Oshawa).
This was important as a "house of entertainment" as early
as the War of 1812, the whole district being then known as
Whitby, the name of the township. In the towns, the Old
Inn at Port Hope and the Albion in Cobourg were early
noted as stopping-places for coaches.

In the forties and fifties the Globe Hotel, Cobourg, was
the best between Toronto and Kingston. Guests at stage-
coach hostelries met around the open fire and spun yarns

[28] Canniff Haight: *Country Life in Canada Fifty Years Ago.* 1885,
pp. 150-1.

of adventure and travel, or exchanged the news and gossip of the day. Let it not be supposed, however, that there was ever much romance about the general run of taverns and inns which dotted the countryside in early days; too often they were the scene of drunkenness, and many early travellers refer to the beds' being so dirty or so full of bugs that it was preferable to lie on the floor, or to travel all night. And even when the coaches were able to operate with any regularity it was quite usual for the passengers to help the driver pry the coach out of the mud with fence rails; while to walk a considerable part of a journey, and almost always up the hills, was an ordinary experience. The roads were at their best during the winter when the ruts and holes were filled up with snow. At this time of year the fastest speed was made, and then only was land travel ever pleasant; at other seasons travelling was usually an ordeal to which one submitted as an inevitable misfortune.

The construction and appearance of a typical stage-coach, (which one traveller referred to as "a mighty heavy, clumsy conveniency, hung on leather springs, and looking for all the world as if elephants alone could move it along"[29]), is well described by Judge Pringle:

"It was strongly built, the carriage part of it adapted to go through rough roads if necessary. The body was closed at the front and back and covered with a stout roof. The sides were open, but protected by curtains that could be let down if rain came on; there was a door at each side, fitted with a sliding window that could be lowered or raised as the weather was fine or stormy. There were three seats inside, each of which was intended for three passengers; those on the front seat sat with their backs to the horses, those on the back and middle seats faced them; the back seat was the most comfortable. Outside there was the driver's seat, and another immediately behind it on the roof; each of these would hold three persons. The best seats in fine weather were those on the outside of the coach, as they commanded a good view of the country on all sides. A traveller who could make interest with the driver and get the seat beside him could get a great deal of information

[29]Bonnycastle, *op. cit.*, Vol. I, p. 217.

COBOURG , CANADA WEST.

ALBION HOTEL.

The Mail Stages for TORONTO KINGSTON &

PETERBORO leave this HOUSE every Morning.

J. A. COWLES.

Reproduced by Courtesy of A. J. Hewson, Esq.

A BUSINESS CARD OF THE ALBION HOTEL, COBOURG,
ABOUT 1840

From Conant's *Life in Canada*

MOODE FAREWELL'S TAVERN, NEAR OSHAWA, IN 1903

A typical inn, well-known to travellers on the Danforth Road as
early as the War of 1812

PASSENGERS AND MAIL CROSSING THE ST. LAWRENCE IN WINTER

If the winter stage could not carry the mail the canoe was called into service. This scene of canoe travel amid ice floes is not exaggerated. (See page 409)

from him about localities and events on his part of the road.

"At the back of the coach body was the baggage-rack for trunks, which were tightly strapped on and protected by a large leather apron. Lighter articles of baggage were put on the roof, which was surrounded by a light iron railing. The coach body, including the baggage-rack, was suspended on strong leather straps, which were stretched on the elaborate framework of the carriage. The whole affair was gaudily painted, and, with its team of four fine horses, looked very attractive and was by no means an unpleasant mode of travelling when the roads were good and the weather fine. Covered sleighs were used in winter, and in spring and fall strong wagons without covers, built to stand bad roads and deep mud."[30]

The type of stage which one met with depended largely upon his luck, however, for when Adam Fergusson travelled over the Cornwall-Prescott route in 1831 he was forced to use a vehicle particularly unadapted for a gentleman of portly dimensions. Concerning the coach and his adventurous journey in it he afterwards wrote:

"I had travelled in coaches and in wagons, but here a vehicle was in waiting which might be termed a cross-breed. It partook both of the wagon and the coach, and was most incommodiously distinguished by the absence of a door, the window forming the only mode of effecting our 'exits and our entrances'.

"A short distance from Cornwall we were brought up, in some very heavy road, by the splinter bar giving way; an accident which, considering that we had to send back to the town for aid, was repaired with marvellous celerity. It soon became evident, however, from this delay, and the general aspect of the road (a heavy clay floated by rain), that we should not sleep at Prescott, and it was some consolation to learn that one of the best-kept taverns in Canada awaited us about midway. . . .

"I have mentioned the awkward provision made in our vehicle for ingress and egress, a provision, by the way, devised for the purpose of excluding water in passing through

[30]Pringle, *op. cit.*, p. 108.

rivers and brooks. Frequent were the requests of our coachman, 'Just to get out a bit', calls which, however prudent and reasonable in themselves, were attended with no slight inconvenience to me, as it proved no joke for a man of my calibre to be bolting out and scrambling in at the window every few miles. Besides this harlequinade our ears were occasionally saluted in more critical circumstances with a shrill cry of, 'Gentlemen, please a little to the right, or to the left', as the case might require, when, our own sensations readily seconding the call, there was an instantaneous and amusing scramble to restore the equilibrium. Broken heads on such occasions are by no means rare, though happily we suffered no material inconvenience beyond the slowness of our progress.

"In one very bad clay-hole with a steep bank our machine fairly stuck fast, and was all but upset. In vain did our excellent horses strive to clear it. The coachman was obliged to repair to a neighbouring farm for a team of oxen, while some of the party provided themselves, *sans ceremonie*, with stakes from the adjoining fence, to be ready with their aid. In due time the oxen arrived, the body of the carriage was lifted off the frame, and the wheels extricated, the whole affair being transacted without any symptoms of bad humour, or, so far as I heard, a single angry malediction. . . . It was evening ere we reached our quarters in a snug, comfortable inn."[31]

Mrs. Anna Jameson, travelling on the rough roads of western Upper Canada in the late thirties, encountered a stage similar to that in which Adam Fergusson made his weary way along the shores of the St. Lawrence. It was "a large oblong wooden box, formed of a few planks nailed together and placed on wheels, in which you enter by the window, there being no door to open and shut, and no springs". In this vehicle the unfortunate travellers went "rolling and tumbling along the detestable road, pitching like a scow amid the breakers of a lake storm".[32]

The mail-stage on the Toronto-Hamilton route in the

[31]Adam Fergusson: *Practical Notes Made During a Tour*. 1834. pp. 85-90. "One of the best-kept taverns in Canada, ... a snug, comfortable inn," was Campbell's Tavern, Matilda Township.
[32]Jameson, *op. cit.*, Vol. II, p. 86 fn.

winter of 1837 was observed by the same lady as it stopped at a tavern in Oakville, and she describes the sleigh and its occupants in her usual lively manner:

"It was a heavy wooden edifice about the size and form of an old-fashioned lord mayor's coach, placed on runners and raised about a foot from the ground; the whole was painted a bright red, and long icicles hung from the roof. This monstrous machine disgorged from its portal eight men-creatures, all enveloped in bearskins and shaggy dreadnoughts, and pea-jackets, and fur caps down upon their noses, looking like a procession of bears on their hind-legs, tumbling out of a showman's caravan. They proved, however, when undisguised, to be gentlemen, most of them going up to Toronto to attend their duties in the House of Assembly."[33]

Even though she was bruised "black and blue" during her stage trips, Mrs. Traill considered that the coach "deserves a much higher character than travellers have had the candour to give it, and it is so well adapted for the roads over which it passes that I doubt if it could be changed for a more suitable one. This vehicle is calculated to hold nine persons, three back, front and middle; the middle seat, which swings on broad straps of leather, is by far the easiest, only you are liable to be disturbed when any of the passengers choose to get out".[34]

In the fifties some of the best stage lines used coaches of the Concord type, much more commodious than the older stage, and carrying sixteen passengers in comparative comfort when the roads were good. Even larger were the omnibuses running on Yonge Street, concerning which more will be said later. All stages followed the general rule, "There is always room for one more", the only advantage in overcrowding being that the passengers were less likely to be hurled from their seats when the vehicle went into a pitch-hole.

It is difficult in a day of fast travel by motor-car to visualise the slow progress of the stage, even when roads were good. From thirty to seventy-five miles a day was the usual rate of speed, and long delays and inconveniences

[33]*Ibid.*, Vol. I, pp. 70-71.   [34]Traill, *op. cit.* pp. 65-66.

of an unforeseen nature were frequent. In the winter of 1828 it took two days to make the stage trip from Montreal to Quebec. The same length of time was necessary for a winter journey between Montreal and Bytown, a change being made at Hawkesbury; though in summer the trip was sometimes accomplished in 36 hours by using steamboat transport chiefly, with stages only over the portages from Montreal to Lachine and from Grenville to Carillon. From Montreal to Toronto was not infrequently a five- or six-day trip. On one occasion Mrs. Jameson left Niagara at 10 a.m. on a journey to Hamilton; after travelling until nearly midnight without any refreshment she finished the forty miles in an almost exhausted condition.[35]

Whatever pleasure there was in stage travel depended upon the state of the coach and the weather, the condition of the roads, the beauty of the scenery, and the frame of mind of the traveller. When all these conditions were satisfactory a journey with congenial companions must have been enjoyable. In the winter season, if the roads were not blocked up by drifts of snow, the sleigh was often able to travel on schedule; but a record was established in the winter of 1840 which stood to the end of coaching days without a parallel.

The scheduled time for the trip from Toronto to Montreal was four and a half days, travel usually being discontinued during the night. The Governor-General, Mr. Poulett Thompson (afterwards Lord Sydenham) was in Toronto, and wished to make a quick trip to Montreal, intending, it is said, to reprieve a prisoner sentenced to death —if he arrived in time. He asked William Weller if he could make a fast trip to Montreal. At this time Weller did not usually act in the capacity of coachman, but, considering it a great honour to drive the Governor, he decided to mount the box himself.

A bed was made in the sleigh for his passenger, and all was in readiness for the start. Before commencing the trip, however, Weller placed a bet of £1,000 that he would reach Montreal within thirty-six hours. The start was timed, and, whirling his twenty-foot lash aloft with a sound like a pistol-shot, Weller commenced his race against time. At the Royal Mail Line stables along the route experienced men were in readiness to effect a quick change of horses and provide all necessities for man and beast. Weller drove the entire distance himself, and won his bet, too, for he pulled up his steaming horses at the Montreal stage-office just thirty-five hours and forty minutes after leaving Toronto—a remarkable time for 360 miles. The Governor-General gave him £100 in payment of the speedy trip, and a suitably-engraved gold watch to commemorate the notable occasion.

Stage-drivers varied, of course, but the characteristics of many of them increased the discomfort of journeys which would have been miserable enough even if the coachmen had been models of conduct. They were frequently in league with innkeepers to bring trade, and many a driver was accustomed to take a drink at each of the taverns along his route: consequently drunken drivers became at times a menace to the travelling public. In 1841 Sir Richard Bonnycastle proceeded westward from Montreal by the steam-and-stage line. From Lachine to Lake St. Louis a steamship covered the route, but from the Cascades the wagon-coach was the means of travel, and the highway "a dangerous ride, close to the high banks of the St. Lawrence and mostly along their very edge, with but few trees or guards to prevent an accident".[36] In the winter of 1848 a drunken stage-driver drove his coach into the St. Lawrence River, and one of the passengers, having clung to the stage all night, had his hands so badly frost-bitten that they had to be amputated.

Other accidents were due to recklessness on the part of the driver, or, perhaps, merely physical exhaustion. The Rev. Anson Green describes the upset of a coach in which he was travelling near Trenton in 1828. The accident occurred because the driver fell asleep, the coach upsetting in a ravine when the unguided horses wandered off the road in search of a drink. The Rev. Green gives a diverting account of the mishap:

"The stupid driver found himself on the opposite bank when he awoke; but we were engulfed in the ditch. We had

[36]Sir Richard Bonnycastle: *The Canadas in 1841.* 1842. Vol. I, p. 87.

three on each seat, one of whom was a very loquacious old maid, and she screamed out fearfully, 'I am killed, I am dead, I really am dead; what shall I do?' The poor creature! Though I had two men on top of me, and my arm in the water, I was sure that I was not dead; and I tried to convince her that she was still alive, but all in vain: nor could I much wonder at the poor creature's fright, for we were as near death as I wished to be.

"The stage door was so tightly fastened that we could not open it; and those who were lying on top of us seemed to be confused and stupid. After a little the driver managed to shove open a small window, through which, one after another, we emerged from our dismal position. We got the poor old crone out also, who, dead as she was, managed to walk across the road to a cottage. Our driver, never more than half awake, gave up in despair. He declared that we could not get that stage out, and he offered to go ten miles for another. But my time was precious, and I told them if they would help me we would be off again in half an hour. By the aid of the horses hitched to the wheels, and rails to pry with, we placed our carriage on the road, mended the broken tongue with the halters, and were soon on our journey."[37]

One traveller was so incensed because a stage-driver had tried to force him to eat breakfast before daybreak that he advocated adding to the Litany: "From all stage-drivers and stage proprietors, Good Lord deliver us."[38]

In the early days attempts to rob the mail-stages were not infrequent. The York mail was robbed in 1821, and there were several unsuccessful attempts in later years; a strong and fearless driver was consequently an advantage. In some districts there was keen competition between stage lines, and a driver of pugilistic fame sometimes drew double the pay of one of more peaceable disposition. The very nature of the business required men inured to every hardship and equal to any emergency; and if some of them failed to negotiate that terror of drivers—the Herriman Hill between Colborne and Grafton—or some other of the innumer-

[37]Green, *op. cit.*, pp. 120-1.
[38]*The Diary of Henry John Jones*, January 23, 1837. (See *Willison's Monthly*, April—September, 1929.)

able hazards of staging days, little blame could be attached to anyone except those responsible for the intolerable roads.

It was not until 1842 that a daily line of stages operated across the province from east to west, and this was inaugurated largely in consequence of requirements with regard to the carriage of the mails. In the early fifties, when the coach lines were most complete, the trunk line extended from Quebec to the Detroit, and was intersected by branch lines in all directions. The stage road from Niagara to London, and the Governor's Road (Dundas Street) were well-travelled, as many as six four-horse stages passing each way daily. Between London and Brantford were more than thirty taverns, all of which did a flourishing business with stage-drivers and their passengers.

Of the branch lines it is possible to mention only a few. The Canada Company, which began to settle the "Huron Tract" in the late twenties, made arrangements to provide for the conveyance of immigrants into the remote sections of the territory. We find that "two good covered Stage Wagons, with Teams of good Horses each, are to be constantly kept travelling between Hamilton, at the Head of Lake Ontario, and through Wilmot to Goderich in the Huron Territory".[39] The fare was to be only $3 from Hamilton to Goderich; and on the arrival of steamboats at the head of Lake Ontario twelve extra wagons were to be available to immigrants intending to settle in the Huron Tract. It would appear, however, that a regular service from Hamilton through Wentworth, Waterloo and Wellington Counties to Galt and Guelph, and on over the Huron Road to Goderich, was not in operation before 1841. Even in 1845 the stage journey from Hamilton to Guelph followed the circuitous route through Galt and Preston.

Northward from the Kingston Road ran stages to all the important towns and villages. The Bletchers, who "kept tavern" three miles north of Port Hope, provided a stage service between Port Hope, Peterborough and Lindsay. Farther west, on Yonge Street, there had been public conveyances at least as early as 1828, when George Playter and his sons established a line. This was purchased by William Weller in 1832, and eight years later he sold his

[39]"A Canadian Settler": *The Emigrant's Informant*. 1834. pp. 66-8.

interest in the service to Charles Thompson of Summerhill. For some ten years Thompson had been a well-known stage-driver over the Toronto-Newmarket-Barrie route, and his connection with the business lasted until 1850. He was early interested in the steamers *Morning* and *Beaver* on Lake Simcoe, and his stages ran in conjunction with them. In 1847 one Shuttleworth started a second service on Yonge Street, running "omnibuses" as far as Richmond Hill. An advertisement of 1850 shows that numerous stages were running up Yonge Street from Toronto:

"A stage in connection with the steamer *Morning* on Lake Simcoe leaves the Simcoe stage office, Liddell's Building, Church Street, daily, Sunday excepted, at 7 o'clock a.m., and at 3 o'clock p.m. Another stage in connection with the steamer *Beaver* on Lake Simcoe leaves the Western Hotel daily at 7 o'clock a.m. . . . . A stage leaves the stage office, Liddell's Building, for Pine Grove daily at 3 o'clock p.m. . . . . There are also stages to Richmond Hill, Thornhill and York Mills leaving the Market Square daily at 4 o'clock p.m."[40]

There were at one time sixty-three taverns to supply the needs of travellers along the Toronto-Barrie route, in addition to 152 taverns and 206 beer shops in Toronto itself, then (1850) a city of about 30,000 people. One of the best-known inns on Yonge Street was the Half-Way House, where horses were changed on the Toronto-Holland Landing route. The proprietors of this hotel succeeded Shuttleworth in the stage business; but the opening of the Northern Railway in 1853 put an end to most of the coaches on Yonge Street. It was still necessary, however, for the mail to be carried by bus as far as Richmond Hill, and this service was continued in turn by John Palmer; Raymond (a hotelkeeper in Richmond Hill); William Cook of the Yorkshire House, Thornhill; and John Thompson, from the early seventies to 1896, when the opening of the electric railway wrote *finis* to the business. For a quarter of a century or more this stage line was almost unique as a survivor among the numerous important routes which had been superseded by the railway.

[40]Quoted in J. Ross Robertson: *Landmarks of Toronto*. 1894-1914. Vol. V, p. 20.

H. B. WILLIAMS' OMNIBUS OF 1849

These buses, charging 6d. fare, operated every ten minutes from the St. Lawrence Market and King and Yonge Streets to the Red Lion Hotel, Yorkville. The first bus was built in Williams' cabinet shop at 140 Yonge Street, near the present Loew's Theatre

SIR JOHN EATON DRIVING CANADA'S FIRST MOTOR-BUS, 1900

This vehicle was known as an Electric Tally-ho

1850-60

H. B. WILLIAMS' BUS, AT THE RED LION HOTEL, 1850

This was one of four ten-passenger omnibuses operated between Toronto and Yorkville, 1850-62. The Red Lion Hotel, Yorkville, was located at 749-763 Yonge Street. In 1861 the Toronto Railway Company commenced a horse-car service. Williams narrowed the gear of his buses so that they would run on the tracks, but after a year's competition he sold out to the Company, and for thirty years horse-cars, together with public cabs and private carriages, were the vehicles of passenger conveyance in Toronto.

A HORSE-CAR OF THE TORONTO STREET RAILWAY

A familiar sight on the streets of Toronto until 1891, when it was superseded by the electric car. At 4 p.m. on September 10, 1861, the first horse-car, with the Artillery Band playing spirited airs on the roof, proceeded down Yonge Street from Yorkville (Bloor Street) to the city, being derailed twice during its maiden journey; a concert and a ball concluded a day of celebration. For many years the driver's wage was $1.20 for a twelve-hour day, and the speed was limited by law to six miles per hour. One or two horses pulled the cars, and usually lasted only a year in the service.

Similarly there were branch lines running off the main roads in all parts of Upper Canada. Even the most remote of settled districts were usually connected in some way or other with the larger settlements towards "the front". In the fifties Renfrew County, far away in "the bush", had a coach line connecting Cobden, at the head of Muskrat Lake, with the Ottawa River; and from Cobden a rowboat service, and later a steamboat, carried passengers and goods to Pembroke. Most of the back township stage lines survived many years after the coming of the railways put an end to the stage-coach along the front; in fact they not infrequently still remain, though usually conducted by motor-car in connection with the mail service.

But the end of the stage as far as the main lines were concerned was approaching slowly but surely, for the Grand Trunk and Great Western Railways were gradually being pushed through the province. In October, 1856, the first through train passed between Toronto and Montreal. The shrill whistle of the Iron Horse sounded the knell of the stage-coach, for there was no possibility of competing with the railway in speed, and the roads were not such as to be conducive to travelling for pleasure. We now have the coach lines returning, but they are motor-coaches travelling over paved highways. Their competition is being keenly felt, too; and perhaps the ghost of the old roadway is now enjoying with malicious glee the present discomfiture of its old rival the railroad!

There was one small part of his extensive business that remained to the stage-driver until the taxicab became common within recent years: this was the transport of passengers from remote railway stations to the centre of the settlements they were intended to serve. Four-horse omnibuses of the type which Shuttleworth introduced on the Toronto-Richmond Hill route could carry about forty passengers in fine weather when the more athletic male travellers might occupy the capacious roof; while smaller and less pretentious buses provided a necessary—if not comfortable —service over the rough roads of town and village.

By 1870 almost all of the important stage routes had been abandoned, and the proprietors whose business had been superseded by the railways gracefully accepted the inevitable and retired to the side roads; but none of them took his medicine as philosophically or expressed his feeling so humorously as did the king of them all—William Weller. He was present at the Grand Dinner in the Town Hall, Peterborough, on December 29, 1854, in honour of the inauguration of the Cobourg and Peterborough Railroad. Many a good speech was delivered, but the enthusiasm reached its climax when he whose business was about to pass away answered the persistent shouts of the audience:

"I know why you have called upon me for a speech,— it is to hurt my feelings; for you know I get my living by running stages, and you are taking the BIT out of my mouth at the same time as you take it out of my horses' mouths. You are comparing in your minds the present times with the past when you had to carry a RAIL, instead of riding one, in order to help my coaches out of the mud. But after all I am rejoiced to see old things passing away and conditions becoming WELLER."[41]

[41]*Cobourg Star*, January 10, 1855.

CHAPTER X

EARLY CANADIAN RAILROADS
THE COBOURG AND PETERBOROUGH RAILWAY

"But, Mousie, thou art no thy lane
In proving foresight may be vain;
The best laid schemes o' mice and men
Gang aft a-gley,
An' lea'e us nought but grief an' pain
For promised joy."

ROBERT BURNS: *To a Mouse.*

ALTHOUGH railroads have been of supreme importance only during the last century, yet we have to look back over three hundred years for their origin. T. C. Keefer, the noted Canadian engineer who was associated in the construction of the great Victoria Bridge at Montreal, neatly describes the crude beginning of railways, about 1630, when "one Master Beaumont ruined himself in coal-mining, but has been immortalised by the biographer of George Stephenson as the first man that formed a railway; for although his rails were of wood, and the wheeled vehicles were drawn by horses, yet the principle of the railway was there. These tramways were in use a century before iron was employed in them, which event is supposed to have taken place about 1738."[1]

The first railway locomotive which might be considered a forerunner of those now in use was invented by the English engineer, George Stephenson, in 1814, although previous to that time Trevithick and others had operated "steam carriages" on roads, much to the terror of those who lived in the vicinity. Stephenson's first locomotive hauled eight loaded coal trucks at the rate of four miles per hour. In 1825 the first passenger railway in the world was in operation, when a line connecting Stockton and Darlington, in Durham County, England, was opened with a great celebration on September 27th. This line was twelve miles long, the rails were laid on a gauge of nearly six feet, and

[1] T. C. Keefer: *Travel and Transportation.* In John Lovell (Ed.): *80 Years' Progress in British North America.* 1863. p. 187.

the carriages or coaches were merely open wagons, much the same as those in use on roads.   In fact the development in passenger cars was long in the nature of imitation of the carriage or stage-coach, rather than anything that even approximated the modern railway coach.

The inhabitants of Canada were not far behind those of England in railway-planning.   As early as 1827 there was a project to connect St. Andrews, on the Bay of Fundy, with Quebec, but the first steam railway actually to be built in British America was a small line constructed in 1830 in the city of Quebec to carry stone from the wharves at Cape Diamond to the Citadel; this was an incline railway operated by a stationary engine.   Several lines were projected in Canada soon after, but the troubled times previous to the Rebellion, and the depression thereafter, prevented most of them from advancing beyond mere plans.

One railway was completed, however, before the Rebellion broke out,—a short portage line connecting St. Johns on the Richelieu River, with La Prairie, a village on the St. Lawrence opposite Montreal.   This fifteen-mile railroad was built to shorten the route to New York by connecting the Molson Line of steamers on the St. Lawrence with a line of boats operating on Lake Champlain; for some years the railway was used only in the summer months.   The importation of an engine from England, and the attempts to operate it, were shrouded in mystery.   An authority states that "the trial trip was made by moonlight in the presence of a few interested parties, and it is not described as a success.   Several attempts were made to get the *Kitten*—for such was the nickname applied to this pioneer locomotive—to run to St. Johns, but in vain; the engine proved refractory and horses were substituted for it".   An American engineer was called in, however, and found that all it needed was "plenty of wood and water".[2]

The opening of the Champlain and St. Lawrence Railroad took place on July 21, 1836, in the presence of the Governor-General, Lord Gosford.   The first train consisted of two cars in which there were benches but no covering overhead; these cars only were pulled by the small engine, while others followed, hauled by horses.   The locomotive

[2]*Tackabury's Atlas of the Dominion of Canada.* 1875. p. 39.

made the first trip in just one minute under an hour, but it was not generally used on the line until 1837.

For many years the locomotives on all railways were characterised by wide smokestacks with wire screens at the top. One of the duties of the fireman was to strike the top of the stack once in a while with a long pole, in order to shake down the cinders and improve the draft. Rails and other equipment were similarly primitive. The first rails of the Champlain and St. Lawrence Railway were made of wood, with flat bars of iron spiked on them. The bars curled up in the heat of summer, and as these "snake-rails" were dangerous, iron rails were soon introduced, to be replaced many years later by steel. The earliest laws enacted in Canada with reference to railways provided that gates should be constructed at all crossings, and were to be kept closed at all times except when wagons desired to cross!

Numerous were the inventions and improvements in railway apparatus which the mechanical geniuses of the day were continually patenting and bringing before the notice of the public. Some of those announced in 1858 may sound humorous to modern ears, but they were the subject of serious attention in a day when travel on a railway was characterised by but few comforts. The people who experienced the unique thrill of a journey to Toronto over the Great Western, the Grand Trunk, or the Ontario and Simcoe Huron Union Railway were advised that their subsequent trips by the new mode of conveyance might be rendered safer or more comfortable by Braid's Spark Arrester, Egan's Car Journal Oiler, Hudsan's Fastener for Car Seats, Webster's Improved Car Link and Draw Car, Fox's Apparatus for Railroad Switching, McDonald's Improved Axle Box, and Crawford's Machine for Arresting Railway Trains. At the same time, among many other devices, it was confidently hoped that traffic conditions would be regulated, and the speed of travel expedited by Porter's Self-acting Railroad Gate, and Thomas' Snow Exterminator![3]

Among railway visionaries of early days there were not

[3] The models of these (and many other) inventions were to be seen in 1858 at the rooms of the Board of Arts and Manufactures for Upper Canada, 79 King Street West, Toronto. Several hundred of them are listed in the *Descriptive Catalogue of the Provincial Exhibition, 1858.* Second Edition, 1858, pp. 65-75.

a few cranks of a harmless nature. Some of these impractical people were, perhaps, merely half a century ahead of their time. A tract written by Sir John Smythe of Toronto was intended to persuade people that a railway to the Pacific would be of great value in case of another war with the United States. His project would provide steam communication between London, England, and China, by "a branch to run on the north side of the Township of Cavan and on the south side of Balsam Lake". This remarkable scheme would continue the railway "in the rear of Lake Huron and in the rear of Lake Superior, twenty miles in the interior of the country of the lake aforesaid; to unite with the railroad from Lake Superior to Winnipeg at the south-west main trading-post of the North-West Company". The value of his plan was, no doubt, greatly enhanced in the eyes of the *hoi polloi* by the signature at the end of "Sir John Smythe, Baronet and Royal Engineer, Canadian Poet, LL.D., and Moral Philosopher".[4]

The first railway constructed in Upper Canada was a short portage road around Niagara Falls from Queenston to Chippawa. This enterprise, known as the Erie and Ontario, was chartered in 1833, but the line was not built until 1839. The grades along the route were too steep for the locomotives of that day, so horse-cars were used upon it, and the railway proved of considerable value in the portage of goods between Lakes Ontario and Erie. A traveller over the line in 1845 wrote of his experiences: "You are whirled along, not by steam, but by three trotting horses at a rapid rate through a wood road till you reach the Falls."[5] In 1854 the railway was rebuilt from Chippawa to Niagara-on-the-Lake, and was operated by steam locomotives; and in later years the line was extended to Fort Erie.

Among the first railway projects in Upper Canada was the construction of a line between the port of Cobourg and Peterborough. As early as 1831 the enterprising citizens of Cobourg, then a small but important village, planned to build a line northwards thirty miles in order to open up the

---

[4]The tract in which this project was placed before the public is quoted in Henry Scadding: *Toronto of Old*. 1873. p. 177.

[5]Sir Richard Bonnycastle: *Canada and the Canadians*. 1846. Vol. I, p. 233.

A RACE ON THE BALTIMORE AND OHIO RAILROAD, 1830

Peter Cooper's locomotive, *Tom Thumb*, is upholding the honour of the steam engine—in spite of the efforts of the drivers and passengers of Stockton and Stokes' horse-car.

W. H. Bartlett

RAILWAY SCENE AT LITTLE FALLS, MOHAWK VALLEY, NEW YORK, 1837

CELEBRATION IN UXBRIDGE AT THE OPENING OF THE
TORONTO AND NIPISSING RAILWAY, SEPTEMBER 14, 1871

COBOURG AND PETERBOROUGH RAILWAY LOCOMOTIVE, 1870
A typical locomotive operating on the nine-mile extension between
the River Trent and the Marmora Iron Mines at Blairton

back country. It was expected that vast amounts of lumber, grain and flour would be hauled to Cobourg harbour and thence shipped to the United States. A rare pamphlet[6] printed in Cobourg in 1832 contains a map showing the route of the proposed railway, and refers to it as an inducement to prospective settlers to choose the Newcastle District.

The original charter of this line was dated March 6, 1834, and provided for a capital of £40,000 in shares of £10 each. The road was to be commenced within two years and finished within eight. The capital was later considerably increased, but twenty years passed before the line was finally opened. The original charter having expired from non-fulfilment of its terms it was necessary to secure another. Promoters revived the charter in 1845, but with the much less ambitious project of substituting a plank road for the railway. The organisation was known as The Cobourg and Rice Lake Plank Road and Ferry Company, the capital of £6,000 might be doubled if necessary, and there was no time limit in which it must be completed. The prime mover in this scheme, and the President of the Company, was William Weller, stage-coach proprietor.

On October 5, 1847, an agreement[7] was signed by which the Company purchased 350,000 board feet of three-inch planks at $5 per M. The roadway was completed and successfully used for a short time, after which it suffered the inevitable fate of plank roads.

In the late forties the depression and unrest following the Rebellion of 1837 had passed away and, aided by the strong incentive of the Guarantee Act of 1849, an era of railway-building was inaugurated. This was furthered by the extensive immigration of settlers, the good harvest of 1850, and the increase of trade incident to the repeal of the Navigation Laws. In 1852 a charter for a railway between Cobourg and Peterborough was again obtained from the government. On February 7, 1853, the first sod was turned in Cobourg amidst great public enthusiasm: the citizens

[6]James Gray Bethune: Schedule of Real Estate in the Newcastle District. 1832.
[7]This interesting agreement is still in existence. A full description of it may be found in E. C. Guillet: Cobourg, in the Cobourg Sentinel-Star, June 12, 1930.

turned out *en masse*, and after a gay parade through the town the festivities were concluded by a grand ball.

A large number of labourers were immediately engaged at the high wage of one dollar a day, and work on the railway proceeded rapidly under the direction of contractors Zimmerman and Balsh and chief engineer Spaulding. The gauge was 5' 6", the same as that of most early railroads in Canada. The route followed the course of a beautiful valley, and in the spring of 1854 the sloping shores of Rice Lake were reached at Harwood and the first section of the line was in operation. Harwood, which had previously consisted of little more than a tavern, now experienced a boom in which land rose sharply in value from $3 to $400 an acre; the little village of Baltimore, half way to Harwood, also developed rapidly, but there was soon to be an equally rapid deflation in values—the usual result of speculation.

During the last months of 1854 the section of the railroad from Harwood to Peterborough was speedily pushed to completion, and a five-mile extension northward to Chemong Lake was planned. By November 15th the Rice Lake bridge had been finished, and the line was in operation from the Indian Village to Cobourg. The charge for passengers was 6s. 3d., and Fisher's stage line connected with the trains and covered the balance of the journey from the north shore of Rice Lake to Peterborough.

The contractors had originally estimated the expenditure on the railway at a price per mile that was soon lost sight of because of many unforeseen obstacles, and the final cost was $1,100,112 for a railroad of twenty-nine and one-half miles. The three-mile trestle supported on piles, which carried the line across Rice Lake, was, as it soon proved, insufficiently braced, and unable to withstand the shoving of the ice and the sweep of the wind. This bridge was undoubtedly a great engineering blunder, from which the Railway never recovered.

The line, however, was opened with great *éclat* on Friday, December 29, 1854, when an inaugural excursion was run to Peterborough. That town had invited the Directors of the Railway and fifty other gentlemen of Cobourg to be their guests at a banquet, and the Company offered a free ticket to all who wished to make the trip.

Over one thousand availed themselves of the invitation, and at 10.30 a.m. twelve well-loaded cars "driven by two power-ful locomotives" left the station near the harbour and pro-ceeded northward at what was then the "great speed of over fifteen miles per hour".[8] Almost all the notables of Co-bourg were on board, and the train proceeded over hill, valley and lake until the merry party reached the station at Peterborough East, where all were found to be safe and sound—much to the surprise of many, we imagine. In fact one young man took no chances on the new type of trans-port, but walked to Peterborough to be present at the celebration!

The northern town was gaily decorated in honour of the auspicious occasion, triumphal arches and banners of good-will having been erected to welcome the guests. Two hundred were accommodated at the grand banquet in the town hall, under the chairmanship of Judge Hall, "a portly and dignified gentleman". The viands are referred to in the *Cobourg Star* as "of the most *recherché* description, comprising fresh cod from Boston, venison from the back-woods, and in fact all the substantials and delicacies of the season. As to the wines they were of the best and costliest kinds".

Following the dinner there were many notable speeches. President Scott of the Company remembered "when the only mode of reaching this spot was by the Otonabee River in a bark canoe, when the name of Peterborough was un-known, when even the woodman's axe had not yet been heard, and when the only inhabitants were the Redman and the wild beast of the forest". The Hon. George S. Boulton referred to the same early period, when he had travelled in the district with his "late lamented friend, the Hon. Peter Robinson, who might be called the father of Peterborough County". The Hon. Ebenezer Perry said he had come to Cobourg in 1815, "when the place was known as Hard Scrabble, and hard scrabbling enough it was, too!"

The addresses were marked by the great enthusiasm of both speakers and audience, laughter and cheers alternating as old times were recalled and recent developments de-scribed; but the most humorous address was that of William

[8]*Cobourg Star*, January 3, 1855.

Weller, owner of the most noted line of stage-coaches in
Canada, the Royal Mail Line on the Kingston Road. He
took the coming of the railway philosophically, stating that
he was "glad to see the old times passing away and conditions becoming WELLER". He hoped that the citizens of
Peterborough would now subscribe for stock in the completed railway, "so that the expense may not be like the
handle of a jug—all on one side".[9] But, although that town
benefited greatly by the railways promoted in Cobourg and
Port Hope, Peterborough never aided in the financing of
either line.

This notable excursion was hardly concluded before the
Company was involved in many difficulties. The trestle
bridge was weakened by the ice during the first winter, and,
though an attempt was later made to fill in the causeway
from shore to shore, work proceeded but slowly in strengthening the structure. For some time an experienced man followed each train across the bridge in a hand-car and minutely examined the whole work; but for several weeks
during the first winter the bridge could not be used. The
cost of the railway, too, had been much greater than
anticipated: £100,000 in bonds was issued, as well as
private stock to the amount of £4,000, and in addition
£125,000 was borrowed by the town of Cobourg from the
Municipal Loan Fund; but as the railway was not in successful operation there was considerable difficulty in meeting interest payments.

In the spring of 1855 the line was able to resume its
business traffic, and many millions of feet of lumber and
large quantities of grain were successfully transported to
Cobourg harbour. The road was equipped by the contractor
with three locomotives, two passenger cars, ten box cars and
thirty platform cars, and more were added from time to
time. For a few years a certain measure of success rewarded the efforts of the citizens of Cobourg through whose
initiative alone the railroad was built. In 1856, between
March 1st and December 31st, 15,364 passengers travelled
on the railway, on which the single fare between Cobourg and Peterborough was $1; during the same period

[9] A full account of the excursion, the banquet, and the celebration
generally, is given in the *Cobourg Star*, January 3 and 10, 1855.

15,634,247 feet of lumber, 58,762 bushels of wheat and 31,586 barrels of flour were transported over the line. The receipts for freight, passenger and mail service amounted to $67,133.53, which was $29,316.00 more than the cost of operating the road; but this profit was less than three *per cent.* of the capital expenditure.

For a short time the harbour of Cobourg was full of ships loading and unloading their cargoes, 14,000,000 feet of lumber and 200,000 bushels of wheat being exported from the port in 1856, in addition to half as much more sent east or west over the Grand Trunk Railway during the last months of the year. This period of prosperity in Canada was due largely to the Reciprocity Treaty of 1854, but it was to be followed by depression and hard times in the early sixties, particularly in the town of Cobourg.

The railway bridge over Rice Lake needed almost constant repairs, and the Directors were continually in financial difficulties. The story is told that on one occasion the sheriff of Northumberland County sat in the last car of one of the regular trains leaving Cobourg. He was recognised by one of the officials, and it was considered that his presence boded no good to the railway; so when the train approached the height of land at Summit, nine miles from Cobourg, there was a sudden retrograde movement in the rear car, and the sheriff was soon making great headway backwards towards Cobourg. He was not the kind of man to be easily daunted, however, so he hired a team and drove to Harwood; but he found on arrival there that all equipment not nailed down had proceeded with the train across Rice Lake into Peterborough County!

The proposed section of the railroad from Peterborough to Chemong Lake was never completed. The historian of Peterborough County says concerning this extension: "The original charter of the Cobourg road empowered that company to extend their line to Chemong (or Mud) Lake, but this right expired in 1854 from non-usage. A charter was then obtained for a separate company having power to form a connection between Peterborough and Chemong Lake, either by a rail or tram road, and passing up either side of the Otonabee River. During 1857-8 this road was commenced as an extension of the Cobourg road, and completed as far as Perry's Mills, about three miles up the river."[10] In later years this section was connected with the Midland Railroad from Port Hope, and the line was pushed through to Lakefield.

In the summer of 1857 Walter Shanley, C.E., inspected the Rice Lake bridge with a view to filling it in as a permanent embankment. This was quite feasible, as the average depth of water was only seventeen and one-half feet; but the cost of the work was estimated at £50,000, and though it was commenced, operations were frequently held up by a change of management and a new policy. The line operated through to Peterborough at intervals for six years, but in 1860 its use, though continued for a time, was dangerous. On September 7, 1860, the Prince of Wales, later Edward VII, travelled over the railway as far as Rice Lake, but crossed the lake by boat, as the bridge was considered unsafe for royalty. Soon afterwards it was entirely closed to traffic and never used again. A man still living, William Burnet of Cobourg, was on the last train to cross the lake, and recalls that the swaying of the bridge was such that many on board feared they would never reach Harwood.[11]

How large a place the Cobourg and Peterborough Railway filled in the municipal politics of Cobourg may easily be imagined. For many years insinuations and accusations with regard to the mismanagement of the line frequently formed the basis of elections. In 1856 the President of the Company was Henry Covert; while after D'Arcy Boulton's attempt in 1857 to place the line on a paying basis the control passed to John H. Dumble, representing the bondholders. He was followed by Messrs. Fowler and Covert, but no one could make the line pay dividends.

A sidelight on early railway financing is afforded by the admission in 1858 of the Minister of Finance, the Hon. William Cayley, that he had advanced £10,000 of public money to the Cobourg and Peterborough Railway Company with whose President, D'Arcy E. Boulton, he was connected by marriage. Similar indefensible conduct, and on a much

[10]Thomas Poole: *Early Settlement of Peterborough and Peterborough County.* 1867. p. 90.
[11]Reminiscences of William Burnet, Cobourg.

From *Picturesque Canada*. 1879   Schell

COBOURG HARBOUR IN THE EIGHTEEN-SEVENTIES

A WRECK ON THE GREAT WESTERN RAILWAY, 1859
A hole 50 feet deep near Dundas washed out by heavy rains

1866.   **FREE.**   **1866.**

COBOURG & PETERBORO'

RAILROAD.

NOT TRANSFERABLE.

Pass ------------------------------------

*until*_____1866, *unless otherwise ordered.*

[TURN OVER.]   ------------------------------------

A RELIC OF EARLY RAILROADING

Reproduced by Courtesy of M. O. Hammond, Esq.

THE REMAINS OF THE COBOURG AND PETERBOROUGH RAILWAY
CAUSEWAY AT HARWOOD, RICE LAKE

larger scale, was characteristic of the financing of the Grand Trunk and other early Canadian railways.

By a change of route the Port Hope, Lindsay and Beaverton Railway now touched Peterborough, and the competition of this line may be said to have been the knockout blow to the success of the Cobourg railroad. In fact an old man confessed some years ago that he and two others were hired in behalf of the rival line to remove the bolts from the Rice Lake trestle, and that their work hastened the disintegration of the bridge in 1861. For some years four-horse sleighs were used during the winter season to transport passengers across the lake from Harwood to Hiawatha Indian Village, and on to the station at Ashburnham, near Peterborough. The Company was in such bad financial condition that necessary repairs to the roadbed were neglected, with the result that the railway was temporarily closed by government inspectors.

It was several years before any attempt was made to operate the road after this disaster. The town of Cobourg became acquainted with the evils of railway speculation, and suffered from the effects of a severe depression. The once busy harbour was described by the *Cobourg Sentinel* in 1863 as "the favourite haunt of the wild duck; it resounds with the crack of the sportsman's rifle instead of with the busy song of the jolly tar".[12] In fact, if a relief measure in connection with the operation of the Municipal Loan Fund had not been passed through the Dominion Parliament in 1858 under the direction of Sir A. T. Galt, the town of Cobourg must have gone bankrupt. Under this legislation the interest only, five *per cent.*, had to be paid, the loss of the principal being assumed by the government; but in spite of such favourable treatment the town was soon in arrears in the payment of interest.

In 1865 an attempt, under J. H. Dumble as Managing-Director, was made to operate the railway by an amalgamation with the Marmora Iron Company. This move had the backing of several wealthy Americans with

[12]*Cobourg Sentinel*, May 2, 1863. A very effective letter written by John Mawe appears in the *Cobourg Sentinel* of June 21, 1864, in which the writer describes the differences between Cobourg in 1857 and the town in 1864. It is literature as humorous as one could wish to read. Almost all of it appears in *Cobourg* in the *Cobourg Sentinel-Star*, February 5, 1931.

mining and smelting interests in Pennyslvania, and the new Company paid $100,000 for the line and its equipment. During this phase of the Railway's life iron ore was brought from Marmora over a small railroad from Blairton to the Trent River, and thence by steamers and scows to Harwood. For a few years a fairly satisfactory revenue was obtained through export trade to the United States, a business total of $94,000 in 1869 leaving a small balance after paying for a number of improvements and all operating expenses.

In 1875 there was another reorganisation, of which William Stanton was President, and a number of others, including Messrs. Chambliss, Barber, Fitzhugh, and Shoenberger, were financially interested. The writer has before him one of the 8% debentures issued at that time. By the terms of the issue the face value was repayable in ten years; but the certificate had twenty interest coupons attached, of which only three were cashed. No more evidence need be given concerning the financial failure of The Cobourg, Peterborough and Marmora Railway and Mining Company!

During this period an interesting event occurred. In the summer of 1874 the Earl and Countess of Dufferin participated in an eleven-hour outing from Cobourg to Harwood on the railway, and thence by steamer to Hastings on the Trent River. The Governor-General and his wife were greatly interested in the Marmora iron mines which they visited on that occasion.

For some years the railway from Cobourg to Harwood continued to be used for occasional traffic, particularly Sunday School picnics and other excursions to the beautiful shores of Rice Lake; but, though the Grand Trunk tried to popularise the line, this type of business could not be expected to pay the expenses of upkeep, and as the roadbed became unsafe from lack of attention the railway finally ceased operations entirely in the eighteen-nineties.

The final episode in the history of the Cobourg and Peterborough Railway, which had opened so auspiciously on December 29, 1854, occurred during the early years of the Great War. The old rails were then taken up and shipped to France, where they were utilized behind the lines to transport ammunition and supplies. The section from the Canadian National Railway to the Cobourg harbour is still used for the carriage of freight and coal; but of the rest nothing remains except the embankment at Harwood, extending three-quarters of a mile into the lake, and the old roadbed—a pleasant walk where one may enjoy the beautiful scenery and contemplate the mistakes of men.

CHAPTER XI

THE GRAND TRUNK RAILWAY

No. 6000

"His body black as Erebus
  Accorded with the hue of night;
His central eye self-luminous
  Threw out a cone of noon-day light,
Which split the gloom and then flashed back
The diamond levels of the track.
No ancient poet ever saw
Just such a monster as could draw
The Olympian tonnage of a load
Like this along an iron road;
Or ever thought that such a birth—
  The issue of an inventor's dream—
  With breath of fire and blood of steam,
Could find delivery on this earth."

E. J. PRATT.[1]

THE development of railways in Canada was greatly retarded by the unsettled conditions prior to the Rebellion of 1837 and the depression which followed. A number of railroads had been projected before the Rebellion, but by 1850 only a few short portage lines, totalling sixty-six miles, had been built in Canada. The most important of these were the Champlain and St. Lawrence, the Erie and Ontario, and an eight-mile line built in 1846-47 around the rapids between Montreal and Lachine.

The Grand Trunk Railway originated in projects to build small sections of railroad between some of the principal cities and towns in Canada East and Canada West. In 1845 it was suggested that a line be built between Toronto and Kingston, and meetings were held at various points along the route to discuss plans. Nothing definite resulted, however, and the proposed Toronto and Kingston Junction Railway never advanced beyond the first plans. Farther east the St. Lawrence and Atlantic Railway Company was organised, and this project eventually formed the nucleus of the Grand Trunk Railway.

The Guarantee Act of 1849 was a strong incentive to railway-building in Canada since it provided for govern-

[1]E. J. Pratt: *No. 6000.* (In the *Canadian National Railways Magazine*, December, 1931, p. 9.)

ment aid to every railroad at least seventy miles in length. As a direct result of the government's attitude the first great period of railway construction in Canada was inaugurated. Between 1850 and 1853 fifty-six charters were issued, and twenty-seven of these were acted upon.

On May 16, 1853, the first railway locomotive in Canada West left Toronto and travelled over the Ontario and Simcoe Huron Union Railroad to Machell's Corners (Aurora). Seven years later "300 locomotives were thundering and bellowing"[2] over the province. During the decade following 1851 city, town, township and county councils borrowed from the Municipal Loan Fund for the construction of railways a total of $6,520,340, and the arrears of interest alone amounted to $2,700,000 in 1861. Between 1849 and 1858, 1,726 miles of railroad were constructed in Canada; and by 1860 there were ten lines of railway, some of them with extensive branches. The length of the railroads in Canada West at that time was 1,383 miles, most of the mileage being included in the two large lines, the Grand Trunk and Great Western.

It was originally planned that a railway should be built from Halifax to the Great Lakes under the ownership of the three Governments concerned,—Nova Scotia, New Brunswick and Canada. Joseph Howe of Nova Scotia led a delegation to England in 1850 and obtained a promise from the British Cabinet that capital would be made available at 3¼ to 3½ per cent. on the security of bonds from the provinces. But this promise was virtually repudiated the following year, without any reason being given except that it was considered that a mistake had been made.

In 1851 an Act of the Parliament of Canada made provision for the construction of a line through Canada East and Canada West. In the same year the Kingston and Montreal Railway Company and the Kingston and Toronto Railway Company were incorporated, both of them in control of Mr. (afterwards Sir) A. T. Galt and those associated with him. At the same time an influential group of English railway contractors, under the direction of Messrs. Jackson, Brassey, Peto and Betts, who had built many lines in Europe, appeared before the Canadian Parliament and

[2]T. C. Keefer: *Travel and Transportation.* In John Lovell (Ed.): *80 Years' Progress in British North America.* 1863. p. 192.

persuaded a majority of the members that it would be safer to entrust the project to them than to the inexperienced Canadian promoters. The former charters, therefore, practically came to an end, and in 1852 a new charter was granted to the Grand Trunk Railway Company of Canada, with an original capitalisation of £3,000,000, but which eventually reached about £12,000,000. An amicable arrangement was made with Galt and his associates, who became members of the Company.

Construction was pushed forward as rapidly as possible. The purchase of the right of way was followed by work on the roadbed, sections of the line being placed in charge of local contractors who worked more or less independently. A man still living, Monroe Lawson of Brighton, describes the procedure:

"I remember watching men surveying for the Grand Trunk Railway. My eldest brother, Clinton, was engaged in clearing the way for the roadbed. The land was purchased from the farmers, and they were given the timber if they would clear it away. Local men were hired to help the gangs of labourers—mostly Irish—in the construction of the road. They employed horses and scrapers for most of the work, a very crude method compared to that used by the next railroad to cross our farm—the Canadian Northern, built just before the Great War and soon after abandoned. The first train that passed over the Grand Trunk in our section was made up of a few small gravel cars, and my sister and I clambered up on the woodshed so we would not miss seeing such a notable event."[3]

In 1855-6 the great trunk line of communication through the Canadas was being pushed to completion. The section from Montreal to Brockville was opened for traffic on November 19, 1855; that from Quebec forty miles eastward to St. Thomas was completed on December 3, 1855; the road between Toronto and Oshawa was open on August 11, 1856; and the 178 miles remaining of the Toronto-Montreal section—that part between Brockville and Oshawa—was ready for traffic on October 27, 1856. The completion of the last section was delayed because of two or three difficult parts which took longer than anticipated. One

[3]Reminiscences of Monroe Lawson, Brighton, in E. C. Guillet: *Cobourg*, in the *Cobourg Sentinel-Star*, June 25, 1931.

of these was the large viaduct at Port Hope, named the Albert Bridge in honour of Prince Albert, consort of Queen Victoria. The first locomotive crossed this bridge on October 13th. Someone with the characteristics of Samuel Pepys noted that the viaduct "was built on 56 piers, had a total length of 1,856 feet and was finished in 1856".[4]

The entrance into Toronto was arranged by an agreement concluded with that city in January, 1856, by which the city agreed to provide all bridges, crossings, etc., within its limits, and to allow the tracks to be constructed on a width of forty feet along what was then the harbour front,— the Old Windmill Line, drawn from a point near the site of old Fort Rouillé to Gooderham's Windmill at the foot of Parliament Street; a considerable part of this region is half a mile from the present Harbour Head Line.

As the railroad was completed in the various districts inaugural excursions and dinner parties to celebrate the notable achievement were interesting events. On Monday, August 25, 1856, the section from Toronto to Oshawa was officially opened when an excursion train of ten carriages, as they were then called, left Toronto and proceeded slowly eastward. The Toronto *Leader*, in describing the trip, said in part: "The greatest interest was manifested in the event by the inhabitants of the different places along the line. Everywhere the train was welcomed by the enthusiastic acclamations of the populace".[5] Similarly, on Monday, September 8th, the Cobourg-Port Hope section was opened by an excursion. The amount of dust encountered at some points led a member of the Company to make the remark that "the guests were unable to see the defects of the road, as so much dust was thrown into their eyes". However, the party finished the day in style by a grand banquet at the Globe Hotel, Cobourg, where all the speakers were complimentary to the directors and engineers of the line, who had succeeded in the face of great obstacles.[6]

On October 18, 1856, the General-Manager of the Grand Trunk issued an announcement of the commencement of service between Montreal and Toronto, and it was widely

[4]W. A. Craick: *Port Hope Historical Sketches.* 1901. p. 50 fn.
[5]Toronto *Leader* quoted in the *Cobourg Star*, September 3, 1856.
[6]*Cobourg Star*, September 10, 1856.

advertised in the press.[7] It contains so much of interest that it is worthy of reproduction in full:

GRAND TRUNK RAILWAY

The public are respectfully informed
that the railway will be opened
throughout to Toronto
On MONDAY, OCTOBER 27.
Trains will run as follows:

THROUGH TRAINS
Stopping at Principal Stations
Will leave Montreal every morning
(Sundays excepted) at 7.30 a.m.,
arriving at Toronto at 9.30 p.m.
Will leave Toronto at 7 a.m., arriving
at Montreal at 9 p.m.

LOCAL TRAINS
Stopping at Stations
Will leave Brockville daily for
Montreal at 8.30 a.m., returning
from Montreal at 3.30 p.m.
Will leave Belleville daily for Brock-
ville at 7 a.m., returning from
Brockville at 3.15 p.m.
Will leave Cobourg daily for Toronto
at 6.30 a.m., returning from
Toronto at 4.45 p.m.

The trains will be run on Montreal
time which is—
8½ mins. faster than Brockville time.
12 mins. faster than Kingston time.
14½ mins. faster than Belleville time.
23 mins. faster than Toronto time.

Freight trains will not run between
Brockville and Toronto during the
first week.

---

[7]The advertisement appeared in all the chief newspapers during the latter part of October, 1856.

Fergus Kyle

OLD AND NEW IN TRANSPORTATION: THE FIRST THROUGH
TRAIN OVER THE GRAND TRUNK RAILWAY AT NAPANEE
STATION, OCTOBER 27, 1856

H. Southam

THE CHAMPLAIN AND ST. LAWRENCE RAILROAD, 1836
A line drawing of a train on the first railway in Canada

OPENING OF THE WELLINGTON, GREY AND BRUCE RAILWAY,
1870
Typical of the enthusiasm which greeted early railway construction

From the *Illustrated London News*, October 6, 1860   G. H. Andrews
THE PRINCE OF WALES LAYING THE LAST STONE OF THE
VICTORIA BRIDGE, 1860

Fares between Toronto and Montreal:
1st class, $10.00; 2nd class, $8.00.
S. P. BIDDER, General Manager.
Montreal, October 18, 1856.

In Montreal extensive plans were made for a celebration on the occasion of the opening of the Toronto-Montreal section. The sum of £10,000 was being raised by public subscription to meet the expenses of the celebration, and the *Gazette* stated that one-fourth of this amount "was subscribed last Friday (October 10th) as a result of the meeting of the principal merchants of the city at the Exchange".[8] On Monday, October 27th, the long-anticipated first through train travelled over the line from Toronto to Montreal, and at almost every station a crowd was assembled to give three cheers for the President and Directors, and to hear complimentary addresses presented and replies given by Chief Engineer A. M. Ross and other important officials. On November 12th and 13th the Montreal celebration took place, with numerous processions, banquets, military reviews and balls. The grand dinner was held in the Company's workshops at Point St. Charles. A newspaper account of the event emphasises the extensive nature of the preparations:

"We need hardly state that the building was fitted up with great taste. There were seventy-four dining tables (exclusive of side tables), covered with 1500 yards or nearly a mile of table cloth! On these tables were 44,000 knives and forks and an equal number of spoons, tumblers and wine glasses. The line of space occupied by the guests was 8,000 feet or about a mile and three-quarters. The chair was occupied by H. Starnes, Esq., Mayor of Montreal, and on his right was His Excellency the Governor-General. . . . . In the evening there was a torchlight procession and other illuminations".

The great event of the second day of the celebration was the grand ball at which "the crush was very great, and hoops suffered considerably. The number present was estimated at between seven and eight thousand. . . . Dancing did not commence in earnest until one o'clock in the morn-

[8] Montreal *Gazette* quoted in the *Cobourg Star*, October 15, 1856.

ing, the room being too crowded to permit it".[9] It is improbable that any event in the history of the Canadas had
occasioned such universal enthusiasm as the completion of
the eastern section of the Grand Trunk Railway.

There is at least one man still living who was a passenger on the first train which passed from Toronto to Montreal. Norman Robertson of Walkerton remembers the chief
characteristics of early railway travel:

"I was a passenger on that history-making train. The
passenger cars of that train were not as comfortable as
those of to-day. Also the 'Miller platform', which now
enables one to pass from one car to another easily, had not
been invented, so, when passing from one car to the next, one
had to step over an opening of some two feet. The rails
on which the wheels ran were of the V pattern and were
not bound together, as now, by fish-plates, the result being
that a jolt was felt as each wheel struck the end of the
next rail.

"On that train the system of checking had not been inaugurated, so that on reaching Toronto there was a general
rush to claim one's trunk. There had been some trouble with
the construction gang in the vicinity of Port Hope, so,
dreading the possibility of meeting an obstruction, the train
ran very slowly after leaving that town. For several years
there were no Sunday trains on this part of the line. The
train coming west from Montreal on Saturday night stopped
at Brockville, and the train from Toronto stopped over at
Belleville". [10]

Ewart Farquhar of Toronto remembers the celebration
by the citizens of the city at that time, and recalls some
further interesting details of early railroading in Toronto
and the province generally:

"The railway track from the east then reached only the
early Fairgreen, between Front Street and the Bay, and
bounded by Berkeley Street on the east. The station, a
substantial structure of stone, was east of Cherry Street,
on the line of the present tracks. The road to Guelph had
also been built and had its station, yard and workshops at
the foot of Bathurst Street. The locomotives required for

[9]*Cobourg Star*, November 19, 1856.
[10]Reminiscences of Norman Robertson, quoted in Fred Williams:
    Do You Know? (Toronto *Mail and Empire*, October 30, 1931.)

this section, coming from the east, were transported from the Berkeley Street terminus to the Bathurst Street end on movable rails over Front Street by means of pinch-bars, a tedious process.

"The first car-building shops were at Niagara-on-the-Lake, the product being sent to the rail-heads by water. Looking back, the fourteen hours required to make the trip to Montreal seems slow, but pioneer railroading was somewhat different from that of the present day. The rails of that day were of iron (not steel), and of inverted V pattern, hollow, less than four inches high, and eighteen feet in length, without fish-plates, and consequently with a space between their ends when in position.

"Locomotives were small and of the wood-burning type, which fuel was often green! The cars were small, of wood construction, and, from the present standpoint, uninviting for a long journey; coupled together by means of link and pins, they were consequently jolty when in motion. Sleeping-cars were unknown, as no all-night travelling was done. In winter the train frequently became snowbound, when the passengers, upon the limited supply of wood fuel becoming exhausted, would take refuge in nearby farmhouses. Under these circumstances the train became a derelict, and had to be rescued by assistance from the divisional points".[11]

When the inaugural train ran from Toronto to Montreal 855 miles of railway had been completed. This included the Toronto-Guelph section which had been purchased and was opened on July 1, 1856, and the Guelph to Berlin (Kitchener) to Stratford division, which was inaugurated by a grand celebration and public holiday on October 8th. The progress between Stratford and Sarnia was much slower; but the twenty-two mile section from St. Mary's to London was ready in 1858, and finally the railway was open to Sarnia in the following year. The most noted contracting engineer on this part of the line was Mr. C. S. (afterwards Sir Casimir) Gzowski.

During the same period the section from Montreal to Portland, Maine, was finished, as were also several extensive links in Canada East, connecting Richmond with Point

[11]Reminiscences of Ewart Farquhar, quoted in Williams, *ibid.*

Levis, and Trois Pistoles with Rivière du Loup. At the same time work was proceeding upon a fifty-mile branch in Canada West between Belleville and Peterborough. In December, 1859, the famous Victoria Bridge, constructed across the St. Lawrence at Montreal by Alexander M. Ross and Robert Stephenson, (son of George Stephenson, the inventor of the railway locomotive), was finished, and the Grand Trunk was then complete. The early plans of the bridge were described by Ross as calling for "a wrought iron box twenty feet deep, sixteen feet wide and about 7,000 feet in length; supported at intervals of about 260 feet by towers òf stone, and open at both ends to admit of trains passing through it, and made of sufficient strength to carry six times the heaviest load hitherto known to travel on railways in this or any other country".[12] The cost of the Victoria Bridge was about $5,000,000, and the total length from one river bank to the other was 9,144 feet. With reference to the speed of travel on the completed line a contemporary publication states that "the journey from Montreal to Chicago can be easily accomplished in about thirty-six hours".[13] There must have been statisticians in those days, too, for we learn that at the inception of the railway there was "on an average a station to every six miles, two men to every three miles, and a locomotive to every four miles".[14]

The Grand Trunk Railway was never a financial success. As usual in early railway-building the cost of construction was much greater than had been anticipated, and the traffic on the line much less than had been confidently expected by the directors. The prospectus of the Company showed a probable dividend of 11½ *per cent.*, and the stock quickly rose to a premium; but it was soon at a discount when it was seen that such exaggerated optimism had no foundation. A contemporary writer states that no "subsequent effort of the Company, with the aid of all the great names now fairly harnessed in, could drag the unwieldy vehicle out of the slough into which, apparently by its own dead weight, it so rapidly sank".[15]

[12]Quoted in Lawrence Oliphant: *Minnesota and the Far West*. 1855. p.33.
[13]John Lovell (Ed.) : *Canada Directory, 1857-8.* 1857. p. 1147.
[14]*Ibid.*   [15]Keefer,*op. cit.,* p. 202.

As early as 1855 the Grand Trunk was too poor to continue construction activities, and asked for a grant from parliament. £900,000 was advanced, upon which interest was later paid out of capital; but soon after the interest was not paid at all, and the government loan became practically a gift. On later occasions, also, the government had to come to the aid of the Company, until eventually £3,111,500 had been contributed towards the railroad.

There was evident in the early period of railway construction in England a general low tone of business morality, and this condition obtained to a considerable extent in the transactions of the Grand Trunk. Many members of parliament used their influence to advocate railways to develop national resources, while at the same time they were in control of, or large shareholders in the proposed roads. Public money was advanced owing largely to their influence, and the profits were to be made by themselves and those associated with them. Several men who abused their positions of public trust made large fortunes in railway speculations, and received titles from the government for railway developments which were advocated chiefly because of the financial benefits which would accrue to themselves. The failure of the Bank of Upper Canada was due mainly to the misuse of the public funds to develop the railway schemes of members of the government.

The Grand Trunk Railway is an example of railroad speculation on a grand and glorious scale, which ended in "a failure so magnificent, complete and disastrous"[16] as to lead to violent recriminations against its projectors and managers, the Canadian Parliament, and each and every person in any way concerned with the enterprise. The Company was conceived and organised in England, and for many years was controlled from London, a condition which effectually eliminates Canadians from the major share of the blame for the failure; at the same time such remote control proved both inefficient and costly. When it was seen that the 11½ *per cent.* dividend was a mere figment of the imagination the directors sought to attribute the lack of it to the absence of western connections, the non-completion of the Victoria Bridge, and the want of sufficient

[16]*Ibid.*, p. 204.

rolling stock; but as each of these conditions was remedied there was no corresponding improvement in the condition of the Grand Trunk.

In its very organisation the Company was defective, for the shareholders did not elect and control the directors, as is always the case in well-regulated corporations. Contracts were commonly awarded without competition, and the contractors' interests were usually opposed to those of the Company in the matter of building a permanently satisfactory roadbed. In places the road was poorly constructed with bad rails, which resulted in the destruction of rolling stock. Stations were often placed where the land was cheapest and speculative possibilities best, or where political support could be purchased, rather than near the business centre of towns. There was general extravagance in salaries and other expenditures, one official receiving $40,000 *per annum*, a princely salary for the times: in short there was mismanagement of the whole enterprise.

After the initial appearance of failure, western connections were suggested as the *sine qua non* of success; so a company was promoted to remedy the lack by constructing a line in Michigan at high cost; this was then leased by the Grand Trunk, even after it was shown that it could not expect to pay running expenses. Another cause of failure was an over-estimate of the probable traffic, a mistake due to the sanguine expectation that transport *via* the lakes would come to an end; but as a matter of fact water transportation long continued to provide keen competition, for it was much cheaper even if slower. For many years empty freight cars characterised westward traffic on the Grand Trunk, and it seemed impossible to avoid this unfortunate condition.

In the original line a gauge of 5' 6" was used, a mistake which entailed further expense in 1872-74 when it was changed to 4' 8½", the standard in use in the United States. Other expenditures were approved to provide for the extension of the system, almost all of the smaller railroads of Ontario eventually becoming part of the Grand Trunk either by purchase, lease, or amalgamation, and often upon extravagant terms. From time to time events of great import occurred, though they had but little effect upon

Reproduced by Courtesy of C. Shedden Laidlaw, Esq.

A DOUBLE-HEADER WOOD-BURNING LOCOMOTIVE, TORONTO
AND NIPISSING RAILWAY

Railroaders will identify the old-timers in this photograph

From the *Illustrated Times*, November 17, 1860

THE GRAND TRUNK RAILWAY AT BELLE ŒIL MOUNTAIN

THE RAILWAY CARRIAGE CONSTRUCTED BY ORDER OF THE DIRECTORS OF THE GRAND TRUNK RAILWAY OF CANADA FOR THE PRINCE OF WALES

From the *Illustrated Times,* November 17, 1860
PRINCE OF WALES' CAR DURING HIS VISIT TO CANADA, 1860

From the *Illustrated London News,* September 29, 1860   G. H. Andrews
VIEW OF OTTAWA IN 1860 FROM BARRACKS HILL, THE SITE
OF THE NEW PARLIAMENT BUILDINGS
The first railway to Ottawa was the Bytown and Prescott, 1854

the financial success of the line. On April 8, 1880, a section from Port Huron to Chicago was opened, the Michigan Central Railroad having had charge of the Grand Trunk traffic in this region previously. In August, 1882, the Great Western Railway, (originally the London and Gore), was also incorporated into the larger line. In 1897-98, a double-track truss bridge, with two outer platforms for electric railway and highway traffic, replaced the old Victoria Bridge across the St. Lawrence. In 1896 the control of the Grand Trunk virtually passed from England to Canada when Charles M. Hays was appointed General-Manager, and later President of the Company; this change in control might have been of greater value had it occurred before a half century of errors had involved the road in a huge debt.

Economic conditions incident to the Great War made the continuance of the Grand Trunk and its subsidiary, the transcontinental Grand Trunk Pacific, impossible under private ownership. Negotiations for purchase of the lines by the Dominion Government resulted in arbitration, and the Grand Trunk Pacific and Grand Trunk were taken over in 1919 and 1921, respectively, the bonds being assumed by the government, and the stock paid for at a price fixed by the arbitrators. These lines, with the Canadian Northern Railway, (taken over in 1918), the Intercolonial, and some smaller roads, were amalgamated into the Canadian National Railway System, which was placed under the direction of an independent and non-political board.

In 1922 Sir Henry Thornton, a noted English[17] railway expert, was appointed President of the National Railways, and he succeeded under adverse conditions in improving temporarily the financial position of this huge system, which totals about 22,500 miles. The Canadian National inherited a great deal of obsolete equipment from the Grand Trunk, and it had to be scrapped; the huge debt which was taken over has also increased the difficulty of attempting to show an operating profit. It would appear that better results might have been obtained if the Grand Trunk obligations had been transferred to the national debt, and the

[17]Sir Henry Thornton was born in the United States, and became a British subject in 1919. During the Great War he held the rank of Major-General and rendered valuable service in organising transport facilities.

Canadian National allowed to commence operations with a clean sheet.

Over-optimism has led to the construction of at least one-third too much railway mileage for the population of Canada; but by eliminating services which do not pay, avoiding the duplication of lines, and in other ways practising the strictest economy, the Canadian railways should be able to weather the storm which the present severe depression has created. Recent revelations before a committee of the House of Commons suggest, however, that much waste and extravagance will have to be eliminated if the system is ever to be operated on a paying basis.

Perhaps the future will see the amalgamation of the Canadian National and Canadian Pacific Railways; but in any case it will be increasingly necessary for the companies to compete with motor-coach and truck lines by entering into that field of transportation for short hauls, using the rails chiefly for a speedy through connection between centres of population, a service in which they are unlikely to be seriously affected by motor competition.

CHAPTER XII

FROM INDIAN COURIER TO AIR MAIL—THE DEVELOPMENT OF THE POSTAL SERVICE

"Made trip from Penetang' to Sault and back (300 miles) with sleigh and two dogs in fifteen days—snow three feet deep. Once made trip in fourteen days. Dig hole in snow with snow-shoes, spread spruce boughs, eat piece cold pork, smoke pipe and go to sleep. Once five days without any food but moss off rocks."

MICHAEL LABATTE, mail courier.[1]

ACCUSTOMED as we are to the telegraph, telephone and radio, it is difficult to appreciate the inconvenience and hardship resulting from the lack of quick means of communication in pioneer days. The postal service was not only very slow, but infrequent and irregular; while at the same time postal rates were prohibitive as far as the great majority of the inhabitants were concerned, 6d. being the charge to carry a single-page letter a few miles, 3s. from Montreal to Bytown (Ottawa), and nearly 6s. from York to England.

As early as 1721 official messengers and other travellers made a practice of carrying letters for private persons between Montreal and Quebec. In 1755 a post office was established at Halifax, which had then direct postal communication with Great Britain. When Canada came under British rule in 1763 Benjamin Franklin, Deputy Postmaster-General for the American Colonies, visited Canada and opened post offices at Quebec, Montreal and Three Rivers; he established courier communication between Montreal and New York, this service being considered as merely an extension into newly-acquired territory. Not until 1791 had the Montreal-Quebec post-road been extended eastward to New Brunswick and westward as far as Kingston.

As a result of the American Revolution the first exclusively Canadian service was established in 1788. This consisted of a monthly courier route from Halifax to Quebec, involving a seven weeks' trip and expenses of about

[1]Reminiscences of Michael Labatte, in A. C. Osborne: *The Migration of Voyageurs from Drummond Island to Penetanguishene.* (Ontario Historical Society, *Papers and Records*, Vol. III, p. 139.)

£200, of which only one-third was met by postal charges. A few years later *maîtres de poste* were appointed to carry the mails in Lower Canada; these men received 6d. a league for their work, and travelled in two-wheeled *calèches* drawn by a single horse.

Previous to the creation of Upper Canada as a separate province there were occasional mails to Kingston, Niagara and Detroit, post offices having been established at these settlements in the late seventeen-eighties to accommodate the Loyalists and the garrisons. The mail was carried by bateau on the St. Lawrence, and in the "King's ships" on Lake Ontario during the navigation season. There was also one "express" each winter, not only to carry military dispatches but also for the convenience of merchants. Mrs. Simcoe describes the winter express as travelling on snowshoes *viâ* Oswego and the south side of Lake Ontario to Niagara, and thence by way of the north shore of Lake Erie to Detroit.[2] One or two Indians often accompanied the messenger as guides. The expedition usually left Montréal in January, carrying whatever mail had accumulated there, and proceeded at about eighteen miles per day on their long journey of at least three months.

A considerable amount of Canadian mail travelled by way of the American postal service, as the following announcement[3] suggests:

"The United States' mail has commenced running between Canadarque (*i.e.,* Canandaigua) and this place: it will arrive on the 1st November, and every other Wednesday successively. Mr. McClallen has taken charge of the post office until a postmaster shall have been appointed. To accommodate the gentlemen of Upper Canada, the letters, etc., for the province will be left with Mr. Edwards, West Niagara. It is necessary that those which are to be forwarded should be left with him every other Thursday by twelve o'clock, succeeding the arrival of the mail.

I. I. ULRICH RIVARDI,
Major Artil. and Eng. Commanding.
Fort Niagara, September 11."

[2] *Diary of Mrs. John Graves Simcoe*, November 5, 1792.
[3] *Upper Canada Gazette*, October 21, 1797.

For many years the section of the postal route west of Niagara was not an official service, but was just as valuable as if it had been, and less costly. Publishers, merchants and stage proprietors sometimes supplemented the service by inaugurating postal systems of their own, usually aided financially by the subscriptions of those who were to benefit. In the Niagara *Canada Constellation* of August 23, 1799, appears a notice of the establishment of postal connections of this kind:

"The printers of the *Constellation* are desirous of establishing a post on the road from their office to Ancaster and the Grand River, as well as another improvement of the same kind at Fort Erie, and for this purpose they propose to hire men to perform the routes as soon as the subscription will allow the expense. . . . In order to establish the business the printers on their part will subscribe generously, and to put the design into execution but little remains for the people to do.

"The benefits that arise from an established certain conveyance of newspapers, letters, etc., are too numerous to particularise; suffice it that the timely receipt of the news (every day important), the ease and cheapness of conveying letters, and the transaction of concerns which would otherwise occasion a journey and expense to town are inducements of sufficient moment to draw forth a quarterly allowance of some few shillings in cash or articles of produce towards its support. Those living near 40-Mile Creek and Ancaster who wish to pay in wheat may pay it to Mr. R. Nellis and Mr. St. Johns."[4]

A private mail service to points in the United States was being operated during the winter of 1799-1800 by Stephen Bates in connection with his stage line. In his advertisement he states that "he will commence as soon as sleighing will admit, and run every two weeks. Passengers will be taken in on reasonable terms."[5] This service was from Niagara to Canandaigua by way of Buffalo.

On August 1, 1801, it was announced that the public coaches would discontinue carrying mail between Niagara, Queenston and Chippawa, since post offices had just been

[4] *Canada Constellation*, August 23, 1799.
[5] *Ibid.*, December 14, 1799.

established and postmasters' stages inaugurated to carry the mail.[6] The change was one of a number of developments in the postal service under the administration of George Heriot. In the same year the first official extension from Niagara to Amherstburg and Detroit was instituted, the mail being carried by schooner from the Detroit River to Fort Erie, by bateau to Chippawa, and by stage to Niagara; for this service the cost per letter was comparatively low, as no oath of allegiance was administered to the captain of the schooner which carried the mail. The military authorities frequently used trusty soldiers as special messengers, thus providing for themselves a speedier and more convenient service.

The government schooners on Lake Ontario were not the only boats to carry mail between Kingston, York and Niagara. In the summer of 1794 Governor Simcoe ordered the purchase of two Schenectady boats, one of which was to ply between Kingston and the Carrying Place, Bay of Quinté, while the other covered the western portion of the route. These boats interchanged official dispatches and occasional passengers, but did not, as a general rule, carry the public mail, which proceeded more irregularly and less speedily than the weekly Schenectady boat service. A public post office was not opened in York until 1799, after which the mail was distributed at a store, or from some other quarters rented for the purpose. Not until 1816 was a special building acquired to serve as an office, and it was merely a log structure.

At the commencement of the new century, probably in the winter of 1800-1, monthly couriers began to cover the route from Kingston to Niagara during the winter, a development made possible by the opening of the Danforth Road from Kingston to Ancaster. This highway was but a bridle-path through the wilderness, but was sufficient for an Indian or white courier to traverse on foot. The *Gazette* carried the following announcement in January, 1802:

"Post office, York, 9th January, 1802—The courier who proceeds on to Niagara this day will on his return from thence remain here one day, when the mail for Lower Canada, as well as for Kingston, will be closed."[7]

[6]*Niagara Herald*, August 1, 1801.
[7]*Upper Canada Gazette*, January 9, 1802.

Seven years later W. Allan, Deputy Postmaster at York, announced that the mail from Quebec would be dispatched for Upper Canada in the first week of each month during the winter, and might be expected to arrive in York "from sixteen to eighteen days later". Between Montreal and Kingston one Anderson carried the mail on his back, and westward from Kingston the route was usually covered by an Indian carrier who "is to go on to Niagara without making any stay (unless found necessary) at this place; so that all persons will have time to prepare their letters by the time he returns from Kingston again".[8] Westward from Niagara the mail was long very irregular. As late as 1807 the winter courier service to Amherstburg was only quarterly. All couriers carried axes to aid them in crossing frozen streams or otherwise clearing their path.

In 1810 a fortnightly service was arranged between Montreal and Kingston, and the following year the same service was continued to Niagara *viâ* York, and on to Amherstburg and Sandwich as often as commercial requirements demanded. During the season of navigation the courier was replaced by bateaux and schooners, which provided a service that gradually improved as the years passed.

In 1815-16 a weekly service was inaugurated between Montreal and Niagara, with a fortnightly extension from Dundas to Amherstburg. Stages carried the mail from Montreal to Kingston, it was then taken by sleigh or on horseback to Niagara, while west from Dundas letters were delivered by a pedestrian courier. The cost of carrying the mails was very great, as may be seen from the fact that the lowest tender the government received for a proposed service of two trips a week between Montreal and Kingston was £3,276 a year, a sum double the anticipated revenue.

In 1816 there were ten post offices in Lower Canada and nine in Upper Canada. The lack of convenient offices caused great hardship among early settlers, for in many cases a two-day trip over difficult trails was necessary to post mail. An interesting document in the Canadian Archives affords another example of hardship resulting from the fewness of offices. It is a petition to the Governor-

8*York Gazette*, January 4, 1809.

General from officers stationed at Stoney Creek during the War of 1812. As the nearest post office was at York, fifty miles away, these men found that they could not write home to England, "having neither agents or acquaintances at Montreal or Quebec who would pay the postage to Halifax, and no post office in this part of the country to receive letters; and if letters are sent to Montreal and the inland postage not paid, they remain there and are never forwarded, and consequently your memorialists' friends will not know whether they are dead or alive. Your Excellency must be sensible of the anxiety of parents when their children are away from them, and particularly in these critical times". They suggested that a bag be made up monthly at the Adjutant-General's office, to be carried free of expense to the point at which the regular postal service commenced.[9]

Important developments in postal connections occurred in 1816 and following years. The opening of the Kingston Road to York in the autumn of that year enabled a more extensive service than had been possible on the Danforth Road, some sections of which were impassable for wheeled vehicles at any season of the year. An office was established at Myers' Creek (Belleville) in 1816, though it was called the Bay of Quinté post office; in 1817 one called Toronto was opened at Smith's Creek (Port Hope); and a third in 1819 at Hamilton (Cobourg). There was but little to indicate where these offices were until the names were changed. In 1817 the postal services were similarly extended to the Eastern Townships of Lower Canada; while another change during the year was the transference of the summer mails from the schooners to the steamship *Frontenac*, which began to operate on the open part of Lake Ontario in June, 1817.

The settlers along the Ottawa River were given a regular postal service in July, 1819, the mails leaving Montreal every Tuesday morning and travelling to Hull and Richmond by way of St. Eustache, St. Andrews and Grenville; Hawkesbury and Perth also had post offices by 1820. The mails were carried to these outlying settlements over a

---

[9]Memorial of the Officers of the Right Division of the Army of Upper Canada to Sir George Prevost, December 3, 1813. Public Archives of Canada, Military Papers, C284, p. 114.

PETITION TO THE GOVERNOR-GENERAL OF OFFICERS OF THE
RIGHT DIVISION OF THE BRITISH ARMY, STATIONED AT
STONEY CREEK DURING THE WAR OF 1812,
ASKING FOR A POSTAL SERVICE

Postage was paid in cash previous to 1851

Air mail

The form of a telegram in 1852. The first telegraph service in
Canada was inaugurated by the Toronto, Hamilton and Niagara
Electro-Magnetic Telegraph Company on December 19, 1846.

SOME DEVELOPMENTS IN COMMUNICATION

newly-broken trail from Brockville, or by way of the Ottawa River. All of the improvements in postal communication during this period were largely due to Daniel Sutherland, Deputy Postmaster-General from 1816 to 1827.

In the early twenties the service in western Upper Canada was exceedingly poor. In 1824 there were only five offices in the Niagara peninsula,—those at Dundas, Grimsby, St. Catharines, Niagara and Queenston,—and in this region 20,000 people lived. In the London District, with a population of 16,588, there were in the same year, post offices at Vittoria, Port Talbot, Burford, Woodstock and Delaware,—one in each of the five counties. The inconvenience arising from these conditions was somewhat lessened in 1825 by the establishment of offices at Hamilton, London,[10] Brantford and St. Thomas. East of York there were at that time twenty-six post offices, but with the exception of the four in the Ottawa district and one other, all of them were along the shores of Lake Ontario or the St. Lawrence River, and those living in the back settlements had to come long distances for their mail. Lists of those for whom letters were waiting in the office were periodically posted there and at other prominent centres, and advertised in the weekly papers, so that no one need make a long trip for mail when there was none.

In 1827 there were forty-nine post offices in Lower Canada and sixty-five in Upper Canada. To these the mail was usually taken once or twice a week, by stage-coach along the front, and by courier to the outlying "back-township" settlements. Perth, for example, had only two mails a week as late as 1835, and the office served a large district. In other remote settlements the service slowly developed. In the late twenties Galt had a post office under that name, though the inhabitants called the village Shade's Mills for some years longer. To the north and west of Galt the new territory opened up for settlement by the Canada Company was gradually supplied with postal connections. In 1831 the mails were carried from Guelph to Goderich every two weeks over the recently-constructed Huron Road. This was typical of the development of the service in new settlements,

[10]The original London post office was located about three miles down the river from the Forks of the Thames, and was removed to London proper in 1826, when the settlement was founded.

infrequent deliveries to widely-scattered offices being the nucleus of a postal system which gradually improved. An interesting service was conducted between Penetanguishene and Sault Ste. Marie. In summer the mail was carried at infrequent intervals by bark canoe; while in winter a *voyageur* made the trip by dog-sled.[11]

During the first half of the nineteenth century postal rates were very high, and the service exceedingly slow and irregular. In the early part of this period letters posted in England in November seldom arrived at York before the following spring; while under the most favourable conditions of later years at least two to three months was necessary. In 1824 three days was the usual time taken for the transfer of mail by stage between York and Niagara. Settlers continually complained of the extreme slowness of the service, stating that when replies to letters were received four or five months later it was usually difficult to understand references to events so far in the past, or to questions long since forgotten.[12] In spite of the poor service, however, the postal rates remained high in Canada. The charge to carry a letter from England to York was $1.12, but by way of New York it was only forty-one cents; consequently many people sent their mail *viâ* the United States, a practice illegal at the time but nevertheless extensively developed.

In the thirties the trunk line of communication extended from Halifax through Quebec, Montreal, Toronto and London to Amherstburg. Branching off the main line were routes to Sorel, Sherbrooke, St. Johns, the Ottawa district, and outlying settlements in the central and western sections of Upper Canada. The Kingston Road and Dundas Street formed the main artery of communication, and the mail was carried by stage-coach whenever the state of the road permitted, and by horseback courier wherever it was impossible for a stage to get through. There were occasional attempts to rob the mail-carrier, the York mail being robbed in 1821.

As late as 1831 the horseback courier had to be called

[11]See the reminiscences of Michael Labatte, at the head of this chapter.
[12]See John Langton: *Early Days in Upper Canada, Letters of John Langton.* 1926. p. 87.

back into service on the Kingston Road, as may be seen from an account of an attempted mail robbery in the *Cobourg Star* of April 5th of that year. The *Star* states that "for some time past, in consequence of the unusually bad state of the roads, the mail between Kingston and York has been conveyed by a single unarmed courier on horseback". In an ironical tone it goes on to say that it could hardly have been expected, "in the present advanced state of our CIVILISATION", that robbers would not take advantage of the circumstances. The attempted robbery took place "on Wednesday night last, as the courier was passing the dense woods between the taverns of Messrs. Smith and Harris, on the road from Mr. Kellogg's to the River Trent". Fortunately, however, the mail-carrier had a stick which he used to good advantage on his assailant, and he continued on his route without much more damage than a hole in the mail-bag made by some sharp instrument in the hands of the robber. The following evening two men were lurking in the same place, but as another traveller accompanied the postman on this occasion no attempt was made. The *Star* concludes: "We since learn that in consequence of the above transaction the necessary precautions have been taken, and the man in future will be always properly armed and attended".[13] This description shows that in 1831 one mail-bag was sufficient to carry the mail for all the settlements between Kingston and York; and that the state of the Kingston Road, and of civilisation generally, left much to be desired, even from the point of view of the inhabitants of that day.

There is an account in the Canadian Archives[14] of a unique robbery of the mails between Kingston and Gananoque in 1839. A group of Americans were the assailants, and they used an island in United States' territory as a base of operations. While the American Government intimated that no great objection would be taken if Canadian police should search the island, yet nothing further resulted, as it was considered that relations between Canada and United States were sufficiently strained at the time owing to the recent "Patriot" raids over the border at Prescott and Windsor.

[13]*Cobourg Star*, April 5, 1831.
[14]Public Archives of Canada, Q416, p. 49.

For many years Weller's Royal Mail Line of stage-coaches was without a rival in land transportation; the brightly-coloured vehicles with the King's coat-of-arms emblazoned on the side were a characteristic sight on the Kingston Road until the coming of the railways forced them out of business. The main line of coaches was from Montreal to Hamilton, with connecting lines branching off into the settled districts on either side. It was not until 1842, however, that there was a daily line of mail-stages operating from the eastern boundary to the Detroit River; this was a result of Deputy Postmaster-General Stayner's requirements with regard to the mails.

The stage seldom arrived on schedule time, for the poor roads made that almost impossible; but when the mail comes and goes only five times a week a few hours' delay is hardly noticeable. The settlements along the front received and dispatched letters each day from Monday to Friday; but the mails to the back townships were much more irregular, being delivered by post-boys on horseback, or by stages, letters and newspapers sometimes taking a week or more to arrive at their destination. Such conditions caused a great deal of criticism of the system of Imperial control, which by its very remoteness proved a great source of dissatisfaction. To send a letter from Toronto to Montreal and receive a reply to it took from two to three weeks; while even as late as 1853 the time occupied in conveying a letter in winter from Quebec to any post office in Canada West beyond Toronto was from eight to eleven days.

Previous to 1851 no postage stamps were used in Canada, and letter postage was usually paid in advance to the postmaster, who made a note to that effect on the letter; in some instances, however, it was collected from the recipient of the mail. Newspaper postage had to be paid in advance by the publisher. Envelopes were not used in the early days, the letter usually being written upon only one side of the page and folded into the shape of an envelope; it was then closed with sealing-wax and addressed. As the postage increased proportionately with the number of pages, it was customary to use a large sheet, write very small upon it, and then continue crosswise once or more over what had been written. Letters executed in this manner were consequently very difficult to decipher, a fact noted by the editor of the *Letters of John Langton*, a recent important historical publication.[15]

The inhabitants of remote regions, those who lived in "the backwoods", as it was termed in pioneer days, often had to go many weeks without their mail. Whenever they found it possible to be absent a day or more from their farms they would make the trip, often on foot, to the nearest post office. Sometimes settlers would arrange to go to the office in alternate weeks to obtain the mail for all in the neighbourhood, and it would be distributed at a bee, a religious service, or some similar gathering. Stories are told of early rural postmasters keeping the mail in their top-hats for convenience in distribution. There was not infrequently considerable negligence in evidence among postmasters, particularly in the rural districts. Cases of letters being opened and read before delivery to the addressee were not uncommon.

Even in later years the mail delivery to outlying points was irregular and uncertain. There was, for example, a regular service from Toronto to Newmarket at the middle of the century, but beyond that village the mail was delivered in a peculiar manner:

"Mail for points farther north was given for delivery to the first reliable settler who happened to come along. This volunteer carrier, the beginning of the rural mail delivery, distributed his letters as he passed up Yonge Street and the Penetang' Road, and handed in the regular mail-bag for Penetang' when he reached that point. Sometimes there were letters still in this bag for settlers along the way, and these had to be sent back as chance offered."[16]

Owing to imperfect addresses it was not always easy to locate the recipients of mail. It was quite usual for letters to arrive from the Old Country addressed "To John Smith who is settled near York, Canada", or "For Patrick O'Shea, who left Cork, Ireland, for Canada". Many others failed to reach their destination because of indecipherable handwriting, or owing to the death of the addressee, or his departure for parts unknown.

[15]Langton, *op. cit.*, p. 5 fn.
[16]Reminiscences of Thomas Craig, in W. L. Smith: *Pioneers of Old Ontario*. 1923. p. 98.

Though the number of post offices vastly increased after the postal service came under Canadian control, yet it was not until recent years that the inhabitants of the rural districts could avoid the inconvenience of having to go several miles for their mail. In 1908 the present system of rural mail delivery was inaugurated. It has been greatly developed since, and has been an important factor in the amelioration of the conditions of Canadian rural life.

Old methods of sorting and transferring mail, and the changes as transportation developed, are well described by Judge Pringle:

"When the mails were carried by stage-coach the bags were in charge of the driver, and were usually put under his seat or on the top of the stage. When a post office was being approached the driver blew his horn lustily to warn the postmaster. On getting to the door he tumbled the mail-bag or -bags off the stage and dragged them into the office, where the postmaster opened and emptied them, selected the matter addressed to his office, and put the rest, with the mail he had to dispatch from his office, into the bags, and delivered them to the driver to be replaced on the stage.

"The changing of the mail sometimes took twenty minutes or more. If the post office was at a place where the horses were changed or the passengers took a meal the delay was not irksome, but otherwise it was by no means pleasant to be detained at the post office door in the severe cold of a winter's night, the heat of a midsummer day, or possibly in a storm of rain or snow. In those days, however, post offices were few and far between, and the detentions were not many.

"Before the opening of the Grand Trunk and other railways the mails were carried on the lake and river steamboats in summer, and for many years were sorted at the principal post offices on the route. A short time before the hour for the arrival of the boat the carrier of the mail would make his appearance at the wharf with a rough-looking horse and still rougher-looking wagon. The moment the boat stopped, the mail-bags were thrown ashore, pitched into the wagon, and driven off at the old horse's best speed to the post office, where the mail was sorted and replaced in the bags and then taken back to the boat.

THE POSTMASTER AT THE CHURCH DOOR

CUNARDERS IN NEW YORK HARBOUR

The first Cunard steamer, the *Britannia* (1840), and the steamship now being built on the Clyde, which will be the world's largest ship. Sir Samuel Cunard was born in Halifax.

"After some years the plan was adopted of putting the mails in charge of a post office clerk, whose duty it was to sort them on the boat, thus saving the delay caused by the trip to the post office and back. This system is in operation on all the railways."[17]

The ocean mails to Canada were carried in sailing-ships even after the steamship had been successfully used for ocean travel; as a result the time necessary for letters to cross the Atlantic was from six to ten weeks. William IV of England died on June 20, 1837, but it was August 2nd before a special courier rode through Upper Canada with the news. In the thirties the average time taken for letters between Liverpool and Quebec was fifty days; but on May 4, 1839, a contract was signed with the Cunard Steamship Line to conduct the service, and on July 1, 1840, the *Britannia* left Liverpool with mail, arriving at Halifax twelve and one-half days later.

Over the route from Halifax to Quebec, a distance of seven hundred miles, postal couriers made the trip in from six to ten days, the best speed being made in winter. Considerable European mail for Toronto and westward points came *viâ* New York, as the winter time between these cities was seven days, while it took two weeks for the mail to travel the 1,212 miles from Halifax to Toronto direct.

During the navigation season the lake steamships carried the mail much more quickly than was possible by the stage-coach. In the winter of 1825-26 the *Canada*, a fast steamship, was built at the mouth of the Rouge River, and engaged in the first regular mail service by water between York and Niagara. Along the St. Lawrence route the mails were carried by stage, bateau or steamship, according to the season of the year and the difficulties to be encountered along the route. In 1842 Donald Bethune of Cobourg received the first contract for a service by water from Toronto to Dickinson's Landing, on the St. Lawrence, twelve miles west of Cornwall. The contract stipulated that Bethune's steamships must cover the distance in thirty-six hours. From Dickinson's Landing the mail was taken by stage to Montreal. John Hamilton's line of steamships was formed in 1837, and was famous in the forties and early

[17]J. F. Pringle: *Lunenburgh, or the Old Eastern District.* 1890. pp. 168-9.

fifties as the Royal Mail Line; these boats made fast time in the carriage of mail and passengers to the main lake ports.

In October, 1856, the Grand Trunk Railway was open between Montreal and Toronto, at which point connections were made with the Great Western Railway to Sarnia. Stage-coach and steamship were almost immediately supplanted in the carriage of the mails by their much speedier rival. A letter which had taken ten and one-half days to travel from Quebec to Windsor in 1853, took only forty-nine hours in 1857, and as the years passed still better time was made. The greater speed entailed a considerable increase in the cost of carriage. In 1853 the government raised the yearly rate for the carriage of mails from $25 to $110 per mile, though it is interesting to know in that connection that practically the entire Board of Directors of the Grand Trunk Railway Company were represented in the Cabinet which made the change. The rate was later reduced, however, to $60 per mile.

The transfer in 1851 of the management of the postal service from Imperial to Canadian control followed upon the almost constant criticism which was so long nearly barren of result. The various provincial governments then assumed charge of the system, and conditions improved almost immediately. The first postage stamps appeared the same year; rates were greatly reduced and made uniform; post offices quadrupled in number within a short period; while revenues from the service increased because of the greater number of letters written. In 1852 the Canadian Post Office handled 3,700,000 letters at a cost of $376,391. In 1860, when the Grand Trunk Railway was in operation, 9,000,000 letters were carried at a cost of $550,000. By 1876 the number of letters carried had increased to 39,000,000; and in 1904, 259,190,000 letters and 27,000,000 postcards passed through the mails. In 1929 $34,885,796 was received from the sale of postage stamps, postcards and other services, including recently introduced devices for prepaying postage in cash; in the same year the conveyance of mail by land, water and air entailed a total expenditure of $14,723,400. There was a notable increase, also, in the number of post offices after the control of the system passed to Canada. In 1840 there were 405 post offices in the Canadas, while in 1861 the number had increased to 1,775. At Confederation the provincial systems were transferred to the Dominion Government, and the Post Office Act of 1867 established a service throughout Canada.

The earliest mail service to Western Canada was by way of the United States. In 1858 the Red River Settlement received letters twice a month, steamships conducting the service in summer from Collingwood to Fort William, and the journey thence to Fort Garry being made by canoe or any other available means. The first post office at Fort William was opened on June 1, 1860, and in winter the mail reached the village through the United States *viâ* Duluth. The service was exceedingly irregular, depending upon the weather and the vagaries of Indian or half-breed courier.

After the West became part of the Dominion of Canada a better mail service was established when the advance of settlement made a means of communication essential. In the eighteen-seventies Fort William received mail once a week, even in the winter, and this continued until the completion in 1885 of the Canadian Pacific Railway from ocean to ocean inaugurated a regular service throughout Canada.

From time to time developments have taken place in parcel post, the issuance of postal money orders, and in Post Office Savings Banks and other similar facilities for the convenience of the public. These auxiliary services have notably expanded since Confederation. On December 25, 1898, Imperial Penny Postage was inaugurated, a notable achievement due largely to the efforts of Postmaster-General the Hon. (later Sir) William Mulock; this proved to be of the greatest value not only in the reduction of the cost of correspondence but also in strengthening the bonds of Empire. Twenty years later, on June 24, 1918, the first air mail service in Canada commenced, a development which will become increasingly important for long-distance communication. In 1929 a total of 430,636 pounds of mail was carried by air without loss or damage. The development of the postal service from Indian courier to air mail in little more than a century is evidence of remarkable progress in our civilisation.

SECTION V
NOTABLE EVENTS

CHAPTER I

THE FIRST PARLIAMENT
OF UPPER CANADA AT NIAGARA, 1792-96

"Honourable gentlemen of the Legislative Council and gentlemen of the House of Assembly:

I have summoned you together under the authority of an Act of the Parliament of Great Britain passed last year, which has established the British Constitution, and all the forms which secure and maintain it, in this distant country. . . . .

The great and momentous trusts and duties which have been committed to the representatives of this province, in a degree infinitely beyond whatever, till this period, have distinguished any other colony, have originated from the British nation, upon a just consideration of the energy and hazard with which its inhabitants have so conspicuously supported and defended the British Constitution."[1]

COLONEL JOHN GRAVES SIMCOE, commander of a Loyalist corps in the American Revolutionary War, was appointed Lieutenant-Governor of the newly-created Province of Upper Canada in 1791, and sailed from Weymouth for Quebec on September 26th of that year, arriving in Canada on November 11th. He was ordered to obey the instructions of the Governor-General, Lord Dorchester, as to the government of his province, but no such instructions appear to have been issued, and the extent of Simcoe's powers was problematical; consequently he tried to make his position as independent as possible.

Simcoe was an ardent admirer of the law and custom of the British constitution. The parliamentary procedure of Great Britain was all excellence in his eyes, and he intended to introduce into Upper Canada "no mutilated constitution, but a perfect Image and Transcript of the British Government and Constitution".[2] The Constitutional Act, which had created the province, contained a provision for the establishment of a hereditary nobility in Canada, but it

[1] Speech of Lieutenant-Governor Simcoe at the opening of the first session of the first parliament of Upper Canada, September 17, 1792. For the full address see John Graves Simcoe: *Letter to Sir Joseph Banks, and Five Official Speeches.* 1890.

[2] See Simcoe's speech at the end of the first session, 1792; also Simcoe to the Duke of Portland, October 30, 1795, *Simcoe Papers*, Vol. IV, p. 115.

was never carried out; even Lord Dorchester, who greatly disliked democracy, advised the Imperial Government that it was unsuited to a country in process of settlement. Simcoe later stated, however, that he had appointed the Lieutenants of Counties chiefly "to give a Constitutional Respectability to the Members of the Legislative Council".[3]

The Lieutenant-Governor put his faith in the aristocratic form of government then characteristic of Britain, and used his full power against republicanism, which had developed in the United States many years previous to the Revolutionary War and had reached its culmination in the constitution adopted by the States of the Union at its close. The population of Upper Canada was predominantly of Loyalist origin at that time; but the Loyalists, while intensely loyal to the king, were accustomed to the more democratic methods of the New England colonies, and wished to introduce them in the home of their adoption. All of them had come from states where municipal institutions—elections and town-meetings—were highly developed, and it was to be expected that they would prefer the same system in Upper Canada. It was Simcoe's task, therefore, to restrain them from approaching the American type of government too closely.

Lieutenant-Governor Simcoe also held the current political theories which insisted upon a close relation between church and state, and an executive entirely independent of the legislature. It was his hope that Upper Canada would contribute to Imperial strength, and it was to gain this end that his policies of immigration and economic development were formed. He disliked the fur trade, however, largely because it savoured of American capitalism and hindered settlement.

Colonel Simcoe had remained at Quebec over the winter of 1791-2, proceeding to his province by bateau in the early summer of 1792. The official party reached Kingston on July 1st, and remained there about three weeks. Simcoe took the oaths of office at Kingston, his first Executive Council having been assembled there for the purpose of administering them. This council was made up of William Osgoode, James Bâby, Alexander Grant, Peter Russell and William

[3]*Simcoe Papers*, Vol. IV, p. 116.

E. Wyly Grier, P.R.C.A., O.S.A.

LIEUTENANT-GOVERNOR JOHN GRAVES SIMCOE

Hon. Alexander Grant   Secretary William Jarvis

Chief Justice Osgoode   Hon. Alexander Macdonell   Hon. Peter Russell

Hon. Robert Hamilton   Hon. D. W. Smith   Hon. James Bâby

MEMBERS OF SIMCOE'S ADMINISTRATION, 1792-6

Robertson, though the last-named did not attend. At Kingston the first steps were taken to organise the Legislative Council. There, too, was issued the Royal Proclamation which divided Upper Canada into counties and set forth the allotment of their representatives to the first parliament; this document established representative government in the province, and the date of its issuance, July 16, 1792, is the occasion which should be remembered as the birthday of our democratic institutions. Great efforts were made by the citizens of Kingston to persuade Simcoe to make their town his capital, but the Governor did not change his plans, and soon after proceeded by the schooner *Onondaga* to Niagara.

When Colonel and Mrs. Simcoe arrived at Niagara on July 26, 1792, the buildings known as Navy Hall were being repaired and renovated for their occupation; this was obviously necessary, for they were little better than sheds. The alterations had not, however, been completed, so three marquees were pitched to provide temporary accommodation. From the point of view of architecture Navy Hall was very plain and ordinary, almost as primitive in construction as the log cabin of the pioneer settler. The buildings were four in number and stood on the shore of Niagara River, just below the site upon which Fort George was built in 1796. They were originally erected for the use of the commanders of the sloops-of-war on Lake Ontario, especially for the housing of stores. Two of the buildings, Freemasons' Hall and Butler's Barracks, were used during the first session of parliament.

The first Legislative Council met in Freemasons' Hall, and was composed of nine members: Chief Justice William Osgoode, James (Jacques) Bâby, Robert Hamilton, Richard Cartwright Jr., John Munro, Alexander Grant, Peter Russell, William Robertson and Richard Duncan, the last two being absentees. Of the seven who attended the council meetings Chief Justice Osgoode was chosen Speaker.

The first Legislative Assembly was composed of sixteen members, some districts sending more than one. The members were as follows: Attorney-General John White (Leeds and Frontenac), John Macdonell (Glengarry), Ephriam Jones (Grenville), David William Smith (Suffolk and

Essex), Hugh Macdonell (Glengarry), William Macomb
(Kent), Jeremiah French (Stormont), Alexander Campbell
(Dundas), Benjamin Pawling (Lincoln), Nathaniel Pettit
(Durham, York and Lincoln), Hazelton Spencer (Lennox,
Hastings and Northumberland), Francis Bâby (Kent),
Isaac Swayze (Lincoln), Joshua Booth (Addington and
Ontario), Parshall Terry (Norfolk and Lincoln), and
Philip Dorland (Prince Edward County, and Township of
Adolphus) ; of these the last three were absentees. Dorland
was a Quaker and refused to be sworn, so his seat was de-
clared vacant and Peter Van Alstine elected to fill the
vacancy. The Speaker of the Assembly was John Mac-
donell.

The Act of the Imperial Government which regulated
the qualifications of voters and members stipulated that
members must own a dwelling-house and lot of the annual
value of £5 sterling. They had to be British subjects, and
not ministers of either the Protestant or the Roman church.
The qualifications of the electors who sent representatives
to the first (and many a later) parliament were very definite
in theory, for any male might vote who was the possessor
of a freehold in land of the value of at least forty shillings
sterling. The spirit of the rule appears to have been, like
the custom of heavy drinking at funeral wakes in Den-
mark, "more honour'd in the breach than the observance".
In Stormont County, for example, the votes polled at the
first and second elections were greater in number than the
population of the county. The explanation lies in the fact
that one's deed did not need to be registered in those primitive days, nor need he have held his land any specified
time prior to the election; so the candidates had agents
stationed below Petite Pointe Maligne to see which could
capture the most bateaumen, and each was given the deed
of a lot of the "backwoods" of the county, recorded his
vote the right way, was served with plenty to eat and drink,
and went on his way rejoicing. The candidate who won in
this instance had been astute enough to prepare beforehand a large supply of printed deeds, and his foresight enabled him to outdistance his opponent quite handily. It
may be said, however, that throughout Upper Canada as
a whole an effort was made to send the best men in each

district, for the inhabitants were not then divided into political parties which might have restricted their freedom of selection.

Of the sixteen members of the first Assembly thirteen were of Loyalist origin, and ten had seen service in the military or naval forces of the Crown. The Speaker, John Macdonell, had been a captain in Butler's Rangers; his brother Hugh, a lieutenant in the King's Royal Regiment of New York. Ephriam Jones was a Loyalist from Massachusetts; and William Macomb a Detroit Loyalist, that town remaining British until 1796. Jeremiah French had served in Sir John Johnson's Regiment during the Revolutionary War. Benjamin Pawling and Nathaniel Pettit were Loyalists from Pennsylvania, while Isaac Swayze and Joshua Booth were New York Loyalists. Hazleton Spencer had been an officer in the King's Royal Regiment, and Parshall Terry had held a commission in Butler's Rangers. Francis Bâby was a son of James Bâby of Detroit, a member of the Legislative and Executive Councils. Peter Van Alstine, who replaced Dorland, was the man who had been in charge of the immigration of Quakers to the Bay of Quinté district. Of the other three members, Alexander Campbell was a Scotchman, John White, the Attorney-General, an Englishman, and D. W. Smith, later Surveyor-General, had been an English soldier.

John White and David William Smith gave the Lieutenant-Governor the best support of any of the members, for they were not favourable to democracy; White, particularly, could see no good in the political attitude of the Loyalist majority. On the whole Simcoe was very disappointed with his Assembly. He would have preferred that they had been aristocrats, who might have seen eye to eye with himself; instead he found most of them to be men who "kept but one table, that is, who dined in common with their servants".[4]

The Governor changed the name of his capital to Newark, and thither the members of the first legislature of Upper Canada journeyed in September, 1792. Some of them travelled by government schooner from Kingston, or made their way by bateau along the shores of Lake Ontario or

[4]Simcoe to Dundas, November 4, 1792; *Simcoe Papers*, Vol. I, p. 249.

Lake Erie, for there were very few roads at that early period; others rode through the woods, following trails or blazed road allowances. Many Indians of the various Six Nations tribes came to the Niagara district to be present during the notable event; while a number of travellers, traders, and farmers from remote parts, all in holiday attire, were to be found at Newark during the first session, which was convened on September 17th.

The ceremonies at the opening of parliament were conducted with pomp and splendour, even though in such primitive surroundings. Governor Simcoe arrived on horseback dressed in full military uniform of scarlet and gold, while his lady was resplendent in white satin, brocaded with wreaths of flowers. A guard of honour from the Northumberland Fusiliers provided an escort. The members and their wives were arrayed in their best, though some of them could not remain for the whole session because it was harvest-time and the crops needed their attention. The proceedings of the session were opened with a prayer by the Chaplain, the Rev. Dr. Addison. A marquee which had formerly belonged to Captain Cook, the noted navigator, was used during the hot September weather for meetings of the Assembly; in fact it is said that on one occasion our first legislators adjourned to a green slope near by, and there, under the shade of some fine old oak trees, with a flat rock for a table, they made the laws and arranged the affairs of the province.

There were five sessions of the first parliament between September, 1792, and June, 1796, their duration being from three to six weeks. Many measures of great practical utility were passed. Owing to the fact that the party system had not yet been developed there was no formal opposition during Simcoe's administration, nor was he able to establish a party in support of his opinions; but in many cases laws were passed with but little opposition, and in some instances the members of the Assembly were unanimous. The interests of that body were frequently opposed to those of the Council. We find, for example, that a bill passed by the Assembly to tax wine was thrown out by the Council, whose members would be more directly affected by such a law; the Council, on the other hand, was desirous of levying a tax on land, but this plan met with disfavour in the Assembly, and there was no such taxation during the first years of the province.

Some further details with reference to land taxes will be of interest here. The opposition to such taxation was quite natural at a time when many Loyalists and government officials had acquired large land grants. Of the members of the Assembly, D. W. Smith appears to have been the only supporter of a land tax; and as he and his father held some 6,400 acres it may be assumed that he was animated by the principle of the thing. In September, 1792, Smith wrote to John Askin of Detroit with reference to the proceedings of parliament:

"We have done little as yet. Ways and means seem the great difficulty—one or two committees for that purpose have proved nearly abortive. I proposed that every landholder pay one farthing per acre *per annum* for all lands above 200 acres, which I conceived would not burden the settlers, but the court party and the popular party were both against me and I stood alone in the house; however, I am still of opinion that a land tax, whether it goes by that name or not, must eventually take place."[5]

Governor Simcoe was in favour of such a tax, but did not succeed in persuading the landholders to alter their views. Two years after he had left the country, the first tax on land in Upper Canada was levied when the Administrator, the Hon. Peter Russell, (who has frequently been referred to as the champion land-grabber of pioneer days), issued a proclamation[6] announcing that all grants of land except those previously pledged would be subject to a fee of sixpence per acre, as well as certain survey charges. An important limitation to the operation of the Act relieved Loyalists and their children from all survey charges, and required them to pay only half the land tax.

An observant traveller, a French duke who was hospitably entertained by Governor and Mrs. Simcoe at Navy Hall in 1795, was present at the opening of the session in the late summer of that year. He found that as it was

[5]D. W. Smith to John Askin, September 28, 1792. See the *Simcoe Papers*, Vol. I, pp. 217 and 237.
[6]The proclamation is dated October 31, 1798.

harvest-time only two members of the Legislative Council out of seven, and only five of the Assembly instead of sixteen, were in attendance. This was not a quorum; but, as a year all but two days had elapsed since the previous session, the Governor decided to open parliament in the hope that other members would shortly arrive by schooner from Detroit and Kingston.[7]   La Rochefoucauld-Liancourt gives a short account of the opening of this session:

"The whole retinue of the Governor consisted in a guard of fifty men of the garrison of the fort.   Dressed in silk, he entered the hall with his hat on his head, attended by his adjutant and two secretaries.   The two members of the Legislative Council gave, by their Speaker, notice of it to the Assembly.   Five members of the latter having appeared at the bar, the Governor delivered a speech modelled after that of the King, on the political affairs of Europe, on the treaty concluded with the United States, which he mentioned in expressions very favourable to the Union, and on the peculiar concerns of Canada."[8]

One of the most serious questions of the day was the marriage problem.   Most of the marriages that had been contracted up to the time of the first parliament had been illegal in that they had not been performed by a clergyman of the Church of England.   There were then very few such clergymen in all Canada, and it had long been customary to have the marriage service read from the Prayer Book by a justice of the peace, the commanding officer of a regiment, or the adjutant or surgeon of the forces; in fact many couples, finding it impossible to have the marriage service regularly performed, were forced to be content with a common law marriage.   A bill to legalize such unions was submitted at the commencement of the first session, but it met with some objections and was withdrawn.   In the second session the Marriage Act was passed, legalising all marriages theretofore contracted in the province.

In connection with the passing of this law concerning irregular marriages it is interesting to know that a few of the members of the first legislature were personally in-

---

[7]Duc de La Rochefoucauld-Liancourt: *Travels through the United States of North America.* 1799. Vol. I, p. 256.
[8]*Ibid.*

J. D. Kelly

OPENING OF THE FIRST PARLIAMENT OF UPPER CANADA BY
LIEUTENANT-GOVERNOR JOHN GRAVES SIMCOE, AT
NIAGARA, SEPTEMBER 17, 1792

Owen Staples, O.S.A.

THE REMAINS OF NAVY HALL, NIAGARA, 1911

From a sketch made in 1842

THE FIRST BROCK MONUMENT AFTER THE EXPLOSION
Benjamin Lett, a Rebellion refugee, is believed to have been
responsible for the outrage

From Heriot's *Travels through the Canadas.* 1807   George Heriot

FORT NIAGARA IN 1804

terested in the Act, as they themselves had contracted such marriages! The lack of registry offices in the early days had caused many important documents to be lost or detroyed, and this wise law confirmed titles to property which would otherwise have been jeopardised. The Act stated that future marriages were to be performed by an Anglican clergyman if there was one within eighteen miles; if not, magistrates or justices of the peace could officiate. The eighteen-mile provision was probably not always as scrupulously observed as upon one occasion in Oxford County when a couple came to Thomas Horner, J.P., to be married. The difficulty was that the parson was only fifteen and one-half miles away; so the wedding party travelled two and one-half miles farther into the woods, and "the bride and bridegroom hopped upon a log, and a minute afterwards jumped therefrom man and wife".[9]

Another Act of great practical value was that respecting millers and their tolls. The first grist-mills were operated by the government as a convenience for the settlers, and a charge was not usually made; but as the number of private mills was increasing, and cases of extortion were not uncommon, it was thought wise to make it illegal for millers to take more than one-twelfth of the grist as payment "for grinding and bolting".

In 1788, three years previous to the creation of the Province of Upper Canada, Lord Dorchester, the Governor-General, had issued a proclamation dividing the territory into four districts, to which he gave the German names Lunenburgh, Mecklenburgh, Nassau and Hesse. At the first parliament these names were changed, respectively, into the Eastern or Johnstown District, the Midland or Kingston, the Home or Niagara, and the Western or Detroit. It is rather humorous that, in fixing a place for the holding of court in each district, far-western Michilimackinac, the great depot of the western fur trade, was chosen as the location for the Detroit District!

The province had been divided into nineteen counties by a proclamation issued by Simcoe at Kingston in 1792, and provision was made at the first parliament for the establishment of courthouses and jails in each. English

[9]Thomas Shenston: *The Oxford Gazetteer*, 1852. p. 32.

institutions were firmly established by the introduction of English civil law and trial by jury; this caused no racial complications of importance, for the French were comparatively few in Upper Canada.

Included in the legislation of the first parliament were acts concerning such important matters as the opening, improvement and maintenance of roads, and the recovery of debts. One Act offered a reward for the killing of bears and wolves, which were then so plentiful as to be a source of considerable trouble and inconvenience to settlers. In 1795 a law was enacted preventing anyone who had borne allegiance to a foreign power from sitting in the Assembly until he had been a resident of Upper Canada for seven years.

Among laws[10] of great value to the people was one inaugurating the Winchester system of weights and measures, another licensing public houses, and others which regulated the militia, the courts, the appointment and payment of officials, and the registration of deeds, wills and mortgages. In the fifth session the currency was regulated, a matter of importance owing to the many types of money then in circulation. But above all the first parliament will be remembered because it dealt a death blow to slavery in Upper Canada by preventing its future expansion, and limiting the term of those who were already slaves. The law stated that no further slaves were to be brought into the province, and that slave-children were to be freed when they reached the age of twenty-five.

Contrary to popular belief, however, it was Governor Simcoe rather than his parliament who was chiefly responsible for the Act concerning slavery. He wished to abolish the evil entirely, but many of the members bitterly opposed the measure introduced by John White, the Attorney-General; some of the opponents of the bill were farmers, who stated that slaves were necessary to carry on their industry. A compromise measure was finally arranged, and it passed both houses, receiving the royal assent at the close

[10]Several of these acts may be found in W. P. M. Kennedy: *Documents of the Canadian Constitution, 1759-1915.* 1918. pp. 227-32. Detailed information concerning the legislation of the first parliament may be found in the standard biographies of John Graves Simcoe.

of the session of 1793; but his advocacy of the Act prevented White from obtaining a seat in any subsequent parliament, for many of the inhabitants considered it an unwarranted interference with their rights of property. Apart from the controversy, however, the fact remains that Governor Simcoe and the first parliament of Upper Canada took the initial steps in the British Empire towards the abolition of slavery.

CHAPTER II

SIR ISAAC BROCK AND QUEENSTON HEIGHTS, 1812

"Nothing in his life
Became him like the leaving of it; he died
As one that had been studied in his death
To throw away the dearest thing he ow'd
As 'twere a careless trifle."
WILLIAM SHAKESPEARE: *Macbeth*, Act i, Sc. 4.

ISAAC BROCK was born on October 6, 1769, in the island of Guernsey, and he spent his boyhood days there. His choice of the army as a career led him into many parts of the world. In 1785 he received a commission as ensign, served in the Channel Islands for several years, and in 1791 was sent to the Barbadoes, British West Indies. When but twenty-eight years of age, in 1797, he purchased a lieutenant-colonelcy, and was serving in Holland as the century closed. During the British attack on Copenhagen, in 1801, Brock was second in command of the land forces, and in the following year his regiment was ordered to Canada, being stationed at York in 1803. Two years later he became a full colonel, and in the following year was made Brigadier in command of the forces in both Upper and Lower Canada, in which he was alternately stationed during the next five years. In 1811 he was in full charge of civil as well as military affairs in Upper Canada, being appointed President and Administrator of the Government in succession to Lieutenant-Governor Gore.

Soon after he arrived in Canada he took part in two dangerous exploits: one of them occurred at night, when, accompanied by twelve men, he pursued six deserters across Lake Ontario in an open boat and captured them near Niagara; and the second was to put down a threatened mutiny at Fort George, a much more serious affair. Colonel Sheaffe was very unpopular because of his severe discipline, and a conspiracy to mutiny and to murder him was accidently discovered among his men. Sheaffe sent word immediately to Colonel Brock, who was then at York.

The vessel which brought him the news took Brock

back at top speed; and with remarkable coolness and intrepidity he soon had the leaders of the trouble handcuffed and in irons. The soldiers who had deserted or conspired to mutiny were tried in Quebec, and seven of them were shot on March 2, 1804. At York, when a letter came announcing the execution, Colonel Brock drew up all his men under arms and read them the letter. He then said in a faltering voice: "Since I have had the honour to wear the British uniform I have never felt grief like this. It pains me to the heart that any member of my regiment should have engaged in a conspiracy which has led to their being shot like so many dogs. . . ." It is said that his men were greatly moved at the touching scene of their Colonel almost in tears.[1] After this unfortunate affair Brock assumed command at Fort George, and there were no more complaints or desertions.

Isaac Brock was not only a soldier, for he was fond of social life, particularly during his stay in York; here he was accustomed to give a ball each year, and it was one of the noted events of the season. Here, too, lived Sophia Shaw to whom Brock became engaged. It is said that he "would travel the worst road in the country—fit only for an Indian mail-carrier—to mix in the society of York".[2]

His fondness for good literature is shown by the following extract from a letter which he wrote in 1811: "I hardly ever stir out, and unless I have company at home my evenings are passed *solus*. I read much, but good books are scarce, and I hate borrowing. I like to read a book quickly, and afterwards revert to such passages as have made the deepest impressions and which appear to me most important to remember, a practice I cannot conveniently pursue unless the book is mine."[3]

Niagara he found rather dull in comparison with York, but he whiled away some of his spare moments playing cribbage or whist, and shooting wild pigeons and partridges. He was an expert and enthusiastic horseman, and spent many an hour in the saddle, gaining an intimate knowledge of the Niagara district. Occasionally he was to be seen

---

[1]See Matilda Edgar: *General Brock*. 1904. p. 63.
[2]Quoted in W. R. Nursey: *The Story of Isaac Brock*. 1908. p. 83.
[3]See Edgar, *op. cit.*, pp. 135-6, for Brock's reading.

among the fishermen, and once at least helped haul in the
nets, "in which were 1,008 whitefish of an average weight
of two pounds, 6,000 being netted in one day".[4] In figure
Brock was tall and athletic. He was of the build that one
expects in a leader, and it was his distinguished appearance
that early marked him out for death at Queenston Heights.
"This is a man", was the remark of the famous Shawanese
Chief, Tecumseh, when he was introduced to Brock.[5]

For many months before the actual outbreak of the War
of 1812 hostilities appeared inevitable, and Brock was very
busy preparing for the defence of the country, a most
difficult task when one considers the slender means at his
disposal. The "handful of regulars and a few thousand
undisciplined militia" were so inferior in numbers to the
armies of the United States that even Brock found it hard
to keep a confident air. "But I talk loud and look big", he
says in a letter to a brother officer.[6] While the American
soldiers exceeded the total population of Canada at that
time, the various states of the Union were not united in the
prosecution of the war; and to this fact, combined with
the difficulties of invading a country without connected
lines of communication, and the conspicuous gallantry of
the militia in defence of it, we owe the remarkable successes
achieved. On June 18, 1812, after weeks of preparation,
the American Congress under President Madison declared
war against Great Britain.

Owing to the very slow means of communication at the
time the first news of the declaration of war reached
Canada in a letter carried by relays of horsemen to a firm
of merchants. The 41st Regiment at Fort George was entertaining American officers at dinner when news of the
declaration arrived, and though the information was announced the dinner proceeded cordially.

At Brock's request the government suspended the Habeas
Corpus Act immediately after the official declaration of war
was received. Suspected individuals in the Niagara district
who refused to take the oath of allegiance were imprisoned
or given forty-eight hours to leave Canada. On July 12,
1812, hostilities commenced when the American forces

[4]Nursey, *op. cit.*, p. 79.   [5]See *ibid.*, pp. 114-17.
[6]Quoted in Edgar, *op. cit.*, p. 215.

under General Hull crossed the Detroit River at Sandwich. Communication was so slow that it was some time before Brock, in York, even heard of the invasion and the bombastic proclamation of General Hull.

On August 6th Brock left York with forty regulars and 260 volunteers and proceeded by land to Long Point, Lake Erie, stopping on the way at the Mohawk Village on the Grand River and obtaining the promise of sixty Indians to follow him. From Long Point this diminutive army proceeded two hundred miles along the shore, using all sorts of boats, and finally after many dangers reached Amherstburg. Hull soon retired to Detroit, and shortly afterwards surrendered the town and his entire army to the British forces which had crossed the river under Brock's direction. Brock had about 730 regulars and militia and some 700 Indians under Tecumseh, but his force was supported by only five guns; to this small army was surrendered by the capitulation of Detroit about 2,500 men, thirty-seven guns, one ship, a large supply of arms and ammunition, and the entire territory of Michigan—almost equal in area to Upper Canada. Colonel Cass, the American Quartermaster-General, wrote to the Secretary of War at Washington: "Confident I am that had the conduct and courage of the General (Hull) been equal to the spirit and zeal of the troops, the event would have been brilliant and successful as it is now disastrous and dishonourable."[7]

This success caused the greatest enthusiasm in Canada and throughout the Empire. Brock became the idol of Upper Canada, and a medal was struck in honour of the victory. The British Government bestowed a knighthood upon him, but he never knew it, for he had died at Queenston Heights before the news reached Canada.

With such of his men as could be spared Brock left for the Niagara frontier, where an invasion was threatened. An armistice was arranged in opposition to his wishes, and this enabled the Americans to strengthen their position at various points along the boundary. When the armistice came to an end some 6,000 of the enemy's troops were concentrated at Niagara.

[7]Colonel Cass to the Secretary of War, quoted in Edgar, *op. cit.*, p. 257.

Early in the morning of October 13th about 1,600 of this force crossed the river at Queenston under a heavy fire from British guns. Captain Ball, whose field gun was planted on the shore over the flats near the town, poured an effective fire on the invaders, sinking a number of boats; but in the half darkness some of the bateaux effected a landing. The noise of the firing awoke Brock, who was at Fort George, and he and his aide-de-camp, Lieut.-Colonel Macdonell, rode hurriedly to Queenston. On the way Brock stopped, without dismounting, at Captain John Powell's house, and Powell's sister-in-law, Sophia Shaw, brought him a "stirrup cup" of coffee and waved him a tender good-bye.

In a letter describing the events of that day Lieutenant Robinson, in later years Chief Justice Sir John Beverley Robinson, wrote: "Several boats were so shattered and disabled that the men in them threw down their arms and came on shore, merely to deliver themselves up as prisoners of war. . . . We hurried to the mountain, impressed with the idea that the enemy's attempt was already frustrated, and the business of the day nearly completed".[8]

Such was not the case, however, for Captain Wool of the United States army had very skilfully led his men to the Heights by way of a fisherman's path on the south side of the mountain. The approach was so steep and narrow that it had not been thought necessary to guard it, and the Americans had reached the summit unobserved and were hidden among the rocks and trees. As a result of their fire on the British battery below, Brock saw that he would have to retire and leave the gun, which was accordingly done. He did not have time even to mount his horse, but led it down the hill to the village, where he reformed his troops, between 100 and 200 men, and prepared to drive the enemy from the Heights. He spoke quietly to the men whom he was about to lead up the slope:

"Men of the 49th, and my brave volunteers, I have heard of your work this morning, and the trying circumstances under which you have been fighting. Now, my lads, as you know, a large body of the enemy has stolen a march on us. They have taken our gun it is true, but they will find it spiked. It is our duty to retake it. Be prepared for

[8]Quoted in Edgar, op. cit., p. 302.

MAJOR-GENERAL SIR ISAAC BROCK, "THE HERO OF UPPER CANADA"

THE BATTLE OF QUEENSTON, OCTOBER 13, 1812

QUEENSTON FROM LEWISTON, 1840
The first Brock Monument may be seen on the Heights

slippery footing. Use every bit of shelter, but when we make the final rush give the enemy no time to think. Pour in a volley; fire low, and when it comes to in-fighting, use the bayonet resolutely and you have them beaten. I know I can depend upon you. . . . There is a foreign flag flying over a British gun. It must not stay there. . . . Don't cheer now, men, but save your breath and follow me."[9]

It was too great a task for so few, but twice he led them upwards, on the second attempt receiving a fatal bullet in the breast, his tall figure and prominent position at the head of his men making him an easy target.[10] His comrades bore him to a house below, where they covered his lifeless form. A few minutes later Lieut.-Colonel John Macdonell was killed while leading another unsuccessful charge. Later in the day General Sheaffe assumed command of the forces, and, with the cry "Revenge the General", the Canadians drove the enemy from the Heights after a sharp encounter. The Americans, under command of Colonel Winfield Scott, fought gallantly; but many were driven over the cliff into the river below, while 925 surrendered after being surrounded, and several hundred were killed or wounded, or withdrew across the river. A number of the enemy resisted for some time in a small log house which long stood part way down the slope; and others, rather than surrender, tried to swim the Niagara and were drowned. In addition to the great loss of Brock, the British had suffered casualties totalling 110, or about one-ninth of the force engaged.

The attitude of the Americans and their reaction to their defeat at Queenston is interesting. Concerning the last phase of the battle, the *Gazette* of Albany, New York, said:

"The battle was renewed by the enemy with great vigour and increased numbers, which compelled the American forces, whose strength and ammunition were nearly ex-

[9]See Nursey, *op. cit.*, p. 172.
[10]The best accounts of Brock's death are contained in two contemporary descriptions of the events of the day. These are (1) the Narrative of Volunteer G. S. Jarvis, 49th Regiment, which is printed in G. Auchinleck: *History of the War between Great Britain and the United States*, 1855, pp. 104-5; and (2) a letter of John Beverley Robinson, dated October 14, 1812, printed in Lady Edgar's *Ten Years of Upper Canada; the Ridout Letters*, 1890, pp. 150-6.

hausted by hard fighting for eleven hours, and with very little intermission, to give way."[11]

The defeat was received in the United States generally as a reflection upon the management of those in charge. A contemporary American periodical, *The War*, was outspoken in its condemnation of the lack of system which it considered the reason for the defeat:

"In recording the unfortunate event we have but one consolation to offer our readers, which is that our troops by their courage in storming the British batteries have conferred the highest reputation on the American arms. . . . It is indeed mortifying that owing to·mismanagement 700 of our regulars and two or three thousand militia should be captured from us by the enemy, without one single object of the war being attained. . . . If it is the determination of the Government to attempt the reduction of Canada, something like a system should be pursued in the operations of the army."[12]

The gallant leader and his aide-de-camp, Macdonell, were buried at the bastion of Fort George, Niagara, a 24-pound American cannon taken at Detroit being placed at Brock's head. Across the river at Fort Niagara the American General, Van Rensselaer, graciously observed the funeral service of his opponent by ordering minute-guns to be fired, and flying the American flag at half-mast over the fort.

In 1816 a copper coin was issued in memory of Brock and widely circulated. On one side is inscribed: "Sir Isaac Brock, the Hero of Upper Canada. Fell October 13, 1812"; and on the reverse: "Success to Commerce and Peace to the World". On March 14, 1815, the Upper Canadian Parliament voted £1,000 towards the erection of a suitable memorial to Sir Isaac Brock, but it was not until 1824 that a monument was raised by the government at Queenston Heights.

The foundation stone of the memorial was laid by Governor Sir Peregrine Maitland, several documents being placed in a hollowed portion of the block. William Lyon Mackenzie inserted a copy of the first issue of his *Colonial*

[11]Albany *Gazette*, quoted in *The War*, October 24, 1812.
[12]*The War*, October 24, 1812.

Advocate; but it was a period of strong political feeling, and "Many days afterwards," says Mackenzie in his *True Blue Almanack*, "when the column was forty-eight feet high, Sir Peregrine Maitland, who was terribly annoyed by the first *Advocate*, ordered his courtier, Thomas Clark, to go and dig it out again. Clark obeyed, and after three days' excavation they exhumed the record with the otter's skin in which it had been wrapped."[13] Under this monument, a Tuscan column 135 feet in height, the remains of Isaac Brock were placed on the 12th anniversary of his death.

Benjamin Lett, an Irish-Canadian who had participated in the Rebellion of 1837 and who had been banished to the United States, planned to revenge himself on the Canadian Government by blowing up Brock's monument. Secretly placing a large amount of powder under the base he accomplished his purpose on Good Friday, April 17, 1840, the column being badly shattered by the explosion. This senseless desecration of Brock's tomb aroused intense anger throughout Canada. Three months later a large meeting of citizens of Upper Canada was held on the Heights, seven steamers coming from Toronto and Hamilton, and others from Cobourg, Kingston and other ports. At this meeting, over which Lieutenant-Governor Sir George Arthur presided, it was determined to establish a fund for the purpose of erecting a new monument.

An interesting and pathetic episode occurred while this meeting was in progress on the Heights. A number of men could be seen grouped together across the river, and a few minutes later they raised a British flag. William Kirby, an eye-witness, writes concerning this incident: "It was known that they were a lot of Canadian refugees who had fled from Canada with Mackenzie and dared not come back. They took this method of showing their respect to Brock, and, it may be, their regret at having risen in rebellion against the Queen. The writer viewed them with an eye of pity and regret, that they should ever have got into such trouble as led to their exile from their own country."[14]

[13] [Mackenzie's] *New Almanack for the Canadian True Blues*. 1834. p. 11. Mackenzie says that he and James Lapraik laid the foundation stone of Brock's monument.
[14] William Kirby: *Annals of Niagara*. 1896. p. 243.

It was not until 1853 that the corner-stone of the present monument was laid. This memorial rises 216 feet above the cliff, or 750 feet above the river, and is a fluted column on a massive pedestal, with a Corinthian capital surmounted by a colossal statue of Brock. The entire cost of the monument was borne by the people of Canada, largely by voluntary subscriptions. Veterans of the War of 1812 were prominent in their enthusiasm for this memorial to their heroic leader, and it is noteworthy that over $1,000 was contributed by Indians, some of whom had fought under Brock.

The new monument was erected some distance from the site of the old, and the body of Brock was again removed and placed under the base. Sir Allan MacNab, a veteran of both the War of 1812 and the Rebellion of 1837, officially unveiled the monument on the 47th anniversary of the hero's death, October 13, 1859, in the presence of a large assembly of Canadian citizens, including many veterans of 1812. The soldiers were drawn up in military array in front of the monument, and Sir Allan delivered an address eulogising Sir Isaac Brock and the troops who fought under him, who did not admit defeat but revenged the death of their great leader by driving the enemy from Canadian soil:

"This monument represents a free-will offering, flowing from emotions which reminiscences of the last war awaken. It commemorates the feelings of the country, inspired by the death of Brock and the brave men who fell with him on these Heights. . . . It grandly illustrates the affection, steadfastly cherished, for the heroic champion who, in the dark hour of our adversity, laid down his life in our cause. It is a splendid and imposing testimony that half a century has not diminished the public esteem for that noble man, nor dimmed the recollection of his noble actions. . . . Friends! This fit emblem of a nation's gratitude is now inaugurated. We here dedicate it to the memory of Sir Isaac Brock and those who fell by his side upon this battlefield—and, through them, to the imperishable memory of all who fell in defence of Canada."[15]

[15]Address of Sir Allan MacNab at the inauguration of the monument, October 13, 1859. See the *Cobourg Star*, October 19, 1859.

In 1860 the Prince of Wales, later Edward VII, laid the corner-stone of a cenotaph which was erected about fifteen yards east of the spot which eye-witnesses designate as the place where Brock was killed. The cenotaph bears the following inscription:

"Near This Spot
Major-General
Sir Isaac Brock, K.C.B.
Provisional Lieutenant-Governor of Upper Canada
Fell on 13th October, 1812,
While Advancing to Repel the
Invading Enemy."

CHAPTER III

THE OCCUPATION OF YORK BY THE AMERICANS, 1813

"About five o'clock on the afternoon of Monday, the 26th, eager watchers on the highlands of Scarboro' catch a first fleeting view of the approaching fleet. . . . At once a vidette mounts horse and is off to town to bring the news and carry the alarm. The signal gun is fired, the bell of St. James' Church is rung as a warning to the townspeople, and every man of the militia drops immediately whatever work he is doing, seizes his gun, and hurries to report for service."

E. J. HATHAWAY.[1]

DURING the War of 1812 the road from Kingston to York was not open for the entire distance. It was consequently a difficult matter to transport supplies from the military and naval headquarters at Kingston to Upper Canada's capital, which had then a population of about seven hundred. Bateaux and schooners were used when it was possible, but in the spring of 1813 the American naval forces had full control of the lake, and cannon and supplies had to be laboriously hauled over the partially-opened roads, or along the beach. Many early settlers near the lake front joined Commissary Wilkins' Corps, which did excellent work under great difficulties. For the assistance of themselves and their oxen the settlers were well paid in army bills, which were redeemed in full at the close of the war.

As the American forces had suffered several defeats during the campaign of 1812 it was to be expected that they would make a determined effort in 1813 to efface the memory of past reverses by present successes. Extensive naval operations on the Lakes were planned, including a raid on Little York.[2] It is remarkable that the British should have

[1]E. J. Hathaway: *Jesse Ketchum and His Times.* 1929. p. 85.
[2]The chief sources concerning the two raids on York in 1813 are as follows: (1) The official reports of the British and American forces engaged in the campaign. (2) Sir R. H. Sheaffe's *Letters.* (Buffalo Historical Society, *Publications,* 1913.) (3) P. Finan: *Recollections of Canada in 1812-13.* 1828. (4) A. N. Bethune: *Memoirs of the Right Rev. John Strachan.* 1870. (5) Matilda Edgar: *Ten Years of Upper Canada; the Ridout Letters.* 1890. (6) American letters, and other matter, in *The War,* a contemporary American periodical. (7) A short account of the events in Robert Gourlay: *A Statistical Account of Upper Canada.* 1822. (8) Letters written by men of importance in York during the raids, and quoted in one or other of the above works.

made so little effort to place the capital in a state of defence: the fortifications were ill prepared for an attack, the guns being half-mounted; and only six hundred white men, including the militia and dockyard workers, were available to resist invasion. Even this small body of defenders would have been 180 fewer if a detachment of the 8th Regiment, on the march from Kingston to Fort George, had not luckily halted at York the day before the attack; while the guns which protected the fortifications were merely three old French 24-pounders, captured in 1760 and all but buried in the earth.

On the 25th of April, 1813, Commodore Isaac Chauncey, in command of a flotilla of American warships, set sail from Sackett's Harbour. The *President Madison,* the *Oneida,* the *General Pike,* and five single-gun schooners made up the fleet. The number of soldiers on board is variously estimated, but it would appear certain that from seventeen hundred to two thousand men were landed near York by bateaux two days later, under the command of Generals Dearborn and Pike. The landing was effected at daybreak on the present site of Sunnyside Beach, eastward from the mouth of the Humber. General Dearborn's dispatch to the Secretary of War at Washington describes the landing as "about three miles westward of the town, and one and a half of the enemy's works. The wind was high and in an unfavourable direction for the boats, which prevented the landing of the troops at a clear field, the site of the ancient French fort Tarento. It prevented also many of the armed vessels taking positions which would have most effectually covered our landing, but everything that could be done was effected".[3]

A small Canadian force under Major Givins appears to have been in the neighbourhood of the remains of old Fort Rouillé, and to have been more influential in preventing a landing there than the wind which Dearborn mentions as the reason for the change of landing-place. Only a few Indians who had been placed in groups in the woods as sharpshooters opposed the disembarkation of the riflemen under Major Forsyth, though a detachment of the Glengarry Light Infantry would have been present had not its

[3]Dearborn to the Secretary of War, York, April 28, 1813.

officers made a mistake in the route of march and led the men into the woods now known as High Park.

The invaders proceeded eastward through the forest towards the fortifications, situated at the eastern end of the present Exhibition grounds. At the same time the ships advanced and directed their fire at the British works and the batteries near the harbour. The enemy was met in the woods by General Sheaffe's small force of regulars and militia, and hard fighting ensued, the Americans being several times repulsed; but the weight of superior numbers prevailed, and the defenders fell back upon the fortifications.

An interesting sidelight on this phase of the battle is contained in a contemporary American periodical, *The War*, purporting to be "a faithful record of the transactions of the War between the United States and Great Britain".[4] A letter is printed in this paper from a field officer in the invading force, in which he belittles the opposition encountered in the woods by saying: "We were there annoyed on our flanks by a party of British and Indians with a six-pounder and two howitzers."[5] The opposition encountered at the landing and in the march eastward through the woods is more honestly described, however, by General Dearborn, who states that "the contest was sharp and severe for nearly half an hour, when the enemy were repulsed by a number far superior to theirs".[6]

The small British force lost almost half its strength in this engagement. An inhabitant of York, Mrs. Breakenridge, who, with other ladies, took refuge at Baron de Hoen's house, four miles up Yonge Street, recalled seeing "the poor 8th Grenadiers come into town on Saturday, and in church on Sunday, with the handsome Captain McNeil at their head; and the next day they were cut to pieces to a man".[7]

During the course of the retreat the British force was further disorganized by the accidental explosion of a portable magazine, which resulted in the death or serious injury

[4]The two bound volumes of this very rare periodical are in the Public Reference Library, Toronto.
[5]*The War*, May 25, 1813.
[6]Dearborn to the Secretary of War, April 28, 1813.
[7]Reminiscences of Mrs. Breakenridge, quoted in John Ross Robertson: *Landmarks of Toronto*. 1894-1914. Vol. I, p. 78. These reminiscences are more extensively quoted in Henry Scadding: *Toronto of Old*. 1873. pp. 433-5.

of a considerable number of men.[8] Sheaffe's regulars retreated along the Garrison Road into the town, then oc-
cupying a small area near the lake shore between the Don
and Church Street. Orders were given to destroy the naval
stores in York and a new ship on the stocks, and it appears
that this was still being done after the surrender of the
town; the enemy consequently made use of this breach of
the rules of war to delay the arrangement of terms of
capitulation.

The American force advanced cautiously towards the
abandoned fortifications, and finding that the fire from the
main fort had suddenly ceased they pushed on to take possession. The next moment there was a terrific explosion,
and over two hundred Americans, including General Pike,
were shot into the air, most of them being killed or seriously wounded; General Pike died a few hours later, and the
American command devolved upon Colonel Prince. The
powder magazine had been fired by an artillery sergeant of
the retreating force to prevent it from falling into the hands
of the enemy; but there appears to have been no intention
of timing the explosion so that it would cause such a terrible
loss of life. General Sheaffe had ordered the firing of the
magazine, but it was merely to destroy the ammunition,
and several Canadians were killed because the explosion
was premature. The American letter quoted above, while
inaccurate in many details, gives an interesting description
of the explosion: "A magazine containing 500 barrels of
powder, many cartloads of stone, and an immense quantity
of iron, shell and shot was blown up. The explosion was
tremendous. The column was raked from front to rear.
Notwithstanding, the troops gave three cheers, instantly
formed column, and marched on towards the town."[9]

General Dearborn immediately landed when he learned
that General Pike had been wounded by the explosion. He
wrote that the American ships entered the harbour with
difficulty owing to adverse winds, and opened "a tremendous
cannonading upon the enemy's batteries, which was kept
up until they were carried or blown up".[10] The blockhouse

---

[8]The horrors of war are well described by P. Finan, who saw the
 blackened and mutilated men being carried into shelter after
 this explosion. See Finan, *op. cit.*, pp. 286-8.
[9]*The War*, May 25, 1813.
[10]See *The War*, May 18, 1813.

on Gibraltar (now Hanlan's) Point was also burned by the enemy. One British ship in the harbour, the *Duke of Gloucester*, fell into the hands of the Americans, and a considerable quantity of ammunition and supplies was also captured.

General Sheaffe did not halt long in York, but hastened eastward so speedily that he left his baggage behind. The Rev. Strachan was a man of different calibre:

"On hearing the tremendous explosion of the magazine, hurried home and found Mrs. Strachan greatly terrified, and off with the children to a neighbour's house. Sent her to a friend's, a little out of town. Go up towards the Garrison, which we had by this time abandoned; find the General (Sheaffe) and his troops in a ravine, the militia scattering. The General determines to retreat to Kingston with the regulars, and leaves the command with Colonel Chewitt and Major Allan, two militia officers; and desires them to make the best conditions they can with the enemy for the protection of the town. Offer my services to assist them."[11]

As Sheaffe proceeded eastward along the Danforth Road with 180 men he made sure that he would not be pursued, for after crossing the Don Bridge, a log structure built in 1806, he ordered it to be burned. The Americans had no intention of following, however, and the British force, "leaving wounded in every farmhouse",[12] eventually reached Kingston. Sheaffe was soon after replaced, for his conduct was not considered creditable, to say the least. It would appear, however, that a large share of the blame ought to be attached to the Imperial Government, which was responsible for the almost indefensible condition of York and the general lack of adequate preparations.

Meanwhile the invaders were in possession of the town, and from three to four o'clock they paraded the streets in triumph. Major Forsyth's rifle corps, "famous for their sharp-shooting and their loose fingers",[13] was then left in charge of York, and the rest of the Americans proceeded to the Garrison, at the foot of the present Bathurst Street.

[11]Letter of John Strachan to a friend in Scotland. See Bethune, *op. cit.*, pp. 47-49.
[12]See *The War*, May 25, 1813.
[13]W. B. Kerr: *The Occupation of York (Toronto) 1813. (Canadian Historical Review*, Vol. V, pp. 10-11.)

Those who remained in the town spent most of the next day or two going from house to house and helping themselves to anything they fancied, a procedure not unusual in war time, particularly when discipline is loose.

The Americans felt very keenly the great loss of men suffered in the explosion; this they believed to have been "previously prepared",[14] and on that account were less inclined to negotiate terms of capitulation, or to enforce the conditions after they had finally been agreed upon and ratified. The Rev. John (afterwards Bishop) Strachan, who had come to York the previous year, was prominent in the negotiations. As the American commander did not ratify the terms of the first conference another was necessary, and Strachan was treated with scant respect by General Dearborn. Commodore Chauncey, however, who acted in a gentlemanly manner throughout the occupation, used his influence upon the General, with the result that the terms, including the parole of prisoners, were ratified. In fact the parole was extended much farther than the British wished, for the enemy sent American sympathisers through the County of York ordering all farmers to come in and be paroled, or their property would be destroyed. Some 500 did so, and were consequently not available for the defence of York on the occasion of the second attack in August.

Before the terms of capitulation were in force, however, the American soldiery had further plundered the town, though no great damage was done. In General Sheaffe's baggage they found a musical snuff-box, which afforded considerable amusement. Half a dozen prisoners were liberated from the jail, and these, with the addition of other evil-disposed citizens of York and the surrounding country, took a hand in the pillage. William Dummer Powell wrote that more plundering was done by "our own people" than by the enemy,[15] and there appears to be no doubt that they were at least equally to blame.

The Rev. Strachan worked courageously day and night moving the wounded from the Garrison to the town; in this difficult work he was ably seconded by Dr. Aspinwall, an American who had settled in York, and by the evening

14Dearborn to the Secretary of War, April 28, 1813.
15Quoted in Kerr, *op. cit.*, p. 14.

of the 29th all the wounded had been transferred to the town. Strachan had frequent cause to complain that the terms of the capitulation were not being respected by the enemy, and on more than one occasion he risked his life to save the property of the townspeople from being plundered.

The Americans who took part in the raid on York were of a calibre greatly inferior to many of those with whom the British were engaged elsewhere during the war. It would appear from all accounts that General Dearborn and his officers had little control over the men, who continued to steal in spite of all orders. A deputation under the militant churchman visited the commander and received back the civil power of the magistrates, and some support in enforcing law and order. As a result the situation was somewhat improved on May 1st, and further pillaging was effectually ended by Dearborn when he ordered the embarkation of his troops, all being on board ship by the 2nd. The ships were wind-bound until the 8th, when they proceeded to Four-Mile Creek, near the mouth of the Niagara River.

A letter written by Thomas Ridout, who was in York when it was captured, and remained there until May 2nd, gives some interesting, though not entirely accurate, details of the occupation. He states that all of the American troops embarked on May 1st, excepting a small party, "who burnt the large blockhouse, government house and officers' quarters. The commissariat magazines were shipped the preceding days. The lower blockhouse and government buildings were burnt on Saturday. Major Givins' and Dr. Powell's houses were entirely plundered by the enemy and some persons from the Humber. . . . Duncan Cameron delivered all the money in the Receiver-General's hands (to the amount, as I understand, of £2,500) over to Captain Elliot of the American navy, the enemy having threatened to burn the town if it was not given up. . . . The public provincial papers were found out, but ordered to be protected, so that nothing was destroyed excepting the books, papers, records and furniture of the upper and lower Houses of Assembly".[16]

[16]Letter of Thomas G. Ridout, dated at Kingston, May 5, 1813. See Edgar, *op. cit.*, pp. 185-6.

Owen Staples, O.S.A.

THE AMERICAN ATTACK ON YORK, APRIL 27, 1813

BRITISH TROOPS BURNING THE DON BRIDGE AT THE TIME OF
THE AMERICAN OCCUPATION OF YORK, 1813

NO. 1 BLOCKHOUSE, TORONTO
This building, the oldest of the group at the foot of Bathurst Street,
is thought to date from 1798

The enemy did not carry away all the gold and documents, for some had been hurriedly removed. Much archives material was taken for safe-keeping up the Don to the homes of John and George Playter, though the Americans sent boats there and took all that could be discovered. Similarly three bags of gold and a large sum in army bills were conveyed by William Roe, an employee in Receiver-General Prideaux Selby's office, to the farm of Chief Justice Robinson, east of the Don Bridge; they were there buried, and, though the army bills were shortly surrendered to the Americans, the gold remained secreted until after they had left York. Roe also removed the Receiver-General's iron chest to the premises of Donald McLean, Clerk of the House of Assembly; but McLean was killed while resisting the invasion of York, and his house and the strong-box plundered, about one thousand silver dollars being removed from the chest.

There is considerable doubt as to how much of the plundering and burning in York was due to the enemy. It is known that General Dearborn seized a considerable amount of flour and provisions and distributed some of it among the poor of the town. £2,000 was taken from the Provincial Treasury, and St. James' Church was entered, as well as the town library; to Commodore Chauncey's credit it may be said that he later collected several boxes of books and sent them back to York. On April 30th the Government Buildings, including the library, were burned, though it is uncertain who set the fire, for we have no statement of an eye-witness. Robert Gourlay says, and the present writer is inclined to believe that his information is correct, that American sailors acting without orders from their officers were to blame for the burning of the buildings, the finding of a scalp in the Parliament House being given as an excuse.[17] If the principles of legal evidence are followed, however, one must agree with a competent writer that the Americans cannot be assumed guilty without weightier evidence than has yet been adduced: "In view of the absence of any direct statement of a personal observer to the effect that the Americans started the fire, we must conclude that the accusation is not proven, and that it is

[17]Gourlay, *op. cit.*, Vol. I, p. 90.

almost as probable that unscrupulous Canadians did it as that the Americans were responsible."[18]

There was, upon the whole, very little serious damage during the American occupation, apart from the destruction of the public records; for the Parliament House, though described by John Strachan as consisting of "two elegant halls",[19] was merely a low wood and brick structure which it would soon have been necessary to replace. It is certain that the Americans considered at the time that the blowing up of the magazine was timed to coincide with their arrival, and were angry and less easily controlled on that account; though, of course, the usual conduct during wars has varied but little from their treatment of York, and has often in similar circumstances been much worse. In fact Gourlay quotes a letter written by Chief Justice Scott to the American Adjutant-General on April 30, 1813, to show that General Dearborn dealt with York much more considerately than had been reported: "On the part of the magistrates of York I gratefully acknowledge the humane attention which has been paid by His Excellency to the present situation of its inhabitants, by pursuing a line of conduct so conducive to the protection of a number of individuals, and so honourable to himself".[20] In retaliation for the burning of York and Newark a British force destroyed the much more valuable public buildings of Washington in 1814.

Incredible though it is, the story has often been repeated that an American officer took the Speaker's wig from the Parliament House and presented it to General Dearborn as a human scalp. Gourlay, a contemporary who could easily learn the truth, states that a scalp was actually found. It had been sent by an officer of the British army to the Clerk of the House, and, as a curiosity, had been thrown into a drawer, where it was discovered by the Americans. They embellished the story by telling their commanders that it

[18]Kerr, *op. cit.*, p. 18.
[19]Open letter of John Strachan to Thomas Jefferson, ex-President of the United States, January 30, 1815. This letter, which was written to defend the burning of Washington by the British in retaliation for the destruction of Newark and the public buildings of York by the Americans, may be found in full in W. F. Coffin: *1812; the War and its Moral.* 1864. Appendix, pp. 273-285.
[20]Quoted in Gourlay, *op. cit.*, Vol. I, p. 92.

was found hanging over the mace.[21] So Commodore Chauncey wrote to the Secretary of the Navy: "A British standard, accompanied with the mace over which hung a human scalp, were taken from the parliament house by one of my officers and presented to me."[22]

Historians have frequently stated that if one wished to see how the Americans were fooled he might inspect the "wig" in the Naval Museum at Annapolis, Maryland, whither it had found its way as a trophy. The curator of the museum states, however, that it has never been in their possession, nor is anything known of its existence since Commodore Chauncey presented it to General Dearborn. The curator remarks that "Captain Chauncey undoubtedly knew the difference between a Speaker's wig and a scalp. For one thing there would be a great difference in size and colour".[23] There remains the possibility that the Americans invented the story as propaganda in order to discredit their enemies; but the writer has no hesitation in accepting in preference Gourlay's explanation, which has upon it all the earmarks of reliability and authenticity.

The battle of York lasted about eight hours, and the British losses were sixty-two killed and seventy-two wounded, mostly regulars. About 250 regulars or militia were captured by the invaders during the engagement. The Americans announced the British losses in killed, wounded and prisoners as 930; while their own were summarised as follows: Killed in battle, 14; wounded in battle, 23; killed by the explosion, 52; wounded by the explosion, 180.[24]

In the Canadian militia, whose gallantry was conspicuous during the engagement, were two men afterwards prominent in public life,—John Beverley Robinson, later knighted and appointed Chief Justice of Upper Canada, and Allan (afterwards Sir Allan) MacNab, Prime Minister

[21]*Ibid.*, p. 91. In other works it is suggested that the scalp was that of one of Major Givins' Indian sharp-shooters, who, hidden in a tree, fired with such deadly effect on the Americans during the debarkation that they scalped him; and that the scalp was associated with the mace because the two eventually found their way to Washington. See Henry Scadding: *Toronto of Old.* 1873. pp. 399-400.

[22]Quoted in Gourlay, *op. cit.*, Vol. I, p. 91.

[23]H. F. Krafft to E. C. Guillet, May 13, 1932.

[24]See *The War*, May 25, 1813.

of the Canadas in 1854; the latter was only fourteen years of age at the time of the attack on York.

The capital suffered another raid a few months later. It had no defenders on this occasion, the militia having been placed on parole during the previous occupation. The second expedition was also under Chauncey, and included Colonel Scott, an unexchanged prisoner of war still on parole. The Americans entered York on July 31st, seizing several hundred barrels of flour in St. George's, Allan's and King's stores. Many other details of this attack are contained in a dispatch written by Sir George Prevost.

"The enemy's fleet of twelve sail made its appearance off York on the 31st. The three square-rigged vessels, the *Pike, Madison* and *Oneida,* came to anchor in the offing; but the schooners continued up the harbour, landed several boats full of troops at the former Garrison, and proceeded from thence to the town, of which they took possession. They opened the jail, liberated the prisoners, and took away three soldiers confined for felony; they then went to the hospital and paroled the few men that could not be removed. They next entered the storehouses of some of the inhabitants, seized their contents, chiefly flour, and the same being private property. Between eleven and twelve that night they returned on board their vessels.

"The next morning, Sunday, the 1st instant, the enemy again landed, and sent three armed boats up the River Don in search of public stores; of which being disappointed, by sunset both soldiers and sailors had evacuated the town, the small barrack, woodyard and storehouse on Gibraltar Point having been first set on fire by them; and at daylight the following morning the enemy's fleet sailed."[25]

The American account of the raid is contained in a letter from Commodore Isaac Chauncey to the Secretary of the Navy. He states that he arrived at York at 3 p.m. on July 31st, and "landed the marines and soldiers under the command of Colonel Scott without opposition, found several hundred barrels of flour and provisions in the public storehouse, five pieces of cannon, eleven boats, and a quantity of shot, shells and other stores, all which were either de-

[25]The dispatch is quoted in Henry Scadding: *Early Notices of Toronto.* 1865. pp. 17-18.

stroyed or brought away. On the 1st inst., just after having received on board all that the vessels could take, I directed the barracks and public storehouses to be burnt; we then re-embarked the men and proceeded for this place, where I arrived yesterday. Between four and five hundred men left York for the head of the lake two days before we arrived there. Some few prisoners were taken, some of whom were paroled; the others have been landed at Fort George."[26]

It is remarkable that the American forces did not consider it strategically important to hold York, and so cut the line of communication between Kingston and Niagara. The invasions of the town were sufficiently serious, however, to check its progress and growth, and many years elapsed before York had recovered from the misfortunes of 1813.

[26]Chauncey to the Secretary of the Navy, August 4, 1813. See *The War*, August 17, 1813.

CHAPTER IV

THE BATTLE OF MONTGOMERY'S FARM, AND THE ESCAPE OF WILLIAM LYON MACKENZIE, 1837

"By His Excellency, Sir Francis Bond Head, Baronet, Lieutenant-Governor of Upper Canada. . . . To the Queen's faithful subjects in Upper Canada. . . .
Be vigilant, patient, and active; leave Punishment to the Laws. Our first object is, to arrest and secure all those who have been guilty of Rebellion, Murder, and Robbery. And to aid us in this, a Reward is hereby offered of one thousand pounds, to anyone who will apprehend and deliver up to Justice, William Lyon Mackenzie."

> Proclamation of Lieutenant-Governor Sir Francis Bond Head, December 7, 1837.

"Mackenzie safely reached the United States, and one cannot help thinking (with him) that it is something to be proud of that no Canadian was base enough to try to sell him for Head's thousand pounds."

> EMILY P. WEAVER.[1]

THE Rebellion of 1837 came to a head in Upper Canada when several hundred of Mackenzie's supporters gathered, early in December, at Montgomery's Hotel.[2] This tavern was a

---

[1] Emily P. Weaver: *The Story of the Counties of Ontario.* 1913. p. 73.
[2] The events relating to the battle of Montgomery's Farm are described from varying points of view by Sir Francis Bond Head, Colonel James Fitzgibbon and William Lyon Mackenzie. All of these "official" accounts are defective to a greater or less extent, and the attempt is made in the present work to get at the truth by using the three conflicting stories as a basis, together with such supplementary material as is available. Bond Head's account (*A Narrative of the Canadian Rebellion.* 1839.) is the least valuable, a fact due largely to the peculiar characteristics of its author. Fitzgibbon's *Appeal to the People of Upper Canada* (1847) is a fair account, though the writer was obsessed with Bond Head's opposition to his every move. William Lyon Mackenzie's description of the battle and his escape are found in the pamphlet, *Mackenzie's Own Narrative of the Late Rebellion* (1838), which he describes as "the only true account"; and in Charles Lindsey's *Life and Times of William Lyon Mackenzie* (1862); these versions are not everywhere reliable. George Coventry's contemporary *Account of the Rebellion of Upper Canada* (Ontario Historical Society, *Papers and Records,* Volume XVII) is an ultra-loyal narrative with little of value that is not more accurately described elsewhere. Charles Durand's *Reminiscences* (1897) contains, particularly in Chapter XI, personal recollections written in a peculiarly rambling style. Perhaps the best short description is found in Samuel Thompson's *Reminiscences of a Canadian Pioneer* (1884), though he probably refreshed his memory by consulting the published accounts. Thompson was merely a shrewd observer who, (among many other curious people, including Dr.

650

large clap-board building, located on the west side of Yonge
Street a little back from the road, between the present
Montgomery and Roselawn Avenues. It had a broad platform in front, and a lamp suspended over a central doorway. John Montgomery, owner of the inn, had rented it to
John Linfoot, but he was boarding there while his home was
being erected close by. In 1837 the hemlock and pine forest
bordering the road had not, in some sections, been removed,
but across from the inn was a cleared space—Montgomery's
farm. Toronto, a city of 12,000 inhabitants, lay four miles
to the south.

Upper Canada was most unfortunate in the type of man
who held the position of Lieutenant-Governor at the time
of the Rebellion. Though he has his defenders, and his
uncompromising attitude may have been to some extent
dictated from London, Sir Francis Bond Head was a most
obstinate man, who persistently refused to take the rebels
seriously. Whatever measures were adopted for the protection of Toronto were due to Colonel James Fitzgibbon,
the hero of Beaver Dams; he roused the people to their
danger, and warned many a citizen "to go to bed every night

John Strachan), "took upon himself to accompany the advancing
force, on the chance of finding something to do, either as a
volunteer or a newspaper correspondent"; his description appears to be unbiassed and authentic, and contains considerable
interesting information not found elsewhere. Thompson appended to Chapter XXIV ·of his *Reminiscences* a narrative
given to him "by a gentleman who, as a young lad, was personally cognizant of the facts described"; this account was written
by Allan McLean Howard, and includes many details of the
movements of Mackenzie's men previous to their dispersal by
the government force. The plans, (insofar as they had any),
and the movements of the rebels are concisely described by
Joseph Gould, who was among those present at the rout of the
"Patriots". (See W. H. Higgins: *The Life and Times of Joseph
Gould*. 1887).

In addition to these primary sources there are a number of accounts of the Rebellion written by competent historians. Among
the best is J. C. Dent's *The Story of the Upper Canadian Rebellion* (2 Volumes, 1885), a work rather strongly biassed
against Mackenzie, but which shows skilful use of all available
sources. It provoked a critique by a man of opposite sympathies, John King, though his *The Other Side of the Story*
(1886) is merely concerned with refutation. In both of these
works rare manuscripts and pamphlets, many of them not now
available, are quoted. The political background of the Rebellion is best covered in W. S. Wallace: *The Family Compact*.
(1920. Chronicles of Canada). Upon the whole, therefore, the
events of the first week of December, 1837, are capable of
exceedingly full treatment.

having arms loaded near his bedside; and on hearing the College bell ring he should run to me to the Parliament House with his arms."[3]

Not only did Bond Head refuse to take steps to protect Toronto, but he sent all the regular troops out of the province, and told Fitzgibbon that if the militia could not defend the country the sooner it was lost the better! Even the staunch loyalist who published *Mackenzie's Own Narrative* (with the sole purpose of discrediting it) wrote: "We are clearly of the opinion that the city might have been captured, sacked and destroyed at any hour during the nights of Sunday, the 3rd, and Monday, the 4th instant, in the total absence of all precaution on the part of the government,—even by a less force than 200 men, under dashing and spirited leaders."[4]

Even when the activities of the rebels made it clear to the perverse Governor that some action would have to be taken he still refused to advance on Mackenzie's force. "O no sir!", said he to Fitzgibbon, "I will not fight them on their ground; they must fight me on mine!" No wonder the Colonel exclaimed (mentally) : "Good Lord! What an old woman I have here to deal with!"[5] In fact such was the obvious neglect of the Lieutenant-Governor throughout his stay in Canada that Lord Durham wrote in his *Report* that "it certainly appeared too much as if the rebellion had been purposely invited by the government, and the unfortunate men who took part in it deliberately drawn into a trap by those who subsequently inflicted so severe a punishment on them for their error."[6]

The rebels were a poorly-organised body of men, many of them without firearms; their leaders, too, could not agree on the tactics to be followed, with the result that continual argument and the ensuing delay spoiled any chance of success. Their general scheme appears to have been "to set fire to the city in sixteen different places, rob the banks, the government and registry offices, take possession of the gar-

[3]Fitzgibbon, *op. cit.*, p. 12.
[4]*Mackenzie's Own Narrative*, Editor's footnote, p. 9.
[5]Fitzgibbon, *op. cit.*, p. 18.
[6]The Earl of Durham's *Report on the Affairs of British North America, January 1, 1839*, pp. 59-60.

WILLIAM LYON MACKENZIE

GOLD MEDAL PRESENTED TO WILLIAM LYON MACKENZIE ON
THE OCCASION OF HIS RE-ELECTION AFTER HIS FIRST
EXPULSION FROM THE LEGISLATIVE ASSEMBLY

From Lindsey's *Life and Times of William Lyon Mackenzie*

THE BATTLE OF MONTGOMERY'S FARM, 1837

From J. C. Dent's *The Story of the Upper Canadian Rebellion*

THE DEATH OF COLONEL MOODIE AT MONTGOMERY'S TAVERN, 1837

rison, and make the Governor prisoner."[7] But the changing (by Dr. Rolph) of the date of the attack on Toronto from Thursday, December 7th, to the preceding Monday was an error which eliminated many who might have taken part in it, and created confusion among the insurgents.

The "Patriots" decided to prevent communication with the city by way of Yonge Street, and on Monday evening killed Colonel Moodie as he defiantly endeavoured to ride past the tavern. During the same night Captain Anthony Anderson, the rebels' most trusted military leader, was shot by Alderman John Powell, who had been captured by Anderson and Shepard while they were on a reconnoitring expedition; Powell had retained two loaded pistols, however, and he suddenly fired at Anderson with deadly effect, and escaped during the ensuing confusion.

Many were the suggestions offered by the rebel leaders as to the best method of surrounding and converging upon the city, but the plan eventually adopted, and put into partial execution about noon on Tuesday, called for the division of the rebel army at Gallows Hill, just south of the present St. Clair Avenue; Lount was then to lead one section down Yonge Street, while Mackenzie, mounted on a small white horse and enveloped in such a voluminous greatcoat that he appeared to many to be bullet-proof, was to advance with another force down what is now Avenue Road. The rebels had reached Gallows Hill when they were halted by Dr. John Rolph and Robert Baldwin, who bore a flag of truce and the Governor's offer of a complete amnesty for all offences, provided that the insurgents immediately dispersed; the rebel leader replied that his demands "should be settled by a National Convention", a proposal which met a definite refusal.[8] A general advance was now prevented by insubordination among the rebels, and a rather general lack of confidence in their leaders. Throughout the week, in fact, disorganisation, indecision, apprehension and cowardice were all contributory causes of the inaction of the "Patriots" at Montgomery's, and their situation was greatly aggravated by the almost entire lack of arms and supplies.

By about 6 p.m. the leaders had once more succeeded in

[7]Duncan Campbell to Malcolm Campbell, dated at Otonabee Township, January 28, 1838. (Unpublished.)
[8]Head, *op. cit.*, pp. 331-2.

getting their followers into some sort of order, and seven
hundred rebels under Samuel Lount attempted a night raid
on Toronto; but the effort was a fiasco, the lack of military
training and discipline being apparent even to themselves.
A half-armed mob, "headed by civilians, and having no confidence in themselves or their military leaders",[9] marched
down Yonge Street, were harangued at the Bloor Street
toll-gate by Mackenzie, and pushed on towards the city,
establishing contact with twenty-seven loyalist soldiers
under Sheriff William B. Jarvis near the present Maitland
Street. Lount's men, armed with rifles, were in front; a
force with pikes came next, and in the rear was a rabble of
useless fellows carrying sticks and cudgels. The engagement was a burlesque:

"After firing once, the loyalists, under Sheriff Jarvis,
started back at full speed towards the city. The front rank
of Lount's men, instead of stepping aside after firing to let
those behind fire, fell down on their faces. Those in the
rear, fancying that the front rank had been cut down by the
muskets of the small force who had taken a random shot
at them, being without arms were panic-stricken; and in a
short time nearly the whole force was on the retreat. Many
of the Lloydtown pikemen raised the cry, 'We shall all be
killed', threw down their rude weapons, and fled in great
precipitation."[10]

The whole affair partook more of boisterous comedy
than of military tactics, for the loyalist detachment was no
better than the rebels, and, perhaps agreeing with Falstaff
that honour would not set to an arm or a leg, or take away
the grief of a wound, its members took to their heels with
all convenient speed, unaware that their opponents were
fleeing as precipitately in the opposite direction. The rebels
left one wounded man behind, and he lay on the ground
until the following morning. Jarvis was forced to follow his
militiamen back to Toronto; while no matter how Mackenzie
argued, coaxed and threatened, he could neither stem the
retreat nor persuade his followers to march again on the
city. They were afraid of everything. A farmer who
lived on Yonge Street observed that "while a detachment
of rebels were marching southwards down the hill, since

---

[9]Lindsey, *op. cit.*, Vol. II, p. 86.   [10]*Ibid.*, p. 87.

known as Mount Pleasant, they saw a wagon-load of cordwood standing on the opposite rise, and, supposing it to be a
piece of artillery loaded to the muzzle with grape or
canister, these brave warriors leaped the fences right and
left like squirrels, and could by no effort of their officers be
induced again to advance."[11] One of those present at the
tavern wrote that Mackenzie proposed to lead another raid
on Toronto if twenty men would follow him, "but he could
not get out of the whole force even such a small number
to go with him." One of Lount's men, named Stiles, would
have shot Mackenzie for imputing cowardice to his followers, if he had not been prevented by others standing
near by.[12]

The rebels' unsuccessful raid appears to have done more
to arouse the authorities in Toronto than had all the argu-
ments of Fitzgibbon. The Governor and his Council appointed him Adjutant-General of the force which was
being raised to defend the city, though he felt that their
efforts were largely directed towards blocking his military
activities. The fire-bells aroused the inhabitants to their
danger, but Fitzgibbon had to waste half an hour of his
valuable time on the evening of the raid in seeing that all
the bells were rung! A rather motley group of men were
mustered by this means, while messengers on horseback rode
their mounts to death in spreading the news throughout the
province and ordering recruits to hasten to the threatened
capital.

Samuel Thompson describes how "the principal buildings
in the city—the City Hall, Upper Canada Bank, the
Parliament Buildings, Osgoode Hall, Government House,
the Canada Company's office—and many private dwellings
and shops, were put in a state of defence by barricading the
windows and doors with two-inch plank, loopholed for
musketry".[13] Toronto's rather formidable appearance was
enhanced by the arrival by steamship of sixty "men of

[11]Samuel Thompson: *Reminiscences of a Canadian Pioneer*. 1884.
pp. 122-3. In A. M. Howard's narrative appended to Chapter
XXIV of this book may be found many details of the high-
handed methods used by Mackenzie and his men during their
occupation of James S. Howard's house, about a mile south of
Montgomery's Tavern.
[12]See letter of P. H. Watson, November 12, 1839, quoted in Lindsey,
op. cit., Vol. II, p. 88 fn.
[13]Thompson, *op. cit.*, p. 123.

EARLY LIFE IN UPPER CANADA

Gore" from Hamilton, under Mr. Speaker MacNab, and of other bodies of militia from Cobourg, Whitby, Scarborough, Niagara, St. Catharines, Oakville, Port Credit and other localities. Some of these men were armed, and the rest were issued muskets and ammunition, which were similarly distributed among all householders who chose to accept them.

In the rebel camp at Montgomery's, meanwhile, all was disorder and indecision. There is every reason to believe, in fact, that extreme excitement reigned among Mackenzie and his followers. Joseph Gould arrived there on Wednesday evening, and was not sanguine of success when he saw how matters stood:

"Mackenzie was then in the act of opening mail-bags and exhibiting their contents. I found that there was no order or discipline; that there had been no picket-guards put out, and that the whole party were liable to be surprised at any moment, and that probably before morning they would be surrounded and cut off. Tired as I was after our long march, I determined to set pickets at once. This I did, and had the guard relieved until morning."[14]

Bond Head's force, which on Tuesday morning had numbered but 300, had been augmented by some 200 during that day, and by the following morning the Governor's fears were further dispelled by the appearance of additional loyal troops. But he had lost that blustering over-confidence which had characterised his earlier actions, and decided to gain time by sending a party up Yonge Street with a flag of truce, as has been previously described; he confidently expected that enough additional men would come into the city during Wednesday to enable an attack on the rebels early the following day. Among the tired farmers who, armed with fowling-pieces, entered Toronto during Thursday were probably some who had really intended to join the rebels in their attack on the city, the change of date not having been communicated to them; these men (according to Mackenzie) came too late to be rebels, and made a virtue of necessity when they joined the loyal force.[15] Be that as it may, the Lieutenant-Governor found some who were enthusiastic

[14]Joseph Gould quoted in W. H. Higgins: *The Life and Times of Joseph Gould.* 1887. p. 107.
[15]*Mackenzie's Own Narrative*, p. 12.

enough: " 'If your Honour will but give us ARMS', exclaimed a voice from the ranks in a broad Irish brogue,
the rebels will find LEGS.' "[16]
The personnel of the government force is a matter of
considerable interest.   Mackenzie, and the "Patriot" writers
generally, contend that the loyal army which gathered at
Toronto consisted chiefly of "Tory college boys, lawyers and
judges",[17] a statement which has more than a grain of truth
in it, for an eye-witness wrote:

"We saw the Lieutenant-Governor in his everyday suit,
with one double-barrelled gun in his hand, another leaning
against his breast, and a brace of pistols in his leathern
belt. Also Chief Justice Robinson, Judges Macaulay, Jones
and McLean, the Attorney-General and the Solicitor-General
with their muskets, cartridge-boxes and bayonets, all standing in the ranks as private soldiers, under the command
of Colonel Fitzgibbon."[18]

Poor Fitzgibbon was not free from worries until the
end, for MacNab wished to attack the rebels in the middle
of the night, and Bond Head was seriously thinking of
placing him in command! On Thursday morning, the 7th
of December, "such an overwhelming force that there remained not the slightest reason for delay"[19] was ready to
march against the rebels. At twelve noon, "with an enthusiasm which it would be impossible to describe", [20] the
march up Yonge Street commenced. William Ryerson describes the troops as consisting of "about 2,000 men, headed
by the Lieutenant-Governor, with Judge Jones, the Attorney-General and Captain Halkett as his aides-de-camp,
and commanded by Colonels Fitzgibbon and Allan N. Mac-
Nab, Speaker of the House".[21] Samuel Thompson, who followed the force northward, gives a more exact estimate,[22]
for the troops numbered only 920, the main body consisting
of 600 men, and the two smaller supporting columns at the
right and left of 200 and 120, respectively. The main force,

[16]Bond Head: *The Emigrant.* 1846. p. 175.
[17]See D. McLeod: *A Brief Review of the Settlement of Upper
      Canada.* . . . 1841. p. 192; and *Mackenzie's Own Narrative*, p. 12.
[18]William Ryerson to Egerton Ryerson, December 5, 1837.   See
      Egerton Ryerson: *The Story of My Life.* 1883. p. 177.
[19]Head's *Narrative*, p. 332.   [20]*Ibid.*
[21]William Ryerson to Egerton Ryerson, December 8, 1837.   See
      Ryerson, *op. cit.,* p. 177.
[22]Thompson, *op. cit.,* p. 125.

accompanied by "music and artillery",[23] was led up Yonge
Street by Sir Francis himself and Colonels Fitzgibbon and
MacNab. The supporting columns, which advanced northward by side roads and through fields to the east and west of
Yonge Street, were commanded by Colonels Samuel P.
Jarvis and William Chisholm, respectively, though Chisholm's command of the left wing appears to have been only
nominal, Judge McLean and Colonel O'Hara being in charge
while Chisholm was sent with a small force to the vicinity
of the Peacock Inn. The two guns which formed the battery
of the main body were in charge of Major Carfrae of the
militia artillery.

The day was remarkably fine, and as the main body
and the west wing marched up Yonge Street and College
(University) Avenue, each force accompanied by a band,
the enthusiasm of the soldiers rose to high pitch.

"The windows and housetops along the chief thoroughfares were crowded by men, women and children, who
waved miniature flags and lustily cheered the cavalcade as
it passed along. The volunteers responded in kind, and the
welkin rang again. Never had the streets of the little
provincial capital presented so stirring an appearance—
not even when the guns of the invader had thundered along
the waterfront in 1813. To many who beheld the scene,
and participated in the enthusiasm which it was eminently
calculated to arouse, this 7th of December was the most
memorable day of their lives."[24]

In a contemporary political pamphlet there is a series of
letters concerning the Rebellion, purporting to be written by
a member of the loyal army but sounding more like Bond
Head himself! In one of them "William Steady" tells his
brother in England of the advance northward: "We found
the rebels posted near 'Gallows Hill' (a very proper place
for them!). They fired; we advanced steadily, and soon
drove them before us like chaff before the wind."[25]   The

[23]Lindsey, op.cit., Vol. II, p. 94.
[24]Dent, op. cit., Vol. II, pp. 119-20 .
[25]"William Steady" to "John Steady", in The True Briton of the
    Nineteenth Century; Canadian Patriots and English Chartists.
    1840. p. 5. Gallows' Hill was, of course, not the gentle rise near
    Montgomery's where the skirmish took place, but a hill some
    distance south, below the present St. Clair Avenue, where the
    loyal army was first observed by the rebel sentinels near the
    tavern.

engagement was, however, a little more extensive than this would indicate. While the loyalists were swinging along Yonge Street to the tune of *Yankee Doodle* (or a march equally appropriate) the disorganised "Patriots" were still discussing their plans. Mackenzie appears to have personally investigated the reported approach of the loyal force, and, having assured himself that the troops were close at hand, he asked his men if they wished to fight. Upon receiving an affirmative answer he ordered most of his poorly-armed followers into a small forest near the hotel, Van Egmond and Lount assuming command of them; others took up a position in an open field across the road, while the rebel leader states that "about 200 of our friends stood at the tavern during the battle, being unarmed."[26] In addition a small force of rebels appears to have been located in the Paul Pry Inn, on the east side of Yonge Street some distance south of Montgomery's.

When MacNab's force reached the brow of the hill just north of what is now Mount Pleasant Cemetery the two guns opened fire. The first shot passed under the eaves and out of the roof of the Paul Pry Inn, and the rebels posted therein immediately took to the woods. Had the supporting columns kept pace with the main loyalist force all the insurgents might have been captured; but those marching through the fields were somewhat behind the others, and the entire force could not therefore converge upon Montgomery's Hotel at the same time. As the fire of the two guns broke upon the rebel force in the open fields they melted away in precipitate retreat, and Fitzgibbon's men entered the tavern. The loyal force suffered a loss of only three wounded, none of them seriously, while one rebel named Wideman was killed in action, and a number wounded, four of them so seriously that they died in hospital. The "Patriots" fled in all directions, and almost all of the leaders escaped capture; but Mackenzie afterwards defended them from charges of cowardice when he wrote: "Never did men fight more courageously. In the face of a heavy fire of grape and canister, with broadside following broadside of musketry in rapid succession, they stood their ground firmly, ... but were at length compelled to re-

[26]*Mackenzie's Own Narrative*, p. 18.

treat."[27] His testimony, however, is rather at variance with his experience, and a better statement is that of John Charles Dent:

"The rebels who fought at Montgomery's were neither better nor worse than other volunteers under like circumstances. They were mostly farm rustics who had never seen a pitched battle, and who had left their homes without any notion of taking part in one. They were not Spartans; Montgomery's farm was not Thermopylae; and assuredly Leonidas was not there. When they were attacked by a force which there was no chance of their successfully opposing, they, after a faint show of resistance, chose the better part of valour. . . . When Mackenzie represented these 'embattled farmers' as withstanding the onslaught of 'an enemy 1,200 strong' . . . . he cast consistency to the winds. . . . He attributes the failure of the attempt on Tuesday night to the arrant cowardice of these very men who, on the following Thursday, are exalted into demigods of valour—into heroes who needed nothing but 'discipline, order, obedience and subordination', in addition to competent leadership, to render them upon the whole more than a match for Cromwell's Ironsides."[28]

A "Patriot" described the battle in the following poetical effusion, typical of many an effort in verse or prose:

"They have met—that small band, resolved to be free
As the fierce winds of Heaven that course o'er the sea—
They have met, in bright hope, with no presage of fear,
Though the bugle and drum of the foemen they hear.
Some seize the dread rifle, some wield the tall pike,
For God and their country—for Freedom they strike,
No proud ensign of glory bespeaks their renown,
Yet the scorn of defiance now darkens their frown.
See the foeman advancing! And now sounds afar
The clang and the shout of disastrous war.
Yes! Onward they come like the mountain's wild flood,
And the Lion's dark talons are dappled in blood."[29]

---

[27]Lindsey, *op. cit.*, Vol. II, p. 95.
[28]Dent, *op. cit.*, Vol. II, pp. 127-8. The quotation from Mackenzie in which he attributes the blame for the defeat upon lack of discipline is from his *Narrative*, p. 18.
[29]From Mackenzie's *Gazette*, quoted in Lindsey, *op. cit.*, Vol. II, p. 95.

In his *Reminiscences* Samuel Thompson recalls many interesting details of the engagement:

"Nothing was seen of the enemy till within half a mile of Montgomery's Tavern. The road was there bordered on the west side by pine woods, from whence dropping rifle-shots began to be heard, which were answered by the louder muskets of the militia. Presently our artillery opened their hoarse throats, and the woods rang with strong reverberations. Splinters were dashed from the trees, threatening and, I believe, causing worse mischief than the shots themselves. It is said that this kind of skirmishing continued for half an hour—to me it seemed but a few minutes. As the militia advanced, their opponents melted away. Parties of volunteers dashed over the fences and into the woods, shouting and firing as they ran. Two or three wounded men of both parties were lifted tenderly into carts and sent off to the city to be placed in hospital. . . .

"Soon a movement was visible through the smoke, on the hill fronting the tavern, where some tall pines were then standing. I could see there two or three hundred men, now firing irregularly at the advancing loyalists, now swaying to and fro without any apparent design. Some horsemen were among them, who seemed to act more as scouts than as leaders. We had by this time arrived within cannon-shot of the tavern itself. Two or three balls were seen to strike and pass through it. A crowd of men rushed from the doors and scattered wildly in a northerly direction. Those on the hill wavered, receded under shelter of the undulating land, and then fled like their fellows. Their horsemen took the side road westward, and were pursued, but not in time to prevent their escape. . . . The march back to Toronto was very leisurely executed, several of the mounted officers carrying dead pigs and geese slung across their saddle-bows as trophies of victory."[30]

Joseph Gould gives the best (if, indeed, not the only) detailed account of the plans of the rebels and their subsequent activities. He states that on Thursday morning they intended to attack Toronto in force, while a feint attack from the east, by way of the Don Bridge, was to be made by Captain Peter Matthews and a few men. Matthews'

[30]Thompson, *op. cit.*, pp. 125-7.

force got under way, but the main body of rebels at Montgomery's was still unorganised when a messenger arrived
from the city with the news of the approach of the loyalists.
Gould's experiences were, no doubt, typical of all, and his
description of them is of additional interest in that he suggests that there was at least one "Patriot"—and an important one, too,—in the loyal force:

"We soon got under arms and started down Yonge Street
to meet them. The troops, however, turned to the west,
and made as though they wanted to get round the west side
to our rear. We hastened through the woods, climbing over
dead hemlock trees and through the underbrush, and rushed
to head them off. We had no arms but our rifles, and
some had only rude pikes and pitchforks. The troops, besides their muskets and plenty of ammunition, had two
small field pieces—one controlled by a friend of ours, and
the other by an enemy. The friend fired grape-shot, and
fired over us into the tops of the trees, cutting off the dead
and dry limbs of the hemlocks, which, falling thickly
amongst us, scared the boys as much as if cannon-balls had
been rattling around us. The other gun was fired low, and
so *careless* that I did not like it. One of the balls struck a
sandbank by my feet and filled my eyes with sand, nearly
blinding me. Another struck one of those dry hemlocks,
scattering the bark and splinters about, and into my face.
Captain Wideman was killed on my left side, and F. Shell
was shot through the shoulder, to the left of the fallen
captain. But we got to the west of the troops. They then
turned and crossed to Yonge Street behind us. It was soon
known that Montgomery's Hotel was on fire and that the
day was lost."

Gould and his companions from Brock, Scott and Uxbridge Townships (Ontario County) were obviously on the
wrong side of Yonge Street to get back home readily, so a
half dozen of them "took to the woods, thinking to go into
the woods and camp out, or go to the States by Hamilton,
or cross home by the woody ridge by way of Stouffville, and
hide until we could go to the States". But they built a
camp-fire in a swamp, and were soon after captured.[31]

[31] See Higgins, *op. cit.*, pp. 106-8. Full details of the activities of the
rebels at Montgomery's may be found in Dent, *op. cit.*, Vol. II,
Chapter XXI *et seq.*

Colonel Fitzgibbon states that his men were almost unmanageable for a time during the pursuit of the rebels towards the tavern, for they advanced "in a stream" in response to the bugle call.[32] The commander and several others pursued Mackenzie, who did not leave the scene of action until the loyalists were close upon him. The rebel leader had left his horse at Price's, but there was no time to get it; his coat and a carpet-bag full of documents were at the tavern. The capture of his papers by the loyal force was unfortunate for the rebels, for among them were lists of all the Radicals who had adhered to his cause; and his error in leaving his records behind when he went out to battle enabled the authorities to apprehend many "Patriots" whose names would otherwise never have been known. As Mackenzie's men scattered in all directions they were hotly pursued by small bodies of soldiers, but most of the prisoners taken were released almost at once and ordered to go home. The loyal force also captured the rebel flag, inscribed "Bidwell, and the glorious minority! 1837, and a good beginning".[33]

One of Fitzgibbon's party pursuing the rebel leader came in sight of him, and saw him abandon his horse and run into the forest. The pursuit was not pressed farther, "for we were without muskets or rifles, and were two or three miles in advance of our men, while rebels were flying through the woods in every direction".[34] The main loyal force did not penetrate more than two miles above the tavern, for the road beyond that point had not been macadamised and was impassable. Sir Francis Bond Head personally ordered the burning of Montgomery's Tavern, and insisted also that David Gibson's home at Willowdale—nearly four miles north of the scene of battle—be consigned to the flames. This was speedily effected by setting fire to the furniture in the lower rooms.

When the day was seen to be lost Mackenzie ran northward, crossing a ploughed field in the rear of Price's house.

---

[32] Fitzgibbon, *op. cit.*, p. 28.
[33] This was an old banner used during an election contest in 1832, the
      figure 7 having been hastily substituted for the figure 2. Its
      use was one of the main reasons for accusing Marshall S.
      Bidwell of complicity in the Rebellion and forcing him into
      exile. See Dent, *op. cit.*, Vol. II, pp. 159-174.
[34] Fitzgibbon, *op. cit.*, p. 28.

After evading the first hot pursuit a few of the leaders stopped a moment to discuss plans of escape. Mackenzie states that "Mr. Fletcher, Colonel Van Egmond, myself, and others held a consultation near Hogg's Hollow, and concluded that it would be useless to reassemble our scattered forces, for that, without arms, success would be doubtful. I instantly determined to pass over to the United States, and accomplished my purpose in three days, travelled 125 miles, was seen by 2,000 persons at least, and with a reward of 4,000 dollars advertised for my head speedily reached Buffalo".[35] As the group broke up, Silas Fletcher insisted that Mackenzie take his overcoat for protection from the cold.

The leader of the abortive insurrection was a ruined man. The hopes of years had been dashed to pieces, and his fine printing establishment, bookstore, home and other property were left to the usual fate of the possessions of rebels. He saw the smoke of burning buildings as he hastened northward on foot, but there was little time to gaze backward and ponder over the desperate fortunes of the "Patriots".

The first man he met was a farmer riding into town, and he proved to be a friend. Mackenzie was soon mounted on his horse, without which escape would have been almost impossible, for when he was ten or twelve miles from Toronto he found himself closely pursued and repeatedly fired at; so he left Yonge Street and fled westward. When he reached Shepard's Mills he stopped to ask the miller whether some horsemen he saw in the distance were friends or foes. A body of Head's cavalry came almost to where he was, but turned off in another direction without suspecting his presence at Shepard's.

[35]*Mackenzie's Own Narrative*, p. 18. In his *Winter Wanderings Ten Years Since* he says his flight occupied five days; there is, in fact, good reason to doubt the accuracy of many of Mackenzie's post-rebellion statements. The ensuing account of his escape, however, is based entirely on his own description of it, for it is obvious that he is the only one who knows what he did. A few names of persons who aided him have been inserted, as well as a little explanatory information with regard to localities through which he passed. Mackenzie's description of his flight was written in 1847 and entitled *Winter Wanderings Ten Years Since*. The account first appeared in the Toronto *Examiner* of October 6, 1847. It was later printed in the Toronto *Globe*, and the essential portions of it are quoted in Lindsey's *Life of Mackenzie*, Vol. II, Chapter V.

A few minutes later he set off again, and soon came up with Colonel Lount and ninety men. Lount favoured dispersing in all directions, but Mackenzie thought that they should ride westward in a body. As a compromise Mackenzie, accompanied by sixteen partially-armed men, continued on foot through Vaughan Township towards the Humber Bridge. A scout was sent in advance and brought back word that the bridge was strongly guarded, so they followed the shore of the river some distance northward, had supper at a friendly farmer's, and crossed the Humber on a small foot-bridge. Finally, in an exhausted condition, they reached the friendly home, near Dixie, of Absalom Wilcox, several of whose sons took part in the revolt; it was then two o'clock Friday morning. Concerning his stay at Wilcox's Mackenzie wrote:

"Blankets were hung over the windows to avoid suspicion, food and beds prepared, and while the Tories were carefully searching for us we were sleeping soundly. Next morning (Friday) those who had arms buried them, and after sending to inquire whether a friend a mile below had been dangerously wounded, we agreed to separate and make for the frontier, two and two together".[36]

Mackenzie and Allan Wilcox set off that morning and hurried to Comfort's Mills, near Streetsville, where they had dinner. Comfort had not heard of the revolt; upon the state of affairs being explained to him, however, he offered Mackenzie money to help him escape, but the leader would not take it. A number of farmers in this locality recognised Mackenzie, but all spoke kindly to him. A young Irishman employed in Comfort's mill, the son of Bernard Doherty, drove the two fugitives westward in a wagon towards Sixteen-Mile Creek.[37] As they proceeded along Dundas Street through the Credit Village (Springfield) they noticed the Lieutenant-Governor's proclamation posted at many points, offering £1,000 reward for Mackenzie's capture, and £500 for the apprehension of David Gibson, Samuel Lount, Jesse Lloyd and Silas Fletcher. A few minutes later they were hotly pursued by mounted troops, and Mackenzie took

[36]Lindsey, *op. cit.*, Vol. II, p. 104.
[37]The creeks were early named according to their distance from Burlington, if on the north shore of Lake Ontario, and from Niagara, if on the south.

the reins when the driver became frightened. They found that the bridge over Sixteen-Mile Creek was guarded by a party under Colonel Chalmers, so they were practically surrounded. Jumping from the wagon and asking a labourer the road to Esquesing (to throw their pursuers off the track), the fugitives made for the woods and hid in the thickets while the soldiers combed the district, approaching very close to them at times; in fact Mackenzie says that they owed their escape to a friendly militiaman who saw them but did not divulge their hiding-place. Capture was avoided here only at the cost of great suffering.

"There was but one chance for escape, surrounded as we were, and that was to stem the stream, and cross the swollen creek. We accordingly stripped ourselves naked, and with the surface ice beating against us, and holding our garments over our heads, in a bitter cold December night, buffeted the current and were soon up to our necks. . . . The cold in that creek caused me the most cruel and intense sensation of pain I ever endured, but we got through, though with a better chance of drowning, and the frozen sand on the bank seemed to warm our feet when we once more trod on it. In an hour and half we were under the hospitable roof of one of the innumerable agricultural friends I could then count on in the country."[38]

At this house they were provided with dry clothes and took a short rest. The help Mackenzie everywhere received made him feel that his sufferings were not entirely in vain, and he always had a warm spot in his heart for those who saved his life.

"I had risked much for Canadians, and served them long and as faithfully as I could—and now, when a fugitive, I found them ready to risk life and property to aid me— far more ready to risk the dungeon, by harbouring me, than to accept Sir Francis Bond Head's thousand pounds. The sons and daughters of the Nelson farmer kept a silent

[38]Lindsey, op. cit., Vol. II, p. 108. It is said that Mackenzie escaped arrest at Oakville, at the mouth of Sixteen-Mile Creek, by being dressed in feminine attire; he makes no reference to it, however, in his account of his flight. Samuel Thompson suggests (Reminiscences, pp. 123-4) that the women's clothes he used were those obtained when a lady traveller's portmanteau was taken from the Dundas Street mail-stage on the previous Tuesday by a small body of men under Mackenzie.

watch outside in the cold, while I and my companion slept."[39]

They did not dare to stay long in the neighbourhood, however, so after an hour's rest they continued their flight, crossing Twelve-Mile Creek on a fallen tree about midnight. During that night they were again pursued, and again escaped into the woods. When the soldiers had gone by, the fugitives continued westward, and during the night passed through Wellington Square, finally reaching, half an hour before dawn, the home of a magistrate whom Mackenzie knew. He told them that his premises had been twice searched on the previous day by troops who were scouring the whole countryside for Mackenzie, and he warned them that it would be unsafe to proceed towards Burlington Bay, where large forces were on the look-out for him; consequently Mackenzie and Wilcox separated, believing that each would have a better chance to escape if they travelled singly.

At daybreak it began to snow and, rather than leave tracks, the rebel leader called at the home of another farmer, who offered to hide him in his barn; fortunately, however, Mackenzie chose to conceal himself in a peas-rick on a high knoll, from which he could see all that went on in the vicinity. He crawled under the stack through holes burrowed by the pigs, and rested there, footsore and hungry. During the day there was a great commotion at the farmhouse, and from his hiding-place Mackenzie actually saw the sheriff, Colonel McDonell, at the head of a posse searching all the buildings in the neighbourhood.

When they had gone on to the next house the excited farmer brought Mackenzie some food, and two bottles of hot water to bathe his feet, at the same time expressing the hope that he would leave before there was another visitation of the soldiery. During the night Mackenzie came out, and, with the help of a small boy who acted as guide, reached by a side-path the home of a friend named King, whose farm was located immediately next to Colonel John Chisholm's, the headquarters of his pursuers. The boy did not betray him, though he might easily have done so, for he worked at the Chisholm's.

[39]*Ibid.*, p. 109.

King provided him with a good supper, and after a short rest they set out on foot towards Dundas, passing a few armed men on the road. His guide left Mackenżie at a friend's house, and here the rebel leader obtained a horse and travelled onward, reaching Dundas, his early home, during the night, and passing on into the mountain country above Hamilton. Some Dutch friends warned him to avoid the well-travelled roads, which were all guarded, and this advice probably saved Mackenzie from capture.

Near Ancaster he procured a fresh horse from an old friend, Jacob Rymal, and proceeded along a concession road for a time, until it appeared safer to take to the woods which at that time covered a considerable part of Binbrook and Glanford Townships. With great difficulty he led his horse through several miles of dense forest and tangled underbrush, eventually reaching the solitary hut of a negro, who directed him on his way. He soon approached a small hamlet where, upon entering a house, he was called by name. Remounting his horse and quietly leaving the vicinity, he lost no time in breaking into a gallop at the first turn of the road, and was soon at a farm ten miles distant. Here he was suspected, not of being an escaped rebel, but a horse thief; for his sudden appearance, with his clothes torn and his face scratched, led this farmer, whose name was Waters, to insist on conducting him to one McIntyre, the nearest magistrate.

Mackenzie might have shot Waters, but instead he decided to try the force of argument and to reveal his identity. Upon discussing the grievances of the people of Upper Canada and mentioning his own name in that connection, he learned that the man was rather friendly to Mackenzie than otherwise; so he said to him: "I am an old magistrate, but at present in a situation of some difficulty. If I can satisfy you as to who I am, and why I am here, would you desire to gain the price of any man's blood?" When it was put that way the farmer naturally answered in the negative, and, upon being shown Mackenzie's pocketbook and the initials on his watch, he agreed to keep silent for twenty-four hours, and guided him for some distance on the road to the frontier.[40]

[40]*Ibid.*, p. 116.

It was Sunday morning, and Mackenzie came upon some men on the way to church; he inquired the road, and then, in order not to excite suspicion, proceeded leisurely for some distance, crossed Twenty-Mile Creek a second time a few minutes later, and once more entered the mountain path. Above him was stationed a military guard, and while in sight of this he "moved on very slowly, as if going to meeting, but afterwards used the rowels to some advantage in the way of propellers. Some persons whom I passed on the road I knew, and some I didn't. Many whom I met evidently knew me, and well was it for me that day that I had a good name. I could have been arrested fifty times before I reached Smithville had the Governor's person and proclamation been generally respected".[41]

His troubles were not yet over, however; for unfriendly people who recognised him put soldiers on his track again, and he avoided his pursuers only by turning off the main road, turning sharply again, and putting his horse in the stable of a friend at Smithville. A few minutes later he saw his pursuers dash along the road he had just left.

Mackenzie remained several hours at this farm, and obtained a slight rest and something to eat. With a companion, Samuel Chandler, who was later exiled to Van Diemen's Land, he then continued his flight, crossing the Twenty-Mile Creek, the Welland Canal and the Chippawa River, and reaching Crowland before daylight. Here they abandoned their horses and continued on foot towards the Niagara River, reaching the farm of Captain Samuel McAfee about nine on Monday morning. Breakfast was prepared for him here, but before eating he thought it best to step outside "to see if the coast was clear. Well for me it was that I did so. Old Colonel Kirby, the Custom House officer opposite Black Rock, and his troop of mounted dragoons in their green uniforms and with their carbines ready, were so close upon me, riding up by the bank of the river, that had I not then observed their approach they would have caught me at breakfast.

"Nine men out of ten, in such an emergency, would have hesitated to assist me; and to escape by land was, at that time, evidently impossible. Mr. McAfee lost not a moment—

[41]*Ibid.*, p. 117.

his boat was hauled across the road and launched in the stream with all possible speed—and he and Chandler and I were scarcely afloat in it and out a little way below the bank when the old Tory Colonel and his green-coated troop of horse, with their waving plumes, were parading in front of Mr. McAfee's dwelling.

"How we escaped here is to me almost a miracle. I had resided long in the district, and was known by everybody. A boat was in the river, against official orders; it was near the shore, and the carbines of the military, controlled by the collector, would have compelled us to return, or have killed me for disobedience. . . . Not a few must have seen the whole movement, and yet we were allowed to steer for the head of Grand Island with all the expedition in our power, without interruption; nor was there a whisper said about the matter for many months thereafter. In an hour we were safe on the American shore."[42]

So ended the perilous escape of William Lyon Mackenzie. Through nerve, ingenuity, and dogged perseverance he had saved his life, for he would undoubtedly have shared the fate of Lount and Matthews had he been apprehended. For sheer melodrama his adventures are unparalleled in Canadian history.

[42]*Ibid.*, p. 121.

CHAPTER V

THE ESCAPE OF REBELLION REFUGEES

"Well, God be thanked for these rebels."
WILLIAM SHAKESPEARE: *Henry IV*, Act iii, Sc. 3.

"We rebelled neither against Her Majesty's person nor her Government, but against Colonial misgovernment. . . . We remonstrated, we were derided. . . . We were goaded on to madness, and were compelled to show that we had the spirit of resistance to repel injuries, or to be deemed a captive, degraded and recreant people. We took up arms not to attack others but to defend ourselves."[1]

IN many sections of Upper Canada there was widespread disaffection during the months preceding the outbreak of the Rebellion of 1837. William Lyon Mackenzie had travelled into many parts of the province, particularly in the more recently-settled districts, and had gained many hundreds of adherents by personal contact. There were many Reformers besides Mackenzie who disseminated political literature which, though often exaggerated in tone, was impossible of entire refutation, and usually hit the nail on the head with annoying vehemence:

"The backwoodsman, while he lays the axe to the root of the oak in the forests of Canada, should never forget that a base basswood is growing in this his native land, which, if not speedily girdled, will throw its dark shadows over the country, and blast its best exertions. Look up, reader, and you will see the branches—the Robinson branch, the Powell branch, the Jones branch, the Strachan branch, the Boulton twig, etc. The farmer toils, the merchant toils, the labourer toils, and the Family Compact reap the fruit of their exertions."[2]

The intensity of political feeling in the province may be gauged by the condition in parts of Northumberland County, which may be considered, upon the whole, a loyal section, furnishing many soldiers at Bond Head's call. In

[1] Letter to Lord Durham from Dr. Wolfred Nelson and others confined in jail at Montreal, June 18, 1838.
[2] *Patrick Swift's Almanac* for 1834, quoted in Henry Scadding: *Toronto of Old*. 1873. pp. 105-6.

a letter from Cobourg to Dr. Egerton Ryerson the Rev.
Anson Green said: "I believe that in Haldimand and
Cramahe Townships there are twenty rebels to one sincere
loyalist. Brother Wilson (son of old Father Wilson) says
that his life has been threatened for circulating the petition
you sent down, and others are in a similar condition."[3]

That Mackenzie and his followers had many friends
throughout the province is best attested by the remarkable
escape of hundreds of "Patriots" who were being tracked
by the authorities; in spite of the fact that their names were
learned from the lists which their leader left behind in
Montgomery's Tavern, and that great rewards were offered
for the apprehension of the leaders, and heavy penalties
laid upon those who harboured them,—even under these
difficulties most of the refugees were able to play hide-
and-seek with the military, and eventually reached the
United States and safety.

Some of the more radical leaders of the Reformers
joined Mackenzie early in December, 1837, at Montgomery's
Tavern, on Yonge Street, but disagreement among the chief
men and the lack of a speedy means of communicating
changes in plans lost the "Patriots" a large number of recruits. There were many, too, who hesitated to take the
final step in revolt and remained at home, suspected by their
loyal neighbours. After Mackenzie's defeat some who had
been luke-warm supporters turned loyalists, while othe
whose sympathies had been more outspoken were subjected
to ill-treatment by the emissaries of the Family Compact, or
its supporters, for there were not a few who were only too
glad to combine revenge and plunder with the duty of in-
vestigating suspicious characters and apprehending refugees. Many Reformers consequently took to the woods or
went into hiding, a strong factor in their persecution frequently being public opinion in their own locality; while
the government policy of terrorism and the general feeling
of unrest incident to the Rebellion led numerous farmers to
sell their land and leave the country. In some districts the
wanton destruction of property was such that the statement
of an American who followed MacNab's punitive expedition

[3] Anson Green to Egerton Ryerson, November 16, 1837. See Egerton
Ryerson: *The Story of My Life*. 1883. p. 176.

through the London District, "The blight of the destroying angle is visible wherever you go,"[4] was not an exaggeration.

Very little was needed to encourage a whole countryside to go rebel-hunting. It was a rumour emanating from Peterborough that William Lyon Mackenzie was in hiding at Lindsay which led to the first of four armed "invasions" of the latter village. Watson Kirkconnell tells the story in his admirable *Victoria County Centennial History*:

"A number of farmers who were with their ox-teams at Purdy's Mill one clear, cool evening were startled to hear a volley of muskets and to see a column of about 300 armed men with a large flag descending the steep river-bank to the north. When the advance guard got on the bridge cheers were raised, trumpets sounded, kettle-drums rattled, the flag waved, and another mighty salvo of musket-fire let off into the upper air. The villagers, some thirty men, women and children in all, rushed from their cabins to see what was happening, and found that their visitors were a detachment of Peterborough militia under Colonel Alexander McDonnell, searching for Mackenzie. As it was too late for the contingent to return home that night, they bivouacked in and around Britton's Tavern, it soon did not matter much which.

"William Purdy had been speaking rather plainly against the Family Compact, and Major Murphy took this opportunity of laying information against him. The miller was accordingly arrested and taken to Cobourg jail. Here he lay without trial for some time, but was at last liberated and told to go home and mind his own business. As a result of this unpleasant experience Purdy decided not to live in Lindsay any longer, and removed to Bath. Of his two sons, Jesse, who had had a severe attack of fever and ague, went with him, while Hazard remained in charge of the mill."[5]

Indignities of a type which remind one of modern college initiations or fraternity "stunts" were sometimes perpetrated by ultra-loyal mobs upon citizens whose political

[4]Toronto *Palladium of British America*, January 8, 1838. See also Charles S. Buck: *Old Sparta and its Neighbourhood*, pp. 51 et seq. This work, the result of a great deal of research, has not yet been published, but its author kindly made the manuscript available to the writer; the pages cited are of the typewritten sheets of the MS.

[5]Watson Kirkconnell: *Victoria County Centennial History*. 1921. pp. 94-5.

activities were disapproved. A certain Mackenzie sympathiser who lived near Cobourg was somewhat more candid than discreet, and as a result he nearly lost his life. A number of citizens decided that they would ship him off to the United States, for whose government he had often expressed admiration. Obtaining a china crate they placed him in it, packed straw around him, and marched towards the harbour. Here someone suggested throwing the crate into the lake, and it was accordingly done. He was not allowed to die, however, but was hauled out before he had been suffocated or drowned. His bath was no doubt intended to cool him off politically as well as physically. Such events sometimes occur in times of great excitement, and this is their only excuse.

The first Rebellion refugee of importance was Dr. John Rolph, a man who had served in the militia during the early part of the War of 1812, and who was early so friendly with that uncompromising loyalist, Colonel Talbot, that he was one of the originators of the Talbot Anniversary celebration. In later years he removed to Dundas, and then to York, giving up his legal practice at that time and restricting his activities to the medical profession, in which he soon reached a position of eminence. He had previously become prominent as a Reformer, and had gradually drifted into the position of partially supporting Mackenzie.

When Dr. Thomas D. Morrison was arrested on the Wednesday morning previous to the battle at Montgomery's a medical student who resided with Rolph rushed to him with the news, and the Doctor immediately decided to escape while there was still a chance. He showed excellent judgment in effecting his departure from York. The student who had informed him of the danger was soon riding westward on Lot (Queen) Street, while Rolph followed leisurely on foot, meeting Chief Justice Robinson on the way. When he reached the point where Dundas Street turns northward he found his young friend awaiting him as had been pre-arranged, and without delay Rolph mounted the horse and proceeded along Dundas Street some twelve miles without molestation.

As he approached the River Credit he encountered a company of loyalist volunteers en route to the Capital. The commander of the troop demanded his destination, and once more the Doctor was equal to the emergency, producing a letter which he had received only the day before requesting his presence at the bedside of a sister seriously ill. This was deemed satisfactory and Rolph was allowed to proceed; but not long afterwards the officer became suspicious and sent two men in pursuit of the fugitive; these soon overtook him and forced him to return with them to Port Credit. Rolph was naturally agitated during his detention, but luck was with him, for a former student of his, Dr. James Mitchell of Dundas, succeeded in persuading the authorities that it was absurd to suppose that Rolph would support Mackenzie, and he was soon once more on his way westward. Mitchell conferred a further benefit by exchanging horses with Rolph, and the Doctor was shortly at the house of Asa Davis, near the village of Wellington Square, Nelson Township, Mackenzie being destined to stop at the same place on the following Saturday during his flight after the battle of Montgomery's Farm. Davis invited him to spend the night there, but he thought it best to push on towards the frontier after an hour's rest. By riding all night he reached the Niagara River near Queenston shortly after daybreak, and soon effected a crossing to the United States, where he remained for five years.[6]

By far the greater number of refugees, however, were those who had taken part in the short battle of Montgomery's Tavern on December 7th, or in other rebel activities, and whose lives and liberty depended upon their evading the authorities. After the skirmish Samuel Lount fled northward on horseback, and by following the second fence behind Price's house he reached a side-line a mile farther north. He then proceeded eastward to Yonge Street, encountering fleeing rebels everywhere. Some of these who had obtained horses joined him, and they stopped for a brief debate on ways and means to escape. As they were making plans dense masses of smoke from the burning tavern arose before their eyes, and they were impelled to break off their parley abruptly and scatter in all directions but southward, most of them going north on

[6]The most complete account of Rolph's experiences is to be found in J. C. Dent: *The Story of the Upper Canadian Rebellion.* 1885. Vol. II, pp. 112-14.

Yonge Street. Mackenzie was not a member of this party, but he, too, running northward over a ploughed field in the rear of Price's house, was soon far from the scene of battle. He came up with Lount between Shepard's Mills and the Humber River, but it was deemed prudent to separate, and each fugitive used his own judgment as to the best way to escape capture.[7]

Lount fled to the northern part of the Township of King, where he had to spend two nights in the woods without shelter. His sole companion was Edward Kennedy, and the two made their way westward from one place of hiding to another. Several times they were almost captured, and they continually suffered untold miseries. On the night of Saturday, December 9th, they took refuge in the home of David Oliphant, a Radical who lived in Eramosa Township; thence they travelled to the vicinity of Guelph, and on through Dumfries, being secreted several days in an almost impenetrable swamp near Galt. They continued their flight to a farmhouse near Glenmorris, where Lount narrowly escaped capture, running out of the back door as a local magistrate entered at the front.

The fugitives proceeded through Burford and Oakland Townships to the village of Waterford, being concealed for a time in a hay-mow near Grover's Tavern. Militia were watching for them everywhere, and they would probably have been captured on several occasions had not the law imposed the penalties of treason upon those convicted merely of harbouring felons. After having remained hidden for two days near Grover's they stole away by night to Mount Pleasant, where they were for over thirty hours concealed in a straw-stack. They next entered West Flamborough, and here they separated for a time, Kennedy taking shelter with his children near Dundas, while Lount was secreted in the houses of Obed Everett, Squire Hyslop, John Hathaway and others. Only the loyalty of their friends and their own unceasing vigilance kept them from capture on numerous occasions.

They were soon forced to flee westward again, being hidden for a time in the house of one Latshaw, near Paris,

[7]It has been thought best to describe Mackenzie's escape at the close of the chapter on the Battle of Montgomery's Farm. See Chapter IV of Section V.

who also assisted in their conveyance by night to the vicinity of Simcoe. Exhausted by fatigue, anxiety and exposure, they determined to attempt to cross Lake Erie. Proceeding to Long Point they embarked in a small boat owned by one Deas, a French-Canadian sympathiser who lived near by. Deas and a boy accompanied them in the frail craft, perhaps for the purpose of bringing the boat back after landing the refugees on the Pennsylvania shore. The hardships they had experienced before were as nothing compared with those which they were about to endure.

"For two days and two nights they buffeted the waves in a vain endeavour to make the opposite shore. Their sufferings were terrible. The bitter blast seemed to penetrate their very marrow, and they had but little clothing to protect them from its fury. Sleep was out of the question, as the weather was rough, and their united efforts were required to manage the boat and keep it clear of water. They were in constant danger of being swamped. Several times the waves passed over them, drenching them to the skin, and chilling them with a chillness which seemed more horrible than death itself. They likewise suffered the pangs of hunger, for their only provision consisted of a piece of pork, which was soon frozen."[8]

At last, when they were almost exhausted, it seemed as if they had not suffered in vain, for the welcome southern shore was near at hand; but fate had decreed that they should not escape. A strong southerly wind suddenly arose, and, though the weakened fugitives fought against it with a renewed vigour born of desperation, they were gradually forced backward into the lake, "and we drifted to the mouth of the Grand River, where we would have frozen to death if a farmer who had watched us drifting on the lake had not taken us prisoners, with the aid of a party".[9] It was suspected that they were smugglers, and they were consequently conveyed to Dunnville, and thence to Chippawa, where they were identified. Kennedy was lodged in the Hamilton jail, while Lount was imprisoned in Toronto, convicted of

---

[8]Dent, *op. cit.*, Vol. II, p. 143.
[9]A narrative of his experiences was published by Kennedy at Dundas in 1849; this rare pamphlet is quoted in Dent, *op cit.*, Vol. II, p. 143 fn. The name of the farmer who effected the capture was Overtrott. He received the reward that had been offered—and also the everlasting dislike of his neighbours.

treason, and, with Peter Matthews, executed on April 12, 1838, at the old jail near the corner of King and Toronto Streets.

Colonel Anthony Van Egmond, a Dutch officer who had seen service under Napoleon, also made his way northward when the flight commenced. Some four miles beyond Montgomery's, near the Golden Lion Inn, Mackenzie and Fletcher came up with him, and were told that Lount was a short distance ahead. Van Egmond was too fatigued to proceed farther and sought shelter on a neighbouring farm, the others continuing their flight by different routes. Van Egmond thought he was safe, but a detachment of militia discovered his hiding-place and conveyed him to Toronto; there, (Mackenzie says), he was placed "in a cell so cold that they had very soon to take him to the hospital—on his way to the grave".[10] A number of other insurgents who had participated in the skirmish at Montgomery's also died in hospital, while Silas Fletcher, Jesse Lloyd and Nelson Gorham succeeded in reaching the United States a short time after the collapse of the Rebellion.

Peter Matthews, who had been detailed to lead sixty men towards the Don Bridge with the object of burning it and stopping the mail-stage from the east, was not long at liberty. His force robbed the mail, and about noon on Thursday crossed the bridge and advanced some distance along King Street into the city; but a detachment of militia under George P. Ridout was dispatched against him from the City Hall, and the rebels beat a hasty retreat, attempting to fire the bridge as they retired. Mrs. Ross, a lady who lived in the vicinity, claims to have quenched the fire, though at the expense of a bullet in her knee.[11] A tavern at the eastern end of the bridge, together with the adjacent stable, driving-shed and toll-gate, was totally destroyed, and during the interchange of bullets the hostler of the inn was fatally shot in the throat.

As one of Matthews' objects was to draw the loyalist force away from the city he did not allow Ridout's men to

[10]Charles Lindsey: *Life and Times of William Lyon Mackenzie*. 1862. Vol. II, p. 103.
[11]See Allan McLean Howard's narrative, appended to Chapter XXIV of Samuel Thompson's *Reminiscences of a Canadian Pioneer*. 1884. p. 133. The story appears to be authentic, for Dr. Widmer of Toronto extracted the bullet from Mrs. Ross' knee!

overtake his force, and was half a mile away when they reached the bridge. Early in the afternoon the news of the defeat at Montgomery's reached these "Patriots", and the rebel band broke up into small knots and took to the woods in different directions. Matthews himself, with some of his neighbours from Pickering, "spent Thursday night, Friday, and a part of Saturday forenoon hiding behind logs and in clumps of bushes in the several ravines which now form part of the picturesque suburb of Rosedale.

"On Saturday evening, a little before six o'clock, they reached the house occupied by John Duncan, on the south half of lot number twenty-five in the third concession of East York, near the town-line between East York and Markham. They were eleven in number, including their leader. They would have been sure of a warm welcome from Mr. Duncan under any circumstances, for he was a Radical of the Radicals; but their welcome was none the less warm from the circumstances that they were well-nigh starved, and stood greatly in need of his assistance. A supper was speedily prepared for them, whereof they heartily partook. . . . 'I know my doom if I am taken', remarked Matthews upon rising from the table,—at the same time drawing his hand significantly across his throat.

"They next required a few hours' repose, after which they intended to make for Pickering, where they hoped to be able to secrete themselves until the storm had blown over, or, at the worst, until they could escape to the States. Beds were made up for most of them on the floor of the principal room of the house. No soporifics were needed to woo them to repose, for probably not one of them had slept for ten consecutive minutes since the previous Wednesday night, and even such fitful snatches as they had been enabled to take had been in the exposed woods and on the cold, hard ground. A small bedroom adjoining was assigned to Matthews, who slept soundly almost as soon as his head touched the pillow. The members of the family sat up, but without keeping any light except such as was afforded by the burning logs in the fireplace."[12]

A heavy snow-storm came on during the evening, an unfortunate circumstance for fugitive rebels, who could

[12]Reminiscences of William Duncan, as recorded in Dent, *op. cit.*, Vol. II, p. 145-6.

easily be tracked by government emissaries. Those at Duncan's were not fated to be caught in this manner, however, for a little before midnight the watchers were disturbed by voices without; a quick glance through the windows showed that the house was surrounded by armed men. The insurgents in the large room were immediately aroused from sleep and a loud knock at the door showed that the fifty or sixty men had no intention of remaining outside. Some of the more impetuous of the rebels were inclined to fight, and shooting followed the entrance of the militia, several persons being slightly wounded.

Matthews was awakened only by the entrance of a militiaman into his room, and the pressure of the muzzle of a rifle against his breast; but the rebel leader was a large and powerful man, and pushed away his armed assailant as one might brush a fly from his sleeve, the soldier striking the opposite wall as though he had been hurled from a catapult. But others rushed in and threw themselves upon him, and further resistance was useless. The insurgents were handcuffed and marched out into the keen winter air, one of them, who had been wounded in the leg, being forced to tramp with the others over twelve miles of rough road to Toronto jail.

David Gibson underwent his share of sufferings, but was fortunate enough eventually to escape. When the skirmish at Montgomery's resulted in the rebels' precipitate retreat, Gibson, who appears to have been in charge of a number of loyalist prisoners detained in or near the tavern, decided upon their release. When this had been accomplished he separated from the other fugitives and struck eastward by devious ways through Scarborough and Pickering Townships. After several days and nights of hardship he reached the home of a friend near the village of Oshawa, and there he remained between four and five weeks, most of the time being spent in a recess in the interior of a straw-stack. A number of refugees were concealed in the vicinity, and, arrangements having been made by their friends, Gibson and several others crossed Lake Ontario in an open boat in January, 1838.

Some men who had taken no part in the Rebellion were persecuted as severely as those who had, a condition due

to the inflamed passions of the times. Marshall S. Bidwell
was one of these unfortunates, and he was forced into exile
by the government, largely because many suspected him of
complicity.[13]   Lieutenant-Governor Head gave him the
chance to retire from the country, and Bidwell left Toronto
on the steamer *Transit* for Niagara, crossing over into the
United States on the 10th of December.

Dr. Thomas D. Morrison's case was somewhat similar,
though he appeared in court on a charge of high treason.
There was no doubt that he was a leading Reformer, but
his complicity in the Rebellion was not definitely proven.
Mackenzie's published account of a meeting in July of
"twelve leading Reformers", on which occasion the plot to
rebel was hatched, was almost enough to implicate Morrison
and send him to the gallows; but the defence counsel successfully broke down the evidence against him, and after
lengthy consideration the jury finally returned a verdict of
"Not Guilty". Morrison had narrowly escaped the fate of
Lount and Matthews, however, and he received a hint that
another charge was being prepared against him; so he
chose the better part of valour and hastened to the United
States, joining his friend, Dr. Rolph, in Rochester.[14] In
1843 he gladly availed himself of the opportunity to return
to Upper Canada.

John Montgomery, owner of the hotel which had been
the rendezvous of the main body of insurgents, was among
the Reformers who were captured soon after the skirmish
but who effected their escape. With a number of others
he was taken in the *Sir Robert Peel* to Fort Henry, Kingston,
the prisoners being in charge of Sheriff Jarvis and a guard
of negroes. The men formed a plot to seize the vessel
en route, but the scheme was abandoned. Montgomery was
sentenced to death, but his sentence was later commuted
to transportation for life. After being at Fort Henry for
some time these prisoners turned their thoughts from the
hope of clemency to the possibility of escape, and formed a
committee of prisoners to make the arrangements. By the
use of a disc nail and a piece of iron ten inches long they

[13]See Note 33 of Section V, Chapter IV. A full account of the
negotiations resulting in Bidwell's banishment may be found in
Dent. *op. cit.*, Vol. II, pp. 159-174.
[14]See Dent, *op. cit.*, Vol. II, pp. 252-5, and his notes at the end of
Chapter XIX (Vol. II, pp. 20 *et seq.*).

laboriously loosened the mortar of a wall four and one-half feet thick. The stage was well set, for the mortar was hidden in a wood-pile, and the noise of the work was smothered at times by two men "who, apparently for their amusement, ... were, with shovel and tongs, beating the stove with all their might, and eliciting thereby roars of laughter from their companions"; Montgomery, meanwhile, was reading the Bible and exhorting his fellow-prisoners to reflect upon the seriousness of the position in which they found themselves.

Between Tuesday and Sunday a hole large enough to crawl through had been made. The prisoners urged the keeper, (who had been married only two or three days before), to accompany his wife to church instead of giving them their daily airing; the same custodian very agreeably sent the men all the biscuit he had in the canteen, and allowed them to hang up blankets, supposedly to keep out mosquitoes but in reality to screen the final preparations for the jail delivery. The escape was exciting:

"When the guard beat the evening tattoo and descended from the ramparts we commenced our escape. We reached the sally port in safety; but here I had the misfortune to fall into the pit and break my leg. One of my companions descended and took my hand, and we were pulled up by the rest. We had decided to be called by numbers, and when we had succeeded in scaling the wall, which we did during a fearful storm, we found No. 10, J. G. Parker, missing. . . . This was a serious defection. Parker was the only man amongst us who knew anything of Kingston, and to his knowledge we had trusted for guidance after leaving the fort. It was a fearful night of storm and lightning, but we decided to take down towards the river, and when daylight came to take to the woods."

Fourteen men made up the party, but it was decided to split up into smaller knots to make detection less likely. Montgomery's group, four in number, finally obtained a boat and crossed to Long Island, avoiding a government vessel sent in search of them. The people on the island were unfriendly, but the refugees carried their boat across, "which was very difficult to do with my broken leg, but I carried paddles and other articles. With great pain, and in a state of exhaustion, we at length succeeded in launching our boat and proceeded to what we felt sure was the mainland. On arriving here we knelt down and thanked God for our safety, and earnestly prayed for that of our companions.

"We soon found, however, that we were again on an island. Re-entering our boat almost famished, our slender provisions (two biscuits a day since leaving the fort) exhausted, we started for Vincent, but were obliged to put ashore, being unable to manage the boat. We pulled her up and went to a house near the shore, and there learned that we were on American ground."

The refugees soon succeeded in obtaining conveyance by boat to Cape Vincent, their conductor being agreeable enough to throw up his hat and give three hearty cheers for the "Patriots"! Montgomery states that "great sympathy and attention were shown us. A public dinner, largely attended, was given in our honour." When they arrived at Watertown they were joined by other groups of escaped prisoners, only two of the party, Watson and Parker, having been recaptured by the Canadian soldiery. They were all hidden by sympathisers until it was known that the Governor of New York State refused to surrender them to the British Government. Thereupon they went on their way rejoicing, though Montgomery was soon after, while in Rochester, knocked down by a team of horses; his skull was fractured and he was unconscious for several weeks, but eventually fully recovered.[15]

Dr. Charles Duncombe, M.P.P., a Rebellion leader in the London District who had taken part in the demonstration at Scotland, in Oakland Township, fled from his pursuers and hid for several weeks wherever he could obtain shelter. A "Patriot" writer states that "after six weeks' hiding in

[15]The quotations referring to Montgomery's escape are from his narrative of his experiences, which may be found in Lindsey, op. cit., Vol. II, Appendix H, pp. 369-73. In 1843 he was pardoned and returned to Upper Canada, erected a new tavern on Yonge Street with the compensation he received under the terms of the Rebellion Losses Act, and survived to a patriarchal age, dying on October 31, 1879, in his 96th year. Those who escaped from Fort Henry at the same time as Montgomery were Edward Kennedy, Wilson Read, Thomas Tracy, Thomas Shepard, John Marr, John Stewart, Stephen Bird Brophy, Michael Shepard, Walter Case, John Anderson and Gilbert Fields Morden.

cellars, dodging in woods and swamps, and suffering every
hardship and privation a person could endure and live,
through the interposition of a kind Providence and the assistance of friends he arrived at Detroit, a mere skeleton".[16]
The same writer, who is not always dependable in the
matter of accuracy, describes how two other leaders, Henry
Fisher and Jesse Paulding, were "sixty-four days in the
woods, the snow knee-deep, before they effected their
escape; during five of which they subsisted on one small
cracker each".[17]

Joshua Doan's experiences were similar to many another
"Patriot" who took part in the activities in this district. He
was for a time concealed in a log granary on Ephraim
Haight's farm, near Sparta, Yarmouth Township, and
Haight put his pursuers off the track and enabled Doan to
escape capture. Samuel Mills was concealed by his father-
in-law, Abner Chase, a recess between the staircase and the
chimney providing a retreat until the hue and cry was over.
One refugee adopted a novel means of preventing his foot-
prints in the snow from being followed, for he walked backwards to his hiding-place in the woods, and his tracks
were consequently rather misleading! Other men, among
them Caleb Kipp and David Harvey, avoided detection by
one subterfuge or another, their friends co-operating by
ingenious schemes to avert the eyes of the soldiery from
places of concealment.[18]

The most extensive escape of refugees is that described
by Thomas Conant, whose grandfather, Roger Conant, had
settled in Darlington Township, Durham County, in 1794.
Roger's son Daniel was the owner of a fleet of schooners
engaged in the trade in lumber, flour and potash with
Niagara and other Lake Ontario ports, and one of his ships,
the *Industry*, was laid up for the winter in a harbour
near Oshawa in December, 1837. The owner was approached by many rebellion refugees and their friends, who
begged him to convey them across the lake, as life was un-

[16]D. McLeod: *A Brief Review of the Settlement of Upper Canada* . . .
       1841. p. 194.
[17]*Ibid.*, p. 195.
[18]For the persecution and plundering of Reformers in the London
       District, and the escape of refugees in 1837-38 (particularly
       those resident in Yarmouth Township), see Buck, *op. cit.*,
       pp. 49-58.

bearable for them in Canada. At first he refused, for he did not wish to involve his family in any trouble which might result; he considered, also, that the time of year made sailing very risky.

So great was the desire of these "Patriots" to escape further persecution that one of them paddled a canoe across Lake Ontario, leaving the Canadian coast near Oshawa about ten o'clock in the evening and arriving on the American shore, near Orchard Beach, at four o'clock the next afternoon. This eighteen-hour trip was the more remarkable because the bow of the canoe had been entirely rotted away, and had to be kept high in the air by placing a heavy stone in the stern.

The refugees renewed their entreaties, and finally Daniel Conant decided to encounter the dangers which appeared certain to follow an attempt to navigate a schooner in winter. The commencement of the adventurous voyage presaged success.

"On the night of the 27th of December, 1837, the little vessel of 100 feet in length quietly slipped from her moorings, and sailed close along the shore of Lake Ontario. It was a bright moonlight night, still, but very cold. Every mile or so she would back her mainsail, and lay to at a signal of a light upon shore that a canoe might put off to the vessel, bearing a Patriot from his hiding in the forest to the side of the boat. . . . Some forty stops, and forty different canoes were paddled out to the vessel and forty Patriots transferred, panting for the land of liberty across Lake Ontario, to the south of them sixty miles or so.

"A fine sailing breeze blew off shore, and, hoisting sail and winging out mainsail and foresail, nothing could bid fairer for a quick and prosperous voyage; and the land of liberty seemed almost gained. Lying upon blankets in the bottom of the vessel were the Patriots, with the hatches closed down tight on account of the intense cold. Quickly and gaily the little vessel sped on, with anxious hearts beating below."[19]

In the morning the mouth of the river at Oswego could be seen in the distance. Despair succeeded joy in the hearts of all when it was seen, as they approached nearer, that a

[19]Thomas Conant: *Upper Canada Sketches.* 1898. pp. 69-70.

large mass of floating ice had been driven into the bay by the same wind which had so fortunately carried the ship across the lake. The men worked valiantly to force a passage through the three miles of ice in front of the harbour; but their exertions were in vain, for after almost superhuman efforts they had proceeded only a quarter of a mile when darkness forced a stop.

During the night the wind fell and the cold increased, so that by morning the ship was firmly frozen in. When they saw what had happened their only hope was that the lower temperature would also make the ice thick enough to enable them to walk to shore. It was found, however, that it was only two inches thick, hardly sufficient to bear a man's weight. But, fearing that the ice-floe might break up at any time, they decided to make the attempt to gain the shore.

Each man took a spar or pole from the ship to aid him in his hazardous journey. Before they had proceeded far one man broke through the ice; the others helped him out, and the grim procession continued. Overcoats, gripsacks and other valuables were thrown away by the refugees as they became too exhausted to carry them farther. When thinner ice was reached a man fell through every few minutes, and he was encrusted with ice soon after being hauled out by his companions; it was not long before the entire group looked like human icicles. Many were on the verge of collapse, but the hope of freedom enabled them to continue. At last, as they approached the shore from which hundreds of Americans were shouting encouragement, it was seen that the pack ice was commencing to move out into the lake.

"Already it had parted from the shore streak of ice and left a space of open water now seven feet wide. Jump it they could not, because their clothes were frozen so hard that they could not spring, and, besides, the ice on the other side of the open space was not thick enough to hold one alighting after the jump. Their last hope sank within them. Death stared them in the face; their wives and friends in Canada would see them no more. Every minute added to the gulf of water between them and the shore ice.[20]

[20]Ibid., pp. 73-4.

From Thomas Conant's *Upper Canada Sketches*   E. S. Shrapnel

REBELLION REFUGEES FROZEN IN AT OSWEGO, 1837
This was the most notable escape of "Patriots" of 1837

Public Archives of Canada   Coke Smyth

ENGAGEMENT IN THE THOUSAND ISLANDS, 1838

From Lindsey's *Life and Times of William Lyon Mackenzie.* 1862   Adrian Sharp

From *A Narrative of the Adventures and Sufferings of Captain Daniel D. Heustis.*
1847

TWO REPRESENTATIONS OF THE BATTLE OF THE WINDMILL

Fortunately one of the sailors who had from the start acted as leader had carried with him a plank in place of a spar. Bridging the open space with his board he called upon all to follow him for their lives, and with a last effort they gained the shore and freedom.

The ship *Industry* was lost and became a wreck. The refugees it had carried across the lake remained for some time in the United States; but after the violent feelings aroused by the Rebellion had subsided all returned to Upper Canada, where many of them occupied prominent positions in later years.

The first proclamation offering amnesty to participants in the Rebellion was issued in October, 1838, and excepted those who had been indicted at the assizes. The men to whom it applied were assured that they might "return to their homes, and that no prosecution for or on account of any offence by them done or committed, and in any way related to or connected with the said revolt, shall be instituted or continued, but that all such prosecutions shall terminate and be forever void, hereby freely offering . . . . our gracious amnesty, pardon and forbearance for and on account of such offence".[21] Those who were excepted from the effects of the proclamation had been indicted at the four special assizes at Toronto, London, Hamilton and Niagara, and numbered twenty-seven, twenty, six and five in the respective districts. They were charged with the crime of high treason, and four proclamations were issued the same day calling upon them to surrender for trial or stand attainted; but, needless to say, not one gave himself up to the mercy of the authorities.[22]

[21]The proclamation was issued by Sir George Arthur on October 22, 1838.

[22]Those who were listed in these proclamations follow:

    (1) At Toronto: John Rolph, physician, William Lyon Mackenzie, printer, John Mantack, labourer, of Toronto; Silas Fletcher, Richard Graham, Jeremiah Graham, Levi Parsons, Henry Stiles, William Fletcher, Daniel Fletcher, of East Gwillimbury; Joseph Borden, Edmond Quirk, Thomas Brown, of King Township; David Gibson, David McCarty, Seth McCarty, Nelson Gorham, Alexander McLeod, Cornelius Willis, and Erastus Clark, of the Township of York; Landon Wurtz of Pickering. James Marshall of Whitchurch; Alem Marr, Joseph Clarkson, Dudley Wilcox, of Markham; Jesse Lloyd of Lloyd Town, and Aaron Munshaw of Vaughan.

    (2) At London: Charles Duncombe of Burford; James Dennis, Peter Delong, Orsimus B. Clark, Abraham Sutton, of Norwich;

No general amnesty[23] of all offences arising out of the events of 1837-38 was proclaimed until February 1, 1849, when a measure was signed by the Governor-General, Lord Elgin, after it had passed unanimously in both Houses. In April of the same year the Rebellion Losses Bill was passed, providing for the payment of claims arising out of the Rebellion in Lower Canada; a similar act had been approved for Upper Canada almost nine years earlier, the proclamation giving the Royal assent to it being issued by Sir George Arthur on October 22, 1840. William Lyon Mackenzie, and most of the other leaders who still remained in exile, returned to Canada soon after the general amnesty, and they found that the policies which they had long advocated and had fought for in 1837-38 were then in large measure a reality; for responsible government had been achieved in their absence—a culmination which would undoubtedly have been more difficult (if not impossible) had they been present during the years of political turmoil out of which it was born.[24]

Eliakim Malcolm, James Malcolm, of Oakland; Lyman Davis of Malahide; Henry Fisher, Norris Humphrey, Jesse Paulding, Samuel Edison the younger, of Bayham; Pelham C. Teeple and Elisha Hall of Oxford West; Joel P. Doan, John Talbot, George Lawton and Solomon Hawes, of Yarmouth; Moses Chapman Nickerson of Woodhouse, and John Massacre of Townsend.

(3) At Hamilton: George Alexander Clark, John Vanarnam, of Brantford Township; Michael Marcellus Mills, merchant, and George Washington Case, of Hamilton; Joseph Fletcher and Angus McKenzie of Nasagaweya Township.

(4) At Niagara: Alonzo Merriman, Aaron Winchester, David Jennings and Chester Jillet, of Pelham; and Thomas Lambert of Gainsborough.

[23]During 1843 Dr. Duncombe, Dr. Rolph, Dr. Morrison, David Gibson, Nelson Gorham and John Montgomery each received a pardon under the Great Seal for complicity in the Rebellion, and all except Dr. Duncombe availed themselves of the privilege of returning to Upper Canada. Rolph and Morrison resumed the practice of medicine in Toronto, Gibson returned to his farm on Yonge Street, Gorham to his home at Newmarket, and Montgomery built a new tavern on the site of the old. (See Note 15, supra.)

[24]The most complete roll of participants in the rebel activities of 1837-8, or those suspected of complicity, is to be found in Lindsey's Life of William Lyon Mackenzie. Appendix I contains the names of all persons "arrested in Upper Canada, and placed in confinement in the prisons of Toronto and other places in the province on a charge of insurrection or treason; the dates of their arrest and discharge; and, if tried, whether by court-martial or civil courts, with the result of such trials severally, from the 5th of December, 1837, to the 1st of November, 1838. At that time twenty-seven were still in

custody." (See Vol. II, pp. 373-398.) The total of this list is 824; and, in addition to the fifty-eight refugees listed above in the four proclamations (See Note 22), there were three others, Jacob Rymal, Joshua Winn and Joshua G. Doan, against whom indictments for high treason had been found, but who had left the country. Of these the first two were from the Home District and the last-named from the London District, Rymal being one of those who had assisted Mackenzie to escape. Joshua Doan was later captured while armed near Sodom, Norwich Township, and he was executed on February 6, 1839. Besides those imprisoned for various terms in Canadian jails there were about one hundred men, including a large number of American members of Hunters' Lodges, who were exiled to Van Diemen's Land (Tasmania), where many of them died amid the terrible conditions of that remote prison colony. Upon the whole, however, the published lists provide but a small proportion of the names of the disaffected, as there were undoubtedly several thousand who were at one time or another "sworn Patriots", but who either were never apprehended or were immediately released during the course of the various rebel activities of 1837-38. Under competent leaders possessed of skill in organisation and tactics the Rebellion of '37 would not have been a fiasco.

CHAPTER VI

THE BATTLE OF WINDMILL POINT, PRESCOTT, 1838

THE STARS OF CANADA

"How fearless is the Patriot's eye;
Nor quails when angry tyrants rave,
And noble 'tis to fight and die,
And fill a freeman's honoured grave.
In such a cause Heav'n smiles above,
To take the children of its love."[1]

WINDMILL POINT, near Prescott in the County of Grenville, is noted for the obstinate defence of four days which was made there, in November, 1838, by insurgents from the United States belonging to a secret society known as the Hunters. The name signified that the members of the lodges were seeking a republican form of government for Canadians, having been deluded into the belief that on their arrival the populace would rise to their support. In the oath which was taken by each Hunter was included the promotion and defence of Republican institutions and ideas throughout the world, and "especially never to rest till all the tyrants of Britain cease to have any dominion or footing whatever in North America".[2]

A convention of the lodges of Ohio and Michigan was held at Cleveland during September, 1838; there a "Republican Government of Upper Canada" was formed, with numerous officials and a long list of officers from "Commander-in-Chief" L. V. Bierce downwards. A Republican Bank was also established by this elaborate secret organisation. There were at least four degrees taken by the Hunters, each including a lengthy oath. They were known to the members as the Snowshoe, the Beaver, the Master Hunter and the Patriot Hunter; of these, privates used the first, commissioned officers two, field officers three, and commanders-in-chief four or more, but all members took the four degrees whether they used them or not. The

[1]Quoted from the Lewiston *Telegraph*, in the Swanton, Vermont, *North American*, May 15, 1839.
[2]See Charles Lindsey: *Life and Times of William Lyon Mackenzie.* 1862. Vol. II, p. 199 fn.

lodges are said to have numbered 1,174, with 80,000 members, and $300,000 at their disposal.

William Lyon Mackenzie was not a member of the organisation, but he was unofficially kept informed of events. He took no direct part in the Hunters' activities, though among other political addresses which he delivered in the United States was one on February 12, 1828, to the citizens of Ogdensburg, later a centre for the raid of Hunters upon Prescott. In fact Canadian refugees, or "Patriots" as they called themselves, held only minor positions in the lodges. It would appear that the members were almost all poor men, many of them young and adventurous, who hoped to improve their condition financially and otherwise by joining the organisation. Those later engaged in the expeditions against Canada were promised 160 acres of land in the country which they hoped to conquer, as well as a cash bounty of $20 each.

During the summer of 1838 there were several disturbances on the St. Lawrence River due to the activity of members of these lodges. The most important of these raids on Canadian territory occurred at midnight on May 30th, when an attack was made on Wells' Island, and the Canadian steamship *Sir Robert Peel* destroyed by marauders. Small vessels were thereupon equipped by the Canadian Government to resist future attacks and to patrol the upper St. Lawrence.

The man in charge of the Prescott expedition of Hunters, "General" J. W. Bierge (or Birge), seems to have been a coward with little or no organising ability. It appears that he assumed command without the approval or knowledge of Bierce. Canadian spies were aware of all the activities of the organisation, and kept the authorities posted concerning developments. During the first ten days of November the Hunters were secretly concentrating at Syracuse, Oswego, Sackett's Harbour and Watertown for an attack on Prescott. They were told by their leaders that nine-tenths of the people of Canada and three-fourths of the troops would rise to their support immediately upon their arrival in the country. The Hunters had control of at least nine steamships on Lake Erie, and of several on Lake Ontario,

including the *United States,* the largest American steamer
on the lake. It appears that the attack on Prescott[3] was
intended to be in concert with others along the border, both
east and west, but the plans miscarried.

On the morning of Sunday, November 11th, about 400
Hunters embarked at Sackett's Harbour in the *United
States,* which then proceeded eastward. The force was considerably augmented at Cape Vincent, French Creek and
Millen's Bay, and at the last-named point two schooners, the
Charlotte of Toronto and the *Charlotte of Oswego,* were
taken in tow by the steamer, whose captain is said to have
been paid $100 by one Daniel George for his share in the
expedition.[4] Most of the men were transferred to the
schooners, which were also loaded with provisions, arms
and ammunition. As soon as the voyage was again under
way the men took from the boxes their swords and pistols,
"many of which were of most beautiful workmanship",[5]
and a few miles above Prescott the schooners were cut
loose; but the cowardice of Bierge and others led to the
desertion of about 200 men, who went on to Ogdensburg in
the steamer.

On the way down the river the leaders of the expedition
discussed plans, but they were not unanimous upon the
procedure to be followed. One of them, "Colonel" Von
Shultz (also spelled Schultz and Shoultz), whose full name is
given as Van Shultz Nils Sezoltevki, was a native of Poland.
This man, who was destined to take the leading part in the
Battle of the Windmill, appears to have been all that could
be desired in a commander in both bravery and ability.

[3]The best account of the Prescott Expedition is in T. B. Hough:
A History of St. Lawrence and Franklin Counties, New York.
1853. The most reliable of the "Patriot" descriptions are those
of Daniel D. Heustis (*A Narrative of the Adventures and
Sufferings of Captain Daniel D. Heustis.* 1847.), and Stephen S.
Wright (*Narrative of the Prescott Expedition,* in Caleb Lyon's
Narrative and Recollections of Van Diemen's Land. 1844.).
Of the other versions of the events most are either taken from
the above, or are exceedingly prejudiced one way or the other.
Lindsey's description in his *Life and Times of William Lyon
Mackenzie* was obtained chiefly from other "Patriot" accounts
now even more rare than those of Heustis and Wright. The
present work is based largely upon the four sources named
above.

[4]See William H. Draper's account in Sir George Arthur's dispatch
to Lord Glenelg, November, 1838.

[5]Hough, *op. cit.,* p. 660.

He hoped to surprise Prescott, being unaware that the inhabitants had been aroused several days previously by rumours of an impending attack. He therefore favoured going at once to McPherson's Wharf, for he expected that if a stop were first made at Ogdensburg, more of the men would desert the ships than would be made up by additional recruits. Von Shultz planned to lead the main body through the centre of Prescott, while "Colonel" Martin Woodruff led the left wing around the north side, and "Colonel" Dorephus Abbey the right wing on the south or river side. The forces were to meet between Fort Wellington and the town, and then to advance on the fort. Had these well-laid plans been attempted the situation might have been even more serious than that which resulted at the windmill; but Bierge and Eustes rejected Von Shultz's plans.

Bierge promised to obtain reinforcements at Ogdensburg and to cross over to the aid of the others on the schooners; but he fell sick with a suddeness that was imputed by his followers to cowardice. The leadership thus fell upon Von Shultz, who took charge of about 170 men on board the *Charlotte of Toronto* and crossed to the Canadian side. The other schooner was in control of Bill Johnson, a notorious character, who managed his ship so poorly that it ran aground on a delta of mud deposited in the St. Lawrence by the Oswegatchie River, which flows into it at that point. The *United States,* manned by "Patriot Hunters", went from Ogdensburg to the assistance of the *Charlotte of Oswego,* but did not succeed in getting her off; later she returned with a larger hawser and a supply of bread and other provisions, but was still unsuccessful in her main purpose.

Meanwhile Von Shultz's schooner floated down to Prescott, and he succeeded in tying up to the wharf; but indecision prevented the "Patriots" from seizing the opportunity to invade the town, and the rope broke before an agreement was reached. The schooner floated on down the river and those on board effected a landing a mile and a half below Prescott, where they took up a position behind stone fences and houses near a large six-storey stone windmill.

The little British steamer *Experiment,* in command of Lieut. Fowell, R.N., opposed the landing with two small cannon, and poured shot into the grounded schooner as well as into the steamer *Paul Pry,* which was attempting to haul her off the sandbar. The *United States* was also prevented by the *Experiment* from approaching Prescott, and soon both steamers retired disabled into American waters. On the last trip of the *United States* a cannon-ball from the *Experiment* entered her wheel-house "and instantly beheaded a young man by the name of Solomon Foster, who stood as a pilot at the wheel".[6] Most of those on board the grounded schooner reached the windmill, and two guns were sent over on a scow. During Monday there was considerable activity on the river, and a number of men effected a crossing back and forth in small boats; but on Tuesday the American naval forces took a hand in the proceedings and seized both schooners.

On Monday news of the invasion had reached Captain Sandom, commander of the Royal Navy at Kingston, and he hastened to the spot with two armed steamers, the *Queen Victoria* and the *Cobourg.* These ships arrived at Windmill Point late Monday night with seventy marines and regulars on board. During the same night Captain George Macdonell arrived at Prescott in command of a detachment of the Glengarry militia, and the men lay on the ground during a heavy rain, expecting an attack at any moment; 140 members of the 9th Provincial Battalion, under Lieut.-Colonel Gowan, also reached Prescott shortly afterwards. On Tuesday morning 300 men of the Dundas militia, under Colonel John Crysler, and a part of the 1st Grenville militia arrived at the scene of action, and the combined companies were organised to drive the invaders from Canadian soil.

The British force advanced and drove in the enemy's pickets, forcing them, after an hour's engagement, to retreat from their outer defences behind stone fences into the large, circular stone mill, one hundred feet in circumference and eighty feet in height. The walls of this structure were three and one-half feet thick, and consequently such gunfire as the ships could bring against them made no impression; in fact, as the stones were set in the shape of a wedge, the

[6] *Ibid.,* p. 663,

artillery merely drove them more firmly into place. The British force decided, therefore, to await the arrival of heavy artillery from Kingston before attempting to dislodge the invaders from their stronghold.

The enemy held an excellent position, and from the small windows of the upper storeys of the mill their sharpshooters kept up a heavy fire upon the British forces, which were situated in an exposed position on rising ground. At 3 p.m. a barn which had been used for shelter by the British was burned by the invaders, and the first phase of the battle ended in at least partial success of the "Patriots"; in fact an American account of the battle says that British officers on horseback "were seen distinctly to fall here and there on the field, and the ranks of the soldiers to waste away under the unequal contest."[7]

The invaders at the windmill had meanwhile built a six-foot stone wall on the exposed side of the mill, and had three cannon in place to defend their position. They had lost thirty-three men who were captured by a flanking movement during Tuesday's engagement, and the rest of the force was in the mill or the neighbouring stone houses. Sandom's naval detachment on board the *Queen Victoria* and the *Cobourg*, with the co-operation of a detachment of Americans from Sackett's Harbour under Colonel Worth, prevented additional Hunters from attempting to cross over from Ogdensburg by capturing all the boats that had been used and patrolling the river. The dead and wounded lay on the field of battle until Wednesday morning, when an hour's truce was arranged to remove them. Both sides engaged in this work for a short time, though the lack of shovels handicapped the "Patriots". During the rest of Wednesday and all day Thursday the opposing forces remained in comparative inaction.

The insurgents now realised the hopelessness of their position, and efforts to arrange a retreat were made both by the men in the windmill and their sympathisers in Ogdensburg, who were practically in control of that town for nearly a week. The "Patriots" sent a man across on a plank to try to effect the desired result; and Colonel Worth of the American force had an interview on board ship with

[7]*Ibid.*, p. 665.

Colonel Young of the British. It was suggested by the American officer that the invaders be allowed to escape if they would retire from their position; this was of necessity refused, "but from an intimation that was dropped, either from inadvertence or design, that the machinery of the *Experiment* (the *Cobourg* and the *Victoria* having gone up the river the night previous) needed repairs that would prevent her being used until two o'clock the next morning, it was very naturally inferred that no means of annoyance would be in the possession of the British during the early part of the night."[8] Therefore the *Paul Pry* was sent over; but a man who accompanied the emissary disembarked first and advised the Hunters to hold their position, as reinforcements and supplies would soon come. The emissary then went ashore himself, but did not succeed in getting the men to retire from the mill.

On Thursday night 117 men made up the force at the windmill, and three of these escaped across the river by canoe. Wright, who took part in the expedition, tells of the sleepless nights when the invaders realised how hopeless was their position after they had been denied help by their cowardly accomplices across the river. They made the best of it, however, and although their ammunition for the three small field guns was soon exhausted, "they loaded the guns with pieces of broken iron, butts and screws that we tore from the doors and fixtures of the mill".[9]

At noon on Friday the 16th, Colonel Dundas and four companies of the 83rd Regiment, with two eighteen-pounders and a howitzer, arrived on the steamboat *William IV*. The British were then ready to put an end to the activities of the invaders. One eighteen-pounder "was posted back of the mill, under Major McBane; a gunboat was posted below the mill, and a heavily-armed steamer above it, so that the shots from these three points might not interfere with each other, and still have the mill in their focus. They were beyond the range of rifle fire, and sufficient to accomplish ere long the demolition of the tower".[10]

While the guns bombarded the mill furiously, a company of regulars, supported by militia, was drawn up on either

[8]*Ibid.*, p. 666.   [9]Wright, *op. cit.*, p. 7.
[10]Hough, *op. cit.*, pp. 667-8.

flank to prevent the escape of the occupants. Von Shultz states in a letter written a few days previous to his execution that his force at that time numbered only 108. His own actions at the last were worthy of a better cause: "As I could get no one to take the defence of the house on our left flank, I went down there myself with ten men. . . . I kept my position, though the roof crumbled to pieces over our heads."[11]

Those in the mill now hoisted a white flag; but the exasperated British kept up the cannonade, and every building near the mill was soon on fire, the raging flames outlining the whole field of battle with a lurid light. Under cover of night Von Shultz and his ten men withdrew from the stone house into the brushwood on the bank of the river, where they were easily captured. Those still in the mill were (Wright says) "without ammunition, betrayed, deserted and disheartened", and proceeded again to send "a flag of truce forth to the British host, as their bugle rang for their first charge". But as the four men with the flag left the mill they were fired on; so they returned, and the Hunters "made ready for a desperate resistance".[12] The British force advanced to within thirty rods, and then halted, much to the surprise of the insurgents, who were called upon to surrender unconditionally. The "Patriots" immediately "disarmed and marched out, defiling between the soldiers of the 83rd who were formed on each side of us".[13]

In the mill the British found several hundred kegs of powder, 200 stand of arms, and many swords, pistols and cartridges; some of the swords were silver-mounted and their handles elaborately carved. A flag, said to have cost $100, was also captured; on it was worked a full-spread eagle surmounted by a star, and beneath the design was wrought in silk: "Liberated by the Onondaga Hunters". It is said to have been presented to Von Shultz "by the patriotic ladies of Onondaga County".[14] In a bakery oven near the mill were found the bodies of two of the invaders, who had hidden there and had been burned to a crisp when the building was set on fire.

[11]Von Shultz to J. R. Parker, December 1, 1838. (See Heustis, *op. cit.*, pp. 57-8; or Lyon, *op. cit.*, pp. 52-3.)
[12]Wright, *op. cit.*, p. 11.   [13]*Ibid.*   [14]Heustis, *op. cit.*, p. 44.

One "Patriot" writer greatly exaggerates the British force which attacked the insurgents and compelled their surrender, stating it to be "5,000 regulars and militiamen; two large gun boats; seven steam boats, each of them armed with heavy cannon, mortars, rockets, carcasses, and every kind of warlike projectiles. To oppose this mighty host the lion-hearted Patriots had only 152 men able to bear arms; they had some artillery, but no ammunition to serve them".[15] The same authority (?) states that the British lost 450 killed, while the invaders suffered a loss of fifteen. His enthusiasm for the cause led also to an imaginative account of Von Shultz's capture:

"At midnight all but their heroic commander were taken. He took possession of the stone house alone, and fired so incessantly that the enemy thought it was full of Patriots. At length they rushed in, and he jumped in their midst. They instantly pounced upon him like a pack of bloodhounds; tore the clothes from his back, robbed him of his hat, watch and vest. This terminated the most extraordinary engagement that ever took place on the continent of North America."[16]

The 157 prisoners were marched to Prescott in a long line, single file and tied to a rope. After being "exhibited to the populace" of the town, where a celebration of the victory was in progress, the men were "crammed into the forecastle of a small steamboat" (the *Brockville*), and proceeded to Kingston.[17] The march to Fort Henry, where they were imprisoned while awaiting trial, is thus described by one of the prisoners: "It was about midnight when we arrived at Kingston. We were tied together in couples, Von Shoultz at the head, a rope passing between us. . . . In this condition, with a line of soldiers on each side, we were marched to Fort Henry, about one mile distant from the landing, the band playing *Yankee Doodle*."[18]

The evidence given at the court-martial brought out the information that the steamboats and schooners of wealthy merchants had been made available to the invaders, who were encouraged by American officials, and, in some cases, supplied with government arms. A judge, a member of

[15]D. McLeod: *A Brief Review of the Settlement of Upper Canada* . . . . 1841. p. 257.
[16]*Ibid.*   [17]Heustis, *op. cit.*, p. 60   [18]*Ibid.*, p. 61.

Congress, and other men of influence were stated to have been members of the lodges, but very few of these took part in the expedition. One prisoner considered that the attack had been "deranged for want of officers".[19] The stories of the men were similar to that of Jeremiah Winnegar, who stated that he "did not expect to fight when he left home; came for the sole purpose of giving liberty to the people of Canada; thought when he was coming that he was doing God service; heard Ministers of the Gospel encouraging the people to support the Patriot Hunters". After he had given his evidence he addressed the court: "I presume many of the Court have families—I have a family as near and dear to me as them—I have left a wife—seven sons and four daughters. . . . Though a poor man, I have the same feelings as others, and my family are dear to me, and, though old, I am their main support—I have now only to throw myself on the mercy of the Court."[20] Winnegar was sentenced by the court-martial to be executed, but he was reprieved, and finally pardoned.

John A. Macdonald, later Prime Minister of Canada, was connected with the trial of Von Shultz (as he was subsequently in the return from exile of M. S. Bidwell) ; but the leader was convicted, and executed on December 8th, ten others, including Abbey, Buckley and Woodruff, being put to death later. Most of the remaining prisoners were young men who little realised the gravity of their offence, about fifty of them being between sixteen and twenty-one years of age. The Rev. Anson Green, a Methodist minister in Kingston at the time, preached to them at the request of Captain Beach, a member of the court-martial. He wrote in his diary: "I never preached to a more attentive and solemn assembly; still there were two God-forsaken looking men who lay upon the floor regardless of what I was saying! (These were afterwards condemned and executed)." He attended two men at their execution, which he describes in considerable detail. Like many other citizens, he "was pleased to learn from Mr. Draper, the Judge Advocate, that but few others would expiate their guilt on the gallows".[21]

[19]Evidence of John B. Kimball. See *Report from the Select Committee of the House of Assembly of Upper Canada*. 1839. p. 27.
[20]Evidence of Jeremiah Winnegar, *ibid.*, pp. 25-6.
[21]Anson Green: *Life and Times*. 1877. p. 224.

Most of the prisoners were eventually pardoned and sent back to the United States; but some were given terms of imprisonment in Canada, or transported to Van Diemen's Land (Tasmania), where there was a penal colony. A number of these exiles later published memoirs of their harrowing experiences, all of the books being now very rare.

At least 150 men were killed or wounded during the invasion, but the losses may have been considerably greater, for it appears unlikely that all the British casualties were publicly admitted. The invaders lost about twenty killed and seventeen wounded, while the British losses were officially announced as two officers and fourteen men killed and about sixty wounded, though the "Patriot" writers claim that their opponents' casualties were much greater.

From all accounts it would appear that the Regulars had to protect the prisoners from the militia of Glengarry, Dundas and Grenville, who were greatly incensed at the invasion; and some of those captured suffered brutal treatment at the hands of countryfolk and militia before the Regulars could prevent it. This was, perhaps, to be expected when such items were found on prisoners as a list of the citizens of Prescott who were to have been hanged upon the capture of the town. A Select Committee of the House of Assembly of Upper Canada reported that "not only were the brave defenders of the province shot down and deliberately murdered by their fiendish assailants, but their dead bodies were mangled and mutilated and hung up as objects of scorn and derision by these inhuman monsters. The body of an intrepid and promising young officer, Lieutenant Johnson of the 83rd Regiment, was thus treated at Prescott".[22] The "Patriot" writers deny all such charges.

Von Shultz appears to have been much the superior in character and ability of those with whom he was associated. One of the members of the Prescott expedition eulogises him: "Von Shultz was an elegant scholar—a good military engineer—and spoke several languages with great fluency. . . . . His whole bearing and conduct were noble. . . . Even regardless of his own sufferings he generously tried to render his companions in arms every service in his power."[23] Historians also speak well of him, one referring to him as a

[22]*Report of Select Committee*, p. 20.
[23]Wright, *op. cit.*, p. 13.

"brave and generous man, a victim of more designing men who led him to the course which brought him to the gallows".[24] Another considered him "a gentleman altogether too good for the company in which he was found".[25]

Von Shultz admitted that he had had a fair trial and deserved his fate, but he wished that Bill Johnson and the other cowards who had misled him and then deserted him might be brought to justice. In a letter to a friend he also acknowledged the kind treatment experienced at the hands of the officers and men of the 83rd Regiment:

"We may fairly say that we owe our lives to them, because, had they not protected us after we surrendered, the militia would surely have killed the greater number of us. The sheriff in whose keeping we are has treated us most kindly, and done everything in his power to better the situation in which we were thrown by the miserable cowardice of General Birge, Bill Johnston and their officers. If our prayers were heard, those base rascals would have been delivered over to the British Government by our own; and we would then meet our own fate with perfect resignation."[26]

Von Shultz left £400 to the dependents of the militia who had been killed. That he should have been robbed of a miniature of his wife Emeline seems an unfortunate addition to the misery of the last days of this misguided man.

At times during the four days' battle of Windmill Point thousands of Americans lined the opposite shore and witnessed the unequal fight. Some of them cheered at every slight advantage gained by the insurgents, but they took care to remain on their own side of the river. For many years the mill, which had been erected in 1822 by a West India merchant, remained a battered and blackened ruin, a reminder of a most unfortunate expedition. In 1873 it was repaired, whitewashed and transformed into a lighthouse, the light being first shown on the anniversary of Waterloo, June 15th. The old building still stands, a noted landmark which calls forth memories of a troubled period in Canadian annals.

[24]D. B. Read: *The Canadian Rebellion of 1837*. 1896. p. 356.
[25]J. C. Dent: *The Story of the Upper Canadian Rebellion*. 1885. Vol. II, pp. 265-6.
[26]Von Shultz to J. R. Parker, December 1, 1838. (See *supra*, Note 11.)

CHAPTER VII

THE FENIAN RAIDS

"Fenianism was a costly and laborious organisation, conceived in secrecy and shrouded in mystery, which was no sooner achieved than it vanished, with nothing to show as the fruit of all its travail."

FRANK H. SEVERANCE.[1]

TOWARDS the close of the American Civil War an anti-British organisation in the United States began to assume a position of importance, and was soon to be the cause of grave anxiety in Canada. The Fenian Brotherhood derived its name from that of the ancient Irish people, and worked in harmony with the Nationalists in Ireland, the purpose being the overthrow of British rule by the repeal of the Act of Union of 1801, or by violent means if the object could not otherwise be attained.

The movement commenced in America about 1857, with Colonel O'Mahoney as organiser and president. The organisation did not become important at the time because of the Civil War, which was soon to break out; but at the close of the War, in 1865, a large number of Irish-Americans, many of them disbanded soldiers, joined the association, which was conducted in secret. Until that time the policy of the Fenians had been to send money and soldiers to Ireland to aid rebellion there. In 1865, however, the Fenian organisation split into two hostile camps, the seceders from the original body being led by Colonel Roberts and "Secretary-of-War" Sweeney. These men called a convention at Cincinnati in September of that year and formed "The Secret Wing of the Fenian Brotherhood", with the policy of invading Canada as a means of indirectly effecting their main purpose. During the succeeding five years this policy formed the platform of the association, and an elaborate organisation was established to give effect to the plan. A mansion in New York flew the Irish flag as the headquarters of Fenianism, large sums of money were subscribed through the purchase of bonds, and the president

[1]Frank H. Severance: *The Fenian Raid of 1866*. (In Buffalo Historical Society, *Publications*, Vol. XXV, p. 266.)

and officials of the "Irish Republic" purchased arms and ammunition, which was hidden in convenient places near the border.

The British Government was fully aware of the machinations of the Fenians, largely through the reports of Major Henri Le Caron, high in command among the Fenians, but who was from the first a British spy. Le Caron was also an important factor in the ultimate failure of the invasions. In Canada there was early prevalent an attitude of indifference concerning the activities of the Fenians, though as early as November, 1861, Major George T. Denison publicly expressed the fear that there would be raids across the border. In later years rumours reached Canada of the elaborate preparations being made in the United States, while Fenian "circles" were stated to be strong in Toronto, Montreal and other centres; but almost up to the eve of the first attack the government was not impressed with the gravity of the situation,—if preparations to meet it be taken as a criterion.

In March, 1866, however, the authorities were sufficiently aroused to order out 10,000 men to meet any emergency that might arise. Soon about 14,000 soldiers were billeted in hotels in Toronto and other centres, and were being drilled and armed; but a few weeks later drill was discontinued. A general feeling of alarm had, however, pervaded the country by this time, and when the first attack occurred at Ridgeway the excitement among the inhabitants was greater than at any time since the Rebellion of '37. Great preparations were made for a period of siege, a large Patriotic Fund was raised by subscription, and some people even removed from the country because of "the Fenian scare", as a popular song[2] put it.

Only those who lived at the time can appreciate the extent of the feeling of alarm which alternately rose and fell during the five years of Fenian activity along the border. A man who resided on the shore of Lake Ontario describes the steps by which the fear increased:

"Fenianism at first did not attract much attention. But as the days went by and rumours increased, gathering force by repetition and transmission, our people began to feel

[2] A version of *Yankee Doodle.*

alarmed. Timorous people became very nervous, and 'the Fenians' was the topic of the day. Not a few persons loaded wagons with all they could put on them, and, climbing on the top of the furniture and bedding, drove away northward."[3]

In the latter part of May, 1866, some 35,000 Fenians are said to have been in readiness along the border; but the United States Government seized a considerable part of their ammunition and supplies, a step which undoubtedly decreased the scope of their activities. A number of raids at various border points had been planned by the Fenian leaders, but only one of importance, that at Ridgeway on the Niagara frontier, actually occurred.

During the last ten days of the month large numbers of men, mostly unarmed, were moving northward, and if asked where they were going they would state that they were bound for California to work in the mines; this explanation became the more ridiculous the closer they approached Buffalo. A participant in the Ridgeway raid wrote many years later that the "Fenian Forty" congregated on the night of May 20, 1866, "in full uniform of the Second Mounted Rifles, armed to the teeth with guns and sabres and all our old accoutrements".[4] Buffalo was chosen as the rendezvous because more Fenians lived there than in any other border city, and also since the extensive shipping in that port provided an easy means of crossing over to Canada at an important and vulnerable point, where there were no Canadian forces within fifty miles. It is thought that the British spy, Major Le Caron, advised "General" John O'Neil (a captain in the Union Army) to cross over to Fort Erie before his full force had come up, thus rendering a valuable service in decreasing the seriousness of the attack.

The Fenian invasions do not bear much comparison with those of the Hunters' Lodges after the Rebellion of '37. The self-styled Patriots of 1838 were largely an unorganised rabble, but the Fenians at Fort Erie formed a well-drilled and well-disciplined force, as the events of their short stay on Canadian soil soon proved; for competent officers, most of them Civil War veterans, were in full control of the men.

[3]Thomas Conant: *Upper Canada Sketches.* 1898. pp. 171-3.
[4]See Buffalo *Courier*, May 29, 1893.

At a late hour in the evening of May 31st the Fenians, many of them well-armed, left their headquarters in Buffalo, ostensibly to go to their homes; but they quietly made their way by devious roads to Black Rock, two miles below Buffalo, where they united and marched to Pratt's Furnace, at which point a tug and canal boats were in readiness to ferry them to Canada. The force, variously estimated at from 650 to 1,340 strong, effected a landing at the Lower Ferry Dock, a mile below Fort Erie.

At 4 a.m. "Colonel" Starr of the invading force raised a green silk Irish flag, amid loud cheers; this banner, now a faded, tattered and torn relic in the possession of the Buffalo Historical Society, was made for the occasion by "The Fenian Sisterhood". O'Neil, the general in command, immediately sent pickets in all directions to reconnoitre. The main force moved into Fort Erie and ordered Dr. Kempson, Reeve of the village, to furnish rations for 1,000 men. After the municipal council had been hurriedly summoned and had made arrangements to do as ordered, a force of Fenians was sent along the Grand Trunk Railway towards Port Colborne, tearing up rails, cutting telegraph wires, and burning Saeurwine's Bridge on the way. The main body, however, moved down to Frenchman's Creek, and camped on Thomas Newbigging's farm, strengthening their position by a barricade of fence rails. Small parties were then sent out in all directions to seize horses and organise cavalry for scouting purposes, though it is stated that only two Fenians were mounted when in action later.[5] Most of Friday, June 1st, passed in this way, many farmers of Bertie Township being forced to give up their horses; while others, hearing of the presence of the Fenians, drove their stock into the great tamarack swamp to the northward.

Early Friday morning General Napier, Commander of the Regulars in Canada West, received news of the crossing. Four hundred of the Queen's Own Rifles had been ordered out the previous evening to be in readiness for eventualities, and these men left Toronto early Friday on the steamship *City of Toronto* for Port Dalhousie, and proceeded to Port Colborne. Lieut.-Colonel J. S. Dennis was in command of the force, and was ordered to entrench himself there and

[5] N. Brewster: *Recollections of the Fenian Raid.* (In Welland County Historical Society, *Publications*, Vol. II, p. 78.)

await reinforcements and further orders; Lieut.-Colonel Alfred Booker was second in command.

Most of the Upper Canadian militia, excepting the cavalry, was ordered out the same morning, but no more troops were sent to the Niagara district immediately for fear that the attack at Fort Erie was merely a feint to draw troops from other border points and then attack in force elsewhere. About noon, however, it was decided to concentrate the forces to drive the Fenians from Fort Erie, and the 16th Regiment and other detachments were sent from Hamilton over the Great Western Railway to St. Catharines. With the arrival of the additional companies Colonel Peacock of the 16th assumed command as the senior officer. His force was made up of a battery of artillery and thirteen companies of volunteer militia under Lieut.-Colonel R. B. Denison; some of these men were sent to Clifton to guard the Suspension Bridge, while others took possession of the bridges near Chippawa, the whole force using St. Catharines as a base of operations.

Rumours reached Colonel Peacock that some 800 Fenians were advancing towards the Suspension Bridge, but it was found that the force had not yet reached Chippawa. He decided, therefore, to proceed by train to Chippawa with several hundred infantry, the battery being ordered to follow by road. He arrived in the vicinity of New Germany just as it was becoming dark, and was there joined by a force of cavalry under Major George T. Denison, which, within twelve hours of leaving Toronto, had travelled forty miles by steamship, twenty miles by train, and twenty-four on the march; this force, the Governor-General's Body Guard, or "Denison's Guerillas" as it was often called, established contact with Fenian outposts in the woods at dark, but owing to the swampy nature of the land, and the lack of knowledge of the enemy's strength and position, the cavalry had to bivouack for the night. The Fenian outpost soon after retired to Fort Erie without firing.

Meanwhile the battle of Lime Ridge had been fought and won by the invaders, who had secretly and very skilfully effected a march from Frenchman's Creek towards Ridgeway. The Canadian force under Dennis and Booker was divided into three parts at the time of the engagement with the enemy, only one section coming into action. This unfortunate circumstance arose out of several misunderstandings. Colonel Peacock's force had attempted to unite with Dennis' troops from Port Colborne, the plan being to meet at Stevensville about 11 a.m. Saturday. Late Friday night Peacock had sent Captain Akers to explain his scheme to Dennis and Booker. But when Akers arrived about 1.30 a.m. he found the forces ready to leave for other points without orders, urged on by one Graham of Fort Erie who arrived with definite news of the location of the Fenian camp at Frenchman's Creek. The three officers then decided that Booker would march there at 8 a.m., while Dennis and Akers, with the Welland Garrison Battery and the Dunnville Naval Company, would reconnoitre the coast in the tug *Robb,* and then land at Fort Erie and attempt to prevent the Fenians' escape.

They notified Colonel Peacock of this scheme, presuming he would agree to meet them at Frenchman's Creek. Colonel Peacock, however, refused, and ordered his original plan to be followed. But Akers and Dennis had already gone in the tug without awaiting the reply; consequently Booker had to advance towards Stevensville without the aid of Akers' engineering knowledge of the best route. Booker's force started about an hour earlier than was necessary, going by train almost as far as Ridgeway. As a result of his leaving ahead of time, a telegram from Peacock ordering an hour's delay arrived at Port Colborne after he had left; but Mr. Stovin, an employee of the railway, recognised its importance, and followed Booker by hand-car, wagon, and on foot, finally reaching the Colonel just as the battle of Lime Ridge was commencing, Peacock's force being miles away at the time.

As Booker's troops, who had left the train near Ridgeway, were marching by the Ridge Road towards Stevensville they came in contact with the Fenian force at Lime Ridge. At the point the battle was fought this ridge was about half a mile wide, gradually rising to a height of thirty or forty feet. Scattered among the fields were orchards and forests which tended to obscure the Fenian position. The invaders had erected several rail-fence barricades, partially hidden by shrubbery, and behind these defences was the main body, with small supporting forces in the neighbouring woods.

Canadian skirmishers of the Trinity College and University Companies drove back the foremost of the Fenians, while the Highland Company cleared the woods of the enemy. The Fenian force then gathered in an orchard, and advanced to the attack led by two or three mounted officers. The Canadian outposts thereupon retired, at the same time shouting: "Look out for cavalry!" Colonel Booker, near the Reserve in the rear, could not see for himself, so he transmitted the information to Major Gillmor, who thereupon ordered his men to "Form square", and the bugler to sound the "Prepare for cavalry". Those in front who had been retiring formed rallying squares, and then fell back on the double to the main body, causing confusion by their precipitate retreat. The rear of the main square was still unformed when the Fenians came within range and fired heavily on the Canadians, killing or wounding a considerable number.

Seeing no cavalry Major Gillmor tried to extend his regiment, but the rear of the square broke away and retreated, the resulting confusion necessitating the command to retire. A member of the Welland Battery who was present at Lime Ridge as a spectator during the early part of the action, and as a participant later, says concerning the retreat: "A majority were willing to renew the fight, but twenty *per cent.* or less made off, and the majority seemed unwilling to make further resistance unless all did so. Thus the action of the minority decided the action of the whole."[6]

Some of the men retreated precipitately, but others, including most of the officers, fought doggedly as they retired, and kept the Fenians at bay, thus covering the retreat of the rest and preventing a complete rout. On the edge of a small wood several officers tried to rally their men but could not do so; consequently the retreat continued, and the force was not reorganised until Port Colborne was reached. The Fenians followed to Ridgeway, and about 400 yards beyond, but made no attempt to pursue the Canadians any farther. A veteran of the American Civil War, an eyewitness of the retreat, states that he met "such a mixed and

[6]A. W. Reavley: *Personal Experiences in the Fenian Raid.* (In Welland County Historical Society, *Publications*, Vol. II, p. 69.)

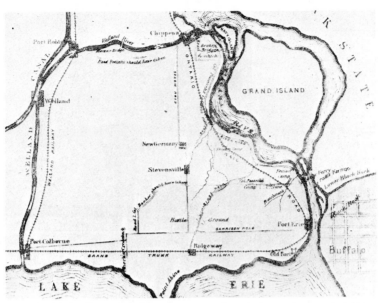

COLONEL DENISON'S MAP OF THE FORT ERIE RAID OF '66

THE "DESPERATE CHARGE" OF THE FENIANS AT RIDGEWAY,
1866

The original caption of this picture announced the total "route" (!) of
the British

From the *Illustrated London News*, January 18, 1868

THE FENIAN ALARM: THE NIGHT GUARD AT PLYMOUTH
The Fenian raids were in co-operation with Nationalists in Ireland

From *L'Opinion Publique*, June 9, 1870

SHARPSHOOTERS OPENING FIRE NEAR COOK'S CORNERS
An event in the Fenian Raid of 1870 in Missisquoi County, Quebec

confused mass as I have never seen elsewhere before or
since. Soldiers and citizens, men, women and children, on
foot and in all varieties of vehicles, with horses, cattle,
sheep and pigs, all mingled together, and all hurrying along
the road south. It brought to my mind Russel's description
of Bull Run."[7]

Colonel Peacock's force, meanwhile, was marching
towards Stevensville, when a messenger from Colonel
Booker arrived with a short note telling of the defeat. The
extreme heat forced Peacock's column to halt soon after,
and it was late in the afternoon before they proceeded from
New Germany, to be joined at dusk by the cavalry under
Major Denison, as described previously.

The third section of the Canadian force, led by Colonel
Dennis and Captain Akers in the tug *Robb,* had recon-
noitred the shore and then landed at Fort Erie, where they
captured a few stragglers. A series of complicated, and, in
some instances, foolish movements ensued, the troops being
divided into several sections. Dennis and some seventy
men encountered the main Fenian force marching towards
Fort Erie after defeating Booker's troops at Lime Ridge;
the small body of Canadians had to retire, though many of
the men, led by Captain King, fought desperately for some
time from within a house in Fort Erie, and inflicted considerable loss on the enemy. Some members of the Welland
Battery, posted in Lewis' Tavern, were captured, but were
allowed to depart soon after. A mounted Fenian officer,
"Colonel" Bailey, was seriously wounded while leading his
men against the small Canadian force, but he later recovered
from his wounds. Colonel Dennis fled earlier in the engagement, hiding in a barn for a time, and finally reaching
Peacock's camp just before daylight, disguised as a
labourer.[8]

At 5 a.m. on Sunday Colonel Peacock ordered his men
to advance into Fort Erie, reinforcements from his former
camp in New Germany being then on the way to support
him. Just as the forces began to move towards the village,
news was received that the Fenians had left, so Denison's
cavalry was ordered to reconnoitre and find out the truth.

[7] Brewster, *op. cit.,* p. 75.
[8] The movements of Dennis and Akers are well described in John H.
    Thompson: *Jubilee History of Thorold.* 1897-8. Chap. VIII.

On reaching the river Major Denison saw a scow "black with men crowded upon it", and was told they were Fenian reinforcements captured by, and fastened to the United States revenue-cutter *Michigan*; upon going out to the boat, however, he learned that it was the main body of Fenians, who had decided to retire to the United States and had been captured by the *Michigan*.[9]

Proceeding towards Fort Erie about 6 a.m. the cavalry observed a few Fenians in the distance, running hither and thither; but almost all were hidden or gone when the troop entered the village. A few prisoners, the wounded, and considerable equipment were taken. Dr. Donelly, the Fenian surgeon, was allowed to leave in a skiff for Buffalo; Father McMahon, their priest, was given the same chance, but remained on the Canadian side and as a result spent some years in jail.

Among those who entered Fort Erie that day was Colonel Garnet Wolseley, the noted British Commander of the Red River Expedition of 1870. The Canadian force of nearly 2,500 men remained about three weeks at the village, for the news of temporary victory had brought some 30,000 Fenians to Buffalo and vicinity. During the stay of the invaders in Canada some of these sympathisers could be seen on the American shore making demonstrations of encouragement. For some days after the main body had withdrawn, occasional Fenians were caught while attempting to escape from hiding-places along the river, the most notable instance being the capture of three in a boat by Major Denison and Sergeant John James, later a Toronto alderman.

The total loss among the Canadian forces during the raid was nine killed or died of wounds, and thirty-one wounded, including five officers. General O'Neil of the Fenians somewhat exaggerated these numbers when he reported that thirty had been killed, 100 wounded and forty-five captured. Three of the Canadian dead were undergraduates of the University of Toronto. The Fenian losses were given by their leader as eight killed and fifteen wounded. The main force of the invaders, captured by the American revenue-

[9]George T. Denison: *Soldiering in Canada*. 1900. p. 105.

cutter *Michigan,* remained two or three days in jail in Buffalo, whereupon the men were released.

The wisdom of the Fenian retirement to the United States cannot be questioned. O'Neil's official report to Colonel W. R. Roberts, President of the Fenian Brotherhood, says that on account of desertions, and owing to the smallness of his force, which was surrounded by ten times their numbers, a retirement was considered necessary: "Thus situated, and not knowing what was going on elsewhere, I decided that the best course was to return to Fort Erie and ascertain if crossings had been made at other points; and, if so, I was content to sacrifice myself and my noble little command for the sake of leaving the way open."[10] Finding that no other crossings had been made, and that the increased vigilance of American revenue-cutters prevented the arrival of reinforcements, the Fenians hastened to escape while it was still possible.

That the invaders behaved remarkably well to the inhabitants of the district about Fort Erie is the testimony of Colonel George T. Denison, who made extensive investigations at the time:

"They have been called plunderers, robbers and marauders, yet, no matter how unwilling we may be to admit it, the positive fact remains that they stole but few valuables, that they destroyed, comparatively speaking, little or nothing, and that they committed no outrages on the inhabitants, but treated everyone with unvarying courtesy. It seems like a perfect burlesque to see a ragged rabble without a government, country or flag affecting chivalrous sentiments and doing acts that put one in mind of the days of knight-errantry."[11]

Men who were captured by the Fenians, and consequently had an excellent chance to observe their actions, corroborate this testimony. One observed that they "took very little from the houses,—chiefly handkerchiefs, stockings, and little items to keep as souvenirs".[12] Another noticed that "their conduct was perfectly orderly. There was no plundering, though the village (Ridgeway) was entirely

[10]Quoted in Henri Le Caron: *25 Years in the Secret Service; the Recollections of a Spy.* 1892. p. 34.
[11]G. T. Denison: *The Fenian Raid on Fort Eric.* 1866. p. 69.
[12]Brewster, *op. cit.,* pp. 76 and 79.

at their mercy"; he also relates the interesting story that as they passed a tavern General O'Neil personally treated each prisoner to a glass of beer, and paid for it![13]

The management, or, rather, mismanagement of the campaign against the Fenians suggests that it was from first to last little more than a comedy of errors. Major Denison was so sure that there would be campaigning in the spring of 1866 that he issued in March of that year a manual of outpost duties for the use of soldiers; but almost everyone else appeared unconcerned about Fenian activities. Many years later Denison wrote:

"During all this time no preparation of any kind for campaigning was made, no organising done, no staff officers appointed, no stores or equipment prepared, and practically everything neglected. The rifle companies all over the country were scattered and had no connection with each other. They were not told off into battalions; and during all March, April and May, in the face of constant and alarming indications of danger, nothing was done."[14]

On the field of battle there was evident a lack of most camping equipment, supplies of food, and many other essentials which would have been available under good organisation. When the forces bivouacked at night they usually lay down in their ranks, without supper, fires, beds or bedding. Denison gave his men at the start of their activities a large biscuit, which some hung around their necks as a souvenir. The breakfast of his corps the next day was unique.

"Just before daybreak on my return to the bivouac, the wagons came up from the rear with some beef and hardtack. The beef was given to us in small chunks. We made fires of the rail fences, and, sticking the small pieces of meat on slivers of wood, we cooked them over the fire by toasting them. When they were cooked and browned on the outside we had to take them in our fingers and eat them, tearing them to pieces with our teeth with the juice running over our hands. We went to the brook near by to get a drink.

[13]W. Ellis: *The Adventures of a Prisoner of War in the Fenian Raid of 1866.* (In *Canadian Defence Quarterly*, Vol. III, 1926, pp. 213 and 215.)
[14]Denison: *Soldiering in Canada*, p. 85.

That was one of the most primitive attempts at a breakfast I ever had."[15]

On Monday, June 4th, after the Fenians had returned to
the United States, some supplies for the Canadian forces
arrived from Toronto, having been obtained in the city
largely by private contribution when it was learned on Sunday that food was scarce; this tided over the period of two
or three days until the commissariat could meet the needs.

Another defect which had a considerable influence on
the conduct of operations against the Fenians was the lack
of good military maps. None of the officers had anything
more than small maps, most of them erroneous and out-of-
date. A still more inexcusable error in organisation was
the failure to send cavalry with the first troops. Perhaps
Colonel Denison, a lifelong cavalryman and a world authority on that branch of the service, was a little biassed in his
opinion of its importance; but in this instance the lack of
cavalry, which he ascribes to "the average stupidity of officials",[16] was undoubtedly prominent among the reasons
for the defeat of the Canadians at Ridgeway. Even more
important than its support of the infantry would have been
its value in scouting; but the Governor-General's Body
Guard was not sent until the day of the battle, and could
not arrive until too late to be of any assistance in avoiding
defeat. The absence of horsemen made it necessary to
depend on conflicting information obtained from civilians,
who were inclined to exaggerate the number of Fenians and
to speak from hearsay rather than knowledge. Had Peacock's force included cavalry he would have been able to
cut off the enemy's escape when Booker notified him of his
defeat. The Fenians were not slow to recognise the need
of horsemen, and took prompt means to obtain a few
mounts on their arrival at Fort Erie; while the fear of
cavalry by the Canadian force under Booker, who had
none of it to support his operations, led directly to the defeat at Lime Ridge.

Colonel Denison's careful and extensive study[17] of the

[15]*Ibid.*, p. 104.   [16]*Ibid.*, p. 88.

[17]Colonel Denison's *The Fenian Raid on Fort Erie* and *Soldiering in
Canada* are used as the basis of the present work, for they
contain, upon the whole, the most reliable account of the military events. Most of the other works of importance on the
subject, as well as reminiscences, are listed in the notes.

events during the raid led him to the conclusion that the failure was in large measure due to the actions of Lieut.-Colonel Dennis, who, without infantry training, was placed in command of the Queen's Own Rifles. His inexperience, and his disobedience of orders, caused Denison to attribute to him and to Captain Akers "the failure of all Colonel Peacock's plans, the defeat of Booker's column, and the defeat and capture of most of Dennis' command".[18] Colonel Denison considered that Dennis and Akers disobeyed Peacock when they went on the expedition in the tug *Robb*; that their landing at Fort Erie, and, still worse, their dividing their small force, were military blunders; while if they had remained on the *Robb* they might have inflicted a heavy loss on the retiring Fenians, and, perhaps, entirely cut off their retreat across the river. In that connection Colonel Denison considered that Peacock's force might have prevented most of the Fenians from escaping had he marched from his camp at New Germany on the receipt of news of Booker's defeat, instead of delaying until 5.30 p.m.

In the matter of responsibility for the defeat at Lime Ridge, Denison found no reason to attach any special blame to any one officer or section of the force which came ·into action. Somerville's account of the battle blames Colonel Booker for the failure, but the value of his estimate is ruined by his admission in a letter that he had been hired to do so by Booker's enemies.[19] The conduct of Booker was later investigated by a Court of Enquiry composed of Lieut.-Colonels Denison, Chisholm and Shanley. They found that he had endeavoured to correct his mistake by giving the order "Re-form column"; but that instead of ordering an advance, which would have enabled the forces to recover their stability, he unfortunately made a second mistake by giving the command to retire. The Court considered, however, that there was "no want of personal coolness" on the part of Colonel Booker, nor any stain on his personal courage and conduct.[20] A similar body, in which Lieut.-Colonel Fairbanks replaced Chisholm, investigated

[18]Denison: *Soldiering in Canada*, pp. 102-3.
[19]See *ibid.*, pp. 117-18.
[20]J. H. Macdonald: *Troublous Times in Canada*. 1910. Appendix,
    pp. 241-2.

the conduct of Dennis, but found that the charges against him were not substantiated; though in this instance Lieut.-Colonel Denison disagreed with the majority and submitted a separate report giving reasons for his belief that the charges were proven.[21]

The Court of Enquiry laid the blame for the defeat upon "disadvantages with which Her Majesty's forces seldom have to contend", which were further intensified by the composition of the force, of which "more than half of the two battalions were youths under twenty years of age, very few accustomed to drill, and many had never shot anything but a blank cartridge."[22]

The bodies of the nine members of the Queen's Own Rifles who had died in action were brought by boat to Toronto and interred with full military honours in St. James' Cemetery. The funeral procession started from the old drill-shed at the foot of Simcoe Street and passed through crowded streets to the cemetery. Some months later a large monument was erected in Queen's Park, Toronto, by the Canadian Government, and unveiled by the Governor-General, Lord Monck.

A veteran of the campaign against the Fenians recalls an interesting incident during the procession from the cemetery to the site of the monument, where the bodies of the dead were to be re-interred. A group of Fenian prisoners was met on the way to Toronto jail, and such a crowd was encountered that many of the soldiers in the procession had to be detached to form a square around the prisoners. A way was then forced through the crowded streets, and the two processions continued to their respective destinations.[23]

At least one romance resulted from the Fenian invasion of Canadian soil, for we learn from a letter in an old newspaper that one of the invaders, Patrick O'Reilly, having been wounded during the battle, made his way with difficulty to a neighbouring farmhouse; there he was hidden and nursed back to health by one of the daughters of the home, and soon after made his escape to the United States. He did

[21]The entire reports of the Courts of Inquiry are printed in Macdonald, *op. cit.*, appendix, pp. 197-255.
[22]*Ibid.*, p. 242.
[23]Reminiscences of Parker Smith, in a letter to the *Cobourg World*, April 9, 1920. See also E. C. Guillet: *Cobourg*, in the *Cobourg Sentinel-Star*, July 16, 1931.

not forget his benefactress, however, but returned a few weeks later to Canada, and the pair eloped across the border.[24] In addition to this actual romance at least one historical novel was penned with the invasions as its *motif*.[25]

The Fenians had planned a simultaneous raid on the Niagara frontier near Queenston, with the intention of raiding St. Catharines; but the only activity occurred on June 4th, when a steamship load of invaders came into the mouth of the river, intending to proceed to Lewiston to pick up some 600 more men, whereupon a crossing was to be made to the Canadian side. The 600 marched from the Falls to Lewiston, but as the ship had not arrived at the appointed time they marched back again; those on the boat later learned that their supporters were not at Lewiston, and so did not proceed farther. The inhabitants along the Canadian shore were being armed and prepared to resist a landing, but nothing further occurred in that district.

Meanwhile an invasion on a much smaller scale than that at Fort Erie had taken place in Quebec, across the Missisquoi border from St. Albans, Vermont. The Fenian force occupied Eccles Hill, just over the border, and used it as a base to pillage Frelighsburg, Cook's Corners and Pigeon Hill, the damage being estimated at $15,000. After a three-day occupation they retreated to the United States on hearing that a British force was approaching.

Many of the Fenian prisoners captured at Ridgeway were discharged at the preliminary hearing and deported to the United States. About forty were sent up for trial, which commenced in Toronto on October 8, 1866. Over twenty of these were found guilty and sentenced to be hanged; but, as the leaders of the expedition had all escaped, it was considered that little good would result from severe treatment of those captured, and their sentences were finally commuted to various terms of imprisonment in Kingston. A few received life sentences, but in 1872 the six then remaining at Kingston were set free. A Canadian militiaman who objected to the clemency of the Canadian

[24]See George Wells: *A Romance of the Raid.* (In Welland County Historical Society, *Publications*, Vol. II, pp. 80-81.)
[25]"Scian Dubh": *Ridgeway, an Historical Romance of the Fenian Invasion of Canada.* 1868.

Government observed that "to add to the annoyance of the volunteers, each Fenian received free transportation to Niagara Falls, and in addition a five dollar bill, with which to celebrate his liberty and make merry with his friends."[26] The Canadian veterans of the campaign were the recipients of silver medals; while one of them states[27] that in later years each man who applied was given 160 acres of land in New Ontario, and still later a cash gratuity of $100.

In March, 1867, there was another "Fenian scare", but, nothing happened at that time, nor until 1870. In that year further raids were planned by General O'Neil, and two invasions across the Quebec border resulted. The more important of the two took place at the same location as the raid of 1866—across the Missisquoi border. Reporters of the Montreal *Witness* were at the scene of the raid, so that full accounts were written of the events by eye-witnesses.[28] On the morning of May 24th there was a large gathering of volunteers at the Military School in Montreal, according to the usual custom on the Queen's birthday. They were "there mysteriously informed that the review on Logan's Farm was postponed on account of the weather, (it was drizzling rain); but that, in accordance with orders from Ottawa, they would have to remain under arms".[29] After some hours had elapsed they were told that Fenians were approaching the border, and that one company from each battalion must proceed to the frontier in the afternoon. The volunteering was enthusiastic, and companies from several regiments of Canadian artillery and infantry set out for the scene of trouble. In addition volunteers and home guards were soon mustered at other points along the frontier.

Meanwhile it was reported that the Fenians were concentrating at St. Albans "from every station and by every northward train".[30] The first invaders began to appear near Eccles Hill on May 23rd, in groups of twelve to twenty men each. On the 24th about 250 were busy arming themselves and making ready to cross the border. They are

[26]Reavley, *op. cit.*, p. 73.   [27]Reminiscences of Parker Smith.
[28]See *The Fenian Raid of 1870, by Reporters*. Published by the Montreal *Witness*, 1870.
[29]*Ibid.*, p. 8.   [30]*Ibid.*, p. 9.

described as "men about 25 years old, the scum of American cities", together with a few others of better class who joined "for the fun of making a raid on Canada".[31]   On the 25th they began their march towards Eccles Hill, which had meanwhile been occupied by Canadian troops. The Fenians had put on their characteristic uniform of blue, green, yellow and grey, and all wore the French military cap. About 200 of them, supplied with forty rounds of ammunition each, advanced across the border, marching "in column with the steadiness of regular troops".[32]

As they approached the hill the Fenians were under fire from the Canadian force, and they returned the shots for a few minutes; then they suddenly "broke in wild disorder and sought the friendly shelter of adjoining houses and lumber piles".[33]   A few skirmishes took place during the next few hours, but the invaders were repulsed wherever any showed a disposition to fight. General O'Neil was captured by an American officer and lodged in jail at St. Albans. On the American side of the border a considerable number of Vermont farmers were waiting with their wagons to carry away the loot that had been promised by the Fenians as payment for their help in bringing up supplies!

A similar raid took place on a much smaller scale in Huntingdon County. The invaders barricaded themselves behind log and rail fences, but when attacked by the 50th Borderers they took "a bee line for the protecting arms of Uncle Sam"[34] with such speed that all escaped capture.

Former Canadians who had removed to the United States were greatly incensed at the Fenian invasions, and particularly at the time of the raid upon Ridgeway. In a number of cities bodies of recruits offered to proceed to Canada and aid in her defence. The Chicago Volunteers, fifty-six in number, actually came to Toronto at their own expense, and their services were accepted by General Napier, though they did not come into action. Their arrival in Toronto aroused great enthusiasm, and a conversazione was held in their honour.[35]

The United States Government was somewhat dilatory

[31]*Ibid.*, p. 15.   [32]*Ibid.*, p. 18.   [33]*Ibid.*, p. 20.   [34]*Ibid.*, p. 54.
[35]For details of the Chicago expedition see *The Fenian Raid at Fort Erie, 1866*, 1866. pp. 36-40. (W. C. Chewett & Co., publishers.)

in taking measures to cope with Fenian activities against Canada; it would appear, in fact, that certain of the highest officials purposely delayed action in order to aid the invaders. Ten days after the Fort Erie raid of '66 President Johnson issued a proclamation forbidding further attacks. Similarly, after the raids of 1870, President Grant took measures to prevent unlawful expeditions from leaving the United States.

There has been no fear of Fenian activity along our borders during the past sixty years. This is due partly to changes in the government of Ireland, which have to a great extent removed the causes which originally prompted Fenianism. But the designs of the invaders of the sixties formed a contributory cause of Confederation, for the provinces realised that the proverb "In Union is Strength" was particularly applicable to themselves. The development of national feeling in Canada was in no small measure due to the fear of invasion from the south.

CHAPTER VIII

THE RIEL REBELLION OF 1870—THE RED RIVER EXPEDITION

"Students of the strategic branch of military science rank the Red River Expedition as one of the most notable examples of an expeditionary force sent into a strange country far from its base of supplies. In this regard it is classed with the landing of Sir Ralph Abercrombie at Alexandria, the first Ashanti expedition, and General Roberts' march to Kandahar."[1]

IN 1869 the vast territories for two centuries under the control of the Hudson's Bay Company reverted to the British Crown and were immediately transferred to the newly-formed Dominion of Canada. The original charter of the great fur-trading Company gave it control of all the land draining into Hudson's Bay, and during the first half of the nineteenth century it had penetrated into the far West, including in its sphere of influence the province of British Columbia.

In the Red River district was located Fort Garry, the Canadian headquarters of the Company, on the site where Winnipeg has since grown to be the metropolis of the West. When the territory was taken over, the Canadian Government immediately sent surveyors to this district, and they proceeded to divide the land into lots, irrespective of the squatters' rights of the Indians and half-breeds then settled in the locality, where they had become accustomed to the mild rule of the Company. At the same time William McDougall was appointed Lieutenant-Governor of the newly-acquired territory and he proceeded to the West by way of the United States, then the only practicable route.

There were at this time two main influences at work in the West,—the Hudson's Bay Company, and the Roman Catholic priesthood. The Company opposed colonisation and settlement as adversely affecting the Indian trade; while the priests hoped that a French Roman Catholic province similar to Quebec would develop, and dominate the

---

[1]Toronto *Mail and Empire*, 1896, quoted in Bruce Harman: *'Twas 26 Years Ago.* 1896. p. 5. (A pamphlet reprinted from the *Mail and Empire*, May 30, 1896.)

HALF-BREEDS TRAVELLING
An expedition to hunt buffalo near Fort Garry. Red River carts were often used in the transport of furs

THE RED RIVER SETTLEMENT

From *L'Opinion Publique*, June 16, 1870

RED RIVER EXPEDITION—TRAINING VOLUNTEERS AT THE
CRYSTAL PALACE, TORONTO

Originally the Palace of Industry, this was the first permanent
Exhibition building, and was located just south of the Provincial
Lunatic Asylum.

From *L'Opinion Publique*, May 12, 1870

INSPECTION OF VOLUNTEERS AT LE CHAMP DE MARS,
MONTREAL, 1870

West. Consequently both opposed European immigration, and united in describing the country as unfit for settlement. The opposition to the new state of affairs was led by Louis Riel, a clever half-breed with a good command of English. Though possibly somewhat lacking in physical courage, he was not deficient in moral determination, and he exerted a great influence over the French-Canadian trappers.

While the priests preached resistance to the Canadian Government, Riel and a few half-breeds made their first move in October, 1869, when they warned the surveyors to desist from their work. Soon afterwards they formed the "Republic of the North-West", and of the Provisional Government which was instituted, Riel was soon President, though at first John Bruce held that position, while Riel was Secretary. As a preliminary step they seized the Hudson's Bay Company stores, and so were able to feed, clothe, arm and pay the insurgents at the Company's expense. Had these stores been better protected, or had they been previously destroyed, it is doubtful if the rebellion could ever have come to a head. The appointment of William McDougall as the first Governor has been generally considered injudicious because of his attitude, described by General Wolseley as "essentially cold-blooded, and entirely wanting in cordiality".[2] Riel's next step was to prevent the Governor's entry into the territory, which was accomplished by the erection of a barricade, defended by half-breeds, on the road between Pembina and Fort Garry.

The inhabitants of the Red River district included a number of English and Scotch settlers. These loyal citizens attempted to upset the Provisional Government, but the result was the imprisonment of several of them, and the execution of Thomas Scott, an Ontario Protestant, on a false charge of breach of parole. Scott was given a "trial" by a half-breed court-martial, and executed a few hours later by a semi-intoxicated firing squad in charge of an American citizen who had seen service in the Northern army in Civil War days. When news of these events reached Ontario, public opinion demanded that an expedition be sent immediately to restore law and order.

[2] Viscount Wolseley: *Narrative of the Red River Expedition.* (In *Blackwood's Magazine*, December, 1870, to February, 1871, p. 215.)

The expeditionary force[3] as finally constituted numbered about 1,400 men, and it was sent at the joint expense of the Imperial and Dominion Governments, the latter paying three-quarters of the cost. The force comprised a detachment of Regulars of the First Battalion 60th Rifles, a battalion of Canadian militia from Ontario and one from Quebec, together with detachments of the Royal Engineers and the Royal Artillery, with two seven-pound bronze mountain guns, and a proportionate number of the Army Service and Army Hospital corps. It was noticeable that the expedition received most of its moral support from Ontario, the people of Quebec being to a large extent antagonistic; only eighty French-Canadians enlisted in the 2nd Rifles, which represented Quebec.

The work of organising and equipping the force began early in May, 1870. General the Hon. James Lindsay was sent out from England to take charge of the organisation; but Colonel Garnet Wolseley, who was placed in command, is very emphatic in stating that ignorance and political jobbery on the part of the Canadian Government prevented the best arrangements from being made, and caused a considerable waste of time and money, as well as untold annoyance.[4]

After passing a rigid physical examination in Toronto the men were marched to the Crystal Palace (the old Palace of Industry), in which they were quartered; this noted building, located south of the Insane Asylum, had been the scene of the brilliant ball given in honour of H.R.H. the

[3]The chief sources of our knowledge of the Red River Expedition are three in number: (1) Viscount Wolseley: *Narrative of the Red River Expedition.* (2) Captain G. L. Huyshe: *The Red River Expedition.* These accounts by the commander of the force and a member of his staff may be considered official, since both writers had access to the documents relative to the expedition. Their narratives are supplemented by (3) Captain Bruce Harman: *'Twas 26 Years Ago,* a shorter description which is important in that it is written from the point of view of a member of the Canadian militia, while the other accounts are those of professional soldiers. In addition to these histories of the force, interesting material has been obtained by the present writer from Lieutenant H. S. H. Riddell's *The Red River Expedition of 1870*; and from the verbal reminiscences of a veteran of the force, William R. Whitelaw of Cobourg, Ontario. Notes 2, 8, 1, 10 and 16, respectively, give detailed information as to the publications in which all of these descriptions of the expedition may be found in print.

[4]Wolseley, *op. cit.*, pp. 225 *et seq.*

PRINCE ARTHUR'S LANDING (PORT ARTHUR) IN 1872

From the *Canadian Illustrated News*, June 15, 1870   "Rev. Mr. W."

RED RIVER EXPEDITION: CAMP AT SAULT STE. MARIE

This is the sketch the making of which led to a false alarm of Fenian activities

From *L'Opinion Publique*, July 7, 1870

THE RED RIVER EXPEDITION: UNLOADING SUPPLIES AT PRINCE ARTHUR'S LANDING

Prince of Wales when he visited Toronto in 1860. After a thorough inspection of the forces and their special equipment for the hazardous journey they entrained on the Northern Railway and proceeded to Collingwood, where on May 21st the first detachment embarked for Thunder Bay. The *Chicora*, the *Arctic* and the *Algoma* were among the steamships which had been obtained to transport the expedition to Lake Superior.

At that time the only canal at Sault Ste. Marie was on the American side and, as it was not expected that a military force could be taken through this channel, an effort was made to effect the three and one-half mile portage of the men and equipment while the boats went through the canal; but the United States Government objected at the time, and only two empty steamships which had been sent in advance of the expedition succeeded in passing through. After a protest by the Dominion Government all restrictions on empty vessels were raised, but not before considerable delay had resulted. During the stay at the Sault a humorous incident enlivened the proceedings. A clergyman appeared one day, making sketches of the tents and other features of the camp. A sentry suspected that he was a Fenian spy, the precursor of a raid on the expedition from across the border, so he immediately called out the whole camp, "much to the disgust of all concerned when the true state of affairs was discovered".[5]

At 10 a.m. on May 25th Colonel Wolseley and the first detachment landed at "The Station" on Thunder Bay, the balance of the expedition arriving at various times up to June 21st, when the last section disembarked. The commander gave the name Prince Arthur's Landing to the place of debarkation, which was about four miles north-west of the mouth of the Kaministiquia River, the name being in honour of the Prince who was then in Canada. Everyone worked until late at night landing oxen, horses, wagons and stores by means of a large scow which drew so little water that it was possible to approach close to shore. The appearance of Prince Arthur's Landing (now Port Arthur) is thus described by the commander of the expedition:

"There was but a small clearance in the woods when we

[5]Harman, *op. cit.*, p. 10. The "Rev. W." 's sketch of the expedition is reproduced on the opposite page.

landed, where a few wooden shanties had been erected, and all around the prospect was extremely desolate. One of those dreadful fires which occasionally sweep over whole districts in Canada, destroying houses, crops, cattle, and sometimes many human lives, had raged over the country between the landing and Shebandowan Lake, destroying small bridges, culverts, and cribwork on the road already partly made between those two points. . . . The forest, which came down to the water's edge all round the bay, presented a pitiful sight. Nature never wears a more sombre appearance than when the fiery element has swept over a forest, burning every leaf, every small branch, and every blade of grass, leaving nothing but the tall dismally-blackened timbers and burnt-up rocks around them."[6]

Colonel Wolseley had been assured by the government that the Dawson Road to Lake Shebandowan would be ready, and portage roads constructed along the route of the expedition by the time the forces were ready to move from Thunder Bay. When he inspected the road the day after his arrival, however, he was able to ride only thirty-one miles, the remainder not having been completed. This was not blamed upon S. J. Dawson, who had charge of communications, but was due to the poor type of men who had been appointed to work under him, and to forest fires and heavy rains which greatly increased the labour beyond expectation. The country was alternately rocky and sandy, a wilderness inhabited only by wandering tribes of Chippawa Indians. Rivers, lakes, rocks and scrub timber were interspersed among burnt-out clearances, called *brûlés*, and at no point along the entire route to Red River were supplies of any kind available. In addition to the physical difficulties were others more annoying. The commander makes frequent references to the loafers who obtained responsible positions by political "pull", to the scarcity of guides, the poorness of drivers, and the inferiority of all military stores supplied by the Canadian Goverment. He attributes considerable of the delay in road-building at Thunder Bay to the influence of a high French-Canadian official who was not anxious to see the expedition succeed.[7]

The Land Transport Corps particularly aroused the ire

[6]Wolseley, *op. cit.*, pp. 237-8.   [7]*Ibid.*, pp. 241-2 and 252-4.

of the officers. One hundred and fifty horses, and half that number of wagons and teamsters, made up the force; but, while the animals were splendid, the teamsters "had been picked up anywhere and everywhere, without any regard to their qualifications; many of them knew no more about driving or about the care of horses than they did about kangaroos. Some had been barkeepers, some clerks, and not a few were 'decayed gentlemen' who had 'seen better times'. They were refractory and difficult to manage, being amenable to no discipline."[8]

After a second inspection of the Dawson Road, Colonel Wolseley decided that it would be preferable to use the Kaministiquia River route to Lake Shebandowan for the carriage of supplies. A great deal of work had first to be done at Prince Arthur's Landing, and for several weeks there was little but work, work, work, from daylight until dark, and often far into the night. The transport of stores, road-building, the construction of stables, storehouses and supply depots, a hospital,—even a redoubt against a possible Fenian attack,—all entailed sustained labour and efficient organisation; but finally, on July 1st, all was in readiness and the expedition set out.

The force travelled in brigades at intervals of a day. In the lead were the Regulars, and the Ontario Rifles and the other units followed, the whole expedition covering a space of 150 miles while in progress. Communications were established between all sections, and Colonel Wolseley travelled from one to another in a birch canoe, keeping all under control for concentration if necessary. There was a commendable feeling of rivalry between the Regulars and Militia as to speed and efficiency, and this existed also among companies in the same unit. The leading detachment travelled 200 miles in nineteen days, building corduroy roads where necessary as they progressed. The difficulties on the way included heavy thunder storms, plagues of flies, forest fires, and every imaginable inconvenience; but all were successfully surmounted. The minute organisation which was characteristic of this expedition is well exemplified in the issuing of veils and mosquito oil as a protection against the ravages of these troublesome flies; ex-

[8]G. L. Huyshe: *The Red River Expedition*. 1871. p. 65.

perience proved, however, that smudges of smoke were more valuable for the purpose, and the other defences were not extensively used.

After the forty-eight mile trip by river and road to Lake Shebandowan there was a section of 310 miles by river and lake to the Lake of the Woods; in this part of the route there were seventeen portages, of which some were more than a mile long and entailed excessive physical labour. From the Lake of the Woods to Fort Garry was just 100 miles by land, but only sixty miles of the road had been built, and the unmade portion was through very bad swamps; consequently it was found impossible to use that route, and the expedition had to travel by the Winnipeg River, which was very difficult of navigation. There were thirty portages in this additional 160 miles.

A total of 126 York boats, weighing from 700 to 900 pounds each, were used to transport the force, and all of these had to be portaged. A typical portage is described by Colonel Wolseley in his account of the expedition. Sixty days' provisions were carried, consisting of salt pork, beans, preserved potatoes, flour, biscuits, pepper, salt, tea and sugar; of these the heaviest to portage was the pork, which was packed in 200-pound barrels. There was, in addition, ammunition, tools, camping and cooking equipment, and a large amount of miscellaneous material, as well as the two guns and their ammunition and equipment.

The method of carriage was that in vogue among the Indians and *voyageurs,* and consisted of "a long strap about three inches wide in the centre, where it is passed across the forehead, but tapering off to an inch in width at the ends, which are fastened round the barrel or parcel to be portaged. Men accustomed to this work will thus carry weights of 400 lbs, and some 500 lbs., across the longest portage, the loads resting on the upper part of the back, and kept there by the strap going round the forehea i. The great strain is thus upon the neck, which has to oe ke₁ʋ very rigid, whilst the body is bent well forward".[9]

The soldiers were gradually trained to use this means of transport, but at first employed somewhat easier methods The officers set the example in carrying loads by the fore-

[9]Wolseley, *op. cit.,* pp. 245-6.

THE HUDSON'S BAY POST AT SAULT STE. MARIE, 1853

LE BOIS BRÛLÉ

Burnt-out clearances (*brûlés*) alternated with rivers, lakes and
rocks over a large part of the route of the Red River Expedition

FORT FRANCES, AT THE MOUTH OF RAINY RIVER

DEUX RIVIÈRES PORTAGE, RED RIVER EXPEDITION, 1870

head strap method, and a large proportion of the men were
soon expert in the work.   A great deal of heavy hauling
was also involved in portaging thirty-foot boats over a
height of 100 feet.   It was usually necessary for each man to
make ten trips over the portages, so that a mile of carriage
necessitated nineteen miles of walking before all the stores
and equipment were transferred.   This was the general
procedure followed in each of the forty-seven portages
which it was necessary to make along the route.   The only
recreations available during this arduous work were fishing and swimming, both of which were greatly enjoyed.

The Deux Rivières Portage was one of the most difficult encountered by the expedition.   A lieutenant of the
60th Rifles states that "in the centre of it was a high rock,
up which a ladder of felled trees had been constructed; and
at the side, steps were cut for the men to carry their loads
up.   Had one of the ropes snapped when hauling the boats
up this ladder, the men at work would doubtless have received very severe injuries, and the boat been broken to a
certainty."[10]

Another very laborious portage was known as the
"Height of Land", because there, between Kashaboiwe Lake
and Lac de Mille Lacs, lay the watershed between Hudson's
Bay and the Gulf of St. Lawrence.   The distance was two
miles, but the portage was cut down by taking advantage of
Summit Pond.   After wading up a narrow creek and
dragging the boats through it, the men reached the Pond at
the western side of which was the portage path.   Two
brigades worked at opposite ends of this carrying-place of
1,900 yards, and so reduced the labour.   To effect the passage of the boats, "a broad road ten feet wide had to be cut
through the woods, and trees laid down at intervals of about
three feet as skids or rollers, on which the boats were dragged over on their keels to keep them from the rocky
ground".[11]

Poplar trees abounded in this region and were the best
for the purposes of the road, as they were green and had a
smooth bark; when it rained, the labour of dragging the

[10]H. S. H. Riddell: *The Red River Expedition of 1870.* (In Literary
    and Historical Society of Quebec, *Transactions*, 1870-2, Vol. III,
    Part 8, p. 117.)
[11]Huyshe, *op cit.*, p. 110.

boats was easier, for the slippery bark was almost as effective as greased rollers. On steep ground the skids were kept in place by the use of strong wooden pegs. It was found best to portage the boats first while the crew were fresh, and the provisions afterwards. Eight men hauled each of the lighter boats, but thirty or forty were frequently necessary to move the larger ones over the steep places. Sometimes the boats contained as much as twenty-four barrels of pork, as well as other provisions and equipment, "and the labour of going backwards and forwards so constantly with heavy loads was very severe."[12] The use of large, rough sledges carrying eight or ten barrels was attempted, but they were too heavy to be of permanent use. Officers and men alike laboured "from five a.m. to eight p.m. with a short interval for breakfast and dinner; nothing to eat but salt pork and biscuit, nothing to drink but tea, they yet looked as healthy and cheery as possible. . . . They had no time to be sick."[13]

The men eagerly anticipated their arrival at Fort Frances on Rainy River, the half-way point. The Hudson's Bay post there consisted merely of a collection of one-storey blockhouses. When the force had almost reached the Fort a gale on Rainy Lake prevented progress for several days, during which the men made rich finds of blueberries which covered the islands. Meanwhile the Chippawa Indians held a great pow-wow at Fort Frances to consider whether the expedition was to be allowed to pass; they finally decided to accede to the government's request, though not before all due formalities had been complied with, and long and monotonous orations in the Indian tongue had been delivered. At Fort Frances Colonel Wolseley left one company of the Ontario Rifles as guard over a depot of supplies and a hospital. An intelligence officer who had been sent in advance to Fort Garry *via* the United States met the expedition at Fort Frances, and reported a panic-stricken population at the Red River settlement. Riel was busy removing plunder to the United States, but the fort was still held by an armed force, and the situation bore a serious and threatening aspect. Orders were therefore given to

[12]*Ibid.*, p. 111.   [13]*Ibid.*, p. 113.

approach Rat Portage with great care, for fear of an ambush or a surprise attack.

The voyage from Fort Frances down the Rainy River was most enjoyable, for there was seventy miles of unbroken navigation with only two small rapids, which could be run. At Rat Portage (Kenora) there was a Hudson's Bay Company post consisting of three log houses with bark roofs, and a palisade. Here the expedition was met by a delegation of English settlers from the Red River, who had travelled there in six large Hudson Bay boats in order to urge the necessity of haste; they requested guns and supplies to prevent an Indian rising that appeared imminent.

The journey down the Winnipeg River between the Lake of the Woods and Lake Winnipeg was 160 miles long, and there was a difference in level of about 340 feet in that distance. Thirty falls and rapids made this section of the voyage a series of beautiful and enchanting scenes, and many a perilous descent was successfully run by the skilled Indian paddlers accompanying the expedition. The first detachment of troops reached Fort Alexander on August 18th, accomplishing the journey from Rat Portage in half the time estimated as necessary. Here news was received that Riel could not organise a force sufficient to resist attack, but that he had ordered the Hudson's Bay Company to stop selling gunpowder or bullets, for fear his men would run short. The Regulars pushed on along Lake Winnipeg towards the mouth of the Red River without waiting for the Militia to come up to Fort Alexander. A number of boats grounded in the shallow water near the mouth, but soon the force was working its way up the river against a heavy wind, proceeding in three lines of boats, in the first of which were the guns, ready for instant action.

On August 23rd the Regulars arrived at the Lower Fort, a building of stone construction with loop-holes throughout and bastions at the corners. As it was only twenty-one and one-half miles by road to Fort Garry, precautions were taken to prevent news reaching Riel that the troops were so close upon him. It appears, however, that the rebel leader had spies posted at various points to keep him informed of the progress of the expedition.

The arrival of the force at the Lower Fort brought out the loyal inhabitants *en masse*: "They received us with the greatest enthusiasm, cheering and waving handkerchiefs. They ran down to the riverside grasping our fellows by the hand, and with tears in their eyes exclaimed, 'God bless you, men! God bless you!', at the same time proffering all sorts of provisions and refreshments."[14]

The Regulars continued by road towards Fort Garry, and bivouacked that night six miles from their destination. It poured rain all night and the road was impassable by morning, so that it was necessary to take to the boats again. Concerning this phase of the expedition the commander wrote:

"This necessary change of plan was annoying, as we had looked forward to advancing upon the Fort in all the pride, pomp and circumstance of war. As we bent over our fires at daybreak, trying to get some warmth for our bodies, and sufficient heat to boil the kettles, a more miserable-looking lot of objects it would be impossible to imagine. Everyone was wet through; we were cold and hungry; our very enemies would have pitied our plight."[15]

After a hurried breakfast of tea and biscuit they again took to the boats, rowing in the rain in three columns towards Fort Garry. A landing was made at Point Douglas, on the left bank, two miles by road from the Fort. The guns were dragged along by a few horses and carts obtained by skirmishers sent in advance, and the forces marched through deep mud in a heavy rain which made it impossible to see far ahead. Word was received *en route* that Riel was still in the fort and intended to fight, and this news raised the spirits of the soldiers, who had long hoped for a battle. As they neared Fort Garry the men were placed in a position that enabled them to command a boat-bridge across the Assiniboine River and prevent the enemy's escape, for the villagers insisted that Riel and his men were still there. Skirmishers advanced in intense excitement, expecting to be fired on any minute; but they soon found that the fort had been evacuated and the gates left open. The men were keenly disappointed, but the rebel guns were hauled out and a royal salute fired from them as the Union

[14]Harman, *op. cit.*, pp. 26-7.   [15]Wolseley, *op. cit.*, pp. 322-3.

Mrs. Edward Hopkins

ADVANCED GUARD CROSSING A PORTAGE, RED RIVER EXPEDITION, 1870

Wolseley's canoe is in the right centre. The original of this illustration was presented to the Dominion of Canada in 1917 by Louisa, Dowager Viscountess Wolseley, in memory of her husband

THE HUDSON'S BAY COMPANY POST AT FORT GARRY, 1870
The site is today in the centre of the city of Winnipeg. In 1870
Winnipeg had a population of slightly more than 200.

H. A. Strong

THE INTERIOR OF FORT GARRY
The artist depicts a scene characteristic of Hudson's Bay trading days

Jack was run up above the fort. There were many evidences of a hasty departure only a few hours previously. In fact Riel and the other leaders were not far distant, and might have been captured if the commander had been given civil authority to issue warrants for their arrest.

The village of Winnipeg was located about 800 yards north of Fort Garry, and connected with it by a straight road. A few whitewashed frame or log buildings made up the settlement, which had a population of about 200. Among the few veterans of the expedition still living is William R. Whitelaw of Cobourg, who recalls the appearance of Winnipeg at that time,—some frame buildings, the Hudson's Bay Company fort, Ashdown's log store, Bannatyne's store, half of which served as the Post Office,—such were the beginnings of the great metropolis of the Middle West![16]

The reaction from the long months of fear and suspense, the absence of police and the former machinery of government, and the fact that whisky was obtainable everywhere, combined to cause considerable trouble in the weeks that followed. Collisions between loyalists and former rebels were hard to prevent, but it was considered best to get along without resort to military rule if at all possible.

The escape of Louis Riel, as learned by Colonel Wolseley,[17] is worth relating. Early in the morning of August 24th, Riel, accompanied by his "Secretary of State", both on stolen horses, left Fort Garry and galloped away through the rain. They crossed the Red River and fled southward, bivouacking on the plains at night. When they awoke in the morning their horses were gone, so they recrossed the river on a raft made from a neighbouring fence, the boards being fastened together by the trousers of Riel's companion. The farmer whose fence they had torn down met them on the opposite side of the river and received in compensation some of the stolen money with which they had filled their pockets before leaving Fort Garry. Two days later, with bare, swollen feet, they reached Pembina, in American territory. As they were not well received there they continued to St. Joseph's, fifty

[16]Reminiscences of William R. Whitelaw. See E. C. Guillet: *Cobourg*, in the *Cobourg Sentinel-Star*, July 23, 1931.
[17]Wolseley, *op. cit.*, pp. 332-3.

miles westward near the border. Riel had previously sent much of his plunder thither, and there the ex-President of "The Provisional Government of the Republic of the North-West" lived for some time.

Meanwhile, between August 29th and September 3rd, Colonel Wolseley and the Regulars left for the east, all returning by the water route except one company, which marched about ninety miles by the Snow Road to the northwest angle of the Lake of the Woods and then took to the boats. They were in barracks at Montreal and Quebec by October. At Red River one militia regiment was quartered in each fort, and during their stay in the district there was some trouble among the members of the force, largely caused by the fact that time hung heavily on their hands. Gambling and drinking among a few of the members and some half-breeds was the beginning of the trouble, which later took on a religious aspect, making it more difficult of settlement. Some of the men became disgruntled because of too frequent drills and inspections; but by the use of great tact the disorders were eventually settled quietly, and no one was severely punished. In the spring of 1871 a further reduction of the force took place, and some of the soldiers, instead of returning east, took up land in the district.

One of the main results of the Riel insurrection was the creation of the Province of Manitoba in 1870, with similar rights of self-government as were enjoyed by the inhabitants of the other provinces. The noted military expedition which so effectively settled the trouble travelled 1,280 miles from Toronto, and accomplished its purpose without the loss of a single life, and with sickness practically unknown. Its success was due to the generalship of its commander, and his thoroughness in all that pertained to the efficiency of the corps. In imitation of the usual custom at lumber camps it was decided that no liquor whatever should be served to the men during the course of the expedition, and this was undoubtedly of paramount importance in the achievement of such magnificent results. Concerning this policy, which had very few precedents in military expeditions, the commander wrote: "By increasing the allowance of tea, and abolishing that of rum, you diminish the supplies to be carried, whilst you add to the health and efficiency of your men."[18] Captain Harman considered that the proof of this statement "was fully exemplified in this expedition, and its success was in a great measure due to the strict temperance discipline of the men. From the time the expedition left Thunder Bay, 1st July, until they arrived at Fort Garry, August 24th, not a drop of liquor was partaken and not a single man seriously ill, and crime unknown."[19]

In a *resumé* of the course of events which culminated in such unusual success General Wolseley wrote:

"So ended the Red River Expedition—an undertaking that will long stand out in our military chronicles as possessing characteristics peculiarly its own. . . . The force sent to the Red River for the purpose of crushing out rebellion there had to advance from its point of disembarkation more than 600 miles through a wilderness of water, rocks and forests, where no supplies were to be had, and where every pound-weight of provisions and stores had to be transported for miles on the backs of the soldiers. . . . By the careful administration of General Lindsay and the officers he had selected to carry out his orders the total expense of the whole Expedition was under £100,000. There was no reckless waste either in material or in money. Such a careful economy was exercised in its organisation, and in administering to its subsequent wants, that it may be safely asserted that no such distance has ever been traversed by an efficient brigade numbering about 1,400 souls, in any of our numerous little wars, at such a trifling cost."[20]

No commander was ever more beloved and respected by his men than was the leader of the Red River Expedition. His valedictory address[21] to the militia regiments under his command shows that he thoroughly reciprocated these sentiments:

"In saying 'good-bye' I beg that each and all of you will accept my grateful recognition of your valuable services. . . . I congratulate you upon the success of our expedition. . . . The credit of this success is due to the gallant soldiers I

[18]Garnet Wolseley: *The Soldier's Pocket-book for Field Service.* 1869. Quoted in Harman, *op. cit.*, p. 24.
[19]Harman, *op. cit.*, p. 24.
[20]Wolseley's *Red River Expedition*, pp. 334-5.
[21]Quoted in Harman, *op. cit.*, pp. 27-8.

had at my back. . . . Nothing but that pluck for which British soldiers are celebrated could have carried you so successfully through the arduous advance upon this place. . . . . I can say without flattery that, although I have served with many armies in the field, I have never been associated with a better set of men."

As a further proof of the high estimation in which he held Canadian troops may be noted his establishment of a corps of Canadian *voyageurs* to participate under his command in the Nile expedition of 1884-85. As a man and as a leader Field Marshall Viscount Wolseley stands out among the great generals in the history of the British army.

BIBLIOGRAPHY

MANUSCRIPT AND UNPRINTED

PUBLIC ARCHIVES OF CANADA

Correspondance Générale, Volumes 91, 93, 95 and 97.
Coventry Papers.
Haldimand Papers.
Manuscripts, 1812-18.
Merritt Papers.
Military Papers.
Mitchell Collection.
Papers on the War of 1812.
Simcoe Papers.
Upper Canada Immigration Papers.
Upper Canada Land Papers.
Upper Canada Sundries.

ARCHIVES OF ONTARIO

Macaulay Papers.
Merritt Papers.
Robinson Papers.
The Diary of John Thomson.

PUBLIC REFERENCE LIBRARY, TORONTO

The Diary of Major R. Mathews.

UNIVERSITY OF TORONTO LIBRARY

GOLDSTEIN, WALTER G.: *Toronto (York) in the War of 1812.* (Ph.D. thesis, 1908.)
HARSTONE, JEAN E.: *The Early History of the County and Town of Peterborough.* (M.A. thesis, 1914.)
LOWER, ARTHUR R.: *The History of the Canadian Timber and Lumber Trade prior to Confederation.* (Ph.D. thesis, 1923.)
STEWART, JEAN C.: *Simcoe as Statesman and Administrator.* (Ph.D. thesis, 1928.)
TALMAN, JAMES J.: *Social Life in Upper Canada, 1815-1840.* (Ph.D. thesis, 1931.)

IN PRIVATE POSSESSION

Maps, ledgers and miscellaneous papers relating to early Upper Canada, and particularly to the Canada Company. (In the possession of E. W. Banting, Esq., Toronto.)
BUCK, CHARLES S.: *Old Sparta and its Neighbours.*
Report Concerning Public Buildings in Upper Canada, 1799. (In the possession of Dr. George Locke, Public Library, Toronto.)
Reminiscences of the Rev. William Tomblin. (In the possession of Mrs. W. J. Garland, Cobourg.)
Letter of Duncan Campbell to Malcolm Campbell, dated at Otonabee Township, January 28, 1838. (In the possession of Miss Annie Campbell, Toronto.)
Agreement between the Cobourg and Rice Lake Plank Road and Ferry Company and Certain Millers. (In the possession of Richard Ley, Esq., Cobourg.)

PRINTED

Works of Reference, Government Publications, etc.

The *Annual Register.*
Chambers' Encyclopaedia.
The *Encyclopaedia Britannica.*
The *Dictionary of Canadian Biography.*
Who's Who in Canada.
The *Dictionary of National Biography.*
Dominion Government, *Reports.*
The *Canada Year Book.*
Public Archives of Canada, *Reports.*
Ontario Government, *Reports.*
Ontario Government, *Archaeological Reports.*
Archives of Ontario, *Reports.*
House of Assembly of Upper Canada, *Journal.*
Ontario Educational Association, *Reports.*
Ontario Land Surveyors, *Reports.*

Reports, Transactions and Papers of Societies

The records of the following societies have been searched for historical material. Where articles have been found which bear directly upon the subject matter of this work they have been listed individually in the bibliography of books and pamphlets.

Algonquin Historical Society.
Brant County Historical Society.
Buffalo Historical Society.
Canadian Historical Association.
Canadian Institute.
Canadian North-West Historical Association.
Celtic Society, Montreal.
Champlain Society.
Cobourg Historical Society.
Elgin Historical Society.
Essex County Historical Society.
Huron Institute.
Lennox and Addington Historical Society.
London and Middlesex Historical Society.
Loyal and Patriotic Society of Canada.
Lundy's Lane Historical Society.
Manitoba Historical and Scientific Society.
Michigan Pioneer and Historical Society.
Niagara Historical Society.
Ontario Historical Society.
Ontario Pioneer and Historical Society.
Ottawa Historical Society.
Quebec Literary and Historical Society.
Royal Society of Canada.
Simcoe County Pioneer and Historical Society.
Thunder Bay Historical Society.
United Empire Loyalist Association of Canada.
United Empire Loyalist Association of Ontario.
Waterloo Historical Society.
Welland County Historical Society.
Wentworth Historical Society.
Women's Canadian Historical Society of Ottawa.
Women's Canadian Historical Society of Toronto.
York Pioneer and Historical Society.

NEWSPAPERS

A study of complete or partial files of the following newspapers has yielded a large amount of invaluable historical material. Those which have been chosen are representative, and include the larger part of the earliest files extant. They are listed chronologically by towns. Reference to a few other publications is made in the notes.

Upper Canada Gazette, or American Oracle. (Published at Niagara, 1793-98; then at York. In 1807 it became the *York Gazette,* and in later years appeared under various names. In 1828 it split into two publications—the *Upper Canada Gazette* and the *U. E. Loyalist.*)

Niagara *Canada Constellation.* (1799-1800.)
Niagara Herald. (1801-1802.)
Kingston Gazette. (1810—.). Later appeared under various names.
Kingston *Upper Canada Herald.* (1819-1851.)
Hallowell Free Press. (Now the *Picton Gazette.* 1830—.)
Cobourg Star. (Now the *Cobourg Sentinel-Star.* 1831—.)
Cobourg Sentinel. (1861-78.)
Cobourg World. (1864—.)
Port Hope Telegraph. (Now the *Guide.* 1831—.)
St. Thomas Journal. (1831—.)
Christian Guardian. (Toronto. Now the *New Outlook.* 1829—.)
Toronto *Examiner.* (1837-55.)
Toronto *Mirror.* (1837-62.)
Toronto *British Colonist.* (1838-58.)
Toronto *Palladium of British America.* (1838-39.)
Toronto *Globe.* (1844—.)
Toronto *Mail and Empire.* (1871—.)
Farmer's Sun. (Toronto. 1890—.)
Swanton, Vermont, *North American.* (1838-41.)
Peterborough Examiner. (1852—.)

PERIODICALS

The following publications have provided considerable historical information not available elsewhere. The articles which are related to the subject matter of this book are listed in the bibliography of books and pamphlets.

American Anthropologist.
Canadian Antiquarian and Numismatic Journal.
Canadian Defence Quarterly.
Canadian Geographical Journal.
Canadian Historical Review.
Canadian Magazine.
Canadian Monthly and National Review.
Canadian National Railways Magazine.
C. S. L. Chart.
Journal of Political Economy.
Methodist Magazine.
National Geographic Magazine.
Ontario Curling Association, *Annuals.*
Queen's University *Bulletins.*
The War. (Published in New York during the War of 1812.)
University Magazine.
Willison's Monthly.

BOOKS, PAMPHLETS AND ARTICLES

In the following list the dates of publication are of the first edition except in a few instances where the original publication is not available. Exceptionally long titles are usually abbreviated. It is hoped that the bibliography will be valuable as a source-book to students of Canadian history; though it is perhaps unnecessary to say that many of the items listed contain comparatively little of value, but have been mentioned to indicate that they have been consulted. A number of general histories have been included since they are frequently the only sources available in the smaller libraries and schools; their contents, however, are for the most part restricted to political, military and constitutional history. Many of the following books and pamphlets are now very rare, and are seldom to be found even in the most extensive public or private collections. Almost all of them are, however, available in one or another of the following public collections: Public Reference Library, Toronto, Legistative Library of Ontario, University of Toronto Library, Victoria University Library, Douglas Library of Queen's University, Library of the Public Archives of Canada, Library of Parliament, Ottawa, Library of Transportation of the University of Michigan, Ann Arbour, U.S.A.

ABBOT, J.: *Philip Musgrave, or Memoirs of a Church of England Missionary in the American Colonies,* 1846.
[ABBOTT, J.]: *The Emigrant to North America.* 1844.
ABDY, E. S.: *Journal of a Residence and Tour in the United States.* 1835.
ADAM, G. M.: *Toronto, Old and New.* 1891.
AHEARN, M. H.: *The Settlers of March Township.* (In Ontario Historical Society, *Papers and Records,* Volume 3.)
ALEXANDER, SIR JAMES: *Transatlantic Sketches.* 1833.
ALEXANDER, SIR JAMES: *L'Acadie, or Seven Years' Explorations in British America.* 2 Volumes. 1849.
ANDERSON, D.: *Canada, or a View of the Importance of the British American Colonies.* 1814.
ANDERSON, JEAN R.: *Mackenzie's Flight.* (In Montreal *Family Herald and Weekly Star,* October 28, 1931.)
[ANGELL, E.]: *Cursory Remarks Upon Emigration.* 1827.
ARFWEDSON, K. D.: *The United States and Canada in 1832, -33 and -34.* 1834.
ARMSTRONG, C.: *A Typical Example of Immigration, 1819.* (In Ontario Historical Society, *Papers and Records,* Volume 25.)
ATKINSON, A. F.: *Present Condition of Upper Canada.* 1849.
AUCHINLECK, G.: *History of the War Between Great Britain and the United States.* 1855.

BÂBY, WILLIAM LEWIS: *Souvenirs of the Past.* 1896.
BANNISTER, J. W.: *Sketches of Plans for Settling in Upper Canada.* 1826.
BEATTY, JOHN: *Diary.* In E. C. Guillet: *The Victoria College Manuscript Discoveries.* (The *New Outlook,* June 17th—July 1st, 1931.)
BELL, PATRICK: *Diary of Life in Canada, 1830-37.* 18?.
BELL, WILLIAM: *Hints to Emigrants.* 1824.
BERNARD, DUKE OF SAXE-WEIMER EISENACH: *Travels through North America in 1825 and 1826.* 1828.
BETHUNE, A. N.: *Memoirs of the Right Rev. John Strachan.* 1870.
BETHUNE, JAMES GRAY: *Schedule of Real Estate in the Newcastle District.* 1832.
BICKET, JAMES: *The Canadian Curler's Manual.* 1840.
BIERGE, J. W.: *An Account of the Prescott Expedition.* 184?.
BIGGAR, E. B.: *The Canadian Railway Problem.* 1917.
BIGOT, FRANÇOIS: *Memoire pour Messire François Bigot. . . .* 2 Volumes. 1763.
BIGSBY, J. J.: *The Shoe and Canoe, or Pictures of Travel in the Canadas.* 2 Volumes. 1850.
BINGHAM, R. W.: *The Cradle of the Queen City: a History of Buffalo.* 1931. (Buffalo Historical Society, Volume 31.)
[BLANE, W. N.]: *An Excursion through the United States and Canada during 1822-23.* 1824.

BLISS, HENRY: *On the Timber Trade.* 1831.
BLISS, HENRY: *The Colonial System.* 1833.
BONNEFONS, J. C.: *Voyage au Canada, 1751-61.* 1887.
BONNYCASTLE, SIR RICHARD: *The Canadas in 1841.* 2 Volumes. 1842.
BONNYCASTLE, SIR RICHARD: *Canada and the Canadians.* 2 Volumes. 1846.
BONNYCASTLE, SIR RICHARD: *Canada as it Is, Was and May Be.* 2 Volumes. 1852.
BORRETT, G. T.: *Out West; Letters from Canada and the United States.* 1865.
BORTHWICK, J. D.: *History of the Montreal Prison . . . ; with an Account of the Fenian Raids of 1866 and 1870.* 1904.
BOUCHETTE, J.: *The British Dominions in North America.* 2 Volumes. 1831.
BOUCHETTE, J.: *A Topographical Description of Lower Canada. . . .* 1815.
BOULTON, D'ARCY: *Sketch of His Majesty's Province of Upper Canada.* 1805.
BOULTON, H. J.: *Short Sketch of the Province of Upper Canada.* 1826.
BOYLE, DAVID: *The Township of Scarborough.* 1896.
BRADLEY, A. G.: *The United Empire Loyalists, Founders of British Canada.* 1932.
BRAID, ANDREW: *John Galt, Canadian Pioneer.* (In Ontario Historical Society, *Papers and Records*, Volume 22.)
BRANT COUNTY *Historical Atlas.* 1875.
BREITHAUPT, W. H.: *Dundas Street and Other Early Roads.* (In Ontario Historical Society, *Papers and Records*, Volume 21.)
BREITHAUPT, W. H.: *The Settlement of Waterloo County.* (In Ontario Historical Society, *Papers and Records*, Volume 22.)
BREITHAUPT, W. H.: *The Railways of Ontario, 1929.* (Reprinted from Ontario Historical Society, *Papers and Records*, Volume 25.)
BREWSTER, N.: *Recollections of the Fenian Raid.* (In Welland County Historical Society, *Publications*, Volume 2.)
BROWN, J. B.: *Views of Canada and the Colonists.* 1844.
BROWN, W. M.: *The Queen's Bush.* 1932.
BRYCE, GEORGE: The *Remarkable History of the Hudson's Bay Company.* 1900.
BRYCE, GEORGE: *A Short History of the Canadian People.* 1887.
BRYDONE, JAMES M.: *Narrative of a Voyage.* 1834.
BUCHAN, W. F.: *Remarks on Emigration.* 18?.
BUCHANAN, A. C.: *Emigration Practically Considered.* 1828.
BUCHANAN, JAMES: *Project for the Formation of a Depot in Upper Canada. . . .* 1834.
BUCKINGHAM, J. S.: *Canada, Nova Scotia, New Brunswick. . . .* 1839.
BURRITT, MRS. ALEXANDER: *The Settlement of the County of Grenville.* (In Ontario Historical Society, *Papers and Records*, Volume 3.)
BURWASH, NATHANAEL: *History of Victoria College.* 1927.
BUTLER, SAMUEL: *The Emigrant's Hand-book of Facts.* 1843.
BUTTERFIELD, C. W.: *History of Brûlé's Discoveries and Explorations.* 1898.

CAMPBELL, F. W.: *The Fenian Invasion of Canada of 1866 and 1870.* 1904.
CAMPBELL, PATRICK: *Travels in the Interior of North America.* 1793.
CAMPBELL, T.: *The Beginning of London.* (In Ontario Historical Society, *Papers and Records*, Volume 9.)
CAMPBELL, W., and BRYCE, G.: *The Scotsman in Canada.* 2 Volumes. 1911.
Canada and Its Provinces. 23 Volumes. 1913. (By "One Hundred Associates"; Adam Shortt and A. G. Doughty, General Editors.)

CANNIFF, WILLIAM: *An Historical Sketch of the County of York.* 18?.
CANNIFF, WILLIAM: *History of the Settlement of Upper Canada.* 1869.
CANNIFF, WILLIAM: *Canadian Steam Navigation.* (In *Tackabury's Atlas of the Dominion of Canada.* 1875.)
CARLETON COUNTY *Historical Atlas.* 1879.
CARNOCHAN, J.: *History of Niagara.* 1914.
CARROLL, JOHN: *Case and His Cotemporaries.* 5 Volumes. 1867-77.
CARROLL, JOHN: *Past and Present.* 1860.
CARRUTHERS, J.: *Retrospect of 36 Years' Residence in Canada West.* 1861.
CARTER, J. S.: *The Story of Dundas County.* 1905.
CARVER, JONATHAN: *Travels through the Interior Parts of North America.* 1797.
CATLIN, GEORGE: *Life Among the Indians.* 18?.
CATLIN, G. B.: *The Story of Detroit.* 1923.
CATTERMOLE, WILLIAM: *Emigration.* 1831.
CELLEM, ROBERT: *Visit of H.R.H. the Prince of Wales in 1860.* 1861.
Centennial of the Settlement of Upper Canada by the United Empire Loyalists. 1884.
CHAGNY, ANDRÉ: *Un Defenseur de la Nouvelle France.* 1913.
CHAMBERLAIN, A. F.: *The Maple Among the Algonkian Tribes.* (In *The American Anthropologist,* January, 1891.)
CHAMBERS, E. T. D.: *The Fisheries of Ontario.* (In *Canada and its Provinces,* Volume 18.)
CHAMPION, THOMAS E.: *The Pioneers of Middlesex.* (In Ontario Historical Society, *Papers and Records,* Volume 9.)
CHAMPLAIN, SAMUEL DE: *Œuvres.* 6 Volumes. 1871.
CHAMPLAIN, SAMUEL DE: *Voyages.* 2 Volumes. (Edited by E. F. Slafter. The Prince Society. 1878-82.)
CHAMPLAIN SOCIETY *Publications.* 22 Volumes. (Issued from time to time.)
CHARLEVOIX, PIERRE F.: *Histoire et Description Générale de la Nouvelle France.* 6 Volumes. 1744.
CHARLEVOIX, PIERRE F.: *Journal d'un Voyage fait par ordre du Roi dans l'Amérique Septentrionale.* 1744.
CHRISTIE, A. J.: *The Emigrant's Assistant.* 1821.
CHRISTMAS, HENRY: *Canada in 1849.* 2 Volumes. 1850.
CHRISTMAS, HENRY: *The Immigrant Churchman in Canada.* 2 Volumes. 1849.
Chronicles of Canada. 32 Volumes. 1914-16.
"CITIZEN OF EDINBURGH, A": *Journal of an Excursion to the United States and Canada.* 1835.
"CITIZEN OF THE UNITED STATES, A": *A Tour through Upper and Lower Canada.* 1799.
CLARKE, CHARLES: *Sixty Years in Upper Canada.* 1908.
CLEARY, F.: *Notes on the Early History of the County of Essex.* (In Ontario Historical Society, *Papers and Records,* Volume 6.)
COBBETT, WILLIAM: *The Emigrant's Guide.* 1829.
COFFIN, W. F.: *1812; the War and its Moral; a Canadian Chronicle.* 1864.
COKE, E. T.: *A Subaltern's Furlough.* 1833.
COLQUHOUN, A. H. U.: *The Career of Joseph Willcocks.* (In *Canadian Historical Review.* 1926.)
CONANT, THOMAS: *Upper Canada Sketches.* 1898.
CONANT, THOMAS: *Life in Canada.* 1903.
CONNON, JOHN R.: *The Early History of Elora and Vicinity.* 1930.
Copies and Extracts of Letters from Settlers in Upper Canada. 1832-3.
COPLESTON, MRS. EDWARD: *Canada: Why We Live in it, and Why We Like it.* 1861.

COPWAY, GEORGE: *Life, History and Travels.* 1847.
COUES, ELLIOTT: *New Light on the Early History of the Greater North-West.* 1897.
COUSINS, GEORGE V.: *Early Transportation in Canada.* (In *University Magazine*, Volume 8.)
COVENTRY, GEORGE: *A Contemporary Account of the Rebellion of Upper Canada.* 1837. (In Ontario Historical Society, *Papers and Records*, Volume 17.)
COWAN, HELEN: *British Emigration to British North America.* 1928.
COWAN, HUGH: *Canadian Achievement in the Province of Ontario.* 1929.
COYNE, J. H.: *Colonel Talbot's Relation to the Early History of London.* (In Ontario Historical Society, *Papers and Records*, Volume 24.)
COYNE, J. H.: *Summary of the Talbot Papers.* (In *Transactions* of the Royal Society of Canada, 1909.)
CRAICK, W. A.: *Port Hope Historical Sketches.* 1901.
CROIL, JAMES: *Dundas County.* 1861.
CROIL, JAMES: *Steam Navigation.* 1898.
CRUIKSHANK, E. A.: *An Episode in the War of 1812.* (In Ontario Historical Society, *Papers and Records*, Volume 9.)
CRUIKSHANK, E. A.: *Early Traders and Trade Routes in Ontario and the West. 1760-83.* (In *Transactions* of the Canadian Institute, Series 4, Volumes 3 and 4.)
CRUIKSHANK, E. A.: *Some Papers of An Early Settler.* 1890-1.
CRUIKSHANK, E. A.: *The Fenian Raid of 1866.* (In Welland County Historical Society, *Publications*, Volume 2.)
CRUIKSHANK, E. A.: *Immigration from the United States into Upper Canada. 1784-1812.* (In Ontario Educational Association, *Reports*, Volume 39.)
CRUIKSHANK, E. A.: *The Early History of the London District.* (In Ontario Historical Society, *Papers and Records*, Volume 24.)
CRUIKSHANK, E. A.: *The Documentary History of the Campaign upon the Niagara Frontier.* 9 Volumes. (In Lundy's Lane Historical Society, *Publications*, 1903.)
CRUIKSHANK, E. A. (Ed.): *The Simcoe Papers.* 4 Volumes. 1923-6.
CRUIKSHANK, E. A.: *Notes on Shipbuilding and Navigation.* (In Ontario Historical Society, *Papers and Records*, Volume 23.)
CUMBERLAND, BARLOW: *The Fenian Raid of 1866.* (In *Transactions* of the Royal Society of Canada, 3rd Series, Volume 4, 1911.)
CUMBERLAND, BARLOW: *The Battle of York.* 1913.
CUMBERLAND, BARLOW: *Canoe, Sail and Steam.* (In *Canadian Magazine*, Volume 42.)
CUMBERLAND, R. W.: *Pioneer Problems in Upper Canada.* (In Queen's University *Bulletins*, No. 46, 1923.)
CUTHBERTSON, GEORGE A.: *Freshwater; a History and a Narrative of the Great Lakes.* 1931.
CUTHBERTSON, GEORGE A.: *The Good Old Days.* (In *C. S. L. Chart*, Volume 17, No. 3. Published by the Canada Steamship Lines.)

DALTON, WILLIAM: *Travels in the United States and Part of Upper Canada.* 1821.
DARLING, STEWART: *Sketches of Canadian Life.* 1849.
DAUBENY, CHARLES: *Journal of a Tour through the United States and Canada in 1837-8.* 1843.
DAVIES, BLODWEN: *Storied York.* 1931.
DAVIN, N. F.: *The Irishman in Canada.* 1879.
DAVIS, ROBERT: *The Canadian Farmer's Travels in the United States of America.* 1837.
DAY, C. M.: *Pioneers of the Eastern Townships.* 1863.
DAY, S. P.: *English America.* 2 Volumes. 1864.

DEFEBAUGH, J. E.: *A History of the Lumber Industry of North America.* 1906.
DENISON, G. T.: *The Fenian Raid on Fort Erie.* 1866.
DENISON, G. T.: *Soldiering in Canada.* 1900.
DENISON, G. T.: *The National Defences.* 1861.
DENT, J. C.: *The Story of the Upper Canadian Rebellion.* 2 Volumes. 1885.
DENT, J. C.: *The Last Forty Years.* 2 Volumes. 1881.
DE ROOS, F. F.: *Personal Narrative of Travels in 1826.* 1827.
Descriptive Catalogue of the Provincial Exhibition, 1858. 1858.
DE VEAUX, S.: *The Falls of Niagara.* 1839.
DICKENS, CHARLES: *American Notes for General Circulation.* 1842.
DICKIE, D. J.: *In Pioneer Days.* 1926.
DICKIE, D. J.: *How Canada Grew Up.* 1926.
DIONNE, N. E.: *Champlain.* 1906. (Makers of Canada Series.)
DIONNE, N. E.: *Hennepin, ses Voyages et ses Œuvres.* 1897.
DIXON, JAMES: *Personal Narrative of a Tour.* 1849.
DOBBIN, F. H.: *An Index to the History of Peterborough.* (In *Peterborough Examiner,* 1923 et seq.)
DOBIE, W. C.: *Sailing Across the Atlantic 60 Years Ago.* (In Thunder Bay Historical Society, *Publications,* Volume 5.)
DORLAND, A. G.: *A History of the Society of Friends in Canada.* 1927.
DOUGHTY, A. G.: *Quebec of Yester-year.* 1932.
DOW, C. M.: *Anthology and Bibliography of Niagara Falls.* 2 Volumes. 1921.
DOYLE, MARTIN: *Hints on Emigration to Upper Canada.* 1832.
"DUBH, SCIAN": *Ridgeway, An Historical Romance of the Fenian Invasion of Canada.* 1868.
DUNCAN, J. M.: *Travels through Parts of the United States and Canada in 1818-19.* 1823.
DUNCUMB, THOMAS: *The British Emigrant's Advocate.* 1837.
DUNHAM, B. M.: *The Trail of the Conestoga.* 1924.
DUNLOP, WILLIAM: *Statistical Sketches of Upper Canada.* 1832.
DUNLOP, WILLIAM: *Two and Twenty Years Ago.* 1859.
DUNLOP, WILLIAM: *Recollections of the American War.* 1905. (A. H. U. Colquhoun, Editor.)
DUNN, J. F.: *Recollections of the Battle of Ridgeway.* (In Welland County Historical Society, *Publications,* Volume 2.)
DURHAM, EARL OF: *Report on the Affairs of British North America.* 1839.

EAYRS, HUGH S.: *Sir Isaac Brock.* 1924.
EBY, EZRA: *A Biographical History of Waterloo Township.* . . . 2 Volumes. 1895-6.
EDGAR, J. D.: *Canada and its Capital.* 1898.
EDGAR, LADY MATILDA: *Ten Years of Upper Canada; the Ridout Letters.* 1890.
EDGAR, LADY MATILDA: *General Brock.* 1904. (Makers of Canada Series.)
ELGIN COUNTY *Historical Atlas.* 1877.
ELGIN HISTORICAL AND SCIENTIFIC INSTITUTE: *Early Settlers and Other Records.* 1911.
ELGIN HISTORICAL AND SCIENTIFIC INSTITUTE: *The Talbot Settlement Centenary Celebration.* 1910.
ELGIN HISTORICAL AND SCIENTIFIC INSTITUTE: *Historical Sketches of the County of Elgin.* 1895.
ELLIOTT, JOHN K.: *Crime and Punishment in Early Upper Canada.* (In Ontario Historical Society, *Papers and Records,* Volume 27.)
ELLIS, W.: *The Adventures of a Prisoner of War in the Fenian Raid Campaign of 1866.* (In *Canadian Defence Quarterly,* Volume 3, 1926.)

"EMIGRANT LADY, AN": *Letters from Muskoka*. 1878.
Emigration, Letters from Sussex Emigrants. 1833.
Emigration, Practical Advice to Emigrants. 1834.
EMIGRATION TO UPPER CANADA. (A collection of articles from British agricultural journals, 1820-1831, in the Ontario Legislative Library.)
"EMIGRANT FARMER, AN": *The Emigrant to North America*. 1844.
"ENGLISH FARMER, AN": *A Few Plain Directions*. 1820.
ERMATINGER, C. O.: *The Talbot Regime*. 1904.
ERMATINGER, EDWARD: *Life of Colonel Talbot, and the Talbot Settlement*. 1859.
EVANS, FRANCIS A.: *The Emigrant's Director and Guide*. 1833.
"EX-SETTLER, AN": *Canada in the Years 1832, -33 and -34*. 1835.

FAIRFLAY, F.: *The Canadas as They Now Are*. 1833.
FAREWELL, J. E.: *Ontario County*. 1907.
(The) *Fashionable Tour: A Guide*. 1830.
(The) *Fenian Raid at Fort Erie, 1866*. 1866.
FERGUSSON, ADAM: *Practical Notes Made During a Tour*. 1834.
FERGUSSON, ADAM: *On the Agricultural State of Canada*. 1832.
FERRIER, A. D.: *Reminiscences of Canada and the Early Days of Fergus*. 1866.
FIDLER, ISAAC: *Observations on the Professions, Literature, Manners and Emigration in the United States and Canada*. 1833.
FINAN, P.: *Journal of a Voyage to Quebec in 1825, with Recollections of Canada in 1812-13*. 1828.
FINCH, I.: *Travels in the United States and Canada*. 1833.
FITZGERALD, JAMES: *A Plan of Settlement and Colonization*. 1850.
FITZGIBBON, JAMES: *An Appeal to the People of Upper Canada*. 1847.
FOTHERGILL, CHARLES: *A Sketch of the Present State of Canada*. 1822.
FOTHERGILL, CHARLES: *Almanac*. 1826.
FOWLER, THOMAS: *The Journal of a Tour through British America*. 1832.
FRASER, ALEXANDER: *The Last Laird of MacNab*. 1899.
FRASER, ALEXANDER: *A History of Ontario*. 1907.
FRASER, JOHN: *Canadian Pen and Ink Sketches*. 1890.
FRASER, MARJORIE J.: *Feudalism in Upper Canada*. (In Ontario Historical Society, *Papers and Records*, Volume 12.)
FRASER, WILLIAM: *Diary*. (In London and Middlesex Historical Society, *Transactions*, Volume 14.)
FRASER, W.: *The Emigrant's Guide, or Sketches of Canada*. 1867.
FRONTENAC, LENNOX AND ADDINGTON COUNTIES *Historical Atlas*. 1878.

GALINÉE, RENÉ B. DE: *Exploration of the Great Lakes, 1669-70*. (In Ontario Historical Society, *Papers and Records*, Volume 4; James H. Coyne, translator and editor.)
GARDINER, H. F.: *Nothing But Names*. 1899.
GARLAND, M. A., AND TALMAN, J. J.: *Pioneer Drinking Habits, and the Rise of the Temperance Agitation in Upper Canada*. (In Ontario Historical Society, *Papers and Records*, Volume 27.)
GARNEAU, F. X.: *Histoire du Canada*. 3 Volumes. 1852.
GATES, WILLIAM: *Recollections of Life in Van Diemen's Land*. 1850.
GEESON, J. E.: *The Old Fort at Toronto*. 1906.
GEIKIE, C.: *Life in the Woods*. 1873.
GIBSON, DAVID: *Conditions in York County a Century Ago*. (In Ontario Historical Society, *Papers and Records*, Volume 24.)
GLASGOW, JOHN: *Fifty-seven Years' Experience of Canadian Life*. (In Wentworth Historical Society, *Papers and Records*, Volume 1.)
GOLDIE, JOHN: *Diary of a Journey through Upper Canada*. 1897.
GORDON, C. W. (Ralph Connor): *The Man from Glengarry*. 1901.
GOUGER, ROBERT: *Emigration for Relief of Parishes*. 1833.

GOURLAY, J. L.: *History of the Ottawa Valley*. 1896.

GOURLAY, ROBERT: *A Statistical Account of Upper Canada*. 3 Volumes. 1822.

GRANT, G. M. (Ed.): *Picturesque Canada*. 2 Volumes. 1879.

GRAY, HUGH: *Letters from Canada*. 1809.

GRECE, CHARLES F.: *Facts and Observations Respecting Canada and the United States*. 1819.

GREELEY, SUSAN B.: *Sketches of the Past*. (In Ontario Historical Society, *Papers and Records*, Volume 23.)

GREEN, ANSON: *Life and Times*. 1877.

GREEN, ERNEST: *The Niagara Portage Road*. (In Ontario Historical Society, *Papers and Records*, Volume 23.)

GREGG, G. R., AND RODEN, E. P.: *Trials of the Fenian Prisoners*. 1867.

GREGG, WILLIAM: *History of the Presbyterian Church in Canada to 1834*. 1885.

GUILLET, EDWIN C.: *Cobourg*. (In the *Cobourg Sentinel-Star*, May 22, 1930—July 28, 1932. This series consists partly of material on the history of Cobourg, but it contains also a great deal of information on early life in Hamilton Township and the old Newcastle District generally. A set of the issues of the *Cobourg Sentinel-Star* in which the articles occur is in the Toronto Public Reference Library, and the files are also available in the Library of Parliament, Ottawa, and in the Legislative Library of Ontario.)

GUILLET, EDWIN C.: *The Victoria College Manuscript Discoveries*. (In the *New Outlook*, March 25—July 1, 1931. Sets of these issues are available in the Public Archives of Canada, in the Toronto Public Reference Library, in the Legislative Library of Ontario, in the University of Toronto Library, and in Victoria University Library. The articles contain a running account of early Methodism in Ontario, and of the lives and times of subscribers to the Upper Canada Academy.)

HAIGHT, CANNIFF: *Country Life in Canada 50 Years Ago*. 1885.

HALDIMAND COUNTY *Historical Atlas*. 1879.

HALE, J. C.: *Instructions to Emigrants*. 1832. (In *Emigration, Letters from Sussex Emigrants*.)

HALL, BASIL: *Travels in America in 1827 and 1828*. 3 Volumes. 1829.

HALL, BASIL: *Forty Etchings, from Sketches made with the Camera Lucida in North America in 1827 and 1828*. 1829.

HALL, FRANCIS: *Travels in Canada and the United States in 1816-17*. 1818.

HALTON COUNTY *Historical Atlas*. 1877.

HAMILTON, THOMAS: *Men and Manners in America*. 2 Volumes. 1833.

Hamilton and the County of Wentworth. 1886.

HANNAY, JAMES: *History of the War of 1812*. 1901.

HARMAN, BRUCE: *'Twas 26 Years Ago: Narrative of the Red River Expedition*. 1896. (Reprinted in pamphlet form from the Toronto *Mail and Empire*, May 30, 1896.)

HARRIS, MRS. AMELIA: *Diary*. (In *London Free Press*, July 14—November 17, 1928.)

HARRIS, DEAN: *Pioneers of the Cross in Canada*. 1930.

HASTINGS AND PRINCE EDWARD COUNTIES *Historical Atlas*. 1878.

HATHAWAY, E. J.: *Jesse Ketchum and His Times*. 1929.

HATHAWAY, E. J.: *The Story of the Old Fort at Toronto*. (In Ontario Historical Society, *Papers and Records*, Volume 25.)

HAW, WILLIAM: *Fifteen Years in Canada*. 1850.

HAWKINS, ERNEST: *Annals of the Colonial Church, Diocese of Toronto*. 1848.

HAYDON, ANDREW: *Pioneer Sketches of the Bathurst District*. 1925.

HAYNES, F. E.: *The Reciprocity Treaty of 1854*. 1892.

HEAD, SIR FRANCIS BOND: *A Narrative of the Canadian Rebellion.* 1839.
HEAD, SIR FRANCIS BOND: *The Emigrant.* 1846.
HEAD, SIR GEORGE: *Forest Scenes and Incidents in the Wilds of America.* 1829.
HEARNE, SAMUEL: *A Journal from Hudson's Bay to the Northern Ocean in the years 1769-1772.* 1795.
HEATON, HERBERT: *History of Trade and Commerce.* 1928.
HEMING, ARTHUR: *The Drama of the Forests.* 1921.
HENNEPIN, LOUIS: *Description de la Louisiane.* 1683.
HENNEPIN, LOUIS: *Nouvelle Découverte d'un Pais plus grand que l'Europe.* 1697.
HENNEPIN, LOUIS: *Nouveau Voyage d'un Pais plus grand que l'Europe.* 1698.
HENRY, ALEXANDER: *Travels and Adventures in Canada and the Indian Territories, 1760-76.* 1807.
HENRY, GEORGE: *The Emigrant's Guide.* 18?.
HERIOT, GEORGE: *History of Canada.* 1804.
HERIOT, GEORGE: *Travels through the Canadas.* 1807.
HERRINGTON, W. S.: *The History of Lennox and Addington.* 1913.
HERRINGTON, W. S.: *Pioneer Life Among the Loyalists of Upper Canada.* 1915.
HERRINGTON, W. S.: *Pioneer Life on the Bay of Quinté.* (In Lennox and Addington Historical Society, *Papers and Records,* Volume 6.)
HEUSTIS, DANIEL D.: *A Narrative of the Adventures and Sufferings of Captain Daniel D. Heustis.* 1847.
HEWITT, GRACE H.: *Early Days in Simcoe County.* 192?.
HICKEY, WILLIAM: *Hints on Emigration to Upper Canada.* 1834.
HIGGINS, W. H.: *Life and Times of Joseph Gould.* 1887.
HILL, S. S.: *The Emigrant's Introduction to the British American Colonies.* 1837.
HILTS, J. H.: *Experiences of a Backwoods Preacher.* 1887.
HOBSON, W. B.: *Old Stage Coach Days in Oxford County.* (In Ontario Historical Society, *Papers and Records,* Volume 17.)
HODGINS, J. G.: *Geography and History of British North America.* 1857.
HODGSON, ADAM: *Letters from North America.* 1824.
HOLLEY, G. W.: *Niagara; its History, Geology, Incidents and Poetry.* 1872.
HOPKINS, J. C.: *The Story of the Dominion,* 1900.
HOPKINS, J. C. (Ed.): *Canada, an Encyclopaedia.* 6 Volumes. 1898.
HOPKINS, J. C.: *Progress of Canada in the Century.* 1900.
HOPKINS, J. C.: *The Story of Canada.* 1922.
HORSEY, AMY: *Early Settlement of Prince Edward County.* (In Women's Canadian Historical Society of Ottawa, *Transactions,* Volume 1.)
HORTON, SIR R. W.: *Ireland and Canada.* 1839.
HOUGH, T. B.: *A History of St. Lawrence and Franklin Counties, New York.* 1853.
HOWARD, MARGARET M.: *Fort Rouillé.* (In Women's Canadian Historical Society of Toronto, *Transactions,* No. 27, 1928-30.)
HOWE, JOHN: *The Emigrant's New Guide.* 1822.
HOWISON, JOHN: *Sketches of Upper Canada.* 1821.
HUNTER, A. F.: *A History of Simcoe County.* 2 Volumes. 1909.
HUNTER, A. F.: *The Ethnographical Elements of Ontario.* (In Ontario Historical Society, *Papers and Records,* Volume 3.)
HUNTER, A. F.: *The Parts of Fort Rouillé and Fort York in the Establishment of Toronto.* (In Ontario Historical Society, *Papers and Records,* Volume 25.)
HUNTER, CHARLES: *Reminiscences of the Fenian Raid of 1866.* (In Niagara Historical Society, *Publications,* 1920.)

HURD, S. P.: *Information for the Use of Persons Emigrating to Upper Canada.* 1832.
HURON COUNTY *Historical Atlas.* 1879.
HUTTON, WILLIAM: *Canada, its Present Condition, Prospects and Resources.* 18?.
HUYSHE, G. L.: *The Red River Expedition.* 1871.

INCHES, JAMES: *Journal of an Excursion in the Year 1834.* 1835.
INCHES, JAMES: *Canada in the Years 1832, -33 and -34.* 1835.
INCHES, JAMES: *Letters on Emigration to Canada.* 1836.
INNIS, H. A.: *The Fur Trade in Canada.* 1930.
INNIS, H. A.: *Peter Pond, Fur Trader and Adventurer.* 1932.
IRVING, WASHINGTON: *Astoria, or an Anecdote of an Enterprise beyond the Rocky Mountains.* 18?.
IZARD, RALPH: *An Account of a Journey. . . . in 1765.* 1846.

JACKMAN, W. T.: *Canadian Railroads.* (In the Toronto *Mail and Empire,* November 28, 1931.)
JAMES, C. C.: *The First Legislators of Upper Canada.* 1902.
JAMESON, ANNA: *Winter Studies and Summer Rambles in Canada.* 3 Volumes. 1838.
JAMESON, E. O.: *The Choates in America.* 1896.
JEFFERYS, C. W.: *Dramatic Episodes in Canada's Story.* 1930.
JOHNSON, WILLIAM: *History of Perth County.* 1903.
JOHNSTON, F. W.: *Notes on North America.* 2 Volumes. 1851.
JOHNSTON, WILLIAM: *Pioneers of Blanshard.* 1899.
JONES, HENRY JOHN: *Diary.* (In *Willison's Monthly,* April-September, 1929.)
JONES, JAMES E.: *Pioneer Crimes and Punishments in Toronto and the Home District.* 1924.
JONES, PETER: *Journal.* 1860.
Journal of a Wanderer. 1844.

KALM, PETER: *Travels into North America.* 2 Volumes. 1772.
KALM, PETER: *A Letter from Mr. Kalm. . . .* (In the *Gentleman's Magazine,* January, 1751.)
KANE, PAUL: *Wanderings of an Artist among the Indians of North America.* 1859.
KEEFER, T. C.: *The Canals of Canada.* 1850.
KEEFER, T. C.: *Travel and Transportation.* (In Lovell: *80 Years' Progress in British North America.* 1863.)
KENNEDY, DAVID: *Incidents of Pioneer Days at Guelph and Bruce County.* 1903.
KENNEDY, W. P. M.: *Documents of the Canadian Constitution, 1759-1915.* 1918.
KENNEDY, W. M. P.: *The Constitution of Canada; an Introduction to its Development and Law.* 1922.
KENNY, F. GERTRUDE: *Some Account of Bytown.* (In Women's Canadian Historical Society of Ottawa, *Transactions,* Volume 1.)
Kent County, Commemorative Biographical Record of. 1904.
KERR, JOHN: *The History of Curling.* 1890.
KERR, JOHN: *Curling in Canada and the United States.* 1904.
KERR, W. B.: *The Occupation of York (Toronto), 1813.* (In *Canadian Historical Review,* Volume 5.)
KILROY, M. C.: *Local Historic Places in Essex County.* (In Ontario Historical Society, *Papers and Records,* Volume 6.)
KING, J.: *The Other Side of the Story.* 1886.
KINGSBURY, BENJAMIN: *The Canadian Movement.* 1847.
KINGSFORD, WILLIAM: *The Early Bibliography of the Province of Ontario.* 1892.
KINGSFORD, WILLIAM: *History of Canada.* 10 Volumes. 1887-1898.
KINGSFORD, WILLIAM: *History, Structure and Statistics of Plank Roads in the United States and Canada.* 1861.

KINGSFORD, WILLIAM: *The Canadian Canals*. 1865.
KINGSTON, W. H. G.: *Western Wanderings, or a Pleasure Tour in the Canadas*. 2 Volumes. 1856.
KINGSTON, W. H. G.: *Emigrant Manuals*. 1851.
KIRBY, WILLIAM: *Canadian Idylls*. 1878.
KIRBY, WILLIAM: *The United Empire Loyalists of Canada*. 1884.
KIRBY, WILLIAM: *Annals of Niagara*. 1896.
KIRKCONNELL, WATSON: *Victoria County Centennial History*. 1921.
KOHL, J. G.: *Travels in Canada, and through the States of New York and Pennsylvania*. 2 Volumes. 1861.

LAFITEAU, J. FRANÇOIS: *Moeurs des Sauvages*. 2 Volumes. 1724.
LAHONTAN, LOUIS A.: *Nouveaux Voyages dans L'Amérique Septentrionale*. 2 Volumes. 1703.
LAMBERT, J.: *Travels through Canada and the United States*. 2 Volumes. 1809.
Lambton County, Commemorative Biographical Record of. 1906.
LANDON, FRED: *London and its Vicinity, 1837-8*. (In Ontario Historical Society, *Papers and Records*, Volume 24.)
LANGTON, JOHN: *Early Days in Upper Canada; Letters of John Langton*. 1926.
LA ROCHEFOUCAULD-LIANCOURT, DUC DE: *Travels through the United States of North America*. 2 Volumes. 1799.
"LATE RESIDENT, A": *The Canadas as They Are Now*. 1833.
LEAVITT, T .W. H.: *History of Leeds and Grenville*. 1879.
LE CARON, HENRI: *25 Years in the Secret Service; the Recollections of a Spy*. 1892.
LETT, W. P.: *Recollections of Bytown and its Old Inhabitants*. 1874.
Letters from Canada. 1862.
Letters from Settlers. 1837(?).
LEVINGE, RICHARD: *Echoes from the Backwoods*. 2 Volumes. 1846.
LEWIS, THADDEUS: *Autobiography*. 1865.
LILLIE, A.: *Canada: Physical, Economic and Social*. 1855.
LINCOLN AND WELLAND COUNTIES *Historical Atlas*. 1876.
LINDSEY, CHARLES: *Life and Times of William Lyon Mackenzie*. 2 Volumes. 1862.
LITTLEHALES, E. B.: *Journal. 1889*. (Henry Scadding, Editor.)
LIZARS, R. AND K.: *In the Days of the Canada Company*. 1896.
LIZARS, R. AND K.: *Humours of '37*. 1897.
LIZARS, K. M.: *The Valley of the Humber*. 1913.
LOGAN, JAMES: *Notes of a Journey through Canada*. 1838.
LONG, JOHN: *Voyages chez Différentes Nations Sauvages de l'Amérique*. 1794.
LOSSING, B. J.: *The Pictorial Field Book of the War of 1812*. 1868.
LOVELL, JOHN (Ed.): *Canada Directory, 1857-8*. 1857.
LOVELL, JOHN (Ed.), and HIND, H. Y., HODGINS, J. G., KEFFER, T. C., MURRAY, W., PERLEY, M. H., and ROBB, C.: *80 Years' Progress in British North America*. 1863.
LOVETT, H. A.: *Canada and the Grand Trunk, 1829-1924*. 1924.
LOWER, A. R. M.: *Immigration and Settlement in Canada, 1812-20*. (In *Canadian Historical Review*, Volume 3.)
LOWER, A. R. M.: *A Sketch of the History of the Canadian Lumber Trade*. (In *Canada Year Book*, 1925.)
LUCAS, SIR C. P.: *The Canadian War of 1812*. 1906.
LUCAS, SIR C. P. (Ed.): *Lord Durham's Report*. 3 Volumes. 1912.
LUNDY, BENJAMIN: *Diary, 1832*. (Edited by Fred Landon. In Ontario Historical Society, *Papers and Records*, Volume 13.)
LYELL, SIR CHARLES: *Travels in North America*. 1845.
LYNCH, JOHN: *Directory of the County of Peel*. 1874.
LYON, CALEB: *Narrative and Recollections of Van Diemen's Land. . . . 1844*.

MCALLISTER, DANIEL: *Reminiscences of the Town of Cobourg.* 1903.
MCDONALD, ARCHIBALD: *Peace River. A Canoe Voyage from Hudson's Bay to the Pacific.* 1872.
MACDONALD, GEORGE SANDFIELD: *The Literary Aspect of the Keltic Settlement in the Counties of Stormont and Glengarry.* (In *Transactions* of the Celtic Society of Montreal, 1884-7.)
MACDONALD, H. S.: *The United Empire Loyalists of the Old Johnstown District.* (In Ontario Historical Society, *Papers and Records*, Volume 12.)
MCDONALD, JOHN: *Emigration to Canada.* 1823.
MCDONALD, JOHN: *Narrative of a Voyage to Quebec, and Journey from thence to New Lanark, Upper Canada.* 1823.
MACDONALD, J. H.: *Troublous Times in Canada.* 1910.
MACDONELL, ALEXANDER: *Journal.* (In Middleton and Landon's *The Province of Ontario*, Volume 2.)
MACDONELL, ALEXANDER: *Reminiscences.* 1888.
MACDONELL, ALEXANDER: *Diary of Governor Simcoe's Journey from Humber Bay to Matchetache Bay, 1793.* 18?.
MACDONELL, J. A.: *Sketches of Glengarry in Canada.* 1893.
MACDONELL, J. A.: *Major-General Sir Isaac Brock.* (In Ontario Historical Society, *Papers and Records*, Volume 10.)
MACDOUGALL, MRS. J. L.: *Renfrew in the Early Days.* (In Women's Canadian Historical Society of Ottawa, *Transactions*, Volume 1.)
MCDOWELL, FRANK: *A Notable Event.* (In the *Canadian National Railways Magazine*, October, 1931.)
MCGREGOR, JOHN: *British America.* 2 Volumes. 1832.
MACHAR, A. M.: *The Story of Old Kingston.* 1908.
MACK, W. G.: *A Letter from the Eastern Townships of Lower Canada.* 1837.
MACKAY, W. A.: *Pioneer Life in Zorra.* 1899.
MCKELLAR, ARCHIBALD: *The Old "Bragh" or Hand-mill.* (In Ontario Historical Society, *Papers and Records*, Volume 3.)
MCKELLAR, ARCHIBALD: *Recollections of Colonel Talbot and his Times.* (In Wentworth Historical Society, *Publications*, Volume 1.)
MCKELLAR, DONALD: *History of the Post Office and Early Mail Service in the Thunder Bay District.* (In Thunder Bay Historical Society, *Publications*, 1912-13.)
MCKELLAR, PETER: *The First Military Expedition to the Red River.* (In Thunder Bay Historical Society, *Publications*, Volume 1.)
MCKELLAR, PETER: *The Red River Expedition.* (In Thunder Bay Historical Society, *Publications*, Volume 2.)
MACKENZIE, SIR ALEXANDER: *General History of the Fur Trade.* 1801.
MACKENZIE, SIR ALEXANDER: *Voyage from Montreal through North America.* 1801.
MACKENZIE, ENEAS: *An Historical View of the United States. . . .* 1819.
MACKENZIE, WILLIAM LYON: *Sketches of Canada and the United States.* 1833.
MACKENZIE, WILLIAM LYON: *Winter Wanderings Ten Years Since.* (In the Toronto *Examiner*, October 6, 1847.)
MACKENZIE, WILLIAM LYON: *Mackenzie's Own Narrative of the Late Rebellion.* 1838.
[W. L. MACKENZIE'S] *New Almanack for the Canadian True Blues.* 1834.
[W. L. MACKENZIE'S] *Caroline Almanack and American Freeman's Chronicle.* 1840.
MCLEAN, S. J.: *An Early Chapter in Canadian Railroad Policy.* (In *Journal of Political Economy*, Volume 6, 1898.)
MCLEAN, S. J.: *The Railway Policy of Canada, 1849-67.* (In *Journal of Political Economy*, Volume 9, 1901.)

MacLennan, John: *The Early Settlement of Glengarry.* (In *Transactions* of the Celtic Society of Montreal, 1884-7.)

McLeod, D.: *A Brief Review of the Settlement of Upper Canada* . . . . 1841.

McMullen, John: *History of Canada.* 1868.

MacMurchy, A., and Reed, T. A.: *Our Royal Town of York.* 1929.

[Macnab, John]: *The Channel-Stane, or Sweepings frae the Rinks.* 4 Volumes. 1883-5.

McNeill, John T.: *Religious and Moral Conditions among the Canadian Pioneers.* (In *Papers* of the American Society of Church History, Volume 8, 1928.)

MacTaggart, John: *Three Years in Canada.* 1829.

MacTaggart, John: *Journal of Dr. Dunlop.* 18?.

McVicar, Robert: *Letters on Emigration.* 1853.

Magrath, T. W.: *Authentic Letters from Upper Canada.* 1833.

Makers of Canada. 21 Volumes. 1906-11.

Marryat, F.: *Diary in America.* 1839.

Marryat, F.: *Second Series of a Diary in America.* 1840.

Marsh, E. L.: *A History of the County of Grey.* 1931.

Marsh, Robert: *Seven Years of My Life, or Narrative of a Patriot Exile.* 1848.

Martin, R. M.: *History, Statistics and Geography of Upper and Lower Canada.* 1838.

Martineau, Harriet: *Retrospect of Western Travel.* 1838.

Mathison, John: *Counsel for Emigrants.* 1835.

Maude, John: *A Visit to the Falls of Niagara in 1800.* 1826.

Mavor, James: *A Chapter of Canadian Economic History.* (In Royal Society of Canada, *Transactions*, 3rd Series, Volume 16.)

May, John: *Bush Life in the Ottawa Valley 80 Years Ago.* (In Ontario Historical Society, *Papers and Records*, Volume 12.)

Meredith, Alden G.: *Mary's Rosedale and Gossip of Little York.* 1928.

Meyer, S. J.: *Narrative of the Prescott Expedition.* 184?.

Middlesex County *Historical Atlas.* 1878.

Middlesex County, History of. 1889.

Middleton, J. E.: *The Municipality of Toronto, a History.* 2 Volumes. 1923.

Middleton, J. E.: *The Romance of Ontario.* 1931.

Middleton, J. E., and Landon, F.: *The Province of Ontario.* 4 Volumes. 1927.

Miller, Linus W.: *Notes of an Exile, on Canada, England and Van Diemen's Land.* 184?.

Molson, John: *From the Canoe to the Railway.* 192?.

Montreal *Witness: The Fenian Raid of 1870, by Reporters.* 1870.

Moodie, Susanna: *Roughing It in the Bush.* 1852.

Moodie, Susanna: *Life in the Clearings Versus the Bush.* 1853.

Moore, George: *Journal of a Voyage.* 1845.

Morehouse, Frances: *Canadian Migration in the Forties.* (In *Canadian Historical Review,* 1929.)

Morgan, H. R.: *Steam Navigation on the Ottawa River.* (In Ontario Historical Society, *Papers and Records,* Volume 23.)

Morgan, J. C.: *The Emigrant's Note Book and Guide.* 1824.

Mudie, Robert: *The Emigrant's Pocket Companion.* 1832.

Muir, R. C.: *The Early Political and Military History of Burford.* 1913.

Mulvaney, C. P.: *Toronto, Past and Present.* 1884.

Mulvaney, C. P., Ryan, C. M., and Stewart, C. R.: *History of the Counties of Peterborough and Haliburton.* 1884.

Murray, C. A.: *Travels in North America.* 1839.

Murray, D. A. B.: *Information for the Use of Emigrants.* 1857.

MURRAY, HUGH: *Historical and Descriptive Account of British North America.* 1839.
MURRAY, JOHN: *The Emigrant and Traveller's Guide.* 1835.
MYERS, J. C.: *Sketches of a Tour.* 1849.

NEAL, F.: *Township of Sandwich, Past and Present.* 1909.
NEILSON, JOSEPH: *Observations upon Emigration to Upper Canada.* 1837.
[NEED, THOMAS]: *Six Years in the Bush.* 1838.
NORFOLK COUNTY *Historical Atlas.* 1877.
Norfolk County, an Illustrated Review. 1931.
NORTHUMBERLAND AND DURHAM COUNTIES *Historical Atlas.* 1878.
NURSEY, W. R.: *The Story of Isaac Brock.* 1908.

OAKES, GARRETT: *Pioneer Sketches.* (In *St. Thomas Weekly Home Journal*, 1876-77.)
O'CALLAGHAN, E. B. (Ed.): *Documents Relative to the Colonial History of the State of New York.* 15 Volumes. 1856-87.
O'CONNOR, DANIEL: *Diary.* 1901.
OGDEN, JOHN C.: *A Tour through Upper and Lower Canada.* 1799.
O'LEARY, THOMAS (Ed.): *Canadian Letters. 1792 and 1793.* (In *Canadian Antiquarian and Numismatic Journal*, Volume 60, 3rd Series.)
OLIPHANT, LAWRENCE: *Minnesota and the Far West.* 1855.
O'NEILL, JOHN: *Official Report on the Attempt to Invade Canada. . . .* 1870.
ONTARIO COUNTY *Historical Atlas.* 1877.
ONTARIO CURLNG ASSOCIATION, *Annuals*, 1876-1932.
OSBORNE, A .C.: *The Migration of Voyageurs from Drummond Island to Penetanguishene.* (In Ontario Historical Society, *Papers and Records*, Volume 3.)
OWEN, E. A.: *The Long Point Settlement.* 1898.
OXFORD COUNTY *Historical Atlas.* 1876.

PALMER, F.: *Early Days in Detroit.* 1906.
PARDOE, A.: *The First Chapter of Upper Canada History.* (In Ontario Historical Society, *Papers and Records*, Volume 7.)
PARKMAN, FRANCIS: *Works.* 20 Volumes. 1897-8.
PATERSON, G. C.: *Land Settlement in Upper Canada, 1783-1840.* (In Ontario Archives, *Reports*, 1920.)
PEEL COUNTY *Historical Atlas.* 1877.
PERTH COUNTY *Historical Atlas.* 1879.
PETERBOROUGH DIRECTORY. 1858.
PICKEN, ANDREW: *The Canadas.* 1832.
PICKERING, JOSEPH: *Inquiries of an Emigrant.* 1831.
PIERCE, LORNE: *William Kirby.* 1929.
PLAYTER, GEORGE F.: *History of Methodism in Canada.* 1862.
PLAYTER, GEORGE F.: *An Account of the Founding of Three Military Settlements. . . . Perth, Lanark, and Richmond.* (In Ontario Historical Society, *Papers and Records*, Volume 20.)
POOLE, THOMAS: *Early Settlement of Peterborough and Peterborough County.* 1867.
PORTER, PETER A.: *Landmarks on the Niagara Frontier.* 1914.
POUCHOT, FRANÇOIS: *Memoir upon the Late War in North America, 1755-60.* 2 Volumes. 1866.
(The) *Present State of the Canadas.* 1835.
PRESTON, T. R.: *Three Years' Residence in Canada, 1837-9.* 1840.
Prince Arthur's Landing, or Port Arthur. 1883.
PRINGLE, J. F.: *Lunenburgh, or the Old Eastern District.* 1890.
"PROJECTOR, A": *A Concise View of the Inland Navigation of the Canadian Provinces.* 1832.

PROUDFOOT, WILLIAM: *Papers and Diary.* (Partially published in *Transactions* of the London and Middlesex Historical Society, 1915, 1917 and 1922; and in Ontario Historical Society, *Papers and Records,* Volumes 26 and 27.)

PRYOR, ABRAHAM: *An Interesting Description of British America.* 1819.

RANKIN, CHARLES: *Exploration of the Garafraxa Road.* (Edited by E. W. Banting and A. F. Hunter. In Ontario Historical Society, *Papers and Records,* Volume 27.)

RATTRAY, W. J.: *The Scot in British North America.* 4 Volumes. 1880-4.

READ, D. B.: *The Canadian Rebellion of 1837.* 1896.

READ, D. B.: *The Life and Times of Major-General Sir Isaac Brock.* 1894.

READ, D. B.: *The Life and Times of General John Graves Simcoe.* 1890.

READ, EVA G.: *History of the County of Carleton.* (In Women's Canadian Historical Society of Ottawa, *Transactions,* Volume 4.)

REAVLEY, A. W.: *Personal Experiences in the Fenian Raid.* (In Welland County Historical Society, *Publications,* Volume 2.)

Reminiscences of Colonel John Clark. (In Ontario Historical Society, *Papers and Records,* Volume 7.)

Reminiscences of Catherine Chrysler White. (In Ontario Historical Society, *Papers and Records,* Volume 7.)

Report from Select Committee of House of Assembly of Upper Canada. 1839.

REVILLE, F. D.: *History of the County of Brant.* 2 Volumes. 1920.

RICE, A. B.: *The History of Welland County.* 1887.

RICHARDSON, JOHN: *Eight Years in Canada.* 1847.

RICHARDSON, JOHN: *The War of 1812.* 1842.

RICKABY, FRANZ: *Ballads and Songs of the Shanty-boy.* 1926.

RIDDELL, H. S. H.: *The Red River Expedition of 1870.* (In Literary and Historical Society of Quebec, *Transactions,* 1870-2, Volume 3, Part 8.)

RIDDELL, WALTER: *Historical Sketch of the Township of Hamilton.* 1897.

RIDDELL, WILLIAM R.: *Old Province Tales, Upper Canada.* 1920.

RIDDELL, WILLIAM R.: *Life of John Graves Simcoe.* 1927.

RIDDELL, WILLIAM R.: *Life of William Dummer Powell.* 1924.

RIDDELL, WILLIAM R.: *The Shivaree and the Original.* (In Ontario Historical Society, *Papers and Records,* Volume 27.)

ROBERTSON, H. H.: *The First Agricultural Society in Wentworth County.* (In Wentworth Historical Society, *Publications,* Volume 7.)

ROBERTSON, J. ROSS: *Landmarks of Toronto.* 6 Volumes. 1894-1914.

ROBERTSON, J. ROSS: *Landmarks of Canada. What Art Has Done for Canadian History.* 2 Volumes. 1917 and 1921.

ROBERTSON, NORMAN: *The History of the County of Bruce.* 1906.

ROGER, CHARLES: *Ottawa, Past and Present.* 1871.

ROGERS, ROBERT: *A Concise Account of North America.* 1765.

ROGERS, ROBERT: *Journal of Major Robert Rogers.* 1765.

ROLPH, THOMAS: *A Brief Account of Upper Canada.* 1836.

ROLPH, THOMAS: *Emigration and Colonization.* 1844.

[ROSE, A. W. H.]: *The Emigrant Churchman in Canada.* 2 Volumes. 1849.

ROSS, A. H. D.: *Ottawa, Past and Present.* 1927.

ROSS, R. B., and CATLIN, G. B.: *Landmarks of Detroit, a History of the City.* 1898.

ROSS, ROBERT B.: *The Patriot War.* 1890. (In the Detroit *Evening News.* Later revised for the Michigan Pioneer and Historical Society.)

ROY, PIERRE-GEORGES: *Les Petites Choses de Notre Histoire.* 6 Volumes. 1919-1931.

ROY, THOMAS: *Remarks on the Principles of Road-making.* 1841.

RUSSELL, A. L.: *The First Military Expedition to the Red River.* (In Thunder Bay Historical Society, *Publications*, 1908-9.)

RUTTAN, HENRY: *Autobiography.* (In *Transactions* of the United Empire Loyalist Association of Ontario, 1899.)

RYERSON, EGERTON: *The Loyalists of America and Their Times.* 2 Volumes. 1880.

RYERSON, EGERTON: *The Story of My Life.* 1883. (J. G. Hodgins, Editor.)

SABINE, LORENZO: *Biographical Sketches of the Loyalists of the American Revolution.* 2 Volumes. 1864.

SANDERSON, J. E.: *The First Century of Methodism in Canada.* 2 Volumes. 1910.

SCADDING, HENRY: *Toronto of Old.* 1873. (The Edition of 1878 contains a number of interesting illustrations omitted from the 1st Edition.)

SCADDING, HENRY: *History of the Old French Fort at Toronto, and its Monument.* 1887.

SCADDING, HENRY: *Early Notices of Toronto.* 1865.

SCADDING, HENRY: *Memoirs of the Four Decades of York, Upper Canada.* 1884.

SCADDING, HENRY, and DENT, J. C.: *Toronto, Past and Present:* *Historical and Descriptive.* 1884.

SCHERCK, M. G.: *Pen Pictures of Early Pioneer Life in Upper Canada.* 1905.

SCHERCK, M. G.: *My Recollections of the Fenian Raid.* (In Welland County Historical Society, *Publications*, Volume 2.)

SCHOOLCRAFT, HENRY R.: *The Indian Tribes.* 6 Volumes. 1851-6.

SCOTT, DUNCAN C.: *John Graves Simcoe.* 1905. (Makers of Canada Series.)

SCOTT, R. W.: *Recollections of Bytown.* 1911.

"SETTLER, A": *Sketch of a Plan. . . .* 1821.

"SETTLER, A CANADIAN": *The Emigrant's Informant.* 1834.

SEVERANCE, F. H.: *The Fenian Raid of 1866.* (In Buffalo Historical Society, *Publications*, Volume 25.)

SEVERANCE, F. H.: *Old Trails on the Niagara Frontier.* 1903.

SHAW, JOHN: *A Ramble through the United States and Canada.* 1856.

SHEAFFE, SIR R. H.: *Letters.* (In Buffalo Historical Society, *Publications*, 1913.)

SHENSTON, THOMAS S.: *The Oxford Gazetteer.* 1852.

SHERWOOD, ADIEL: *A Memoir of Early Settlement.* (In Leavitt: *History of Leeds and Grenville*, pp. 18-21. Also in Ontario Historical Society, *Papers and Records*, Volume 2.)

SHIRREFF, CHARLES: *Thoughts on Emigration.* 1831.

SHIRREFF, PATRICK: *A Tour through North America.* 1835.

SHORTT, A.: *Life of the Settler in Western Canada before the War of 1812.* (In Queen's University *Bulletins of History*, Volume 12.)

SHUTTLEWORTH, E. B.: *The Windmill and its Times.* 1924.

SIMCOE, MRS. JOHN GRAVES: *Diary.* 1911.

SIMCOE, JOHN GRAVES: *Letters to Sir Joseph Banks, and Five Official Speeches.* 1890.

SIMPICH, FREDERICK: *Ontario, Next Door.* (In *National Geographic Magazine*, August, 1932.)

SKELTON, ISABEL: *The Backwoodswoman.* 1924.

SKELTON, OSCAR D.: *The Railway Builders.* 1920. (Chronicles of Canada.)

SLEIGH, (LIEUTENANT-COLONEL): *Pine Forests and Hacmatack Clearings.* 1853,

Small Houses of the Late 18th and Early 19th Centuries in Ontario. (Published by the Department of Architecture, University of Toronto.)

SMALLFIELD, W. E., and CAMPBELL, R.: *The Story of Renfrew.* 1919.

SMITH, D. W.: *A Short Topographical Description of His Majesty's Province of Upper Canada. . . .* 1799.

SMITH, GOLDWIN: *Canada and the Canadian Question.* 1891.

SMITH, J. H.: *Historical Sketch of the County of Wentworth and the Head of the Lake.* 1897.

SMITH, MICHAEL: *A Geographical View of the Province of Upper Canada.* 1813.

SMITH, MICHAEL: *A Geographical View of the British Possessions in North America.* 1814.

SMITH, WILLIAM: *History of Canada.* 2 Volumes. 1815.

SMITH, WILLIAM: *History of the Post Office in British North America.* 1920.

SMITH, W. H.: *Canadian Gazetteer.* 1846.

SMITH, W. H.: *Canada, Past, Present and Future.* 2 Volumes. 1851.

SMITH, W. L.: *Pioneers of Old Ontario.* 1923. (Supplementary volume to Makers of Canada Series.)

SNIDER, C. H. J.: *Wooden Waggons and Iron Rails.* (In *Canadian National Railways Magazine*, October, 1931.)

SNIDER, C. H. J.: *Schooner Days.* (In current Saturday issues of the Toronto *Evening Telegram*.)

SNIDER, C. H. J.: *In the Wake of the 1812-ers.* 1913.

SNIDER, C. H. J.: *The Story of the Nancy and Other Eighteen-twelvers.* 1926.

SNOW, SAMUEL: *The Exile's Return: or Narrative of Samuel Snow. . . .* 1846.

SOMERVILLE, ALEXANDER: *Narrative of the Fenian Invasion of Canada.* 1866.

SQUAIR, JOHN: *History of Darlington and Clark.* 1927.

STACEY, C. P.: *Fenianism and the Rise of National Feeling in Canada.* (In *Canadian Historical Review*, Volume 12.)

STANSBURY, PHILIP: *Pedestrian Tour in North America.* 1822.

STEELE, J. S.: *Reminiscences of a Pioneer.* (In Simcoe County Pioneer and Historical Society, *Papers*, 1911.)

STEELE, MILLIE and ELLEN: *Diary of a Voyage from London to Upper Canada in 1833.* (In Ontario Historical Society, *Papers and Records*, Volume 23.)

[STEWART, ALEXANDER]: *The Life and Trial of William H. King, M.D., for Poisoning his Wife at Brighton.* 1859.

STEWART, FRANCES: *Our Forest Home.* 1889.

STRACHAN, JAMES: *A Visit to the Province of Upper Canada in 1819.* 1820.

STRICKLAND, SAMUEL: *Twenty-seven Years in Canada West.* 2 Volumes. 1853.

STUART, C.: *The Emigrant's Guide to Upper Canada.* 1820.

Sussex Emigrants for Canada. 1833. (Letters.)

Sussex Emigrants in Upper Canada. 1833. (Continuation of Letters.)

SUTCLIFFE, ROBERT: *Travels in North America, 1804-6.* 1811.

SYMONS, JOHN: *The Battle of Queenston Heights.* 1859.

TALBOT, E. A.: *Five Years' Residence in the Canadas.* 2 Volumes. 1824.

TALMAN, JAMES J.: *Agricultural Societies of Upper Canada.* (In Ontario Historical Society, *Papers and Records*, Volume 27.)

TASKER, L. H.: *The United Empire Loyalist Settlement at Long Point, Lake Erie.* (In Ontario Historical Society, *Papers and Records*, Volume 2.)

TAYLOR, C. C.: *Toronto Called Back.* 1886.

TAYLOR, J.: *Narrative of a Voyage to, and Travels in Upper Canada.* 1846.
TEEFY, L.: *Historical Notes on Yonge Street.* (In Ontario Historical Society, *Papers and Records,* Volume 5.)
Testimonial of Roger Bates. (In Ontario Historical Society, *Papers and Records,* Volume 7.)
TEXTOR, L. E.: *A Colony of Emigrés in Canada, 1798-1816.* 1905.
THELLER, E. A.: *Canada in 1837-8.* 2 Volumes. 1841.
THOMAS, CYRUS: *History of Argenteuil and Prescott Counties.* 1896.
THOMPSON, JOHN H.: *Jubilee History of Thorold.* 1897-8.
THOMPSON, SAMUEL: *Reminiscences of a Canadian Pioneer.* 1884.
THORNTON, JOHN: *Diary of a Tour.* 1850.
THWAITES, R. G.: *The Jesuit Relations and Allied Documents.* 73 Volumes. 1896-1901.
[TODD, H. C.]: *Notes upon Canada and the United States of America.* 1835.
TOLFREY, FREDERICK: *The Sportsman in Canada.* 2 Volumes. 1845.
TRAILL, CATHARINE P.: *The Backwoods of Canada.* 1836.
TRAILL, CATHARINE P.: *Canadian Crusoes.* 1850.
TRAILL, CATHARINE P.: *The Female Emigrant's Guide.* 1854.
TRAILL, CATHARINE P.: *Pearls and Pebbles.* 1894.
TREMENHEERE, H. S.: *Notes on Public Subjects Made during a Tour in the United States and Canada.* 1852.
(The) *Trent Valley Canal.* (In the Toronto *Mail and Empire,* June 6, 1896.)
TROUT, J. M.: *The Railways of Canada.* 1871.
(The) *True Briton of the Nineteenth Century; Canadian Patriots and English Chartists.* 1840.
TUDOR, HENRY: *Narrative of a Tour in North America, 1831-2.* 1834.
TUPPER, F. B.: *Life and Correspondence of Major-General Sir Isaac Brock.* 1845.

VAN RENSSELAER, SOLOMON: *A Narrative of the Affair at Queenstown.* 1836.
VAN TYNE, CLAUDE H.: *The Loyalists in the American Revolution.* 1902.
VIGNE, G. T.: *Six Months in America.* 1832.

WADDILOVE, W. J.: *The Stewart Missions.* 1838.
WAKEFIELD, P.: *Excursions in North America.* 1806.
WAIT, BENJAMIN: *Letters from Van Diemen's Land.* 1843.
WALLACE, F. W.: *Wooden Ships and Iron Men.* 1924.
WALLACE, M. W.: *The Old Stage Road along Lake St. Clair.* (In Ontario Historical Society, *Papers and Records,* Volume 25.)
WALLACE, W. S.: *The Family Compact.* 1915. (Chronicles of Canada Series.)
WALLACE, W. S.: *The United Empire Loyalists.* 1914. (Chronicles of Canada Series.)
WALLACE, W. S.: *The Growth of Canadian National Feeling.* 1927.
WALLACE, W. S.: *A Dictionary of Canadian Biography.* 1926.
WALLING, H. F. (Ed.): *Tackabury's Atlas of the Dominion of Canada.* 1875.
Walton's Almanac. 1837.
WARBURTON, ELIOT: *Hochelaga, or England in the New World.* 2 Volumes. 1846.
WARNOCK, ROBERT: *A Sketch of the County of Halton, Canada West.* 1862.
WARR, G. W.: *Canada as it Is.* 1847.
WATT, A.: *The Case of Alexander McLeod.* (In *Canadian Historical Review,* Volume 12, June, 1931.)
WEAVER, EMILY P.: *The Story of the Counties of Ontario.* 1913.
WEIR, F. G.: *Scugog and its Environs.* 1927.

WELD, ISAAC: *Travels through the States of North America*. 1799.
Welland County, the History of. 1887.
WELLINGTON COUNTY *Historical Atlas*. 1906.
WELLS, G.: *A Romance of the Raid*. (In Welland County Historical Society, *Publications*, Volume 2.)
WELLS, G.: *The Fenian Raid in Willoughby*. (In Welland County Historical Society, *Publications*, Volume 2.)
WELLS, W. B.: *Canadiana, Containing Sketches of Upper Canada*. 1837.
WENTWORTH COUNTY *Historical Atlas*. 1875.
WESTON, RICHARD: *A Visit to the United States and Canada*. 1833.
WILCOX, L.: *A Sketch of the Early Settlement of the Town of York*. 18?.
WILKIE, DAVID: *Sketches of a Summer Trip to New York and the Canadas*. 1837.
WILLCOCKS, JOSEPH: *Diary*. (In Middleton and Landon's *The Province of Ontario*, Volume 2.)
WILLIAMS, FRED.: *Do You Know?* (In current issues of the Toronto *Mail and Empire*.)
WILLIAMS, THOMAS: *Memories of a Pioneer*. (In Simcoe County Pioneer and Historical Society, *Papers*, 1908.)
WILLIS, N. P.: *American Scenery*. 2 Volumes. 1840.
WILLIS, N. P.: *Canadian Scenery*. 2 Volumes. 1842.
WILSON, C. H.: *The Wanderer in America*. 1824.
WILSON, SIR DANIEL: *Toronto of Old*. (In *Canadian Monthly and National Review*, Volume 4.)
WINSOR, JUSTIN: *Narrative and Critical History of America*. 8 Volumes. 1884-9.
WOLSELEY, GARNET (later Viscount): *The Soldier's Pocket Book for Field Service*. 1869.
WOLSELEY, VISCOUNT: *Narrative of the Red River Expedition*. (In *Blackwood's Magazine*, December, 1870—February, 1871.)
WOOD, WILLIAM: *All Afloat*. 1920. (Chronicles of Canada Series.)
WOOD, W. R.: *Past Years in Pickering*. 1911.
WOODS, R. S.: *Harrison Hall and its Associations, or a History of the Western Peninsula*. 1896.
WRIGHT, STEPHEN S.: *Narrative of the Prescott Expedition*. (In Caleb Lyon's *Narrative and Recollections of Van Diemen's Land*. ... 1844.)
WRIGHT, A. W.: *Memories of Mount Forest and Surrounding Townships*. 1928.
WRIGHT, A. W.: *Pioneer Days in Nicholl*. 1924.
WRIGHT, FRANCES: *Views of Society and Manners in America*. 1822.
WRIGHT, PHILEMON: *An Account of the First Settlement of the Township of Hull*. 1832. (In Andrew Picken: *The Canadas*, Appendix, pp. XI to XXXIII.)
WRONG, GEORGE M.: *A Canadian Manor and its Seigneurs; the Story of a Hundred Years, 1761-1861*. 1928.

YEIGH, FRANK: *Ontario's Parliament Buildings*. 1893.
YEIGH, MRS. K. W.: *Letters of Colonel Talbot*. (In *St. Thomas Journal*, February 4, 11, 18 and 25, 1893.)
YORK COUNTY *Historical Atlas*. 1878.
York County History. 1885.
YOUNG, JAMES: *Reminiscences of Galt and Dumfries*. 1880.

KEY TO THE INDEX

The index is an exhaustive one, but attention to the following rules and principles upon which it is based will enable the most effective use:

1. To save continual repetition and confusion the following subjects are treated in one place only:

    (a) INDIANS. The life and characteristics of the Indians are listed alphabetically under this one general head and not elsewhere; but in addition separate tribes are indexed under their names.

    (b) SAILING-SHIPS. The names of all sailing-vessels referred to in the text are listed alphabetically under this head and not elsewhere.

    (c) STEAMSHIPS. These are treated in the same manner as sailing-ships.

    (d) SONGS AND DANCE MUSIC. Listings are made under this heading and not elsewhere.

    (e) REGIMENTS and other military or naval units are similarly listed under that head and not elsewhere.

    (f) TRANSPORTATION AND TRAVEL. Under this head are listed more or less chronologically the various elements in the development of transportation and conditions of travel; but in this instance it has been considered advisable to cross-reference the items fully.

    (g) Place-names which have varied from time to time are indexed fully under their present appellation: references to York, for example, are found under Toronto. Wherever essential, however, the variants are cross-referenced.

2. Persons are listed under their surnames and Christian names, all distinctions of rank or office being omitted except where they indicate a man's profession, or where he is referred to in that capacity. This procedure is varied only when confusion in names might otherwise occur, or where the Christian name is not available.

3. An elaborate Table of Chapter Contents has been compiled to enable one to see at a glance what each of the various sections of the book contains. Consequently it should not be necessary to depend exclusively upon the index for the references to the component parts of social and economic life, pioneer processes and industries, and the events of political, constitutional and military history. These have been listed individually, however, and cross-referenced wherever it has been considered of value.

4. Incidental references to other countries are frequent, but they are listed in the index only where such reference is of special value apart from the context in which it occurs. Similarly the continual references to the various Great Lakes and to the St. Lawrence River have been omitted as of little or no independent value.

5. All inns, taverns and mills, many of which formed the nucleus of settlements, are fully indexed under the names of their owners; and the persons concerned are listed separately where there is any additional information about them.

6. Newspapers are listed under the place and name of the publication except in four instances,—the *Upper Canada Gazette*, the *Colonial Advocate*, the *Christian Guardian*, and the *Farmer's Sun,*— in which cases the place of publication has no particular significance, or changed during the life of the paper. In the bibliography may be found the main particulars concerning the establishment and the changes in names of publications.

7. The authors of books or essays quoted or cited in this work are indexed under their names, but the source of the reference is not repeated. Artists and their works are listed in the forematter, but are not repeated in the index.

INDEX